African Philosophy

SELECTED READINGS

Albert G. Mosley
Ohio University

Prentice Hall, Englewood Cliffs, New Jersey 07632

Library of Congress Cataloging-in-Publication Data

Mosley, Albert G.
   African philosophy : selected readings / Albert G. Mosley.
      p.   cm.
   Includes bibliographical references.
   ISBN 0–02–384181–8
   1. Philosophy, African.   I. Title.
   B5305.M67   1995
   199′.6—dc20   95–2731
                                                     CIP

Acquisitions Editor: Ted Bolen
Editorial Assistant: Meg McGuane
Production Editor: Tony VenGraitis
Buyer: Lynn Pearlman
Cover Design: Bruce Kenselaar

©1995 by Prentice-Hall, Inc.
A Simon & Schuster Company
Englewood Cliffs, New Jersey 07632

Printed in the United States of America

10   9   8   7   6   5   4   3   2   1

ISBN 0-02-384181-8

Prentice-Hall International (UK) Limited, *London*
Prentice-Hall of Australia Pty. Limited, *Sydney*
Prentice-Hall Canada Inc., *Toronto*
Prentice-Hall Hispanoamericana, S.A., *Mexico*
Prentice-Hall of India Private Limited, *New Delhi*
Prentice-Hall of Japan, Inc., *Tokyo*
Simon & Schuster Asia Pte. Ltd., *Singapore*
Editora Prentice-Hall do Brasil, Ltda., *Rio de Janeiro*

To the memory of
Harry, Joella, and William Mosley

Contents

Preface

When I first began teaching a course in African philosophy during the early 70s, the major European influences in metaphysics and epistemology included Frazier, Levy-Bruhl, Evans-Prichard, Tempels, and Horton. The major African influences included Blyden, Crummell, Du Bois, Senghor, Diop, Mbiti, and Nkrumah. The views of this latter group were especially popular among sympathizers of African nationalism because they represented a pride in Africa and the desire to be free of European hegemony. However, during the late 70s and 80s there arose among African intellectuals a critical response to attempts by both Europeans and Africans to ascribe a peculiar nature to the African character. This critique was made by Africans of varying persuasions and their critique of nationalist ideologies, in turn, stimulated countercritiques. I have tried to provide a selection of readings that chronicles this development. In addition, there is a healthy debate in contemporary African philosophy on many other issues, as indicated by the selections on magic, witchcraft, aesthetics, and morality. Nonetheless, I am aware of significant omissions and I hope future collections will help make this literature more widely available.

Each of the selections provided is preceded by a short synopsis. The synopsis is intended to motivate reading the selection by alerting the reader to the selection's general direction and orientation. Critical discussion should make it clear that reading the synopsis is no substitute for reading the selection itself.

This text would not have come into being were it not for my friend and colleague Gene Blocker. He has encouraged and assisted me at every stage of the process, and I am deeply indebted to him for his help. A special note of gratitude also to Don Borchert, who has supported my efforts in every way a chairperson and a friend could. I also wish to thank my current editor, Ted Bolen, and his staff at Prentice Hall; my copyeditor Luanne Dreyer Elliott; and Maggie Barbieri, my first editor at Macmillan. A special thanks to my reviewers, Kwasi Wiredu, Jeff Crawford, and Victor Wan-Tatah. Their detailed comments and suggestions were influential in shaping this work's final form. A very special thanks to my friend Jeff Crawford for reading the final draft and helping counterbalance my cryptic extremes. Also, my appreciation to Ohio University for its support and to Harvey Whitney, Jason Hightower, Chris Citro, and Travis Regier for their many hours of bibliographical and editorial work. Chris Citro played an indispensable role in tracing down publishers, keeping track of correspondences, and obtaining documents. I am also deeply indebted to Alice Donohoe and Christina Dalesandry for their gracious and generous assistance at every stage in this project.

Finally, I would like to thank my wife, Kathleen, for her support, love, and many suggestions; and my children, Amelia and Charles, for keeping me from being too serious even in the most serious of times.

Acknowledgments

Kwame Anthony Appiah, "The Uncompleted Argument: Du Bois and the Illusion of Race" originally published in *Critical Inquiry*. Copyright © 1985 by The University of Chicago Press. Reprinted with permission of the author.

H. Gene Blocker, "On the Distinction between Modern and Traditional African Aesthetics." Printed with permission of the author.

P. O. Bodunrin, "Magic, Witchcraft, and ESP: A Defence of Scientific and Philosophical Skepticism" *Second Order* 2(1–2), 1978, pp. 36–50. Reprinted with permission of the publisher.

Lucien Levy-Bruhl, From *How Natives Think*. Copyright © 1986 by Princeton University Press. Reprinted by permission of Princeton University Press.

Parker English and Nancy Steele Hamme, "Morality, Art, and African Philosophy: A Response to Wiredu." Printed with permission of the authors.

Jeffrey Crawford, "Cheikh Anta Diop, the 'Stolen Legacy,' and Afrocentrism." 1993. Printed with permission of the author.

Kwame Gyekye, From *An Essay on African Philosophical Thought—The Akan Conceptual Scheme* (New York: Cambridge University Press, 1987), pp. 195–212.

Barry Hallen and J. O. Sodipo, "Excerpts from *Knowledge, Belief, and Witchcraft:* Analytical Experiments in African Philosophy" from *Knowledge, Belief, and Witchcraft* (London: Ethnographica Press, 1986), pp. 96–118.

Robin Horton, "African Traditional Thought and Western Science" in *Rationality,* Bryan R. Wilson, ed. (Oxford, England: Basil Blackwell, 1970).

Paulin Hountondji, "The Particular and the Universal." *The Sapina Newsletter*, Bulletin of the Society for African Philosophy in North

America 2,(2–3), May–December 1989, pp. 1–66. Originally published in *Bulletin de la Sociéte Française de Philosophie*, 81(4), 1987, pp. 145–189

Abiola Irele, "Contemporary Thought in French Speaking Africa" from *Africa and the West: The Legacies of Empire*, Isaac Mowoe and Richard Bjornson, eds. (New York: Greenwood Press, 1986).

David James, " 'The Instruction of Any' and Moral Philosophy" Printed with permission of the author.

John Mbiti, From *African Religions and Philosophy,* 2ed. (New York: Heinemann Publishers, Ltd., 1981). Reprinted with permission of the publisher.

Albert G. Mosley, "Negritude, Nationalism, and Nativism: Racists or Racialists?" Printed with permission from the author.

Sophie Oluwole, "On the Existence of Witches" *Second Order* 2,(1–2), 1978, pp. 20–35. Reprinted with permission of the publisher.

Innocent C. Onyewuenyi, "Traditional African Aesthetics: A Philosophical Perspective" *International Philosophical Quarterly*, September 1984, pp. 237–244. Reprinted with permission of the publisher.

Oyekan Owomoyela, "African and the Imperative of Philosophy: A Skeptical Consideration." *African Studies Review* 30, 1. March 1987, pp. 79–100.

Leopold S. Senghor, "On Negrohood: Psychology of the African Negro." *Diogenes* 37, Spring 1962, pp. 1–15.

Placide Tempels, From *Bantu Philosophy*. (Paris: Présence Africaine, 1959) Colin King, Translator. Reprinted with permission of the publisher.

Kwasi Wiredu, "How Not to Compare African Thought with Western Thought" 1980. Reprinted by permission of the author.

————— , "Custom and Morality: A Comparative Analysis of Some African and Western Conceptions of Morals." Reprinted by permission of the author.

▲ Introduction to *African Philosophy: Selected Readings*

This anthology presents key documents chronicling the debate about the nature of the African and the nature of African philosophy. It brings together texts by Africans, African-Americans, Europeans, and European-Americans which provide philosophical insights about the nature of traditional and modern African culture. V. Y. Mudimbe points out in his book *The Invention of Africa* (Bloomington, IN: Indiana University Press, 1988) how our concept of "the African" has evolved through the interaction between Africans and Europeans over the last six centuries. The African slave trade and colonialism has been especially relevant in shaping the concept of the African.

Throughout the world, from ancient to modern times, those enslaved have been a living symbol of social impotency. The fact that Africans and Native Americans were the primary source of slaves in the colonization of the Americas branded them as worthy of a special kind of contempt. The racist justification for the enslavement of Africans, Native Americans, and other aboriginal people portrayed them as inferior varieties of the human species, if not lower species altogether, which could be used much as beasts of burden to achieve the ends determined by the higher races. The African became a living example of Aristotle's definition of the natural slave, and it was considered right and natural for the African to be held as property, exploited, and treated as a thing. Africans who did not become slaves, who escaped the kidnappings and raids, were nonetheless contaminated by their blood ties to those who had been subjected, and for the most part were still considered naturally inferior to the European, and subject to European domination.

As a result, Africans and people of African descent have had to grapple with a peculiar array of problems deriving from the ideology and practices of slavery and colonization. These problems have shaped how Africans perceive themselves, how they are perceived by others, and the kinds of practices Africans have evolved in response to the encounter with the West (see David B. Davis: *The Problem of Slavery in Western Culture,* Ithaca: Cornell University Press, 1966; and Orlando Patterson: *Slavery & Social Death,* Cambridge: Harvard University Press, 1982).

The initial set of readings (Section I.A) provides a broad sample of readings in what has come to be called ethnophilosophy: the attempt to articulate a metaphysical and epistemological framework that reflected the essential unity of African cultures. This program generated a sharp response from a more critically minded and technically trained generation of African philosophers. The second set of readings (Section I.B) exemplifies this critique of ethnophilosophy. The dutiful repetition of traditional customs and practices, merely because they were done this way in the past, is rejected as stifling and maladaptive. Philosophy, for the critics of ethnophilosophy, is a technical discipline just as algebra and chemistry are. In the third set of articles, the critique of ethnophilosophy is in turn taken to task for accepting Western models too uncritically.

The next set of readings (Section II) is meant to illustrate how the techniques of modern philosophy can be applied to an issue clothed in exoticism, that of magic and witchcraft. The appeal to a world of ancestors, divinities, witches, and spiritual healers is given a sympathetic reading in terms of possible psychosomatic and psychical effects. Such prospects are then critically appraised.

The final set of readings (Section III) looks at some contemporary debates in the area of morality and aesthetics. The distinguished Ghanian philosopher Kwasi Wiredu develops some bold claims about the relationship between morality and religion in traditional and modern African societies and is challenged on this issue by an American philosopher and art historian who use traditional Akan art as a historical record of traditional Akan moral beliefs. The concluding two articles explore the nature of traditional African aesthetic beliefs. Three of the articles in Section III are previously unpublished, demonstrating the growing interest in and continuing development of African philosophy.

Ethnophilosophy

In the numerous taxonomies of the varieties of humankind produced during the Enlightenment era (roughly the late 1600s through the early 1800s), typically, Europeans were considered superior to non-Europeans and, within Europe, Anglo-Saxons were held to be superior to Celts, Franks superior to Gauls, etc. Irrespective of the manner in which particular subraces were related, Caucasians were generally considered the most superior and Africans the most inferior of races.

Among the literate, it was widely believed that every species and subspecies, every race and subrace, was ordered in accordance with the Great Chain of Being, in which God was the most perfect form of being, followed by the angels, man, then the apes, and so on, down to the lowest form of life. And just as man was given dominion over all the lower forms of being, so the European was given dominion over the lower races. Such a view provided the ideological justification for slavery, colonialism, and imperialism.

Edward Blyden and W.E.B. Du Bois were African-Americans who, at the end of the nineteenth century, confronted the racist view of the relationship between Africans and Europeans. Born in the first generation after the abolition of slavery (Blyden in the West Indies and Du Bois in Massachusetts), both men were well educated and exceptionally literate. They were thoroughly familiar with the views on race current in the latter part of the nineteenth century and devoted their lives and talents to countering racist practices and arguments.

In contrast to a racist view of the relationship between Africans and Europeans, Blyden and Du Bois embraced a racialist view of that relationship. According to the racialist point of view, each race was different and had unique qualities that could be duplicated by no other race. The races complemented one another, so that what one lacked, the other provided. Only by the cultivation of its unique qualities could any particular race make its contribution to the progress of world civilization. And this was as true of the African (or black) race as it was of the European (or white) and Oriental (or yellow) races. While some advocated inter-marriage and the creation of superior hybrids from the different races (e.g. Frederick Douglass), Blyden and Du Bois argued that Africans needed to turn inward and perfect their unique capabilities through interaction with one another.

The relativism inherent in the racialist point of view is reflected in Levy-Bruhl's contention that there is a basic difference in the mentalities of European and non-European races. Lucien Levy-Bruhl (1857–1939) was a French philosopher who taught at the Sorbonne from 1896 to 1927. In opposition to many earlier anthropologists and students of human culture, Levy-Bruhl argues that non-Western people were not simply less competent at rational modes of thought than western people. It is not, he holds, that non-Europeans cannot think as logically as Europeans. Rather, the thought patterns of non-Europeans follow a different "logic" from that of Europeans. Non-Europeans are not simply less adept at avoiding contradictions than Europeans. Instead of adhering to the law of non-contradiction (one cannot maintain that both of two inconsistent propositions are true) as Europeans do, non-Europeans operate in accordance with "the law of participation," which imposes quite a different set of constraints from the law of noncontradiction.

In a similar fashion, the Belgian priest Father Placide Tempels argues in his famous book *Bantu Philosophy* (Paris: Presence Africaine, 1952) that Africans have a different metaphysical view of reality from Europeans. The ontology of the African world is made up of forces rather than things, and these forces ebb and flow, diminish and increase. Losses and gains are relevant, not in terms of strict quantities, but in terms of their effect in augmenting or diminishing the life forces of those involved.

Tempels' argument is similar to that of the American linguist, Benjamin Whorf, who argues in his book *Language, Thought, and Reality* (NY: MIT Press, 1956) that the structure of a language shapes the way its users structure reality. Whorf argues that the grammar of Native American languages is structurally distinct from that of Indo-European languages, and gives rise to a metaphysic of fields and forces rather than of discrete things colliding. Alex Kagame, a Rwandian philosopher and linguist, assesses and extends Tempels' claims in his books *La Philosophie Bantu-Rwandaise de l'Etre* (Brussels: Academie Royaledes Sciences Coloniales, 1956; and *La Philosophie Bantu Comparee* (Paris: Presence Africaine, 1976) Tempels' views have been combined with those of Kagame and applied to Africans in the Americas by the Belgium ethnographer Jahnhein Janz in his book *Muntu* (NY: Grove Press, 1990).

John Mbiti, a Kenyan philosopher and clergyman, adopts an explicitly ethnographic approach to demonstrate that there are certain basic similarities between different ethnic groups throughout Africa, and that these similarities manifest a concept of time and person that differs radically from that characteristic of modern Europe. He argued that the African concept of time was phenomenal rather than mechanistic. The passage of time was noted in terms of the individual's phenomenal experiences of concrete events, rather than in terms of the mechanistic processes characteristic of clocks. Moreover, he contrasts time that is relevant to the living (*Sasa*) with time that is beyond relationship with the world of the living (*Zamani*) and uses this distinction to show how traditional Africans distinguished the living, the living dead, and the nonliving dead. Within this context, he explains ancestor worship, healing, divination, witchcraft, and other puzzling aspects of traditional African culture. Mbiti's view of the relationship between an African concept of time and the continued existence of the dead is meant to show the rational coherence of African belief systems and to challenge their portrayal as inferior, irrational, and incomprehensible.

The doctrine of "Negritude" was a sustained attempt by Leopold S. Senghor, Aime Cesaire, Leon Damas, and others to reconstruct the distinct character of the African way of knowing. Leopold S. Senghor, first president of Senegal and primary expositor of "negritude," argues that the African is sensual rather than intellectual and gains knowledge by participating in (rather than by analyzing) the object of attention. Senghor emphasizes the importance of the subjective point of view, in contrast to emphasis on objectivity, and identifies negritude with an affectual/emotive attitude toward the world.

This section ends with a discussion of the work of Cheik Anta Diop of Senegal by Jeffrey Crawford and a commentary on an ancient Egyptian text by David James. Diop claims that the ancient Egyptians were an African people but that this fact was obscured by the racist nature of modern European scholarship. Diop employs detailed textual analyses to demonstrate that the main themes of Greek philosophy derive from concepts already present in Egyptian cosmologies. Moreover, Diop proposes to show direct relationships between the language of ancient Egypt and modern African languages such as Wolof, and he makes similar claims regarding the social institutions of ancient Egypt and the social institutions of precolonial subSaharan Africa. Because of the existence of such links between ancient Egyptian culture and contemporary African cultures, Diop concludes that African philosophy must include as careful a study of the Egyptian hieroglyphic literature as Western philosophy does of Greek philosophy. In the selection provided, the European philosopher Jeffrey Crawford reviews Diop's claims, compares them to the "stolen legacy" theory of George James, and assesses their relevance to the current debate concerning Afrocentrism.

In support of the position that ancient Egyptian literature had a clear philosophic content, the final paper in this section presents a text, *Instruction of Any,* which dates from the eighteenth Dynasty of the New Kingdom, sometime around the fourteenth century B.C. This work portrays a scribe and his son engaged in a spirited debate concerning the nature of moral instruction. The philosopher David James argues in his commentary that, though a thousand years earlier, *Instruction of Any* is in every sense as philosophical a text as the early Socratic dialogues of Plato.

Ethiopians have also maintained a long tradition of written literature, which is now becoming available in translation. A focus on the literature of ancient Egypt and medieval Ethiopia provides a significant alternative to the exclusive use of orally transmitted folk beliefs as the ground of African philosophy. This shift in attention from oral to written African texts marks a shift from African philosophy viewed as the universal acceptance of certain unconscious principles by members of the African race, to a view of African philosophy engaged in a critical examination of the assumptions on which such an ethnic approach to African philosophy is based.

Africa and the Africans

Edward W. Blyden

Edward W. Blyden (1832–1912) was born in the West Indian island of St. Thomas and, after being denied educational opportunities in the United States, settled in West Africa in 1851 as a permanent resident of Liberia and Sierra Leone. He was to a great extent self-taught and was an extraordinarily literate and prolific defender of the inherent potential of the Negro race.

Blyden begins this essay by outlining the effect of the slave trade on African historical development, detailing the means by which African traditional rulers were co-opted and the people made vulnerable and insecure. If Africa was to free itself from the anarchy imposed by the slave trade, Blyden held that the slave trade would first have to be abolished. A second condition for Africa's ascent from anarchy would be the return of talented and educated Africans from the diaspora, who would help lead indigenous Africans into the modern world. Because Europeans had no natural affinity to Africa's climate nor immunity to many of its diseases, Blyden believed that Europeans in Africa often developed disparaging views about the African, views that reflected more the European's deteriorating health than the African's true nature. This Blyden took to be another reason why only Africans could be effective leaders for Africa.

Blyden was especially concerned to refute the idea that the African was a degenerate or embryonic form of the European. Instead, he argued that the African had capacities and potentialities that were different from those possessed by the European race and that these capacities needed only to be nurtured by contact with the achievements of modern civilization. The abolition of the slave trade would check the deleterious effect of European civilization on Africa, and the return of Africa's most talented daughters and sons would allow it to display its peculiar talents and gifts to the world.

An excellent summary of Blyden's work is given in Chapter 4 of V. Y. Mudimbe's The Invention of Africa.

The abolition of slavery in the United States was not an isolated phenomenon. It was an important link in the great chain of events which are leading up to the regeneration of Africa. A Negro writer of the present day on Africa and African questions, therefore, can neither forget American slavery nor the great American Emancipation. He must, ever and anon, like the manumitted Hebrews of old, recall the 'house of bondage', not only as the *fons et origo malorum* to a large portion of his race, but as the type and representative of all the oppression which has everywhere afflicted the Negro in the countries of his exile. He must also remember the great deliverance, when the door of his prison-house was forcibly opened, and five millions of his race marched out into the open air of personal freedom, not only as the starting point for a large section of his people on a loftier and nobler career, but as an important step towards the amelioration and reconstruction of his fatherland—as Heaven's intervention in the solution of a great and intricate problem as the pledge and proof of God's providential care and beneficent purposes for Africa and the African.

Before the abolition of slavery in the United States, it was generally taken for granted that, as things had been, so far as the Negro was concerned, so they would continue to be; that there was no other destiny for Africa than to be the hunting-ground for unprincipled men of all other countries, and no other destiny for the Negro than to continue in servitude to the man-hunters and their abettors. And many an intelligent Christian thought he saw in the Bible clear warrant for this view.

But hardly had the Negro come out of the house of bondage in America, when traditional views on the subject of his destiny began to fade away among the unwholesome superstitions of the past. Events began to direct attention to his ancestral home. The emancipation of millions of people of a foreign and uncongenial race, in a country governed by republican institutions, could not but awaken serious reflections in the minds of the thoughtful. Here was a new problem for solution, and one which, to the minds of many, presented terrible contingencies. They could not conceive of five millions of blacks living among thirty millions of whites in any other relation than that of servitude, especially when servitude had been the uniform antecedent relation. But that relation had been abruptly severed. The five millions of slaves were now free men.

There were several proposals made for the disposition of this unwelcome and inconvenient element. Many thought that they should be sent to the Great West, and be formed into a 'territory' of the United States. Others held that they should be absorbed into the body politic under reconstruction laws. Others proposed their concentration as free men and independent in the Gulf States. Not a few advocated their deportation to the West Indies, or Central America. A small number contended that an endeavour should be made to return them to the land of their fathers. For several years, this last proposition was ridiculed and contemned, but it could not long be suppressed. It was founded upon a principle inherent in humanity. It appealed to the irresistible instincts and sympathy of race, and it has recently gained an immense popularity among the blacks. Organizations for emigration to Africa, called "Exodus Associations," are being formed among them. While we write this, we learn that near two hundred thousand are ready to leave for Africa. Those of the Negroes in the United States who comprehend this movement and aid it, and avail themselves of it, will be elevated, and will save their posterity from perpetual degradation, or, possibly, extinction. Those who ignore it, and fight against it, will be baffled and thwarted in all their attempts at elevation in the land of their former oppressors, if they are not altogether crushed by the odds against them. This is the teaching of all history.

In the meanwhile, events have been co-operating for the opening of Africa. Scarcely had the emancipation proclamation been promulgated, when Livingstone disappeared from the civilized world, and lost himself in the wilds of Africa, just as the intensest interest had been excited in the work of exploration which, as an humble missionary, he had begun. In attempts to ascertain the whereabouts of the lost traveller, more and more of the country was revealed to the outside world; and in the fifteen years which have elapsed since the abolition of slavery in America, more has been learned of Africa by the civilized world than was ever previously known. Explorers from all the leading nations are entering the country from every quarter. One of the Sovereigns of Europe turns aside from the cares of State, and from the great questions now interesting Europe, to give his personal influence to stimulate the work of African exploration and civilization. The Royal Geographical Society has shown its increased interest and determination in the matter, by instituting an "African Exploration Fund," to be appropriated "to the scientific examination of Africa (especially the central part of the continent), in a systematic and organized manner."[1] A proposition has been laid before the American Congress for a preliminary survey of the countries east of Liberia, with a view to the construction of a railroad from Monrovia to Central Africa. In Africa itself, magnificence and beauty are being disclosed where the most forbidding natural features were expected. More than a dozen lakes have been discovered in regions formerly supposed to contain only "trackless deserts of shifting sand." The continent has been crossed from east to west by youthful and enthusiastic explorers. So that the exiled African, returning to the land of this ancestors, will not be journeying to a country of which he has no knowledge. The general ignorance of this continent, which only a few years ago prevailed, when it used to be said that "our maps of the moon were more correct and complete than those of interior Africa," can never again exist.

---

[1] Circular issued by the Royal Geographical Society, 1877.

But, while every effort is made to explore and describe the country, very little attempt is made to study the Man of Africa. It is very natural that adventurous travellers should deem it the most important part of their mission to describe the country, to spend their time in telling of what the outside world is consciously and confessedly ignorant, and of which, therefore, there is the greatest anxiety to gather information. The geographical problem presses for solution. As to the Man, there is not this anxiety. The outside world thinks it knows the Man of Africa. Has not the Negro been seen as a labourer in every part of the world? Has he not for centuries been on the plantations in all the Western hemisphere? Have not numerous travellers written about him, and has he not been minutely described by scientific men, from his skull to his heels? But it is beginning to be apprehended now by the more thoughtful, that, after all, the Man of Africa is not understood. There is now more thinking, writing, learning, and talking about Africa than ever before. Still the notions of Europeans are extremely vague about the Man. On two points only they seem to be clear, viz., first, as to the irrepressible or inextinguishable character of the Man—that he will not fade away or become extinct before Europeans, as the American and Australian aborigines have done; and, secondly, that in any calculations looking to the material improvement or aggrandisement of his native home, he cannot be wisely ignored. Further than this, all is dark to the European mind. Only the Negro will be able to explain the Negro to the rest of mankind.

We have travellers in Africa belonging to all the principal nations of the world, and all, in a greater or less degree, indulge in strains of disparagement of the Man. And this not as a rule, and not even generally, from a desire to be unfair, but partly from preconceived notions of the Negro, imbibed from reading or hear-say in the course of their preparation for their journey; partly from the influence of their atmospheric surroundings in the field of their investigations; and partly, also, on the principle that it is easier to pull down than to build up; and that there is a sort of fame attached to the great destroyer. The names of the builders of mighty pyramids may be forgotten with the ages, while the name of the destroyer of a magnificent temple has lingered in the memory of generations.

There is no possibility of entering Africa, either from the east or west, without passing through a belt of malarious country by which the strongest constitutions are affected. A pernicious miasma receives strangers at the threshold of the continent. Their whole nervous system becomes disordered—the action of the liver is deranged. They become the prey of melancholy in its literal, etymological sense, and in this abnormal state of mental impressibility they take the most gloomy views of the people, and reproduce their own preconceived or favourite types of the African. In a letter to the *New York Herald,* Dr Livingstone says:

The irritability produced by disease made me pigheaded. The same cause operates with modern travellers, so that they are unable to say a civil word about the natives. Savages seldom deceive you, if put upon their honour; yet men turn up the whites of their eyes, as if deception showed an anomalous character in the African. Modern travellers affect a tone of moral superiority that is nauseous.

And in his works he frequently warns the reader against accepting, without qualification, the statements of some African travellers about the natives. Dr Johnson says, "Every man is a rascal as soon as he is sick."

While, therefore, we duly appreciate the geographical or material results of the labours of modern explorers of Africa; while we cannot but admire their gigantic physical and moral courage, the inextinguishable faith in themselves and their destiny which sustained them in their perilous labours, we cannot admit that the philosophical results of their efforts have been satisfactory. When they attempt to transcend the physical or material, there is contradiction and confusion. There is want of clearness in the pictures they draw; and the most skillful and accurate delineator has succeeded in producing but clumsy daguerreotypes or distorted photographs of the superficial life of the people. The European world is, as yet, only in the infancy of its studies in African psychology. No European statesman or philanthropist has, as yet, even attempted to grapple with it. Far more difficult of settlement than the sources of the Nile, the intellectual character and susceptibility of the Negro will probably, for ages yet, elude the grasp and comprehension of the most sagacious European. Livingstone was the first of modern Europeans to approach the source of the Nile and indicate its locality; so, likewise, he has come nearer than any other European to understanding the Man of Africa. And, like all true philosophers, he never dogmatises as to the results of his investigations in that direction. He of all travellers made the Man an object of his study, and the benefit of the Man the ultimate aim of his labours. "When one travels," he said, "with the specific object in view of ameliorating the condition of the natives, every act becomes ennobled."[2]

In his letter to James Gordon Bennett, under date November 1871, he says: "If my disclosures regarding the terrible Ujijian slavery should lead to the suppression of the East Coast slave-trade, I shall regard that as a greater matter by far than the discovery of all the Nile sources together."

The African is now judged by the specimens in exile and along a coast—more spoilt and debauched than benefited by foreign intercourse—just as the physical character of the interior was inferred, in former times, from the lowlands and swamps seen along the margin of the continent. No Roderick Murchison has arisen yet in the intellectual world to lay down with any definiteness the character of the mental

[2] *Last Journals*, vol. i, p. 13.

landscape of the Negro. No Professor Hall has yet descried the remote satellite of his genius. Livingstone has come the nearest to fulfilling the office of such a philosopher. He had the first and most important prerequisite to proficiency in that class of study, viz., sympathy with his subject. He not only loved Africa, but the African. He had an instinctive appreciation of the peculiarities and varieties of African character, and so remarkable a power of blending his observations into a harmonious whole, that he was able, in no little degree, to emancipate himself, notwithstanding his physical sufferings, from the trammels of his race-prejudices, and with that insight and discrimination which a correct sympathy gives, to select the materials for his delineation of African character—dealing with Africans not only in their abnormal and degraded forms, upon which most travellers love to dwell, but studying the deeper aspects and finer capacities of the people. He has thus become the popular and most trustworthy teacher of the best portion of the Christian world with regard to the African.

Nearly all other modern travellers have regarded the Man of Africa with contempt, in comparison with the natural features—the physical grandeur and material resources—of the country. *Solum melius populo.* Mr Herbert Spencer, with the aid of his friends, has prepared a basis for a work on African Sociology, in the shape of a classified compilation of materials taken from the works of writers on Africa. But as his facts have been drawn so largely from second-hand sources, and from the writings of travellers whose observations were confined to very small localities, and made under the disturbing influence of disease, we cannot expect that the work, when completed, though it will be one of considerable merit and a monument of industry, will be a trustworthy guide. The author will have relied, to a very large extent, upon isolated cases and *ex parte* statements.

It has been to us a source of surprise and regret to notice that the *Westminster Review,* usually so fair and candid in dealing with the Negro, should have allowed itself—chiefly under the guidance of Sir Samuel Baker—to carry on a discussion on Africa and the African in the spirit and temper manifested in its article on "Slavery in Africa" (April 1877). The Reviewer endorses as correct the superficial and contemptuous estimate of Negro character as given by Sir Samuel Baker. With the writings of Livingstone before him, and with numerous admissions in favour of the African from Sir Samuel Baker himself, the Reviewer yet makes every available use of Baker's works, not to accept his liberality, but to emphasise the suggestions of what we cannot but characterize as his inveterate prejudices.

The intelligent Negro traveller in foreign lands comes across four classes of Europeans. First, the class who are professionally philanthropic. These, at the sight of the Negro, go into ecstasies over this "man and brother," and put themselves to all sorts of inconvenience to prove to this unfortunate member of the human race that they believe God hath made of one blood all nations of men, &c. The second class is composed of those who, at the sight of the Negro, have all their feelings of malice, hatred, and all uncharitableness excited, and who adopt every expedient and avail themselves of every occasion to give exhibitions of their vehement antagonism. The third class regard him with contemptuous indifference, and care to exhibit neither favour nor dislike, whatever his merit or demerit. The fourth class consists of those who treat him as they would a white man of the same degree of culture and behaviour, basing this demeanour altogether upon the intellectual or moral qualities of the man. To the cultivated Negro, of course, the last class is the most interesting to meet, and if he had his choice between classes first and second, he would choose the second. Writers on Africa and the African race may be divided into very much the same classes; and the race has scarcely suffered more from the violent antagonism of its foes than from the false and undue admiration of its friends.

Before pointing out some of the errors of the *Westminster* Reviewer, we will take a brief survey of the past and present history of the African slave-trade, and see how far it has introduced waste and disorder into Africa, and prevented the progress of the people. Of course we have no detailed account of the proceedings of the slave-hunters who captured the unfortunate creatures represented on Egyptian monuments; but we have pretty full accounts of the origin and character of the modern slave-trade, and we give here a summary from an able and well-informed source:

> Within two centuries after the suppression of slavery in Europe, the Portuguese, in imitation of those piracies which existed in the uncivilized ages of the world, made their descents on Africa, and committing depredations on the coast, first carried the wretched inhabitants into slavery. This practice, thus inconsiderable at its commencement, became general, and our ancestors, together with Spaniards, French, and most of the maritime powers of Europe, soon followed the piratical example; and thus did the Europeans revive a custom which their own ancestors had so lately exploded from a consciousness of its impiety. The unfortunate Africans fled from the coast, and sought, in the interior parts of the country, a retreat from the persecution of their invaders; but the Europeans still pursued them, entered their rivers, sailed up into the heart of the country, surprised the Africans in their recesses, and carried them into slavery. The next step which the Europeans found it necessary to take was that of settling in the country, of securing themselves by fortified posts, of changing their system of force into that of pretended liberality; and of opening by every species of bribery and corruption a communication with the natives. Accordingly they erected their forts and factories, landed their merchandise, and endeavoured by a peaceful deportment, by presents, and by every appearance of munificence, to allure the attachment and confidence of the Africans. Treaties of peace and commerce were concluded with the chiefs of the

country, in which it was agreed that the kings on their part should from this period sentence *prisoners of war* and convicts to European servitude; and that the Europeans should supply them in return with the luxuries of Europe.[3]

Thus began that horrible traffic which for generations has distracted the African continent. The discovery of America stimulated the traffic and intensified its horrors.

Africans were deported to slaughter virgin forests, to test the capability of virgin soils, and to enrich both hemispheres with sugar, tobacco, cotton and wines. And it is due to the terrors of its harbourless coast, the malaria of its mangrove swamps, its burning deserts, its dangerous beasts and reptiles, its impenetrable jungles, its wary tribes prepared either for fight or flight, that Africa was not entirely depopulated to satisfy the greed of Christian nations for slaves, during the last four centuries.

Though, under the pressure of enlightened Christian sentiment, the traffic has been abandoned by Christian nations, still the continent is made to bleed at almost every pore. Notwithstanding all that has been written and said on this subject, those who have seen anything of the horrors of the traffic—which no pen can adequately describe—are solemnly impressed with the necessity of urging continually upon the public mind, with every possible emphasis and reiteration, the importance of its suppression. Livingstone says:

When endeavouring to give some account of the slave-trade of East Africa it was necessary to keep far within the truth, in order not to be thought guilty of exaggeration; but in sober seriousness the subject does not admit of exaggeration. To overdraw its evils is a simple impossibility. The sights I have seen, though common incidents of the traffic, are so nauseous, that I always strive to drive them from my memory. In the case of most disagreeable recollections I can succeed, in time, in consigning them to oblivion; but the slaving scenes come back unbidden, and make me start up at dead of night, horrified by their vividness.

Sir Samuel Baker, in his *Albert Nyanza,* describes an attack made upon a village for slaves, as follows:

Marching through the night, guided by their Negro hosts, they bivouac within an hour's march of the unsuspecting village, doomed to an attack about half an hour before the break of day. Quietly surrounding the sleeping villages, they fire the grass huts in all directions, and pour volleys of musketry through the flaming thatch. Panic-stricken, the unfortunate victims rush from the burning dwellings, the men are shot down like pheasants in a *battue,* while the women and children are kidnapped and secured,

---

[3] *Rees's New Cyclopædia;* art. "Slavery."

the herds of cattle are driven away, and the human victims lashed together, forming a living chain, while a general plunder of the premises ensues.

In his *Ismalia* he says:

> It is impossible to know the actual number of slaves taken from Central Africa annually. . . . The loss of life attendant upon the capture and subsequent treatment of the slaves is frightful. The result of this forced emigration, combined with the insecurity of life and property, is the withdrawal of the population from the infested districts. The natives have the option of submission to every insult, to the violation of their women and the pillage of their crops, or they must either desert their homes or seek independence in distant districts, or they must ally themselves with their oppressors to assist in the oppression of other tribes. Thus the seeds of anarchy are sown throughout Africa. The result is horrible confusion, distrust on all sides, treachery, devastation and ruin.[4]
>
> Graves and numerous skeletons (says Cameron) testified to the numbers whose lives had been sacrificed on this trying march, whilst slave-clogs and forks still attached to some bleached bones, or lying by their side, gave only too convincing a proof that the demon of the slave-trade still exerted his influence in this part of Africa.[5]

Schweinfurth, the German traveller, who travelled for some time in charge of the Nile slavers, and witnessed their diabolical proceedings, says that the "traders of Darfoor and Kordofan are as coarse, unprincipled, and villainous a set as imagination can conceive."

An avenging Nemesis must surely follow in the footsteps of such unparalleled atrocity and wickedness.

The *Westminster* Reviewer, with all these facts before him, and after quoting from Livingstone a statement which justly attributes the backward condition of Africans to the disturbing influence of the slave-trade, chooses to select the very lowest tribes upon which to make his unfavourable comments, and from which to infer the character of the whole race, and seems to suppose that he has clenched and riveted his disparaging work by introducing the following sketch of the Negro as furnished to his hand by Sir Samuel Baker:

> Negroes seldom think of the future; they cultivate the ground at various seasons, but they limit their crops to their natural wants; therefore an unexpected bad season reduces them to famine. They grow a variety of cereals, which, with a minimum of labour, yield upon their fertile soil a large return. Nothing would be easier than to double the production, but this would entail the necessity of extra store-room, which means extra labour. Thus, with happy indifference, the native thinks lightly of to-morrow. He eats and drinks while his food lasts, and when famine arrives he endeav-

---

[4] *Ismailia,* vol. i, pp. 4, 5.
[5] *Across Africa,* vol. ii, p. 256.

ours to steal from his neighbours . . . nothing is so distasteful to the Negro as regular daily labour, thus nothing that he possesses is durable. His dwelling is of straw or wattles, his crops suffice for support from hand to mouth; and as his forefathers worked only for themselves and not for posterity, so also does the Negro of to-day. Thus, without foreign assistance, the Negro a thousand years hence will be no better than the Negro of to-day, as the Negro of to-day is in no superior position to that of his ancestors some thousand years ago.

Such is the indictment against a whole race drawn by an amateur philanthropist, who only saw portions of the people in one corner of the continent, where, by his own account, they are so harassed and persecuted by the slave-traders that progress is impossible. None more eloquently or truthfully than Sir Samuel Baker has described the horrors of the slave-trade and its blighting effects upon the country and people. "What curse," he asks, "lies so heavily upon Africa?" He answers:

> It is the internal traffic in slaves. All idea of commerce, improvement, and the advancement of the African race must be discarded until the traffic in slaves shall have ceased to exist.

In a curious paragraph the Reviewer apparently apologises for the slavers by involving the native chiefs who sell slaves in equal, if not greater, guilt; but in the very next sentence he recovers his mental equilibrium and sense of justice, and tells us of:

> Crafty slave-dealers, who, under various pretexts, set chief against chief, knowing that whichever wins they will be the gainers, obtaining thereby the numerous slaves they covet.

There is nothing surprising in the fact that, under such circumstances, Africans sell each other. Who was it that sold those Angles whom Gregory saw in the slave-market at Rome? Is it not well known that Saxon husbands and parents sold their wives and daughters? Did not slavery prevail in every country in Europe?

Now, suppose that during the days of European ignorance and darkness, when the people sold their own children, the large alien populations of Asia had agreed to make constant incursions into Europe and stimulate the traffic in slaves. Suppose the result of the battle of Marathon had been different and Europe had become the vassal of Asia, and Asiatic hordes had entered its territory for the purposes for which both Europeans and Asiatics have entered Africa, and had continued their depredations to this period, what would be the condition of Europe today?

It cannot have escaped the most superficial reader of African history that the savages introduced by the slave-trade have had a distinctly marked effect not only on the personal or tribal character of the inhabitants, but on their social organization—on the whole industrial and economic life of the country. Their condition for centuries has been one of restless anarchy and insecurity.

Both Livingstone and Baker describe regions free from the slave-trade, where the people were superior and had many of the elements of progress; but they enjoy only a sort of insular immunity with all the disadvantages of such a position. Their dwelling-places are like islands in piratical seas, kept, as it were, constantly under martial law, with the means of defence always carried about or accessible at a moment's notice—forever on the alert to hold their own against the traders who menace them from every quarter. These regions the cowardly marauders avoid. Speaking of the warlike Baris, Sir Samuel Baker says:

> I discovered that these people had never had any communication with the slave-traders, who were afraid to molest so powerful a tribe.

Mr Stanley, in his address at Cape Town in November last, when fresh from his great achievement of the discovery of the course of the Lualaba-Congo River, described certain inaccessible localities as follows:

> I can assure you that on this map—and it will probably be the last part of Africa to be explored—there is a part close to Zanzibar which every expedition takes good care to avoid. It lies between Mombassa and Lake Victoria, and there lives there the ferocious tribe of the Wahomba. An expedition of a thousand men could go there and penetrate the country, but with an ordinary travelling expedition it would be impossible. Then there is the Somab country; I should like to see what travellers would make of that. And there is another district which would tax the skill of the best explorer. From the north end of Lake Tanganyika to the south end of Lake Albert Nyanza there is a pretty and very interesting district, but it is a country where you will have to fight if you want to explore it. Here is another district close to the West Coast, and yet in two hundred years the Portuguese have been unable to explore it. Between St. Paul and a part called Ambriz, a distance of only sixty miles, there is no communication by land, and yet it is Portuguese territory. There are martial as well as pacific tribes.[6]

Still, formidable as are the "martial" tribes, the exigencies of their condition are a perpetual bar to progress.

> We can scarcely enter into the feelings (says Livingstone) of those who are harried by marauders. Like Scotland in the twelfth and thirteeeth centuries, harassed by Highland Celts on one side and English Marchmen on the other, and thus kept in the rearward of civilization, these people have rest neither for many days nor for few.[7]

[6] *Times,* 30 November 1877.
[7] *Last Journals,* vol. ii, 143.

The Reviewer, after pulling the Negro down to the lowest possible point in the scale of being, to which Sir Samuel Baker in his aggressive dogmatism and satirical humour has reduced him, suggests the uselessness of endeavouring to educate him, in the ordinary sense and by the ordinary methods, we presume, of European education, He says:

> That the Negro is not incapable of civilization, has indeed been proved, yet the testimony of Dr Livingstone would tend to show that education with the Negro does not necessarily fit him for helping to elevate his race. "Educated blacks from a distance" (says Livingstone) "are to be avoided; they are expensive, and are too much of gentlemen for your work."

With regard to the character of the "education" which the Negro has received, and is now, as a general thing, receiving from his European teacher, and to the estimate which the Negro, as he rises in civilization, intelligence, and culture, will put upon that "education," we venture to refer the Reviewer to articles dealing with this subject in *Fraser's Magazine* for November 1875, and May and October 1876.

Then, as if struck by the injustice of his general line of argument, the Reviewer believes himself to have fallen upon instances which must beyond all cavil substantiate his conclusions. He proceeds:

> If it should be considered unfair to judge of the Negro in his present condition in his native land, ruined and demoralized as it undoubtedly is by the slave-trade, no objection can be raised to an inference drawn from his condition as a free man in our colonies, or in those native free states to which he has been consigned by a freedom-loving people. If we look at the present state of Hayti, Sierra Leone, and Liberia, the attempts of the Negro at self-government are not encouraging; these attempts seem generally to end in anarchy, in a burlesque of everything civilized, and constant revolutions.

Then, as if still conscious of the unfairness of his position, the Reviewer adds:

> It could, perhaps, hardly be otherwise; we can scarcely expect people down-trodden for ages to develop at once, on recovering their freedom, a love of order and an aptitude for civilization, which have been with us the slow growth of many centuries. All impartial writers are agreed in considering the *sudden* emancipation of the Negro as a great political blunder.

But the evil in so-called Negro civilized communities lies deeper than anything suggested by the Reviewer—deeper than the down-trodden condition for centuries of the people—deeper, far deeper than their "sudden emancipation."

Among the evils wrought by the slave-trade, none has been more damaging to Africa and the Negro race than the promiscuous manner in which the tribes have been thrown together and confounded in the lands of their exile. And in dealing with the Negro question European writers overlook this fact altogether. There are Negroes and Negroes. The numerous tribes inhabiting the vast continent of Africa can no more be regarded as in every respect equal than the numerous peoples of Asia or Europe can be so regarded. There are the same tribal or family varieties among Africans as among Europeans. And the Reviewer does not seem to be ignorant of this. He says:

> We must not lose sight of the fact that there are many races in Africa—that the typical Negro with prognathous jaw and woolly hair, who has been so eagerly sought as a slave in all ages, is quite as distinct from the Kaffir, and from many of the races described by travellers in the interior, as from the dimunitive Bushman, the feeble remnant of an older race now extinct.

This is true: there are the Foulahs inhabiting the region of the Upper Niger, the Mandingoes, the Housas, the Bornous of Senegambia, the Nubas of the Nile region, of Darfoor and Kordofan, the Ashantees, Fantees, Dahomians, Yorubas, and that whole class of tribes occupying the eastern and middle and western portions of the continent north of the equator. Then there are the tribes of Lower Guinea and Angola, so much ridiculed by Winwood Reade and Monteiro; all these, differing in original bent and traditional instincts, have been carried as slaves to foreign lands and classed as one. And in speaking of them they are frequently characterized in one or two sentences. Now it should be evident that no short description can include all these people; no single definition, however comprehensive, can embrace them all. Yet writers are fond of selecting the prominent traits of single tribes with which they are best acquainted, and applying them to the whole race. So the Reviewer makes a disparaging inference as to the character and capacity of all Africans from the want of success which has attended the efforts of so-called Negro communities in Christian lands, who, under the government of Europeans, show no marked ability; or who, as in the case of Hayti and Liberia, have set up for themselves, as alleged, ill-contrived, unsuitable, or unstable governments.

In the first place, these Negroes, as far as they are purely African, do not represent even the average intellectual or moral qualities of the African at home. The Africans who were carried into slavery were mostly of the lowest orders—of the criminal and servile classes—the latter of whom had lived for generations at home with "half their worth conveyed away," and who, it was not to be supposed, would improve in manly qualities under the circumstances to which they were introduced in foreign lands. Only here and there a leading mind—a real Man—was carried into captivity. And where these did not succumb under the new conditions, and become "the foul hyena's prey," they invariably took prominent positions among their own people. In the United States and the

West Indies there were numbers, whose descendants may be seen to this day wearing the mark of superiority, who were neither criminal nor servile in their antecedents. These inspired the respect, confidence, and even admiration of the oppressors of their race; and, for their sakes, the dominant class would have made large concessions to the African; but as no rule could be established to meet exceptional cases, they were obliged to deal with all according to the regulations established for the majority.

And where under the lead of the superior few of the race, as in Hayti, or, under the philanthropic suggestions of the benevolent among their oppressors, they are assisted in the establishment of a separate nationality, as in Liberia, still the specific gravity of the majority has a continual tendency to hamper and thwart the efforts of the minority.

There is a perpetual struggle between the very few who are aiming to forward the interests of the many, and the *profanum vulgus,* largely in the majority.

If any cannot imagine such differences between Negroes and Negroes, perhaps their imagination may be stimulated if we call their attention to differences equally marked which grew up between white men and white men in a highly civilized country. Travellers in the Southern States of America, before the abolition of slavery, described two classes of whites—"white trash" as they were sometimes called. They were described by all writers, especially Mr Frederick Law Olmstead, as

> Loafers, squatters, dwellers in the woods, hangers-on among the cities, amounting to several millions, and forming, in fact, a numerical majority, and about as ignorant, squalid and brutal as could well be imagined. The dislike which the planters felt to the neighbourhood of the poor whites on account of their thievish habits and contagious idleness induced them to buy out the poor whites as fast almost as they settled near them.

Yet these people enjoyed equal social and political rights with the wealthiest or best educated whites. Now, suppose, by some means, the comparatively wealthy few had been reduced to an equal pecuniary condition with the "white trash," the latter retaining the numerical superiority, and they had been required or had undertaken to form an independent state on democratic principles, without extraneous stimulus or repression, what should we naturally expect to be the result?

The cruel accidents of slavery and the slave-trade drove all Africans together, and no discrimination was made in the shambles between the Foulah and the Timneh, the Mandingo and the Mendi, the Ashantee and the Fantee, the Eboe and the Congo—between the descendants of nobles and the offspring of slaves, between kings and their subjects—all were placed on the same level, all of black skin and woolly hair were "niggers," chattels, having no rights that their oppressors were bound to respect. And when, by any course of events, these people attempt to exercise independent government, they start in the eyes of the world as

Africans, without the fact being taken into consideration that they belong to tribes and families differing widely in degrees of intelligence and capacity, in original bent and susceptibility.

But the laws affecting other portions of humanity are not supposed by certain writers to affect the Negro. He is an exceptional being, made, if not now by the consent of enlightened men for perpetual servitude, at least for the finger of scorn to point at. Learned reviewers, masters of style, and apparently the ablest minds, do not think it an unworthy amusement to rail at the Negro—to make him the object, if not always of energetic vituperation and invective, of satirical humour and practical jokes. In reading through the African experience of Sir Samuel Baker, as furnished by himself, especially in his *Ismailia,* one cannot help noticing that however panegyrical the terms in which a benefactor may be introduced on the stage, he is never dismissed without whatever shortcomings he may have had being brought into prominence. He is sure not to let go without a parting touch of satirical disparagement. In describing the departure from Khartoum (8 February 1870), he says with a sneer, "I had had to embrace the governor, then a *black* pacha, a *rara avis in terris.*" This habit of indulging in caricature for the sake of amusement easily leads to a spirit of misrepresentation and calumny.

In speaking of the love of music for which Africans are everywhere noted, Sir Samuel Baker says, with a touch of exaggeration:

> The natives are passionately fond of music. I believe the safest way to travel in these wild countries would be to play the cornet without ceasing, which could insure a safe passage. A London organ-grinder would march through Central Africa followed by an admiring and enthusiastic crowd, who, if his tunes were lively, would form a dancing escort of most untiring materials. . . . A man who, in full Highland dress, could at any time collect an audience by playing a lively air with the bagpipe, would be regarded with great veneration by the natives, and would be listened to when an archbishop by his side would be totally disregarded.

After quoting this passage, a grave American divine, in an elaborate article on Africa in an American Review, could see nothing from which to infer any noble qualities in the Negro, and could not let the opportunity pass without indulging in the conventional giggle. Continuing Baker's joke, he still further degrades the impression, in order, apparently, to develop the smile into a "broad grin." He says:

> An African's religion finds vent at his heels. Songs and dances form no inconsiderable part of the worship at a Southern coloured campmeeting. If we were constructing a ritual for the race we should certainly include this Shaker element.[8]

---

[8] *Methodist Quarterly Review* (New York); January 1876.

"An African's religion" is inferred from what takes place at "a Southern coloured camp-meeting." "A ritual for the whole race" must "include the Shaker element." We would assure the reverend doctor that such a "ritual" would be an egregious failure. The "Shaker element" prevails chiefly, if not entirely, among Negroes or "coloured" people, who have been trained under the influence of the denomination of which Dr Wentworth himself is a distinguished ornament. But only a comparatively small number of Africans are shouting Methodists. The greater portion of the race who are not Pagans are either Mohammedans or Roman Catholics, and *their* "religion" does not "find vent at their heels." The traveller in Africa will find himself in need of far more solid acquirements when passing through Mohammedan districts, than the ability to play the cornet, organ, or bagpipe. It is due, however, to the qualities whose presence is implied by the African's love of music that bilious and irritable travellers pass through their country not only with impunity, but receiving the kindest treatment.

> Wo man singt, da lass dich ruhig nieder,
> Böse Menschen haben keine Lieder.

And here we cannot but call attention to a fact which, in the intelligent Negro, undermines his admiration of foreign races, viz., that his race, numerically the weakest, has been through the ages selected for oppression and ridicule by the other branches of the human family. If there are, according to the present estimate, twelve hundred millions of human beings upon the earth, two hundred millions of whom are Africans, we have in the treatment which Africans have received from the rest of mankind one of the remarkable illustrations of the advantage the strong are prone to take of the weak. Ten hundred millions against two hundred millions. Ten persecuting, abusing, ridiculing two. And this has been the case in all the ages, ten against two. And yet, men, apparently thoughtful, affect to wonder that Negroes have appeared in all the historic periods as slaves—have been represented on all the monuments of Egypt as carried in chains in triumphal processions.

But in spite of all, the Negro race has yet its part to play—a distinct part—in the history of humanity, and the continent of Africa will be the principal scene of its activity. The mistake which Europeans often make in considering questions of Negro improvement and the future of Africa, is in supposing that the Negro is the European in embryo—in the undeveloped stage—and that when, by and by, he shall enjoy the advantages of civilization and culture, he will become like the European; in other words, that the Negro is on the same line of progress, in the same groove, with the European, but infinitely in the rear. The *Saturday Review,* not long since, in a remarkable leading article on American politics, in which some curious inaccuracies occurred, made the following statement:

> On their own continent, Africans seem to be irreclaimable, but after two or three generations of servitude they begin to resemble inferior Europeans. The slave-trade may perhaps eventually prove to have been the first cause of Negro civilization. The mimetic instinct of the Negro race tends, like the similar faculty in children, to accelerate the process of unconscious education.[9]

This view proceeds upon the assumption that the two races are called to the same work and are alike in potentiality and ultimate development, the Negro only needing the element of time, under certain circumstances, to become European. But to our mind it is not a question between the two races of inferiority or superiority. There is no absolute or essential superiority on the one side, nor absolute or essential inferiority on the other side. It is a question of difference of endowment and difference of destiny. No amount of training or culture will make the Negro a European; on the other hand, no lack of training or deficiency of culture will make the European a Negro. The two races are not moving in the same groove, with an immeasurable distance between them, but on parallel lines. They will never meet in the plane of their activities so as to coincide in capacity or performance. They are not *identical,* as some think, but *unequal;* they are *distinct* but equal; an idea that is in no way incompatible with the Scriptural truth that God hath made of one blood all nations of men.

> All are architects of Fate,
>   Working in these walls of time;
> Some with massive deeds and great,
>   Some with ornaments of rhyme.
> Nothing useless is, or low;
>   Each thing *in its place* is best;
> And what seems but idle show
>   Strengthens and supports the rest.[10]

The African at home needs to be surrounded by influences from abroad, not that he may change his nature, but that he may improve his capacity. Hereditary qualities are fundamental, not to be created or replaced by human agencies, but to be assisted and improved. Nature determines the *kind* of tree, environments determine the *quality* and *quantity* of the fruit. We want the eye and ear of the Negro to be trained by culture that he may see more clearly what he does see, and hear more distinctly what

[9] *Saturday Review,* 24 March 1877.
[10] *Longfellow.*

he does hear. We want him to be surrounded by influences from abroad to promote the development of his latent powers, and bring the potentiality of his being into practical or actual operation. He has capacities and aptitudes which the world needs, but which it will never enjoy until he is fairly and normally trained. Each race is endowed with peculiar talents, and watchful to the last degree is the great Creator over the individuality, the freedom and independence of each. In the music of the universe each shall give a different sound, but necessary to the grand symphony. There are several sounds not yet brought out, and the feeblest of all is that hitherto produced by the Negro; but only he can furnish it. And when he does furnish it in its fullness and perfection, it will be welcomed with delight by the world.

When the African shall come forward with his peculiar gifts, he will fill a place never before occupied. But he must have a fair opportunity for his development. Misunderstood and often misrepresented even by his best friends, and persecuted and maligned by his enemies, he is, nevertheless, coming forward, gradually rising under the influences of agencies seen and unseen.

It is the fashion of some friends of the African to deplore his past, or lack of past, and to infer from this fact an 'inferior faculty of self-development' in the race.

But, with the facts before us, we cannot admit the fairness of such an inference as these sympathizing critics of the race are disposed to draw. No one who has paid any attention to the subject at all will aver that there is any possibility of development without the interference of a higher type of intelligence or energy, which must either come from without or must be assisted by favourable conditions within, in order to become continuous or general. Mr Stanley, having become, on a second journey through Africa, better acquainted with the people, takes a far more accurate view of them than he was disposed to do when he passed through the country in his hasty and impatient search for Livingstone.

In his address at Cape Town, above referred to, he endeavoured to show the kinship in habits, propensity and feeling between the black man and the white man, illustrating this by several comparisons between Central Africa at present and the Homeric age.[11] And in his address in London, before the Royal Geographical Society, in February last, he remarked "It has been said that the African is unimprovable and irredeemable; but that I wholly and utterly deny."

It is a fact that a description of the condition of things in portions of Central Africa truthfully given would read like an account of the earlier ages of Greece and Rome. We have ourselves visited remote and sequestered districts about the head-waters of the Niger, where we have

[11] *Times,* 30 Nov. 1877.

found Negro Mohammedan students devoting themselves to literature with an indifference to the outside world which reminded us of the habits of the monks in the middle ages, who, in retirement and seclusion, pursued literature for its own sake;[12] and if the proceedings of chiefs in council which we have witnessed were written down in plain, unadorned style, the account would read like descriptions in Cæsar's Commentaries of the doings of the Celts in the days of their unsophisticated habitudes. Now, if Greeks, Romans, or Celts had been smothered in the cradle of their civilization by extraneous violence perpetuated to this time, is it unreasonable to suppose that they would be found at this day in much the same condition that Stanley found some of the African tribes? That these tribes have ever advanced so far is astounding, considering what they have had to contend against.

Through the labours of Mr Herbert Spencer and other thinkers in that line, it has now come to be regarded as an elementary fact among scientific men that societies are determined in their growth by their environment, whether physical or human. "The self-development of a society is limited by its environment." In primitive and rudimentary societies there may occur exceptional cases of individual power, where mental energy may introduce changes and begin improvements; but if surrounding circumstances are hostile, the influence will die with the introducer, and the improvements will not be perpetuated. We are told by Mr Spencer that among the Karens "now and then a little Napoleon arises, who subdues a kingdom to himself and builds up an empire. The dynasties, however, *last only with the controlling mind.*"[13] There have been similar experiences in Africa. Changes of vast importance have taken place in the interior as a result of internal activity—of individual intelligence and energy; but instead of being perpetuated, they have been destroyed by the hostile influences from without. Dr Barth tells of the ruins of the ancient capital of Bornou, Ghasreggomo, about 13° N.lat., 12° E. long., situated in the finest country in Bornou, with a rich alluvial soil; a country which formerly teemed with hundreds of villages and was laid out in cornfields, but which is now (or was when he saw it) almost deserted, and covered with dense forests and impenetrable jungle, and has become the haunt of the monkey and the hog, the elephant and the lion. Barth noticed also the admirable brick structures of the ruins of former towns in this neighbourhood, so much more durable than the frail buildings of the present day. All this is proof that there was a beginning of social advancement and well-being in the days of security; but Negro slaves were wanted for the Caucasians in North Africa and Southeastern Europe; *razzias* were encouraged, the slave-hunting Tawareks invaded the

---

[12] See Barth's *Travels in Central Africa;* vol. iii, p. 373.
[13] *Principles of Sociology;* p. 485.

country, and all progress was checked. And this is only one instance out of thousands which might be recited. Thus the African has gone on from generation to generation furnishing, in remote ages, materials to swell the triumphal processions of Egyptian kings, and, in modern times, strong arms for the plantations of the Western hemisphere, and is taunted by his persecutors (and his friends) with his inability to rise against this pressure.

In no part of Central Africa have any human agencies from without exerted any uplifting power; no planetary influences, according to mediæval theory, have operated to produce any variation from the regular type; and, as we have just seen, there is no internal tendency in any individual or race, as a rule, to vary from the ancestral organism. Africa needs wholesome interference from without. There has been interference, but it has been for the most part an interference of violence which, through the centuries, has prevented the survival of any variation from the original type, which would have pushed forward improvements in the country. And now that the effort of the enlightened portion of humanity is to suppress the violent interference and introduce agencies for the improvement of the people, it is of the greatest possible importance that the people be understood. From the want of appreciation of their capacities and susceptibilities, innumerable are the theories proposed for the amelioration of their condition. Sir Samuel Baker advocates military discipline. He says:

> I believe that if it were possible to convert the greater portion of African savages into disciplined soldiers, it would be a most rapid stride toward their future civilization. A savage who has led a wild and uncontrolled life must first learn to obey authority before any great improvement can be effected.[14]

He would apply force everywhere. Civilize Africa by force. They must be 'regimented' under captains of industry who will compel them to their task. The scourge and the sword must carry out the views which Sir Samuel thinks good. He concludes a glowing account of one of his military expeditions with the following flourish:

> The Bari war was now over; on every side the natives had been thoroughly subdued.[15]

Subdued! yes, possibly, but not brought over to respect and affection. It is surprising that Sir Samuel Baker should not have been able to see that his proceedings among the Baris, judging from his own "unvarnished

[14] *Ismailia;* vol. i, p. 302.
[15] *Ibid.,* vol. ii, p. 428.

tale," were nothing of which to boast. "It is probable," Livingstone generously says, "that actual experience will correct the fancies which he (Sir Samuel) now puts forth as to the proper mode of dealing with Africans."[16] We cannot help feeling that the erroneous theories held by travellers as to the African seduce them often into serious blunders and grievous wrongs, making the nationality and religion they represent an opprobrium, and exposing themselves or their successors to needless peril.

It is owing, in a great measure, to the inadequate theories held by those who undertake to deal with the African, whether as friend or foe, that while in the colonies along the coast European influence and teaching furnish new elements of commercial and religious life, they are helpless to raise the people above the "mimetic" stage, and endow them with creative or reproductive power. What we want is, that the foreign information introduced should properly *educate* the people—that is, should be so assimilated as to develop, and be fertilized by, native energy. We want to see the foreign leaven so introduced as to spread beyond the coast, transcend the malarious regions of the continent, and, taking possession of the healthier and nobler tribes of the interior, leaven the whole lump. In order to bring about these results, those who from abroad assume to be teachers and guides should study the people so as to be able to deal scientifically and not empirically with them. By this we mean that they should study the laws of growth as they affect or pertain to the Negro race. The present practice of the friends of Africa is to frame laws according to their own notions for the government and improvement of this people, whereas God has already enacted the laws governing in these affairs, which laws should be carefully ascertained, interpreted, and applied; for until they are found out and conformed to, all labour will be ineffective and resultless. We may be told that this is a very difficult, if not impossible task, for the European to perform, and that it is very far to look ahead to the time when the Negro shall be able to do this work for himself. This may be so; but what we are aiming to show, is, that in this direction, and this direction only, lies the hope of Africa's future. Her ultimate usefulness and happiness will be secured, so far as human instrumentality can bring them about, on this line; and this is a subject to be carefully studied, especially by the missionary, if Christianity is to take root at all in Africa, or to be to the native anything more than a form of words. A little common sense will do more for this country than a great deal of moral preaching and the loftiest philanthropic purpose without that elementary but rare quality.

We do not expect to see this continent, or any large portions of it, under one government, either foreign or indigenous. But we do expect

[16] *Last Journals,* vol. ii, p. 155.

to see, following the extinction of the slave-trade, and the introduction from abroad of facilities for internal communication, the increase of free principles. We expect to see the native tribes or communities so evenly balanced among themselves as to bury for ever in oblivion even the tradition of tribal or individual aggression, with a public sentiment so elevated and purified that the general sense against wrong or injustice of any kind will preponderate and render impossible the existence of single malefactors who now have it in their power to distract extensive regions and check the operations of husbandry. And we should expect to see in Africa all the progress we have indicated above as the result of a few years of internal tranquillity and order, which the continent has *never* within the memory of man enjoyed. There will be an exhibition of virtues not dreamt of in the Caucasian world, a sudden development of energies latent for ages. "Ethiopia shall *suddenly* stretch forth her hands unto God."

Next, then, to the exploration of the country, the most important preliminary to the general civilization of the African tribes is the suppression of the slave-trade. And it is fit that the nations of Europe should unite for the extinction of the horrible traffic. Shem and Japheth have largely participated in the guilt of the enslavement of Ham. Shem, having lagged behind Japheth in the march of enlightenment, persists in the perpetration of the hideous wrong. But, under pressure, the dilatory brother is being urged on to his duty.

Africa has been spoiled by all the races alien to her, and, under their stimulating example, by her own sons. Other races have passed through the baptism of slavery, as a stepping-stone to civilization and independence, but none has toiled under the crushing weight of a servitude so protracted and inflicted from so many sources. Millenniums mark the period of the bondage and humiliation of Africa's children. The four quarters of the globe have heard their groans and been sprinkled and stained with their blood. All that passed by have felt at liberty to contemn and plunder. The oppressors of this race have been men with religion, and men without religion—Christians, Mohammedans, and Pagans. Nations with the Bible, and nations with the Koran, and nations without Bible or Koran—all have joined in afflicting this continent. And now the last of her oppressors, tearing from her bosom annually half a million of her children, are nations with the Koran. All travellers tell us that when the Arab traders in East Africa are suppressed the work will be done. This will, no doubt, be accomplished before very long. The Viceroy of Egypt is pledged to England to suppress the traffic, and in a given time to abolish slavery altogether.

It was a long time before the Christian world discovered, or rather admitted, the wrong in the slave-trade; and we are persuaded that just as the truth in Christianity produced, though tardily, a Wilberforce and a

Clarkson, so the truth in Islam will raise up—is now raising up—Muslim philanthropists and reformers who will give to the Negro the hand of a brother, and perhaps, outstripping their Christian brethren in liberality, accord him an equal share in political and social privileges—a liberality in dealing with weaker races which some Europeans confess themselves unable to exercise.

Dr Livingstone seems to have thought that there might be some possibility of a Muslim Wilberforce, if we may judge from his immortal prayer, written, according to Mr Waller, just one year before his death, and recorded on the tablet near his grave in Westminster Abbey, and which, in conclusion, is here most fervently reiterated:

> All I can add in my loneliness is, may Heaven's rich blessing come down on every one—American, English, or Turk, who will help to heal the open sore of the world.[17]—Amen.

---

[17] *Last Journals,* vol. ii, p. 182.

The Conservation of Races

William Edward Burghardt Du Bois

W. E. B. Du Bois (1868–1963) was born in Great Barrington, Massachusetts, and died in Accra, Ghana. Throughout his life he battled against racist restrictions on opportunities for Africans and equally for recognition of the unique genius of the African race. A principal organizer of the First and Second Pan African Conferences, a founder of the National Association for the Advancement of Colored People (NAACP) and editor of its magazine, The Crisis, social science researcher, university lecturer, prolific author, and activist, Du Bois is a complex figure whose ideas continued to develop as he grew older. In this essay, written when he was in his early thirties, Du Bois addresses the issue of racial differences and their implications for Africans. He is prepared to accept the prevailing taxonomy of mankind into the African, European, and Oriental races, but he denies that physical characteristics alone determine membership in a particular race. The true basis of the difference between races is spiritual and psychical, and each race should strive to articulate its peculiar message in the development of civilization. Like Blyden, Du Bois identifies slavery and the slave trade as the principal factors that have inhibited Africa's development. For Du Bois, the African was not an inferior or immature version of the European, and it was the duty of the African-American to take the lead in realizing the African ideal in the development of modern civilization. He admonished Africans to band together in order to realize their special talents and eliminate their special vices.

The American Negro has always felt an intense personal interest in discussions as to the origins and destinies of races: primarily because back of most discussions of race with which he is familiar, have lurked certain assumptions as to his natural abilities, as to his political, intellectual and moral status, which he felt were wrong. He has, consequently, been led to deprecate and minimize race distinctions, to believe intensely that out of one blood God created all nations, and to speak of human brotherhood as though it were the possibility of an already dawning to-morrow.

Nevertheless, in our calmer moments we must acknowledge that human beings are divided into races; that in this country the two most extreme types of the world's races have met, and the resulting problem as to the future relations of these types is not only of intense and living interest to us, but forms an epoch in the history of mankind.

It is necessary, therefore, in planning our movements, in guiding our future development, that at times we rise above the pressing, but smaller questions of separate schools and cars, wage-discrimination and lynch law, to survey the whole question of race in human philosophy and to lay, on a basis of broad knowledge and careful insight, those large lines of policy and higher ideals which may form our guiding lines and boundaries in the practical difficulties of every day. For it is certain that all human striving must recognize the hard limits of natural law, and that any striving, no matter how intense and earnest, which is against the constitution of the world, is vain. The question, then, which we must seriously consider is this: What is the real meaning of Race; what has, in the past, been the law of race development, and what lessons has the past history of race development to teach the rising Negro people?

When we thus come to inquire into the essential difference of races we find it hard to come at once to any definite conclusion. Many criteria of race differences have in the past been proposed, as color, hair, cranial measurements and language. And manifestly, in each of these respects, human beings differ widely. They vary in color, for instance, from the marble-like pallor of the Scandinavian to the rich, dark brown of the Zulu, passing by the creamy Slav, the yellow Chinese, the light brown Sicilian and the brown Egyptian. Men vary, too, in the texture of hair from the obstinately straight hair of the Chinese to the obstinately tufted and frizzled hair of the Bushman. In measurement of heads, again, men vary; from the broad-headed Tartar to the medium-headed European and the narrow-headed Hottentot; or, again in language, from the highly-inflected Roman tongue to the monosyllabic Chinese. All these physical characteristics are patent enough, and if they agreed with each other it would be very easy to classify mankind. Unfortunately for scientists, however, these criteria of race are most exasperatingly intermingled. Color does not agree with texture of hair, for many of the dark races have straight hair; nor does color agree with the breadth of the head, for the yellow Tartar has a broader head than the German; nor, again, has the science of language as yet succeeded in clearing up the relative authority of these various and contradictory criteria. The final word of science, so far, is that we have at least two, perhaps three, great families of human beings— the whites and Negroes, possibly the yellow race. That other races have arisen from the intermingling of the blood of these two. This broad division of the world's races which men like Huxley and Raetzel have introduced as more nearly true than the old five-race scheme of Blumenbach, is nothing more than an acknowledgment that, so far as purely physical characteristics are concerned, the differences between men do not explain all the differences of their history. It declares, as Darwin himself said, that great as is the physical unlikeness of the various races of men their likenesses are greater, and upon this rests the whole scientific doctrine of Human Brotherhood.

Although the wonderful developments of human history teach that the grosser physical differences of color, hair and bone go but a short way toward explaining the different roles which groups of men have played in Human Progress, yet there are differences—subtle, delicate and elusive, though they may be—which have silently but definitely separated men into groups. While these subtle forces have generally followed the natural cleavage of common blood, descent and physical peculiarities, they have at other times swept across and ignored these. At all times, however, they have divided human beings into races, which, while they perhaps transcend scientific definition, nevertheless, are clearly defined to the eye of the Historian and Sociologist.

If this be true, then the history of the world is the history, not of individuals, but of groups, not of nations, but of races, and he who ignores or seeks to override the race idea in human history ignores and overrides the central thought of all history. What, then, is a race? It is a vast family of human beings, generally of common blood and language, always of common history, traditions and impulses, who are both voluntarily and involuntarily striving together for the accomplishment of certain more or less vividly conceived ideals of life.

Turning to real history, there can be no doubt, first, as to the widespread, nay, universal, prevalence of the race idea, the race spirit, the race ideal, and as to its efficiency as the vastest and most ingenious invention for human progress. We, who have been reared and trained under the individualistic philosophy of the Declaration of Independence and the laisser-faire philosophy of Adam Smith, are loath to see and loath to acknowledge this patent fact of human history. We see the Pharaohs, Caesars, Toussaints and Napoleons of history and forget the vast races of which they were but epitomized expressions. We are apt to think in our American impatience, that while it may have been true in the past that closed race groups made history, that here in conglomerate America *nous avons changer tout cela*—we have changed all that, and have no need of this ancient instrument of progress. This assumption of which the Negro people are especially fond, can not be established by a careful consideration of history.

We find upon the world's stage today eight distinctly differentiated races, in the sense in which History tells us the word must be used. They are, the Slavs of eastern Europe, the Teutons of middle Europe, the English of Great Britain and America, the Romance nations of Southern and Western Europe, the Negroes of Africa and America, the Semitic people of Western Asia and Northern Africa, the Hindoos of Central Asia and the Mongolians of Eastern Asia. There are, of course, other minor race groups, as the American Indians, the Esquimaux and the South Sea Islanders; these larger races, too, are far from homogeneous; the Slav includes the Czech, the Magyar, the Pole and the Russian; the Teuton includes the German, the Scandinavian and the Dutch; the English include the Scotch, the Irish and the conglomerate American. Under Romance nations the widely-differing Frenchman, Italian, Sicilian and Spaniard are comprehended. The term Negro is, perhaps, the most indefinite of all, combining the Mulattoes and Zamboes of America and the Egyptians, Bantus and Bushmen of Africa. Among the Hindoos are traces of widely differing nations, while the great Chinese, Tartar, Corean and Japanese families fall under the one designation—Mongolian.

The question now is: What is the real distinction between these nations? Is it the physical differences of blood, color and cranial measurements? Certainly we must all acknowledge that physical differences play a great part, and that, with wide exceptions and qualifications, these eight great races of to-day follow the cleavage of physical race distinctions; the English and Teuton represent the white variety of mankind; the Mongolian, the yellow; the Negroes, the black. Between these are many crosses and mixtures, where Mongolian and Teuton have blended into the Slav, and other mixtures have produced the Romance nations and the Semites. But while race differences have followed mainly physical race lines, yet no mere physical distinctions would really define or explain the deeper differences—the cohesiveness and continuity of these groups. The deeper differences are spiritual, psychical, differences—undoubtedly based on the physical, but infinitely transcending them. The forces that bind together the Teuton nations are, then, first, their race identity and common blood; secondly, and more important, a common history, common laws and religion, similar habits of thought and a conscious striving together for certain ideals of life. The whole process which has brought about these race differentiations has been a growth, and the great characteristic of this growth has been the differentiation of spiritual and mental differences between great races of mankind and the integration of physical differences.

The age of nomadic tribes of closely related individuals represents the maximum of physical differences. They were practically vast families, and there were as many groups as families. As the families came together to form cities the physical differences lessened, purity of blood was replaced by the requirement of domicile, and all who lived within the city bounds became gradually to be regarded as members of the group; *i.e.,* there was a slight and slow breaking down of physical barriers. This, however, was accompanied by an increase of the spiritual and social differences between cities. This city became husbandmen, this, merchants, another warriors, and so on. The *ideals of life* for which the different cities struggled were different. When at last cities began to coalesce into nations there was another breaking down of barriers which separated groups of men. The larger and broader differences of color, hair and physical proportions were not by any means ignored, but myriads of minor differences disappeared, and the sociological and historical races of men began to approximate the present division of races as indicated by physical researches. At the same time the spiritual and physical differences of race groups which constituted the nations became deep and decisive. The English nation stood for constitutional liberty and commercial freedom; the German nation for science and philosophy; the Romance nations stood for literature and art, and the other race groups are striving, each in its own way, to develope for civilization its particular message, its particular ideal, which shall help to guide the world nearer and nearer that perfection of human life for which we all long, that

"one far off Divine event."

This has been the function of race differences up to the present time. What shall be its function in the future? Manifestly some of the great races of today—particularly the Negro race—have not as yet given to civilization the full spiritual message which they are capable of giving. I will not say that the Negro race has as yet given no message to the world, for it is still a mooted question among scientists as to just how far Egyptian civilization was Negro in its origin; if it was not wholly Negro, it was certainly very closely allied. Be that as it may, however the fact still remains that the full, complete Negro message of the whole Negro race has not as yet been given to the world: that the messages and ideal of the yellow race have not been completed, and that the striving of the mighty Slavs has but begun. The question is, then: How shall this message be delivered; how shall these various ideals be realized? The answer is plain: By the development of these race groups, not as individuals, but as races. For the development of Japanese genius, Japanese literature and art, Japanese spirit, only Japanese, bound and welded together, Japanese inspired by one vast ideal, can work out in its fullness the wonderful message which Japan has for the nations of the earth. For the development of Negro genius, of Negro literature and art, of Negro spirit, only Negroes bound and welded together, Negroes inspired by one vast ideal, can work out in its fullness the great message we have for humanity. We cannot reverse history; we are subject to the same natural laws as other races, and if the Negro is ever to be a factor in the world's history—if among the gaily-colored banners that deck the broad ram-parts of civilization is to hang one uncompromising black, then it must be placed there by black hands, fashioned by black heads and hallowed by the travail of 200,000,000 black hearts beating in one glad song of jubilee.

For this reason, the advance guard of the Negro people—the 8,000,000 people of Negro blood in the United States of America—must soon come to realize that if they are to take their just place in the van of Pan-Negroism, then their destiny is *not* absorption by the white Americans. That if in America it is to be proven for the first time in the modern world that not only Negroes are capable of evolving individual men like Toussaint, the Saviour, but are a nation stored with wonderful possibilities of culture, then their destiny is not a servile imitation of Anglo-Saxon culture, but a stalwart originality which shall unswervingly follow Negro ideals.

It may, however, be objected here that the situation of our race in America renders this attitude impossible; that our sole hope of salvation lies in our being able to lose our race identity in the commingled blood of the nation; and that any other course would merely increase the friction of races which we call race prejudice, and against which we have so long and so earnestly fought.

Here, then, is the dilemma, and it is a puzzling one, I admit. No Negro who has given earnest thought to the situation of his people in America has failed, at some time in life, to find himself at these cross-roads; has failed to ask himself at some time: What, after all, am I? Am I an American or am I a Negro? Can I be both? Or is it my duty to cease to be a Negro as soon as possible and be an American? If I strive as a Negro, am I not perpetuating the very cleft that threatens and separates Black and White America? Is not my only possible practical aim the subduction of all that is Negro in me to the American? Does my black blood place upon me any more obligation to assert my nationality than German, or Irish or Italian blood would?

It is such incessant self-questioning and the hesitation that arises from it, that is making the present period a time of vacillation and contradiction for the American Negro; combined race action is stifled, race responsibility is shirked, race enterprises languish, and the best blood, the best talent, the best energy of the Negro people cannot be marshalled to do the bidding of the race. They stand back to make room for every rascal and demagogue who chooses to cloak his selfish deviltry under the veil of race pride.

Is this right? Is it rational? Is it good policy? Have we in America a distinct mission as a race—a distinct sphere of action and an opportunity for race development, or is self-obliteration the highest end to which Negro blood dare aspire?

If we carefully consider what race prejudice really is, we find it, historically, to be nothing but the friction between different groups of people; it is the difference in aim, in feeling, in ideals of two different races; if, now, this difference exists touching territory, laws, language, or even religion, it is manifest that these people cannot live in the same territory without fatal collision; but if, on the other hand, there is substantial agreement in laws, language and religion; if there is a satisfactory adjustment of economic life, then there is no reason why, in the same country and on the same street, two or three great national ideals might not thrive and develop, that men of different races might not strive together for their race ideals as well, perhaps even better, than in isolation. Here, it seems to me, is the reading of the riddle that puzzles so many of us. We are Americans, not only by birth and by citizenship, but by our political ideals, our language, our religion. Farther than that, our Americanism does not go. At that point, we are Negroes, members of a vast historic race that from the very dawn of creation has slept, but half awakening in the dark forests of its African fatherland. We are the first fruits of this new nation, the harbinger of that black to-morrow which is yet destined to soften the whiteness of the Teutonic to-day. We are that people whose subtle sense of song has given America its only American music, its only American fairy tales, its only touch of pathos and humor amid its mad money-getting plutocracy. As such, it is our duty to conserve our physical powers, our intellectual endowments, our spiritual ideals; as a race we must strive by race organization, by race solidarity, by race unity to the realization of that broader humanity which freely recognizes differences in men, but sternly deprecates inequality in their opportunities of development.

For the accomplishment of these ends we need race organizations: Negro colleges, Negro newspapers, Negro business organizations, a Negro school of literature and art, and an intellectual clearing house, for all these products of the Negro mind, which we may call a Negro Academy. Not only is all this necessary for positive advance, it is absolutely imperative for negative defense. Let us not deceive ourselves at our situation in this country. Weighted with a heritage of moral iniquity from our past history, hard pressed in the economic world by foreign immigrants and native prejudice, hated here, despised there and pitied everywhere; our one haven of refuge is ourselves, and but one means of advance, our own belief in our great destiny, our own implicit trust in our ability and worth. There is no power under God's high heaven that can stop the advance of eight thousand thousand honest, earnest, inspired and united people. But—and here is the rub—they *must* be honest, fearlessly criticising their own faults, zealously correcting them; they must be *earnest*. No people that laughs at itself, and ridicules itself, and wishes to God it was anything but itself ever wrote its name in history; it *must* be inspired with the Divine faith of our black mothers, that out of the blood and dust of battle will march a victorious host, a mighty nation, a peculiar people, to speak to the nations of earth a Divine truth that shall make them free. And such a people must be united; not merely united for the organized theft of political spoils, not united to disgrace religion with whoremongers and ward-heelers; not united merely to protest and pass resolutions, but united to stop the ravages of consumption among the Negro people, united to keep black boys from loafing, gambling and crime; united to guard the purity of black women and to reduce that vast army of black prostitutes that is today marching to hell; and united in serious organizations, to determine by careful conference and thoughtful interchange of opinion the broad lines of policy and action for the American Negro.

This, is the reason for being which the American Negro Academy has. It aims at once to be the epitome and expression of the intellect of the black-blooded people of America, the exponent of the race ideals of one of the world's great races. As such, the Academy must, if successful, be

a. Representative in character.
b. Impartial in conduct.
c. Firm in leadership.

It must be representative in character; not in that it represents all interests or all factions, but in that it seeks to comprise something of the *best* thought, the most unselfish striving and the highest ideals. There are scattered in forgotten nooks and corners throughout the land, Negroes of same considerable training, of high minds, and high motives, who are unknown to their fellows, who exert far too little influence. These the Negro Academy should strive to bring into touch with each other and to give them a common mouthpiece.

The Academy should be impartial in conduct; while it aims to exalt the people it should aim to do so by truth—not by lies, by honesty—not by flattery. It should continually impress the fact upon the Negro people that they must not expect to have things done for them—they MUST DO FOR THEMSELVES; that they have on their hands a vast work of self-reformation to do, and that a little less complaint and whining, and a little more dogged work and manly striving would do us more credit and benefit than a thousand Force or Civil Rights bills.

Finally, the American Negro Academy must point out a practical path of advance to the Negro people; there lie before every Negro today hundreds of questions of policy and right which must be settled and which each one settles now, not in accordance with any rule, but by impulse or individual preference; for instance: What should be the attitude of Negroes toward the educational qualification for voters? What should be our attitude toward separate schools? How should we meet discrimi-nations on railways and in hotels? Such questions need not so much spe-cific answers for each part as a general expression of policy, and nobody should be better fitted to announce such a policy than a representative honest Negro Academy.

All this, however, must come in time after careful organization and long conference. The immediate work before us should be practical and have direct bearing upon the situation of the Negro. The historical work of collecting the laws of the United States and of the various States of the Union with regard to the Negro is a work of such magnitude and impor-tance that no body but one like this could think of undertaking it. If we could accomplish that one task we would justify our existence.

In the field of Sociology an appalling work lies before us. First, we must unflinchingly and bravely face the truth, not with apologies, but with solemn earnestness. The Negro Academy ought to sound a note of warning that would echo in every black cabin in the land: *Unless we con-quer our present vices they will conquer us;* we are diseased, we are de-veloping criminal tendencies, and an alarmingly large percentage of our men and women are sexually impure. The Negro Academy should stand and proclaim this over the housetops, crying with Garrison: *I will not equivocate, I will not retreat a single inch, and I will be heard.* The Acad-emy should seek to gather about it the talented, unselfish men, the pure and noble-minded women, to fight an army of devils that disgraces our manhood and our womanhood. There does not stand today upon God's earth a race more capable in muscle, in intellect, in morals, than the American Negro, if he will bend his energies in the right direction; if he will

> Burst his birth's invidious bar
> And grasp the skirts of happy chance,
> And breast the blows of circumstance,
> And grapple with his evil star.

In science and morals, I have indicated two fields of work for the Academy. Finally, in practical policy, I wish to suggest the following *Academy Creed:*

1. We believe that the Negro people, as a race, have a contribution to make to civilization and humanity, which no other race can make.

2. We believe it the duty of the Americans of Negro descent, as a body, to maintain their race identity until this mission of the Negro peo-ple is accomplished, and the ideal of human brotherhood has become a practical possibility.

3. We believe that, unless modern civilization is a failure, it is en-tirely feasible and practicable for two races in such essential political,

economic and religious harmony as the white and colored people of America, to develop side by side in peace and mutual happiness, the peculiar contribution which each has to make to the culture of their common country.

4. As a means to this end we advocate, not such social equality between these races as would disregard human likes and dislikes, but such a social equilibrium as would, throughout all the complicated relations of life, give due and just consideration to culture, ability, and moral worth, whether they be found under white or black skins.

5. We believe that the first and greatest step toward the settlement of the present friction between the races—commonly called the Negro Problem—lies in the correction of the immorality, crime and laziness among the Negroes themselves, which still remains as a heritage from slavery. We believe that only earnest and long continued efforts on our own part can cure these social ills.

6. We believe that the second great step toward a better adjustment of the relations between the races, should be a more impartial selection of ability in the economic and intellectual world, and a greater respect for personal liberty and worth, regardless of race. We believe that only earnest efforts on the part of the white people of this country will bring much needed reform in these matters.

7. On the basis of the foregoing declaration, and firmly believing in our high destiny, we, as American Negroes, are resolved to strive in every honorable way for the realization of the best and highest aims, for the development of strong manhood and pure womanhood, and for the rearing of a race ideal in America and Africa, to the glory of God and the uplifting of the Negro people.

▲ How Natives Think

Lucien Levy-Bruhl

Lucien Levy-Bruhl (1857–1939), one of the leading ethnologists of his time, was a French philosopher who taught at the Sorbonne from 1896 to 1927. He developed a theory of non-Western cultures that rejected the view, current in the work of anthropologists such as Frazier and Tylor, that myth, magic, and spiritual agency were simply protoscientific notions that had failed to evolve into the scientific form current in modern European cultures. Rather, he argued that traditional beliefs in non-Western cultures were based on concepts that were not intellectual and were not subject to the usual laws of logic.

Levy-Bruhl holds that the manner in which concepts are formed and used varies from culture to culture, and he terms such concepts "collective representations." Whereas the most important concepts in Western culture are learned primarily in academic settings and have a long history of intellectual development, the most important concepts in non-Western cultures are typically learned in rites and rituals that involve intense affective and psychomotor experiences. Such concepts are mystical rather than intellectual and refer to forces, actions, and entities that are real, but imperceptible to the senses. Concepts learned through rites and rituals are not organized in accordance with the laws of logic, and allow for things to be both themselves and something else simultaneously. Thus, there is no contradiction in classifying an entity as being both a person and also a bird, in believing that a person can be in two different places simultaneously, or in insisting that a causal connection exists between a person and an image of the person and between a dream and real-life events.

For Levy-Bruhl, primitive people have a different concept of causality that allows for the existence of spiritual agency, so that purely physical explanations are never sufficient. Mystical causation is not grasped by rational inference but rather by acts of divination. Notwithstanding their differences, however, both are modes of discernment that have evolved within the social settings of their respective cultural settings. Mystical connections felt within an affective realm is as socialized for primitive cultures as is the intellectual realm for modern cultures. In traditional cultures, emotional significance is as important as logical consistency is in modern cultures, and spiritual agency is as causally effective as empirical agency. Medicine, sorcery, witchcraft, dreams, divination, and ancestor worship are the means through which mystical forces operate in traditional cultures. And knowledge of supernatural reality requires participatory involvement not mere logical understanding. Indeed, the aim of myths, rites, and ceremonies is to create a felt participation between the individual and the mystical elements of that culture. Ecstasy and possession are forms in which such felt participation manifest themselves.

    As we shall see, Levy-Bruhl's characterization of traditional non-Western cultures exerted a profound effect on the interpretation of African culture given by Tempels, Senghor, and many others. His ideas evolved during his lifetime and continue to be used in the work of contemporary anthropologists such as Tambiah, Lloyd, and others.*

COLLECTIVE REPRESENTATIONS IN PRIMITIVES' PERCEPTIONS AND THE MYSTICAL CHARACTER OF SUCH

I

Before undertaking an investigation of the most general laws governing collective representations among undeveloped peoples, it may be as well to determine what the essential characteristics of these representations are, and thus avoid an ambiguity which is otherwise almost inevitable. The terminology used in the analysis of mental functions is suited to functions such as the philosophers, psychologists, and logicians of our civilization have formulated and defined. If we admit these functions to be identical in all human aggregates, there is no difficulty in the matter; the same terminology can be employed throughout, with the mental reservation that "savages" have minds more like those of children than of adults. But if we abandon this position—and we have the strongest reasons for considering it untenable—then the terms, divisions, classifications, we make use of in analysing our own mental functions are not suitable for those which differ from them; on the contrary, they prove a source of confusion and error. In studying primitive mentality, which is a new subject, we shall probably require a fresh terminology. At any rate it will be necessary to specify the new meaning which some expressions already in use should assume when applied to an object differing from that they have hitherto betokened.

---

    * See Tambiah, Stanley J.: *Magic, Science, Religion, and the Scope of Rationality* (NY: Cambridge University Press, 1990); Lloyd, G.E.R.: *Demystifying Mentalities* (NY: Cambridge University Press, 1990)

This is the case, for instance, with the term "collective representations."

In the current parlance of psychology which classifies phenomena as emotional, motor, or intellectual, "representation" is placed in the last category. We understand by it a matter of cognizance, inasmuch as the mind simply has the image or idea of an object. We do not deny that in the actual mental life every representation affects the inclinations more or less, and tends to produce or inhibit some movement. But, by an abstraction which in a great many cases is nothing out of the ordinary, we disregard these elements of the representation, retaining only its essential relation to the object which it makes known to us. The representation is, *par excellence,* an intellectual or cognitive phenomenon.

It is not in this way, however, that we must understand the collective representations of primitives. Their mental activity is too little differentiated for it to be possible to consider ideas or images of objects by themselves apart from the emotions and passions which evoke these ideas or are evoked by them. Just because our mental activity is more differentiated, and we are more accustomed to analysing its functions, it is difficult for us to realize by any effort of imagination, more complex states in which emotional or motor elements are *integral parts* of the representation. It seems to us that these are not really representations, and in fact if we are to retain the term we must modify its meaning in some way. By this state of mental activity in primitives we must understand something which is not a purely or almost purely intellectual or cognitive phenomenon, but a more complex one, in which what is really "representation" to us is found blended with other elements of an emotional or motor character, coloured and imbued by them, and therefore implying a different attitude with regard to the objects represented.

Moreover, these collective representations are very often acquired by the individual in circumstances likely to make the most profound impression upon his sensibility. This is particularly true of those transmitted at the moment when he becomes a man, a conscious member of the social group, the moment when the initiation ceremonies cause him to undergo new birth,[1] when the secrets upon which the very life of the group depends are revealed to him, sometimes amid tortures which subject his nerves to the most severe tests. It would be difficult to exaggerate the intense emotional force of such representations. The object is not merely discerned by the mind in the form of an idea or image; according to the circumstances of the case, fear, hope, religious awe, the need and the ardent desire to be merged in one common essence, the passionate appeal to a protecting power—these are the soul of these representations, and make them at once cherished, formidable, and really *sacred* to the

---

[1] Vide Chap. VIII. pp. 352–3.

initiated. We must add, too, that the ceremonies in which these representations are translated into action, so to speak, take place periodically; consider the contagious effect of the emotional excitement of witnessing the movements which express them, the nervous exaltation engendered by excessive fatigue, the dances, the phenomena of ecstasy and of possession,—in fact everything which tends to revive and enhance the emotional nature of these collective representations. At any time during the intervals between the occurrences of these ceremonies, whenever the object of one of these representations once more arises in the consciousness of the "primitive," even should he be alone and in a calm frame of mind at the moment, it can never appear to him as a colourless and indifferent image. A wave of emotion will immediately surge over him, undoubtedly less intense than it was during the ceremonies, but yet strong enough for its cognitive aspect to be almost lost sight of in the emotions which surround it. Though in a lesser degree, the same character pertains to other collective representations—such, for instance, as those transmitted from generation to generation by means of myths and legends, and those which govern manners and customs which apparently are quite unimportant; for if these customs are respected and enforced, it is because the collective representations relating to them are imperative and something quite different from purely intellectual phenomena.

The collective representations of primitives, therefore, differ very profoundly from our ideas or concepts, nor are they their equivalent either. On the one hand, as we shall presently discover, they have not their logical character. On the other hand, not being genuine representations, in the strict sense of the term, they express, or rather imply, not only that the primitive actually has an image of the object in his mind, and thinks it real, but also that he has some hope or fear connected with it, that some definite influence emanates from it, or is exercised upon it. This influence is a virtue, an occult power which varies with objects and circumstances, but is always real to the primitive and forms an integral part of his representation. If I were to express in one word the general peculiarity of the collective representations which play so important a part in the mental activity of undeveloped peoples, I should say that this mental activity was a *mystic* one. In default of a better, I shall make use of this term—not referring thereby to the religious mysticism of our communities, which is something entirely different, but employing the word in the strictly defined sense in which "mystic" implies belief in forces and influences and actions which, though imperceptible to sense, are nevertheless real.

In other words, the reality surrounding the primitives is itself mystical. Not a single being or object or natural phenomenon in their collective representations is what it appears to be to our minds. Almost everything that we perceive therein either escapes their attention or is a matter of indifference to them. On the other hand, they see many things there of which we are unconscious. For instance, to the primitive who belongs to a totemic community, every animal, every plant, indeed every object, such as the sun, moon, and stars, forms part of a totem, and has its own class and sub-class. Consequently, each individual has his special affinities, and possesses powers over the members of his totem, class, and sub-class; he has obligations towards them, mystic relations with other totems, and so forth. Even in communities where this form does not exist, the group idea of certain animals (possibly of all, if our records were complete) is mystic in character. Thus, among the Huichols, "the birds that soar highest . . . are thought to see and hear everything, and to possess mystic powers, which are inherent in their wing and tail feathers." These feathers, carried by the shaman, "enable him to see and hear everything both above and below the earth . . . to cure the sick, transform the dead, call down the sun, etc."[2] The Cherokees believe that fishes live in companies like human beings, that they have their villages, their regular paths through the waters, and that they conduct themselves like beings endowed with reason.[3] They think, too, that illnesses—rheumatic affections in particular—proceed from a mystic influence exercised by animals which are angry with the hunters, and their medical practices testify to this belief.

In Malaya and in South Africa the crocodile, and in other places the tiger, leopard, elephant, snake, are the object of similar beliefs and practices, and if we recall the myths of which animals are the heroes, in both hemispheres, there is no mammal or bird or fish or even insect to which the most extraordinary mystic properties have not been attributed. Moreover, the magic practices and ceremonies which, among nearly all primitive peoples, are the necessary accompaniment of hunting and fishing, and the sacrificial rites to be observed when the quarry has been killed, are sufficiently clear testimony to the mystic properties and powers which enter into the collective representations relating to the animal world.

It is the same with plant life. It will doubtless suffice to mention the *intichiuma* ceremonies described by Spencer and Gillen, designed to secure, in mystic fashion, the normal reproduction of plants,—the development of agrarian rites, corresponding with the hunting and fishing ceremonial, in all places where primitive peoples depend wholly or partly on the cultivation of the soil for their subsistence—and lastly, the highly unusual mystic properties ascribed to sacred plants, as, for instance, the soma in Vedic India, and the *hikuli* among the Huichols.

Again, if we consider the human body, we shall find that each organ

[2] C. Lumholtz, *Unknown Mexico,* ii. pp. 7–8.
[3] J. Mooney, "The Sacred Formulas of the Cherokee," *E. B. Rept.,* vii. p. 375.

of it has its own mystic significance, as the widespread practice of cannibalism and the rites connected with human sacrifices (in Mexico, for instance) prove. The heart, liver, kidney, the eyes, the fat, marrow, and so on, are reputed to procure such and such an attribute for those who feed on them. The orifices of the body, the excreta of all kinds, the hair and nail-parings, the placenta and umbilical cord, the blood, and the various fluids of the body, can all exercise magic influences.[4] Collective representations attribute mystic power to all these things, and many widespread beliefs and practices relate to this power. So, too, certain parts of plants and animals possess peculiar virtues. "*Badi* is the name given to the evil principle which . . . attends (like an evil angel) everything in his life. . . . Von de Wall describes it as the 'enchanting or destroying influence which issues from anything; for example, from a tiger which one sees, from a poisonous tree which one passes under, from the saliva of a mad dog, from an action which one has performed.'"[5]

.   .   .   .

From these facts and many similar ones which we might quote, we can draw one conclusion: primitives perceive nothing in the same way as we do. The social *milieu* which surrounds them differs from ours, and precisely because it is different, the external world they perceive differs from that which we apprehend. Undoubtedly they have the same senses as ours—rather more acute than ours in a general way, in spite of our persuasion to the contrary—and their cerebral structure is like our own. But we have to bear in mind that which their collective representations instill into all their perceptions. Whatever the object presented to their minds, it implies mystic properties which are inextricably bound up with it, and the primitive, in perceiving it, never separates these from it.

To him there is no phenomenon which is, strictly speaking, a physical one, in the sense in which we use the term. The rippling water, the whistling wind, the falling rain, any natural phenomenon whatever, a sound, a colour,—these things are never perceived by him as they are by us, that is, as more or less compound movements bearing a definite relation to preceding and to subsequent movements. His perceptive organs have indeed grasped the displacement of a mass of material as ours do; familiar objects are readily recognized according to previous experience; in short, all the physiological and psychological processes of perception have actually taken place in him as in ourselves. Its result, however, is immediately enveloped in a state of complex consciousness, dominated by collective representations. Primitives see with eyes like ours, but they do not perceive with the same minds. We might almost say that their perceptions are made up of a nucleus surrounded by a layer of varying den-

[4] K. Th. Preuss, "Der Ursprung der Religion und Kunst," *Globus*, lxxxvi. p. 20; lxxxvii. p. 19.

[5] W. W. Skeat, *Malay Magic*, p. 427.

sity of representations which are social in their origin. And yet such a simile seems somewhat clumsy and inexact, for the primitive has not the least feeling of such a nucleus and surrounding layer; it is we who separate them; we, who by virtue of our mental habits cannot help distinguishing them. To the primitive the complex representation is still undifferentiated.

The profound difference which exists between primitive mentality and our own is shown even in the ordinary perception or mere apprehension of the very simplest things. Primitive perception is fundamentally mystic on account of the mystic nature of the collective representations which form an integral part of every perception. Ours has ceased to be so, at any rate with regard to most of the objects which surround us. Nothing appears alike to them and to us. For people like ourselves, speaking the language familiar to us, there is insurmountable difficulty in entering into their way of thinking. The longer we live among them, the more we approximate to their mental attitude, the more do we realize how impossible it is to yield to it entirely.

It is not correct to maintain, as is frequently done, that primitives associate occult powers, magic properties, a kind of soul or vital principle with all the objects which affect their senses or strike their imagination, and that their perceptions are surcharged with animistic beliefs. It is not a question of *association*. The mystic properties with which things and beings are imbued form an integral part of the idea to the primitive, who views it as a synthetic whole. It is at a later stage of social evolution that what we call a natural phenomenon tends to become the sole content of perception to the exclusion of the other elements, which then assume the aspect of beliefs, and finally appear superstitions. But as long as this "dissociation" does not take place, perception remains an undifferentiated whole. We might call it "polysynthetic," like words in the languages spoken by certain primitive peoples.

Finally, the same considerations apply equally to another class of phenomena—dreams—which occupy an important place in the primitive mind. To primitives the dream is not, as it is to us, simply a manifestation of mental activity which occurs during sleep, a more or less orderly series of representations to which, when awake, the dreamer would give no credence, because they lack the conditions essential to objective validity. This last characteristic, though it does not escape the primitives, seems to interest them but slightly. On the other hand, the dream, to them, is of far greater significance than to us. It is first a percept as real as those of the waking state, but above all it is a provision of the future, a communication and intercourse with spirits, souls, divinities, a means of establishing a relation with their own special guardian angel, and even of discovering who this may be. Their confidence in the reality of that which the dreams makes known to them is very profound. Tylor, Frazer, and the representatives of the English school of anthropology have brought together a vast number of facts which bear witness to this, collected by investigators of primitive peoples of the most diverse types. Shall I, too, quote some? In Australia "Sometimes a man dreams that someone has got some of his hair or a piece of his food, or of his 'possum rug, or indeed anything almost that he has used. If he dreams this several times he feels sure of it and calls his friends together, and tells them of his dreaming too much about 'that man,' who must have something belonging to him. . . . Sometimes natives only know about having their fat taken out by remembering something of it as in a dream."[6]

To the North American Indians, dreams, natural or induced, have an importance which it would be difficult to overestimate. "Sometimes it is the rational mind which is wandering, whilst the mind which feels continues to animate the body. Sometimes the familiar spirit gives wholesome advice upon what is about to happen; and sometimes it is a visit from the soul of the object of which one dreams. But in whatsoever fashion the dream may be conceived, it is always regarded as a sacred thing, and as the most usual method employed by the gods of making their will known to men. . . . Frequently it is an order from the spirits."[7] In Lejeune's *Relations de la Nouvelle France,* it is stated that the dream is "the god of the heathens"; and an observer of our own times says: "Dreams are to savages what the Bible is to us, the source of Divine revelation—with this important difference that they can produce this revelation at will by the medium of dreams."[8] Consequently the Indian will at once carry out what has been commanded or simply indicated to him in a dream. Mooney tells us that among the Cherokees, when a man dreams that he has been bitten by a snake, he must follow the same treatment as if he had really been bitten, for it is a witch-snake that has done the injury, and if he did not, swelling and ulceration would ensue, possibly even many years later.[9] In the *Relations de la Nouvelle France* we read that "a warrior, having dreamed that he had been taken prisoner in battle, anxious to avert the fatal consequences of such a dream, called all his friends together and implored them to help him in this misfortune. He begged them to prove themselves true friends by treating him as if he were an enemy. They therefore rushed upon him, stripped him naked, fettered him, and dragged him through the streets with the usual shouts and insults, and even made him mount the scaffold. . . . He thanked them warmly, believing that this imaginary captivity would ensure him against

[6] Howitt, "On Australian Medicine-men," *J.A.I.,* xvi. 1, pp. 29–30.

[7] Charlevoix, *Journal d'un Voyage dans l'Amérique Septentrionale,* iii. pp. 353–5.

[8] A. Gatschet, *The Klamath Language,* p. 77 (Contributions to *North American Ethnology,* ii. 1).

[9] "Myths of the Cherokee," *E. B. Rept.,* xix. p. 295.

being made prisoner in reality.... In another case, a man who had dreamed he saw his hut on fire, did not rest till he had witnessed its burning in reality.... A third, not believing that his dream would be sufficiently realistic if he were burned in effigy insisted on having fire applied to his legs, as is done with captives about to undergo capital punishment.... It was fully six months before he recovered from the burns."[10]

The Malays of Sarawak never doubt their blood-relationship with a certain animal, if they have dreamed about it. "Wan's great-great-grandfather became blood-brother to a crocodile.... Wan had several times met this crocodile in dreams. Thus in one dream he fell into the river where there were many crocodiles about. He climbed on to the head of one which said to him, 'Don't be afraid,' and carried him to the bank. Wan's father had charms given him by a crocodile and would not on any account kill one, and Wan clearly regards himself as being intimately related to crocodiles in general."[11]

In short, to conclude with a peculiarly happy dictum of Spencer and Gillen: "What a savage experiences during a dream is just as real to him as what he sees when he is awake."[12]

To explain these phenomena, are we to rely upon the current theory which refers them to a psychological illusion constantly obtaining among primitives? They would be unable to distinguish an actual perception from one which, though powerful, is merely imaginary. In all cases of life-like representation, the belief in the objectivity of this representation would appear. Accordingly, the apparition of a dead person would induce the belief that he was actually present. The representation of one's own self, in a dream, acting, travelling, conversing with persons who are at a distance or who have disappeared, would convince one that the soul does indeed leave the body during sleep and travels whither it feels conscious of going. "The supreme confusion in the thought of non-civilized individuals," says Powell, "is the confusion of the objective with the subjective."

Without disputing the general accuracy of the psychological law which is invoked here, I should like to point out that it does not wholly account for the way in which primitives represent their dreams, and the use to which they put them. In the first place, they distinguish very clearly between perceptions which come to them through dreams from those they receive in the waking state, however similar they may otherwise be. They even recognize different categories of dreams, and attribute a varying degree of validity to them. "The Ojibbeways have divided

---

[10] *Années,* pp. 46–8 (1661–2).

[11] Hose and Macdougall, "Relations between Men and Animals in Sarawak," *J.A.I.,* xxi. p. 191.

[12] Spencer and Gillen, *The Northern Tribes of Central Australia,* p. 451.

dreams into various classes, and given each a special name. The excellent Bishop Baraga, in his lexicon of that language, has collected the Indian names for a bad dream, an impure dream, an ominous dream, as well as for a good or happy dream."[13] "The Hidatsa have much faith in dreams, but usually regard as oracular only those which come after prayer, sacrifice, and fasting."[14] It is therefore with full knowledge of the circumstances and due reflection that primitives accord the one kind of perception as complete a credence as the other. Instead of saying, as people do, that primitives believe in what they perceive in the dream, *although* it is but a dream, I should say that they believe in it *because* it is a dream. The "illusion" theory does not suffice. How do we account for the fact that, knowing well that the dream *is* a dream, they should nevertheless rely upon it? This cannot be explained as a mere psychological process effected in the individual. Here again, we are obliged to take into account the collective representations which make both the perception and the dream something entirely different for the primitive from what they would be for us.

Our perception is directed towards the apprehension of an objective reality, and this reality alone. It eliminates all that might be of merely subjective importance, and in this it is in contrast with the dream. We do not understand how anything that is seen in a dream can be placed on a par with that which we see in the waking state: and if such a thing does occur we are forced to believe that it is the result of a very strong psychological illusion. But with the primitives there is no such violent contrast as this. Their perception is oriented in another fashion, and in it that which we call objective reality is united and mingled with, and often regulated by, mystic, imperceptible elements.

·   ·   ·   ·   ·   ·   ·   ·   ·   ·   ·   ·   ·

Thus not only does the time sequence in phenomena of the most impressive kind often remain unperceived by the primitive's mind, but he frequently believes firmly in an order of succession which is not borne out by experience, for experience can no more undeceive primitives than it can teach them. In an infinite number of cases, as we have seen, their minds are impervious to experience. Therefore when they make the cassocks of the missionaries responsible for the drought, or attribute an epidemic to a portrait, it is not merely the sequence in point of time which impresses their minds and becomes a causal relation to them. The mental process is a different and rather more complex one. That which we call experience and the natural order of phenomena does not find in primitives, minds prepared to receive and be impressed by it. On the contrary, their minds are already preoccupied with a large number of

[13] Kohl, Kitchi Gama: *Wanderings 'round Lake Superior*, p. 236.
[14] Dorsey, "Slovan Cults," Bureau of American Ethnology, Smithsonian Institute, Report XI, p. 516.

collective representations, by virtue of which objects, whatever they may be, living beings, inanimate objects, or articles manufactured by man, always present themselves charged with mystic properties. Consequently while these minds are very often unheedful of the objective relations, they pay great attention to the mystic connections, whether virtual or actual. These preformed connections are not derived from the experience of the present, and experience is powerless against them.

II

Let us then no longer endeavour to account for these connections either by the mental weakness of primitives, or by the association of ideas, or by a naïve application of the principle of causality, or yet by the fallacy *post hoc, ergo propter hoc;* in short, let us abandon the attempt to refer their mental activity to an inferior variety of our own. Rather let us consider these connections in themselves, and see whether they do not depend upon a general law, a common foundation for those mystic relations which primitive mentality so frequently senses in beings and objects. Now there is one element which is never lacking in such relations. In varying forms and degrees they all involve a "participation" between persons or objects which form part of a collective representation. For this reason I shall, in default of a better term, call the principle which is peculiar to "primitive" mentality, which governs the connections and the preconnections of such representations, *the law of participation.*

At the moment it would be difficult to formulate this law in abstract terms. It will be sufficiently defined in the course of this chapter, although that which we desire to define scarcely enters the ordinary framework of our thought. However, in default of a wholly satisfactory formula, we can make an attempt to approximate it. I should be inclined to say that in the collective representations of primitive mentality, objects, beings, phenomena can be, though in a way incomprehensible to us, both themselves and something other than themselves. In a fashion which is no less incomprehensible, they give forth and they receive mystic powers, virtues, qualities, influences, which make themselves felt outside, without ceasing to remain where they are.

In other words, the opposition between the one and the many, the same and another, and so forth, does not impose upon this mentality the necessity of affirming one of the terms if the other be denied, or vice versa. This opposition is of but secondary interest. Sometimes it is perceived, and frequently, too, it is not. It often disappears entirely before the mystic community of substance in entities which, in our thought, could not be confused without absurdity. For instance, "the Trumai (a tribe of Northern Brazil) say that they are aquatic animals.—The Bororo (a neighbouring tribe) boast that they are red araras (parakeets)." This does not merely signify that after their death they become araras, nor that araras are metamorphosed Bororos, and must be treated as such. It is something entirely different. "The Bororos," says Von den Steinen, who would not believe it, but finally had to give in to their explicit affirmations, "give one rigidly to understand that they are araras *at the present time,* just as if a caterpillar declared itself to be a butterfly."[15] It is not a name they give themselves, nor a relationship that they claim. What they desire to express by it is actual identity. That they can be both the human beings they are and the birds of scarlet plumage at the same time, Von den Steinen regards as inconceivable, but to the mentality that is governed by the law of participation there is no difficulty in the matter. All communities which are totemic in form admit of collective representations of this kind, implying similar identity of the individual members of a totemic group and their totem.

From the dynamic standpoint also, the creation of entities and phenomena, the manifestation of such and such an occurrence, are the result of a mystic influence which is communicated, under conditions themselves of mystic nature, from one being or object to another. They depend upon a participation which is represented in very varied forms: contact, transference, sympathy, telekinesis, etc. In many aggregates of an undeveloped type the abundance of game, fish, or fruit, the regularity of the seasons, and the rainfall, are connected with the performance of certain ceremonies by individuals destined thereto, or to the presence or to the well-being of a sacred personality who possesses a special mystic power. Or yet again, the newborn child feels the effects of everything its father does, what he eats, etc. The Indian, out hunting or engaged in warfare, is fortunate or unfortunate according to whether his wife, left behind in the camp, eats, or abstains from eating, certain foods, or is doing or not doing certain things. The collective representations abound in relations of this nature. What we call the natural relation of cause and effect passes unnoticed, or is of but slight importance. It is the mystic participations which are in the front rank, and frequently occupy the whole field.

On this account the mentality of primitives may be called *prelogical* with as good reason as it may be termed *mystic*. These are two aspects of the same fundamental quality, rather than two distinct characteristics. If we take the content of the representations more particularly into account, we shall call it mystic—and, if the connections are the chief consideration, we pronounce it prelogical. By *prelogical* we do not mean to assert that such a mentality constitutes a kind of antecedent stage, in point of time, to the birth of logical thought. Have there ever existed groups of human or pre-human beings whose collective representations have not yet been subject to the laws of logic? We do not know, and in any case, it

[15] K. von den Steinen, *Unter den Naturvölkern Zentralbrasiliens,* pp. 305–6.

seems to be very improbable. At any rate, the mentality of these undeveloped peoples which, for want of a better term, I call *prelogical,* does
not partake of that nature. It is not *antilogical;* it is not *alogical* either. By
designating it "prelogical" I merely wish to state that it does not bind itself down, as our thought does, to avoiding contradiction. It obeys the
law of participation first and foremost. Thus oriented, it does not expressly delight in what is contradictory (which would make it merely absurd in our eyes), but neither does it take pains to avoid it. It is often
wholly indifferent to it, and that makes it so hard to follow.

As has been said, these characteristics apply only to the collective
representations and their connections. Considered as an individual, the
primitive, in so far as he thinks and acts independently of these collective representations where possible, will usually feel, argue and act as
we should expect him to do. The inferences he draws will be just those
which would seem reasonable to us in like circumstances. If he has
brought down two birds, for instance, and only picks up one, he will ask
himself what has become of the other, and will look for it. If rain over-
takes and inconveniences him, he will seek shelter. If he encounters a
wild beast, he will strive his utmost to escape, and so forth.

.   .   .   .

THE FUNCTIONING OF PRELOGICAL MENTALITY

I

It would be idle to institute any comparison between the discursive
processes of prelogical mentality and those of our thought, or to look for
any correspondence between the two, for we should have no grounds on
which to base a hypothesis. We have no *a priori* reason for admitting
that the same process is used by both. The discursive operations of our
rational thought—the analysis of which has been made familiar to us
through psychology and logic—require the existence and the employment of much that is intricate, in the form of categories, concepts, and
abstract terms. They also assume an intellectual functioning, properly so
called, that is already well-differentiated. In short, they imply an ensemble of conditions which we do not find existing anywhere in social aggregates of a primitive type. On the other hand, as we have seen, prelogical
mentality has its own laws, to which its discursive operations must necessarily submit.

In order to determine what these operations are, and how they are
accomplished, our only resource is to describe and analyse them according to the direct connections we have observed between the collective
representations. This is a most difficult task, both on account of the char-

acter of these same operations, and of the incompleteness of the documents at our disposal. The attempt I am about to make, therefore, will undoubtedly yield an imperfect and very unfinished outline only, but it will not have been useless if it shows that the operations of prelogical mentality depend upon the law of participation, and cannot be explained apart from it.

Before we begin to analyse these operations, we must first of all say something about the co-existence of the laws of contradiction and participation. Are we to suppose that certain operations are governed entirely by the first, and others just as exclusively by the second, of these laws? Do we imagine, for instance, that every individual representation is the result of thought that is already logical, whilst collective representations alone submit to a law peculiar to prelogical mentality? Water-tight compartments of this kind are inconceivable, if only because it is very difficult—indeed almost impossible—to trace a distinct line of demarcation between individual and collective representations. What can be more individual, to all appearances, than sense-perceptions? Nevertheless we have noted the extent to which the primitive's sense-perceptions are enveloped in mystic elements which cannot be separated from them and which undoubtedly are collective in their nature. The same may be said of most of the emotions experienced and of most of the movements which take place almost instinctively at the sight of a certain object, even quite an ordinary one. In these communities as much as in our own, perhaps even more so, the whole mental life of the individual is profoundly *socialized.*

We must therefore expect to see the influence of the law of participation exercised, not only pre-eminently in what we have called collective representations, but also making itself felt more or less emphatically in all mental operations. Conversely, the effect of the law of contradiction is already more or less strong and constant, first of all in operations which would be impossible without it (such as numeration, inference, etc.) and then also in those which are governed by the law of participation. There is nothing but what is changing and unstable, and this is one of the greatest difficulties with which we have to contend. In the mentality of primitive peoples, the logical and prelogical are not arranged in layers and separated from each other like oil and water in a glass. They permeate each other, and the result is a mixture which is a very difficult matter to differentiate. Since the laws of logic absolutely exclude, in our own thought, everything that is directly contrary to itself, we find it hard to get accustomed to a mentality in which the logical and prelogical can be co-existent and make themselves equally perceptible in mental processes. The prelogical element which our collective representations still contain is too small to enable us to reconstruct a mental state in which the prelogical, when dominant, does not *exclude* what is logical.

What strikes us first of all is that prelogical mentality is little given to analysis. Undoubtedly in a certain sense every act of thought is synthetic, but when it is a question of logical thought this synthesis implies, in nearly every case, a previous analysis. Relations are expressed by judgments only after the food for thought has first been well digested, and subjected to elaboration, differentiation, and classification. Judgment deals with ideas which have been rigidly defined, and these are themselves the proof and product of previous logical processes. This previous work, in which a large number of successive analyses and syntheses occur and are recorded, is received ready-made by every individual in our communities when he first learns to talk, by means of the education inseparably bound up with his natural development; so much so indeed that certain philosophers have believed in the supernatural origin of language. In this way the claims of logical thought are urged, established, and then confirmed in each individual mind by the uninterrupted constraining force of his social environment, by means of language itself and of what is transmitted by language. This is a heritage of which no member of our community is deprived, and which none would ever dream of refusing. Logical discipline is thus imposed upon his mental operations with irresistible force. The fresh syntheses which it effects must submit to the definitions of the concepts employed, definitions which the previous logical operations have legitimatized. In short, his mental activity, in whatever form it may be exercised, must submit to the law of contradiction.

The conditions under which prelogical mentality operates are altogether different. There is no doubt that it, too, is transmitted socially by means of language and concepts without which it could not be exercised. It also implies work which has been previously accomplished, an inheritance handed down from one generation to another. But these concepts differ from ours,[16] and consequently the mental operations are also different. Prelogical mentality is essentially synthetic. By this I mean that the syntheses which compose it do not imply previous analyses of which the result has been registered in definite concepts, as is the case with those in which logical thought operates. In other words, the connecting-links of the representations are given, as a rule, with the representations themselves. In it, too, the syntheses appear to be primitive and, as we have seen in our study of perception, they are nearly always both undecomposed and undecomposable. This, too, explains why primitive mentality seems both impervious to experience and insensible to contradiction in so many instances. Collective representations do not present themselves separately to it, nor are they analysed and then arranged in

[16] Vide Chap. III. pp. 126–7.

logical sequence by it. They are always bound up with preperceptions, preconceptions, preconnections, and we might almost say with prejudgments; and thus it is that primitive mentality, just because it is mystical, is also prelogical.

But, someone may object, if the mental operations of uncivilized peoples differ from logical thinking in their mode of functioning, if their paramount law is the law of participation, which *a priori* allows of these preconnections and participations of participations which are so infinitely varied, if their mentality does finally escape the control of experience, will it not appear to us unbridled and unregulated, and just as purely arbitrary as it is impenetrable? Now in nearly all inferior races we find, on the contrary, that the mentality is stable, fixed and almost invariable, not only in its essential elements, but in the very content and even in the details of its representations. The reason is that this mentality, *although* not subordinate to logical processes, or rather, precisely *because* it does not submit to them, is not free. Its uniformity reflects the uniformity of the social structure with which it corresponds. Institutions fix beforehand, so to speak *ne varietur,* the combinations of collective representations which are actually possible. The number of the connecting-links between the representations and the methods by which they are connected are predetermined at the same time as the representations themselves. It is especially in the preconnections thus established that the predominance of the law of participation and the weakness of the strictly intellectual claims are made manifest.

Moreover, collective representations as a rule form part of a mystical complex in which the emotional and passionate elements scarcely allow thought, as thought, to obtain any mastery. To primitive mentality the bare fact, the actual object, hardly exists. Nothing presents itself to it that is not wrapped about with the elements of mystery: every object it perceives, whether ordinary or not, moves it more or less, and moves it in a way which is itself predestined by tradition. For except for the emotions which are strictly individual and dependent upon immediate reaction of the organism, there is nothing more *socialized* among primitives than are their emotions. Thus the nature which is perceived, felt, and lived by the members of an undeveloped community, is necessarily predetermined and unvarying to a certain extent, as long as the organized institutions of the group remain unaltered. This mystical and prelogical mentality will evolve only when the primitive syntheses, the preconnections of collective representations are gradually dissolved and decomposed; in other words, when experience and logical claims win their way against the law of participation. Then, in submitting to these claims, "thought," properly so called, will begin to be differentiated, independent, and free. Intellectual operations of a slightly complex kind will become possible, and the logical process to which thought will gradually attain, is both the necessary condition of its liberty and the indispensable instrument of its progress.

II

In the first place, in prelogical mentality memory plays a much more important part than it does in our mental life, in which certain functions which it used to perform have been taken from it and transformed. Our wealth of social thought is transmitted, in condensed form, through a hierarchy of concepts which co-ordinate with, or are subordinate to, each other. In primitive peoples it consists of a frequently enormous number of involved and complex collective representations. It is almost entirely transmitted through the memory. During the entire course of life, whether in sacred or profane matters, an appeal which without our active volition induces *us* to exercise the logical function, awakens in the primitive a complex and often mystic recollection which regulates action. And this recollection even has a special tone which distinguishes it from ours. The constant use of the logical process which abstract concepts involve, the, so to speak, *natural* use of languages relying upon this process, disposes our memory preferably to retain the relations which have preponderating importance from the objective and logical standpoint. In prelogical mentality both the aspect and tendencies of memory are quite different because its contents are of a different character. It is both very accurate and very emotional. It reconstructs the complex collective representations with a wealth of detail, and always in the order in which they are traditionally connected, according to relations which are essentially mystic. Since it thus, to a certain extent, supplements logical functions, it exercises the privileges of these to a corresponding degree. For instance, a representation inevitably evoked as the result of another frequently has the quality of a conclusion. Thus it is, as we shall see, that a sign is nearly always taken to be a cause.

The preconnections, preperceptions, and preconclusions which play so great a part in the mentality of uncivilized peoples do not involve any logical activity; they are simply committed to memory. We must therefore expect to find the memory extremely well developed in primitives, and this is, in fact, reported by observers. But since they unreflectingly assume that memory with these primitives has just the same functions as with us, they show themselves both surprised and disconcerted by this. It seems to them that it is accomplishing marvellous feats, while it is merely being exercised in a normal way.

.   .   .   .

This extraordinary development of memory, and of a memory which faithfully reproduces the minutest details of sense-impressions in the correct order of their appearance, is shown moreover by the wealth of vocabulary and the grammatical complexity of the languages. Now the very men who speak these languages and possess this power of memory are (in Australia or Northern Brazil, for instance) incapable of counting beyond two or three. The slightest mental effort involving abstract reasoning, however elementary it may be, is so distasteful to them that they immediately declare themselves tired and give it up. We must admit therefore, as we have already said, that with them memory takes the place (at very great cost, no doubt, but at any rate it does take the place) of operations which elsewhere depend upon a logical process. With us, in everything that relates to intellectual functions, memory is confined to the subordinate rôle of registering the results which have been acquired by a logical elaboration of concepts. But to prelogical mentality, recollections are almost exclusively highly complex representations which succeed each other in unvarying order, and in which the most elementary of logical operations would be very difficult (since language does not lend itself thereto).

.   .   .   .

Our concepts are surrounded by an atmosphere of logical potentiality. This is what Aristotle meant when he said that we never think of the particular as such. When I imagine Socrates as an individual, I think of the man Socrates at the same moment. When I see my horse or my dog, I certainly perceive their special characteristics, but these also as belonging to the species horse or dog. Strictly speaking, their image may be imprinted on my retina and appear to my consciousness as quite distinctive, as long as I am not paying attention to it. But directly I apprehend it, it is inseparable from everything connoted by the terms "horse" and "dog"—that is, not only from an infinite number of other potential images like the first, but also from the sustained consciousness which I have both of myself and of a possible, logically ordered, conceivable world of experience. And since each of my concepts can be broken up into others which in their turn can be analysed, I know that I can pass from these to others by definite stages which are the same for all minds resembling my own. I know that logical processes, if they be correct, and their elements drawn from experience as they should be, will lead me to definite results which experience will confirm, however far I may pursue them. In short, logical thought implies, more or less consciously, a systematic unity which is best realizable in science and philosophy. And the fact that it can lead to this is partially due to the peculiar nature of its concepts, to their homogeneity and ordered regularity. This is material which it has gradually created for itself, and without which it would not have been able to develop.

Now this material is not at the command of the primitive mind. Primitive mentality does indeed possess a language, but its structure, as a rule, differs from that of our languages. It actually does comprise abstract representations and general ideas; but neither this abstraction nor this generalization resembles that of our concepts. Instead of being surrounded by an atmosphere of logical potentiality, these representations welter, as it were, in an atmosphere of mystic possibilities. There is no homogeneity in the field of representation, and for this reason logical generalization, properly so called, and logical transactions with its concepts are impracticable. The element of generality consists in the possibility—already predetermined—of mystic action and reaction by entities upon each other, or of common mystic reaction in entities which differ from each other. Logical thought finds itself dealing with a scale of general concepts varying in degree, which it can analyse or synthesize at will. Prelogical thought busies itself with collective representations so interwoven as to give the impression of a community in which members would continually act and react upon each other by virtue of their mystic qualities, participating in, or excluding, each other.

V

Since abstraction and generalization mean this for prelogical mentality, and its preconnections of collective representations are such, it is not difficult to account for its classification of persons and things, strange as it frequently appears to us. Logical thought classifies by means of the very operations which form its concepts. These sum up the work of analysis and synthesis which establishes species and genera, and thus arranges entities according to the increasing generality of the characters observed in them. In this sense classification is not a process which differs from those which have preceded or will follow it. It takes place at the same time as abstraction and generalization: it registers their results, as it were, and its value is precisely what theirs has been. It is the expression of an order of interdependence, of hierarchy among the concepts, of reciprocal connection between persons and things, which endeavours to correspond as precisely as possible with the objective order in such a way that concepts thus arranged are equally valid for real objects and real persons. It was the governing idea which directed Greek philosophical thought, and which inevitably appears as soon as the logical mind reflects upon itself and begins consciously to pursue the end to which it at first tended spontaneously.

But to the primitive mind this predominating concern for objective validity which can be verified is unknown. Characteristics which can be discerned by experience, in the sense in which we understand it, characteristics which we call objective, are of secondary importance in its eyes, or are important only as signs and vehicles of mystic qualities. Moreover, the primitive mind does not arrange its concepts in a regular order. It perceives preconnections, which it would never dream of changing, between the collective representations; and these are nearly always of greater complexity than concepts, properly so called. Therefore what can its classifications be? Perforce determined at the same time as the preconnections, they too are governed by the law of participation, and will present the same prelogical and mystic character. They will betoken the orientation peculiar to such a mind.

The facts already quoted are sufficient proof of this. When the Huichols, influenced by the law of participation, affirm the identity of corn, deer, hikuli and plumes, a kind of classification has been established between their representations, a classification the governing principle of which is a common presence in these entities, or rather the circulation among these entities, of a mystic power which is of supreme importance to the tribe. The only thing is that this classification does not, as it should do in conformity with our mental processes, become compacted in a concept which is more comprehensive than that of the objects it embraces. For them it suffices for the objects to be united, and felt as such, in a complexity of collective representations whose emotional force fully compensates, and even goes beyond, the authority which will be given to general concepts by their logical validity at a later stage.

In this way the classifications to which Durkheim and Mauss have called our attention, noting their very different characteristics from those which distinguish our logical classifications, may again be explained. In many undeveloped peoples—in Australia, in West Africa, according to Dennett's recent book,[17] among the North American Indians, in China and elsewhere—we find that all natural objects—animals, plants, stars, cardinal points, colours, inanimate nature in general—are arranged, or have been originally arranged, in the same classes as the members of the social group, and if the latter are divided into so many totems, so, too, are the trees, rivers, stars, etc. A certain tree will belong to such and such a class, and will be used exclusively to manufacture the weapons, coffins, etc., of men who are members of it. The sun, according to the Aruntas, is a *Panunga* woman, that is, she forms part of the sub-group which can only intermarry with members of the *Purula* sub-group. Here we have something analogous with that which we have already noticed about associated totems and local relationship, a mental habit quite different from our own, which consists in bringing together or uniting entities preferably by their mystic participations. This participation, which is very strongly felt between members of the same totem or the same group, between the ensemble of these members and the animal or plant species which is their totem, is also felt, though undoubtedly to a lesser degree, between the totemic group and those who have the same location in

---

[17] *At the Back of the Black Man's Mind* (London, 1906).

space. We have proofs of this in the Australian aborigines and in the North American Indians, where the place of each group in a common campingground is very precisely determined according to whether it comes from north or south or from some other direction. Thus it is felt once more between this totemic group and one of the cardinal points, and consequently between this group and all that participates in it, on the one hand, and this cardinal point and all that participates in it (its stars, rivers, trees, and so forth), on the other.

In this way is established a complexity of participations, the full explanation of which would demand exhaustive acquaintance with the beliefs and the collective representations of the group in all their details. They are the equivalent of, or at least they correspond with, what we know as classifications: the social participations being the most intensely felt by each individual consciousness and serving as a nucleus, as it were, around which other participations cluster. But in this there is nothing at all resembling, save in appearance, our logical classifications. These involve a series of concepts whose extent and connotation are definite, and they constitute an ascending scale the degrees of which reflection has tested. The prelogical mind does not objectify nature thus. It *lives* it rather, by feeling itself participate in it, and feeling these participations everywhere; and it interprets this complexity of participations by social forms. If the element of generality exists, it can only be sought for in the participation extending to, and the mystic qualities circulating among, certain entities, uniting them and identifying them in the collective representation.

In default of really general concepts, therefore, primitive mentality is conversant with collective representations which to a certain extent take their place. Although concrete, such representations are extremely comprehensive in this respect, that they are constantly employed, that they readily apply to an infinite number of cases, and that from this point of view they correspond, as we have said, with what categories are for logical thought. But their mystic and concrete nature has often puzzled investigators. These did indeed note its importance and could not fail to draw attention to it, though at the same time they realized that they were face to face with a method of thinking which was opposed to their own mental habits. Some examples in addition to those already quoted will help to make us realize these representations, which are general without however being at the same time abstract.

In the Yaos,[18] Hetherwick notes beliefs which appear incomprehensible to him. He cannot understand how it is that the *lisoka* (the soul, shade or spirit) can be at once both personal and impersonal. In fact, af-

[18] Hetherwick, "Some Animistic Beliefs among the Yaos of Central Africa," *J.A.I.*, xxxii. pp. 89–95.

ter death the *lisoka* becomes *mulungu.* This word has two meanings: one, the soul of the dead, the other, "the spirit world in general, or more properly speaking the aggregate of the spirits of all the dead." This would be conceivable if *mulungu* meant a collective unity formed by the union of all the individual spirits; but this explanation is not permissible, for at the same time *mulungu* signifies "a state or property inhering in something, as life or health inheres in the body, and it is also regarded as the agent in anything mysterious. 'It is *mulungu*' is the Yao exclamation on being shown anything that is beyond the range of his understanding." This is a characteristic trait which we shall find in all collective representations of this nature: they are used indifferently to indicate a person or persons, or a quality or property of a thing.

To get out of the difficulty, Hetherwick distinguishes between what he calls "three stages of animistic belief: (1) the human *lisoka* or shade, the agent in dreams, delirium, etc.; (2) this *lisoka* regarded as *mulungu,* and an object of worship and reverence, the controller of the affairs of this life, the active agent in the fortunes of the human race; (3) *mulungu* as expressing the great spirit agency, the creator of the world and all life, the source of all things animate or inanimate." It seems as if Hetherwick, like the French missionaries of old in New France, tends to interpret what he observes by the light of his own religious beliefs, but he adds, in good faith: "And yet between these three conceptions of the spirit nature no definite boundary line can be drawn. The distinction in the native mind is ever of the haziest. No one will give you a dogmatic statement of his belief on such points."

If Hetherwick did not get from the Yaos the answers he wanted, it may possibly have been because the Yaos did not understand his questions, but it was largely because he did not grasp their ideas. To the Yaos the transit from the personal soul, before or after death, to the impersonal soul or to the mystic quality which pervades every object in which there is something divine, sacred and mystic (not supernatural, for on the contrary nothing is more natural to primitive mentality than this kind of mystic power) is not felt. To tell the truth, there is not even such transit: there is "identity governed by the law of participation" such as we found in the case of the Huichols, entirely different from logical identity. And through the perpetual working of the law of participation, the mystic principle thus circulating and spreading among entities may be represented indifferently as a person or subject, or a property or power of the objects which share it, and consequently an attribute. Prelogical mentality does not consider there is any difficulty about this.

Bantu Philosophy

Father Placide Tempels

In this influential work, the Belgian priest Father Placide Tempels attempts to articulate the basis of the African view of reality. For Tempels, the essential difference between European and African views of reality is that the basic ontological categories of European civilization are composed of things with fixed natures, as molecules are composed of atoms, amino acids of molecules, and people of amino acids. On the other hand, the basic categories in Bantu thought are dynamic forces that ebb and flow. These dynamic forces are of different kinds: divine forces, celestial forces, terrestrial forces, human forces, animal forces, plant forces, and fire, water, and mineral forces. Evil is the use of such forces to diminish the vital force of a particular person or group, whereas good is the use of such forces to amplify vital force.

These different kinds of forces interact with one another, resulting in the augmenting or diminishing of their respective vital energies. Magical knowledge and technique is the means the Bantu use to manipulate the interaction of vital forces. There is a chain of spiritual beings or forces between God (from which all other forces emanate) and man, and between man and minerals. Through divination and communication with one's ancestors, a person can learn the nature of the forces he or she encounters and learn how to manipulate them.

The closer a category of force is to God, the greater its knowledge of the interaction of vital forces. Thus, the divinities are closer to God than the ancestors, the ancestors are closer than the elders, the elders are closer than the young, and specialists are closer than ordinary men and women. Because of the white man's technological superiority, the Bantu regarded him as a superior human force, at least on the level of the elders, and against which their magic was powerless. Nonetheless, so long as they confined its use to themselves and their natural environment, knowledge of vital forces was as efficacious as was knowledge of physical forces for Europeans.

Tempels' argument is similar to that of the American linguist, Benjamin Whorf, who argues in his book Language, Thought, and Reality *(NY: MIT Press, 1956) that the structure of a language shapes the way its users structure reality. Whorf argues that the grammar of Native-American languages is structurally distinct from that of Indo-European languages, and gives rise to a metaphysic of fields and forces rather than of discrete things. Alex Kagame, a Rwandian philosopher and linguist, assesses and extends Tem-*

pels' claims in his books La Philosophie bantu-rwandaise de l'etre *(Brussels: Academie Royale des Sciences Coloniales, 1956; and* La Philosophie bantu comparee *(Paris: Presence Africaine, 1976). Tempels' views have been combined with those of Kagame, and applied to Africans in the Americas by the Belgian ethnographer Jahnhein Janz in his book* Muntu *(NY: Grove Press, 1990).*

I . . . invite the reader of this study to put out of his mind while reading it both his western philosophical thought and any judgments which he may have already made concerning Bantu and primitive peoples. I ask him to abandon received ideas and to apply his mind to getting hold of the significance of what is here said, trying to grasp Bantu thought from within and not allowing himself to be diverted into criticism of my way of setting it out or of my choice of terms. I ask him even to reserve judgment concerning the evaluation to be put upon the theory and, before he pronounces judgment upon it, to have patience to consider the proofs and applications of it which will ultimately be given. After that he may propound his criticisms and attack either the theory itself or the way in which it is set out.

Let us do as the Africans do. When they hold a palaver it is a rule that whoever is arguing a case should suffer an interruption. Even when he stops speaking, the judge will say to him, "Have you finished speaking?"; and only after that gives the floor to the opposing side.

Bantu Behaviour: It Is Centred in a Single Value: Vital Force.[1]

Certain words are constantly being used by Africans. They are those which express their supreme values; and they recur like variations upon a **leitmoti[f]** present in their language, their thought, and in all their acts and deeds.

This supreme value is **life, force, to live strongly,** or **vital force.**

The Bantu say, in respect of a number of strange practices in which we see neither rime nor reason, that their purpose is to acquire **life, strength** or **vital force, to live strongly,** that they are to make life stronger, or to assure that force shall remain perpetually in one's posterity.

[1] The French terms are la force, vivre fort, force vitale. Despite precedents, I am still affronted by the phrase "vital force"; but if the Reader, equally jarred, is driven in his search for an alternative to ponder the whole context of the concept involved in Fr. Tempels' book, he may in the end conclude that his time has not been ill-spent. [Trans.]

Used negatively, the same idea is expressed when the Bantu say: we act thus to be protected from misfortune, or from a diminution of life or of being, or in order to protect ourselves from those influences which annihilate or diminish us.

Force, the **potent life, vital energy** are the object of prayers and invocations to God, to the spirits and to the dead, as well as of all that is usually called magic, sorcery or magical remedies. The Bantu will tell you that they go to a diviner to learn the words of life, so that he can teach them the way of making life stronger. In every Bantu language it is easy to recognize the words or phrases denoting a **force,** which is not used in an exclusively bodily sense, but in the sense of the integrity of our whole being.

The **bwanga** (which has been translated "magical remedy") ought not, they say, to be applied to the wound or sick limb. It does not necessarily possess local therapeutic effects, but it strengthens, it increases the vital force.

In calling upon God, the spirits, or the ancestral spirits, the heathen ask above all, "give me force." If one urges them to abandon magical practices, as being contrary to the will of God and therefore evil, one will get the reply, "wherein are they wicked?" What we brand as magic is, in their eyes, nothing but setting to work natural forces placed at the disposal of man by God to strengthen man's vital energy.

When they try to get away from metaphors and periphrases, the Bantu speak of God himself as "the Strong One," he who possesses Force in himself. He is also the source of the Force of every creature. God is the "Dijina dikatampe": the great name, because he is the great Force, the "mukomo," as our Baluba have it, the one who is stronger than all other.

The spirits of the first ancestors, highly exalted in the super-human world, possess extraordinary force inasmuch as they are the founders of the human race and propagators of the divine inheritance of vital human strength. The other dead are esteemed only to the extent to which they increase and perpetuate their vital force in their progeny.

In the minds of Bantu, all beings in the universe possess vital force of their own: human, animal, vegetable, or inanimate. Each being has been endowed by God with a certain force, capable of strengthening the vital energy of the strongest being of all creation: man.

Supreme happiness, the only kind of blessing, is, to the Bantu, to possess the greatest vital force: the worst misfortune and, in very truth, the only misfortune, is, he thinks, the diminution of this power.

Every illness, wound or disappointment, all suffering, depression, or fatigue, every injustice and every failure: all these are held to be, and are spoken of by the Bantu as, a diminution of vital force.

Illness and death do not have their source in our own vital power, but result from some external agent who weakens us through his greater force. It is only by fortifying our vital energy through the use of magical recipes, that we acquire resistance to malevolent external forces.

We need not be surprised that the Bantu allude to this vital force in their greetings one to another, using such forms of address as: "You are strong," or "you have life in you," "you have life strongly in you"; and that they express sympathy in such phrases as "your vital force is lowered", "your vital energy has been sapped." A similar idea is found in the form of sympathy, "wafwa ko!" which we translate "you are dying"; and by reason of our mistranslation, we are quite unable to understand the Bantu and find them given to ridiculous exaggeration when they continually say that they are "dead" of hunger or of fatigue, or that the least obstacle or illness is "killing" them. In their own minds they are simply indicating a diminution of vital force, in which sense their expression is reasonable and sensible enough. In their languages, too, are words like "kufwa" and "fukwididila," indicating the progressing stages of loss of force, of vitality, and the superlative of which signifies total paralysis of the power to live. It is quite erroneous for us to translate these words by "to die" and "to die entirely."

This explains what has, indeed, been true, that the thing which most inhibits pagans from conversion to Christianity and from giving up magical rites is the fear of attenuating this vital energy through ceasing to have recourse to the natural powers which sustain it.

In 1936 I gave my Normal Class students at Lukonzolwa (Lake Moëro) as an essay subject, "Obstacles to conversion among pagan peoples." To my astonishment, so far from setting out a list of practices, all of them declared that the great obstacle could be summed up in a conviction that to abandon the customs appointed by their ancestors would lead to death. The objection, therefore, was rather a matter of principle than of practice, their fear being grounded in the "truths" of Bantu ontology.

These various aspects of Bantu behaviour already enable us to see that the key to Bantu thought is the idea of vital force, of which the source is God.[2] Vital force is the reality which, though invisible, is

[2] The Revd. Sister Carmela, of the Sœurs Missionnaires de Notre Dame d'Afrique supplies important confirmation from Bunia, in Ituri (Belgian Congo: ". . . Here the African never speaks of "vital force." When anyone speaks to him about it, he replies, "Yes, it is exactly like that with us"; and he smiles with satisfaction. And they say one to another, "She knows us."

But among them the facts are such that everyone knows them and nobody needs to talk about them. For example, they say, we never speak of the "force of life" because with us life and force are one and the same thing. If one is less strong, one does not speak of life. Neither does one say that life "is becoming stronger"; one feels it; one has an impression of it.

And, if favourable external conditions make you stronger, it will be said that you have power . . .

Evidently vital force is to the African mind the great and important thing.

They have also some small idea of being, but as some quite higher thing. For exam-

supreme in man. Man can renew his vital force by tapping the strength of other creatures.

Bantu Ontology.

The General Notion of Being.[3] We have seen that the Bantu soul hankers after life and force. The fundamental notion under which being is conceived lies within the category of forces.

Metaphysics studies this reality, existing in everything and in every being in the universe. It is in virtue of this reality that all beings have something in common, so that the definition of this reality may be applied to all existent forms of being.

To arrive at this reality common to all beings, or rather, which is identical in all beings, it is necessary to eliminate all forms of reality which belong to one category only among beings.

We pay attention to the elements only, but to all the elements, which are common to all beings. Such elements are, e.g. the origin, the growth, the changes, the destruction, or the achievement of the beings, passive and active causality, and particularly the nature of the being as such supporting those universal phenomena. These elements constitute the object of metaphysical knowledge, that is to say, of knowledge embracing **all** the physical or the real.

Metaphysics does not treat of the abstract or the unreal: these are but its notions, its definitions, its laws, which are abstract and general, as the notions, definitions and laws of every science always are.

Christian thought in the West, having adopted the terminology of Greek philosophy and perhaps under its influence, has defined this reality common to all beings, or, as one should perhaps say, being as such; "the reality that is," "anything that exists," "what is." Its metaphysics has most generally been based upon a fundamentally static conception of being.

Herein is to be seen the fundamental difference between Western thought and that of the Bantu and other primitive people. (I compare only systems which have inspired widespread "civilizations").

We can conceive the transcendental notion of "being" by separating

---

ple, a woman reflecting upon injustice on the part of a stronger party: "God is." She does not say. "God lives!" Since our Africans are unable to obtain justice they say, "God is!"

The Bahema, Alur, Walenda all have the same philosophy as the Bantu. The forms of religion change, yes; but the basis of it is exactly the same."

[3] "The chief value of your book consists, I think, in your demonstration of the difference which exists between Africans and Whites in the way in which they conceive of being. That is a fine discovery indeed, the fruit of your penetrating and patient analysis, which deserves all praise. It constitutes a contribution of which we must take full account in order the better to enter into African thought and the better to understand them. On this point your work seems to me to be impressive beyond any possibility of contradiction." Achille, Card. Lienart.

it from its attribute, "Force," but the Bantu cannot. "Force" in his thought is a necessary element in "being," and the concept "force" is inseparable from the definition of "being." There is no idea among Bantu of "being" divorced from the idea of "force." Without the element "force," "being" cannot be conceived.

We hold a **static** conception of "being," they a **dynamic**.

What has been said above should be accepted as the basis of Bantu ontology: in particular, **The concept "force"** is bound to **the concept "being"** even in the most abstract thinking upon **the notion of being**.

At least it must be said that the Bantu have a double concept concerning being, a concept which can be expressed: "being is that which has force."

But I think we must go further. Our statement of Bantu philosophy should press as closely as possible its distinctive characteristics. It seems to me that we shall not attain this precision by formulating the notion of being in **Bantu thought** as "**being** is that which **possesses** force."

I believe that we should most faithfully render the Bantu thought in European language by saying that Bantu speak, act, live as if, for them, beings were forces. Force is not for them an adventitious, accidental reality. Force is even more than a necessary attribute of beings: **Force is the nature of being, force is being, being is force.**[4]

When we think in terms of the concept "being," they use the concept "force." Where we see concrete beings, they see concrete forces. When we say that "beings" are differentiated by their essence or nature, Bantu say that "forces" differ in their essence or nature. They hold that there is the divine force, celestial or terrestrial forces, human forces, animal forces, vegetable and even material or mineral forces.

The reader will be able to form his own opinion at the end of this study as to the validity, the exact worth of this hypothesis: **in contradistinction to our definition of being as "that which is," or "the thing insofar as it is," the Bantu definition reads, "that which is force," or "the thing insofar as it is force," or "an existent force."** We must insist once again that "force" is not for Bantu a necessary, irreducible attribute of being: no, the notion "force" takes for them the place of the notion "being" in our philosophy. Just as we have, so have they a transcendental, elemental, simple concept: with them "force," with us "being."

It is because all being is force and exists only in that it is force, that the category "force" includes of necessity all "beings": God, men living and departed, animals, plants, minerals. Since being is force, all these be-

---

[4] It can rightly be said that the Bantu regard being as exclusively or essentially a "principle of activity." This term is borrowed from our scientific and therefore more philosophical terminology. One must on that account be careful not to understand it in relation to our static concepts of being, but in accordance with Bantu thought wherein this same principle is regarded as realising itself more or less in itself.

ings appear to the Bantu as forces. This universal concept is hardly used by the Bantu, but they are susceptible to philosophical abstractions though they express them in concrete terms only. They give a name to each thing, but the inner life of these things presents itself to their minds as such specific forces and not at all as static reality.[5]

It would be a misuse of words to call the Bantu "dynamists" or "energists," as if the universe were animated by some universal force, a sort of unique magical power encompassing all existence, as certain authors seem to believe, judging from their treatment of "mana," "bwanga," or "kanga." Such is an European presentation of a primitive philosophy that is but imperfectly understood. The Bantu make a clear distinction and understand an essential difference between different beings, that is to say, different forces. Among the different kinds of forces they have come to recognize, just as we do, unity, individuality but individuality clearly understood as meaning individuality of forces.[6]

That is why it seems to me necessary to reject as foreign to Bantu philosophy the dualism of good and evil as two forces; and also what has been called "common being" or "community of nature," when these terms are so used as to eliminate the individuality of forces.

In the category of visible beings the Bantu distinguish that which is perceived by the senses and the "thing in itself." By the "thing in itself" they indicate its individual inner nature, or, more precisely, the **force** of the thing. They are expressing themselves in figurative language when they say "in every thing there is another thing; in every man a little man." But one would grossly deceive oneself in wishing to attribute to this piece of imagery any exact verbal expression of the Bantu notion of being. Their allegory merely brings into relief the distinction they make between the contingent, the visible phenomenon of being or of force, and the intrinsic visible nature of that force.

When "we" differentiate in man the soul and the body, as is done in certain Western writings, we are at a loss to explain where "the man" has gone after these two components have been separated out. If, from our European outlook, we wish to seek Bantu terms adequate to express this manner of speaking, we are up against very great difficulties, especially if we are proposing to speak about the soul of man. Unless under European influence, the Bantu do not thus express themselves. They distinguish in man body, shadow and breath. This breath is the assumed man-

---

[5] A missionary to the Ubangi (Belgian Congo) writes to me: "My researches in linguistics confirm in my mind how universally African your study is. Among the Ngbaka the "substantive" indicates a thing less as "that" than as "thus." We contemplate the "being" of the thing, they its "force." It is the extent, more or less, to which a thing is vital force that constitutes for them the "being" of the thing."

[6] The Du. reads, "units or individuals standing by themselves, each of them being a force apart." [Trans.]

ifestation, the evident sign, of life, though it is mortal and in no way corresponds with what we understand by the soul, especially the soul as subsisting after death, when the body with its shadow and its breath will have disappeared. What lives on after death is not called by the Bantu by a term indicating part of a man. I have always heard their elders speak of "the man himself," "himself," "aye mwine"; or it is "the little man" who was formerly hidden behind the perceptible manifestation of the man; or the "muntu," which, at death, has left the living.

It seems to me incorrect to translate this word "muntu" by "the man." The "muntu" certainly possesses a visible body, but this body is **not** the "muntu." A Bantu one day explained to one of my colleagues that the "muntu" is rather what you call in English the "person" and not what you connote by "the man." "Muntu" signifies, then, vital force, endowed with intelligence and will. This interpretation gives a logical meaning to the statement which I one day received from a Bantu: "God is a great muntu" ("Vidye i muntu mukatampe"). This meant "God is the great Person"; that is to say, **The** great, powerful and reasonable living force.

The "bintu" are rather what we call **things**: but according to Bantu philosophy they are beings, that is to say **forces not endowed with reason, not living.**

All Force Can Be Strengthened or Enfeebled. That Is to Say, All Being can Become Stronger or Weaker. We say of a man that he grows, develops, acquires knowledge, exercises his intelligence and his will; and that in so doing he increases them. We do not hold that by these acquisitions and by this development he has become more a man; at least, not in the sense that his human **nature** no longer remains what it was. One either has human nature or one hasn't. It is not a thing that is increased or diminished. Development operates in a man's qualities or in his faculties.

Bantu ontology—or, to be more exact, the Bantu theory of forces—is radically opposed to any such conception. When a Bantu says "I am becoming stronger," he is thinking of something quite different from what we mean when we say that our powers are increasing. Remember that, for the Bantu, being is force and force being. When he says that a force is increasing, or that a being is reinforced, his thought must be expressed in our language and according to our mental outlook as "this being has grown as such," his nature has been made stronger, increased, made greater. What Catholic theology teaches concerning, in particular, the supernatural realities of grace, that it is a supernal reinforcement of our being, that it is able to grow and to be strengthened in itself, is an idea similar to what the Bantu accept in the natural order as true of all being, of all force.

This is the sense in which it seems that we should understand the expressions which have been quoted to show that the behaviour of the

Bantu is centred on the idea of vital energy: "to be strong," "to reinforce your life," "you are powerful," "be strong;" or again, "your vital force is declining, has been affected."

It is in this sense also that we must understand Fraser, when he writes in the "Golden Bough," "The soul like the body can be fat or thin, great or small"; or again, "the diminution of the shadow is considered to be the index of a parallel enfeeblement in the vital energy of its owner."[7]

The same idea again is envisaged by M. E. Possoz when he writes in his "Elements of Negro Customary Law:" "For the African, existence is a thing of variable intensity"; and further on when he mentions "the diminution or the reinforcement of being."

We must speak next of the existence of things or of forces. The origin, the subsistence or annihilation of beings or of forces, is expressly and exclusively attributed to God. The term, "to create" in its proper connotation of "to evoke from not being" is found in its full signification in Bantu terminology (**kupanga** in Kiluba). It is in this sense that the Bantu see, in the phenomenon of conception, a direct intervention of God in creating life.

Those who think that, according to the Bantu, one being can entirely annihilate another, to the point that he ceases to exist, conceive a false idea. Doubtless one force that is greater than another can paralyse it, diminish it, or even cause its operation totally to cease, but for all that the force does not cease to exist. Existence which comes from God cannot be taken from a creature by any created force.

The Interaction of Forces: One Being Influencing Another. We speak of the mechanical, chemical and psychical interactions between beings. Realists and idealists meet in recognizing yet another causality conditioning being itself, the cause of the existence of being as such. It is a metaphysical causality which binds the creature to the Creator. The relationship of the creature to the Creator is a constant. I mean to say that the creature is by his nature permanently dependent upon his Creator for existence and means of survival. We do not conceive of any equivalent relationship between creatures. Created beings are denoted in scholastic philosophy as substances, that is to say, beings who exist, if not by themselves, at any rate in themselves, **in se, non in alio.** The child is, from birth, a new being, a complete human being. It has the fulness of human nature and its human existence as such is independent of that of its progenitors. The human nature of a child does not remain in permanent causal relationship with that of its parents.

This concept of separate beings, of substance (to use the Scholastic term again) which find themselves side by side, entirely independent one

---

[7] The references are to pp. 179 and 191 of the abridged (1 vol. edition). [Trans.]

of another, is foreign to Bantu thought. Bantu hold that created beings preserve a bond one with another, an intimate ontological relationship, comparable with the causal tie which binds creature and Creator. For the Bantu there is interaction of being with being, that is to say, of force with force. Transcending the mechanical, chemical and psychological interactions, they see a relationship of forces which we should call ontological. In the **created force** (a contingent being) the Bantu sees a causal action emanating from the very nature of that created force and influencing other forces. One force will reinforce or weaken another. This causality is in no way supernatural in the sense of going beyond the proper attributes of created nature. It is, on the contrary, a metaphysical causal action which flows out of the very nature of a created being. General knowledge of these activities belongs to the realm of natural knowledge and constitutes **philosophy** properly so called. The observation of the action of these forces in their specific and concrete applications would constitute Bantu natural science.

This interaction of beings has been denoted by the word "magic." If it is desired to keep the term, it must be modified so that it is understood in conformity with the content of Bantu thought. In what Europeans call "primitive magic" there is, to primitive eyes, no operation of supernatural, indeterminate forces, but simply the interaction between natural forces, as they were created by God and as they were put by him at the disposal of men.

In their studies of magic, authors distinguish "imitative magic," "sympathetic magic," "contagious magic," "magic of expressed desire," etc. Whatever the resemblance, contact, or the expression of desire, does not arise out of the essence of what is indicated by magic, that is to say, the interaction of creatures. The very fact that there should have been recourse to different terms to distinguish the "kinds"[8] of magic, proves that any attempt to penetrate to the real nature of magic has been given up in favour of a classification in terms of secondary characters only.

The child, even the adult, remains always for the Bantu a man, a force, in causal dependence and ontological subordination to the forces which are his father and mother. The older force ever dominates the younger. It continues to exercise its living influence over it. This is said to give a first example of the Bantu conception in accordance with which the "beings-forces" of the universe are not a multitude of independent forces placed in juxtaposition from being to being. All creatures are found in relationship according to the laws of a hierarchy that I shall describe later. Nothing moves in this universe of forces without influencing

---

[8] Fr. "espèces" (inverted commas in the original). The word is used in two senses: **a)** referring to the different "kinds" of magic named by older anthropologists and quoted above; **b)** indicating that these "kinds" are in truth manifestations or "appearances" only of the inadequately conceived reality.

other forces by its movement. The world of forces is held like a spider's web of which no single thread can be caused to vibrate without shaking the whole network.

It has been maintained that "beings" only acquire "power" to act upon other beings or forces through the intervention of spirits and manes. This contention emanates from European observers, it does not exist in the minds of Africans. The dead intervene on occasion to **make** known to the living the nature and quality of certain forces, but they do not thereby **change** that nature or those qualities which are preordained as belonging to that force. Africans expressly say that creatures are forces, created by God as such; and that the intervention of spirits or manes changes nothing: such changes are a White man's idea.

The Hierarchy of Forces: Primogeniture. As with Indian castes and as the Israelites distinguished the "pure" from the "impure," so beings are differentiated in Bantu ontology into species according to their vital power ("levenskracht") or their inherent vital rank ("levensrang"). Above all force is God, Spirit and Creator, the **mwine bukomo bwandi.** It is he who has force, power, in himself. He gives existence, power of survival and of increase, to other forces. In relation to other forces, he is "He who increases force."[9] After him come the first fathers of men, founders of the different clans. These archipatriarchs were the first to whom God communicated his vital force, with the power of exercising their influences on all posterity. They constitute the most important chain binding men to God. They occupy so exalted a rank in Bantu thought that they are not regarded merely as ordinary dead. They are no longer named among the manes; and by the Baluba they are called bavidye, spiritualised beings, beings belonging to a higher hierarchy, participating to a certain degree in the divine Force.[10]

After these first parents come the dead of the tribe, following their order of primogeniture. They form a chain, through the links of which the forces of the elders exercise their vitalising influence on the living generation. Those living on earth rank, in fact, after the dead. The living belong in turn to a hierarchy, not simply following legal status, but as or-

---

[9] Du. "versterker." [Trans.]

[10] The language of the Bantu would cause one to think that they identify the founders of the clan with God himself. It so happens that they call both by the same name. There is, however, no identification, but a simple comparison, a practice analogous to that in which a Chief's deputy is treated as the Chief himself, since he is his sensory manifestation and his speech is often the word of him who sent him.

We often hear an African say to someone who has befriended him: "You are my father and mother, you are my supreme Chief. You are my God." Often, too, Africans have called me "Syakapanga" (Creator). They were in this way expressing their conviction that I was His word-bearer, His messenger to them.

dered by their own being in accordance with primogeniture and their vital rank; that is to say, according to their vital power.

But man is not suspended in thin air. He lives on his land, where he finds himself to be the sovereign vital force, ruling the land and all that lives on it: man, animal, or plant. The eldest of a group or of a clan is, for Bantu, by Divine law the sustaining link of life, binding ancestors and their descendants. It is he who "reinforces" the life of his people and of all inferior forces, animal, vegetable and inorganic, that exist, grow, or live on the foundation which he provides for the welfare of his people. The true chief, then, following the original conception and political set up of clan peoples, is the father, the master, the king; he is the source of all zestful living; he is as God himself. This explains what the Bantu mean when they protest against the nomination of a chief, by government intervention, who is not able, by reason of his vital rank or vital force, to be the link binding dead and living. "Such an one cannot be chief. It is impossible. Nothing would grow in our soil, our women would bear no children and everything would be struck sterile." Such considerations and such despair are entirely mysterious and incomprehensible so long as we have not grasped the Bantu conception of existence and their interpretation of the universe. Judged, however, according to the theory of forces, their point of view becomes logical and clear.

After the category of human forces come the other forces, animal, vegetable and mineral. But within each of these categories is found a hierarchy based on vital power, rank and primogeniture.

From that it follows that an analogy can be found between a human and a lower group (e.g. in the animal class), an analogy based on the relative place of these groups in relation to its own class. Such would be an analogy founded on primogeniture or upon a pre-determined order of subordination. A human group and an animal species can occupy in their respective classes a rank relatively equal or relatively different. Their vital rank can be parallel or different. A Chief in the class of humans shows his royal rank by wearing the skin of a royal animal. The respect for this ranking in life, the care not to place oneself higher than one's legitimate place, the necessity not to approach the higher forces as if they were our equals, all that can supply the key to the so much disputed problem of "tabu" and "totem."

The Created Universe Is Centred on Man: The Present Human Generation Living on Earth Is the Centre of All Humanity, Including the World of the Dead. The Jews had no precise views of the beyond, nothing more than that of compensation in the future life for earthly merit. The idea of bliss became known to them a short time only before the coming of Christ. "Sheol" was a desolate region; and sojourn there seemed a gloomy business, offering little enough to attract those who had the good fortune to be still living on earth.

In the minds of the Bantu, the dead also live; but theirs is a diminished life, with reduced vital energy. This seems to be the conception of the Bantu when they speak of the dead in general, superficially and in regard to the external things of life.

The General Laws of Vital Causality. After what we have said upon the question of "force beings"[11] grouped in respect of their natures, of intensity of life class by class, and of the precedence according to primogeniture, it will be now clear that, among clan peoples, the universe of forces is organically constructed in what we can call an ontological hierarchy. The interaction of forces and the exercise of viral influences occurs, in fact, according to determined laws. The Bantu universe is not a chaotic tangle of unordered forces blindly struggling with one another. Nor must we believe that this **theory of forces** is the incoherent product of a savage imagination, or that the action of the same force can be now propitious and now pernicious, without a determining power to justify the fact. Doubtless there are force influences acting in this unforeseeable manner, but this assertion does not allow the conclusion that action occurs in a manner scientifically unpredictable, in a totally irrational mode. When a motor-car breaks down, one can say that this event was not determined in advance by what constitutes the essential nature of a motor-car, but we do not on that account believe ourselves obliged to deny the correctness and validity of the laws of mechanics. On the contrary, the breakdown itself can be explained only by adequate application of these very laws. The same is true of the laws of the interaction of forces. There are possible and necessary actions, other influences are metaphysically impossible by reason of the nature of the forces in question. The possible causal factors in life can be formulated in certain metaphysical, universal, immutable and stable laws.

These laws can, I think, be set out as follows:

I. Man (living or deceased) can directly reinforce or diminish the being of another man.
   Such vital influence is possible from man to man: it is indeed necessarily effective as between the progenitor a superior vital force,—and his progeny—an inferior force. This interaction does not occur only when the recipient object is endowed, in respect of the endowing subject, with a superior force, which he may achieve of himself, or by some vital external influence, or (especially) by the action of God.

II. The vital human force can directly influence inferior forcebeings (animal, vegetable, or mineral) in their being itself.

---

[11] Fr. "êtres-forces."

III. A rational being (spirit, manes, or living) can act indirectly upon another rational being by communicating his vital influence to an inferior force (animal, vegetable, or mineral) through the intermediacy of which it influences the rational being. This influence will also have the character of a necessarily effective action, save only when the object is inherently the stronger force, or is reinforced by the influence of some third party, or preserves himself by recourse to inferior forces exceeding those which his enemy is employing.

Note: Certain authors claim that inanimate beings, stones, rocks, or plants and trees are called by the Bantu "bwanga," as exercising their vital influence on all that comes near them. If this were authenticated, it would open the question: "do lower forces act by themselves upon higher forces?" Some authors say that they do. For my part, I have never met any African who would accept this hypothesis. **A priori,** such an occurrence would seem to me to contradict the general principles of the theory of forces. In Bantu metaphysic the lower force is excluded from exercising by its own initiative any vital action upon a higher force. Besides, in giving their examples, these authors ought to recognize that often a living influence has been at work, for example, that of the manes. Likewise certain natural phenomena, rocks, waterfalls, big trees, can be considered—and are considered by the Bantu—as manifestations of divine power; they can also be the sign, the manifestation, the habitat of a spirit. It seems to me that such should be the explanation of the apparent influences of lower forces on the higher force of man. Those lower beings do not exercise their influence of themselves, but through the vital energy of a higher force acting as cause. Such an explanation accords in all cases with Bantu metaphysic. Such manifestations belong to the third law enunciated above.

BANTU WISDOM OR CRITERIOLOGY[12]

What Is Bantu Wisdom?

It consists in the Bantu's discernment of the nature of beings, of forces: true wisdom lies in ontological knowledge. The Sage "par excellence" is God, who knows every being, Who comprehends the nature and the quality of the energy of each.[13]

God **is** Force, possessing energy in himself, the mover of all other forces. He knows all forces, their ordering, their dependence, their po-

---

[12] Criteriology: Du. kennisleer, Fr. criteriologie. See N.E.D. "the doctrine of a criterion (of knowledge, etc.) quoting one example of it from the "Atheneum," 14th July, 1884: "the relation of thought to reality as regards its validity." [Trans.]

[13] I abe Shayuka uyuka dyuba ne bufuku: Thou art the Father or knowledge, thou knowest the day and the night.

tential and their mutual interactions. He knows, therefore, the cause of every event. **Vidye uyukile:** God knows. Such is the ultimate reference of the Baluba in face of every insoluble problem, before every inescapable evil; and each time that human wisdom is taken to the court of reason.

In the administration of justice, when all human presumptions agree to crush an innocent litigant deprived of means to prove his case, he will protest: **Vidye uyukile!** God knows: God, who knows every deed and the true man in the intimacy of his being, knows my innocence.

When the **manga,** the magic strengtheners of being, fail, the remedy maker will say **Vidye wakoma,** God is strong.[14] This means: He is stronger than my remedies. But those pagans who, while accepting the principle of vital interactions, do not believe in certain concrete applications or proposed remedies will say, in resigning themselves to an evil, the cause of which is escaping them: Vidye uyukile: God knows (yet he allows it).

Nothing in fact happens without the permission of the Strongest One. The sentence "He knows" certainly means "He understands the occurrence," but it means more often, "He has his reasons."

God knows. He gives man "power" to know. Let us remember that all being is force, that each of its faculties is a force. There is, therefore, the force of knowing, just as there is a force of willing. Therefore men have the power of knowing. There are above all the ancestors, the **ba-vidye,** and among them the elders, dead or living, who know. "It is they who started things."

True knowledge, human wisdom, then, will equally be metaphysical: it will be the intelligence of forces, of their hierarchy, their cohesion and their interaction.

I have stated the primacy of ancestors, the elders. In fact, just as the vital human force (its being) does not exist by itself, but is and remains essentially dependent upon its elders, so the power to know is, like being itself, essentially dependent upon the wisdom of the elders.

How often in a village, when one wishes to question Bantu about some happening—a law suit or a custom, or even some geographical or geological data—does not one provoke the reply: "We younger ones do not know: it is the elders who know." That happens even when the matter in question is, as we think, something which they know all about. Nevertheless, as they think, they do not know, because they are young, because they do not know of or by themselves. Ontologically and juridically the elders who hold the ascendancy are the only ones to know fully, in the last resort. Their wisdom exceeds that of other men. It is in this

---

[14] Du. "wanneer **manga**—"magische" versterkingsmiddelen—niet baten zal de **manga**-man zeggen: Vidye wakoma, God is sterk, d.i. sterker dan **mijn manga.**"

sense that the old say: "The young cannot know without the elders." "If it were not for the elders," the Bantu say again, "if the young were left to themselves, the village would get nowhere. The young would no longer know how to live: they would have neither customs, laws, nor wisdom any longer. They would stray into disaster."

Study and the personal search for knowledge does not give wisdom. One can learn to read, to write, to count: to manage a motor car, or learn a trade; but all that has nothing in common with "wisdom." It gives no ontological knowledge of the nature of beings. There are many talents and clever skills that remain far short of wisdom.

That is how the Bantu speak of their traditional wisdom.

Let us now see how we Europeans would set out to give a reasoned exposition of Bantu wisdom and of their system of criteriology.

Metaphysics, or the Philosophy of Forces, Is Within the Capacity of Every Bantu.

The philosophy of forces is a theory of life, a **weltanschaung**. It is possible that it may have been devised to justify a given behaviour, or that a particular adaptation of nature may have conditioned this behaviour, but always the philosophy of forces strictly governs in fact the whole of Bantu life.

It explains the human motivations of all Bantu customs. It decrees the norms in accordance with which personality in the individual shall be kept unaltered or allowed to develop.[15] This does not mean that every Bantu is able to enumerate the cardinal truths of his philosophy, but it is not less true that the "muntu" who neglects to orientate his life in accordance with the ancient norms laid down by Bantu wisdom will be treated as "kidima" by his fellows: that is to say as a sub-human, a man of insufficient mind to count as a "muntu." The normal "muntu" knows his philosophy, he recognizes the forces in beings.[16] He knows about the growth of beings and their ontological influences. He notes the operation of the general laws of cause and effect between living forces which we treated above in the chapter on Bantu ontology. This ontology, inasmuch as it remains universal and truly philosophical knowledge, is the common property of the whole Bantu society. This universal wisdom is ac-

---

[15] Du. "Maar het is toch zeker, dat een **muntu**, die zijn leven niet richt naar algemeene lijnen van de eeuwenoude Bantu filosofie, door de Bantu zelf voor **kidima** uitdemaakt wordt, voor een mensch die niet voldoende verstand bezit om als volledig, normaal mensch door de gaan, dus voor een minus habens." "This does not mean that every **muntu** can say off hand the ten cardinal truths of his philosophy of life, but it is certain that a **muntu** who does not order his life according to the general rules of the age old Bantu philosophy will be called **kidima** by the Bantu themselves as a man who has not enough brains to be considered a normal person, therefore as a minus habens." [Trans.]

[16] Better, according to the Du. "beings as forces," "wesens als krachten." [Trans.]

cepted by everyone, it is not subjected to criticism, it has currency, in regard to its general principles, as imperishable Truth.

The ethnological views which have been set out in this book do not constitute a secret knowledge confined to a few savants or initiates. We have set down only the popular wisdom of the common man.

Bantu Philosophy Is Based on Internal and External Evidence.

If the Bantu so generally accept their present beliefs free from doubt, that is because—they say—their wisdom is engendered in them at the same time as their living force by their parents and ancestors, who continue to instruct them by means of divination. Songs, fables, mythological traditions and ceremonies of initiation assure instruction in Bantu thought. However, they draw other arguments from their own experience. Since their ancestors proceeded from God himself, should not they have a longer knowledge than they themselves? Besides, their ancestors lived by this philosophy, preserved and handed down life through their recourse to these natural forces, and saved the Bantu people from destruction. Consequently their wisdom seems sound and sufficient. Moreover, this practical wisdom is so completely adapted by the elders to the needs of life that no problem is, so to speak, left unanswered; and that a prescription is provided for every eventuality: this, to the minds of the Bantu, affords proof of the fundamental and realistic soundness of their philosophy. Thus Mgr. Leroy says in "La Religion des Primitifs" that the Bantu seems himself engaged in a constant struggle with the forces of nature which surround him; and he emerges from this struggle, now as victor, now as vanquished. He establishes every day the existence of hidden forces in plants and herbs. For primitive minds, these considerations furnish adequate grounds of proof of the validity of their philosophy of forces and of the concept of beings as forces. To see that natural forces are sometimes potent and sometimes ineffective is enough to justify to him the inference that a being, that is to say a force, can now strengthen and now weaken, that a being's force can become inoperative, that the **bwanga** can "depart," "grow cold," or be "trampled under foot," as they put it.

So the criteriology of the Bantu rests upon external evidence, upon the authority and dominating life force of the ancestors. It rests at the same time upon the internal evidence of experience of nature and of living phenomena, observed from their point of view. No doubt, anyone can show the error of their reasoning; but it must none the less be admitted that their notions are based on reason, that their criteriology and their wisdom belong to rational knowledge.

The Bantu Differentiate Philosophy
from the Natural Sciences.

The transcendental and universal notions of being and of its force, of action, and of the relationships and reciprocal influences of beings make up Bantu philosophy. This domain is accessible to the ordinary intelligence of every normal "muntu."

If one desired to ridicule this philosophy or to give a childish caricature of it, objecting that its concepts do not rest upon the discipline of rigorous scientific experience, it would be as well to take care not to commit oneself to arguments more ridiculous than the pretended stupidity of these primitive peoples themselves.

Is our philosophy based upon scientific experiment? Does it depend upon chemical analysis, on mechanics, or on anatomy? Natural sciences can no more refute a system of philosophy than they can create one. Our elders used to possess a systematised philosophy which the most advanced modern sciences have not broken down. Moreover, our ancestors came by their knowledge of being at a time when their experimental scientific knowledge was very poor and defective, if not totally erroneous. The tool of empirical science is sense experience of visible realities, while philosophy goes off into intellectual contemplation of general realities concerning the invisible nature of beings. But no instrument exists for measuring the soul, though this fact does not exclude the possibility that experiences may occur in order to furnish intelligence with reasonable proof of the existence of the spiritual principle in life. It is the intellect that creates science. Indeed the experiments of the natural sciences, as also the generalizations of the philosopher ought to be made methodically and with discernment and analysed in accordance with sound logical reasoning. This presupposes always that one does not question the objective worth of intellectual knowledge. Happily, primitive peoples are no more tortured with doubt than our subévolués on the subject of the reality of intellectual knowledge, nor of the validity of human reasoning.

The subjective point of view of the Bantu founds the general principle and notion of being on the argument of authority and on their own observation of the constitution of the universe. That, I presume, is why this conception can be found among all the so-called non-civilized peoples. For the same reason it persists among educated natives and converts to Christianity.

The general conception of being which one may hold and the knowledge of the particular qualities of each individual being are two distinct things. It is not the duty of philosophy as such to include the defining of a particular being by describing its specific essence, energy, faculties, influences and properties. This belongs to the sphere of the natural sciences. And one can pose the question whether, within the natural sciences, unanimity has been achieved and the last word said upon the nature of the different natural forces which have so far been discovered.

Among the Bantu likewise, the same divergence of views and the same ignorance is to be found in regard to the imperfect knowledge of concrete objects with which they are in actual contact. They agree that many mysteries remain to be elucidated. Who but God can know everything, say our Bantu. God can give a name to each thing because he knows all beings. That is why the practical application of Bantu philosophy to the daily needs of life, to magical practices, differs from tribe to tribe and from district to district. It also explains why, in comparing different territories, apparently contradictory proceedings can be observed, which none the less are but varied applications of the same general Bantu philosophical principles.

Beings, however, are known by their individual natures. So, as has already been observed above, the Bantu distinguish the external appearance of visible beings from the force and inner nature of beings themselves. But the inner, invisible force can concentrate or manifest itself more particularly in one part of the visible being. The vital force can be intensified and compacted and can exteriorise itself at what we may call a nodal point or vital centre. This vital centre, this nodal point, this particularised manifestation or sign of the vital force, is called "kijimba" by the Baluba. A wild beast may be pierced by ten arrows without dying, while another beast succumbs to the first shot. This is because the one arrow has touched the vital centre, or one of its vital centres.

Why is the crocodile so formidable a beast? Where is its murderous vital force centred if not in its ever-watchful eye that nothing escapes? And the symbol, the instrument endowed with the destructive vital force of Master Lion: where is it located? Obviously it must be in its ferocious tooth.

It is, then, very natural, from the Bantu point of view, that if anyone wishes to take for himself, or to make use of, the vital force of an inferior being, he should try to procure for himself a like "kijimba" which signifies and materialises the vital relation between the other being and himself.[17] It is, moreover, the "kijimba" that one finds as the chief element, the active principle, the source of energy in every "bwanga." Knowledge of certain specified forces and particularly of the corresponding "bijimba" is spread in a relatively uniform manner among all Bantu. There are certain "bijimba" of especially powerful beings whose function is to add their force to the carrying out of certain habitual activities such as hunting or fishing. In these occupations one has expressly to measure

---

[17] The Du. adds: "Wordt elke levenshandeling bij de Bantu, elk levensvertand niet met een signum bëwezen en bekrachtigd?" "Is not every transaction which is undertaken by Bantu, every engagement they enter into, indicated and ratified by a visible token?" [Trans.]

one's vital power against that of another living being. There is a struggle of the vital forces of the hunter and the prey. One must, therefore, be strong in combat and arm oneself with all the forces of attack, even those belonging to lower beings, in order to assure oneself of power to destroy the prey.

There are certain general laws which enable one to know and to discover the vital forces and influences of certain beings. These are the "principles" which some authors present as active principles, principles of causality of the magic. In fact they are not the active causes in "magic" or in the employment of natural forces. They are simple signs which allow us to discover and know these natural forces. So one has read: "similia similibus curantur." Ethnologists explain this by declaring that a force acts by likeness and by agreement. I have, I think, sufficiently explained that this likeness cannot be the causal foundation of vital influence. But the resemblance between the murderous force of the lion or of the crocodile and the intentions which actuate the hunter or the fisherman lead the Bantu to believe that the forces of these great carnivores can be used in the exercise of the trade of hunter or fisherman; or rather, in the struggle in which they engage respectively against the prey and the fish.

Another law says that the living being exercises a vital influence on everything that is subordinated to him and on all that belongs to him. That is why every injury to anything depending upon a person will be regarded, as has already been said, as a diminution of the being of that person himself. "All property is rich in mysterious influences," said Burton in "L'âme luba." The fact that a thing has belonged to anyone, that it has been in strict relationship with a person, leads the Bantu to conclude that this thing shares the vital influence of its owner. It is what ethnologists like to call "contagious magic, sympathetic magic"; but it is neither contact nor "sympathy" that are the active elements, but solely the vital force of the owner, which acts, as one knows, because it persists in the being of the thing possessed or used by him.

A third law allows the Bantu to recognize and discover vital forces or vital influences in certain cases. A living man's words or his gesture are considered, more than any other manifestation, to be the formal expression or sign of his vital influence. From that, if words or gestures lead to favourable or unfavourable effects as they are applied to a predetermined person, one may deduce therefrom that such a person exercises his vital influence, for good or ill, upon such other person. What one is in the habit of calling "magic of expressed wish," or "magic of mimicry," or "imitative magic," indicates this kind of handiwork; but here, again, there are neither words nor mimicry that exercise a power, but only signs that externalise the action of the vital influence and make it known to third parties.

These three principles (maybe others will be discovered) fix the rules of research and of knowledge of concrete forces and of vital influences emanating from particular objects. They are in some kind the laws of the Bantu's knowledge of the natural sciences; they are canons of judgment and in no way causes.

The Cleavage Between the Domains of Certain Knowledge and of Uncertain Science among the Bantu.[18] From what has been said we can note the cleavage between those principles and laws considered by the Bantu to be absolute and immutable and the domains of particular knowledge in which one feels one's way in relativity, uncertainty and speculation.

The general notions treated in Chapter II of this book are regarded by Bantu as absolute and invariable. Their philosophical and ontological conceptions, so far as they are applicable to being in itself have, for the Bantu, absolute and necessary validity, admitting of no exceptions. It would, therefore, be fundamentally erroneous to suggest that the conceptions and principles of the Bantu are essentially variable, uncertain and arbitrary. Exactly the reverse is true, at least if one is able to adopt correctly their subjective point of view. Their metaphysic, like ours, proclaims universal and unchangeable laws.

Even the general laws of natural science, of physics, and in particular the three canons of judgment regarding knowledge of force-beings and their influence, have for the Bantu a quality of general validity.

Nevertheless, when one comes down to the level of particular knowledge, the Bantu agree that one is in the realm of speculation and guessing, of skill and deftness.

And so, to know what particular vital influence has attacked a man to cause his sickness, one consults a specialist in the science of the interference of forces. In the same way, to know what "kijimba" will be able to restore such an one, it is not enough to rely on one's own knowledge, any more than to rely upon the counsel of the first person whom one may meet. In such cases, the wise thing to do is to consult a diviner. Just as not every one can read cards or be a palmist, so not everyone can be a diviner. The exercise of this skill presupposes special knowledge or, more precisely, the force to know.

Is Bantu Wisdom Natural, Super-normal or Super-natural?

We call natural, such knowledge as man can acquire by the normal exercise of his faculties. Super-normal knowledge exceeds the needs and

[18] The contrast between the two terms "certain knowledge" and "uncertain science" comes out more sharply, perhaps, in English than in French, but cf. Lalande, op. cit. p. 71 "approximatif." The Du. is simpler: "Wat staat vast en wat is wisselvallig en onzeker in de kennis bij de Bantu?" "What is absolute and what is uncertain in Bantu knowledge?" [Trans.]

capacities of a human being, but not of a being created with a higher order of intelligence. Supernatural knowledge surpasses the capacity of every kind of created being.

From what has been said above, especially as to the knowledge of the "force-being" among the Bantu, it seems that their philosophy, like ours, makes no claim to be more than the natural intellectual knowledge of beings. The general principles of the knowledge of forces and of influences also belongs to the realm of natural, empirical knowledge of the Bantu. Since the particular knowledge of the forces which have determined a given event, or the knowledge of a thing in its concrete nature and in its capacity for acting in respect of certain predetermined persons are only, for the Bantu, (it seems to me) natural knowledge deeper than usual; it is only in certain cases, when the direct or indirect intervention of God or of some other superior being is postulated, that one can speak of super-normal knowledge.

These are deductions from the principles of Bantu philosophy as they have been propounded above. They are worth just as much as the hypothesis of their ontology itself is worth. I believe, however, that these considerations entitle us to reckon as worthless the omnibus expressions that hamper ethnological research when people are pleased to label established facts with such epithets as "mysterious" and with qualifications of "supernatural knowledge" or "indeterminate influences" and many like terms. In general, among the Bantu, we meet only with knowledge that can be routine or specialised, without ceasing on that account to be natural knowledge. In their view it is only in certain cases that one seems to be able to run up against supernormal knowledge.

It seems convenient to insert here a parenthesis on what is generally called "initiation" in ethnological literature. The "kilumbu" or "nganga," that is to say the man who possesses a clearer than usual vision of natural forces and their interaction, the man who has the power of selecting these forces and of directing them towards a determinist usage in particular cases, becomes what he is only because he has been "seized" by the living influence of a deceased ancestor or of a spirit,[19] or even because he has been "initiated" by another "kilumbu" or "nganga." The general principles of Bantu ontology carry the corollary that every man can be influenced by a wiser one. Any one who is thus "seized," passes into a trance at the moment when the spirit or **vidye** possesses him, and it is at this moment that the neophyte acquires his superior force whereby to know and to direct forces. But in this phenomenon there is no question of initiation. Initiation occurs only when a candidate for "kilumbu" or "nganga" goes to find "a man with manga" and asks to be trained in his art. Should initiation, then, consist in what the master "nganga" tells his

[19] Fr. "influence vitale d'un ancêtre prédécédé ou d'un esprit . . ." [Trans.]

disciple (his child in **manga,** as the Baluba say) of the secrets of "sorcery and magic"? The "nganga" can only teach his apprentice the different manipulations and ceremonies of his art, he can give him adequate training in the behaviour he ought to adopt in the higher life for which he is intended; he can teach him the means to get himself into the desired state such that he can acquire force and knowledge, but, as I venture to think, it does not lie within his power to **give** force or knowledge. To possess the real knowledge and power of **manga,** there will not be, according to the view of the Bantu, any initiation in the English sense of the term. Only when the "master-nganga" has completed his work of educating the neophyte does the time arrive for his pupil to receive his power and his knowledge in the course of what has been wrongly called the "initiation ceremony." I presume that it is universal in the Bantu world that in the course of this ceremony the initiate enters into a trance, loses consciousness and becomes as if dead to his ordinary human life, to be reborn from this catalepsy endowed with the superior force and the exalted knowledge of "nganga" or "kilumbu." It is indeed under the living influence of his master that he is educated and reborn to this higher living force, but the force and the power which live in him come from a deceased ancestor or from a spirit, under the influence of whom his master equally acquired his power and his knowledge. Only in this way can one explain the case of one or another pupil who cannot be induced into trance or rapture. His master is obliged to send him away, saying to him "you are unsuitable." It is therefore evident that a vital force must intervene superior to that of the master of forces, and that it is wrong to speak of "initiation."

These relationships, vital influences of the dead upon the living, are daily bread to the Bantu. In a greater or less degree these phenomena are familiar to every **muntu:** they live in communion with their dead and this living influence of the dead should not be adjudged supernormal according to the canons of our philosophy, but as a natural occurrence, as the normal ordering of events in the world of forces of Bantu philosophy. This is the point of view of the Bantu which the ethnologist should adopt.

Is there among the Bantu a Knowledge which Is Not Magical, that Is to Say, that Is Not Knowledge of Force? Is Their Wisdom Critical?

It has been claimed (Alliert: "Le non-civilisé et nous") that the African reasons half as we do (that is to say in accordance with a critical reasoning associated with the nature of things) and that he then abandons all reasoning and gives himself up to magic.

Thus it is indicated, for example, that Africans show themselves to be intelligent and reasonable in the weaving of their nets, the making of their traps and, more generally, in all their hunting crafts. They know what tools they should use to make efficient instruments, they employ an infallible logic to contrive their ambushes. Then suddenly, as some authors claim, they give up all reasoning in order to depend for the success of their hunt on the help of the spirit of hunting or of the huntsman's **bwanga.** I think all the same that it is unsound to divide primitive man into two and to dub him inscrutable, illogical, or mysterious. It is possible that in gathering grasses, in retting them and in making baskets, fish-traps and other utensils out of them, the African sees no ontological agency at work. These are utilitarian crafts outside the sphere of wisdom or of vital force. Yet, one hears them say that these skills are given to them with their vital force. But they make a clear distinction between the aptitude to make a material object well and the power to devise instruments to overcome and capture other living beings. The first is mere child's play, the second a vital work. We need not, then, be surprised to see the African go about his professional aptitudes "magically," or to learn that he thinks while doing so of the vital forces which he is going to encounter. A man who is going to build a canoe would never for a moment cease to keep in mind his philosophy of forces. Any simple skill, moreover, as well as the practice of magic, is shot through and through with this dynamic conception of beings. This conception, however, is quite a different thing from magic, which is nothing but an evil practice equally prevalent amongst those who have a more static conception of beings and those whose philosophy is dynamic. Coppersmiths and black-smiths think that they will not be able to smelt the ore, thereby changing the nature of the material treated, unless they dutifully appeal to a higher force which can dominate the vital force of the "earth" which they claim thus to change into metal. As for the huntsman, he is convinced that it is through a higher vital force that he has the genius at his command whereby to construct his weapons efficiently; and the dexterity to use them effectively in his combat with his captured prey. He thinks that it is his vital influence, reinforced by the power of the tutelary spirit of hunts-men which has led the prey into his gins. It would be difficult to find an activity or an event of any importance in the lives of Africans which is not associated with their philosophy of forces by reason of their beliefs concerning vital influences.

The knowledge of Africans is not two-pronged.[20] They do not have a separate criteriology of the philosophy of forces, side by side with the reasoning of a rational, critical philosophy. The philosophy of forces

---

[20] Fr. "bifide": lit. "cleft into two divisions." The context here will not stand the technical "dualistic." The English "bifid" (N.E.D.) is too unfamiliar, as also is "bifurcate." "Two-pronged" suggests the required basic union with separation. [Trans.]

seems to them to inhere in their knowledge as a whole. They have no other conception of the world. Their philosophy directs all their activities and their inactivities. All consciously, their human behaviour is conditioned by their knowledge of being as force.

Can we say that our philosophy alone is a realist or critical knowledge, while theirs is not? If we understand by a critical philosophy, a philosophy founded upon observation of reality and upon deductions which can be drawn from human experience, I claim that Bantu philosophy is, from their point of view and for the ends indicated above, a critical philosophy as rightly so called in our western systems. In their eyes, their philosophy rests upon internal and external evidence. If it were not so, it would be necessary to conclude that for lack of rational ends, their system would be the product of the merest fancy. But then the compact logic of their system would become an inexplicable miracle.

For the rest, it may be asked whether it is possible to have a philosophy worthy of the name that is not the product of critical thinking. It is another matter to verify whether their observations have been made correctly; or whether their deductions do not conceal errors of reasoning. A system of philosophy may be called "critical" even if it should be proved fallacious. If the term "critical philosophy" be reserved exclusively for an exact and true concept of being, one system only of philosophy can exist; and it cannot be tolerated that differing systems of thought should have the word "philosophy" applied to them.

▲ African Religions and Philosophy

John Mbiti

In his acclaimed work African Religions and Philosophy, *Professor John Mbiti of Kenya continues the view that Africans utilize a different ontology than that current in the modern West. This ontology consists of five categories: God, spirits, man, animals and plants, and phenomena and non-living objects. In addition to these, there is a force permeating the universe, which a few medicine men, priests, and rainmakers have the ability to tap and manipulate.*

The key to understanding this ontology is the African concept of time, which is based on the concrete experience of phenomena rather than on a correlation with recurrent mechanical process (e.g. clocks). Mbiti presents a model of African time in which it consists of an endless past (called the Zamani), a present (called the Sasa), and a very short future. Instead of experiencing time as moving forward into an infinite future, Africans experience time as moving backward from the Sasa to the Zamani. Even after death, a person continues to be a part of the present, or Sasa, as long as they are remembered by those who are alive and can be recognized by name. But when there is no one who personally remembers a dead person, then that individual passes from the Sasa to the Zamani, and enters a state of collective immortality. Rituals commemorating the dead are thus an important way of allowing them to retain their personal identity and remain a part of the present.

In accordance with this view of time, there is a continuum of spirits between man and God consisting of the living, the living dead, the long dead, national heroes who have become deified, spirits who have never lived, and finally, God. It is believed that spirits can communicate directly with God and often may possess the living and speak through them. In addition to the unseen world of spirits, there is also believed to be a mystical force or power that can be manipulated by magical means, both to help and to harm the living. Because spirits have a more direct access to this power, it is important that the living appease the dead and appeal to them for help and aid. For the African, there are no accidents: every event has both a physical cause and a spiritual cause, and each must be identified for a full understanding of any event.

*Mbiti's work has been widely discussed and debated. For recent treat-
ments, see Kwame Gyekye* An Essay in African Philosophical Thought *(NY:
Cambridge University Press, 1987), V.Y. Mudimbe* The Invention of Africa:
Gnosis, Philosophy, and the Order of Knowledge *(Bloomington, IN: Indiana
University Press, 1988), and D.A. Masolo* African Philosophy in Search of
Identity *(Bloomington, IN: Indiana University Press, 1994).*

THE CONCEPT OF TIME

Religion is a difficult word to define, and it becomes even more difficult
in the context of African traditional life. I do not attempt to define it, except to say that for Africans it is an ontological phenomenon; it pertains
to the question of existence or being. We have already pointed out that
within traditional life, the individual is immersed in a religious participation which starts before birth and continues after his death. For him
therefore, and for the larger community of which he is part, to live is to
be caught up in a religious drama. This is fundamental, for it means that
man lives in a religious universe. Both that world and practically all his
activities in it, are seen and experienced through a religious understanding and meaning. Names of people have religious meanings in them;
rocks and boulders are not just empty objects, but religious objects; the
sound of the drum speaks a religious language; the eclipse of the sun or
moon is not simply a silent phenomenon of nature, but one which speaks
to the community that observe it, often warning of an impending cata-
strophe. There are countless examples of this kind. The point here is that
for Africans, the whole of existence is a religious phenomenon; man is a
deeply religious being living in a religious universe. Failure to realize
and appreciate this starting point, has led missionaries, anthropologists,
colonial administrators and other foreign writers on African religions to
misunderstand not only the religions as such but the peoples of Africa.

Africans have their own ontology, but it is a religious ontology, and
to understand their religions we must penetrate that ontology. I propose
to divide it up into five categories, but it is an extremely anthropocentric
ontology in the sense that everything is seen in terms of its relation to
man. These categories are:

1. *God* as the ultimate explanation of the genesis and sustenance of both
   man and all things
2. *Spirits* consist of extra-human beings and the spirits of men who died a
   long time ago
3. *Man* including human beings who are alive and those about to be born

4. *Animals and plants,* or the remainder of biological life

5. *Phenomena and objects without biological life*

Expressed anthropocentrically, God is the Originator and Sustainer of man; the Spirits explain the destiny of man; Man is the centre of this ontology; the Animals, Plants and natural phenomena and objects constitute the environment in which man lives, provide a means of existence and, if need be, man establishes a mystical relationship with them.

This anthropocentric ontology is a complete unity or solidarity which nothing can break up or destroy. To destroy or remove one of these categories is to destroy the whole existence including the destruction of the Creator, which is impossible. One mode of existence presupposes all the others, and a balance must be maintained so that these modes neither drift too far apart from one another nor get too close to one another. In addition to the five categories, there seems to be a force, power or energy permeating the whole universe. God is the Source and ultimate controller of this force; but the spirits have access to some of it. A few human beings have the knowledge and ability to tap, manipulate and use it, such as the medicine-men, witches, priests and rainmakers, some for the good and others for the ill of their communities.[1]

To see how this ontology fits into the religious system, I propose to discuss the African concept of time as the key to our understanding of the basic religious and philosophical concepts. The concept of time may help to explain beliefs, attitudes, practices and general way of life of African peoples not only in the traditional set up but also in the modern situation (whether of political, economic, educational or Church life). On this subject there is, unfortunately, no literature, and this is no more than a pioneer attempt which calls for further research and discussion.

Potential Time and Actual Time

The question of time is of little or no academic concern to African peoples in their traditional life. For them, time is simply a composition of events which have occurred, those which are taking place now and those which are inevitably or immediately to occur. What has not taken place or what has no likelihood of an immediate occurrence falls in the category of "No-time." What is certain to occur, or what falls within the rhythm of natural phenomena, is in the category of inevitable or *potential time.*

The most significant consequence of this is that, according to traditional concepts, time is a two-dimensional phenomenon, with a long

---

[1] This is approximately what the anthropologists call *mana* but it has nothing to do with Tempels' "vital force."

past, a *present* and virtually *no future.* The linear concept of time in western thought, with an indefinite past, present and infinite future, is practically foreign to African thinking. The future is virtually absent because events which lie in it have not taken place, they have not been realized and cannot, therefore, constitute time. If, however, future events are certain to occur, or if they fall within the inevitable rhythm of nature, they at best constitute only *potential time,* not *actual time.* What is taking place now no doubt unfolds the future, but once an event has taken place, it is no longer in the future but in the present and the past. *Actual time* is therefore what is present and what is past. It moves "backward" rather than "forward"; and people set their minds not on future things, but chiefly in what has taken place.

This time orientation, governed as it is by the two main dimensions of the present and the past, dominates African understanding of the individual, the community and the universe which constitutes the five ontological categories mentioned above. Time has to be experienced in order to make sense or to become real. A person experiences time partly in his own individual life, and partly through the society which goes back many generations before his own birth. Since what is the future has not been experienced, it does not make sense; it cannot, therefore, constitute part of time, and people do not know how to think about it—unless, of course, it is something which falls within the rhythm of natural phenomena.

In the east African languages in which I have carried out research and tested my findings, there are no concrete words or expressions to convey the idea of a distant future. We shall illustrate this point by considering the main verb tenses in the Kikamba and Gikuyu languages. (See table on page 91.)

The three verb tenses which refer to the future (numbers 1–3), cover the period of about six months, or not beyond two years at most. Coming events have to fall within the range of these verb tenses, otherwise such events lie beyond the horizon of what constitutes actual time. At most we can say that this short future is only an extension of the present. People have little or no active interest in events that lie in the future beyond, at most two years from now; and the languages concerned lack words by which such events can be conceived or expressed.

Time Reckoning and Chronology

When Africans reckon time, it is for a concrete and specific purpose, in connection with events but not just for the sake of mathematics. Since time is a composition of events, people cannot and do not reckon it in vacuum. Numerical calendars, with one or two possible exceptions,

Analysis of African Concept of Time, as Illustrated by a Consideration of Verb Tenses among the Akamba and Gikuyu of Kenya

Tense	Kikamba	Gikuyu	English	Approximate Time
1. Far Future or Remote Future	Ningauka	Ningoka	I will come	About 2 to 6 months from now
2. Immediate or Near Future	Ninguka	Ninguka	I will come	Within the next short while
3. Indefinite Future or Indefinite Near Future	Ngooka (ngauka)	Ningoka	I will come	Within a foreseeable while, after such and such an event.
4. Present or Present Progressive	Ninukite	Nindiroka	I am coming	In the process of action, now
5. Immediate Past or Immediate Perfect	Ninauka (ninooka)	Nindoka	I came (I have just come)	In the last hour or so
6. Today's Past	Ninukira	Ninjukie	I came	From the time of rising up to about two hours ago
7. Recent Past or Yesterday's Past	Nininaukie (nininookie)	Nindirokire	I came	Yesterday
8. Far Past or Remote Past	Ninookie (ninaukie)	Nindokire	I came	Any day before yesterday
9. Unspecified Tene (Zamani)	Tene ninookie (Nookie tene)	Nindookire tene	I came	No specific time in the "past"

Sasa — braces grouping rows 4–8

Zamani — braces grouping rows 1–9

91

do not exist in African traditional societies as far as I know. If such calendars exist, they are likely to be of a short duration, stretching back perhaps a few decades, but certainly not into the realm of centuries.

Instead of numerical calendars there are what one would call *phenomenon calendars,* in which the events or phenomena which constitute time are reckoned or considered in their relation with one another and as they take place, i.e., as they constitute time. For example, an expectant mother counts the lunar months of her pregnancy; a traveller counts the number of days it takes him to walk (in former years) from one part of the country to another. The day, the month, the year, one's life time or human history, are all divided up or reckoned according to their specific events, for it is these that make them meaningful.

For example, the rising of the sun is an event which is recognized by the whole community. It does not matter, therefore, whether the sun rises at 5 A.M. or 7 A.M., so long as it rises. When a person says that he will meet another at sunrise, it does not matter whether the meeting place takes at 5 A.M. or 7 A.M., so long as it is during the general period of sunrise. Likewise, it does not matter whether people go to bed at 9 P.M. or at 12 midnight: the important thing is the event of going to bed, and it is immaterial whether in one night this takes place at 10 P.M. while in another it is at midnight. For the people concerned, time is meaningful at the point of the event and not at the mathematical moment.

In western or technological society, time is a commodity which must be utilized, sold and bought; but in traditional African life, time has to be created or produced. Man is not a slave of time; instead, he "makes" as much time as he wants. When foreigners, especially from Europe and America, come to Africa and see people sitting down somewhere without, evidently, doing anything, they often remark, "These Africans waste their time by just sitting down idle!" Another common cry is, "Oh, Africans are always late!" It is easy to jump to such judgments, but they are judgments based on ignorance of what time means to African peoples. Those who are seen sitting down, are actually *not wasting* time, but either waiting for time or in the process of "producing" time. One does not want to belabour this small point, but certainly the basic concept of time underlies and influences the life and attitudes of African peoples in the villages, and to a great extent those who work or live in the cities as well. Among other things, the economic life of the people is deeply bound to their concept of time; and as we shall attempt to indicate, many of their religious concepts and practices are intimately connected with this fundamental concept of time.

The day in traditional life, is reckoned according to its significant events. For example, among the Ankore of Uganda, cattle are at the heart of the people. Therefore the day is reckoned in reference to events pertaining to cattle. Thus approximately:

6 A.M. is milking time (*akasheshe*).

12 noon is time for cattle and people to take rest (*bari omubirago*), since, after milking the cattle, the herdsmen drive them out to the pasture grounds and by noon when the sun is hot, both herdsmen and cattle need some rest.

1 P.M. is the time to draw water (*baaza ahamaziba*), from the wells or the rivers, before cattle are driven there to drink (when they would pollute it, or would be a hindrance to those drawing and carrying the water).

2 P.M. is the time for cattle to drink (*amasyo niganywa*), and the herdsmen drive them to the watering places.

3 P.M. is the time when cattle leave their watering places and start grazing again (*amasyo nigakuka*).

5 P.M. is the time when the cattle return home (*ente niitaha*), being driven by the herdsmen.

6 P.M. is the time when the cattle enter their kraals or sleeping places (*ente zaataha*).

7 P.M. is milking time again, before the cattle sleep; and this really closes the day.[2]

The month. Lunar rather than numerical months are recognized, because of the event of the moon's changes. In the life of the people, certain events are associated with particular months, so that the months are named according to either the most important events or the prevailing weather conditions. For example, there is the "hot" month, the month of the first rains, the weeding month, the beans harvest month, the hunting month, etc. It does not matter whether the "hunting month" lasts 25 or 35 days: the event of hunting is what matters much more than the mathematical length of the month. We shall take an example from the Latuka people, to show how the events govern the approximate reckoning of months:

> *October* is called "The Sun," because the sun is very hot at that time.
>
> *December* is called "Give your uncle water," because water is very scarce and people become thirsty readily.
>
> *February* is called "Let them dig!" because it is at this time that people begin to prepare their fields for planting, since the rains are about to return.
>
> *May* is known as "Grain in the ear," for at that time grain begins to bear.
>
> *June* is called "Dirty mouth," because children can now begin to eat the new grain, and in so doing get their mouths dirty.
>
> *July* is known as "Drying grass," because the rains stop, the ground becomes dry and the grass begins to wither.
>
> *August* is "Sweet grain," when people eat and harvest "sweet grain."
>
> *September* is known as "Sausage Tree," because at this time the sausage

---

[2] Cf. J. Roscoe *The Northern Bantu* (1915), p. 139 f., which is not completely accurate. My version is an improvement on Roscoe's.

tree (*kigalia africana*) begins to bear fruit.[3] (The fruit looks like a huge sausage, hence the name.)

And so the cycle is complete, the natural phenomena begin to repeat themselves once more and the year is over.

The year is likewise composed of events, but of a wider scale than those which compose either the day or the month. Where the community is agricultural, it is seasonal activities that compose an agricultural year. Near the equator, for example, people would recognize two rain seasons and two dry seasons. When the number of season-periods is completed, then the year is also completed, since it is these four major seasons that make up an entire year. The actual number of days is irrelevant, since a year is not reckoned in terms of mathematical days but in terms of events. Therefore one year might have 350 days while another year has 390 days. The years may, and often do, differ in their length according to days, but not in their seasons and other regular events.

Since the years differ in mathematical length, numerical calendars are both impossible and meaningless in traditional life. Outside the reckoning of the year, African time concept is silent and indifferent. People expect the years to come and go, in an endless rhythm like that of day and night, and like the waning and waxing of the moon. They expect the events of the rain season, planting, harvesting, dry season, rain season again, planting again, and so on to continue for ever. Each year comes and goes, adding to the time dimension of the past. Endlessness or 'eternity' for them is something that lies only in the region of the past, i.e. something in tense number 9 of our chart multiplied endless times. (When Christians speak of eternity in Kikamba or Gikuyu, they say "tene na tene," i.e. "tene and tene," or the period or state of tense number 9 multiplied by itself. This means that what is 'eternal' lies beyond the horizon of events making up human experience or history.)

The Concept of Past, Present and Future

We must discuss further time dimensions and their relationship with African ontology. Beyond a few months from now, as we have seen, African concept of time is silent and indifferent. This means that the future is virtually non-existent as *actual* time, apart from the relatively short projection of the present up to two years hence. To avoid the thought associations of the English words past, present and future, I propose to use two Swahili words, "Sasa" and "Zamani."

In our chart of the verb tenses, Sasa covers the "now-period" of

---

[3] Cf. L. F. Nalder, ed., *A tribal survey of Mongalla Province* (1937), p. 11 f., from which this has been adapted.

tenses 1 to 7. Sasa has the sense of immediacy, nearness, and "now-ness"; and is the period of immediate concern for the people, since that is "where" or "when" they exist. What would be "future" is extremely brief. This has to be so because any meaningful event in the future must be so immediate and certain that people have almost experienced it. Therefore, if the event is remote, say beyond two years from now (tense number 4), then it cannot be conceived, it cannot be spoken of and the languages themselves have no verb tenses to cover that distant "future" dimension of time. When an event is far in the future, its reality is com-pletely beyond or outside the horizon of the Sasa period. Therefore, in African thought, the Sasa "swallows" up what in western or linear con-cept of time would be considered as the future. Events (which compose time) in the Sasa dimension must be either about to occur, or in the process of realization, or recently experienced. Sasa is the most mean-ingful period for the individual, because he has a personal recollection of the events or phenomena of this period, or he is about to experience them. Sasa is really an experiential extension of the Nowmoment (tense number 4) stretched into the short future and into the unlimited past (or Zamani). Sasa is not mathematically or numerically constant. The older a person is, the longer is his Sasa period. The community also has its own Sasa, which is greater than that of the individual. But for both the community and the individual, the most vivid moment is the NOW point, the event of tense number 4. Sasa is the time region in which peo-ple are conscious of their existence, and within which they project them-selves both into the short future and mainly into the past (Zamani). Sasa is in itself a complete or full time dimension, with its own short future, a dynamic present, and an experienced past. We might call it the *Micro-Time* (Little-Time). The Micro-Time is meaningful to the individual or the community only through their participating in it or experiencing it.

Zamani is not limited to what in English is called the past. It also has its own "past," "present" and "future," but on a wider scale. We might call it the *Macro-Time* (Big Time). Zamani overlaps with Sasa and the two are not separable. Sasa feeds or disappears into Zamani. But be-fore events become incorporated into the Zamani, they have to become realized or actualized within the Sasa dimension. When this has taken place, then the events "move" backwards from the Sasa into the Zamani. So Zamani becomes the period beyond which nothing can go. Zamani is the graveyard of time, the period of termination, the dimension in which everything finds its halting point. It is the final storehouse for all phe-nomena and events, the ocean of time in which everything becomes ab-sorbed into a reality that is neither after nor before.

Both Sasa and Zamani have quality and quantity. People speak of them as big, small, little, short, long, etc., in relation to a particular event or phenomenon. Sasa generally binds individuals and their immediate environment together. It is the period of conscious living. On the other hand, Zamani is the period of the myth, giving a sense of foundation or "security" to the Sasa period; and binding together all created things, so that all things are embraced within the Macro-Time.

The Concept of History and Pre-history

Each African people has its own history. This history moves "backward" from the Sasa period to the Zamani, from the moment of intense experience to the period beyond which nothing can go. In traditional African thought, there is no concept of history moving "forward" towards a future climax, or towards an end of the world. Since the future does not exist beyond a few months, the future cannot be expected to usher in a golden age, or a radically different state of affairs from what is in the Sasa and Zamani. The notion of a messianic hope, or a final destruction of the world, has no place in traditional concept of history. So African peoples have no "belief in progress," the idea that the development of human activities and achievements move from a low to a higher degree. The people neither plan for the distant future nor "build castles in the air." The centre of gravity for human thought and activities is the Zamani period, towards which the Sasa moves. People set their eyes on the Zamani, since for them there is no "World to Come," such as is found in Judaism and Christianity.

Both history and pre-history are dominated by the myth. There are innumerable myths all over the continent of Africa explaining items like the creation of the universe, the first man, the apparent withdrawal of God from the world of mankind, the origin of the tribe and its arrival in its present country, and so on. People constantly look towards the Zamani, for Zamani had foundations on which the Sasa rests and by which it is explainable or should be understood. Zamani is not extinct, but a period full of activities and happenings. It is by looking towards the Zamani that people give or find an explanation about the creation of the world, the coming of death, the evolution of their language and customs, the emergence of their wisdom, and so on. The 'golden age' lies in the Zamani, and not in the otherwise very short or non-existent future.

Such history and pre-history tend to be telescoped into a very compact, oral tradition and handed down from generation to generation. If we attempt to fit such traditions into a mathematical time-scale, they would appear to cover only a few centuries whereas in reality they stretch much further back; and some of them, being in the form of myths, defy any attempt to describe them on a mathematical time-scale. In any case, oral history has no dates to be remembered. Man looks back from whence he came, and man is certain that nothing will bring this world to a conclusion. According to this interpretation of African view of history, there are innumerable myths about Zamani, but no myths about any end of the world, since time has no end.[4] African peoples expect human history to continue forever, in the rhythm of moving from the Sasa to the Zamani and there is nothing to suggest that this rhythm shall ever come to an end: the days, months, seasons and years have no end, just as there is no end to the rhythm of birth, marriage, procreation and death.

The Concept of Human Life in Relation to Time

Human life has another rhythm of nature which nothing can destroy. On the level of the individual, this rhythm includes birth, puberty, initiation, marriage, procreation, old age, death, entry into the community of the departed and finally entry into the company of the spirits. It is an ontological rhythm, and these are the key moments in the life of the individual. On the community or national level, there is the cycle of the seasons with their different activities like sowing, cultivating, harvesting and hunting. The key events or moments are given more attention than others, and may often be marked by religious rites and ceremonies. Unusual events or others which do not fit into this rhythm, such as an eclipse, drought, the birth of twins and the like, are generally thought to be bad omens, or to be events requiring special attention from the community, and this may take the form of a religious activity. The abnormal or unusual is an invasion of the ontological harmony.

Death and Immortality

As the individual gets older, he is in effect moving gradually from the Sasa to the Zamani. His birth is a slow process which is finalized long after the person has been physically born. In many societies, a person is not considered a full human being until he has gone through the whole process of physical birth, naming ceremonies, puberty and initiation rites, and finally marriage (or even procreation). Then he is fully "born," he is a complete person.

Similarly, death is a process which removes a person gradually from the Sasa period to the Zamani. After the physical death, the individual continues to exist in the Sasa period and does not immediately disappear from it. He is *remembered* by relatives and friends who knew

[4] The only possible exception to this statement comes from the Sonjo of Tanzania who think that the world will one day shrink to an end. This is not, however, something that dominates their life, and they go on living as though the idea did not exist. It is known that at one point in their history, this volcanic mountain (known in Maasai as Oldonyo Lengai: Mountain of God) erupted and caused an "end of the world" in their small country. This event may have been retained in the form of a myth which has been transferred to the unknown future, as a warning about possible future eruptions. See R. F. Gray *The Sonjo of Tanganyika* (1963) who, however, does not offer an explanation of this myth.

him in this life and who have survived him. They recall him by name, though not necessarily mentioning it, they remember his personality, his character, his words and incidents of his life. If he "appears" (as people believe), he is recognized *by name.* The departed appear mainly to the older members of their surviving families, and rarely or never to children. They appear to people whose Sasa period is the longest.

This recognition by name is extremely important. The appearance of the departed, and his being recognized by name, may continue for up to four or five generations, so long as someone is alive who once knew the departed personally and by name. When, however, the last person who knew the departed also dies, then the former passes out of the horizon of the Sasa period; and in effect he now becomes completely *dead* as far as family ties are concerned. He has sunk into the Zamani period. But while the departed person is remembered by name, he is not really dead: he is alive, and such a person I would call the *living-dead.* The living-dead is a person who is physically dead but alive in the memory of those who knew him in his life as well as being alive in the world of the spirits. So long as the living-dead is thus remembered, he is in the state of *personal immortality.* This personal immortality is externalized in the physical continuation of the individual through procreation, so that the children bear the traits of their parents or progenitors. From the point of view of the survivors, personal immortality is expressed or externalized in acts like respecting the departed, giving bits of food to them, pouring out libation and carrying out instructions given by them either while they lived or when they appear.

This concept of personal immortality should help us to understand the religious significance of marriage in African societies. Unless a person has close relatives to remember him when he has physically died, then he is nobody and simply vanishes out of human existence like a flame when it is extinguished. Therefore it is a duty, religious and ontological, for everyone to get married; and if a man has no children or only daughters, he finds another wife so that through her, children (or sons) may be born who would survive him and keep him (with the other living-dead of the family) in personal immortality. Procreation is the absolute way of insuring that a person is not cut off from personal immortality.

The acts of pouring out libation (of beer, milk or water), or giving portions of food to the living-dead, are symbols of communion, fellowship and remembrance. They are the mystical ties that bind the living-dead to their surviving relatives. Therefore these acts are performed within the family. The oldest member of the family is the one who has the longest Sasa period, and therefore the one who has the longest memory of the departed. He it is who performs or supervises these acts of remembrance on behalf of the entire family, addressing (when the occasion demands it) the symbolic meal to all the departed (living-dead) of the family, even if only one or two of the departed may be mentioned by name or position (e.g. father, grandfather). There is nothing here about the so-called "ancestor worship," even if these acts may so seem to the outsiders who do not understand the situation.

With the passing of time, the living-dead sink beyond the horizon of the *Sasa* period. This point is reached when there is no longer anyone alive who remembers them personally by name. Then the process of dying is completed. But the living-dead do not vanish out of existence: they now enter into the state of *collective immortality*. This is the state of the spirits who are no longer formal members of the human families. People lose personal contact with them. The departed in this state become members of the family or community of the spirits, and if they appear to human beings they are not recognized by name and may cause dread and fear. Their names may still be mentioned by human beings, especially in genealogies, but they are *empty names* which are more or less without a personality or at best with only a mythological personality built around fact and fiction. Such spirits have no personal communication with human families; in some societies, however, they might speak through a medium, or become guardians of the clan or nation, and may be mentioned or appealed to in religious rites of local or national significance. In other societies such spirits are incorporated into the body of intermediaries between God and man, and human beings approach God through them or seek other help from them. In reality, these spirits of the departed, together with other spirits which may or may not have been once human beings, occupy the ontological state between God and men. Beyond the state of the spirits, men cannot go or develop. This then is the destiny of man, as far as African ontology is concerned. African religious activities are chiefly focused upon the relationship between human beings and the departed; which really means that man tries to penetrate or project himself into the world of what remains of him after this physical life. If the living-dead are suddenly forgotten, this means that they are cast out of the Sasa period, and are in effect excommunicated, their personal immortality is destroyed and they are turned into a state of non-existence. And this is the worst possible punishment for anyone. The departed resent it, and the living do all they can to avoid it because it is feared that it would bring illness and misfortunes to those who forget their departed relatives. Paradoxically, death lies "in front" of the individual, it is still a "future" event; but when one dies, one enters the state of personal immortality which lies not in the future but in the Zamani.

Space and Time

Space and time are closely linked, and often the same word is used for both. As with time, it is the content which defines space. What matters most to the people is what is geographically near, just as Sasa embraces the life that people experience. For this reason, Africans are particularly tied to the land, because it is the concrete expression of both their Zamani and their Sasa. The land provides them with the roots of existence, as well as binding them mystically to their departed. People walk on the graves of their forefathers, and it is feared that anything separating them from these ties will bring disaster to family and community life. To remove Africans by force from their land is an act of such great injustice that no foreigner can fathom it. Even when people voluntarily leave their homes in the countryside and go to live or work in the cities, there is a fundamental severing of ties which cannot be repaired and which often creates psychological problems with which urban life cannot as yet cope.

Discovering or Extending the Future Dimension of Time

Partly because of Christian missionary teaching, partly because of western-type education, together with the invasion of modern technology with all it involves, African peoples are discovering the future dimension of time. On the secular level this leads to national planning for economic growth, political independence, extension of educational facilities and so on. But the change from the structure built around the traditional concept of time, to one which should accommodate this new discovery of the future dimension, is not a smooth one and may well be at the root of, among other things, the political instability of our nations. In Church life this discovery seems to create a strong expectation of the millennium. This makes many Christians escape from facing the challenges of this life into the state of merely hoping and waiting for the life of paradise. This strong millennial expectation often leads to the creation of many small independent churches centred around individuals who symbolize, and more or less fulfil, this messianic expectation.

The discovery and extension of the future dimension of time possess great potentialities and promises for the shaping of the entire life of African peoples. If these are harnessed and channelled into creative and productive use, they will no doubt become beneficial; but they can get out of control and precipitate both tragedy and disillusionment.

The traditional concept of time is intimately bound up with the entire life of the people, and our understanding of it may help to pave the way for understanding the thinking, attitude and actions of the people. It is against this background that I shall attempt to introduce and examine their religious systems and philosophy.

.   .   .   .

SPIRITUAL BEINGS, SPIRITS AND THE LIVING-DEAD

The spiritual world of African peoples is very densely populated with spiritual beings, spirits and the living-dead. Their insight of spiritual realities, whether absolute or apparent, is extremely sharp. To understand their religious ethos and philosophical perception it is essential to consider their concepts of the spiritual world in addition to concepts of God. We have repeatedly emphasized that the spiritual universe is a unit with the physical, and that these two intermingle and dovetail into each other so much that it is not easy, or even necessary, at times to draw the distinction or separate them. Although the spiritual world plays such an important role in African life, no serious studies have been made on the subject.[5] This is one of the weakest links in the study of African religions and philosophy.

The spirits in general belong to the ontological mode of existence between God and man. Broadly speaking, we can recognize two categories of spiritual beings: those which were created as such, and those which were once human beings. These can also be subdivided into divinities, associates of God, ordinary spirits and the living-dead. Our time analysis is here very useful in helping us to place the spiritual beings in their proper category, and to grasp the logic behind their recognition by African peoples. We can now take a closer look at these beings that populate the spiritual realm.

Divinities and God's Associates

I am using the word "divinity" to cover personifications of God's activities and manifestations, of natural phenomena and objects, the so-called "nature spirits," deified heroes and mythological figures. Sometimes it is difficult to know where to draw the line, especially since different writers loosely speak of 'gods', 'demigods', 'divinities', 'nature spirits', 'ancestral spirits' and the like.

Divinities are on the whole thought to have been created by God, in the ontological category of the spirits. They are associated with Him, and often stand for His activities or manifestations either as personifications or as the spiritual beings in charge of these major objects or phenomena of nature. Some of them are national heroes who have been elevated and deified, but this is rare, and when it does happen the heroes become associated with some function or form of nature. Concrete examples will make these points clearer.

[5] Reference to spirits is found in many of the books listed in the bibliography at the end of this work, but as a rule the subject is given little space.

It is reported that the Ashanti have a pantheon of divinities through whom God manifests Himself. They are known as *abosom;* are said to "come from Him" and to act as His servants and intermediaries between Him and other creatures. They are increasing numerically; and people hold festivals for major tribal divinities. Minor divinities protect individual human beings; and it is believed that God purposely created the *abosom* to guard men.[6] Banyoro divinities are departmentalized according to people's activities, experiences and social-political structure. They include the divinities of war, of smallpox, of harvest, of health and healing, of the weather, of the lake, of cattle and minor ones of different clans. The same pattern of divinities is reported among Basoga, Edo and others.

The Yoruba have one thousand and seven hundred divinities (*orisa*), this being obviously the largest collection of divinities in a single African people. These divinities are associated with natural phenomena and objects, as well as with human activities and experiences. They are said to render to God "annual tributes of their substance in acknowledgment of His Lordship." Parallel to the Yoruba social-political structure, these divinities form a hierarchy. *Orisa-nla* is 'the supreme divinity' in the country, and acts as God's earthly deputy in creative and executive functions. *Orunmila* is reputed to be an omnilinguist divinity who understands "every language spoken on earth," and who represents God's omniscience and knowledge. This divinity shows itself among men through the oracle of divinition, and has the fame of being a great doctor. *Ogun* is the owner of all iron and steel, being originally a hunter who paved the way for other divinities to come to earth, for which reason they crowned him as "Chief among the divinities." He is ubiquitous, and is the divinity of war, hunting and activities or objects connected with iron. *Sango* represents the manifestation of God's wrath, though legend makes him a historical figure in the region of Oyo near Ibadan. He is the divinity of thunder and lightning, and there is a cult for him. These are but a few of the Yoruba divinities, an interesting study of which can be found in Idowu's book.[7]

·   ·   ·   ·   ·   ·   ·   ·   ·   ·   ·   ·   ·   ·

Spirits

Myriads of spirits are reported from every African people, but they defy description almost as much as they defy the scientist's test tubes in the laboratory. Written sources are equally confusing. We have tried to include under the term 'divinity', those spiritual beings of a relatively

[6] Busia in D. Forde (ed.) *African Worlds* (Oxford: Oxford University Press, 1954), p. 191 f.

[7] Idowu, E. B. *Olodumare: God in Yoruba Belief* (London: Longmans, 1962) pp. 55–106.

high status. If we pursue the hierarchical consideration, we can say that the spirits are the "common" spiritual beings beneath the status of divinities, and above the status of men. They are the "common populace" of spiritual beings.

As for the origin of spirits, there is no clear information what African peoples say or think about it. Some spirits are considered to have been created as a "race" by themselves. These, like other living creatures, have continued to reproduce themselves and add to their numbers. Most peoples, however, seem to believe that the spirits are what remains of human beings when they die physically. This then becomes the ultimate status of men, the point of change or development beyond which men cannot go apart from a few national heroes who might become deified. Spirits are the destiny of man, and beyond them is God. Societies that recognize divinities regard them as a further group in the ontological hierarchy between spirits and God. Man does not, and need not, hope to become a spirit: he is inevitably to become one, just a child will automatically grow to become an adult, under normal circumstances. A few societies have an additional source of the spirits, believing that animals also have spirits which continue to live in the spirit world together with human and other spirits.

Spirits are invisible, but may make themselves visible to human beings. In reality, however, they have sunk beyond the horizon of the Zamani period, so that human beings do not see them either physically or mentally. Memory of them has slipped off. They are "seen" in the corporate belief in their existence. Yet, people experience their activities, and many folk stories tell of spirits described in human form, activities and personalities, even if an element of exaggeration is an essential part of that description. Because they are invisible, they are thought to be ubiquitous, so that a person is never sure where they are or are not.

Since the spirits have sunk into the horizon of the Zamani, they are within the state of collective immortality, relative to man's position. They have no family or personal ties with human beings, and are no longer the living-dead. As such, people fear them, although intrinsically the spirits are neither evil nor good. They have lost their human names, as far as men are concerned—i.e. those that once were human beings. To men, therefore, the spirits are strangers, foreigners, outsiders, and in the category of 'things'. They are often referred to as 'ITs'. Viewed anthropocentrically, the ontological mode of the spirits is a depersonalization and not a completion or maturation of the individual. Therefore, death is a loss, and the spirit mode of existence means the withering of the individual, so that his personality evaporates, his name disappears and he becomes less and not more of a person: a thing, a spirit and not a man any more.

Spirits as a group have more power than men, just as in a physical

sense the lions do. Yet, in some ways men are better off, and the right human specialists can manipulate or control the spirits as they wish. Men
paradoxically may fear, or dread, the spirits and yet they can drive the
same spirits away or use them to human advantage. In some societies only
the major spirits (presumably in the category of divinities) are recognized,
and often these are associated with natural phenomena or objects.

Although the spirits are ubiquitous, men designate different regions
as their places of abode. Among some societies like the Abaluyia, Banyarwanda and Igbo, it is thought that the spirits dwell in the under-
ground, netherworld, or the subterranean regions. The Banyarwanda say,
for example, that this region is ruled by "the one with whom one is forgotten"; and the Igbo consider it to be ruled by a queen. The idea of the
subterranean regions is suggested, obviously, by the fact that the bodies
of the dead are buried and the ground points to, or symbolizes, the new
homeland of the departed. A few societies like some Ewe, some Bushmen and the Mamvu-Mangutu, situate the land of the spirits above the
earth, in the air, the sun, moon or stars.

The majority of people hold that the spirits dwell in the woods,
bush, forest, rivers, mountains or just around the villages. Thus, the spirits are in the same geographical region as men. This is partly the result of
human self-protection and partly because man may not want to imagine
himself in an entirely strange environment when he becomes a spirit.
There is a sense in which man is too anthropocentric to get away from
himself and his natural, social, political and economic surroundings.
This then makes the spirits men's contemporaries: they are ever with
men, and man would feel uncomfortable if the ontological mode of the
spirits were too distant from his own. This would mean upsetting the
balance of existence, and if that balance is upset, then men make sacrifices, offerings and prayers, to try and restore it. In effect, men visualize
their next ontological stage, in form of spirits, but geographically it is not
another stage. The world of the spirits, wherever it might be situated, is
very much like the carbon copy of the countries where they lived in this
life. It has rivers, valleys, mountains, forests and deserts. The activities of
the spirits are similar to those of human life here, in addition to whatever
other activities of which men may not know anything.

Yet, in certain aspects, the spirit world differs radically from the human world. It is invisible to the eyes of men: people only know or believe
that it is there, but do not actually "see" it with their physical eyes. But
more important, even if the spirits may be the depersonalized residue of
individual human beings, they are ontologically "nearer" to God: not eth-
ically, but in terms of communication with Him. It is believed that
whereas men use or require intermediaries, the spirits do not, since they
can communicate directly with God. We have already shown that in
many African societies the spirits and the living-dead act as intermedi-

aries who convey human sacrifices or prayers to God, and may relay His reply to men. We have also seen that in some societies it is believed that God has servants or agents whom He employs to carry out His intentions in the universe. The spirits fill up the ontological region of the Zamani between God and man's Sasa. The ontological transcendence of God is bridged by the spirit mode of existence. Man is forever a creature, but he does not remain forever man, and these are his two polarities of existence. Individual spirits may or may not remain for ever, but the class of the spirits is an essential and integral part of African ontology.

Becoming spirits is, in a sense, a social elevation. For this reason, African peoples show respect and high regard for their living-dead and for some of the important spirits. Spirits are "older" than men, when viewed against the Sasa and Zamani periods—they have moved completely into the Zamani period. Their age which is greater than that of human beings compels the latter to give them respect along the same pattern that younger people give respect to older men and women, whether or not they are immediately members of the same family. In relation to the spirits, men are the younger generation, and social etiquette requires that they respect those who have fully entered and settled in the Zamani period.

Spirits do not appear to human beings as often as do the living-dead, and where mention of their appearances is made it is generally in folk stories. They act in malicious ways, as well as in a benevolent manner. People fear them more because of their being "strangers" than because of what they actually are or do. They are said to have a shadowy form of body, though they may assume different shapes like human, animal, plant forms or inanimate objects. People report that they see the spirits in ponds, caves, groves, mountains or outside their villages, dancing, singing, herding cattle, working in their fields or nursing their children. Some spirits appear in people's dreams, especially to diviners, priests, medicine-men and rain-makers to impart some information. These personages may also consult the spirits as part of their normal training and practice. In many societies it is said and believed that spirits call people by name, but on turning round to see who called them there would be nobody. This sounds like a naughty game on the part of the spirits who probably derive a lot of fun from it. In folk stories it is told that the spirits sleep in the daytime and remain awake at night.

As the spirits are invisible, ubiquitous and unpredictable, the safest thing is to keep away from them. If they, or the living-dead, appear too frequently to human beings people feel disturbed. Then the spirits possess men, and are blamed for forms of illness like madness and epilepsy. Spirit possession occurs in one form or another in practically every African society. Yet, spirit possession is not always to be feared, and there are times when it is not only desirable but people induce it through special dancing and drumming until the person concerned experiences spirit possession during which he may even collapse. When the person is thus possessed, the spirit may speak through him, so that he now plays the role of a medium, and the messages he relays are received with expectation by those to whom they are addressed. But on the whole, spirit possessions, especially unsolicited ones, result in bad effects. They may cause severe torment on the possessed person; the spirit may drive him away from his home so that he lives in the forests; it may cause him to jump into the fire and get himself burnt, to torture his body with sharp instruments, or even to do harm to other people. During the height of spirit possession, the individual in effect loses his own personality and acts in the context of the "personality" of the spirit possessing him. The possessed person becomes restless, may fail to sleep properly, and if the possession lasts a long period it results in damage to health. Women are more prone to spirit possession than men. Exorcism is one of the major functions of the traditional doctors and diviners; and when spirits "endanger" a village, there are usually formal ceremonies to drive away the notorious spirits. In some societies family spirits have to be moved ceremoniously when the villagers move from one place to another. This insures that the family spirits and especially the living-dead, move with members of their human relatives and are not forsaken when there is nobody to "remember" them in their personal immortality.

Human relationships with the spirits vary from society to society. It is, however, a real, active and powerful relationship, especially with the spirits of those who have recently died—whom we have called the living-dead. Various rites are performed to keep this contact, involving the placing of food and other articles, or the pouring of libation of beer, milk, water and even tea or coffee (for the spirits who have been "modernized"). In some societies this is done daily, but most African peoples do it less often. Such offerings are given to the oldest member of the departed—who may still be a living-dead, or may be remembered only in genealogies. This is done with the understanding that he will share the food or beverage with the other spirits of the family group. Words may or may not accompany such offerings, in form of prayers, invocations or instructions to the departed. These words are the bridge of communion, and people's witness that they recognize the departed to be still alive. Failure to observe these acts means in effect that human beings have completely broken off their links with the departed, and have therefore forgotten the spirits. This is regarded as extremely dangerous and disturbing to the social and individual conscience. People are then likely to feel any misfortune that befalls them is the logical result of their neglect of the spirits, if not caused by magic and witchcraft.

For spirits which are not associated with a particular family, offerings may be placed in spirit shrines where these exist. Such shrines belong to the community, and may be cared for by priests. Some of the spirits who are accorded this honour are venerated according to their functions, for example the spirits of the water may receive offerings when people want to fish or sail in the water; and the spirits of the forests may be consulted when people want to cut down the forest and make new fields. Here we merge with the category of the divinities, which we have already described above.

The Living-Dead

The departed of up to five generations are in a different category from that of ordinary spirits which we have been considering. They are still within the Sasa period, they are in the state of personal immortality, and their process of dying is not yet complete. We have called them the living-dead. They are the closest links that men have with the spirit world. Some of the things said about the spirits apply also to the living-dead. But the living-dead are bilingual: they speak the language of men, with whom they lived until "recently"; and they speak the language of the spirits and of God, to Whom they are drawing nearer ontologically. These are the 'spirits' with which African peoples are most concerned: it is through the living-dead that the spirit world becomes personal to men. They are still part of their human families, and people have personal memories of them. The two groups are bound together by their common Sasa which for the living-dead is, however, fast disappearing into the Zamani. The living-dead are still 'people', and have not yet become 'things', 'spirits' or 'its'. They return to their human families from time to time, and share meals with them, however symbolically. They know and have interest in what is going on in the family. When they appear, which is generally to the oldest members of the household, they are recognized by name as "so and so"; they enquire about family affairs, and may even warn of impending danger or rebuke those who have failed to follow their special instructions. They are the guardians of family affairs, traditions, ethics and activities. Offence in these matters is ultimately an offence against the forebearers who, in that capacity, act as the invisible police of the families and communities. Because they are still 'people', the living-dead are therefore the closest link between men and God: they know the needs of men, they have "recently" been here with men, and at the same time they have full access to the channels of communicating with God directly or, according to some societies, indirectly through their own forebearers. Therefore people may involve them in family affairs more often for minor needs of life than they approach God. Even if the living-dead may not do miracles or extraordinary things to remedy the need, men experience a sense of psychological relief when they pour out their hearts' troubles before their seniors who have a foot in both worlds.

All this does not mean that the relationship between men and the living-dead is exclusively paradisal. People know only too well that following physical death, a barrier has been erected between them and the living-dead. When the living-dead return and appear to their relatives, this experience is not received with great enthusiasm by men; and if it becomes too frequent, people resent it. Men do not say to the living-dead: "Please sit down and wait for food to be prepared!"; nor would they bid farewell with the words: "Greet so-and-so in the spirit world!" And yet these are two extremely important aspects of social friendliness and hospitality among men in African communities. The food and libation given to the living-dead are paradoxically acts of hospitality and welcome, and yet of informing the living-dead to move away. The living-dead are wanted and yet not wanted. If they have been improperly buried or were offended before they died, it is feared by the relatives or the offenders that the living-dead would take revenge. This would be in the form of misfortune, especially illness, or disturbing frequent appearances of the living-dead. If people neglect to give food and libation where this is otherwise the normal practice, or if they fail to observe instructions that the living-dead may have given before dying, then misfortunes and sufferings would be interpreted as resulting from the anger of the living-dead. People are, therefore, careful to follow the proper practices and customs regarding the burial or other means of disposal of dead bodies, and make libation and food offerings as the case might be. In some societies, special care of the graves is taken, since the living-dead may be considered to dwell in the area of the graves, some of which are in the former houses of the departed.

Attention is paid to the living-dead of up to four or five generations, by which time only a few, if any, immediate members of their families would still be alive. When the last person who knew a particular living-dead also dies, then in effect the process of death is now complete as far as that particular living-dead is concerned. He is now no longer remembered by name, no longer a 'human being', but a spirit, a thing, an IT. He has now sunk beyond the visible horizon of the Zamani. It is no more necessary to pay close attention to him in the family obligation of making food offerings and libation, except, in some societies, within the context of genealogical remembrances or in the chain of the intermediaries. By that time also, additional living-dead have come into the picture and deserve or require more attention from the living. Those who have "moved on" to the stage of full spirits, merge into the company of spirits, and people lose both contact with and interest in them. They are no longer in the human period of the Sasa, even if they may continue to be men's contemporaries. Their plane of existence is other than that of men, they are ontologically spirits and spirits only. In some societies it is believed that some living-dead are "reborn." This is, however, only partial re-incarnation since not the entire person is reborn as such, but only certain of his characteristics or physical distinctions.

· · · · · · · · · · · · · ·

MYSTICAL POWER, MAGIC, WITCHCRAFT AND SORCERY

On the subject of magic and witchcraft in Africa there is a great deal of literature.[8] And yet, one is struck and disappointed by the large amount of ignorance, prejudice and falsification which keeps coming out in modern books, newspapers and conversation on this subject. Discussion is centred on two camps at opposite ends. The larger camp has those who expose their own ignorance, false ideas, exaggerated prejudices and a derogatory attitude which belittles and despises the whole concept of mystical power. The other is represented by a few scholars who seriously consider African views, fears, uses and manipulation of this power. Most of the distorted ideas have come through European and American popular writers, missionaries and colonial administrators. Every African who has grown up in the traditional environment will, no doubt, know something about this mystical power which often is experienced, or manifests itself, in form of magic, divination, witchcraft and mysterious phenomena that seem to defy even immediate scientific explanations. . . .

. . . [T]he whole psychic atmosphere of African village life is filled with belief in . . . mystical power. African peoples know that the universe has a power, force or whatever else one may call it, in addition to the items in the ontological categories which we discussed in chapter three. It is difficult to know exactly what it is or how it functions. Even where allowance is made for conjuring tricks, obvious cheating, superstition, manipulation of hidden means of communication and other skilled use of laws of nature, one is left and confronted with phenomena which as yet cannot be scientifically explained away. The incidents I described above are not very dramatic, and yet they cannot be dismissed as trickery, hypnotism or purely the result of psychological conditions of those who experience them. To my knowledge, there is no African society which does not hold belief in mystical power of one type or another. It shows itself, or it is experienced, in many ways.

[8] G. Bloomhill *Witchcraft in Africa* (Cape Town 1962), p. 164 f.

There is mystical power in words, especially those of a senior person to a junior one, in terms of age, social status or office position. The words of parents, for example, carry "power" when spoken to children: they "cause" good fortune, curse, success, peace, sorrows or blessings, especially when spoken in moments of crisis. The words of the medicine-man work through the medicine he gives, and it is this, perhaps more than the actual herb, which is thought to cause the cure or prevent misfortunes. Therefore, formal "curses" and "blessings" are extremely potent; and people may travel long distances to receive formal blessings, and all are extra careful to avoid formal curses. The specialists whom we discussed in the previous chapter have much mystical power both as individuals and by virtue of their professions or offices.

There is mystical power which causes people to walk on fire, to lie on thorns or nails, to send curses or harm, including death, from a distance, to change into animals (lycanthropy), to spit on snakes and cause them to split open and die; power to stupefy thieves so that they can be caught red-handed; power to make inanimate objects turn into biologically living creatures; there is power that enables experts to see into secrets, hidden information or the future, or to detect thieves and other culprits. African peoples know this and try to apply it in these and many other ways. For that reason, they wear charms, eat "medicines" or get them rubbed into their bodies; they consult experts, especially the diviners and medicine-men to counteract the evil effects of this power or to obtain powerfully "charged" objects containing the same power. Some may even pay fantastic amounts of wealth to have a reasonable access to it, in one form or another. The majority, if not all, fear it, and many of them have encountered it in their normal life. This mystical power is not fiction: whatever it is, it is a reality, and one with which African peoples have to reckon. Everyone is directly or indirectly affected, for better or for worse, by beliefs and activities connected with this power, particularly in its manifestation as magic, sorcery and witchcraft. Without going into any exhaustive discussion, we may now draw our attention to magic, sorcery and witchcraft.

Magic is generally considered under "good magic" and "evil magic." The use of good magic is accepted and esteemed by society. It is chiefly the specialists, and particularly the medicine-man, diviner and rainmaker, who use their knowledge and manipulation of this mystical power for the welfare of their community. It is used in the treatment of diseases, in counteracting misfortunes, and in warding off or diluting or destroying evil "power" or witchcraft. The diviner or medicine-man provides amounts of mystical power to people in form of charms, amulets, powder, rags, feathers, figures, special incantations or cuttings on the body. He uses it to protect homesteads, families, fields, cattle and other property. If you go into African homesteads you might see, for example, a forked post standing in the middle of the compound, or a piece of pot on the roof of the house, or a few lines of ashes strewn across the gate as you enter the homestead; and if you go to the fields you might spot a horn sticking out of the ground, or an old gourd hanging on a tree. If you see babies, they probably will have coils round the neck or wrist, their hair might be shaved off except for small locks left standing on the otherwise bare heads, or the locks might be knotted. These and many hundreds of other articles or visible signs, are pointers to people's belief in the mystical power: some are protective measures, others are intended to bring good health, fortune or prosperity. It is forbidden and feared in many African societies, to "praise" somebody else's children or property, for to do so may cause the mystical power to harm or destroy the child or property. One needs eyes to see, to "read" and to understand the meaning of signs, objects and articles that may be found in African homes, fields, possessions and even on their bodies.

No doubt there are people who believe that protection or prosperity comes from these objects which they wear or otherwise use. This would be magic. But others believe and acknowledge that the objects in themselves have no inherent power as such. Instead, these objects represent and symbolize power which comes from God. This power may directly be supplied by God, or it may be through the spirits, the living-dead or as part of the invisible force of nature in the universe. The objects can also lose their effectiveness, and the owner must then get new ones or if possible get old objects recharged like a car battery. At this point religion and magic merge, and there is no clear way of separating them, any more than magic has been separated from Christianity or Islam at certain points.

Some individuals spend a great deal of their wealth and effort to obtain this type of magical protection and means of prosperity. Some dealers are real experts in the business, but there are others who supply cheap, false articles for the sake of gain. The commonest specialist is the medicine-man, of whom we have already spoken. He uses "good magic," as do also the diviner and rainmaker who function chiefly for the good of society. These specialists tell that the mystical power which they tap and use, comes ultimately from God; and as we have seen, part of their profession involves praying to God, directly or through the intermediary of the living-dead and spirits, to solicit His help. As such, this is "spiritual" power functioning through physical means; and as we have seen for African peoples the two worlds are one universe. The spirits have more access to this power than do human beings. It is perhaps this which adds to the stature of the departed, even if these died as children, for upon death, the living-dead enter into a higher "dynamic" hierarchy than that of the living. As a rule also, younger people will rarely attempt to use this power against older members of their community, unless it is in taking counter measures. The older a person is, and the higher his social status is, the more he is thought or expected to have this mystical power, either in himself or through the possession of the necessary objects in which it may be stored.

It is to be noted in passing that some of the independent Churches, particularly in southern and western Africa, have men and women who specialize in dealing with this power.

Evil magic involves the belief in and practice of tapping and using this power to do harm to human beings or their property. It is here that we find sorcery at work, in addition to other related practices. We must point out, however, that a great deal of belief here is based on, or derives from, fear, suspicion, jealousies, ignorance or false accusations, which go on in African villages. People fear to leave around their hair, nails, clothes or other articles with which they are normally in direct contact in case their "enemies" will use them and work evil magic against them. The hair, or nails may be burnt or pricked or otherwise used in a "harmful" way, and thus cause infliction on the person from whom they come. It is feared that an enemy might put thorns on a person's foot print, and thus cause harm to him. This is what James Frazer distinguishes as "contagious magic." His other useful category is "homoeopathic magic," which in African societies could be illustrated with endless examples. This involves the belief that what happens to an object which looks like another will affect the latter. For example, an enemy might make a doll which represents a particular person, and by burning or pricking that doll it is believed that the person would be harmed accordingly. These two categories of magical beliefs and practices function, however, in both good and evil ways. It is when used maliciously that this mystical power is condemned as "black magic," "evil magic" or "sorcery."

Technically speaking, however, "sorcery" involves the use of poisonous ingredients, put into the food or drink of someone. But this is an academic finesse. For African people's sorcery stands for anti-social employment of mystical power, and sorcerers are the most feared and hated members of their communities. It is feared that they employ all sorts of ways to harm other people or their belongings. For example, they send flies, snakes, lions or other animals to attack their enemies or carry disease to them; they spit and direct the spittle with secret incantations to go and harm someone; they dig up graves to remove human flesh or bones which they use in their practices; they invoke spirits to attack or possess someone. African peoples feels and believe that all the various ills, misfortunes, sicknesses, accidents, tragedies, sorrows, dangers and unhappy mysteries which they encounter or experience, are caused by the use of this mystical power in the hands of a sorcerer, witch or wizard. It is here that we may understand, for example, that a bereaved mother whose child has died from malaria will not be satisfied with the scientific explanation that a mosquito carrying malaria parasites stung the child and caused it to suffer and die from malaria. She will wish to know why the mosquito stung her child and not somebody else's child. The only satisfactory answer is that "someone" sent the mosquito, or worked other evil magic against her child. This is not a scientific answer, but it is reality for the majority of African peoples. We may easily get rid of mosquitoes and prevent many diseases; but there will always be accidents, cases of barrenness, misfortunes and other unpleasant experiences. For African peoples these are not purely physical experiences: they are "mystical" experiences of a deeply religious nature. People in the villages will talk freely about them, for they belong to their world of reality, whatever else scientists and theologians might say. Nothing harmful happens "by chance": everything is "caused" by someone directly or through the use of mystical power. If you have your ears open, you will hear the names of people being blamed for misfortunes, sickness, accidents and other forms of suffering, in every village. It is mainly women who get blamed for experiences of evil kind; and many a women has suffered and continues to suffer under such accusations, sooner or later.

Sorcerers, evil magicians, witches and medicine-men or diviners occasionally employed for this purpose, are believed to send flies, bats, birds, animals, spirits and magical objects (like the "magic snake" which does not bleed) to achieve their ends; they harm with the "evil eye"; they dig evil medicine in the ground where the victim will pass; they put magic objects in the homes or fields of their victim; or send "death" from a distance; they might change into animals in order to attack their victims; or they place harmful medicines where the victim would come into contact with it. All this means that in the villages people cannot feel completely "safe." It also means that even the smallest experience of misfortune and sorrow is blamed on the misuse of this mystical power. For that reason, people resort to medicine-men and diviners to supply them with protective objects. The principle or logic at work here is that the good use of this power will counteract the evil use, and thus keep the user relatively safe, so long as his "medicine" is more powerful than that of his enemy. Charms, amulets, medicines drunk or rubbed into the body, articles on the roof or in the fields, cuts, knots, and many other visible and invisible, secret and open precautions, are used in all communities for seriously religious intentions, to secure a feeling of safety, protection and assurance. In this perspective we see the importance of diviners and medicine-men who, in addition to supplying the objects of cure and protection, may also perform rituals to cleanse people or homesteads subjected to attacks from this mystical power. They also give medicines to cure or "cool" those who are believed to use that power for evil purposes. Formerly the workers of this type of evil were severely punished by their communities, through stoning, beating, paying of fines and death. Even today one fairly often reads in newspapers of people being attacked, and occasionally killed, on accusation or suspicion of practising evil magic.

A modern trend in the use of mystical power is seen in the activities of "money doublers." This racket is reported in western Africa, though it may be starting elsewhere as well. Money doublers cheat people by telling them to leave sums of money at agreed places, promising that by "miraculous" magical ways they will "double" the money, and the owners can then collect the larger amount after a while. When people return to collect their money, they find the bags or boxes either empty or filled up with sand, leaves, stones or other worthless material. Even educated people, including Church pastors, are reported to fall victim to "money doublers."

Anthropologists and sociologists use the term "witchcraft" in a specialized way. According to them witches, who are mainly women, are people with an inherent power by means of which they can abandon their bodies at night and go to meet with similar people (other witches) or to "suck" or "eat away" the life of their victims. Some societies, like the Azande, can even pin-point the spot in the witch's body where "witchcraft" is located. If we press this usage of the term witch and witchcraft, we would find that actually some African societies do not hold this belief. It would also mean that some witches do not realize that they are witches; and this makes witchcraft an infectious or hereditary tendency. Some women suspect themselves to be witches while in actual fact they are not. They may also find themselves meeting with other "witches" at night, physically at least, to plan their activities or share their experiences. I confess that this part of the story hinges close to fiction, and it may well turn out to be extremely difficult to substantiate.

Witchcraft is a term used more popularly and broadly, to describe all sorts of evil employment of mystical power, generally in a secret fashion. African societies do not often draw the rather academic distinction between witchcraft, sorcery, evil magic, evil eye and other ways of employing mystical power to do harm to someone or his belongings. Generally the same word is used for all these English terms; and the same person is accused or suspected of employing one or more of these ways of hurting members of his community. In popular usage the term "witchcraft" is employed to designate the harmful employment of mystical power in all its different manifestations. I am inclined to use the term "witch" or "witchcraft" in this broader sense; and here theologians may wish to part company with anthropologists. In any case, it is easier to say "bewitch" than "evil magicize" or "sorcerize" in describing the use of this power to harm another person. Whatever terminology wins in the end one thing is absolutely certain, that African peoples believe that there are individuals who have access to mystical power which they employ for destructive purposes. In a non-scientific environment belief of this type cannot be "clean" from fear, falsehood, exaggeration, suspicion, fiction and irrationality. Whatever reality there is concerning witchcraft in the broad and popular sense of the term, the belief in it is there in every African village, and that belief affects everyone, for better or for worse. It is part of the religious corpus of beliefs.

We may conclude this chapter by summarizing a few major points. African peoples are aware of a mystical power in the universe. This power is ultimately from God, but in practice it is inherent in, or comes from or through physical objects and spiritual beings. That means that the universe is not static or "dead": it is a dynamic, "living" and powerful universe.

Access to this mystical power is hierarchical in the sense that God has the most and absolute control over it; the spirits and the living-dead have portions of it; and some human beings know how to tap, manipulate and use some of it. Each community experiences this force or power as useful and therefore acceptable, neutral or harmful and therefore evil. On the credit side, mystical power is employed for curative, protective, productive and preventive purposes. For this reason, Africans wear, carry or keep charms, amulets and a variety of other objects, on their bodies, in their possessions, homesteads and fields. Medicine-men and diviners are the main dealers in the use, manufacture and distribution of these articles of "medicine" or power. On the negative side, it is used to "eat" away the health and souls of victims, to attack people, to cause misfortunes and make life uncomfortable. The witches, wizards, sorcerers, evil magicians and people with an evil eye, are the ones who employ this power for anti-social and harmful activities. From time to time, each community undertakes to "smell-out" or hunt the sorcerers and witches, punish them, "cool" them off, cure them and counteract their activities. Everyone, however, keeps constant guard against the wicked doings of these "evil workers," whether they are real or imaginary.

A good number of people spend large amounts of their wealth to obtain access to this power. Expert users spend years to acquire their knowledge and skill some of which is obviously secret and unknown to outsiders. Such experts have their own "science" in dealing with this mystery of the universe. There are reports of fantastic experiences and phenomena attributed to this mystical power; and some of them defy both repetition and explanation by means of modern science.

The subject of mystical power, magic, sorcery and witchcraft, with all the beliefs that accompany it, has other dimensions besides the religious. There are social, psychological and economic aspects which add to the complexity of discussing and understanding this subject.

· · · · · · · · · · · · · · ·

▲ On Negrohood: Psychology of the African Negro*

Leopold S. Senghor

Leopold Senghor is an acclaimed poet, essayist, philosopher, and political activist. He was born in 1906 in Joal, Senegal and served as that country's first president. During the 1930s Senghor, with Leon Damas of French Guiana and Aime Cesaire of Martinique, played a major role in articulating the basic ideas that have come to be known as "Negritude." Negritude is predicated on the existence of a basic difference between European whites and African Negroes, a difference that manifests itself in the cultural forms characteristic of each race.

Senghor considers the propensity to produce the cultural forms characteristic of one's race to be partially inherited, a result of the physiological makeup of the individual. This difference in physiology is also supposed to manifest itself in terms of the characteristic manner in which members of a particular race developed their knowledge of reality. Thus, the European typically visualizes what is to be known, and then attempts to analyze it into its basic constituents. The African, on the other hand, adopts a more kinesthetic attitude toward the object of attention and attempts to "participate" in the internal rhythms of the object.

As a result of the paradoxes of quantum mechanics, Darwinian evolution, and mathematical logic, Senghor felt that Europeans were becoming more aware of the limitations of the scientific approach to reality and were beginning to recognize the need to cultivate an aesthetic appreciation of reality. This requires using the body to produce emotional responses that allow the knower to participate in a kind of mystical union with the known. It is this affective attitude toward the world that is the essence of the African way of knowing, the essence of Negritude.

For a treatment of the relationship between Negritude and African Socialism, see Chapter 7 of Segun Gbadegesin African Philosophy: Traditional Yoruba Philosophy and Contemporary African Realities *(NY: Peter Lang, 1991). For Negritude's relationship to the Harlem Renaissance, see Chapter 1 of D.A. Masolo* African Philosophy in Search of Identity *(Bloomington: Indiana University Press, 1994).*

* Translated by H. Kaal.

How surprised the psychologists of the French army were when they discovered that Senegalese conscripts were more sensitive to the vicissitudes of the climate, and even to extreme heat, than the soldiers of "met-
ropolitan" France; that they reacted to the least changes in the weather,
and even to such barely discernible events as minute inflections of the
voice. These warriors who had passed for brutes—these heroes—turned
out to have the sensitivity of women. It is often said, and not without reason, that *the Negro is a man of Nature.* The African negro, whether peasant, fisherman, hunter or herdsman, lives outdoors, both off the earth and
with it, on intimate terms with trees and animals and all the elements,
and to the rhythm of seasons and days. He keeps his senses open, ready
to receive any impulse, and even the very waves of nature, without a
screen (which is not to say without relays or transformers) between subject and object. He does, of course, reflect; but what comes first is form
and color, sound and rhythm, smell and touch. As Aimé Césaire, the poet
of negrohood, chants:

> Hail to the royal Kaicedrat!
> Hail to those who have invented nothing,
> To those who have explored nothing,
> To those who have subdued nothing,
> But abandoned themselves to the grip of the essence of every thing,
> Ignorant of the surface, but gripped by the movement of every thing,
> Not caring to subdue, but to play the game of the world.
>
> Truly the elder sons of the world:
> Open to all the breezes of the world,
> The brotherly air of all the breezes of the world;
> A bed without a drain for all the waters of the world,
> Sparkling with the sacred fire of the world;
> Flesh of the flesh of the world, palpitating with the very movement
>   of the world.[1]

In these often-cited verses, the poet contrasts the Negro with the
White, the African with the European. I am well aware that contrast sim-
plifies the problem. But the contrast is significant, as shown by the fact
that Jean-Paul Sartre takes it up in *Orphée noir,* where he contrasts the
black peasant with the white engineer.[2] It is the attitude towards the *object*—towards the external world, the *Other*—which characterizes a people, and thereby their culture.

Let us consider first the European White in his attitude towards the
object. He is (or at least was from the time of Aristotle to the "stupid
nineteenth century") an *objective intelligence.* As a man of action, war-

---

[1] *Cahier d'un retour au pays natal,* Gallimard.
[2] Preface to the *Anthologie de la nouvelle poésie nègre et malgache de langue
française,* P.U.F., p. xxxi.

rior, bird of prey, pure vision, he first of all distinguishes himself from the object. He keeps it at a distance, immobilizes it outside time and in some sense outside space, fixes it and slays it. Armed with precision instruments, he dissects it mercilessly so as to arrive at a factual analysis. Learned, but moved by practical considerations, the European White uses the Other, after slaying it, for practical ends: He treats it as a *means*. And he *assimilates* it in a centripetal motion; destroys it by feeding on it. "The Whites are cannibals," a wise old man of my country said to me a few years ago, "they do not respect life." It is indeed this kind of diet which they call "the humanization of nature" and, more accurately, "the domestication of nature." "But," added the wise old man who had seen, heard and thought much, "they do not realize, those Whites, that life cannot be domesticated, and especially not God, who is the source of all life and in whom all life resides." And he concluded: "It is life which humanizes and not death. I am afraid all this will turn out badly. The Whites, in their destructive folly, are in the end going to bring misfortune upon us." Of course, the wise old man used figurative language which I have rendered badly.

The African negro is as it were locked up in his black skin. He lives in a primordial night, and does not distinguish himself, to begin with, from the object: from tree or pebble, man or animal, fact of nature or society. He does not keep the object at a distance, does not analyze it. After receiving its impression, he takes the object, all alive, into his hands—like a blind man, anxious not to fix it or to kill it. He turns it over and over in his supple hands, touches it, *feels* it. The African negro is one of those worms created on the Third Day: a pure sensory field. It is in his subjectivity and at the end of his antennae, like those of an insect, that he discovers the *Other*. And at this point, he is *e-moved** to the roots of his belly and carried, in a centrifugal motion, from subject to object on the waves which the Other emits.

Contemporary physicists have discovered underneath matter a universal energy: the waves and radiations of matter. This is more than a fantasy. Pierre Teilhard de Chardin has, as is well known, drawn revolutionary conclusions from it, and distinguished between *tangential* or material, and *radial* or psychic, energy. I wonder whether the subject does not perceive both forms of energy in the electric waves which agitate the nerve cells. This would partly explain the behavior of the African negro. At any rate, American psychologists have noted that the reflexes of the

---

* The French *émotion* and its English equivalent (the noun "emotion") may suggest that an emotion is an outward movement. To bring out this suggestion, the author inserts a hyphen between prefix and stem. His *é-motion* will accordingly be rendered as "e-motion." While the same suggestion may be carried by the French *émouvoir*, its English equivalent (the verb "to move," in the sense in which a person can be moved to tears, joy, etc.) carries at best the suggestion that an emotion is a movement. To suggest the outward direction, the author's *é-mouvoir* will be rendered by the artificial "to e-move."—TR.

Negro are more natural and sure, because more in agreement with the object. Hence negroes were employed during the Second World War in industry and in the technical services of the army at a higher percentage than they represented in the population. This means that, by their very physiological makeup (which should not, however, make us lose sight of their psychic heredity and social experience), their behavior is more *lived,* in the sense that it is a more direct, a more concrete, expression of sensation and stimulation, which come from the object with its original force and quality. The impression is retained in the "living moment" to be transformed into sensation and representation which, in turn, form the basis of behavior with its social background. And thus the Negro—the African negro, to return to him—reacts more faithfully to stimulation by the object: he espouses its rhythm. This carnal sense of *rhythm,* that of movement, form and color, is one of his specific characteristics. For rhythm is the very essence of energy. It is rhythm which is at the bottom of imitation, which plays such a prominent role in the "generative" or "creative" activities of man: in memory, language and art.

Let us pause for a moment to illustrate this proposition about the rhythm of a movement in music and dance. When I see a team in action, at a soccer game for example, I take part in the game with my entire body. When I listen to a jazz tune or an African negro song, I have to make every effort not to break into song or dance, for I am now a "civilized" person. George Hardy wrote that the most civilized negro, even in a dinner jacket, always stirred at the sound of a tom-tom. He was quite right. The reason for all this is that team play reproduces the gestures natural to man, and that African negro music and dance (which are one, like music and dance in general) reproduce the movements of the human body, which are in turn attuned to the movements of the brain and of the world: to heart-beat, respiration, the rhythms of marching and making love, ebb and flow, the succession of days and seasons, and in general, all the rhythms of the universe. As Pierre Teilhard de Chardin wrote, man is first of all a "cosmic phenomenon."[3] It is this cosmic rhythm, with its variations and modulations, which the object emits; this, which makes a pleasurable impression on the nerve cells; this, which our behavior is a response to. When this rhythm is disturbed and the object emits a discordant rhythm, it produces a disagreeable sensation and elicits a defensive reaction. When the rhythm is either missing or unnatural, which is always true of plainsong, and often of European music, the African negro still reacts, but by imposing his own rhythm. After the First World War, we used to "jazz up" the plainsong, to the great indignation of Father Jeuland. "Don't act like negroes," he chided us. The conclusion to be drawn from all this is that the rhythm of the object is certainly transmitted to

[3] Letter of Sept. 21, 1952.

the body of the subject through his nerve cells, at which point—at the height of emotion—the rhythms of the heart and lungs fall in step with it, as illustrated by music and dance.[4] It has been observed that the rhythm of a movement, in the case of music and dance, is less transformed by the brain than any other rhythm. The reason is probably that it is more in agreement with the physiological rhythms. The brain plays as it were only the role of a relay station. A friend of mine, an African negro poet, confessed to me that every form of beauty hit him in the root of his belly and made a sexual impression on him. Not only the music, dance and masks of the Negro, but also a painting by Giotto and a Florentine palace. This went even further than might be thought; for the symbolic imagery of High Mass, visual as well as auditory, produced in him the same impression. Above all, let no one decry this as eroticism. *Sensuality* would be the more accurate term. But *spirituality* would be better still; for the spirituality of the Negro is rooted in sensuality: in his physiology.

Let us stay with the *e-motion* of the African negro, and take up the thread of fantasy. Here, then, is the subject who leaves his I to *sympathize* with the *Thou,* and to identify himself with it. He dies to himself to be reborn in the Other. He does not assimilate it, but himself. He does not take the Other's life, but strengthens his own with its life. For he lives a communal life with the Other, and in *sym-biosis* with it: He knows [and is thus born with] it.* Subject and object are dialectically confronted in the very act of knowledge [and thus of common birth]. It is from a long caress in the night, from the intimacy of two bodies confounded with one another, from the act of love, that the fruit of knowledge is born. "I want you to feel me," says a Senegalese elector when he wants his deputy to know him well and to distinguish him from others. To greet, in Wolof, is *neyu;* and a distinguished old man tells me that the word has the same etymology as *noyi,* "to breathe to oneself," to feel. "I think, therefore I am," wrote Descartes, who was the European *par excellence.* The African negro could say, "I feel, I dance the Other, I am." Unlike Descartes, he has no need for a "verbal utensil" (to use a term my teacher, Ferdinand Brunot, invented) to realize his *being,* but for an *objective complement.* He has no need to think, but to live the Other by dancing it. In dark Africa, people always dance because they feel, and they always dance someone or something. Now to dance is to discover and to *re-create,* to identify oneself with the forces of life, to lead a fuller life, and in short, to *be.* It is, at any rate, the highest form of knowledge. And thus, the knowledge of the African negro is, at the same time, discovery and creation—re-creation.

---

[4] Cf. "Physiologie de l'art," by Tanneguy de Quénétain, *Réalités,* No. 141, Oct. 1957.
* The French *connaître* (to know) may suggest that knowledge is common birth. To bring out this suggestion, the author writes *connaître* (to know) as *co-naître* (literally: to be born with). Since there is no English equivalent which would carry this suggestion, the literal and the suggested sense will have to be conveyed by different words.—TR.

Some young negro intellectuals, who have read Marx absentmindedly, and who are only beginning to rid themselves of the inferiority complex with which the colonialists inoculated them, have reproached me for having reduced the knowledge of the African negro to pure emotion, and for having denied that the African negro is endowed with reason and technical knowledge. They have read me as absent-mindedly as, before me, the "scientific socialists." All the evidence shows that there are two cultures, that of the European White and that of the African negro. The question is how these differences and the reasons for them are to be explained, and this my critics have not yet done. Let me refer them to their own sources: "Reason has always existed," wrote Marx to Arnold Ruge, "but not in a rational form." Engels, still more explicit, observed in his preparatory notes for *AntiDühring*: "Two kinds of experience, the one external, material, and the other internal: the laws and the forms of thought. The forms of thought, too, are partly transmitted through heredity. A mathematical axiom, for example, is self-evident to a European. But certainly not to a Bushman or an Australian negro."[5] This could hardly be put better; and this reflection confirms what was said before. Reason is one, in the sense that it is made for the apprehension of the Other, that is, of objective reality. Its nature is governed by its own laws, but its modes of knowledge, its "forms of thought," are diverse and tied to the psychological and physiological makeup of each race.

The vital force of the African negro, that is, his surrender to the Other, is thus inspired by reason. But reason is not, in this case, the *visualizing* reason of the European White, but a kind of *embracing* reason which has more in common with *logos* than with *ratio*. For *ratio* is compass, T-square and sextant; it is measure and weight. *Logos* on the other hand was the living word before Aristotle forged it into a diamond. Being the most typical human expression of a neural and sensory impression, *logos* does not mold the object (without touching it) into rigid logical categories. The *word* of the African negro, which becomes flesh as we shall see presently when we come to language, restores objects to their primordial color, and brings out their true grain and veins, their names and odors. It perforates them with its luminous rays so as to make them again transparent, and penetrates their sur-reality, I mean, their *sub-reality*,* in its primeval wetness. *The reason of classical Europe is analytic through utilization, the reason of the African negro, intuitive through participation.*

The phrase "the reason of classical Europe" is deliberate. For we now find the European Whites themselves—artists, philosophers, even scientists—going to the school of participant reason. We are witnessing a

[5] Translated from the German of the Moscow edition, 1946, p. 40.
* That is, their underlying reality.—TR.

true revolution in European epistemology, which has been taking place since the turn of the century. Gaëtan Picon has described this change in his introduction to *Panorama des idées contemporaines*[6] under the title "On the Style of the Contemporary Spirit."

The new method, and hence the new theory, of knowledge arose out of the latest scientific discoveries: relativity, wave mechanics, quantum mechanics, non-Euclidian geometries. And also out of new philosophical theories: phenomenology, existentialism, Teilhardism. It was a response to the need to outgrow the scientific positivism of the nineteenth century and even dialectical materialism. European dialectics (for there is also the dialectics of the African negro) was still too abstract, even in Marx's and Engels's hands, and too close to logic, which it had absorbed, with its concepts and categories, inductions and deductions. It was also determinist. Nowadays, whether we look at science, philosophy or art, we find discontinuity and indeterminism at the bottom of everything, of the mind as well as the real, where they reveal themselves after the most detailed and at the same time the most passionate investigations. All disciplines break up into more specific disciplines. "There are several geometries," writes Gaëtan Picon, "several possible kinds of logic, mentality and irreducible psychological structures."[7] The mind, as well as the real, manifests itself through varied and conflicting images.

Since the object appeared henceforth as "discontinuous and indeterminate reality,"[8] Europeans were led to abandon their method of *objectivity* which had prevailed among them for two thousand years. As Gaston Bachelard has emphasized in *Le nouvel esprit scientifique,* a new situation calls for a new method. Gaëtan Picon adds specifically: "Since time immemorial, Western philosophical tradition has insisted on the distance between object and observer; since time immemorial, it has tried to escape the confused struggle in which looks and objects are confounded in their very nature, and to substitute contemplation for embrace."[9] Similarly for the scientific tradition, not to mention the artistic one. The new method in science, philosophy and art is at the opposite end from this "visual realism." "We witness a general retreat of the idea of objectivity. Everywhere, we find the researcher implicated in his own researches, and revealing things only by veiling them. The light of knowledge is no longer that unchanging clarity which would light on the object without touching it and being touched by it; it is a troubled flame sparked by their *embrace,* a lightning produced by *contact,* a *participation,* a *communion.* Modern philosophy wants to be experience, a living

---

[6] Gallimard. *Cf.* G. Bachelard, *Le nouvel esprit scientifique,* P.U.F., and P. Guaydier, *Les grandes découvertes de la physique moderne,* Corréa.

[7] *Op. cit.,* p. 11.

[8] *Ibid.,* p. 25.

[9] *Ibid.,* p. 26.

identity of knowledge and the known, of life and thought, of life and reality. The sciences of man are opposed to explanation and comprehension: To grasp the sense of a fact of human nature is to grasp oneself in it,
and it in oneself."[10] It is not significant that Gaëtan Picon uses the same
words I used a moment ago—the words I underlined: "embrace," "contact," "participation," "communion" and "identity?" The very same
words are used by anthropologists in their studies of African and
Melanesian cultures, as by Frobenius, Griaule and Leenhardt.[11] My
friend, the painter Pierre Soulages, confessed after reading my article on
the aesthetics of the African negro:[12] "This is really the aesthetics of the
twentieth century."

Thus nowadays the European White is no longer content to see, dis-
sect, measure and weigh the object he wants to know. He must also touch
it, taste it, and penetrate to its core: he must *feel* it, as the African negro
does. To know, for example, a fact of human nature, whether in psychology or in sociology, is no longer to know it at second hand, as Lucien
Lévy-Bruhl did. No matter how much of a genius one may be, it is no
longer enough to examine it from the outside and to gather figures about
it; one has to *live* it. To know the Caledonians, Maurice Leenhardt had to
live among them; and Marcel Griaule, who lived several months a year
among the Dogon, felt the need to have himself initiated so that he would
know them. Father Libermann urged his missionaries to "become negroes among negroes" as the surest means of getting to know them "to
win them over to Jesus Christ." This method, which consists in living the
object, is that of the phenomenologists and existentialists. It is a matter of
participating in the object in the act of knowledge; of going beyond concepts and categories, appearances and preconceptions produced by education, to plunge into the primordial chaos, not shaped as yet by discursive reason. It is, as Kierkegaard wrote in his *Journal,* a matter of "letting
one's thoughts appear with the umbilical cord of first love." It is the
attitude of a wide-eyed child; the attitude of the African negro. Knowledge is then no artificial product of discursive reason made to cover up
reality, but discovery through emotion, and not so much discovery as *rediscovery*. Knowledge coincides here with the *being* of the object in its
originating and original reality, in its discontinuity and indeterminacy:
in its life.

We are thus led back to the emotion of the African negro—to *negrohood,*
which Jean-Paul Sartre defines as "a certain affective attitude towards the

[10] *Ibid.,* p. 27.
[11] *Cf.* Maurice Leenhardt, *Do Kamo: La Personne et le mythe dans le monde
mélanésien,* Gallimard.
[12] *Diogenes,* No. 16, Oct. 1956.

world."[13] This would be the place to cite other illustrious witnesses, like the Count of Keyserling who speaks of the "stormy vitality" and the "great emotional warmth of black blood." But I prefer to go back to my childhood memories of bygone evenings. How many tears were shed for indomitable heroes. And because the listeners saw in this trait the sign of a noble soul. As my mother, who was a fine and sensitive person said, and who cried abundantly at each retelling, "It is not human not to cry." But here is a scene from daily life: a meeting of two parents, or two friends, who have not seen each other for a long time. The litany of greetings has initially a banal rhythm:

> Are you at peace?
> Only at peace.
> Is your father at peace?
> Only at peace.
> Is your mother at peace?
> Only at peace.
> Is everyone at home at peace?
> Only at peace.

This is followed by an exchange of news, about parents, friends, fields and herds. Then old memories are brought up. When certain facts are recalled and dear faces evoked, emotion takes hold of their bodies. They embrace each other and hold hands for a long time. Then the litany of greetings begins again. But this time the rhythm is more pronounced; it is the very rhythm of a poem. Their breasts are distended, their throats constricted. The emotion is there and makes them burst into sobs and shed heavy tears.

What then is an *emotion?* At first sight, it can be translated into a certain attitude of the body. The classical theories, those of James and Janet, present an emotion with little variation as "a physiological disorder," as "a response less well adapted to the given situation," and as "check-mate behavior"—or better, as "the consciousness of bodily manifestations."[14] It is, of course, true that an emotion is accompanied by bodily manifestations which are perceived from the outside as agitations. But let us examine things more closely. To repeat, the object produces, by way of the sense organs, an excitation which is translated into an impression and produces a muscular reaction—a response. This is the brute, immediate reaction, that of an animal. A human reaction is, as we have seen, rarely such a simple muscular reaction. Thao, who combines phenomenology with dialectical materialism, has discovered the complexity of the problem by analyzing it. After emphasizing the role which

---

[13] *Orphée noir: Anthologie de la nouvelle poésie nègre et malgache de langue française,* by L. S. Senghor, p. xxix.

[14] Jean-Paul Sartre, *Esquisse d'une théorie des émotions,* Hermann et Cie, pp. 16–7.

experience of the environment plays in behavior, he concludes: "The behavior of joy, fear and anger is defined in such a way that the sense of the sensation is no longer simply experienced in the privacy of the inner sense, but appears, like a phantom, as an object that attracts, repels or irritates. An emotion is not the purely subjective movement of a want; it includes the sense of the object as an 'emoving' object."[15] I am well aware, and I have emphasized above, that for the African negro more than for anyone else, an emotion is primarily "the subjective movement of a want"—a movement closely connected with his physiology. Hence his sense of rhythm and the spontaneity of his reflexes. But it is also something else.

Sartre defines an emotion as "an abrupt fall of consciousness into the world of magic."[16] But what is in turn the world of magic? It is the world beyond the visible world of appearances. The latter is rational only because it is visible and measurable. The world of magic is, for the African negro, more real than the visible world: it is *sub-real*. It is animated by invisible forces which govern the universe and whose specific characteristic is that they are, through sympathy, harmoniously related to one another as well as to visible things, or appearances. As Eliphas Lévy writes, "there is only one dogma of magic, and this is that the visible is a manifestation of the invisible, or in other words, that the perfect word is embodied in measurable and visible things in exact proportion to the things that cannot be measured with our senses or seen with our eyes."[17] Since African negroes are deeply religious, we should for the sake of precision speak in their case of the *mystical* rather than of magic. Magic (to which we shall return) is only the ashen, desecrated, residue of the mystical view according to which *caeli enarrant gloriam Dei*.

But let us return to the example given a little while ago. Here is a mother who sees her son again after several years. He, a student returning from France, has the emotion of being abruptly thrust backwards, outside the real world of today and into the world prior to the "French presence." His mother is no longer a civil-law mother who has less rights than a father, but a traditional African mother who, underneath her social obligations, is tied to her son by the umbilical cord of sentiment, which is the life force of the clan. For in black Africa, a child has the blood and belongs to the clan of his mother. "it is the belly which ennobles," says a Serer proverb. The student's mother is, then, overcome by emotion. She touches the face of her son, searching, as if she were blind or as if she wanted to draw nourishment from it. Her body, "immediately enlivened by consciousness,"[18] reacts: She cries now and dances the

---

[15] *Phénoménologie et matérialisme dialectique*, pp. 259–60.
[16] *Op. cit.*, p. 49.
[17] Quoted by André Breton in *Art magique*, Club français du livre, p. 14.
[18] Jean-Paul Sartre, *Op. cit.*, p. 41.

dance of return: the dance of possessing her son who returned. And the maternal uncle, who belongs to the family because he has the same blood as the mother, accompanies the dance by clapping his hands. The mother is no longer part of the world of today, but belongs to the mystical, and mythical, world of long ago, which is part of the world of dreams. She believes in that world, for she lives in it now and is possessed by it. As Sartre writes: "In emotion, consciousness is degraded and abruptly transforms the determinist world we live in into a world of magic."[19]

Let us push the analysis further ahead. We shall discover that the tissue of society itself, the relations among men, and above all, the relations between men and nature, consist of magical bonds. This is where, in Alain's words, "the spirit languishes among things." Even those structures of European society that are at first glance technical and rational, turn out under analysis to be founded on human, and hence on psychological, relations in which imagination, the daughter of desire, plays an essential part—a part whose importance has been emphasized by surrealists and psychoanalysts alike. Remo Cantoni, an Italian communist, has written in the periodical *Esprit*:[20] "Marxism has gained political strength by having turned into a popular millenary and apocalyptic faith, for it can absorb the enormous energies of religious faith." We find thus that "faith," which is known to be connected with magic, underlies a society founded on discursive reason and technology, and in short, on determinism, and gives this society the creative power to produce *myths* which are the real bread of the masses.

This is even truer of African negro society. Technical activities (to which we shall return) are here always tied to cultural and religious activities: to art and magic, if not to the mystical. The latter activities are always given precedence over the former, and especially over productive labor. We have here a society founded essentially on human relations, and perhaps even more on relations between men and "gods." It is an *animistic* society, I mean, a society content with the "necessities of life," and less interested in "terrestrial nourishment" than in spiritual nourishment, or more precisely, a society which does not separate natural from supernatural wants. Here, the facts of nature and especially "the facts of society are not things."[21] Concealed behind them are the cosmic forces— the forces of life—which govern and animate the appearances, endowing them with color and rhythm, life and sense. It is this *meaning* which forces itself upon consciousness and elicits an emotion. To be still more precise, an emotion is the seizure of one's entire being—both of consciousness and body—by the world of indeterminism; it is the irruption

[19] *Ibid.,* p. 45.
[20] May-June 1948.
[21] This is the title of a work by Jules Monnerot (Gallimard).

of the world of the mystical—or of magic—into the world of determinism. What emoves an African negro is not so much the external aspect of an object as its profound reality: its *sub-reality,* and not so much the *sign* as its *sense.* What emoves him in a dancer's mask is, across the "image" and its rhythm, the spontaneous vision of a "god," and what emoves him in water is not that it flows, liquid and blue, but that it cleanses and purifies. To the extent that the sensible aspect, with its individual characteristics, is clearly perceived through the sense organs and nerves, it is only the sign of the sense of the object. Body and consciousness, sign and sense, constitute the same ambivalent reality. But the emphasis lies on the sense.

This means that an emotion, under its initial aspect as a fall of consciousness, is on the contrary *the rise of consciousness to a higher state of knowledge.* It is "consciousness of the world,"[22] "a certain way of apprehending the world."[23] It is an integrated consciousness, for "the 'emoved' subject and the 'emoving' object are united in an indissoluble synthesis,"[24] and to repeat, in a dance of love. I have said that emotion is a higher form of knowledge. In support, let me quote this reflection by one of the great scientific minds of the twentieth century. "The most beautiful emotion we can experience," wrote Albert Einstein, "is the mystical. This is the source of all art and of true science."

It is, at any rate, this gift of emotion which explains *negrohood,* which Sartre, to repeat, defines as "a certain affective attitude towards the world," and which I have defined as "the totality of the cultural values" of the African negro. The two definitions do not conflict. It is in fact the *emotive attitude* towards the world which explains all the cultural values of the African negro: religion, social structures, art and literature, and above all, the genius of their languages.

[22] Jean-Paul Sartre, *Op. cit.,* p. 29.
[23] *Ibid.,* p. 30.
[24] *Ibid.,* p. 30.

Cheikh Anta Diop, the "Stolen Legacy," and Afrocentrism

Jeffrey Crawford

Jeffrey Crawford is the current chair of the Department of Philosophy at Central State University in Wilberforce, Ohio. In the following selection, Crawford considers some of the influential views of the Senegalese scholar, scientist, and political activist Cheikh Anta Diop. Diop adds a historical dimension to ethnophilosophy by locating the roots of African philosophy in the civilization of ancient Egypt. His work has been heralded by some Afrocentrists as showing that the ancient Egyptians were an African people, that there are direct linguistic and cultural relationships (religious beliefs, kinship structures, etc.) linking ancient Egypt to precolonial and contemporary Africa, and that the flowering of Greek philosophy between 600–300 B.C. was built on prior Egyptian intellectual achievements. Diop argues that facts supporting these links have been misrepresented by modern racist scholarship, a claim also made by George G. M. James in his book Stolen Legacy *(NY: Philosophical Library, 1954) and more recently by Martin Bernal in* Black Athena: The Afroasiatic Roots of Classical Civilization, *vol. 1 (New Brunswick, N.J.: Rutgers University Press, 1987).*

Crawford focuses primarily on Diop's version of the claim that ancient Greek philosophy was "stolen" from ancient Egypt (the "stolen legacy" theory), comparing it with George G. M. James' presentation of that thesis. Crawford claims that a major advantage of Diop's version over James' was Diop's ability to read and translate the hieroglyphic literature himself, while James was limited by depending on translations from secondary sources. Crawford concludes that, whether we call ancient Egyptian thought philosophy or myth, Diop makes a strong case that the ancient Greek philosophers were clearly influenced by the intellectual legacy of ancient Egypt. Crawford ends his essay with a survey of current versions of Afrocentrism and an assessment of Diop's significance for Afrocentrism.

Between the early 1950s and his death in 1986, the Senegalese scholar Cheikh Anta Diop (b. 1923) argued for a number of controversial claims. These included: that Egypt was essentially an African civilization; that its founders and sustainers were of the same racial groups that are currently dominant in sub-Saharan Africa, i.e., they were Black; that they had developed the mathematics, science, and philosophy, which were the basis for the Greek intellectual takeoff of the sixth century B.C.; that beneath the superficial cultural diversity of Africa lay a substrate of cultural unity that derived from ancient Egypt; and that a federated state could be built on this unity and provide the necessary size and clout for African development in the postcolonial era.[1]

Diop has not been alone in arguing for these views, though perhaps no one else has done so as comprehensively. Henri Frankfort presented evidence for the African roots of Egyptian culture in his *Kingship and the Gods*.[2] Kwame Nkrumah was one of many who has seen traditional African cultures as a partial basis for building Pan-African political unity.[3] Recently, Martin Bernal's *Black Athena* stirred controversy in the academy by advocating Egypt's cultural primacy in fostering Greek development.[4]

It is noteworthy that Diop's work, which goes farther than Bernal's in challenging Greek originality, has gained little attention among American scholars. Not so in all quarters, however. Mamadou Diouf and Mohamad Mbodj claim in their "The Shadow of Cheikh Anta Diop" that for some time among African scholars to question Diop's work was synonymous with antipatriotism, while referring to it was obligatory and repeating "its great principles, often without any real knowledge of the work itself, was a certificate of nationalism and Pan-Africanism."[5] But perhaps Diop's work has gained most attention among African-Americans, particularly Afrocentric scholars, for many of whom it is taken as foundational. Although Afrocentrism is a broad set of tendencies and not a single unified approach, a core consensus exists among its proponents that Diop is correct in considering Egypt as the key to understanding sub-Saharan African culture, on the one hand, and the true roots of European culture, on the other. Diop strongly argues, and Afrocentrists agree, that the Greeks saw as far as they did by standing on the shoulders of Egyptian giants. Further, Afrocentrists share Diop's commitment to using scholarship in the interests of African people and as part of a process of worldwide human development.[6]

Coming of age as the colonial sun set, Diop was part of an intellectual/political radiation that included Fanon, Senghor, Nkrumah, Kenyatta, Nyerere, and Awolowo. Diop's countryman Alioune Diop founded the literary journal *Présence Africaine* (and the broader publishing activities that developed) in 1947 with the goals of rehabilitating "the collective memory of the peoples of Africa [and bringing] new life to Africans from inside their culture"; making African culture familiar to the rest of the world; and reinstating "the Black" as a participant in the universal oeuvre of human culture.[7] Cheikh Anta Diop shared these goals and sought to develop an intellectual framework for restoring Africa and Africans to world cultural history. Trained as a physicist, but called to a battlefield of culture and history, Diop thought and wrote on a grand scale, attempting to integrate findings from chemistry and physics, anthropology, archaeology and linguistics, ancient historians, Egyptian cultural history, and more. Diop recast the world with Africa at its center, the birthplace of humankind and of human culture. Naming his last book *Civilization or Barbarism,* he reversed the roles of the civilized and barbaric, rejected the limits of Western historical writing and intellectual traditions concerning Africa, and laid what he saw as a basis for an "authentic anthropology."[8]

Clearly, Diop's project invites diverse interpretations and responses. One perspective on his work is that it was primarily an attack on the ideological racism that had developed during the transatlantic slave trade and had been perfected under colonialism. For if the Egyptians were Black, and the cultures of the rest of Africa shared essential features with Egyptian culture, and if the Greek intellectual miracle was based on African cultural achievements, then the Black race can hardly be the backward, uncivilized and congenitally inferior species portrayed by racist ideology.

Identifying and attacking racism and claiming credit where credit is due are tendencies deeply rooted in Afrocentric literature. Diop's argument against racism and his basic historical framework, as well as many of his specific conclusions, are often accepted as unquestionable tenets within the Afrocentric tradition. His work is seen as revealing what has been hidden about Africa, as well as what has been intentionally distorted, and for many, Diop provides the model for intellectual work by and about Africans.[9]

THE STOLEN LEGACY THEORY

Diop's attack on racism has two main prongs. One prong is the view that the avowedly great accomplishments of ancient Egypt are attributable to Nile Valley Blacks, people of basically the same racial identity as those groups now dominant in sub-Saharan Africa. Further, that contemporary cultures of sub-Saharan Africa share essential features with ancient Egypt is shown by an analysis of linguistic and social forms. Using the results of such analysis, contemporary sub-Saharan African cultures can be seen as different evolutionary developments of ancient Egyptian culture. Viewed through this lens, sub-Saharan African culture is not a chaos of cultural diversity and strangeness. Rather, it shares basic systematic features of structure, philosophy, and worldview which give it coherence, intelligibility, and value.

The second main prong, and the one addressed most centrally in this paper, is the "stolen legacy theory." On Diop's version of the theory, it was Nile Valley Blacks who invented the science, mathematics, and philosophy, properly so-called, for which the Greeks have received credit. His most fully developed case for the theory is found in Chapters 16 and 17 of *Civilization or Barbarism,* which account for more than one third of the entire work.[10] To better understand Diop's case, and appreciate its appeal within the Afrocentric tradition, it will be helpful to compare his version to that offered by George G. M. James in his *Stolen Legacy,* from which the theory takes its name.[11]

James argues for the stolen legacy theory on at least four fronts. According to James, the Egyptian intellectual elite were educated in the Egyptian Mystery System. In this system, the myth of Osiris's death and resurrection served as metaphors for initiates moving through stages of personal and spiritual growth, beginning as novices and some few attaining the level of adepts. James's sources for his information about ancient Egyptian culture are primarily Masonic, and his account is therefore open to the charge that he has uncritically read Masonry backward onto Egyptian institutions.[12] In contrast, Diop's account of Egypt is drawn much more directly from Egyptian material, in many cases from his own, or others', translations of Egyptian texts.

James used the Greek and Roman historians as uncritically as he did Masonic sources. He does not discuss, or seem to notice, the alternative and contradictory accounts often found in these sources, and he provides no criteria for preferring one account to another. With the faith of a true believer, James appears to have selected whatever account best fit his purposes. Although Diop is also open to the charge of using ancient sources uncritically, he acknowledges, as James does not, that the accounts of the ancient historians need to be approached with caution and sifted through carefully.

Although both James and Diop argue that Plato, and some earlier Greek philosophers, studied for long and definite periods in Egypt, claims that may best remain speculative, James's writing is beset with anachronisms that Diop avoids. For instance, James asserts that most of Aristotle's corpus was copied from books in the library at Alexandria. He does not seem to notice that, given the date when the city was founded and the library built, Aristotle would have had at most a year before his death to accomplish his Great Act of Plagiarism.[13] Also, on the first page of *Stolen Legacy,* James claims that "After nearly five thousand years of prohibition against the Greeks, they were permitted to enter Egypt." Thus, James has the Greeks, before there were Greeks, trying to get into

Egypt, before there was an Egypt, at least according to dates taken as standard by most historians. Nor does James give an argument for why the standard dates should be changed. Diop avoids such anachronisms and documents references to Egyptian texts when he argues for direct Greek appropriations.

A fourth line of argument James develops is the idea that Greek social and political life was too chaotic to have spawned philosophy.[14] As James develops this part of his case, it becomes clear that he thinks of the Greeks as largely passive. For James, the diversity of early Greek thought does not reflect an internal process of discovery but derives from their imperfect understanding of, or their only partial initiation into, the Egyptian Mysteries. His case presupposes that there was only one system of thought in Egypt, although only a few were exposed to or able to grasp its entirety, and that this system of thought was also true.

Diop's case differs from James's on all these points. For Diop, the diversity of Greek thought derived partly from the diversity of the Egyptian thought, which influenced the Greeks, and partly from Greek originality. Further, I find no evidence that Diop thought the Egyptians had discovered some immutable truths we should all be busy trying to rediscover.[15]

James's conclusions about the stolen legacy, if not all the specifics of his arguments, have become standard within Afrocentrism. Diop's case for the theory offers even greater appeal to Afrocentrists because he avoids the more glaring of James's errors. Diop, trained in nuclear physics and literate in a range of disciplines, brought a scientist's eye to the subject, pursuing his arguments in more detail and with more logical rigor and circumspection than James. We can ask, of course, whether Diop is reading science backward where James read Masonry, but Diop allows the discussion to be joined at a higher level and on a different set of issues. James, an "old scrapper" in Jacob Carruthers's term, sensed something racist in the state of scholarship, and *Stolen Legacy* is his full-bore, true-believer attack in defense of the race. He may not have floated like a butterfly, but academically he stung like one. Diop stings more like a bee.[16]

Civilization or Barbarism covers myriad topics and was intended to be expansive. Thus, as with much of Diop's work, his account of the Stolen Legacy theory is open to alternative readings. His core claims, however, are fairly clear. Contrary to prevailing Western opinion, Egypt was neither prescientific, nor prephilosophical. Rather, the elite of the Egyptian intelligentsia consisted of consciously self-reflective systematizers who engaged in abstract, metalevel theorizing. Further, the conceptual format of pre-Socratic philosophy was Egyptian, having been developed in the great Egyptian cosmological systems. This conceptual format was adopted by Plato and Aristotle with some additional borrowing from Egypt, as is demonstrated, for instance, by parallels (plagiarisms?) between Egyptian cosmological texts and the *Timaeus.* Thus, for Diop, Egyptian work in mathematics, mechanics, cosmology, and other fields was suitably advanced to be properly called science and philosophy, and the Greeks were both influenced by and appropriated much Egyptian work.

The heart of Diop's case concerning philosophy is a series of textual and conceptual parallels between Egyptian material and Greek philosophical thought, beginning with the pre-Socratics and continuing through Aristotle. He argues that the format of Greek thought, the problems they posed, and the conceptual framework within which they worked were Egyptian. According to Diop, the following basic conceptual moves had all been developed in Egypt before philosophy was a twinkle in Greek eyes: (1) looking for a simple set of principles to explain the diversity of appearance; (2) understanding the cosmos as resulting from opposing forces in dynamic tension; (3) viewing the natural world and human persons as involving various levels of ensoulment; (4) thinking of the creation as resulting from rational agency copying or actualizing ideal and eternal forms.

According to Diop, long before the age of Greek ascendancy, the Egyptians had developed four different but interrelated cosmological systems: the Hermopolitan, Heliopolitan, Theban and Memphite.[17] Although the systems varied in their details, they shared essential features. "According to these systems, the universe was not created *ex nihilo,* . . . but there . . . always existed an uncreated matter," the equivalent of non-being or chaos. This eternal and uncreated matter, according to Diop, "contained at the archetypal state (Plato) all the essences of the . . . future beings" that would later be created.[18] *Nun,* the primordial uncreated matter of Egyptian cosmology, would become the basis for the materialistic tendencies in Greek philosophy, while *Ra,* the divine act, or actor, would support its idealistic tendencies.

Within Egyptian thought, Diop argues, "each principle of explanation of the universe is doubled by a divinity."[19] The primitive matter presupposed in Egyptian cosmogony "also contained the law of transformation, the principle of the evolution of matter through time, equally considered as a divinity: *Khepera.*"[20] As a principle, "the law of becoming" actualizes the archetypes already existing in potentiality within matter. Diop sees here the basis of Plato's theory of reminiscence and Aristotle's theory of potentiality and actuality. As the process of becoming unfolds and eternal uncreated matter goes through "the stages of organization . . . [t]he first consciousness . . . emerges from the primordial *Nun;* it is God, *Ra,* the demiurge (Plato) who is going to complete creation."[21]

The early stages of Egyptian cosmogony are essentially materialistic, and according to Diop, they form the basis for Greek and Latin atomism. "But with the appearance of the demiurge, Ra, Egyptian cosmogony takes a new direction" for "as soon as Ra conceives beings, they emerge into existence."[22] Here we have the basis for creation by the word, a form to be taken over by the revealed religions and by nominalists in contemporary Western philosophy. *Ra* (the original of Plato's demiurge) emerges from *Nun,* as the first consciousness and completes the creation. *Ra,* as did *Ptah* in the very early Memphite theology, and as would others, creates "through the word (Islam and Judeo-Christian religions), the logos (Heraclitus)," the thought that steers all things through all things.[23]

In the Heliopolitan cosmogony, Ra creates the divine pairs:

1. *Shu* and *Tefnut* = air (space) and humidity (water).
2. *Geb* and *Nut* = earth and heaven (light fire).[24]

Diop equates these divine pairs with the four elements of the pre-Socratics. In the Hermopolitan cosmogony, divine pairs of opposites represent the opposing principles of nature that are supposed to be at the origin of things:

Kuk and Kuket + . . . darkness and light.
Nun and Nunet + . . . matter and nothingness [chaos].
Heh and Hehet = . . . the infinite and the finite.
Amon and Amonet = . . . the noumenon and the phenomenon.
Niaou and Niaouet = . . . the void and the replete.[25]

Diop concludes that even this summary account makes clear "all that Greek philosophy owes to the Egyptian thought of the Nile Valley's Blacks: Heraclitus theory of opposites, Aristotle's dialectics . . . the diverse cosmogonies of the pre-Socratic philosophers."[26]

Throughout his case, Diop maintains that to be considered philosophy, thought must meet certain restrictive criteria. Not every system of thought that embodies a worldview and establishes patterns for perception and rules for interpreting experience is a philosophical system. Thought must be conscious of itself as thought, that is, metalevel thought, and presumably discourse must occur. Further, myth must be separated from concept; that is, to be philosophical, thought must recognize a distinction between myth and principle. Neither criterion is an absolute, but points in a direction and reflects tendencies. Philosophy is not something that is totally absent one day and completely present the next. Rather, it emerges in an evolutionary process through which thought becomes conscious of itself and myth is separated from concept. Diop notes that even Greek philosophy sometimes fails the criterion of adequate separation of myth from concept.[27] According to Diop, philosophy emerged in Egypt the same way that it has emerged anywhere it has emerged. It was not always present, or not always present to the same degree, but rather now to a greater and now to a lesser degree.

Diop holds that the Egyptians established parallel systems of explanation, one more mythic, more focused on personifications, on divinities; the other less mythic, anthropomorphic, and personal, more focused on abstract principles. Further, both these systems carried over into the African cultures that radiated out of Egypt, just as both these systems shaped Greek culture on many levels. For it is clear that although *Civilization or Barbarism* concentrates on Egyptian influence on Greek philosophy, Diop follows Herodotus in the view that Greek religion and culture in general were influenced through early Egyptian colonization of the Greek mainland.

Diop's position is that as Thales, Anaximander, and Anaximines sought a first principle they were exploring possibilities first conceived in Egypt. Egyptians were the first to see the world order as emerging from a watery chaos, from the limitless, from air. Prior to Anaximander, the Egyptians had conceptualized the world order as emerging from opposites in dynamic tension, "making reparations onto one another."[28] For Diop, one would have to be blinded by ideology (racism), not to see and acknowledge the Egyptian influence on this first generation of Greek philosophers. The second generation of Greek philosophers, Pythagoras, Heraclitus, and Parmenides, took matters a step further, were "more abstract," more interested in the soul, in persons, and in what could or could not be known. Still, the basic possibilities they explored were Egyptian possibilities. Herodotus was justified in seeing Pythagoras's beliefs in immortality and metempsychosis as Egyptian.[29] Heraclitus's vision of flux, governed by the Logos, was *Nun,* the watery chaos, reconceived as fire, but governed by *Ra,* he who "spoke" order out of chaos. Similar points can be made for others of the pre-Socratics.[30]

According to scholarly works such as Maurice Cornford's *From Religion to Philosophy* (Princeton, NJ: Princeton University Press, 1991) and John Mansley Robinson's *Introduction to Early Greek Philosophy* (Boston: Houghton, Mifflin, 1968), philosophy in Greece emerged by demythologizing, depersonifying, moving away from anthropomorphic conceptions of causality. For Diop, this same model can be applied to the Egyptians as well as the Greeks. Moreover, Diop does not deny that the early Greek philosophers abstracted from the concrete and mythic of their own cultures. They did. But they abstracted from the myths of Egyptian culture as well.

The Greeks plagiarized but were not mere plagiarizers; they played off of whatever came their way and clearly played off each other. But, however original they may have been, philosophy no more sprang fullgrown from Greek foreheads than analytic philosophy was a strictly twentieth-century invention or than baroque music or jazz were invented with no significant antecedents. And this holds not just for the pre-Socratics, but for Plato—that canon to which all subsequent Western philosophical works are but footnotes.

According to Diop, Plato's cosmogony in the *Timaeus* is a makeover of the Heliopolitan cosmogony.[31] His case for this claim is three-pronged: (1) the form of the *Timaeus* faithfully reproduces that of the Heliopolitan cosmogony; (2) some exact phrases in Plato's work can be found in Egyptian texts; (3) some puzzling passages in Plato can be understood best if interpreted as deriving from an Egyptian background.

Diop begins by claiming that Plato's

> world is made according to a perfect, immutable model, as opposed to the perpetual becoming of matter (being born and dying) which is the true materialization of imperfection: the demiurge (we would say Ra of the Heliopolitan cosmogony), the worker who creates the sensible beings always has his eyes fixed on his model, which is an absolute, beautiful, perfect idea, the archetype, the eternal essence of being, which he copies.[32]

Diop sees the Egyptian concept of *Nun* in Plato's idea that the archetypes subsist in the original stuff of the world, *Nun* being the uncreated primordial matter that contains all things "already created in potentiality and awaiting their actualization."[33] That is, Diop's position is that Plato has taken over the basic form of the Heliopolitan cosmogony in the *Timaeus,* that his understanding of creation is the same as that found in the prior Egyptian tradition.

Plato's world was one founded on rational law, according to Diop, because his world derived from "the Egyptian Heliopolitan cosmogony where the essences . . . lay in the uncreated primordial matter" but were accessible to the intellect, "which alone can think and grasp the archetypes, the essences of beings."[34] For Diop, Plato's demiurge, "the perfect causality of the world," shares, "point by point," the essential characteristics of the Heliopolitan god, *Ra.* Quoting from the *Timaeus* that the demiurge brings order to disorder and that it could never be permitted for "the best to make anything but that which is most beautiful," Diop concludes that the passage he quotes

> could be taken for an excerpt (without reference) from the Heliopolitan cosmogony: as a matter of fact, in the cosmogony the *Nun,* the chaotic primordial matter, was first the site of an indescribable disorder and it is the action of the god Khepera, through time, that will actualize the essence of *Ra,* who brought order by completing creation, in beauty and goodness. This is the reason why order (*Hu*), justice or truth (*Maat*) are of divine essence for the ancient Egyptians as they are for Plato.[35]

Diop continues that the influence of Egyptian cosmogony on Plato carried over into his theory of the tripartite soul.

The immortality of the individual's soul and that of the world, as affirmed in the *Timaeus,* is ontologically founded on the Egyptian cosmogony, because the individual *Ka,* meaning the perimeters of the intellect, are indestructible elements of the universal *Ka.* They are alien to the body. Joined to the *Ba,* the individual's sensible soul, and to the physical support which is the body, they form the living human being.[36]

Diop admits that "Plato does not always copy to the letter the Egyptian texts that were written two thousand years before him," but that he can be seen as an interpreter of such texts. As examples of such interpretation, Diop cites passages in the *Timaeus* in which the demiurge fashions souls, sows them on the Earth, moon, and stars, and "after having sown, [leaves] to the young gods the task of making perishable bodies," while "the God who had regulated all this remained in his accustomed state," resting. Plato's young gods are the syzygies of Egyptian cosmogony, the pairs of opposites cited previously, while *Nun* is the God whose accustomed state is rest.[37]

Diop's case concerning Aristotle elaborates on themes established in his treatment of the pre-Socratics and Plato.[38] Thus, Diop argues that Aristotle's criticism of the pre-Socratics shows that they were indeed following an Egyptian model. Yet according to Diop, Aristotle followed that same model, for

> there is no doubt that the theory of the dialectical movement due to the action of opposite couples (thesis, antithesis, synthesis) originates from the Hermopolitan cosmogony, which explains all the phenomena of the universe by the action of the law of opposites.[39]

While Aristotle criticizes the ancients "when all is said and done [he] accepts the opposites as principles."[40] Thus, according to Diop, for Aristotle,

> matter is accidental non-being, while privation, meaning the absence of form, is non-being in itself. . . . Thus we have the following two opposites: form and privation (absence of form), joined together by matter, a subject that desires form. . . . It is almost a transposition on the physical plane of Plato's pair of terms [from the *Timaeus*], joined together by a geometric or arithmetic mediator.[41]

Diop continues with quotes from Aristotle's *Physics* and *Metaphysics,* concluding that throughout

> we find the concepts of the Egyptian cosmogony, rejuvenated, embellished perhaps, but always recognizable: the theory of opposites of the Hermopolitan school, the creation in potentiality and in actuality, the pure form, meaning the eternal essence, the archetype, as last reality and final cause of the world's evolution, all [of which] sends us back to Egypt.[42]

Diop's case may be summarized as follows: Given the extent to which Egyptian and Greek thought parallel each other, and the large number of claims by ancient authorities for Egyptian influence on the Greeks, it is only reasonable to conclude that there was cultural contact and influence. Further, while the Greeks were chauvinistic about their own culture, and ambivalent in their assessment of Egypt, admiration of Egypt was common in elite Greek circles, and many looked to Egypt for their cultural inspiration. Given this combination of structural parallels, testimonial evidence of contact and influence, and favorable Greek attitudes toward Egypt, only an ideologist, or one mislead by ideologists, would deny that Egypt played a significant role in the origins and development of Greek philosophy.

Part of the attractiveness of Diop's work for those who question the standard view of Greek origins, is that if he has proven his point for the pre-Socratics, then his case also applies to Plato, Aristotle, and the rest of Western philosophy. For if the Western philosophical tradition is in any significant sense a series of footnotes to Plato, and if Plato was working within a tradition whose basic conceptual format was Egyptian, then the Western philosophical tradition is a series of footnotes to Egypt.

One response to such a suggestion is that Diop's position, while intriguing, is a case yet to be made, and even if made is little more than a possible way of understanding Bertrand Russell's claim that "Greek philosophy arose due to the contact of the Greek Mind with the great civilizations of Egypt and Babylonia."[43] Others may proclaim Diop's work as a new orthodoxy, the revealed truth as proven by Diop's reading of Plato and Herodotus's reading of Pythagoras as mere plagiarists of Egyptian material.[44]

Certainly, Diop provides an opportunity to think through a range of methodological issues about the nature of philosophy, myth, and magic, as well as broader questions about the relationship of oral and written traditions to philosophical thought. Defined restrictively, as it has been in many recent Western traditions, philosophy is a peculiar cultural phenomenon: institutionalized bickering about the bases and meanings of fundamental societal beliefs, values, and practices, *canonizing* particularly prized forms of argumentation grouped under the term *reason*. Perhaps not much of that has been recorded around the world or through time, though some degree of reasoned disagreement and critical self-reflection may be found in every culture. Such critical discourse may be encoded in a range of cultural expressions not normally identified with philosophy, including folktales and humor. Clearly, one role of trickster figures is to go against the grain. Between around 600–300 B.C., the Greeks appear to have institutionalized critical self-reflection on central cultural beliefs in novel ways, ways in which one could make a living, gain status and followers, open a school, be a freelance teacher for hire, or be condemned to death. However, such a view of Greek philosophy, as a peculiarly institutionalized mode of thought, is perfectly consistent with Diop's contention that the Greeks pursued their critical reflections within an Egyptian format.

Diop's work provides a useful framework for a conceptual content analysis of Greek philosophy. As the details of his case are developed, it seems likely that, just as many central Christian concepts and symbols have been found to originate in Egypt, so many philosophical ideas may be acknowledged to have Egyptian roots as well. On such a view, the Greeks may not have been passive copiers, but if they saw far, critiqued their own cultural traditions, and considered alternative possibilities for understanding the world, it was partly because they had been exposed to various systematized accounts of being first coherently developed by the Egyptians.

It is important to keep in mind that Diop's case should also be understood in its role as an attack on racism. This explains why Diop argues that their mathematical and grammatical teaching and writing presuppose that the Egyptians had created a metalanguage and had conceptualized grammars and mathematical logic.[45] With this claim he is attacking the idea that African people do not think abstractly, or do not do so with the facility of Europeans. In this, he is attacking one of the central beliefs of ideological racism, a belief encoded in interpretations in which the Egyptians had "recipes" and "rules of thumb," that is, techniques for solving certain problems but not real theories or proofs. The latter, so argued eighteenth- and nineteenth-century scholars, would have to wait on the Greeks, for the Black race was not naturally capable of such thought, but rather was a breed apart and a breed inferior.

For similar reasons, Diop rejects the interpretation of Egyptian cosmology as merely myth. In this, he opposes scholars such as Henri Frankfort who saw Egypt as great, and who even saw it as African, but who did not see its cosmological corpus as philosophy.[46] Diop argues that some Egyptians, from a very early date, had a demythologized conception of cosmology and had in his words, "accomplished, to a sufficient degree, the separation of myth from concept."[47]

Clearly, Diop is not claiming that myth and mythological thinking are philosophical thinking. The former are characterized by a world in which experience is permeated by personal powers, a world consisting only of I–Thou relationships, rather than of both I–Thou and I–It relationships.[48] In separating myth from concept, the ancient Egyptians moved away from anthropomorphism, toward a world understood as deriving from nonpersonal principles. Diop's claim that the Egyptians were practicing philosophy in the sense of understanding and experiencing the world as resulting from abstract principles and laws is by extension the claim (1) that Black people think as abstractly and systematically as white people and (2) that there is evidence that they did so before white people.

Diop's case here may seem excessive, were ours not a world with a fully raciated and ranked social reality. Why the scramble to find philosophy in Africa? Perhaps for the same reason there is a scramble to find rhythm in European quarters. What has been denied is prized, and in the case of philosophy, what has been denied has also been claimed as a defining characteristic of being human. Paradoxically, the scramble for rhythmic sensibility among Europeans has much the same urgency as mastery of abstract, systematic, rational thought among African intellectuals.

Of course, what Diop is objecting to is the idea, no longer explicitly espoused in responsible scholarship, but still encoded in the corpus and the commentary, that Africans are just not up to philosophical thinking. By linking *Black African* to *Egyptian* and *Egyptian* to *Origin of Philosophy,* Diop is linking terms and concepts that heretofore had been seen as oxymoronic.[49]

Some suggest that Diop's and others' focus on racism in scholarship is outdated,[50] but we must be wary of accepting such reassurances. To illustrate the need for caution, one need only consider basic history of philosophy texts by such authors as Robert Brumbaugh, Merrill Ring, John Mansley Robinson, and D. W. Hamlyn.[51] Each of these authors either fails to mention, or explicitly denies, any significant Egyptian influence on Greece. Brumbaugh includes maps of Pythagoras's and Plato's voyages, and none of the lines go to Egypt. And all with no argument. Such examples show the need for critical vigilance and the value of scholarly debate. Clearly, Diop cannot be rightly accused of railing only against outdated or fictional historians of Greek philosophy.

Diop's work will further those tendencies in the history of philosophy that have seen the Greeks as original, but not isolated; tendencies that see philosophy as innately human, rather than innately Greek or Western. True believers will take Diop as gospel, as proving more than he has, or even more than he himself claimed. Others will reject Diop out of hand as mere ideology. Most creatively, perhaps, Diop can be taken as providing material and possibilities to be explored, an aid to rethinking the stories on which we were raised.

What is philosophy? On more restrictive definitions, there may not be enough evidence to say that the Egyptians were doing it or that they had, to return to Diop's words, sufficiently separated myth from concept. Even on a restrictive definition, however, Diop's case suggests that the format within which the Greeks demythologized was partly an Egyptian format. Diop argues that the Egyptians started a process of separating myth from concept that the Greeks continued. Whether one agrees with this specific claim or not, Diop raises challenges and possibilities that go

beyond other stolen legacy cases. His work deserves serious consideration both because of the quality of his argument and the importance of
his conclusions.

AFROCENTRISM

Scholars who characterize themselves as Afrocentric are among those
who already take Diop's work seriously, indeed, who sometimes take it as
paradigmatic. Leonard Jeffries, for instance, Professor of Africana Studies, City College of New York, writes that "Diop's *Civilization or Barbarism* is truly an extraordinary scientific and scholarly masterpiece,"
concluding that it "will undoubtedly become a classic of Afrocentric
Scholarship."[52] And it makes sense that Afrocentrists would hail his
work. For beyond the stolen legacy theory, *Civilization and Barbarism* argues for a number of other claims central to Afrocentrism. Chief among
these are the views (1) that sub-Saharan African culture derives from
Egypt, and thus shares in the dual mythic/philosophical explanatory systems of Egypt, and (2) that these Egyptian roots account for an underlying cultural unity beneath superficial cultural differences.

Because part of the Afrocentric project is to develop an account of
an African cultural system that crossed the Atlantic with captives in the
slave trade and that persists throughout the diaspora, Diop is perceived
as a gifted and formidable ally. Because of the range of disciplines on
which his work drew—including linguistics, anthropology and economic
history—Diop's work is taken as providing empirical evidence for claims
that are highly controversial but that few have the detailed knowledge to
successfully dispute. Not many scholars have enough expertise to dispute Diop's claims that contemporary Wolof and Bambara words have
clear etymological roots in ancient Egyptian. And those competent in
that area would probably not be able to assess his account of the central
role of matriarchy in the Asian (read African) mode of production. And
it is unlikely that the latter would be competent to discuss his critique of
the standard Western view of Egyptian mathematics.

It is important to remember that Afrocentrism is a work in progress
and not a well-defined or restrictive tradition. Some in the tradition—
Karenga, Asante, and Akbar,[53] for example—tend to argue that core
Egyptian values and concepts should be adopted by African people
where and in whatever circumstances they may find themselves, because
such values and concepts suit African people. Other Afrocentrists do not
claim to be accurately rediscovering Egyptian truths but take inspiration
from Egyptian material in constructing worldviews that reject and move
beyond Eurocentric options.

Diop's work seems to support both tendencies: those that move toward a kind of racial essentialism (Karenga, Asante, Akbar) and those that reject racial or cultural essentialism but that draw on a wide range of African material to challenge Western intellectual hegemony and propose alternatives. For Diop, there is an essential thread of history, language, and psychology that links Africans with ancient Egypt even into the New World. However, his account of the basis for such a common thread is materialistic, grounded in similar modes of production. His position seems to be that though such a thread exists, because the material basis of culture is being revolutionized, there is no choice but for Africans to strike out into new cultural waters beyond the matrix laid down in the Asian mode of production.[54]

Diop may be a cultural essentialist, as are most Afrocentrists, but his materialism puts him at odds with some of Afrocentrism's foremost proponents. Molefi Asante identifies *Nommo,* the word as a shared act of community, as central to the African cultural system. Unlike Diop, Asante gives no account of the basis for such a trait, and he certainly does not seem to think *Nommo* derives from a certain form of social reproduction.[55]

In another example of divergence within the camp, Na'im Akbar's account of the Ka, Ba, and Zed bears little resemblance to Diop's account, although this account is central to Diop's case that similar Greek concepts had derived from Egypt.[56] Could it be that Akbar is following a different model? Broadly speaking, however, Diop's work joins and furthers a process through which detailed positions will be worked out on a number of issues. Certainly, his case concerning philosophy will aid and abet those who doubt that philosophy sprang Athena-like, fully developed from the foreheads of the Greeks. And some Afrocentrists are likely to hail Diop as having proven that the Greeks were nothing but plagiarists, proclaiming a new orthodoxy such that all who disagree with it are automatically "racists." But such a new orthodoxy will not go far or serve its proponents well in the academy.

The addition of the concept of *African* to that of *philosophy* has already been the occasion for much fruitful philosophy, for it has lead to high-quality critical dialogue aimed at clarifying conceptual issues and exploring historical relations. Diop's work has certainly influenced Afrocentrists scholars and deserves more attention from the academy than it has received.

Notes

1. Cheikh Anta Diop's major historical works include *Precolonial Black Africa* (Westport, CT: Lawrence Hill, 1987); *The African Origins of Civilization: Myth or Reality* (Westport, CT: Lawrence Hill, 1974); *The Cultural Unity of Black Africa: The Economic and Cultural Basis for a Fed-

erated State (Westport, CT: Lawrence Hill, 1978); and *Civilization or Barbarism: An Authentic Anthropology* (Westport, CT: Lawrence Hill, 1991). All these works were originally published in French by Presence Africaine, Paris. Diop also published several briefer historical essays highlighting his major contentions in the journals *Nile Valley Civilizations* and the *Journal of African Civilizations.*

2. Henri Frankfort, *Kingship and the Gods* (Chicago, 1948).

3. Kwame Nkrumah, *Consciencism,* Monthly Review Press, 1970.

4. Martin Bernal, *Black Athena: The Afroasiatic Roots of Classical Civilization,* vol. 1 (New Brunswick, NJ: Rutgers University Press, 1987). An indication of the interest Bernal's work aroused is the fall 1989 issue of *Arethusa,* which was devoted entirely to responses to Bernal's work and includes his replies to those responses.

5. In *The Surreptitious Speech: Presence Africaine and the Politics of Otherness, 1947–1987,* edited by V. Y. Mudimbe (Chicago: University of Chicago Press, 1992), pp. 118–35.

6. The theme of African leadership in world transformation takes many forms and is a theme that can be found in the writings and speeches of Martin Luther King, Jr., W.E.B. DuBois, Malcolm X, and others.

7. Christiane Yande Diop, in the Introduction of *The Surreptitious Speech,* xiii.

8. The signification here, of course, is on traditions of Western anthropology, which viewed the African as the curiosity to be explained.

9. "The Shadow of Cheikh Anta Diop," in *The Surreptitious Speech* details some continental responses to his work. See also Jacob Carruthers' *Essays in Ancient Egyptian Studies* (Los Angeles, 1984) and Habib Sy's "At the forefront of the African Renaissance in Philosophy" and Theophile Obenga's "African Philosophy of the Pharaonic Period," in *Egypt Revisited,* edited by Ivan Van Sertima, *Journal of African Civilization* (1989) 277–85, 286–324.

10. *Civilization or Barbarism,* 231–376.

11. George G. M. James, *Stolen Legacy* (New York: Philosophical Library), 1954. This is the citation given by Bernal in his *Black Athena.* I have had several copies of *Stolen Legacy* over the years, and my current copy has no publication or copyright information. I believe James originally published the book himself, and since then, it has circulated in a variety of ways. Currently, it is available in Afrocentric or African-oriented book stores.

12. See Jeff Crawford, "How to Study Ancient African Philosophy," *Proceedings of the Ohio Philosophical Association* (April 1991): 114–27. The works referred to there include Albert Mackey, *An Encyclopedia of Freemasonry,* (Philadelphia: Everts, 1896) and C. H. Vail *Ancient Mysteries.* I have not been able to find bibliographical information on Vail's book, but the language used in James's quotes makes it clear that Vail

gives a Masonic reading to Egyptian institutions. Largely through *Stolen Legacy,* this reading of Egypt has gained some popularity. In scholarly circles, Henry Olela follows James's lead in his *From Ancient Africa to Ancient Greece: An Introduction to the History of Philosophy* (Atlanta: The Select Publishing Corporation, 1981). On a popular level, I believe the following quotes from an article by Darren V. Bolden, "Knowledge of Self" *Black Excellence* (Sept./Oct. 1990): 22–25, reflects James's influence: "Any knowledgeable Black person knows that all of the famed Greek philosophers were students of the Egyptians." Bolden concludes that the examples he cites are "an indication of white-washing African greatness through 'Stolen Legacies.'"

13. *Stolen Legacy,* 129–30.

14. *Stolen Legacy,* 21–26.

15. While Diop's work is open to alternative readings, I do not think he is a foundationalist in the sense that what was known in the beginning was better and truer than what we know now. Afrocentrism, at least on some of its presentations, does seem to endorse the idea of original truths, which have been lost, distorted, or stolen over the years. Of course, the idea that first man possessed original truths, which have since been lost is widespread and not peculiar to any particular cultural group or social movement.

16. Bernal quotes Carruthers on p. 436 of *Black Athena.* Carruthers groups Diop with others who form an extension of the "old scrappers" but who have developed the multidisciplinary skills necessary to make their cases stick. These *new* old scrappers, unlike mainline or conservative, but academically sophisticated Black scholars, are *race* men (and women) for whom the academy is a cultural battlefield.

17. *Civilization or Barbarism,* 310.

18. *Civilization or Barbarism,* 310.

19. *Civilization or Barbarism,* 310.

20. *Civilization or Barbarism,* 310.

21. *Civilization or Barbarism,* 310–11.

22. *Civilization or Barbarism,* 311.

23. *Civilization or Barbarism,* 311.

24. *Civilization or Barbarism,* 311.

25. *Civilization or Barbarism,* 313.

26. *Civilization or Barbarism,* 313.

27. *Civilization or Barbarism,* 309.

28. Anaximander's single sentence that has come down to us, as quoted in John Mansley Robinson, *An Introduction to Early Greek Philosophy* (Boston: Houghton Mifflin, 1968), 34.

29. See Herodotus's *Histories,* Book Two, 121–125. While Herodotus does not name Pythagoras, there is little doubt that he was among those intended when after describing the Egyptian theory of transmigration

of souls Herodotus wrote: "This theory has been adopted by certain Greek writers, some earlier, some later, who have put it forward as their own. Their names are known to me, but I refrain from mentioning them."

30. *Civilization or Barbarism*, 309–13.

31. *Civilization or Barbarism*, 337–ff.

32. *Civilization or Barbarism*, 337.

33. *Civilization or Barbarism*, 337.

34. *Civilization or Barbarism*, 337.

35. *Civilization or Barbarism*, 339.

36. *Civilization or Barbarism*, 339–40.

37. *Civilization or Barbarism*, 341.

38. *Civilization or Barbarism*, 353–8.

39. *Civilization or Barbarism*, 353.

40. *Civilization or Barbarism*, 356.

41. *Civilization or Barbarism*, 357.

42. *Civilization or Barbarism*, 357.

43. Bertrand Russell, *The History of Western Philosophy*, 7.

44. See note 29, for the reference to Herodotus.

45. *Civilization or Barbarism*, 327.

46. Frankfort, *Kingship and the Gods* (Chicago, 1948).

47. *Civilization or Barbarism*, 309.

48. For more on the view that ancient Egyptian culture embodied an I–Thou relationship with the world, see particularly Henri Frankfort et al., *Before Philosophy: The Intellectual Adventure of Ancient Man*. The introductory essay by H. and H. A. Frankfort, "Myth and Reality," 11–38, is a classic statement of the position. On the view espoused by the Frankforts, and standard in most literature dealing with such matters, early man, and contemporary savage man, was prelogical, experiencing the world through mythopoeic consciousness. An alternative position on what distinguishes traditional cultures from scientific or modern Western cultures is proposed by Robin Horton, "African Traditional Thought and Western Science," in this volume. In Horton's view, people in traditional cultures are fully as rational and systematic in their thought as Westerners raised on science. However, while it is the very essence of scientific thinking to consider alternative explanatory strategies for experience, i.e., Western science is an "open" universe, such is forbidden in traditional cultures, i.e., they are "closed."

49. For more on this theme see Lucius Outlaw, "African, African American, Africana Philosophy," *The Philosophical Forum* 24 no. 1–3 (Fall–Spring 1992–93): 63–93; and Gene Blocker's "African Philosophy," *African Philosophical Inquiry* 1. no. 1 (January 1987): 1–7.

50. Kwame Anthony Appiah makes such a claim in his review of Clinton M. Jean's *Behind the Eurocentric Veils* in *The Times Literary Supplement* (February 12, 1993): 24–25.

51. Robert Brumbaugh, *The Philosophers of Greece,* (Albany, NY: SUNY, 1981); Merrill Ring, *Beginning with the Pre-Socratics* (Palo Alto, CA: Mayfield, 1987); John Mansley Robinson, *An Introduction to Early Greek Philosophy* (Boston: Houghton Mifflin, 1968); D. W. Hamlyn, *A History of Western Philosophy* (New York: Viking, 1987). My point is not that these texts, all but the last of which I have used in courses, are worthless or bankrupt. They simply reflect the standard view, which needed no argument when they were written, of Greek originality. Whether argument will be needed, or whether the standard view will change remains to be seen.

52. Jeffries is quoted on the back cover of *Civilization or Barbarism.*

53. See Maulana Karenga, "Towards a Sociology of Maatian Ethics: Literature and Context," in *Egypt Revisited,* edited by Ivan Van Sertima; Molefi Kete Asante, *Afrocentricity,* (Trenton, NJ: Africa World Press, 1988), *Kemet, Afrocentricity, and Knowledge* (Trenton, NJ: Africa World Press, 1990), and *The Afrocentric Idea,* (Philadelphia: Temple University Press, 1987); Na'im Akbar, "Nile Valley Origins of the Science of the Mind," in *Proceedings of the Nile Valley Conference, Atlanta,* edited Ivan Van Sertima, New Brunswick, NJ: 1985), 120–32. A special edition of *Journal of African Civilizations,* vol. 6, 2, November 1984.

54. Diop develops his theory of history in "Laws Governing the Evolution of Societies: Motor of History in Societies of AMP and the Greek City-State," Part Two of *Civilization or Barbarism,* 109–228. "AMP" refers to the Asian Mode of Production, which Diop says should more accurately be the "African" Mode of Production. His reflections on the current scene are in Chapters Fourteen and Fifteen, "How to Define Cultural Identity" and "Toward a Method for an Approach to Intercultural Relations."

55. See *The Afrocentric Idea,* 17–18.

56. See Akbar's "Nile Valley Origins of the Science of the Mind," in *Proceedings of the Nile Valley Conference.*

"The Instruction of Any" and Moral Philosophy

David James

Written on papyrus sometime before or during the fourteenth century B.C., the Instruction of Any *dates from the Eighteenth Dynasty of the New Kingdom. The Epilogue of this work portrays the scribe, Any, and his son, Khonshotep, engaging in a lively dialogue concerning the nature of moral instruction. Early in the discussion Any compares moral instruction to training an animal or shaping a tool. Khonshotep objects, insisting instead that discussion and inward acceptance by the pupil is essential for the development of moral character. Any responds by progressively altering his position. David James' commentary attempts to show how issues regarding the very nature of moral instruction are present in the dialogue. For James,* The Instruction of Any *is a self-reflective work in which the characters Any and Khonshotep personify dialectically developed positions on the issue in question. This, he concludes, is sufficient for it to be considered a true work of moral philosophy—centuries before the Socratic dialogues.*

Centuries before the birth of Socrates, moral instructions from father to son were written on papyrus in ancient Egypt. The *Instruction of Any* dates from the Eighteenth Dynasty of the New Kingdom. It was written before or during the fourteenth century, B.C. Like many instructions, the body of moral instruction in the *Instruction of Any* is framed by a Prologue and an Epilogue. The Epilogue portrays Any and his son, Khonshotep, engaging in a spirited discussion of a number of fascinating issues: What is moral instruction? How is moral instruction possible? Does it require force? Is it like training an animal? Like learning a language? Is it a gift of the gods? By raising such questions and proposing answers, the Epilogue, I argue, deserves to be considered as moral philosophy.

The single most important moral concept of the ancient Egyptians was a person's heart. The heart was the inward seat of morality and moral character, much like Socrates' later notion of a *daimon* or inner voice.[1] It was thought that the heart could speak after death and accuse its owner of injustice, and so a special prayer addressed to the heart to forestall any postmortem negative testimony was often inscribed on an amulet laid on the chest during embalmment. Another famous and ubiquitous image of the heart from the Egyptian *Book of the Dead*, contemporary with the *Instruction of Any*, depicts the judgment of the dead. A scale weighs the heart of the deceased, which must exactly balance justice or *Maat* for the dead to obtain immortality.[2] We encounter a reference to the heart in Khonshotep's first speech in the Epilogue:[3]

1 *The scribe Khonshotep answered his father, the scribe Any:*
2 I wish I were like (you),
3 As learned as you!
4 Then I would carry out your teachings,
5 and the son would be brought to his father's place.
6 Each man is led by his nature,
7 You are a man who is a master,
8 Whose strivings are exalted,
9 Whose every word is chosen.
10 The son, he understands little
11 When he recites the words in the books.
12 But when your words please the heart,
13 The heart tends to accept them with joy.
14 Don't make your virtues too numerous,
15 That one may raise one's thoughts to you;
16 A boy does not follow the moral instructions,
17 Though the writings are on his tongue!

Thirty-five centuries have elapsed, yet Khonshotep's youthful impatience shines forth here with perfect clarity. Khonshotep first puts his difficulty with his father's instructions in terms of their different level of understanding. Any is a learned scribe, while he, his son, "understands little." But Khonshotep's problem with Any's instructions goes beyond his evident impatience with rote recitation of poorly understood maxims. Khonshotep says that his father's words do not "please the heart." As we have noted, for Any and Khonshotep the heart is the seat of conscience and moral character. To please the heart involves, beyond understanding, personal acceptance and commitment. There are too many instructions, Khonshotep complains; Any has made his "virtues too numerous." Even when these instructions remain "on the tongue," they will not guide action. Even if remembered and understood, too many exacting moral instructions demand too much to be accepted. The generation gap here lies as much in the heart as in the head.

18 *The scribe Any answered his son, the scribe Khonshotep:*
19 Do not rely on such worthless thoughts,

20 Beware of what you do to yourself!
21 I judge your complaints to be wrong,
22 I shall set you right about them.
23 There's nothing [superfluous in] our words,
24 Which you say you wished were reduced.
25 The fighting bull who kills in the stable,
26 He forgets and abandons the arena;
27 He conquers his nature,
28 Remembers what he's learned,
29 And becomes the like of a fattened ox.
30 The savage lion abandons his wrath,
31 And comes to resemble the timid donkey.
32 The horse slips into its harness,
33 Obedient it goes outdoors.
34 The dog obeys the word,
35 And walks behind its master.
36 The monkey carries the stick,
37 Though its mother did not carry it.
38 The goose returns from the pond,
39 When one comes to shut it in the yard.
40 One teaches the Nubian to speak Egyptian,
41 The Syrian and other strangers too.
42 Say: "I shall do like all the beasts,"
43 Listen and learn what they do.

Any first puts responsibility for understanding and accepting moral instruction squarely back on Khonshotep's court. To be unready for moral instruction is "what you do to yourself," solely a matter of Khonshotep's own choice. It is up to Khonshotep, Any insists, to make himself a successful moral pupil. Any models moral instruction on animal training. Bulls and lions overcome aggressive instincts to kill and are thus tamed. The horse, the dog, the monkey, and the goose forget their wild natures and learn obedience to their master. In lines 40–41 Any makes a different comparison: Moral instruction is also like teaching a foreigner to speak Egyptian. Returning to the main message at the end—and perhaps pointedly failing to distinguish Egyptian-speaking foreigners from tame animals—Any exhorts Khonshotep to make a resolve and act on it: Become a pupil like the animals, readily submitting to instruction which will tame his untutored, wild nature.

44 *The scribe Khonshotep answered his father, the scribe Any:*
45 Do not proclaim your powers,
46 So as to force me to your ways;
47 Does it not happen to a man to slacken his hand,
48 So as to hear an answer in its place?
49 Man resembles the god in his way
50 If he listens to man's answer.
51 One (man) cannot know his fellow,
52 If the masses are beasts;
53 One (man) cannot know his teachings,

54 And alone possess a mind,
55 If the multitudes are foolish.
56 All your sayings are excellent,
57 But doing them requires virtues;
58 Tell the god who gave you wisdom:
59 "Set them on your path!"

Khonshotep rejects force as a method of moral instruction. Any should not "proclaim [his] powers" to force Khonshotep to follow his instructions. Human moral conviction involves hearing an answer, participation in moral conversations and listening to reasons. It involves, as we saw in Khonshotep's first speech, acceptance by the heart (lines 12–13). According to Khonshotep, when we listen to and "hear an answer," we resemble a god rather than a beast. For Khonshotep, this linguistic capacity is a god-like power of human beings. Seeing a fundamental link among language, knowledge, and a divine aspect of human nature is familiar in postPlatonic philosophy. But we must keep in mind that the *Instruction of Any* is, by nearly a millennium, a *pre*Platonic text.[4]

Khonshotep's attack on Any's animal training model of moral instruction moves their dialogue to a higher philosophical level. Khonshotep's language model of moral instruction affirms that moral instruction is based upon the pupil's ability to hear, discuss, and accept maxims of instruction. As already noted, Any compares moral instruction with learning a language in lines 40–41. This admission is the entering wedge for Khonshotep's reply. Interpreting Khonshotep's speech as a *reductio* argument captures the logic of his speech with maximal charity and rigor.

1. Suppose moral instruction is like animal training.
2. Moral instruction is like animal training only if men are beasts. [line 52]
3. Moral instructors and pupils are beasts. [from (1) and (2)]
4. But unlike men, beasts cannot listen to or hear answers. [implication of lines 47–50]
5. Moral instruction is a kind of knowledge communicated in a language one can listen to and hear. [the "entering wedge' of lines 40–41 and restated in lines 47–50]
6. Moral instructors cannot communicate moral instructions to pupils. [from (3), (4) and (5); lines 53–55]
7. Therefore, moral instruction is impossible. [from (5) and (6); lines 51–52]
8. But moral instruction is possible. [Any certainly assumes this, and Khonshotep never seriously doubts it]
9. Therefore, (1) is false: Moral instruction is *not* like animal training.

Khonshotep ends his second speech by challenging Any to tell (not ask!) the god who gave Any wisdom to help moral pupils find the path to moral wisdom. Perhaps Khonshotep really holds that, since listening and hearing moral instruction involves a god-like power of understanding, accepting moral instructions is helped by, or may even require, the assistance of the god. An ironic reading seems more likely, however, because Khonshotep's impatient and often angry challenge to parental authority seems constant throughout the Epilogue. Moreover, in his next speech Any responds with anger to Khonshotep, telling him to "turn [his] back to these many words that are not worth being heard." Any clearly takes lines 56–59 as another challenge rather than a serious affirmation of his god-like wisdom. By setting himself up as a moral authority and defending a view of moral instruction which regards others as akin to animals needing training, Any is in effect elevating himself to divine status. Khonshotep's ironic point is that Any is quite far from divine status, quite far from one who the gods made wise. Though Khonshotep says that Any's "sayings are excellent," he really means the reverse of this.

60 *The scribe Any answered his son, the scribe Khonshotep:*
61 Turn your back to these many words,
62 That are not worth being heard.
63 The crooked stick left on the ground,
64 With sun and shade attacking it,
65 If the carpenter takes it, he straightens it,
66 Makes of it a noble's staff,
67 And a straight stick makes a [horse] collar.
68 You foolish heart,
69 Do you wish us to teach,
70 Or have you been corrupted?

In lines 61–62 and 68–70 Any attacks Khonshotep and suggests that Khonshotep's challenges indicate the moral corruption of his heart. Yet in this speech Any also clearly changes his own position. Any abandons the animal model of moral instruction and now, presumably under the force of Khonshotep's criticisms, puts forward a new story about moral instruction in lines 63–67. Any apparently no longer considers Khonshotep's arguments altogether "not worth being heard."

What is Any's new story? A stick's shape is warped from alternating shade and sun. Similarly, moral instruction now is seen to begin with a pupil who has a nature shaped by conflicting environmental influences. Alternation of sun and shade causes the stick to shrink and expand, and ultimately to bend. A carpenter can still produce a good product from this stick, just as a moral instructor can produce a good product from a moral pupil whose nature has been warped by conflicting influences earlier in his life. The moral instructor must be skilled in overcoming the results of childhood influences which may have corrupted the pupil's heart.

A straightened stick can be made into a noble's staff or into a horse collar. A staff suited for a noble should be of the highest quality, made useful and attractive by the craftsman. Similarly, the well-trained heart has an inner quality which is noble and useful to the state. Any's second image is quite different. A horse collar restrains and guides a horse who needs to be led. Without a good collar the horse may wander astray. Though this image recalls the animal training model, here Any compares moral instruction to making the collar, not taming the horse. This is a major difference. A horse is directed by wearing a collar but a horse collar can always be taken off. Unlike the process of taming, which totally remakes the internal constitution of a domesticated animal, a collar directs the natural impulses of the horse rather than totally remaking or destroying them.

Both images of what can be done with the bent stick modify the animal training model by recognizing the existence of an already present heart or moral nature in the pupil. The new craftsman model acknowledges some truth in Khonshotep's position and moves somewhat closer to it. The final exchange between Khonshotep and Any, though enigmatically brief, continues to indicate a convergence of their views.

> 71   "Look," said [Khonshotep], "you my father,
> 72   You who are wise and strong of hand:
> 73   The infant in his mother's arms,
> 74   His wish is for what nurses him."
> 75   "Look," said [Any], "when he finds his speech,
> 76   He says, 'Give me bread.'"

Various interpretations suggest themselves. Khonshotep may just be comparing the infant who seeks nourishment with the moral pupil, suggesting that moral instruction should be built on, and responsive to, the neediness of human beings. Or it may be that Khonshotep is mounting a final attack on moral perfectionism by recommending that moral instructors should limit themselves to instructions which satisfy the most basic needs "for what nurses" pupils. Instructors should not demand moral perfection through instructions which call on the pupil to renounce or restrain his most basic needs. Both readings are plausible and they are compatible.

However, the fact that Khonshotep mentions an infant's mother and her connection to her infant strongly suggests a third interpretation which enriches rather than invalidates other possibilities. The nursing mother gives loving nurture and she does not base her relationship to her child on force. The values of gentleness, attentiveness, and responsiveness which characterize nursing are the values Khonshotep has argued for throughout the Epilogue. Even more important is that in the body of his instructions Any explicitly recommends that a father's care for his son should be based on maternal values:

> Double the food your mother gave you,
> Support her as she supported you;

> She had a heavy load in you,
> But she did not abandon you.
> When you were born after your months,
> She was yet yoked (to you),
> Her breast in your mouth for three years.
> As you grew and your excrement disgusted,
> She was not disgusted, saying: "What shall I do!"
> When she sent you to school,
> And you were taught to write,
> She kept watching over you daily,
> With bread and beer in her house,
> When as a youth you take a wife,
> Any you are settled in your house,
> Pay attention to your offspring,
> Bring him up as did your mother.[5]

Khonshotep in his last speech [lines 71 and 72] is reminding his father to be consistent, to heed his own moral instructions. Since Any maintains that a father should "pay attention to [his] offspring [and] bring him up as did [his own] mother," Any cannot consistently maintain either the animal model or the craftsman model of moral instruction.

According to Miriam Lichtheim, "Any's concluding answer [in lines 75–76] apparently means that when a child is old enough to speak he asks to be nourished materially and spiritually."[6] Perhaps, but there are other meanings as well. Taken literally, Any's point may be that as children change, their desires change: First they wanted mother's milk, now they want bread. Maybe this is meant as a reply to Khonshotep's claim that moral instruction should hearken to fundamental needs and desires. To ask for bread is to seek to satisfy a basic need, but one which has been modified by experience. As the craftsman model says, moral instruction modifies innate nature.

But father and son may be closer to agreement here than this would suggest. Sometimes what is not said is as important as what is said. Only in this final speech does Any refrain from berating Khonshotep for his worthless words, corruption, and irresponsibility. Could it be that Any now agrees with Khonshotep, or at least has begun to listen to him? Is he trying to act on his own earlier instruction to treat one's son as one was treated by one's mother?

It is significant that Any says that children do not learn speech; they "find" speech. If pupils "find" speech, then speech is in some sense waiting to be found. Here Any, for the first time, explicitly acknowledges the naturalness of speech as a human characteristic. When the son says, "Give me bread," he is united to both parents by his neediness and dependency. Either parent may give him bread. Any thus indicates that fathers can nurture, and at the same time he now seems to accept that we are not just bundles of appetites, needing to be tamed by force. Growth and speech together transform the infant into a child who can communicate new needs and be fed by both father and mother. It now appears that Any agrees with Khonshotep that moral instruction must hearken to and respect the pupil's needs and nature as a language user if it is to succeed. While differences remain, a reconciliation between father and son, a partial convergence of their views on moral instruction, is the note on which the Epilogue ends.

What are we to make of the *Instruction of Any?* Too many different activities by too many different people at too many different times have been called "moral philosophy" to expect a definition of the term via necessary and sufficient conditions. "Moral philosophy" is a family resemblance term. To assess borderline cases we need to note how many important features they share with undoubted examples of moral philosophy. Although this process is inevitably somewhat circular and stipulative, it is probably the best we can do.

The early Socratic dialogues of Plato are undoubted cases of moral philosophy. We have found the Epilogue of the *Instruction of Any* to be quite similar, a self-reflective dialogue on the possibility of moral instruction. Khonshotep and Any are lively characters whose personal relationship mirrors their changing philosophical stances. The *Instruction of Any* contains profound philosophical positions, dialectical development, reasoned arguments, and irony. Such traits, which are found in the *Crito,* the *Meno,* and other Socratic inquiries, suffice to make the *Instruction of Any* a work of moral philosophy. The history of moral philosophy is accordingly transformed: Thales was not the first philosopher, nor was Socrates the first moral philosopher, nor was Plato the first to compose artful philosophic dialogue. Historically, Africa should be moved from the margins to the center of moral philosophy.[7]

Notes

1. S.G.F. Brandon, *The Judgment of the Dead,* Scribners (1967): 29 and 37. The whole of Chapter 1 is relevant. See also Marian Goodlander, "Significant Trends in Ancient Egypt," *The Personalist* 31 (1950): 23. Goodlander cites the use of "heart" in the *Instruction of Ptahhotep* (ca. 2200 B.C.): "It is the heart which makes its possessor a hearkener or one not hearkening."

2. E.A.W. Budge, *The Book of the Dead: The Hieroglyphic Transcript of the Papyrus of Ani,* University Books (1960): 437–457 and 568–596. The prayers concerning the heart are in Chapters 26–30. The famous judgment of the dead, with its weighing of the heart, is in Chapter 125.

3. This and all subsequent quotations from the *Instruction of Any* are from Miriam Lichtheim, *Ancient Egyptian Literature, Volume II: The New Kingdom,* University of California Press (1976): 135–146. Lichtheim notes that the text presents great difficulties to the translator, but as a

philosopher rather than an Egyptologist I must rely on her translation. I have numbered the lines of the Epilogue for ease of reference. A selection from Lichtheim's translation which includes the entire Epilogue is in Daniel Bonevac, William Boon and Stephen Phillips, *Beyond the Western Tradition: Readings in Moral and Political Philosophy,* Mayfield (1992): 16–18.

4. Was Plato, perhaps, a student of Egypt's philosophy? An affirmative answer is defended by Martin Bernal, *Black Athena: The Afroasiatic Roots of Classical Civilization,* Rutgers University Press (1987); and Molefi Kete Asante, *Kemet, Afrocentricity and Knowledge,* Africa World Press (1990).

5. On the New Kingdom's kinder and gentler family values, as found in this passage, see John A. Wilson, "Egypt: The Values of Life," in *The Intellectual Adventure of Ancient Man,* Henri Frankfort, et. al., University of Chicago Press (1946): 113.

Another passage, this one near the end of the body of the *Instruction of Any,* is also quite relevant:

Do not control your wife in her house,
When you know she is efficient;
Don't say to her: "Where is it? Get it!"
When she has put it in the right place.
Let your eye observe in silence,
Then you recognize her skill;
It is joy when your hand is with her,
There are many who don't know this.
If a man desists from strife at home,
He will not encounter its beginning.
Every man who founds a household
Should hold back the hasty heart.

6. Lichtheim, Volume II: 146.

7. I began work on this paper during the 1992 Faculty and Curriculum Development Workshop in African American Studies at Old Dominion University. I want to thank ODU colleagues who participated in the workshop and the workshop directors, Charles E. Jones, Janis Sanchez, and John Hudgins, for their stimulation and encouragement.

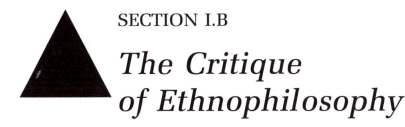

SECTION I.B

The Critique
of Ethnophilosophy

Kwasi Wiredu of Ghana was one of the first African philosophers to insist on the importance of taking a critical stance toward African traditional beliefs. In his "How Not to Compare African Thought with Western Thought" he argues that traditional African belief systems were just one of many prescientific world views, from which Europe had, to a greater degree than Africa, freed itself. And if Africa was to take its place in the modern world, it must be prepared to be critical of its own traditional beliefs. Ancestor worship and witchcraft are examples of practices cited as based primarily on superstition. In Wiredu's view, Africans will have modernized their thinking processes only when they are prepared to subject such beliefs to rational inquiry. Modernity requires that the African take as critical a stance to traditional African beliefs as Europeans have taken to traditional European beliefs.

Paulin Hountondji of Benin is the philosopher most associated with the critique of ethnophilosophy. Hountondji makes a strong case against what he calls "unanimism"—the view that all African people can be characterized by a particular metaphysical and epistemological orientation. Because of its unanimist orientation, ethnophilosophy ignores the multiplicity of cultures that exist in Africa and their many differences. Moreover, he argues that philosophy requires a critical orientation to received views and the development of a scientific attitude toward the world. But none of these practices are cultivated in the oral transmission of traditional beliefs. Because of these deficiencies, Hountondji concludes that ethnophilosophy itself is not a form of philosophy, though it may provide one of the sources for the development of African philosophy.

In line with the attack on ethnophilosophy by Hountondji and Wiredu, Kwame Anthony Appiah (Ghana) critically assesses the claims of African-American nationalists such as Blyden and Du Bois, and African nationalists such as Nkrumah. Appiah argues that these African nationalists never developed an acceptable definition of the notion of race. This, he claims, is because race is a pseudo-concept that is more hinderance than help in meeting the problems faced by the people of Africa.

The next three selections critique the critics of ethnophilosophy, thereby exemplifying the dialectical nature of the development of African philosophy. Albert G. Mosley subjects Kwame Anthony Appiah's arguments as presented in his recent book *In My Father's House—Africa in the Philosophy of Culture* (NY: Oxford University Press, 1992) to careful inspection. Appiah's classification of racism into extrinsic and intrinsic varieties, his claim that Blyden and Du Bois were intrinsic racists, and his claim that the concept of race has neither biological nor sociohistorical legitimacy are all examined and challenged in Mosley's response.

Oyekan Owomoyela of Nigeria provides a comprehensive summary of the ethnophilosophical position and its critique by Wiredu, Hountondji, Bodunrin, and others. He points out that the deference to the past so associated with traditional culture is true more in name than in fact, and he argues that ideas need not be written in order to be critically assailed and altered. The belief in a mystical world of spirits may be pre-scientific, but it may be a needed antidote to the scientific approach to nature. Africa's conquest by the West does not mean that African belief systems are inferior to modern European beliefs, and Owomoyela reaffirms that different civilizations may exemplify different virtues and different vices.

Abiola Irele, a Nigerian specializing in Francophone literature, provides a magisterial overview of philosophy in Francophone Africa. He presents the work of Senghor, Kagame, and Diop as examples of ethnophilosophy and reviews the arguments of their major critics, including Albert Franklin, Stanislas Adotevi, Franz Fanon, Marcien Towa, and Paulin Hountondji. In the final section of his paper, Irele examines V. Y. Mudimbe's *The Invention of Africa* (Bloomington, IN: Indiana University Press, 1988) and concludes with a warning that Mudimbe, Hountondji, and others should be wary of uncritically accepting the hegemony of Western models of science and philosophy.

▲ How Not to Compare African Thought with Western Thought[1]

Kwasi Wiredu

Kwasi Wiredu is a Ghanaian philosopher, former chair of the Department of Philosophy of the University of Ghana, and currently teaches at the University of South Florida. He has published extensively in the area of African philosophy, and the selection provided here is one of the most cited and debated in the literature.

In this article, Wiredu argues that a failure to appreciate the nature of traditional Western thought has encouraged the tendency to identify Western thought with modern Western thought. Because African cultures in the modern world are the existing approximations to a prescientific stage of intellectual development, the contrast drawn by ethnophilosophers between African and Western modes of thought has really been between traditional and modern modes of thought.

He chides educated Africans for uncritically adhering to traditional African beliefs and practices, and warns that exhortations for Africans to uncritically preserve their traditional beliefs may be counterproductive to Africa's progress. If Africa is to develop its resources, then beliefs and practices that have no rationale, and practices that are economically and socially detrimental, must be critically assessed and replaced by more appropriate ones. In this regard, he stresses the need to cultivate written over oral modes of communicating, arguing that literacy is a necessary condition for the transition from a prescientific to a scientific phase of human development.

The modernization of Africa must involve not only Africa's physical resources but its modes of thought as well. The influence of the Western philosophical tradition on African traditional cultures is no less important than the impact of Greek and Roman thought on the barbaric tribes of Western Europe. This does not mean that traditional African cultures have nothing to contribute to the evolution of world civilization and, to illustrate, Wiredu suggests that Westerners could learn much from African systems of morality that are not based on appeal to the command of spiritual entities and forces. This is a suggestion that Wiredu develops in a later essay in this volume.

Many western anthropologists and even non-anthropologists have often been puzzled by the virtual ubiquity of references to gods and all sorts of spirits in traditional African explanations of things. One western anthropologist, Robin Horton, has suggested that this failure of understanding is partly attributable to the fact that many western anthropologists "have been unfamiliar with the theoretical thinking of their own culture."[2] I suggest that a very much more crucial reason is that they have also apparently been unfamiliar with the folk thought of their own culture.

Western societies too have passed through a stage of addiction to spiritistic explanations of phenomena. What is more, significant residues of this tradition remain a basic part of the mental make-up of a large mass of the not so-sophisticated sections of Western populations. More importantly still, elements of the spiritistic outlook are, in fact, deeply embedded in the philosophical thought of many contemporary westerners—philosophers and even scientists.

Obviously it is a matter of first rate philosophical importance to distinguish between traditional, i.e., pre-scientific, spiritistic thought and modern scientific thought by means of a clearly articulated criterion (or set of criteria). Indeed, one of the most influential and fruitful movements in recent Western philosophy, namely the logical positivist movement, may be said to have been motivated by the quest for just such a criterion. Also anthropologically and psychologically it is of interest to try to understand how traditional modes of thought function in the total context of life in a traditional society. Since African societies are among the closest approximations in the modern world to societies in the pre-scientific stage of intellectual development, the interest which anthropologists have shown in African thought is largely understandable.

Unfortunately instead of seeing the basic non-scientific characteristics of African traditional thought as typifying traditional thought in general, Western anthropologists and others besides have tended to take them as defining a peculiarly African way of thinking. The ill-effects of this mistake have been not a few.

One such effect is that the really interesting cross-cultural comparisons of modes of thought have tended not to be made. If one starts with the recognition that all peoples have some background of traditional thought—and remember by *traditional* thought here I mean pre-scientific thought of the type that tends to construct explanations of natural phenomena in terms of the activities of gods and kindred spirits—then the interesting and anthropologically illuminating comparison will be to see in what different ways spiritistic categories are employed by various peoples in the attempt to achieve a coherent view of the world. In such specific differences will consist the real peculiarities of, say, African traditional thought in contradistinction from, say, Western traditional thought. Such comparisons may well turn out to hold less exotic excitement for the Western anthropologist than present practice would seem to suggest. In the absence of any such realization, what has generally happened is that not only the genuine distinguishing features of African traditional thought but also its basic non-scientific, spiritistic, tendencies have been taken as a basis for contrasting Africans from Western peoples. One consequence is that many Westerners have gone about with an exaggerated notion of the differences in nature between Africans and the peoples of the West. I do not imply that this has necessarily led to anti-African racism. Nevertheless, since in some obvious and important respects, traditional thought is inferior to modern, science-oriented thought, some Western liberals have apparently had to think hard in order to protect themselves against conceptions of the intellectual inferiority of Africans as a people.

Another ill-effect relates to the self-images of Africans themselves. Partly through the influence of Western anthropology and partly through insufficient critical reflection on the contemporary African situation, many very well placed Africans are apt to identify African thought with *traditional* African thought. The result has not been beneficial to the movement for modernization, usually championed by the very same class of Africans. The mechanics of this interplay of attitudes is somewhat subtle. To begin with, these Africans have been in the habit of calling loudly, even stridently, for the cultivation of an African authenticity or personality. True, when such a call is not merely a political slogan, it is motivated by a genuine desire to preserve the indigenous culture of peoples whose confidence in themselves has been undermined by colonialism. But it was a certain pervasive trait of this same culture that enabled sparse groups of Europeans to subjugate large masses of African populations and keep them in colonial subjection for many long years and which even now makes them a prey to neo-colonialism. I refer to the *traditional* and non-literate character of the culture, with its associated technological underdevelopment. Being traditional is, of course, not synonymous with being non-literate. A culture can be literate and yet remain traditional i.e., non-scientific, as the case of India, for example, proves. India has a long tradition of written literature, yet it was not until comparatively recent times that the scientific spirit made any appreciable inroads into the Indian way of life. But, of course, a culture cannot be both scientific and non-literate, for the scientific method can only flourish where there can be recordings of precise measurements, calculations and, generally, of observational data. If a culture is both non-scientific and non-literate, then in some important respects it may be said to be backward in a rather deep sense. We shall in due course note the bearing of the non-literate nature of the traditional African culture on the question of just what African philosophy is.

What is immediately pertinent is to remark that unanalyzed exhortations to Africans to preserve their indigenous culture are not particularly useful—indeed, they can be counterproductive. There is an urgent need in Africa today for the kind of analysis that would identify and separate the backward aspects of our culture—I speak as an anxious African—from those aspects that are worth keeping. That such desirable aspects exist is beyond question, and undoubtedly many African political and intellectual leaders are deeply impregnated by this consideration. Yet the analytical dimension seems to be lacking in their enthusiasm. So we have, among other distressing things, the frequent spectacle of otherwise enlightened Africans assiduously participating in the pouring of libation to the spirits of our ancestors on ceremonial occasions, or frantically applauding imitation of the frenzied dancing of "possessed" fetish priests—all this under the impression that in so doing they are demonstrating their faith in African culture.

In fact, many traditional African institutions and cultural practices, such as the ones just mentioned, are based on superstition. By "superstition" I mean a rationally unsupported belief in entities of any sort. The attribute of being superstitious attaches not to the content of a belief but to its mode of entertainment. Purely in respect of content the belief, for example, in abstract entities in semantic analysis common among many logistic ontologists in the West is not any more brainy then the traditional African belief in ancestor spirits. But logisticians are given to arguing for their ontology. I happen to think their arguments for abstract entities wrong-headed;[3] but it is not open to me to accuse them of superstition. When, however, we come to the traditional African belief in ancestor spirits—and this, I would contend, applies to traditional spiritistic beliefs everywhere—the position is different. That our departed ancestors continue to hover around in some rarefied form ready now and then to take a sip of the ceremonial schnapps is a proposition that I have never known to be rationally defended. Indeed, if one were to ask a traditional elder, "unspoilt" by the scientific orientation, for the rational justification of such a belief, one's curiosity would be quickly put down to intellectual arrogance acquired through Western education.

Yet the principle that one is not entitled to accept a proposition as true in the absence of any evidential support is not Western in any but an episodic sense. The Western world happens to be the place where, as of now, this principle has received its most sustained and successful application in certain spheres of thought, notably in the natural and mathematical sciences. But even in the Western world there are some important areas of belief wherein the principle does not hold sway. In the West just as anywhere else the realms of religion, morals and politics remain strongholds of irrationality. It is not uncommon, for example, to see a Western scientist, fully apprised of the universal reign of law in natural phenomena, praying to God, a spirit, to grant rain and a good harvest and other things besides. Those who are tempted to see in such a thing as witchcraft the key to specifically *African* thought—there is no lack of such people among foreigners as well as Africans themselves—ought to be reminded that there are numbers of white men in today's London who proudly proclaim themselves to be witches. Moreover, if they would but read, for example, Treyor-Roper's historical essay on "Witches and Witchcraft,"[4] they might conceivably come to doubt whether witchcraft in Africa has ever attained the heights to which it reached in Europe in the sixteenth and seventeenth centuries.

It should be noted, conversely, that the principle of rational evidence is not entirely inoperative in the thinking of the traditional African. Indeed, no society could survive for any length of time without conducting a large part of their daily activities by the principle of belief according to the evidence. You cannot farm without some rationally based knowledge of soils and seeds and of meteorology; and no society can achieve any reasonable degree of harmony in human relations without a *basic* tendency to assess claims and allegations by the method of objective investigation. The truth, then, is that rational knowledge is not the preserve of the modern West[5] nor is superstition a peculiarity of the African peoples.

Nevertheless, it is a fact that Africa lags behind the West in the cultivation of rational inquiry. One illuminating (because fundamental) way of approaching the concept of "development" is to measure it by the degree to which rational methods have penetrated thought habits. In this sense, of course, one cannot compare the development of peoples in absolute terms. The Western world is "developed," but only relatively. Technological sophistication is only an aspect, and that not the core, of development. The conquest of the religious, moral and political spheres by the spirit of rational inquiry remains, as noted earlier, a thing of the future even in the West. From this point of view the West may be said to be still underdeveloped. The quest for development, then, should be viewed as a continuing world-historical process in which all peoples, Western and non-Western alike, are engaged.

There are at least two important advantages in looking at development in this way. The first is that it becomes possible to see the movement towards modernization in Africa not as essentially a process in which Africans are unthinkingly jettisoning their own heritage of thought in the pursuit of Western ways of life, but rather as one in which Africans in common with all other peoples seek to attain a specifically *human* destiny—a thought that should assuage the qualms of those among thoughtful Africans who are wont to see modernization as a foreign invasion. The relation between the concepts of development and modernization ought to be obvious. Modernization is the application of the results of modern science for the improvement of the conditions of human life. It is only the more visible side of development; it is the side that is more immediately associated with the use of advanced technology and novel techniques in various areas of life such as agriculture, health education and recreation. Because modernization is not the whole of development there is a need to view it always in a wider human perspective. Man should link the modernization of the conditions of his life with the modernization of all aspects of his thinking. It is just the failure to do this that is responsible for the more unlovable features of life in the West. Moreover, the same failure bedevils attempts at development in Africa. Rulers and leaders of opinion in Africa have tended to think of development in terms of the visible aspects of modernization—in terms of large buildings and complex machines, to the relative neglect of the more intellectual foundations of modernity. It is true that African nations spend every year huge sums of money on institutional education. But it has not been appreciated that education ought to lead to the cultivation of a rational[6] outlook on the world on the part of the educated and, through them, in the traditional folk at large. Thus it is that even while calling for modernization, influential Africans can still be seen to encourage superstitious practices such as the pouring of libation to spirits in the belief that in this kind of way they can achieve development without losing their Africanness. The second advantage of seeing development in the way suggested above is that the futility of any such approach becomes evident. To develop in any serious sense, we in Africa must break with our old uncritical habits of thought; that is we must advance past the stage of traditional thinking.

Lest these remarks appear rather abstract, let us consider a concrete situation. Take the institution of funerals in Ghana, for example. Owing to all sorts of superstitions about the supposed career of the spirits of departed relatives, the mourning of the dead takes the form of elaborate, and, consequently expensive and time consuming social ceremonies. When a person dies there has first to be a burial ceremony on the third day; then on the eighth day there is a funeral celebration at which customary rites are performed; then forty days afterwards there is a fortieth day celebration (*adaduanan*). Strictly, that is not the end. There are such occasions as the eightieth day and first anniversary celebrations. All these involve large alcohol-quaffing gatherings. Contrary to what one might be tempted to think, the embracing of Christianity by large sections of Ghanaian population has not simplified funeral celebrations; on the contrary, it has brought new complications. Christianity too teaches of a whole hierarchy of spirits, started from the Supreme Threefold Spirit down to the angels both good and refractory down further to the lesser spirits of deceased mortals. Besides, conversion to Christianity in our lands has generally not meant the exchange of the indigenous religion for the new one, but rather an amalgamation of both, which is made more possible by their common spiritistic orientation. Thus, in addition to all the traditional celebrations, there is nowadays the neo-Christian Memorial Service, replete with church services and extended refreshments, a particularly expensive phase of the funeral process. The upshot is that if a close relation of a man, say his father, died, then unless he happens to be rich, he is in for very hard financial times indeed. He has to take several days off work, and he has to borrow respectable sums of money to defray the inevitable expenses.

The extent of the havoc that these funeral habits have wrought on the national economy of Ghana has not been exactly calculated, but it has become obvious to public leaders that it is enormous and that something needs urgently to be done about it. However, the best that these leaders have seemed capable of doing so far has been to exhort the people to reform their traditional institutions in general and cut down on funeral expenses in particular. These appeals have gone unheeded; which is not surprising, if one recalls that these leaders themselves are often to be seen ostentatiously taking part in ceremonies, such as the pouring of libation, which are based on the same sort of beliefs as those which lie behind the funeral practices. It has so far apparently been lost upon our influential men that while the underlying beliefs retain their hold, any verbal appeals are wasted on the populace.

The ideal way to reform backward customs in Africa must, surely, be to undermine their superstitious belief-foundations by fostering in the people—at all events, in the new generation of educated Africans—the spirit of rational inquiry in all spheres of thought and belief. Even if the backward beliefs in question were *peculiarly* African, it would be necessary to work for their eradication. But my point is that they are not African in any intrinsic, inseparable sense; and the least that African philosophers and foreign well-wishers can do in this connection is to refrain, in this day and age, from serving up the usual congeries of unargued conception about gods, ghosts, and witches in the name of *African philosophy.* Such a description is highly unfortunate. If at all deserving of the name "philosophy," these ideas should be regarded not as a part of African philosophy simply, but rather as a part of *traditional* philosophy in Africa.

This is not verbal cavilling. The habit of talking of African philosophy as if all African philosophy is *traditional* carries the implication,

probably not always intended, that modern Africans have not been trying, or worse still, ought not to try, to philosophize in a manner that takes
account of present day development in human knowledge, logical, mathematical, scientific, literary, etc. Various causes have combined to motivate this attitude. African nationalists in search of an African identity,
Afro-Americans in search of their African roots and Western foreigners in
search of exotic diversion—all demand an African philosophy that shall
be fundamentally different from Western philosophy, even if it means the
familiar witches' brew. Obviously, the work of contemporary African
philosophers trying to grapple with the modern philosophical situation
cannot satisfy such a demand.

The African philosopher writing today has no tradition of written
philosophy in his continent[7] to draw upon. In this respect, his plight is
very much unlike that of say, the contemporary Indian philosopher. The
latter can advert his mind to any insights that might be contained in a
long-standing Indian heritage of written philosophical meditations; he
has what he might legitimately call *classical* Indian philosophers to in-
vestigate and profit by. And if he is broad-minded, he will also study
Western philosophy and try in his own philosophizing to take cognizance of the intellectual developments that have shaped the modern
world. Besides all this, he has, as every people have, a background of un-
written folk philosophy which he might examine for whatever it may be
worth. Notice that we have here three levels of philosophy: we have spoken of a folk philosophy, a written traditional[8] philosophy and a modern
philosophy. Where long-standing written sources are available folk philosophy tends not to be made much of. It remains in the background as a
sort of diffused, immanent, component of community thought habits
whose effects on the thinking of the working philosopher is largely unconscious.[9] Such a fund of community thought is not the creation of any
specifiable set of philosophers; it is the common property of all and
sundry, thinker and non-thinker alike, and it is called a *philosophy* at all
only by a quite liberal acceptation of the term. Folk thought, as a rule,
consists of bald assertions without argumentative justification, but philosophy in the narrower sense must contain not just theses. Without argumentation and clarification, there is, strictly, no philosophy.

Of course, folk thought can be comprehensive and interesting on its
own account. Still its non-discursiveness remains a drawback. For example, according to the conception of a person found among the Akans of
Ghana, (the ethnic group to which the present writer belongs), a person
is constituted by *nipakua* (a body) and a combination of the following
entities conceived as spiritual substances:[10] (1) *okra* (soul, approximately), that whose departure from a man means death, (2) *Sunsum,* that
which gives rise to a man's character, (3) *ntoro,* something passed on
from the father which is the basis of inherited characteristics and, finally,

(4) *mogya,* something passed on from the mother which determines a man's clan identity and which at death becomes the *saman* (ghost). This last entity seems to be the one that is closest to the material aspect of a person; literally, *mogya* means blood. Now, in the abstract, all this sounds more interesting, certainly more imaginative, than the thesis of some Western philosophers that a person consists of a soul and body. The crucial difference, however, is that the Western philosopher tries to argue for his thesis, clarifying his meaning and answering objections, known or anticipated; whereas the transmitter of folk conceptions merely says: "This is what our ancestors said."[11] For this reason folk conceptions tend not to develop with time. Please note that this is as true in the West and elsewhere as it is in Africa.

But in Africa, where we do not have even a written traditional philosophy, anthropologists have fastened on our folk world-views and elevated them to the status of a continental philosophy. They have then compared this "philosophy" with Western (written) philosophy. In other, better placed, parts of the world, if you want to know the philosophy of the given people, you do not go to aged peasants or fetish priests or court personalities; you go to the individual thinkers, in flesh, if possible, and in print. And as any set of individuals trying to think for themselves are bound to differ among themselves, you would invariably find a variety of theories and doctrines, possibly but not necessarily, sharing substantial affinities. Since the reverse procedure has been the only one that has seemed possible to anthropologists, it is not surprising that misleading comparisons between African traditional thought and Western scientific thought have resulted. My contention, which I have earlier hinted at, is that African traditional thought should in the first place only be compared with Western folk thought. For this purpose, of course, Western anthropologists will first have to learn in detail about the folk thought of their own peoples. African folk thought may be compared with Western philosophy only in the same spirit in which Western folk thought may be compared also with Western philosophy, that is, only in order to find out the marks which distinguish folk thought in general from individualized philosophizing. Then, if there be any who are anxious to compare African philosophy with Western philosophy, they will have to look at the philosophy that Africans are producing today.

Naturally Western anthropologists are not generally interested in contemporary African philosophy. Present day African philosophers have been trained in the Western tradition, in the continental or Anglo-American style, depending on their colonial history. Their thinking, therefore, is unlikely to hold many peculiarly African novelties for anyone knowledgeable in Western philosophy. For this very same reason, African militants and our Afro-American brothers are often disappointed with the sort of philosophy syllabus that is taught at a typical modern department of philosophy in Africa. They find such a department mainly immersed in the study of Logic, Epistemology, Metaphysics, Ethics, Political Philosophy, etc., as these have been developed in the West, and they question why Africans should be so engrossed in the philosophy of their erstwhile colonial oppressors.

The attentive reader of this discussion should know the answer by now: The African philosopher has no choice but to conduct his philosophical inquiries in relation to the philosophical writings of other peoples, for his own ancestors left him no heritage of philosophical writings. He need not—to be sure, he must not—restrict himself to the philosophical works of his particular former colonial oppressors, but he must of necessity study the written philosophies of other lands, because it would be extremely injudicious for him to try to philosophize in self-imposed isolation from all modern currents of thought, not to talk of longer-standing nourishment for the mind. In the ideal, he must acquaint himself with the philosophies of all the peoples of the world, compare, contrast, critically assess them and make use of whatever of value he may find in them. In this way it can be hoped that a tradition of philosophy as a discoursive discipline will eventually come to be established in Africa which future Africans and others too can utilize. In practice the contemporary African philosopher will find that it is the philosophies of the West that will occupy him the most, for it is in that part of the world that modern developments in human knowledge have gone farthest and where, consequently, philosophy is in closest touch with the conditions of the modernization which he urgently desires for his continent. In my opinion, the march of modernization is destined to lead to the universalization of philosophy everywhere in the world.

The African philosopher cannot, of course, take the sort of cultural pride in the philosophical achievements of Aristotle or Hume or Kant or Frege or Hussérl of which the Western student of philosophy may permit himself. Indeed an African needs a certain level-headedness to touch some of these thinkers at all. Hume,[12] for example, had absolutely no respect for black men. Nor was Marx,[13] for another instance, particularly progressive in this respect. Thus any partiality the African philosopher may develop for these thinkers must rest mostly on considerations of truth-value.

As regards his own background of folk thought, there is a good reason why the African philosopher should pay more attention to it than would seem warranted in other places. Africans are a much oppressed and disparaged people. Some foreigners there have been who were not even willing to concede that Africans as a traditional people were capable of any sort of coherent[14] world-view. Those who had the good sense and the patience and industry to settle down and study traditional African thought were often, especially in the 19th and early 20th centuries, colonial anthropologists who sought to render the actions and attitudes of our forefathers intelligible to the colonial rulers so as to facilitate their governance. Although some brilliant insights were obtained, there were also misinterpretations and straightforward errors. Africans cannot leave the task of correction to foreign researchers alone. Besides, particularly in the field of morality, there are non-superstition-based conceptions from which the modern Westerner may well have something to learn. The exposition of such aspects of African traditional thought specially befits the contemporary African philosopher.

Still, in treating of their traditional thought, African philosophers should be careful not to make hasty comparisons.[15] Also they should approach their material critically; this last suggestion is particularly important since all peoples who have made any breakthrough in the quest for modernization have done so by going beyond folk thinking. It is unlikely to be otherwise in Africa. I should like to repeat, however, that the process of sifting the elements of our traditional thought and culture calls for a good measure of analytical circumspection lest we exchange the good as well as the bad in our traditional ways of life for dubious cultural imports.

It should be clear from the foregoing discussion that the question of how African thought may appropriately be compared with Western thought is not just an important academic issue but also one of great existential urgency.

Notes

1. This paper first appeared in *Ch'indaba* and is reprinted here by permission of the author.
2. Robin Horton, "African Traditional Thought and Western Science," in *Rationality* ed. Bryan Wilson (Oxford: Basil Blackwell). Originally published in *Africa* 37, nos. 1 & 2 (1967). Also appears on page 301 of this book.
3. My reasons for this remark will be found in my series of articles on "Logic and Ontology," *Second Order: an African Journal of Philosophy* 2, no. 1 (January 1973) and no. 2 (July 1973): 3, no. 2 (July 1974); 4, no. 1 (January 1975).
4. *Encounter* 28, no. 5 (May 1967) and no. 6 (June 1967).
5. Note that "the West" and "Western" are used in a cultural, rather than ideological sense in this discussion.
6. I am aware that my insistence in the overriding value of rationality will be found jarring by those Westerners who feel that the claims of rationality have been pushed too far in their countries and that the time is overdue for a return to "Nature" and the exultation in feeling, intuition and immediacy. No doubt the harsh individualism of Western living

might seem to lend support to this point of view. But in my opinion the trouble is due to too little rather than too much rationality in social organization. This, however, is too large a topic to enter into here.

7. The Arab portions of Africa are, of course, an exception, though even there what we have is the result of the interaction between indigenous thought and Greek influences.

8. "Traditional" here still has the pre-scientific connotation. Of course, if one should speak of *traditional* British empiricism, for example, that connotation would be absent.

9. Since such effect do, in fact, occur, this threefold stratification should not be taken as watertight.

10. See, for example, W. E. Abraham, *The Mind of Africa* (Chicago: University of Chicago Press, 1967).

11. However, the circumstances that in Africa, for example, our traditional thought tends not to be elaborately argumentative should be attributed not to any intrinsic lack of the discursive spirit in our ancestors but rather to the fact that their thoughts were not written down.

12. Hume was able to say in his *Essays* (London: George Routledge & Sons, Ltd), footnote on pages 152 and 153 in the course of the essay on "National Characters:" "I am apt to suspect the Negroes to be naturally inferior to the Whites. There scarcely ever was a civilized nation of that complexion, nor any individual, eminent either in action or speculation. . . . In Jamaica, indeed they talk of one Negro as a man of parts and learning; but it is likely that he is admired for slender accomplishments, like a parrot who speaks a few words plainly." Obviously considerable maturity is required in the African to be able to contemplate impartially Hume's disrespect for Negroes and his philosophical insights, deploring the former and acknowledging and assimilating the latter. A British philosopher, Michael Dummett, was recently placed in a not altogether dissimilar situation when, himself a passionate opponent of racialism, he discovered in the course of writing a monumental work on Frege (*Frege: Philosophy of Language,* Duckworth, London, 1973),—a work which he had, indeed, suspended for quite some time in order to throw himself heart and soul into the fight against racial discrimination in his own country, Britain,—that his subject was a racialist of some sort. (See his own remarks in his preface to the above-mentioned book.) It would have argued a lack of balance in him if he had scrapped the project on the discovery. In any event he went ahead to complete the work and put all students of the philosophy of logic in his debt.

13. Marx is known once, in a burst of personal abuse of Lassalle, in a letter to Engels, to have animadverted: "This combination of Jewry and Germany with a fundamental Negro streak. . . . The fellow's self assertiveness is Negro too." Quoted in J. Hampden Jackson, *Marx, Proudhon and European Socialism* (London: English Universities Press, 1951), p. 144. It

is sometimes understandable for a man to chide his own origins, but to condemn a downtrodden people like this is more serious. Would that black men everywhere had more of the self assertiveness which Marx here deprecates. The Akans of Ghana have a proverb which says: "If the truth happens to lie in the most private part of your own mother's anatomy, it is no sin to extract it with your corresponding organ." African enthusiasts of Marx, (or of Hume, for that matter) may perhaps console themselves with the following less delicate adaptation of this proverb. "If the truth happens to lie in the mouth of your racial traducer it is no pulillanimity to take it from there."

14. Coherent thought is not necessarily scientific thought. Traditional thought can display a high degree of coherence; and certainly African traditional thought is not lacking in coherence.

15. I ought perhaps to point out that the kind of comparison between African thought and Western thought that has been criticized in this discussion is the sort which seeks to characterize the given varieties of thinking as wholes. My remarks do not necessarily affect the comparison of isolated propositions.

▲ The Particular and the Universal

Paulin Hountondji

Paulin Hountondji was born in the Republic of Benin and is currently its Minister of Education. His book African Philosophy *(Bloomington, IN: Indiana University Press, 1987) is a collection of previously published articles, in which he spells out his view of the nature of philosophy in general and of African philosophy in particular. It provides an extended critique of the belief that the commonly held beliefs of traditional African people constitute a philosophy.*

Philosophy, for Hountondji, is a method and process of critical analysis. He begins by critically analyzing Tempels, Levy-Bruhl, Kagame, Mbiti, and others who have proposed to exhibit the philosophical assumptions underlying traditional African cultures. He argues that, rather than exhibiting traditional cultures as they really were, they exhibit them relative to the interests they bring to their descriptions. Thus, Tempels' real interest was to provide colonialists with insights into the African character so as to make governing Africans easier. Hountondji rejects the myth that there is some hidden and unconscious philosophy that all Africans adhere to, and calls this belief the fallacy of unanimism. Ethnophilosophy is misguided because it seeks a nonexistent collective philosophy imbedded within the folk beliefs of traditional people.

Hountondji points out that ethnophilosophy was often used to valorize Africans for the very same traits that Westerners used to degrade them. Blackness was associated with the emotional and corporeal to provide a clear distinction between African and European modes of thinking and being. African intellectuals valorized traditional African culture as offering solutions neglected and unavailable in Western culture. They "have wrongly believed that [African philosophy] lies in our past, needing only to be exhumed and then brandished like a miraculous weapon in the astonished face of colonialist Europe" (53).

For Hountondji, philosophy exists only as a form of debate, in which theses are critically assessed. Essential to this process is writing, for only if ideas are recorded can energy be directed toward assessing them rather than merely recounting them. The "first and most basic requirement of philosophy . . . is the broad, democratic practice of writing—a necessary, if not sufficient, condition" (101). Further, he writes, "oral tradition favors the consolidation of knowledge into dogmatic, intangible systems, whereas archival transmission promotes better the possibility of a critique of knowledge between individuals and from one generation to another" (103).

In the following article, "The Particular and the Universal," Hountondji continues his critique of the program to describe and reconstruct authentic traditional African systems of thought, drawing on the distinction between science and ethnoscience. He distinguishes two kinds of ethnoscience. One is descriptive, as ethnobotany would attempt to describe the botanical taxonomy and beliefs of a traditional culture. But to the extent that ethnophilosophy is primarily descriptive, it is not itself a form of philosophy. He accuses cultural nationalism of attempting to reduce the many currents of African culture into a fixed system derived from the golden past, instead of recognizing that African culture is, and always has been, diverse and pluralistic.

The other sense of ethnoscience involves the application of current scientific techniques to the study of some aspect of a traditional culture, as ethnolinguistics would apply modern linguistics to the language of a "primitive" group. In this sense, ethnophilosophy might apply current philosophical techniques to the study of traditional African folk beliefs, with no assumption that those beliefs are themselves an unadulterated carryover from the past. The knowledge so gained would not be valuable in itself, to be preserved and presented like museum pieces. Rather, the value of this form of ethnophilosophy would derive from the degree to which it provides fruitful insights regarding current problems.

Let the French Society of Philosophy be thanked for this invitation that honors me, and that, quite frankly, also honors the entire community of African philosophy. Let the Society be congratulated for this beginning, for its interest in the intellectual struggles that exist outside of the Hexagon, under different skies, in different contexts.

By entitling this exposé "The Particular and the Universal," I hoped to suggest that through its unique history, through the specificity of its themes and problems, the intellectual debate that exists today in black Africa uncovers, in certain ways, one of philosophy's oldest questions. This current debate discloses and perhaps reawakens it. The abrupt claim to an "African philosophy," the critique of this claim led by certain authors, including myself, in the name of a specific concept concerning philosophy and the current needs of Africa, the counter-critique, vigorously suscitated by this critique, and the concomitant development of what I have formerly called learned ethnophilosophy, that is to say, a reconstruction of traditional systems of thought, still as conjectural and as fragile, but less naive than that of the pioneers, and especially, doubled by a theoretical counteroffensive attempting to assure its own legitimacy, this long discussion, already aged of more than forty years, where a multitude of philosophical, political ethnographical, or purely rhetorical arguments intersect, is at base no other than a new, original form of the ancient debate between Socrates and Protagoras, Socrates and Gorgias, Socrates and Callicles. On the one hand, the defenders of the principle of contradiction who were called philosophers, such as Plato and Aristotle, and on the other, those skillful manipulators of language who were called sophists. That this debate has never been settled is only proof of its constant and variegated reappearance in the history of thought. And, that it could not be settled is of course, as Aristotle in his own way acknowledges in the Gamma book of *Metaphysics,* that the sophistry is in one sense as irrefutable as the principle of contradiction is not demonstrable; because the debate between those who defend and oppose the principles of logic is not in itself a logical debate, a debate that would be situated in a theoretical framework as such—in a theoretical framework limited precisely by these principles—rather a more dense confrontation, an affrontation where two language practices are opposed, two strategies and virtually two value systems, and where the significance of theory in general, the value of this infinite research called philosophy, is directly placed into question. If there is a lesson here reminiscent of the Aristotelian critique of the Sophists, it is precisely the following: good faith is not summoned, it either exists, or it does not, the search for truth cannot demonstrate its own necessity as a task, the valorization of the universal is rooted in free choice.

And this is why Aristotle, not being able to refute the Sophists, instead attempted to situate them outside of the game, that is to say, outside of the debate; not being able to oppose them through logical arguments, he opposed them through dialectical arguments; not being able to prove his own theoretical position—the practical value of theory in general—it sufficed him to place the actual crux of the debate on trial, so as to know the actual possibility of communication, in as much as it elicits a task of univocity for each interlocutor:

"To not signify that one thing is one," writes the author of *Metaphysics,* "is to signify nothing at all."

If I evoke this debate here, it is because the quarrel concerning ethnophilosophy in contemporary Africa is also, in a way, a quarrel opposing two practices of language, one that plays on ambiguity, and especially the ambiguities of the word "philosophy," and the other that, on the contrary, attempts to sustain this same task of univocity beyond the multiplicity of meanings of the word "philosophy" and their corresponding practices. Hence, it is the meaning of the word "philosophy" that is first placed into question. Beyond what might seem at first glance to be a simple quarrel of words, are also serious theoretical and methodological problematics that are placed into question concurrently, questions of ideology and politics, in the most profound sense of these words, in terms of what politics designate, beyond the immediate preoccupations of a strategical and tactical order, in terms of the conditions for conquering the empowered, the global vision that we have of our society's destiny and even more generally, of human fate.

Now let's move to ethnophilosophy.

The term itself is less recent than one would think. For many readers, both Africans and non-Africans, it contains a pejorative sense, being linked to the critique of a certain approach, of a certain type of analysis of traditional systems of thought, a critique that was used especially in the 70s. Later, I will return to the legitimacy of this pejorative usage and the fecundity of this critique.

First, it is useful to recognize that this word is quite old. One finds it, for example, in a text published in London in 1957, the year of the former Gold Coast's independence, entitled, *Ghana: Autobiography of Kwame Nkrumah.* The Ghanian leader mentions how, after having received his Master of Philosophy (M.A.) at the University of Pennsylvania in February of 1943, he registered at the same university with the intention of preparing his doctoral thesis on the subject of ethnophilosophy. The thesis remained incomplete until his departure for London in 1945. The word appears spontaneously, without the slightest hesitation or justification in the author's work which suggests that it must have had frequent usage in American university circles where Nkrumah was educated. This neologism would be linked then to the flourishing in the United States of what is today called the ethnosciences. Hence, ethnophilosophy as a project would be the extension of the domain of thought in general, of the inventory of bodies of knowledges called "primitive," already undertaken during this period in terms of plants and animals by two pilot disciplines: ethnobotany and ethnozoology.

In fact, this is the most general sense of the word. Ethnophilosophy is this specialization of ethnology which is tasked with studying the "philosophy" of so-called primitive, archaic, or traditional peoples—in any case, peoples who are the object of ethnology. I will not delay here by delving into an inevitable problem which concerns the specific difference distinguishing these peoples from others, the study of which is reserved for sociology: I mean, the problem of the real meaning of the notion of primitivity (of archaism, or of traditionality) applied to certain societies, the problem of the validity of the separation instated by ethnology as a specialized science. What would be interesting to study further here concerns the position held by ethnophilosophy in relation to other specialties of ethnoscience and in relation to philosophy, the real status of this discipline, its presuppositions, its theoretical and ideological justifications, the extent of its domain and its limitation.

Today, there are many ethnosciences. Their number has increased dramatically in the past decade. Everything is happening as if the anthropologists only recently discovered the existence of bodies of constituted knowledges in oral civilizations which required on their part a systematic effort of exploration. Hence, today one finds the following terminology in contemporary literature, not including ethnobotany and ethnozoology which were previously cited: ethnobiology, ethnopsychiatry, ethnomedicine, ethnomineralogy, ethnopsychoanalysis, ethnopsychology, ethnomusicology, ethnolinguistics, ethnomethodology, ethnohistory, ethnosociology, ethnotypology, ethnodemographics, ethnotechnology, and even ethno-epistemology and ethnocuisine all being terms that respectively designate either disciplines being constituted, or emerging theoretical projects.

What is remarkable is that in order to describe the precise meaning of these terms, one must move at least in two directions. In the first case, ethnoscience is the inventory of knowledges of the so-called primitive peoples, about an object or a given domain of objects: ethnozoology, as inventory of knowledges of animals; ethnobotany, as inventory of knowledges of plants; ethnobiology, as inventory of knowledges of living beings; ethnomineralogy, as inventory of knowledges of inanimate beings, etc. On the other hand, the second case does not deal with an inventory of constituted knowledge but with the application of some given sciences in order to apply a particular aspect of a discipline to so-called "primitive" culture: hence, ethnolinguistics, though not able to articulate the inventory of the linguistic knowledge of so-called primitive peoples, defines the application of linguistics and other various methodological knowledges honed by modern science in terms of the language practice of these said peoples; ethnodemographics is no longer the inventory of demographic knowledges of the people in question, but is instead the application of knowledges and methodological approaches yielded by demographics to the peoples in question.

In the first stated case, ethnoscience reveals itself as a descriptive knowledge, a knowledge of pure restitution, a metaknowledge, where the knowing subject understands, at least at first, that its role is reduced to a minimum and is satisfied with recording this constituted knowledge and quasi-science in the tradition. The second case, however, deals with an active knowledge, a knowledge based on a practice which is itself presumed unreflected, a construction for which ethnology is solely responsible. Because it joins these two distinct significations on common ground, ethnoscience resembles an ambiguous concept, and so, we have to pose an essential question: that of the locality of knowledge, the question of where knowledge situates itself, where the construction is operated and from which a corpus results, the question of knowing whether this construction manifests itself in the culture under study or whether this construction is the work of the ethnologist.

It is inevitably tempting at this point to say that nothing is so simple, that in situations delineated are limit cases and hence not comparable to real-life situations. In one sense, yes, it is true that even in the cases of ethnobotany and ethnozoology it is never a question of simply recording a prerequisite knowledge, but more a question of a critical inventory, indeed, a veritable reconstitution. Inversely, the ethnosciences that present themselves as original constructions would voluntarily recognize that they do not study completely thoughtless practices, but that they almost always find theoretical beginnings linked to these practices, sometimes much more than simple beginnings, and that they cannot stop themselves from taking these "indigenous theories" (as they call them) seriously. For this reason, certain disciplines are quite difficult to classify in either one of these two categories of ethnoscience. Hence, ethnopsychiatry, an inventory of traditional theories whose goal is to produce mental health, is also necessarily and simultaneously an inventory of traditional theories on mental health. What imposes this dual status is the undeniable efficiency of at least certain therapies as ordered practices and their necessary reference to perfectly conscious conceptual elaborations. Ethnomedicine is in the same situation. So is ethnohistory since, by being a branch of history which is in general applied to the study of the history of so-called illiterate peoples and being in this sense a constructed knowledge, it encounters, methodically questions, and exploits to its own needs the oral traditions of the people under study, the knowledge that they themselves have produced about their own history and becomes at the same time a knowledge simply recorded, a knowledge of restitution. In the same way ethnomusicology, the theory of musical practices in so-called traditional societies, cannot not lend at the same time an attentive ear to the "indigenous" theories of these practices to the extent that these theories necessarily accompany artistic activity.

More generally, any knowledgeable theory of traditional *savoir faire* cannot create a situation where it is not at the same time an accompanying theory of knowledge, a theory of "indigenous" theories, integrating with these "indigenous" theories a relation of variable nature, that can move from a pure and simple transferring to critical analysis and interpretations. And, if this is so, it is because savoir faire is never not thought out, but is always a vehicle of knowledge because man everywhere is, in every sense, at base an animal that talks and that already in his speech, above and beyond all possible breaks and ruptures that one can imagine, is the seed of what might one day become under certain determined conditions, theory, *episteme,* science up to, and including, the most modern of sciences.[2]

That given, one could accept it as correct. However, it should not be thought that our question concerning knowledge, that of the locus of knowledge, has been pushed away or that a peremptory response has been given. By observing that knowledge is fundamentally nowhere, or more exactly, that it is everywhere, on both sides, and that all ethnosciences refer to a pre-existing knowledge in the culture under study, by thus acknowledging the circulation of a knowledge that moves constantly from the culture-object to the scientific corpus of anthropologists, upon the condition of, in certain cases, a newly elaborated theoretical work, the problem will not be solved, it will be simply displaced by that fact that it has been transformed. The question remains: how according to which modalities, why, and to whose profit does this circulation of knowledge function? What are the terms? Is there a complete circulation, that is to say, a final return to the original point, or is there instead a sort of dispossession with no return? And what, finally, is the status of ethnosciences? What are the effects? What is their function in relation to more traditional knowledges and to other sciences? Inversely, what is the status of these traditional knowledges in relation to ethnosciences and to modern science which in general integrates and moves past ethnoscience? What was missing from them, what is still missing from them and hence prevents them from becoming authentic sciences? Have they, or have they not evolved in the past and if not, why? If they have, how and to what end?

These questions and many related ones will reappear in the discussion of ethnophilosophy. We will not only re-encounter them. We will find them inscribed in the larger framework and not only as a minute point. Why? Because ethnophilosophy is certainly not a specialty of ethnoscience among others, but is the common base of the ethnosciences, the system of theoretical and methodological presuppositions, indeed of ideological presuppositions, that render them possible, and therefore the space where all the difficulties of ethnoscience crystallize and become comprehensible to the naked eye.

Though the word was used, as I have said, at least in 1957, and comes to us most likely, I suppose, from the United States in the 40s, the pejorative connotation of this word is nonetheless more recent. In his *Essay on the Philosophical Problematic in Contemporary Africa,* published in Yaoundé in 1971, my colleague Marcien Towa from Cameroon uses it to designate what seems to him to be a perfect example of methodological confusion. The negritude philosopher, he says, begins by describing the deeds and cultural values of his people with the same desire for objectivity and scientific detachment as the ethnologist; then, he briskly changes attitudes and begins to defend and reclaim these values as a philosopher would defend and reclaim a thesis without however, having taken the time to justify them as a philosopher would have done. It is this hybrid method, this veritable confusion of genres, that Towa denounces under the word "ethnophilosophy."

I have used this word in the past in an article written in 1969, which appeared in *Diogenes* in 1970, and which was to constitute the first chapter of "African Philosophy: Myth or Reality?" in order to designate the same type of analysis by placing into question not only the confusion of methods but also the status of the object that one is attempting to restore: the "African philosophy," the so-called primitive philosophy, understood as a system of collective thought, spontaneous, implicit, inalterable, to which all the members of a given society would adhere. In my opinion, such a hypothesis seemed to translate a unanimous prejudice, a prejudice according to which everyone would agree on everything in societies of this type.

Actually, if the word "ethnophilosophy" is older than one thought, so is the critique of ethnophilosophy. We are familiar with Césaire's severe lesson in his *Discourse on Colonialism* published in 1950 which stood against the potential political usage of the notion of a Bantu philosophy.[3] We are familiar with Albert Franklin's no less remarkable critique of *Black Orpheus* by Jean-Paul Sartre published in 1952 in the collection *The Black Students Speak*.[4] We are familiar with the striking articles of the late Ugandan poet Okot p'Bitek, published in the journal *Transition* following the publication of the English version of Tempels' *Bantu Philosophy* and which was to reappear in *Africa's Cultural Revolution,* a text by the same author.[5] We are familiar with Frantz Crahay's brilliant critique published in *Diogenes* in 1965 under the title, "The Conceptual Take-off: Conditions of a Bantu Philosophy."[6] Today, thanks to the work of Father Smet of the Catholic Divinity School in Kinshasa, we are also familiar with some of the first reactions expressed in the days which followed the publication of *Bantu Philosophy,* some of which truly showed great public disdain for Tempels in the name of certain political and religious positions which were among the most retrograde of the time and others which, on the contrary, quickly espoused the missionary's perspective, whereas a small number was already formulating what we might call the critique of ethnophilosophy in a language exemplary by its rigor and balance.[7] At least one article by Father Edmond-Eloi Boelart should be mentioned here: an article which was published in 1949 in *Aequatoria,* a journal of the Catholic Mission of Coquilhatville, the contemporary Mbandaka in Zaire, "La Philosophie Bantoue selon le R. P. Tempels"; also, another text of great finesse and lucidity published by the Jesuit priest Léon de Sousberghe in 1951 in *Zaire,* a Belgian journal, entitled "A Propos de 'La Philosophie Bantoue'".[8]

The critique of ethnophilosophy is thus also quite old. What is new is neither the word nor the thing but the conjunction of the word and the thing, the use of the word "ethnophilosophy" to no longer designate a science or a project of the future, but to indicate a discipline that is already being constituted. The first attempts to do so roused certain doubts as to its viability and theoretical consistency; the use of the concept was

consequently no longer prospective and optimistic, but instead retrospective and polemical.

It is perhaps not by chance that this polemical usage comes from a
Francophone space. It is in this space in fact more than in the English
speaking countries that ethnophilosophy has been deployed in its least
acceptable form. There, ethnophilosophy isolates the belief system in relation to their material context and presents them abstractly as if they
supported themselves by the sole virtue of their internal coherence.
Pierre Alexandre accurately observes this: this tendency is typically
Francophone and, in this sense, one could oppose the work of Tempels
and the Griaule school[9] to the work of the Anglo-Saxon Africanists
whose approach, being much more pragmatic, rarely isolates the traditions of thought and does not insist on their abstract systematicity, but
instead resituates them in their empirical context. So, it must be that if
the word "ethnophilosophy" comes from America, ethnophilosophy itself as an attempt to produce an abstract reconstruction of thought systems comes to us from the Francophone space. Consequently there is
nothing surprising if the word had been reinvented in this space in order
to stigmatize, to denounce and to permit a transcending of this type of
approach. It was menacing and was beginning to become invasive in
Africa, in the scientific practice of the regional philosophers and anthropologists. There is, in effect, something fascinating about this model.
Some of our best minds in Africa have submitted to it. It became urgent
to react. We did it and hence reinstated a debate that is still going on.

Before continuing, it is necessary to say a few words on the reasons
for ethnophilosophy. Ethnophilosophy has its reasons that are not
forcedly bad and that are even, on the whole, quite generous. It struggles
against a given situation, it condemns the prejudices that we continue to
condemn still, it has adversaries who, in most cases, are also our own.
Thus, its purpose has a polemical significance that one must begin by recognizing even if one must challenge both the methods employed and the
strategy in place. The objective is still fundamentally to rehabilitate the
so-called primitive culture, to bring out its own cohesiveness and depth
in order to dissipate the usual notions concerning the primitive mentality.

The desire to rehabilitate, common to all ethnophilosophical discourses is, however, still linked to more particular objectives which vary
according to the author. In each case, it is necessary to examine these objectives, to question the author's reasons, the stated intentions and, upon
occasion, the motives in order to understand the genesis, the conditions
of the possibility, the real attitude and limits of the project of ethnophilosophy concurrently.[10]

The attitudes that we have just described are not only expressed in
the essays of *L'Essor du Congo,* a daily newspaper published in Elisa-

bethville. These same attitudes are taken up again in the *Bantu Philosophy,* itself where the author attempts to reveal the practical and theoretical implications while affirming his essential thesis: that the Bantu possess a philosophy. What is remarkable though, is the presence of the same ambiguity, the same desire to defend the Africans without the participation of the Africans themselves.

First, to defend them. Tempels' primary thesis is that the average behavior of the Bantu should not only be accredited to a psychological motive, like fear, but that it should be perceived as a rational behavior, based on a coherent system of concepts. This is his way of saying that the Black man is a real man, that the great sin of the colonizer was to reduce him to a child or to a subhuman, to scorn him, to believe that he is inferior and to treat him accordingly. There is no reason to doubt Tempels' sincerity when he invites the White community to a courageous self-critique, when he accounts for the blunders of the colonial administration, of its ignorance concerning the cultural values and practices of the Bantu, of its oblivion to man, like its gratuitous violence, the crisis that has shaken the colony for many years. The ultimate play of the debate is of an established symbol: "He who feigns the lack of a system of thought in the primitive peoples, refuses their status as humans."[11]

Thus, the major ideological question concerns the humanity of the Black people and, more generally, of the "primitive" peoples. Acknowledging this humanity, and thus (*dixit* Tempels) a Bantu philosophy, is the first condition, the necessary and quasi-sufficient condition, of a normalization of race relations and of a resolution of the political crisis in the colony: "The distance separating the Whites and the Blacks will subsist and grow larger as long as we refuse to recognize the healthy aspirations of their being."[12]

Clearly, the responsibility of the crisis is the burden of the White community and the colonial administration. The Black man wants to be respected and is justified in his desire. Tempels designates himself as the voice of the Black people and as the echo of their legitimate demands: "What they desire above all, (is) . . . the White man's acknowledgement and his respect for the dignity of humanity, for simple human value."[13]

While he takes up the cause for Blacks in general however, the missionary cannot disguise his ill-tempered snarl against *one* category of Blacks, the so-called "évolués." The Belgian colonization invented this new artificial class from every other, a sort of *groupe-tampon,* serving as intermediary between the White community and the indigenous masses. This modern African elite, however, is only a caricature of the authentic elite in Tempels' opinion, a class of strangers and of degenerates who desperately attempt to mimic the White man without ever succeeding in assimilating his profound thoughts.

In order to understand the meaning and real significance of this critique, it is necessary to know that the rebellions and popular uprisings originated in this class of people, that the "agitators" of the rebellion, those who today we could call the African political leaders, came from the heart of this class. Tempels' relentless opposition to these "embittered people," his zeal in denigrating and in ridiculing them is not innocent. They are, according to him, "materialists who have lost their footing in their own ancestral traditions without being able to grasp Western philosophy and thought." One still sees the most childish beliefs in these people crouched under a thin layer of disguise as Whites: subsequent to inquiry, hasn't one discovered in some of them "a notebook where magic formulas are scribbled from beginning to end . . ." copied from the notebook of another "évolué" who transcribed them himself?[14]

Thus the "évolués" are, too often, false Europeans. Worse, they are also false Bantu, denounced as such, and consequently despised by the "elders of the bush":

> "I heard some older wise men repeating . . . : 'These are men of *lupeto* and of *money*.' They explained to me that these young people living with white men knew nothing but money, that was the only thing with any value in their life; they abandoned the wise Bantu vitality and respect for life for a philosophy of money; money is their only ideal; money is their goal, the supreme norm and goal of their acts."[15]

Here's the clincher: the critique no longer comes from the missionary, but instead comes from the peasants themselves, from the indigenous Bantu masses. Of course, Tempels could have heard other signals in the bush, other evaluations of these "evolved" people. But this one suited him fine: he only heard this one.

Thus, the political Bantuism begins with an abrupt separation in the heart of the indigenous masses, between the authentics and the inauthentics, the pure and the impure, the real and the false Bantu and with an attempt to isolate the first ones from the second ones . . .[16]

The brutal reminder of educational obligations and of human advancement, the demand for a real "spiritual direction," calling the colonizer to lead the Blacks instead of simply exploiting them, the insistence on specific tasks of managing the people including, among other things, schooling, acclimating to the European law (or, modernization of the customary law), and more fundamentally and more importantly, dialogue with the other, listening patiently and methodically, respect for what he is and for his human aspirations, this reminder and requirement would yield, in the context of a savage atmosphere, a passably subversive sound while it indicated by its insufficient politic the extreme limits of human generosity imprisoned in colonial ideology. . . .

Politics however are not Tempels' unique motivation. Faith is another force, equally important and determining. Further on we will see that finally these two motivating forces are actually the same. It would be convenient though, to first clarify the situation by distinguishing between the two.

The missionary's wish is to speak to his catechism pupils in a language that has significance for them, to adapt the process of christianizing to their own mentality, to their native system of concepts.

Obviously, beyond their political preoccupations, the major problem of *Bantu Philosophy* uncovers what was formerly called, in that same period, the "missiology": the theory of the missionary practice, reflections on the ways and means of a successful evangelization.[17]

In any case, what is certain is that generally all of Tempels' work prior to the *Bantu Philosophy,* with the exception of a small article where a scientific approach is clear, were dedicated to these questions concerning "missiology," or more simply, of pastorals.[18] The objective of the *Bantu Philosophy* was two-fold—theoretical and practical—indeed, triple: beyond its scientific ambition which we have until now only minimally dealt with, the work had moreover a two-fold practical ambition: political and religious. Now, this triumvirate goal will continue simplifying itself after the battle concerning *Bantu Philosophy,* rearranging and tightening Tempels' discourse uniquely around the religious preoccupation. This is to say that the importance of this motivating factor in this work published in 1945 could not be overestimated.

Of course, we must avoid oversimplifying the work of 1945 after the fact. The political preoccupation, partially absent from the writings of the second Tempels, where instead the mystique of human love as the royal path towards God and as an authentic realization of the faith—this political preoccupation, that appeared increasingly insignificant to the prophet of the *Jama,* is not only present but also, as we have shown, decisive in the *Bantu Philosophy.*

But what is the relation between these two preoccupations? Tempels' text leaves no doubt on this subject: the political motivation was already subordinate to the religious motivation in his *Bantu Philosophy.*

One discovered in the process of this trial that there was a supreme miracle, an unexpected concordance and sort of pre-established harmony between Bantu thought and the doctrine of the Catholic Church:

> "The Bantu paganism, the ancient Bantu wisdom aspires with all of its Bantu spirit towards the soul of Christian spirituality. It is only in Christianity that the Bantu will discover the peace of the secular nostalgia and the complete satisfaction of their most profound aspirations. The Bantu civilization will either be Christian or it will not."[19]

Politico-ideologies still somewhat religious and deterministic in the case of Tempels, ethnophilosophy's justifications are also, of course, scientific: knowledge is their target; more specifically, their aim is to produce a new intelligence concerning cultural deeds. After having insisted on the lateral motivations for so long, at present we need to say something about its specific theoretical motivation.

These days, the thesis of a "primitive philosophy" is still a polemical thesis, led against a theory which the authors concerned reject passionately: the work of prelogism. It is inscribed in a long discussion where the work of Lévy-Bruhl on the primitive mentality constitutes an essential reference point.

In the introduction to *Mental Functions in Inferior Societies,* the French philosopher had clearly indicated the polemical significance of his own theses. These theses targeted the "English anthropological school" as represented by Tylor and Frazer, two of its most eminent representatives. Lévy-Bruhl severly questioned two fundamental postulates of this school: the postulate concerning a universal human nature, identical in both time and space, and the adjoining postulate of a primitive philosophy, of a reasoned and coherent vision of the universe that would preside over the deeds and attitudes of the "savage" and would be of the same nature, though of an inferior development than the philosophies of the "civilized." Lévy-Bruhl inversed this double postulate. On the one hand, he admits a difference in the nature of the modern man and the "primitive"; on the other, he substitutes the thesis of a particular psychic nature, the primitive mentality, for the one concerning animism, understood as an elementary form of philosophy.

As one knows, the shock was significant. Lévy-Bruhl's theses were bitterly discussed here, at the French Society of Philosophy, and we are all familiar with the long process of the author's self-rectification that followed and which culminated in his *Notebooks,* published posthumously.

Works on "African philosophy" must be perceived, in turn, as a part of this famous debate, one way among others of refuting the thesis of prelogism by realigning with Tylor's theses destroyed by the French ethnologist. They give Tylor's theses a new vitality.

It is true that in *Bantu Philosophy* Lévy-Bruhl is not quoted. Tempels however, constantly incriminates a very close author: Raoul Allier, whose two-volume *Psychology of Conversion* published in 1925 is often cited by Tempels in addition to an essay which appeared two years later entitled *The Non-civilized and Us: Irreducible Difference or Inherent Identity?*.[20]

Thus *Bantu Philosophy* was able to present itself in its essential intention as a realization, indeed the only authentic realization of an ethnological project, in the most complete sense, that is to say, of a science that facilitates a real "understanding" of primitive peoples with what such an understanding supposes by "philosophical penetration." And once conquered, this penetration was to serve as the key to all secrets, to understanding all behaviors of primitive man. The relation of *Bantu Philosophy* to *Elements of Black Customary Law*[21] was therefore neither contingent nor exclusive. Beyond juridical anthropology, ethnophilosophy was both able to and supposed to mingle with all sectors of social and cultural anthropology and with all the human sciences in general in a fundamental relation.

The project being defined as such, we will not insist on the particular results of Tempels' analysis. Let us remember only that for him, the supreme value of the Bantu, his existential ideal, the first object of his prayers and invocations is life, potent life, the force of life, the vital energy; and that on this initial observation, Tempels thinks himself able to constitute six theses that he deems the essential ontology of the Bantu.

First thesis: the equivalence of being and force. . . .

Second thesis: Variable intensity of being, according to which "all forces can reinforce or weaken themselves . . . every being can become stronger or weaker."

Third thesis: the interaction of forces that states that a being can influence another and that there exists "beyond mechanical, chemical or psychological interaction . . . a relationship of forces that we should name "ontological." . . .

Fourth thesis: hierarchy of forces in which "all beings are segregated by species and class according to the power/strength of each (levenskracht)." . . .

Fifth thesis: creation is centered around the human being and, more precisely, on the reproduction of the living.

Sixth thesis: the interaction of forces is not actualized arbitrarily, but according to strict laws that are based on the hierarchy of forces. . . .[22]

Such is the Bantu ontology in its perfect simplicity as seen by Tempels. Other aspects of Bantu thought are based on this theory of forces and are exposed in the four following chapters: their "criteriology," or theory of knowledge, their "theory of muntu," where one can see the equivalent of a psychology, their ethics that value everything that aspires to reinvigorating life, and devalue everything that destroys it, or weakens it; their philosophy of law that doesn't preoccupy itself so much with material reparations of injuries than with the "restoration of life" through compensations that sometimes have little in common with the real damage. To conclude all of this, a final chapter indicated by its prolific title: "Bantu Philosophy and Our Mission to Civilize".

Tempels' construction is only cited here as an example. It is undoubtedly a privileged example since it functioned and continues to do so for more than one author, beyond criticisms of detail, beyond diverse theoretical and methodological readjustments like an analytical model requisitioning complementary analyses, for example. It is also a privileged example resulting from the extraordinary success of the book, the profound impact that it had on influential African intellectuals like Alioune Diop, founder of the journal *Présence Africaine,* who devoted a fervent preface to the Parisian edition of *Bantu Philosophy* and also managed to snatch the most laudatory appreciations from authors like Bachelard, Louis Lavelle, Gabriel Marcel, Jean Wahl, Albert Camus and Griaule to mention only some of the most well known.[23]

It must be understood, however, that in the history of ethnophilosophy, Tempels' book is neither the first nor, of course, the last; that, beyond its motifs and particular destiny and, in certain surprising ways, beyond the paradox that one could call the Tempels' effect, *Bantu Philosophy* remains one approach among others of a more general project: the project of a reconstruction by diverse methods and with a degree of systematicity varying with the particular case of what is called with more or less theoretical scruples, the "philosophy of the primitive." Hence, it is important that when one judges Tempels either favorably or unfavorably, one must specify if the respective judgement is specific to *Bantu Philosophy,* or if it is more general, extending itself to include other works of a similar sort. What happens generally is that one polarizes oneself on *Bantu Philosophy,* judging this book alone and not the positive and negative aspects of the theoretical project witnessed by the book. This undoubtedly reveals nothing in terms of the value of some of these critiques like those of Césaire and others. The fecundity appears only to be radicalized. This implies that beyond the arbitrary appearances of strengths and weaknesses of Tempels' short essay, one must pay attention to that which in these strengths and weaknesses is inevitably linked to the initial project itself.

We are familiar with Césaire's severe sarcasm. Contrary to the enthusiasm expressed by a number of Black intellectuals by the discovery of their "philosophy," the Caribbean poet not only finds the conclusions of the missionary's analysis negligent, but also politically dangerous. In summing up this critique, which is not only the first but also—in a deliberately political sense—the most radical to be addressed to *Bantu Philosophy,* we lose much of its flavor and polemical sharpness. Beyond the metaphysical subtleties and everything else that was able to seduce so many readers, Césaire's intuition gets right to the point. The *Discourse on Colonialism*[24] did not focus on such and such form of colonialism, or on such and such form of management of colonial administration. It primarily questioned colonialism in general and thus in a scrutinizing and ruthless manner re-examined the varied discourses of a number of authors, of a number of highly respected figures and at times, of leading scientific, literary, religious and political figures who were then supposed objective and sacrosanct, but who in reality, like everyone else, took, as Césaire said, "leurs vessies pour des lanternes."

It is in this context that authors like Griaule and Tempels are also questioned, in a willingly excessive language marked by a desire to establish a distinct and rigid boundary; Griaule and Tempels are "ethnographs, metaphysicians and specialists of Dogons, eccentric Belgian theologians," thinkers who in terms of the question concerning the people's right, the only one at issue, affirm the same ideas and objectively reinforce, through practice, the same positions as others who were more directly implicated: "gouverneurs sadiques et préfets tortionnaires, (. . .) colons flagellants et banquiers goulus, (. . .) macrotteurs politiciens lèche-chèques et magistrats aux ordres, (. . .) tous suppôts du capitalisme, tous tenants déclarés ou honteux du colonialisme pillard, tous responsables, tous haissables, tous négriers, tous redevables désormais de l'aggressivité révolutionnaire."[25]

And Césaire in his necessary aggression quotes from one of his targets (among others) "from R. P. Tempels, a missionary and Belgian, his vaseuse and mephitique Bantu philosophy discovered opportunistically, as Hinduism by others, in order to oppose communist materialism, which supposedly is threatening of turning Blacks into "moral vagabonds."

The invective alone could not, however, convince. It was necessary to justify it, to move from accusation to critique. This is also what Césaire does. And since one must resist the temptation to cite profusely, let's say that voluntary abstraction, that parenthetical silence in Tempels' essay of colonial reality and of what characterized it in the Congo during the same time period: pillage, torture, exploitation, humiliation, oppression, expropriation of the indigenous peoples—to the profit of an exclusive valorization of their traditional thought:

> "Quelle générosité, mon Père! Et quel zèle! (. . .) La pensée des Bantous étant ontologique, les bantous ne demandent de satisfaction que d'ordre ontologique. Salaires décents! Logements confortables! Nourriture! Ces Bantous sont de purs esprits, vous dis-je: Ce qu'ils désirent avant tout et par dessus tout, ce n'est pas l'amélioration de leur situation économique ou matérielle, mais bien la reconnaissance par le Blanc et son respect pour leur dignité d'homme, pour leur pleine valeur humaine. En somme, un coup de chapeau à la force vitale bantoue, un clin d'oeil à l'âme immortelle bantoue. Et vous êtes quitte! Avouez que c'est à bon compte!"[26]

The critique is severe, and should be nuanced undoubtedly in light of what we know today regarding Tempels' militant activity and the political positions of the co-authors of *Dettes de Guerre*. One cannot think that the author of "Social Justice" seriously wanted to say what Césaire makes him say here, that he really did not see the necessity, the urgency of an "economic or material" amelioration of the local peoples, but that only material reclamations, as important as they were, appeared to him to be the result of a more fundamental requirement, that is, one of respect.

Despite these limitations however, the critique maintains all of its significance, even today: colonial racism, the Whites' scorn for the "indigenous" people was not the cause, but the consequence of the pillage. So, the most radical requirement was not, could not have been only the refusal of this scorn and the exigency of respect. If the colonized himself thinks the contrary, it is because his perception is rooted in a mystified conscience. By acting only on this perception to the point of celebrating it, instead of delineating its limits and insufficiencies, Tempels, in fact, consecrated the mystification.

There is a more serious matter. With the same apparent objectivity, with a tone that pretends to be that of a simple observation, Tempels notes in his book that the White man, a new phenomenon moving in the world of the Bantu, had been integrated by the Bantu at a level particularly high, as a superior human force, transcending the vital force of all Black people. But this statement cannot be innocent. Silence signifies approbation and Césaire makes no mistake there:

> "Qu'en tête de la hiérarchie des forces vitales bantoues, prenne place le Blanc, et le Belge singulièrement, et plus singulièrement encore Albert ou Léopold, et le tour est joué. On obtiendra cette merveille: *le Dieu bantou sera garant de l'ordre colonialiste belge et sera sacrilège tout Bantou qui osera y porter la main.*"

This argument is unique. It confirms the preceding while revealing its significance: one is not only accountable for what one says, one is just as responsible for one's silence, that from the moment that one no longer speaks, one consecrates, either directly or indirectly, the established order.

Césaire however, quite scrupulous and somehow shaken by his own critique, tries immediately to limit its extent by specifying that: "It is clear that here one attacks not the Bantu philosophy, but the usage that certain will undertake in order to achieve some political goal."

The distinction could be useful in preserving, upon occasion, the positive results of the attempt for cultural rehabilitation, and reserving the possibility to inscribe them in another political horizon or in a politically neuter political horizon, one that is purely theoretical. To look more closely however, the political use denounced by Césaire was not arbitrary, but a necessity inscribed in Tempels' method; indeed, in the project itself of a reconstitution of the Bantu "philosophy." Because, if it was correct to show in the life of the so-called primitive, or semi-primitive cultures, a coherent system of thought, the use of the word "philosophy" to designate this system of thought was nonetheless not innocent; instead it was the expression of a will to consecrate this thought, to suspend it in time, to reaffirm its permanence and indispensable character. Yet this path was not the only one possible. There was at least another one that consisted in questioning, beyond the frozen appearances of beliefs and other thought structures, the genesis of these structures, the history that produced them, though sometimes dissimulated, but in certain cases also readable to the naked eye.

The theme of the White man's superiority offers a good illustration of the difference between the two approaches: Tempels' philosophical approach, if we can call it that, first consists in acting on the belief in the idea of this superiority, shared not only among the Whites, but also among Blacks, while furtively attempting to justify it, to ground it by making it appear as a necessary consequence of a Bantu ontology; then, the critical approach, which would consist in an attempt to replace this belief in the ensemble of its context, the colonial domination, which alone truly explains it by facilitating an understanding of its genesis and allows an understanding of its transitory character.

Now, it is true that for the anthropologists, the word "philosophy" always designates a system of thought supposed permanent, a sum of theoretical and ideological invariants. The use of this word to indicate a way of thinking is hence still an index of a fixed presupposition, a desire to suspend, to solidify beliefs. Possibly, in this sense, one can even add to a doctrinal corpus supposed stable (for example, the ontology of vital force), ideological traps and other mirages produced by the accidents of history.

In this sense, the subtle distinction between Bantu philosophy and the political use of this philosophy becomes obvious. It is precisely in the invention of a Bantu "philosophy," in the baptism which names the Bantu spiritual heritage a philosophy, that one must perceive a political choice. Thus Césaire's critique goes even further than he himself thought. In its analysis of systems of thought, Césaire's critique warns against the temptation to take the temporary for the definitive, against any and all reductive readings, against the illusion of immobility, against the evacuation of the dialectic. Instead, it invites us to always replace spiritual productions into their material contexts, the context of struggle for production and survival, one of social and political struggles. Moreover, it indicates that all analyses and theoretical work should be placed into perspective by asking them, even against their project, questions about their practical implications, the issue of their pertinence with respect to the actual social struggles.

Such is, in general, the political game of the critique of ethnophilosophy. Beyond the particular positions of this or that author, who could be, on occasion, more or less progressive according to the political problems posed, ethnophilosophy in general remains a fundamentally conservative discourse. By naming "philosophy" the ensemble of dominating collective representations in a given society at a given moment of its history, these representations are given a metaphysical consecration, turning a fact into a law and from then prohibiting all criticism. Similarly, this naming often consecrates the ongoing ideological alienation present in these collective representations, the distorted vision of the real, the interiorization by the oppressed themselves of their oppressor's system of values.

Finally, it is insignificant that the oppression originates on the inside or outside of a system, that it comes from another race or from the same, that it accompanies colonial domination or internal processes of subjugation and exploitation, be it pre- or post-colonial. The "philosophy" of a people, in the sense understood by an anthropologist, is always the direct or indirect reflection of structures of domination which prevail in the moment (s)he studies it. By celebrating it, the anthropologist comforts, in his or her way, these same structures of domination.

From this perspective, nothing is more equivocal than the cultural nationalism, the ferocious, and in the principle legitimate will to rehabilitate one's culture unjustly denigrated. But in its lucid forms, this will yield quite easily to a temptation to defend indiscriminately all of the aspects of the culture as a whole, including the most retrograde and, more seriously, it facilitates a desire to generalize, to extend to the entire society and to establish in an absolute fashion the cultural values that in reality only belong to the sphere of dominating social classes. The cultural nationalist plays the game of the dominating classes. And this is why if it functions in periods of resistance as a powerful force of collective mobilization, it loses its role outside of these moments and so, can constitute, on the contrary, an obstacle impeding consciousness of the society, its cleavages and its real contradictions.

Thus, it is because of a serious misunderstanding that for quite awhile now our critique of ethnophilosophy, mine and that of some colleagues, has been accused of Westernism or Eurocentrism. We were reproached for reserving the monopoly and the merit of philosophy for Europe. The situation though is much more complicated. On the one hand, philosophy is not the only possible form of cohesiveness, but simply one way, among others, of thinking. And we have no reason to postulate its existence in our societies as if it were a condition *sine qua non* of dignity and of collective respectability. On the other hand, if it could at first glance appear very "African" to reclaim an African philosophy, one should know that in reality this reclamation once again only takes up in turn a requirement initially formulated by Western ethnology for reasons that are potentially disturbing; that beyond this it could objectively be a way of legitimizing the established disorder and the relations of power that prevail in a given society; that consequently, the choice is not between a Eurocentrist opinion and another that would be African, but between two ways of treating culture in general, be it European or African, two different approaches of which one, when considering a part as a whole, aims to reduce, to simplify, to unify; and the other which, instead, wills itself resolutely pluralistic, attentive to internal contradictions, to the intense dialectic that pierces each and every culture.

Two questions remain, however. First: beyond the animated history of ideas and opinions, beyond the pluralistic shock of doctrines, always revealed in one society, was it the most "primitive"; aren't there, despite everything, consistencies? And if so, how do we treat these consistencies without falling into excessive reductionism? Secondly, once we have pushed the ethnological concept of philosophy aside, once we have refused to give metaphysical consecration to the collective representations, is there really no sense in speaking about an African philosophy? To speak of it in terms of the past, like a form of discourse effectively accredited by history, but also, and perhaps especially, in relation to the present and future, like a task that must be valued?

The critique of ethnophilosophy might have given the impression that we were negating the existence of constants, the existence of invariants in the cultural tradition of each people, or at least, that one was reducing these constants to simple material givens devoid of any intellectual value. In fact, this is not so, and one wouldn't know how to move to such an extreme without betraying reality. The movement of ideas has always had its limits, the social debate always develops itself on the basis of a minimum consensus that gives it its meaning and renders the diverse positions present intelligible, even when they are most contradictory. Consequently, nothing prohibits that one may be increasingly interested in the limitations of the movement than on the movement itself, may take the collective representations as the object of study, place their logic into question, and question their mode of functioning, their degree of generality (which is not forcedly the same for all), finally their differentiating relation vis-à-vis the different positions expressed.[27]

Yet, *voilà:* at no moment will the reconstituted collective representations be established as a philosophy. Instead, one should admit that that current system of thought, present in all personal thought is always, precisely, the obstacle to surmount, the anonymous unthinkable of which the critical interrogation should constitute, when possible, the beginning of philosophy. The analysis of these representations should consequently be pursued outside of all apologetic perspectives, whose only goal should be to identify, to objectively know the system of intellectual constraints in which everyone finds himself caught, often without noticing, and without even suspecting its existence. It is not by locking oneself within a system that one becomes a philosopher. Instead, it is by the burden of liberating oneself, even if this liberation, a liberation that is constantly starting over, is never fully realized, and even if one always has the right, once these collective prejudices are placed on trial, to confirm them upon the occasion, each for himself, by rationally justifying them, in part or completely, and by making them lose their status of prejudice by the same hand.

Finally, a last question: is there no significance in speaking about an African philosophy? This is again one of those misunderstandings that the critique of ethnophilosophy has resulted in. In fact, the goal of this critique was simply to distance from a concept of philosophy created expressly, something like an invested counter-sense and nonetheless consecrated in all ethnological literature by the word "philosophy." But once this counter-sense is dissipated, the question remains and could be worded in these terms: what is it in Africa that is termed philosophy in the international cultural tradition?

The real difficulties hence begin to appear. First, though, this major difficulty: in this tradition, the plurality of notions and practices of philosophy, the polysemy of this concept. From this polysemy, the ethnologists' ruse had been precisely to want to complicate it one notch by illicitly introducing a supplementary meaning to it. It was, however, easy to see that it wasn't working like the other meanings, that it was, compared to them, radically heterogeneous, that it was destroying the system of possible meanings and the ordered variation that permitted passing from one to the next, and which was in every sense a counter-sense. But once the subterfuge was played out, one could once again, in a new manner, meditate on philosophy in Africa of yesterday; question, today and tomorrow, the place of philosophy, that is to say the place of that specific activity from where the diverse practices flow, the practices recognized elsewhere as philosophy, namely in the countries from where, historically, the word philosophy has reached us.

Thus posed, the question remains open. I am satisfied to respond by referring to the present: there exists today an African philosophy in a non-ethnological sense of the term, a production, a philosophical and pluralistic research, irreducible to some collective unthinkable. But how old is this research? What is its historical depth? What works have already expressed it in the past, and what was their destiny, their value, the weaknesses of these works, their real relation to African problems, their degree of insertion in the living path of our history?[28]

That is a deluge of questions to which I cannot, for myself, respond, but on the subject of which many important works currently exist and still continue to appear. In any case, what one can affirm is that whatever the final response, questions of this genre could only loom over the threshold of a theoretical moment completely new in relation to that of ethnophilosophy. In effect, philosophy, in the sense given by ethnologists, has precisely no history. The project, even the idea of a history of African thought, supposes the complete liquidation of the ancient problematic space, the end of this type of research and of its exclusive valorization of constants.

That said, the knowledge of the past cannot be known as an end in itself, but has meaning only insofar as it nurtures a current project. The real question, in this perspective, is to know whether or not we need a philosophy in Africa today, and why. To this question, I also thought that I would be able to provide a start, but only the beginning of a response. I valued the necessity to relativize, to correctly replace the desire of philosophy, to finally stop overestimating it, expecting it to deliver more than it could: for example, a definitive response to what Kant called transcendental problems, and the assuaging of the religious anxiety which is universally human; or, in another schema, the solution-miracle to the practical problems of liberation and development, on the subject of which the philosopher sees himself too often interpellated as philosopher, as if he had more competence than others in solving these problems. I valued that instead it was necessary to every possible extent to get out of philosophy so as to confront the real problems, to apply an adequate treatment to these problems dictated by their own constitution; and so, the philosophical exigency could only reappear in its correct place, summoned by necessity, by the progress of knowledge, as a condition of progress and even of a wider opening; instead of a philosophy, which, by working its own vacuousness, "functions" still as a consecration of prejudice and a major impediment to a real knowledge.

To conclude, let's return to our initial question concerning the place of knowledge. After what we have just said on the topic of collective representations, it is clear that the question itself is highly equivocal and that in order to clarify it, one must begin at least by distinguishing between representation and knowledge, the latter appearing as a specification of the former, a form of representation particularly elaborated, without prejudice of modalities, of the nature and conditions of this process of elaboration.

So clearly that in one sense, ethnoscience, as an inventory of traditional knowledges, knowledge of respectful restitution of elaborated conceptions produced in a culture being studied, is fundamentally different from ethnophilosophy which, not being able to resign itself to being an inventory of beliefs and other collective representations, often succumbs to the temptation of borrowing from the people being studied the conviction of the ethnologist, and sees itself obliged, in every case, to give to these representations the appearance of a knowledge, to project a cohesiveness onto it, a form of elaboration that is, from the start, foreign.

Thus, ethnophilosophy is always a constructed knowledge that would like to be taken as a knowledge of restitution. In this sense, the greatest fault of the ethnologist is not, as one would have you believe, to want to appropriate a collective wisdom where the people studied would remain the veritable authors; on the contrary, it is the projection of an imaginary "wisdom/knowledge" onto the people, a system of representations constructed from fragments by the ethnologist, even if this construction at least partially uses certain materials borrowed from the people. Hence, Father Tempels' *Bantu Philosophy* is not the philosophy of the Bantu, but the philosophy of Tempels himself; the "Bantu-Rwanda philosophy of being" is not really inherent, as Kagame attempts to show, in the Kinyarwanda language, but is a construction that Kagame himself is responsible for. The "locus" of philosophy is, in this case, the singularity of the author, and the culture studied, a simple pretext, which is a support more imaginary than real in this arbitrary construction. In the seemingly generous gesture that hastens itself to establish as philosophy an ensemble of given collective representations, in this metaphysical consecration of a spontaneous mode of thought, a gap in reality is opened where the most personal convictions of the knower-analyst are swallowed up, the system of his own philosophical and religious choices appear; at the same time and in the same gesture, the collective representations, which are transfigured from this moment on, seem able to remain motionless and to escape from the living critique in their own society.[29]

Finally, be it a question of philosophy or of science, the real problem, the inevitable task of today, is to create the conditions for a real appropriation or, at the right moment, a reappropriation of knowledge by each society. The inventory of traditional knowledges on plants and animals cannot be an end in itself, no more than the most general inventory of collective representations. But, apart from the fact that this inventory must keep a great distance from all apologetic discourse, it must also constitute the starting point of an actualization, of a verification and each time possible, of a critical validation of these knowledges, thanks to the most proven methods of modern botany and zoology with the goal of a harmonious integration into the movement of scientific research, taken up by the society itself from this moment on.

The critique of ethnophilosophy hence overflows into a larger project: a project concerning a collective appropriation by Africa of the international scientific heritage, inseparable from an active reappropriation of her own knowledges and traditional savoir-faire. The facile apology of our systems, beliefs and other collective representations only leads to an impasse. What we need most today is not to offer our cultures as spectacle to others, nor to ourselves; what we need is a renewed creativity on every level, in every sphere.

Notes

1. *Ghana: Autobiography of Kwame Nkrumah,* London, Thomas Nelson, 1957.

2. There is no attempt here to make an issue about what is better in con-

temporary epistemology, notedly the insistance on the discontinuous course of knowledge, and the irreducible specificity of modern science, meaning Galilean. One cannot, however, avoid noticing the surreptitious slippage, too frequent in certain analyses, of this correct description towards a naive claim that science as Western "property," a distinctive character of European culture.

3. Aimé Césaire, "Discours sur le colonialisme," Paris, 1950, New edition, *Présence Africaine,* Paris, 1955. These citations refer to the 1976 printing.

4. Albert Franklin, "La Négritude: réalité ou mystification? Réflexions sur 'Orphée Noir'", in "Les étudiants noirs parlent," *Présence Africaine,* no. 14, 1952, p. 287–303. Reprinted in A. J. Smet, *Philosophie Africaine. Textes choisis. II et bibliographie sélective.* Kinshasa, Presses Universitaires du Zaire, 1975, p. 299–313.

5. Okot p'Bitek, "Bantu Philosophy?," *Transition,* no. 13, 1964; Id., "A reply to R. G. Harris's "Cool, Sober and Methodical'," *Transition,* no. 16, 1964. The two articles are reprinted in Okot p'Bitek, *Africa's Cultural Revolution,* Introduction by Ngugi wa Thiong'o, Nairobi, MacMillan books for Africa, 1973, p. 58–68.

6. Franz Crahay, "Le décollage conceptuel: conditions d'une philosophie bantoue," *Diogène,* Paris, no. 52, 1965, p. 61–84.

7. R. P. Placide Tempels, *La Philosophie bantoue,* Elisabethville, 1945, ed. Lovania, reprinted in a revised version at Présence Africaine editions, Paris, 1949. Our quotations come from the *Présence Africaine* 1961 edition. We use "Bantu" everywhere (invariably) instead of the French spelling "bantoue" that will only occasionally appear in some quotations. On the history and the successive versions of *La philosophie bantoue,* one will read with interest A. J. Smet, "Le père Placide Tempels et son oeuver publiée," *Revue africaine de théologie* (Kinshasa), t. I, 1977, no. 1, p. 77–128. The controversy suscitated in the heart of the Catholic hierarchy by this book, see Id., "Les débuts de la controverse autour de 'La philosophie bantoue' du P. Tempels, quelques lettres inédites," *Revue africaine de théologie,* vol. 5, no. 10, October 1981, p. 165–181.

8. Cf. Edmond-Eloi Boelart, "La philosophie bantoue selon le R. P. Placide Tempels," *Aequatoria* (Coquilhatville), no. 9, 1946, p. 81–90; reprinted in A. J. Smet, *Philosophie africaine . . . ,* vol. II, op. cit., p. 274–287. Cf. also Léon de Sousberghe, "A propos de 'La philosophie bantoue'," Zaire (Bruxelles), vol. 5, 1951, p. 821–828; reprinted in A. J. Smet, ibid., p. 288–297.

9. Cf. Pierre-Alexandre, *Les Africains,* Paris, ed. Lidis, 1981, p. 516 (coll. Histoire ancienne des peuples). Speaking of francophone authors, the author thinks about Marcel Griaule and his school first, and only by extension does he consider Tempels. In fact, if the author of *Bantu Philosophy* was originally Flemish, he didn't participate any less in a cul-

ture largely dominated by the French language of the colonial administration in the Congo. It is probably not an accident that the *Bantu Philosophy* was first published in a French version, 1945, one year before the
publication of the original text.

10. For example, it is not without significance to affirm that *La philosophie bantoue,* by Father Tempels, published in 1945 in Elisabethville,
now Lubumbashi, in Zaire, is strictly a contemporary of a number of political and polemical articles, five total, published anonymously by Tempels, in 1944 and 1945, in a daily paper in Elisabethville, *L'Essor du
Congo.* Even the titles of these articles are revealing: "La philosophie de
la rébellion," "Justice Sociale," "L'administration des indigènes. Solution: un administrateur dans chaque territoire," "A propos des mariages
indigènes," finally, "Pour la protection légale du mariage de nos indigènes." These articles respectively appeared in *L'Essor du Congo* from
August 31, 1944, February 15, 17, September 1, November 3, 1945. The
first three were partially reprinted in *Dettes de Guerre* (see infra, n. 11),
the last two in *Kongo-Overzee* (Anvers). Placide Tempels, *Ecrits
polémiques et politiques,* anastatic reproduction, Faculté de théologie
catholique de Kinshasa, 1979, coll. Cours et Documents, 3.

The political bantuism could have appeared highly subversive to the
most conservative elements of the colonial society and, on the contrary
terribly retarded in the eyes of the most demanding democrats at the
same time. Essential ambivalence that will lead once again, in its own
way, to the ethnophilosophical discourse.

11. *La philosophie bantoue,* op. cit., p. 15.

12. Ibid, p. 18.

13. Ibid, p. 116.

14. Ibid, p. 19.

15. Ibid, p. 118.

16. Important nuance: the "évolués" themselves are not rejected as a
group. The line of demarcation crosses them also, opposing to all, those
who "seem completely materialized in the example of so many colonizers," those, more numerous still, "who keep some of the human dynamic
that comes from their fathers," and who are "currently so profoundly
suspicious or embittered and will be the most zealous collaborators of
the White man as soon as they know that he only works for the complete
and total evolution of their human person" (*La philosophie bantoue,* p.
116). But this only confirms our reading: Tempels' tactic, the logic of his
discourse as a political discourse, targets to isolate, among the Bantu
population, its most active elements, its natural spokespersons, its political leaders, whether real of potential; to isolate them and to discredit
them, thus creating a clean place for the "well-intentioned" Europeans
(this expression appears frequently throughout the text) who would like,

like him and with him, to establish himself as the spokesman for the Black community.

17. Father P. Charles, professor of theology at the University of Louvain and member of the Royal Academy of Colonial Sciences was one of the most well known artisans of this theory. Tempels was supposed to meet him during his long "vacation" in Belgium (1946–1949), like he was supposed to, during the same period, become friends with the priest, Joseph Cardijn, the founder of the Young Catholic Workers and future cardinal, and a Chinese academic so famous for his reverberating conversion to Christianity and his entry in the order of St. Benedict, Dom Célestin Lou-Tsen-Tsiang, author of *Souvenirs et pensées* (Bruges, Desclée de Brouwer, 1945). On all these points, as with the curious relation between Tempels and a nun that he refers to as "Sister X," Willy de Craemer, op. cit., p. 31–37, would be read with interest.

18. The article in question is a project of theoretical renewal of linguistics in light of Bantu philosophy: "L'étude des langues bantoues à la lumière de la philosophie bantoue," *Présence Africaine,* vol. 5, 1948, p. 755–760. The questions of missiology and of pastoral are taken up in "Cathéchèse bantoue," already cited, in *La christianisation des philosophies paiennes,* (Anvers, 1949), and in various texts collected in an important work, *Notre rencontre,* Centre d'études pastorales, Limete-Léopoldville, 1962, p. 207, *Notre Rencontre,* vol. II, pro manuscripto, ibid., 1962. The publisher refused to publish, the second volume which was never officially printed.

19. Ibid.

20. Raoul Allier. *La psychologie de la conversion chez les peuples non-civilisés.* Paris, Payot, t. I, 1925, p. 595; t. II p. 509.

Id., *Le non-civilisé et nous: différence irréductible ou identité foncière?* Paris, Payot, 1927, p. 317.

The confrontation between the two authors alone merits a special study. This will not be our purpose.

21. Emile Possoz, *Eléments de droit coutumier nègre,* Elisabethville, Ed. Lovania, 1943.

La philosophie bantoue, op. cit., p. 24: "Abstenons-nous provisoirement de tout jugement, pour ne faire que de l'ethnologie. Essayons avant tout de comprendre la pensée des Bantous (. . .). Sans pénétration philosophique, l'ehtnologie n'est que folklore" (underlined in the text).

22. Ibid, p. 40.

23. Cf. "Témoignages sur 'La philosophie bantoue' du Père Tempels," *Présence Africaine,* no. 7, 1949.

24. Aimé Césaire, op. cit., 1976 edition, p. 31–32.

25. Ibid, p. 36–37.

26. Ibid, p. 36.

27. Examples exist of similar studies. Cf. Marc Augé, *Théorie des pouvoirs et idéologie: étude de cas en Côte d'Ivoire,* Paris, Hermann, 1975. Cf. also Paulin Hountondji, "Langues africaines et philosophie: la thèse relativiste," *Les Etudes Philosophiques* (Paris), 1982, no. 4, p. 393–406.

28. Cf. Antonius-Guilielmus Amo Afer of Axim in Ghana. *Translation of his works,* Halle-Wittenberg, Martin-Luther University, 1968, p. 254. See my commentary in P. Hountondji, *Sur la "philosophie africaine,"* Paris, F. Maspero, 1977, chap. 5, p. 129–170.

On all of these authors, an interesting book by the priest Henri Grégoire, *De la littérature des Nègres,* Paris, 1808.

The Uncompleted Argument: Du Bois and the Illusion of Race

Kwame Anthony Appiah

Kwame Anthony Appiah is a Ghanian philosopher currently in the African-American Studies Department at Harvard University. In Dusk of Dawn: An Essay toward an Autobiography of a Race Concept *(NY: Harcourt Brace, 1940) W. E. B. Du Bois proposed to show how his concept of race had evolved from his earlier views in "The Conservation of Races" (1897; this volume, Chapter 2). Appiah does a close reading of these texts, and concludes that Du Bois' subsequent sociohistorical concept of race was of little improvement over his earlier biospiritual concept of race. Appiah also reviews work in contemporary human biology to argue that there is little empirical support for the concept of race in modern science.*

It appears that race is a concept designed primarily to justify dominance—dominance of Europeans over non-Europeans, and certain Europeans over other Europeans. If we reject the legitimacy of dominance then we no longer have a need for racial concepts. Appiah concludes that the quest of African nationalists such as Du Bois for a form of personality and culture reflecting the African's peculiar racial nature is quixotic and doomed to failure. Appiah's In My Father's House: Africa in the Philosophy of Culture *(NY: Oxford University Press, 1992) is a brilliant extension of the argument presented in this selection.*

INTRODUCTION

Contemporary biologists are not agreed on the question of whether there are any human races, despite the widespread scientific consensus on the underlying genetics. For most purposes, however, we can reasonably treat this issue as terminological. What most people in most cultures or-

dinarily believe about the significance of "racial" difference is quite remote, I think, from what the biologists *are* agreed on. Every reputable biologist will agree that human genetic variability between the populations
of Africa or Europe or Asia is not much greater than that within those
populations; though *how much* greater depends, in part, on the measure
of genetic variability the biologist chooses. If biologists want to make interracial difference seem relatively large, they can say that "the proportion of genic variation attributable to racial differences is . . . 9–11%."[1] If
they want to make it seem small, they can say that, for two people who
are both Caucasoid, the chances of difference in genetic constitution at
one site on a given chromosome are currently estimated at about 14.3
percent, while for any two people taken at random from the human population, they are estimated at about 14.8 percent. (I will discuss why this
is considered a measure of genetic difference in section 2.) The statistical
facts about the distribution of variant characteristics in human populations and subpopulations are the same, whichever way the matter is expressed. Apart from the visible morphological characteristics of skin,
hair, and bone, by which we are inclined to assign people to the broadest
racial categories—black, white, yellow—there are few genetic characteristics to be found in the population of England that are not found in similar proportions in Zaire or in China; and few too (though more) which
are found in Zaire but not in similar proportions in China or in England.
All this, I repeat, is part of the consensus (see "GR," pp. 1–59). A more
familiar part of the consensus is that the differences between peoples in
language, moral affections, aesthetic attitudes, or political ideology—
those differences which most deeply affect us in our dealings with each
other—are not biologically determined to any significant degree.

　These claims will, no doubt, seem outrageous to those who confuse
the question of whether biological difference accounts for our differences
with the question of whether biological similarity accounts for our similarities. Some of our similarities as human beings in these broadly cultural respects—the capacity to acquire human languages, for example, or,
more specifically, the ability to smile—*are* to a significant degree biologically determined. We can study the biological basis of these cultural capacities and give biological explanations of our exercise of them. But if
biological difference between human beings is unimportant in these explanations—and it is—then racial difference, as a species of biological
difference, will not matter either.

　In this essay, I want to discuss the way in which W.E.B. Du Bois—
who called his life story the "autobiography of a race concept"—came
gradually, though never completely, to assimilate the unbiological nature
of races. I have made these few prefatory remarks partly because it is my
experience that the biological evidence about race is not sufficiently
known and appreciated but also because they are important in discussing
Du Bois. Throughout his life, Du Bois was concerned not just with the

meaning of race but with the truth about it. We are more inclined at present, however, not to express our understanding of the intellectual development of people and cultures as a movement toward the truth; I shall sketch some of the reasons for this at the end of the essay. I will begin, therefore, by saying what I think the rough truth is about race, because, against the stream, I am disposed to argue that this struggle toward the truth is exactly what we find in the life of Du Bois, who can claim, in my view, to have thought longer, more engagedly, and more publicly about race than any other social theorist of our century.

Du Bois' first extended discussion of the concept of race is in "The Conservation of Races" (1897), a paper he delivered to the American Negro Academy in the year it was founded. The "American Negro," he declares, has "been led to . . . minimize race distinctions" because "back of most of the discussions of race with which he is familiar, have lurked certain assumptions as to his natural abilities, as to his political, intellectual and moral status, which he felt were wrong." Du Bois continues: "Nevertheless, in our calmer moments we must acknowledge that human beings are divided into races," even if when we "come to inquire into the essential difference of races we find it hard to come at once to any definite conclusion." For what it is worth, however, the "final word of science, so far, is that we have at least two, perhaps three, great families of human beings—the whites and Negroes, possibly the yellow race."[2]

Du Bois is not, however, satisfied with the final word of nineteenth-century science. For, as he thinks, what matter are not the "grosser physical differences of color, hair and bone" but the "differences—subtle, delicate and elusive, though they may be—which have silently but definitely separated men into groups" ("CR," p. 75).

> While these subtle forces have generally followed the natural cleavage of common blood, descent and physical peculiarities, they have at other times swept across and ignored these. At all times, however, they have divided human beings into races, which, while they perhaps transcend scientific definition, nevertheless, are clearly defined to the eye of the historian and sociologist.
>
> If this be true, then the history of the world is the history, not of individuals, but of groups, not of nations, but of races. . . . What, then, is a race? It is a vast family of human beings, generally of common blood and language, always of common history, traditions and impulses, who are both voluntarily and involuntarily striving together for the accomplishment of certain more or less vividly conceived ideals of life. ["CR," pp. 75–76]

We have moved, then, away from the "scientific"—that is, biological and anthropological—conception of race to a sociohistorical notion. Using this sociohistorical criterion—the sweep of which certainly encourages the thought that no biological or anthropological definition is possible—Du Bois considers that there are not three but eight "distinctly differentiated races, in the sense in which history tells us the word must be used" ("CR," p. 76). The list is an odd one: Slavs, Teutons, English (both in Great Britain and America), Negroes (of Africa and, likewise, America), the Romance race, Semites, Hindus and Mongolians.

> The question now is: What is the real distinction between these nations? Is it the physical differences of blood, color and cranial measurements? Certainly we must all acknowledge that physical differences play a great part. . . . But while race differences have followed mainly physical race lines, yet no mere physical distinctions would really define or explain the deeper differences—the cohesiveness and continuity of these groups. The deeper differences are spiritual, psychical, differences—undoubtedly based on the physical, but infinitely transcending them. ["CR," p. 77]

Each of the various races is

> striving, . . . in its own way, to develop for civilization its particular message, its particular ideal, which shall help to guide the world nearer and nearer that perfection of human life for which we all long, that "one far off Divine event." ["CR," p. 78]

For Du Bois, then, the problem for the Negro is the discovery and expression of the message of his or her race.

> The full, complete Negro message of the whole Negro race has not as yet been given to the world.
> The question is, then: how shall this message be delivered; how shall these various ideals be realized? The answer is plain: by the development of these race groups, not as individuals, but as races. . . . For the development of Negro genius, of Negro literature and art, of Negro spirit, only Negroes bound and welded together, Negroes inspired by one vast ideal, can work out in its fullness the great message we have for humanity.
> For this reason, the advance guard of the Negro people—the eight million people of Negro blood in the United States of America—must soon come to realize that if they are to take their just place in the van of Pan-Negroism, then their destiny is *not* absorption by the white Americans. ["CR," pp. 78, 79][3]

Du Bois ends by proposing his Academy Creed, which begins with words that echo down almost a century of American race relations:

> 1. We believe that the Negro people, as a race, have a contribution to make to civilization and humanity, which no other race can make.
> 2. We believe it the duty of the Americans of Negro descent, as a body, to maintain their race identity until this mission of the Negro people is accomplished, and the ideal of human brotherhood has become a practical possibility. ["CR," p. 84]

What can we make of this analysis and prescription?

On the face of it, Du Bois' argument in "The Conservation of Races" is that "race" is not a scientific—that is, biological—concept. It is a sociohistorical concept. Sociohistorical races each have a "message" for humanity—a message which derives, in some way, from God's purpose in creating races. The Negro race has still to deliver its full message, and so it is the duty of Negroes to work together—through race organizations—so that this message can be delivered.

We do not need the theological underpinnings of this argument. What is essential is the thought that through common action Negroes can achieve, by virtue of their sociohistorical community, worthwhile ends which will not otherwise be achieved. On the face of it, then, Du Bois' strategy here is the antithesis in the classic dialectic of reaction to prejudice.

The thesis in this dialectic—which Du Bois reports as the American Negro's attempt to "minimize race distinctions"—is the denial of difference. Du Bois' antithesis is the acceptance of difference, along with a claim that each group has its part to play; that the white race and its racial Other are related not as superior to inferior but as complementaries; that the Negro message is, with the white one, part of the message of humankind.

I call this pattern the classic dialect for a simple reason: we find it in feminism also—on the one hand, a simple claim to equality, a denial of substantial difference; on the other, a claim to a special message, revaluing the feminine Other not as the helpmeet of sexism, but as the New Woman.

Because this is a classic dialectic, my reading of Du Bois' argument is a natural one. I believe that it is substantially correct. But to see that it is correct, we need to make clear that what Du Bois attempts, despite his own claims to the contrary, is not the transcendence of the nineteenth-century scientific conception of race—as we shall see, he relies on it—but rather, as the dialectic requires, a revaluation of the Negro race in the face of the sciences of racial inferiority. We can begin by analyzing the sources of tension in Du Bois' allegedly sociohistorical conception of race, which he explicitly sets over against the scientific conception. The tension is plain enough in his references to "common blood"; for this, dressed up with fancy craniometry, a dose of melanin, and some measure for hair-curl, is what the scientific notion amounts to. If he has fully transcended the scientific notion, what is the role of this talk about "blood"?

We may leave aside for the moment the common "impulses" and the voluntary and involuntary "strivings." These must be due either to a shared biological inheritance, "based on the physical, but infinitely transcending" it; to a shared history; or, of course, to some combination of these. If Du Bois' notion is purely sociohistorical, then the issue is common history and traditions; otherwise, the issue is, at least in part, a common biology. We shall know which only when we understand the core of Du Bois' conception of race.

The claim that a race generally shares a common language is also plainly inessential: the "Romance" race is not of common language nor, more obviously, is the Negro. And "common blood" can mean little more than "of shared ancestry," which is already implied by talk of a "vast family." At the center of Du Bois' conception, then, is the claim that a race is "a vast family of human beings, . . . always of common history [and] traditions." So, if we want to understand Du Bois, our question must be: What is a family of common history?

We already see that the scientific notion, which presupposes common features in virtue of a common biology derived from a common descent, is not fully transcended. A family can, it is true, have adopted children, kin by social rather than biological law. By analogy, therefore, a vast human family might contain people joined not by biology but by an act of choice. But it is plain that Du Bois cannot have been contemplating this possibility: like all of his contemporaries, he would have taken for granted that race is a matter of birth. Indeed, to understand the talk of "family," we must distance ourselves from its sociological meaning. A family is almost always culturally defined only through either patrilineal or matrilineal descent. But if an individual drew a "conceptual" family tree back over five hundred years and assumed that he or she was descended from each ancestor in only one way, it would have more than a million branches at the top. Although, in such a case, many individuals would be represented by more than one branch—that far back we are all going to be descended from many people by more than one route—it is plain that either a matrilineal or patrilineal conception of our family histories drastically underrepresents the biological range of our ancestry. Biology and social convention go startlingly different ways. Let's pretend, secure in our republicanism, that the claim of the queen of England to the throne depends partly on a single line from one of her ancestors nine hundred years ago. If there were no overlaps in her family tree, there would be more than fifty thousand billion such lines, though there have never been that many people on the earth; even with reasonable assumptions about overlaps, there are millions of such lines. We chose one line, even though most of the population of England is probably descended from William the Conqueror by *some* uncharted route. Biology is democratic: all parents are equal. Thus, to speak of two people as being of common ancestry requires that, before some historical point in the past, a large proportion of the branches in their respective family trees coincided.[4]

Already, then, Du Bois requires, as the scientific conception does, a common ancestry (in the sense just defined) with whatever—if anything—that ancestry biologically entails. But apparently this does not commit him to the scientific conception, for there are many groups of common ancestry—ranging from humanity in general to narrower groups such as the Slavs, Teutons, and Romance people taken together—which do not, for Du Bois, constitute races. Thus, Du Bois' "common history," which must be what is supposed to distinguish Slav from Teuton, is an essential part of his conception. The problem is whether a common history can be a criterion which distinguishes one group of human beings—extended in time—from another. Does adding a notion of common history allow us to make the distinctions between Slav and Teuton or between English and Negro? The answer is no.

Consider, for example, Du Bois himself. As the descendant of Dutch ancestors, why doesn't his relation to the history of Holland in the fourteenth century (which he shares with all people of Dutch descent) make him a member of the Teutonic race? The answer is straightforward: the Dutch were not Negroes; Du Bois is. But it follows from this that the history of Africa is part of the common history of Afro-Americans not simply because Afro-Americans descended from various peoples who played a part in African history but rather because African history is the history of people of the same race.

My general point is this: in order to recognize two events at different times as part of the history of a single individual, we have to have a criterion for identity of the individual at each of those times, independent of his or her participation in the two events. In the same way, when we recognize two events as belonging to the history of one race, we have to have a criterion for membership in the race at those two times, independent of the participation of the members in the two events. To put it more simply: sharing a common group history cannot be a criterion for being members of the same group, for we would have to be able to identify the group in order to identify *its* history. Someone in the fourteenth century could share a common history with me through our membership in a historically extended race only if something accounts both for his or her membership in the race in the fourteenth century and for mine in the twentieth. That something cannot, on pain of circularity, be the history of the race. Whatever holds Du Bois' races together conceptually cannot be a common history; it is only because they are bound together that members of a race at different times can share a history at all. If this is true, Du Bois' reference to a common history cannot be doing any work in his individuation of races. And once we have stripped away the sociohistorical elements from Du Bois' definition of race, we are left with the true criterion.

Consequently, not only the talk of language, which Du Bois admits is neither necessary (the Romance race speaks many languages) nor sufficient (Afro-Americans and Americans generally speak the same language) for racial identity, must be expunged from the definition; now we have seen that talk of common history and traditions must go too. We are left with common descent and the common impulses and strivings that I put aside earlier. Since common descent and the characteristics which flow from it are part of the scientific conception of race, these impulses are all that remain to do the job that Du Bois had claimed for a sociohistorical conception: namely, to distinguish his conception from the biological one. Du Bois claims that the existence of races is "clearly defined to the eye of the historian and sociologist" ("CR," p. 75). Since biology acknowledges common ancestry as a criterion, whatever extra insight is provided by sociohistorical understanding can be gained only by observing the common impulses and strivings. Reflection suggests, however, that this cannot be true. For what common impulses—whether voluntary or involuntary—do the Romance people share that the Teutons and the English do not?

Du Bois had read the historiography of the Anglo-Saxon school, which accounted for the democratic impulse in America by the racial tradition of the Anglo-Saxon moot. He had read American and British historians in earnest discussion of the "Latin" spirit of Romance peoples; and perhaps he had believed some of it. Here perhaps may be the source of the notion that history and sociology can observe the differing impulses of races.

In all these writings, however, such impulses are allegedly discovered to be the a posteriori properties of racial and national groups, not criteria of membership in them. It is, indeed, because the claim is a posteriori that historical evidence is relevant to it. And if we ask what common impulses history has detected which allow us to recognize the Negro, we shall see that Du Bois' claim to have found a criterion of identity in these impulses is mere bravado. If, without evidence about his or her impulses, we can say who is a Negro, then it cannot be part of what it is to be a Negro that he or she has them; rather, it must be an a posteriori claim that people of a common race, defined by descent and biology, have impulses, for whatever reason, in common. Of course, the common impulses of a biologically defined group may be historically caused by common experiences, common history. But Du Bois' claim can only be that biologically defined races happen to share, for whatever reason, common impulses. The common impulses cannot be a criterion of group membership. And if that is so, we are left with the scientific conception.

How, then, is it possible for Du Bois' criteria to issue in eight groups, while the scientific conception issues in three? The reason is clear from the list. Slavs, Teutons, English, Hindus, and Romance peoples each live in a characteristic geographical region. (American English—and, for that matter, American Teutons, American Slavs, and American Romance people—share recent ancestry with their European "cousins" and thus share a relation to a place and certain languages and traditions.) Semites and Mongolians each inhabit a rather larger geographical region also. Du Bois' talk of common history conceals his superaddition of a geographical criterion: group history is, in part, the history of people who have lived in the same place.[5]

The criterion Du Bois actually uses amounts to this: people are members of the same race if they share features in virtue of being descended largely from people of the same region. Those features may be physical—hence Afro-Americans are Negroes—or cultural—hence Anglo-Americans are English. Focusing on one sort of feature—"grosser . . . differences of color, hair and bone"—defines "whites and Negroes, possibly the yellow race" as the "final word of science, so far." Focusing on a different feature—language or shared customs—defines instead Teutons, Slavs, and Romance peoples. The tension in Du Bois' definition of race reflects the fact that, for the purposes of European historiography (of which his Harvard and University of Berlin training had made him aware), it was the latter that mattered; but for the purposes of American social and political life, it was the former.

The real difference in Du Bois' conception, therefore, is not that his definition of race is at odds with the scientific one. It is, rather, as the classic dialectic requires, that he assigns to race a moral and metaphysical significance different from that of his contemporaries. The distinctive claim is that the Negro race has a positive message, a message not only of difference but of value. And that, it seems to me, is the significance of the sociohistorical dimension: the strivings of a race are, as Du Bois viewed the matter, the stuff of history.

> The history of the world is the history, not of individuals, but of groups, not of nations, but of races, and he who ignores or seeks to override the race idea in human history ignores and overrides the central thought of all history. ["CR," p. 75]

By studying history, we can discern the outlines of the message of each race.

"CRISIS": AUGUST 1911

We have seen that, for the purpose that concerned him most—understanding the status of the Negro—Du Bois was thrown back on the scientific definition of race, which he officially rejected. But the scientific definition (Du Bois' uneasiness with which is reflected in his remark that races "perhaps transcend scientific definition") was itself threatened as he spoke at the first meeting of the Negro Academy. In the later nineteenth century most thinking people (like too many even today) believed that what Du Bois called the "grosser differences" were a sign of an inherited racial essence which accounted for the intellectual and moral deficiency of the "lower" races. In "The Conservation of Races" Du Bois elected, in effect, to admit that color was a sign of a racial essence but to deny that the cultural capacities of the black-skinned, curly-haired members of humankind were inferior to those of the white-skinned, straighter-haired ones. But the collapse of the sciences of racial inferiority led Du Bois to deny the connection between cultural capacity and gross morphology—the familiar impulses and strivings of his earlier definition.

We can find evidence of his change of mind in an article in the August 1911 issue of the *Crisis*.

> The leading scientists of the world have come forward[6] . . . and laid down in categorical terms a series of propositions which may be summarized as follows:
> 1. (a) It is not legitimate to argue from differences in physical characteristics to differences in mental characteristics. . . .
> 2. The civilization of a . . . race at any particular moment of time offers no index to its innate or inherited capacities.[7]

These results have been amply confirmed since then. And we do well, I think, to remind ourselves of the current picture.

Human characteristics are genetically determined, to the extent that they are determined, by sequences of DNA in the chromosome—in other words, by genes.[8] The region of a chromosome occupied by a gene is called a locus. Some loci are occupied in different members of a population by different genes, each of which is called an allele; and a locus is said to be polymorphic in a population if there is at least one pair of alleles for it. Perhaps as many as half the loci in the human population are polymorphic; the rest, naturally enough, are monomorphic.

Many loci have not just two alleles but several, and each has a frequency in the population. Suppose a particular locus has n alleles, which we can call 1, 2, and so on up to n; then we can call their frequencies $x_1, x_2, \ldots$, to x_n. If we consider two randomly chosen members of a population and look at the same locus on one chromosome of each of them, the probability that they'll have the same allele at that locus is just the probability that they'll both have the first allele (x_1^2), plus the probability that they'll both have the second (x_2^2), plus the probability that they'll both have the nth (x_n^2). We can call this number the expected homozygosity at that locus: for it is just the proportion of people in the population who would be homozygous at that locus—having identical alleles at that locus on each of the relevant chromosomes—provided the population is mating at random.[9]

Now if we take the average value of the expected homozygosity for all loci, polymorphic and monomorphic (which, for some reason, tends to get labeled J), we have a measure of the chance that two people, taken at random from the population, will share the same allele at a locus on a chromosome taken at random. This is a good measure of how similar a randomly chosen pair of individuals should be expected to be in their biology *and* a good (though rough) guide to how closely the populations are genetically related.

I can now express simply one measure of the extent to which members of these human populations we call races differ more from each other than they do from members of the same race. For example, the value of J for Caucasoids—based largely on samples from the English population—is estimated to be about 0.857, while that for the whole human population is estimated at 0.852.[10] The chances, in other words, that two people taken at random from the human population will have the same characteristic at a locus, are about 85.2 percent, while the chances for two (white) people taken from the population of England are about 85.7 percent. And since 85.2 is 100 minus 14.8 and 85.7 is 100 minus 14.3, this is equivalent to what I said in the introduction: the chances of two people who are both Caucasoid differing in genetic constitution at one site on a given chromosome are about 14.3 percent, while, for any two people taken at random from the human population, they are about 14.8 percent. The conclusion is obvious: given only a person's race, it is hard to say what his or her biological characteristics will be, except in respect of the "grosser" features of color, hair, and bone (the genetics of which are, in any case, rather poorly understood)—features of "morphological differentiation," as the evolutionary biologist would say. As Nei and Roychoudhury express themselves, somewhat coyly, "The extent of genic differentiation between human races is not always correlated with the degree of morphological differentiation" ("GR," p. 44).

To establish that race is relatively unimportant in explaining biological differences between people, where biological difference is measured in the proportion of differences in loci on the chromosome, is not yet to show that race is unimportant in explaining cultural difference. It could be that large differences in intellectual or moral capacity are caused by differences at very few loci and that, at these loci, all (or most) black-skinned people differ from all (or most) white-skinned or yellow-skinned ones. As it happens, there is little evidence for any such proposition and much against it. But suppose we had reason to believe it. In the biological conception of the human organism, in which characteristics are determined by the pattern of genes in interaction with environments, it is the presence of the alleles (which give rise to these moral and intellectual capacities) that accounts for the observed differences in those capacities in people in similar environments. So the characteristic racial morphology—skin and hair and bone—could only be a sign of those differences if it were (highly) correlated with those alleles. Furthermore, even if it were so correlated, the causal explanation of the differences would be that they differed in those alleles, not that they differed in race.

Since there are no such strong correlations, even those who think that intellectual and moral character are strongly genetically determined must accept that *race* is at best a poor indicator of capacity.

But it was earlier evidence, pointing similarly to the conclusion that "the genic variation within and between the three major races of man . . . is small compared with the intraracial variation" ("GR," p. 40) and that differences in morphology were not correlated strongly with intellectual and moral capacity, which led Du Bois in the *Crisis* to an explicit rejection of the claim that biological race mattered for understanding the status of the Negro:

> So far at least as intellectual and moral aptitudes are concerned, we ought to speak of civilizations where we now speak of races. . . . Indeed, even the physical characteristics, excluding the skin color of a people, are to no small extent the direct result of the physical and social environment under which it is living. . . . These physical characteristics are furthermore too indefinite and elusive to serve as a basis for any rigid classification or division of human groups.[11]

This is straightforward enough. Yet it would be too swift a conclusion to suppose that Du Bois here expresses his deepest convictions. After 1911, he went on to advocate Pan-Africanism, as he had advocated Pan-Negroism in 1897, and whatever Afro-Americans and Africans, from Ashanti to Zulu, share, it is not a single civilization.

Du Bois managed to maintain Pan-Africanism while officially rejecting talk of race as anything other than a synonym for color. We can see how he did this by turning to his second autobiography, *Dusk of Dawn,* published in 1940.

"DUSK OF DAWN"

In *Dusk of Dawn*—the "essay toward an autobiography of a race concept"—Du Bois explicitly allies himself with the claim that race is not a scientific concept.

> It is easy to see that scientific definition of race is impossible; it is easy to prove that physical characteristics are not so inherited as to make it possible to divide the world into races; that ability is the monopoly of no known aristocracy; that the possibilities of human development cannot be circumscribed by color, nationality, or any conceivable definition of race.[12]

But we need no scientific definition, for

> all this has nothing to do with the plain fact that throughout the world today organized groups of men by monopoly of economic and physical

power, legal enactment and intellectual training are limiting with determination and unflagging zeal the development of other groups; and that the concentration particularly of economic power today puts the majority of mankind into a slavery to the rest. [*D,* pp. 137–38]

Or, as he puts it pithily a little later,

the black man is a person who must ride "Jim Crow" in Georgia. [*D,* p. 153]

Yet, just a few pages earlier, he has explained why he remains a Pan-Africanist, committed to a political program which binds all this indefinable black race together. The passage is worth citing extensively.

Du Bois begins with Countée Cullen's question, "What is Africa to me?" and answers,

Once I should have answered the question simply: I should have said "fatherland" or perhaps better "motherland" because I was born in the century when the walls of race were clear and straight; when the world consisted of mut[u]ally exclusive races; and even though the edges might be blurred, there was no question of exact definition and understanding of the meaning of the word. . . .

Since then [the writing of "The Conservation of Races"] the concept of race has so changed and presented so much of contradiction that as I face Africa I ask myself: what is it between us that constitutes a tie which I can feel better than I can explain? Africa is, of course, my fatherland. Yet neither my father nor my father's father ever saw Africa or knew its meaning or cared overmuch for it. My mother's folk were closer and yet their direct connection, in culture and race, became tenuous; still, my tie to Africa is strong. On this vast continent were born and lived a large portion of my direct ancestors going back a thousand years or more. The mark of their heritage is upon me in color and hair. These are obvious things, but of little meaning in themselves; only important as they stand for real and more subtle differences from other men. Whether they do or not, I do not know nor does science know today.

But one thing is sure and that is the fact that since the fifteenth century these ancestors of mine and their other descendants have had a common history; have suffered a common disaster and have one long memory. The actual ties of heritage between the individuals of this group, vary with the ancestors that they have in common [with] many others: Europeans and Semites, perhaps Mongolians, certainly American Indians. But the physical bond is least and the badge of color relatively unimportant save as a badge; the real essence of this kinship is its social heritage of slavery; the discrimination and insult; and this heritage binds together not simply the children of Africa, but extends through yellow Asia and into the South Seas. It is this unity that draws me to Africa. [*D,* pp. 116–17]

This passage is affecting, powerfully expressed. We might like to be able to follow it in its conclusions. But we should not; since the passage seduces us into error, we should begin distancing ourselves from the appeal of its argument by noticing how it echoes an earlier text. Color and hair are unimportant save "as they stand for real and more subtle differences," Du Bois says here, and we recall the "subtle forces" that "generally followed the natural cleavage of common blood, descent and physical peculiarities" of "The Conservation of Races." There it was an essential part of the argument that these subtle forces—"impulses" and "strivings"—were the common property of those who shared a "common blood"; here, Du Bois does "not know nor does science" whether this is so. But if it is not so, then, on Du Bois' own admission, these "obvious things" are "of little meaning." If they are of little meaning, then his mention of them marks, on the surface of his argument, the extent to which he cannot quite escape the appeal of the earlier conception of race.

Du Bois' yearning for the earlier conception which he prohibited himself from using accounts for the pathos of the gap between the unconfident certainty that Africa is "of course" his fatherland and the concession that it is not the land of his father or his father's father. What use is such a fatherland? What use is a motherland with which your own mother's connection is "tenuous"? What does it matter that a large portion of his ancestors have lived on that vast continent, if there is no subtler bond with them than brute—that is, culturally unmediated—biological descent and its entailed "badge" of hair and color?

Even in the passage that follows Du Bois' explicit disavowal of the scientific conception of race, the references to "common history"—the "one long memory," the "social heritage of slavery"—only lead us back into the now familiar move of substituting a sociohistorical conception of race for the biological one; but that is simply to bury the biological conception below the surface, not to transcend it. Because he never truly "speaks of civilization," Du Bois cannot ask if there is not in American culture—which undoubtedly *is* his—an African residue to take hold of and rejoice in, a subtle connection mediated not by genetics but by intentions, by meaning. Du Bois has no more conceptual resources here for explicating the unity of the Negro race—the Pan-African identity—than he had in "The Conservation of Races" half a century earlier. A glorious non sequitur must be submerged in the depths of the argument. It is easily brought to the surface.

If what Du Bois has in common with Africa is a history of "discrimination and insult," then this binds him, by his own account, to "yellow Asia and . . . the South Seas" also. How can something he shares with the whole nonwhite world bind him to only a part of it? Once we interrogate the argument here, a further suspicion arises that the claim to this bond may be based on a hyperbolic reading of the facts. Du Bois' experience of "discrimination and insult" in his American childhood and as an adult citizen of the industrialized world was different in character from that experienced by, say, Kwame Nkrumah in colonized West Africa; it is absent altogether in large parts of "yellow Asia." What Du

Bois shares with the nonwhite world is not insult but the *badge* of insult; and the badge, without the insult, is the very skin and hair and bone which it is impossible to connect with a scientific definition of race.

CONCLUDING UNSCIENTIFIC POSTSCRIPT

Du Bois died in Nkrumah's Ghana, led there by the dream of Pan-Africanism and the reality of American racism. If he escaped that racism, he never completed the escape from race. The logic of his argument leads naturally to the final repudiation of race as a term of difference and to speaking instead "of civilizations where we now speak of races." The logic is the same logic that has brought us to speak of genders where we spoke of sexes, and a rational assessment of the evidence requires that we should endorse not only the logic but the premises of each argument. I have only sketched the evidence for these premises in the case of race, but it is all there in the scientific journals. Discussing Du Bois has been largely a pretext for adumbrating the argument he never quite managed to complete.

I think the argument worth making because I believe that we—scholars in the academy—have not done enough to share it with our fellow citizens. One barrier facing those of us in the humanities has been methodological. Under Saussurian hegemony, we have too easily become accustomed to thinking of meaning as constituted by systems of differences purely internal to our endlessly structured *langues*.[13] Race, we all assume, is, like all other concepts, constructed by metaphor and metonymy; it stands in, metonymically, for the Other; it bears the weight, metaphorically, of other kinds of difference.

Yet, in our social lives away from the text-world of the academy, we take reference for granted too easily. Even if the concept of race is a structure of oppositions—white opposed to black (but also to yellow), Jew opposed to Gentile (but also to Arab)—it is a structure whose realization is, at best, problematic and, at worst, impossible. If we can now hope to understand the concept embodied in this system of oppositions, we are nowhere near finding referents for it. The truth is that there are no races: there is nothing in the world that can do all we ask "race" to do for us. The evil that is done is done by the concept and by easy—yet impossible—assumptions as to its application. What we miss through our obsession with the structure of relations of concepts is, simply, reality.

Talk of "race" is particularly distressing for those of us who take culture seriously. For, where race works—in places where "gross differences" of morphology are correlated with "subtle differences" of temperament, belief, and intention—it works as an attempt at a metonym for culture; and it does so only at the price of biologizing what is culture, or ideology. To call it "biologizing" is not to consign our concept of race to biology. What is present there is not our concept but our word only. Even the biologists who believe in human races use the term "race," as they say, "without any social implication" ("GR," p. 4). What exists "out there" in the world—communities of meaning, shading variously into each other in the rich structure of the social world—is the province not of biology but of hermeneutic understanding.

I have examined these issues through the writings of Du Bois, with the burden of his scholarly inheritance, and have tried to transcend the system of oppositions which, had Du Bois accepted it, would have left him opposed to the (white) norm of form and value. In his early work, Du Bois took race for granted and sought to revalue one pole of the opposition of white to black. The received concept is a hierarchy, a vertical structure, and Du Bois wished to rotate the axis, to give race a "horizontal" reading. Challenge the assumption that there can be an axis, however oriented in the space of values, and the project fails for loss of presuppositions. In his later work, Du Bois—whose life's work was, in a sense, an attempt at just this impossible project—was unable to escape the notion of race he had explicitly rejected. We may borrow his own metaphor: though he saw the dawn coming, he never faced the sun. And we must surely admit that he is followed in this by many in our culture today; we too live in the dusk of that dawn.

Notes

1. Masatoshi Nei and Arun K. Roychoudhury, "Genetic Relationship and Evolution of Human Races," *Evolutionary Biology* 14 (1983): 11; all further references to this work, abbreviated "GR," will be included in the text.

2. W.E.B. Du Bois, "The Conservation of Races," *W.E.B. Du Bois Speaks: Speeches and Addresses,* 1890–1919, ed. Philip S. Foner (1897; New York, 1970), pp. 73, 74, 75; all further references to this work, abbreviated "CR," will be included in the text.

3. This talk of racial absorption (and similar talk of racial extinction) reflects the idea that Afro-Americans might disappear because their genetic heritage would be diluted by the white one. This idea might be considered absurd in any view propounding the notion of a racial essence: either a person has it or they don't. But this way of thinking conceives of racial essences as being like genes, though Mendelian genetics was not yet "rediscovered" when Du Bois wrote this piece. Du Bois is probably thinking of "passing for white"; in views of inheritance as the blending of parental "blood," the more that black "blood" is diluted, the more it is likely that *every* person of African descent in America *could* pass for white. That, of course, would be a kind of extinction of the Negro. It is interesting that those who discussed this issue assumed that it would not cause the extinction of the white race also and the creation of a "hy-

bridized" human race. But, as I say, such speculation is ruled out by the rise of Mendelian genetics.

4. I owe this way of thinking about the distance between social and biological ancestry to chapter 6 of R. B. Le Page and A. Tabouret-Keller's forthcoming book, *Acts of Identity.* I am very grateful to Professor Le Page for allowing me to see a typescript.

5. This seems to me the very notion that the biologists have ended up with: a population is a group of people (or, more generally, organisms) occupying a common region (or, more generally, an environmental niche), along with people largely descended from that original group who now live in other regions. See Nei and Roychoudhury, "Gene Differences between Caucasian, Negro, and Japanese Populations," *Science* 177 (Aug. 1972): 434–35, and "Genetic Relationship," p. 4.

6. This claim was prompted by G. Spiller; see *Papers in Inter-Racial Problems Communicated to the First Universal Races Congress Held at the University of London, July 26–29, 1911,* ed. Spiller (1911; Secaucus, N.J., 1970).

7. Du Bois, "Races," *Crisis,* August 1911, pp. 157–58.

8. Strictly we should say that the character of an organism is fixed by genes, along with sequences of nucleic acid in the cytoplasm and some other features of the cytoplasm of the ovum. But these latter sources of human characteristics are largely swamped by the nucleic DNA and are, in any case, substantially similar in almost all people. It is the latter fact that accounts, I think, for their not being generally mentioned.

9. It follows from these definitions that where a locus is monomorphic, the expected homozygosity is going to be one.

10. These figures come from Nei and Roychoudhury, "Genetic Relationship," and I have used the figures derived from looking at proteins, not blood-groups, since they claim these are likely to be more reliable. I have chosen a measure of "racial" biological difference that makes it look spectacularly small, but I would not wish to imply that it is not the case, as these authors say, that "genetic differentiation is real and generally statistically highly significant" (pp. 8, 11, 41). I would dispute their claim that their work shows the existence of a biological basis for the classification of human races; what it shows is that human populations differ in their distributions of genes. That is a biological fact. The objection to using this fact as a basis of a system of classification is that far too many people don't fit into just one category that can be so defined.

11. Du Bois, "Races," p. 158.

12. Du Bois, *Dusk of Dawn: An Essay toward an Autobiography of a Race Concept* (1940; New York, 1975), p. 137. All further references to this work, abbreviated *D,* will be included in the text.

13. Post-structuralism is not a step forward here, as Terry Eagleton has observed (see *Literary Theory: An Introduction* [Oxford, 1983], pp. 143–44).

Negritude, Nationalism, and Nativism: Racists or Racialists?

Albert G. Mosley

This article reviews the claims of Negritude by Senghor and Cesaire and the claims of African Nationalists such as Blyden and Du Bois in order to distinguish racist from racialist points of view. It then presents Kwame Anthony Appiah's argument in My Father's House: Africa in the Philosophy of Culture *(NY: Oxford University Press, 1992) that Senghor, Blyden, and Du Bois were "intrinsic racists" and that the concept of race is a pseudo-concept. In contrast, Mosley provides good reason to believe that Appiah's notion of "intrinsic racism" is the truly bogus concept. Mosley presents models of races among non-humans in order to illustrate a valid use of the concept of race, and argues that racialist views of human beings are neither unintelligible nor inherently incoherent.*

Appiah also suggests that the pursuit of indigenous traditional cultural forms of knowledge is inherently flawed because the reconstruction of traditional beliefs and practices relies on texts created by colonialists, explorers, and missionaries, and natives writing at the time. Each of these sources makes essential use of Western categories, which infects the descriptions of traditional beliefs and practices with terms laden with Eurocentric concerns.

In rebuttal, Mosley argues for the existence of indigenous sources of knowledge about traditional practices, for the legitimacy of recognizing and cultivating important aspects of indigenous culture, and for the legitimacy of using the language of the hegemonic culture to describe the limits of that hegemony. He concludes that Appiah's treatment of negritude, African nationalism, and nativism is seriously flawed.

NEGRITUDE AND NATIONALISM

Leopold Senghor, with Aime Cesaire, is one of the originators of the term *negritude* and chief exponent of perhaps its most radical version. In an article published in *Diogené* (no. 37) in 1962 entitled "On Negritude: The Psychology of the African Negro," Senghor wrote that the European

> distinguishes the object from himself. He keeps it at a distance. He freezes it out of time and, in a way, out of space. He fixes it, he kills it. With his precision instruments he dissects it in a pitiless factual analysis. As a scientist, yet at the same time prompted by practical considerations, the European makes use of the *Other* that he has killed in this way for his practical ends. He makes a *means* of it.

On the other hand, the African

> does not begin by distinguishing himself from the object, the tree or stone, the man or animal or social event. He does not keep it at a distance. He does not analyze it. Once he has come under its influence, he takes it like a blind man, still living, into his hands. He does not fix it or kill it. He turns it over and over in his supple hands, he fingers it.

And of the African-American he claims that

> American psychological workers have found that the reflexes of Negroes are surer and more natural because they are more closely related to the object. Hence the employment of Negroes during the Second World War in industry and the technical services, beyond the proportion which they represent of the population. . . . this means that the Negro by the very fact of his physiology has reactions which are more *lived,* in the sense that they are more direct and concrete expressions of the sensation and of the stimulus, and so of the object itself with all its original qualities and power.

This indicates, for Senghor, that the African both on the continent and in the diaspora

> reacts more faithfully to the stimulus of the object. He is wedded to its rhythm. This physical sense of rhythm, rhythm of movements, forms and colors, is one of his specific characteristics, for rhythm is the essence of energy itself. It is rhythm which is at the basis of imitation and which plays a determining role in man's generic activity and in his creative activity: in memory, language and art.

He goes on to say the following:

> One of my friends, an African poet, confessed to me that all forms of beauty strike him at the root of the belly, and give rise to a sexual feeling. This not only with music, dancing or African mask, but with a painting by Giotto or

a Florentine palace. It goes even further, for the symbolic image, visual and auditory, of a High Mass has the same effect on him. Some one will raise the cry of eroticism. It would be more accurate to talk of sensuality. But the African's spirituality is rooted in his sensuality: in his physiology.

In taking this stance, Senghor appears to be confirming the racist's view of the African and African-American as oriented more toward the concrete than to the abstract. In this way, racists reinforced their claim that Africans should not be given extensive education, because they were not mentally equipped to deal with abstractions. Rather, it was argued, Africans were best suited for manual labor and, indeed, were better at it than the European. Likewise, the claim that Africans were naturally more sensual excused white men for the use they made of black women and justified their brutal treatment of black men (lynching, castration, whipping) to deter them from sexually abusing white women.

While acknowledging such associations, Senghor maintained:

> It is a fact that there is a white European civilization and a black African civilization. The question is to explain their differences and the reasons for these differences, which my opponents have not yet done.

Senghor's explanation of the difference is that reason manifests itself in different ways in different races. Among Africans, reason manifests itself as a "reason-by-embrace," a participation of the knower into the object known. But for the European, reason is the "eye-reason" of logic and precise measurement.

For many, Senghor's views generate concern because the idea that different racial, ethnic, or national groups have different genetically determined social tendencies is one that was used prominently to justify the enslavement and exploitation of Africans. Racists of the eighteenth and nineteenth century argued that the different races of mankind were arranged hierarchically, with the African or black race at the bottom—closest to beasts of burden—and with the Caucasian or white race at the top—the most advanced of the human species.

J. F. Blumenbach, professor of natural history at Gottingen, was the first to use the term *Caucasian* to describe the white race, which he held to be the first and most beautiful race and from which all others races were degenerate offshoots. Part of the belief that the people of the Caucasoids were the first race derived from the belief that Noah's ark had landed at Mount Ararat in the Southern Caucasus. This scheme of the origins of the original Europeans—the Aryans—placed Germans closer to the origins of mankind than other Europeans (Bernal 1987, 219–20).

Arthur de Gobineau (1816–1882), considered to be the father of racism, divided human races into three types: White, Black, and Yellow.

I understand by white men the members of those races which are also called Caucasian, Semitic or Japhetic. By black men I mean the Hamites; by yellow the Altaic, Mongol, Finnish and Tartar branches. (Biddiss 1970, 119)

He wrote of Africans:

The black variety is the lowest and lies at the bottom of the ladder. The animal character lent to its basic form imposes its destiny from the moment of conception. It never leaves the most restricted intellectual zones. If its faculties for thinking are mediocre or even nonexistent, it possesses in its desire and as a consequence in its will an intensity that is often terrible. Many of the senses are developed with a vigor unknown in the other two races: principally taste and smell. It is precisely in the greed for sensations that the most striking mark of its inferiority is found. (Bernal 1987, 241)

Gobineau believed, however, that civilization advanced only by the intermixture of the races, an intermixture that inevitably raised the level of other races while diluting the white race:

The two most inferior varieties of the human species, the black and yellow races, are the crude foundation, the cotton and wool, which the secondary families of the white race make supple by adding their silk; while the Aryan group, circling its finer threads through the noble generations, designs on its surface a dazzling masterpiece of arabesques in silver and gold. (Biddiss 1970, 119)

It is such an intermixture of the races that produces the arts:

Artistic genius, which is equally foreign to each of the three great types, arose only after the intermarriage of White and Black. (Biddiss 1970, 119)

Negritude rejects the negative evaluations of the traits considered typical of the African personality and emphasizes their positive character. For Senghor, the African's sensuality is the basis, not of brutal instincts, but of sublime spirituality: "the spirituality of the Negro is rooted in sensuality: in his physiology" (Senghor 1962, 5). Modes of thought and ways of knowing are "partially transmitted through heredity" and "are diverse and tied to the psychological and physiological makeup of each race" (Senghor 1962, 7). This mode of knowing, this "embracing reason," in which the knower participates intimately and physiologically with the known, is one that differs from the analytical reason characteristic of Europe but is equally important for human development. Senghor argued that Europeans were themselves being forced to acknowledge the limitations of their mode of knowing through their own researches in mathematical logic and quantum physics and had begun "going to the school of participant reason" (Senghor 1962, 8).

Senghor and Cesaire's early views on the relationship between races are presaged in the work of Johann Gotfried Herder. Herder argued that a nation reflected the racial genius of the people of a particular geographical and historical context. Once impregnated with this particular trait, the people maintained it, no matter how they might be divided by artificial borders. Herder further held that "all peoples, not merely Germans, should be encouraged to discover and develop their own genii" (Bernal 1987, 206). Herder denied the hierarchical ranking of mankind into four or five races, with blacks at the bottom and whites at the top. Rather, for Herder, each *Volk* had its own role to play in making its contribution to human civilization, a role that no other group could fulfill.

We may characterize Herder's view (following Frederickson, discussed later) as "racialist," to distinguish it from the "racist" views of Gobineau. But even the "racialist" formulation of racial differences was a double-edged sword, for the claim continued to be made that the Anglo-Saxons' or Aryans' special gift was to lead, to conquer, to break new ground, while the special gift of the African Negro was to serve, to forgive, and to exhibit the virtues of the true Christian. Thus, Frederick Schlegel argued that it was the Aryan race descending from the mountains that conquered not only India, but Egypt as well. And it was the Aryans that led these civilizations to their greatest achievements. It was thus the inescapable destiny of the Aryans to lead (Bernal 1987, 230ff).

Such views on the nature of racial differences were also prominent in the debate concerning the social role of African slaves and freedmen in the Americas. The historian George Fredrickson characterized this debate as follows:

> The biological school saw the Negro as a pathetically inept creature who was a slave to his emotions, incapable of progressive development and self-government because he lacked the white man's enterprise and intellect. But those who ascribed to the priority of feeling over intellect sanctioned both by romanticism and evangelical religion could come up with a strikingly different concept of Negro "differences." Whereas scientists and other "practical" men saw only weakness, others discovered redeeming virtues and even evidences of black superiority. (Frederickson 1971, 101)

Frederickson calls this latter doctrine "romantic racialism," and cites evidence to show that it was a popular view among northern abolitionists of the nineteenth century. Some went so far as to argue that the Negro was in fact a superior race to the Anglo-Saxons, because they were natural Christians, carrying within, much more than the Caucasian, "the germs of a meek, long-suffering, loving virtue" (1971, 106). In 1845, James Russell Lowell, a Garrisonian abolitionist wrote:

> We have never had any doubt that the African race was intended to introduce a new element of civilization, and that the Caucasian would be benefitted greatly by an infusion of its gentler and less selfish qualities. The Cau-

casian mind, which seeks always to govern at whatever cost, can never come to so beautiful or Christian a height of civilization, as with a mixture of those seemingly humbler but truly more noble qualities which teach it to obey. (Frederickson 1971, 107)

Theodore Tilton, editor of the New York *Independent,* wrote in 1863:

> In all the intellectual activities which take their strange quickening from the moral faculties—which we call instincts, intuitions—the negro is superior to the white man—equal to the white woman. It is sometimes said . . . that the negro race is the feminine race of the world. This is not only because of his social and affectionate nature, but because he possesses that strange moral, instinctive insight that belongs more to women than to men. (Frederickson 1971, 115)

Both racism and racialism tend to assume that the social potential of a particular group derive from racially determined factors peculiar to that group. These factors constitute influences over which individuals have little personal control. The views differ primarily in that racists portray such factors hierarchically, with certain predispositions superior to others; while racialists view such factors as complementary, with each predisposition having its relative strengths and weaknesses.

Given this distinction, it is easy to see how Senghor's racialist views could be confused with the racist views of someone like Gobineau. Each view accepts the assumption that biological characteristics determine social characteristics, and they differ only in the racist viewing certain social characteristics (aggressive, analytical) as being absolutely superior to other social characteristics (participatory, intuitive), while the racialist viewed all social characteristics as only relatively superior. Some forms of racism and racialism further assume a biological connection between racial type and "mode of cognition." Cesaire accepted such a connection in his early years, and Senghor has maintained such a belief.

In both racism and racialism, character differences between groups are to be traced to and explained by reference to specific racial differences between the groups. While the concept of race has evolved from a religious to a biological to the current ethnic conception, the practice of viewing race as determinative of social character has continued.

Racialist and racist views argued that a biological connection to a particular "race" was necessary for certain kinds of social achievements. For Negritude, as for many other African nationalists, only the African could teach the African. Thus, Edward Blyden held that "each of the races of mankind has a specific character and specific work" (Blyden 1967, 277). And in "The Conservation of Races," Du Bois wrote that mankind was divided into races, and each race was characterized by, to use Crummell's term, "distinct proclivities." As such, the destiny of the Negro American was not absorption by white Americans; rather, it was in

Negroes working with Negroes to produce their own distinctive nations and national cultures.

THE CRITIQUE OF NATIONALISM

In his book *In My Father's House: Africa in the Philosophy of Culture,* Kwame Anthony Appiah (1992) defines "racialism" as the belief that all the members of a particular race "share certain traits and tendencies with each other that they do not share with members of any other race. These traits and tendencies characteristic of a race constitute, on the racialist view, a sort of racial essence . . . [which] account for more than the visible morphological characteristics—skin color, hair type, facial features" (1992, 13). Appiah denies that racialism itself is dangerous: "Provided positive moral qualities are distributed across races, each can be respected, can have its 'separate but equal' place."

While racism presupposes racialism, it differs from racialism in that it attributes the most valuable personal and social qualities to one race, while limiting the presence of valuable social traits in other races. Racism thus establishes a hierarchy of qualities, reflecting a hierarchy of races. Racialism also assumes that different qualities reflect the causal influence of different races, but it denies that any one set of qualities is absolutely superior or that any one race is superior to all others. Appiah aptly summarizes the "Africa for the African" position of Du Bois, Blyden, and Crummell as "the acceptance of difference along with a claim that each group has its part to play, that the white and the Negro races are related not as superior to inferior but as complementaries; the Negro message is, with the white one, part of the message of humankind" (Appiah 1992, 24).

Although negritude is most often associated with the name of Senghor, the first to actually coin the term "negritude" was Aime Cesaire, of Martinique. Initially, both Senghor and Cesaire attributed the differences between African and European cultures to the influence of race. But while Senghor maintained a belief in a biological basis for the peculiar orientation attributed to African culture, Cesaire altered his views and came to hold that negritude was not biologically but historically determined:

> I do not in the slightest believe in biological permanence, but I believe in culture. My Negritude has a ground. It is a fact that there is a black culture: it is historical; there is nothing biological about it. (Arnold 1981, 37)

While maintaining the importance of art and poetry as an antidote to logic and science, Cesaire accounted for the orientation of blacks toward the arts as an adaptation of traditional African orientations to the historical conditions imposed by the slave trade, slavery, colonialism, and segregation.

Du Bois's concept of race likewise evolved from a biological to a sociohistorical form. Thus, in 1947 Du Bois seemed quite clear about his notion of race: The Negro race is all those forced to bear the insult of being slaves or the descendants of slaves during the Industrial Revolution of Western Europe. Du Bois writes:

> [S]ince the fifteenth century these ancestors of mine and their descendants have had a common history; have suffered a common disaster and have one long memory. The actual ties of heritage between the individuals of this group vary. . . . But . . . the real essence of this kinship is its social heritage of slavery; and this heritage binds together not simply the children of Africa, but extends through yellow Asia and into the South Seas. It is this unity that draws me to Africa. (1940, 41, 116–7)

And in *The Crisis,* Du Bois (1947) writes:

> The so called American Negro group . . . while it is in no sense absolutely set off physically from its fellow Americans, has nevertheless a strong, hereditary cultural unity born of slavery, of common suffering, prolonged proscription, and curtailment of political and civil rights. . . . Prolonged policies of segregation and discrimination have involuntarily welded the mass almost into a nation within a nation.

Appiah acknowledges that Du Bois changed his view of race from a biologically based to a culturally based conception, but he nonetheless considers this insufficient to avoid a basic flaw. As such, Appiah asserts that the passage from *Dusk of Dawn* "seduces us into error" by substituting a sociohistorical conception of race for a biological one. This, for Appiah, "is simply to bury the biological conception below the surface, not to transcend it" (Appiah 1992, 41).

Appiah characterizes the views of these African nationalists as Sartre had characterized negritude—as forms of antiracist racism. To justify labeling Senghor, Blyden, Crummell, and Du Bois as racists, Appiah proposes a distinction between what he calls "extrinsic" and "intrinsic" racism. *Extrinsic racism* associates valuable social traits with membership in a particular race. To illustrate, being a member of the white race would be conceived of as causally determining whether one would be a bearer of certain superior qualities. *Intrinsic racism,* on the other hand, makes no necessary association between being a member of a particular race and having certain valuable social qualities. For the intrinsic racist, the very fact that one is of a particular race gives one preferential advantages, just as being a human gives one preferential advantages over nonhumans.

Appiah argues that nationalists were "intrinsic racists" because they considered Africans to be more like members of a family than like bearers of similar traits. The fact that a particular individual, *b*, is a member of *B*'s family gives *b* preferential access to *B*'s wealth over individuals who are not members of *B*'s family, independently of whether *b* has any behavioral or social traits in common with *B*. But I wish to argue that Appiah's "intrinsic racism" is a bogus concept because, as he has characterized it, "intrinsic racism" is not a form of racism at all.

The "intrinsic racist" views other members of his or her race as members of the same family, and on that basis alone, irrespective of talent or merit, gives the "family member" preferential treatment over members of other "families" (or "races"). Thus, the preferential treatment of a member of one's own family over a nonfamily member need not be based on the belief that members of one's own family are superior to members of other families. Preferential treatment of a member of one's own family could as well be based on a moral duty of gratitude and/or a prudential rule favoring reciprocal altruism between (alleged) relatives. But there need be no assumption that members of one's own family are superior to members of other families.

But as we have seen, the assumption of superiority is central to the definition of a racist. As such, Appiah's notion of "intrinsic racism" is not a form of racism at all. Nor is it a form of racialism, because it contains no suggestion that valuable social qualities are selectively distributed between groups. Preferential treatment for a member of a particular family requires no assumptions that the individual is the bearer of certain traits associated with that family. On the other hand, Crummell, Blyden, Du Bois, and Senghor were racialists because they did believe that the African harbored special talents, which made possible certain contributions to world civilization that only the African could provide.

Despite whatever weaknesses racialism might harbor, one of the primary concerns of African nationalism and negritude was to deny racist claims of superiority, even as they acknowledged claims of racial differences. Racialism attempted to acknowledge racially determined differences while divesting those differences of any implication of absolute superiority or inferiority. To characterize the negritude and African Nationalist movements as racist, as Appiah does, is to accuse them of an error they were designed to oppose. To do this using the notion of "intrinsic racism" amounts to an attempt to rewrite history by selectively redefining its central concepts. I believe Appiah is seriously in error in characterizing Senghor, Cesaire, Crummell, Blyden, and Du Bois, as racists. They espoused a form of racialism, not racism.

This is not to imply, however, that racialism is itself without error. A commonly cited weakness of racialism is the suggestion that racial type is a necessary or sufficient condition for the display of certain behavioral and social traits. To say that being a member of race X is sufficient for having (the potential for) trait x does not preclude race Y and race Z from also having (the potential for) trait x. Both racism and racialism require viewing race as a necessary condition for possessing (the potential for) certain traits to achieve selective distribution of traits by race.

To illustrate, if being a member of the Caucasian race were considered a necessary condition for being intelligent/analytical, then while all Caucasians need not be intelligent/analytical, all intelligent/analytical type persons would have to be Caucasian. Similar comments apply if negritude is interpreted in this way. As J. O. Sodipo points out, if the racialism of negritude is taken literally, then Wordsworth and the romantic poets of Europe must be regarded as Africans (Sumner, 290). And, as we have seen, this is a conclusion suggested by both Senghor and Gobineau.

From Cesaire we learn that it is no accident that Senghor's views seem so close to Gobineau's. In an interview in 1967 Cesaire says this about the influence of Gobineau on himself and Senghor:

> Yes, we read Gobineau, Senghor and I. It was essentially to refute him, since he was the great French theoretician of racism. But at the same time, I must admit, Senghor liked him a great deal. His liking was understandable; he was grateful to Gobineau for saying: "Art is black." The Black is an artist. If there are artists in Western civilization, it is because there are nonetheless a few drops of Negro blood in them. Consequently the attitude toward Gobineau was very ambivalent. (Arnold, p. 41)

One way of avoiding this difficulty is to view the association between race and social traits in statistical rather than categorical terms. This involves viewing race X as displaying a significantly higher frequency of the occurrence of trait x, rather than as being the exclusive bearer of trait x. Thus, to use the typical traits cited by racists and racialists, a population with a higher proportion of Africans might show a higher proportion of artists, musicians, and athletes; while a population with a higher proportion of Europeans might show a higher proportion of scientists, mathematicians, and engineers. Nonetheless, many Africans might be scientists, mathematicians, and engineers, and many Europeans might be artists, musicians, and athletes.

Racialism affirms that certain kinds of social behavior are selectively linked to certain races and explains this link in terms of causal connections. But, of course, correlation does not necessarily imply causation. And it might be that the correlation between racial type and behavioral type is purely coincidental, a mere artifact of chance. Or the correlation might be the result of some further cause, perhaps of a religious, economic, or other sociohistorical nature.

Thus, the association between members of the African race and the display of an aesthetic orientation could be explained by reference to the systematic exclusion of Africans from the development of analytic skills and their confinement to opportunities in the "arts." On the other hand, the higher frequency of the display of analytic skills among Europeans could be explained by the preferential treatment accorded Europeans for opportunities to develop such skills. Certainly, then, there might be conditions that might cause race X to display a disproportionate frequency of behavior x, without race itself being a cause of the behavior x. On the other hand, if the frequency of x is a defining characteristic of race X, then the relationship between race X and trait x is stipulative rather than causal: Race X just is that race in which x occurs with a higher frequency than in other races.

Despite these caveats, the possibility of a selective distribution of behavioral traits causally determined by race cannot be ruled out as impossible. The fact of such, were it established, could be used to justify a racist orientation, on the assumption that certain selectively distributed traits were inherently superior to other selectively distributed traits. But this is certainly not the position of the African nationalists we have reviewed, nor of the negritudists.

Appiah's error in characterizing nationalism and negritude as racist is compounded by his misguided critique of a basic assumption of both racism and racialism. This critique calls into question the very existence of races and hence the differential distribution of traits between races. Appiah denies the possibility of developing an adequate conception of "race," and urges that we "transcend" such usage altogether.

A major reason Appiah cites for rejecting the concept of race altogether is the dilemma that the offspring of two different races would be equally of both races or a hybrid that was a member of no race. But it is not clear why this in itself is reason to reject racial classifications. The existence of cases that do not fit an accepted taxonomic schema has never, in itself, been a sufficient reason for rejecting that schema. More concretely, the fact that there might be more mongrels than purebreds is no argument against the existence of different breeds of dogs.

Indeed, a good model of a racialist schema would be the case of breeds of dog (see Smith 1975). While each breed may be superior to other breeds in certain respects, no breed is superior to all other breeds in all respects. And though it might be typical of breed X that it exhibit trait x, this might be neither a necessary nor a sufficient condition for a particular individual's being a member of that breed. And though the offspring of two distinct breeds might itself be a member of neither, it might still be possible to account for some of the mongrel's behavior/morphology by reference to the behavior/morphology of its immediate progenitors—to traits distinctive of the breed of its parents. Thus, pit-bulls (or dalmatians) have traits that are distinctive to their breed, and although we might not want to say that having a pit-bull (or dalmatian) parent is sufficient to cause a particular dog to be aggressive (or white with black spots), we might explain its aggressiveness (or being white with black spots) by pointing out that the dog is the immediate progeny of a breed that is typically aggressive (white with black spots).

Theodore Dobzhansky defined races as "Mendelian populations which differ in the incidence of some genetic variants in their gene pools" (1962, 239), and he illustrated the concept in terms of different races of the fruit fly *drosophila* that had adapted to different elevations of the Sierra Nevada mountains of California. Differences between races are not determined by distinguishing individuals with different traits into correspondingly different classes. Rather, racial differences apply only at the level of the population, in terms of the relative frequency of traits between populations. "Mankind," he writes, "is a polytypic species composed of a cluster of races, Mendelian populations with more or less different gene pools" (232).

The analogy being drawn between races of *homo sapien, canis carnivore,* and *drosophila* is not meant to denigrate human beings, but rather is meant to illustrate that biologists apply the same classificatory principles to humans, dogs, birds, and fruitflies. To the extent that we accept the existence of different breeds of domesticated dogs, and different varieties of fruitflies, I see no reason to deny the existence of different races of human beings. All that is necessary in either case is that a population (race or breed) be genetically isolated and that the frequency of certain traits be selected for.

Usually, the traits used to distinguish different races of mankind are the visible morphological ones such as skin color, eye color, hair type, nose and lip shape, etc. But such traits are not always the most important one's in distinguishing races, and recent research in human biology has used a number of traits that can only be discerned by instrumental analysis but that provide more reliable indicators. Appiah is aware of such developments and uses the genetically determined propensity to produce certain protein types to reach the following conclusion:

> the chances of two people who are both "Caucasoid" differing in genetic constitution at one site on a given chromosome are about 14.3 percent, while, for any two people taken at random from the human population, they are about 14.8 percent. (1992, 36)

In other words, two individuals chosen at random from two different races have only a 0.5% greater probability of differing in the kinds of proteins they produce than two individuals chosen at random from within the same race. His general point is that, because variations within a race are almost as great as variations between different races, divisions between races are based on differences so minuscule as to be insignificant.

In a footnote to this discussion, Appiah's bias and selective use of data are scarcely veiled. He writes:

> These figures come from Nei and Roychoudhury, "Genetic relationship and Evolution of Human Races." I have used figures derived from looking at proteins, not blood groups, since they claim these are likely to be more reliable. I have chosen a measure of "racial" biological difference that makes it look spectacularly small, but I would not wish to imply that it is not the case, as these authors say, that "genetic differentiation is real and generally statistically highly significant" (41). I would dispute their claim that their work shows there is a biological basis for the classification of human races: what it shows is that human populations differ in their distributions of genes. That is a biological fact. The objection to using this fact as a basis of a system of classification is that far too many people don't fit into just one category that can be so defined. (1992, 196)

One marvels at Appiah's verbal sophistry, for as Dobzhansky has pointed out, races are just populations within a species that differ in their distributions of gene frequencies. Nei and Roychoudhury use both protein and blood group data to conclude that "the genetic differentiation of human races is of the same order of magnitude as that found in local races of other organisms" (1983, 41) and that "the races of each of Caucasoid, Asian, Mongoloid, and Negroid form a separate cluster" (40). That there are many individuals who do not clearly fit into one race or another is never an issue.

While Nei and Roychoudhury acknowledge that interracial genetic variation is small when compared with intraracial genic variation, they stress that "the genetic differentiation is real and generally statistically highly significant." At the same time, they warn that two populations that look alike (e.g., Australian aborigines and South African Bushmen) might nevertheless be strikingly dissimilar in terms of protein and blood type frequencies. Thus, "genetic distance between populations is not always correlated with morphological difference" (41). To return to our previous analogy, just because a dog looks like a dalmatian does not mean that it really is one. But it also does not mean that there are no dalmatians.

The claim that concepts of race have a biological legitimacy is not meant to suggest that current concepts of race are based primarily on biological considerations. Indeed, the conceptions of race institutionalized by slavery and colonization were designed primarily around socioeconomic considerations. The conception of an African as any individual with at least one traceable African ancestor (the "one-drop rule") is absurd as a means of differentiating distinct biological groups. It is like claiming that having one traceable dalmatian progenitor makes a dog a dalmatian. But such a rule did make sense in a society in which the most valuable form of property was in the form of human beings held as slaves.

The "one-drop rule" definition of the African race was devised to support the establishment and maintenance of slavery and segregation. Whereas in the rest of the Americas, slavery was replenished by new imports from Africa, in the United States, the primary means of replenishing slaves was by birth. Rules stipulating that only Africans could be treated as property, that any person who had at least one traceable African ancestor was of the African race, and that the child of a slave was a slave were critical to the program of replenishing slaves by birth and maintaining the exploitation of freed slaves.

> Freedmen's status was not an end to the process of marginalization but merely the end of one phase of that marginalization, slavery, which itself had several stages. Freedmen's status began a new phase, but the ex-slave was still a marginal person. (Patterson 1982, 249)

It is in this context that the current conception of the African or Negro or black race evolved. And although such a conception may make little biological sense, it makes perfect sense when seen as a historical means of establishing and maintaining European supremacy (Patterson 1982, 176).

It is in such a historical context that Du Bois was considered an African, even though he was the product of a mixed father and a mixed mother. Clearly, the conception of race he lived was not a purely biological one, for biologically, he was as much European as African (and perhaps more so). But Du Bois did not attempt to evade identification as an African and deftly used the intellectual tools of his time to transform the view of the African as intrinsically inferior to the European.

In contrast, Appiah wishes to divest the world of the concept of race by denying that the notion plays any constructive part in dealing with the problems Africa faces. Further, because African-Americans (e.g., Blyden and Du Bois) conceived of their relationship to Africa primarily in terms of their belonging to the same race, he considers that relationship to be as tenuous and infertile as the concept of race on which it is built.

Appiah holds that Africans and African-Americans have experienced different degrees of involvement with European cultural values, and so have been affected by European expansionism in very different ways. The vast majority of Africans, he argues, experienced European expansionism only tangentially, at the periphery of their lives. Only those Africans sent to be educated in the West approximated the degree of alienation experienced by slaves and their progeny.

Appiah believes that African nationalists, because most have been influenced by African-Americans, have a romanticized view of Africa, deriving from the European concept of the African. The European conceived of the African as "the other," the opposite to the domineering and analytical bent of Europe; and negritude enshrined this view of the African as a virtue, the natural antidote to European militarism and will to dominance.

African nationalists held that African cultural institutions should reflect the uniqueness of the African character. In the field of literature, this claim to uniqueness is presented under the guise of "nativism": the view that African literature must take a peculiarly African form. For Appiah, this involves accepting the European stereotype of the African while merely reversing its value. The nationalist/negritudist/nativist conception of the African remains that provided by the European.

Some nativists (e.g., Okot p'Bitek, Mazisi Kunene, Robert Mungoshi) have advocated writing in traditional African languages to recreate the values implicit in traditional life. But Appiah believes this offers little hope because, he argues, our very conception of traditional African ways is shaped by the European reconstruction of African traditional life. Appiah illustrates his point with a case he should know best, that of his own group, the Ashanti.

For Appiah, what we know of the laws and customs of traditional Ashanti is best summarized in Rattray's book *Ashanti Law and Constitution.* But, clearly, Rattray brought to his study of the Ashanti European assumptions that became embedded within his description of traditional Ashanti law and customs. This means that the nativist, in accepting such views of traditional life, is unwittingly adopting a European view of traditional African life.

During the rigors of the slave trade and colonialism, Europeans created chieftainships and tribal allegiances where none had existed before. More often than not, the traditional chiefs were chosen, not by Africans, but by Europeans, to represent Africans to Europeans to the explicit advantage of Europeans. The traditional chiefdoms recognized by Europeans were often as much a creation of the European as of the African. Rattray's book is supposed to describe the traditional world of the Ashanti, but it is as much a reflection of Europe's effect on Africa as it is of an Africa unadulterated with European cultural impositions. Thus, while nativists may want to go back to tradition, Appiah argues that the only tradition they have to go back to is the tradition as reconstructed by Europeans.

Appiah holds that the very idea that there should be a literature that is peculiarly African is a Western idea. He considers the conceptual progenitor of nativists and African nationalists to be Herder, who held that every race had an essence that was expressed through its literature. But for Appiah, the nativist attempt to realize such a form of literature is doomed to failure, much as the attempt to find a good witch is doomed. For as there are no witches, the search for a good one is quixotic and self-abortive. And as there are no races, the nationalist quest for a racially determined culture can never be completed.

For Appiah, both the racialist and the nativist inherit their orientations from a European perspective in which a racial essence is manifested in the form of its nation-state and in the form of its literature. For this reason, Appiah considers African nationalism to be just as wrongheaded as European racism. Because nativists use European concepts of race to justify their rejection of European racism, Appiah is able to charge that "Few things are less native than nativism" (1992, 60). Rather, he argues, nativism is the continuation of a European problematic. It never escapes Western categories. "The cultural nationalists are blind that their nativist demands inhabit a western architecture."

> The very notion of Pan Africanism was founded on the notion of the African, which itself was developed, not on the basis of any genuine commonality between them, but on the basis of the European concept of the African. The very category of the Negro is a European concept, invented by the European so as to justify his domination of them. The very course of African Nationalism has been to make real the imaginary identities to which Europe has subjected us. (Appiah 1992, 62)

Because African nationalists, nativists, and negritudists have defended their position by reference to the doctrines of Herder, Appiah assumes that they have no other basis for such views. We are left with the suggestion that African nationalists and nativists have no orientation except that derived from European influences. But this view must certainly be rejected. There is no reason to believe that traditional intellectuals such as Ogotomeli of the Dogon (interviewed by M. Griaule in *Conversations with Ogotomeli,* Oxford: Oxford University Press, 1965), the Luo sages interviewed by H. Odera Oruka (1990) of Kenya, the Yoruba Babalowa interrogated by Hallen and Sodipo (1986) of Nigeria, and the Akan Onyansafo interviewed by Kwame Gyekye of Ghana were inaccessible to African nativists.

The Kenyan philosopher H. Odera Oruka, has coined the term "philosophical sagacity" to describe the result of traditional intellectuals reflecting on African traditional beliefs. Such individuals are not only wise in the customs and beliefs of their people, they are also wise in assessing the efficacy of such practices and beliefs. Oruka cites his father as such a sage and in his book *Sage Philosophy* (1990) provides interviews with many other such individuals.

Barry Hallen and John Sodipo have also engaged in extensive interviews with the Onisegun sages of Nigeria. In so doing, they uncover a critical, empirical epistemological orientation that is seldom attributed to traditional cultures. They conclude that "the conceptual systems of alien languages—including those of so-called traditional cultures—have implicit in them alternative epistemological, metaphysical, moral, etc. systems that are of philosophical interest in their own right" (1986, 84). To illustrate, they provide a comparative investigation of "witchcraft" and its closest yoruba equivalent "àjẹ́." But there is no reason to believe that their interest in this subject is merely the projection of a European phenomena onto traditional African beliefs.

It is likewise with Appiah's countryman and fellow Akan, Kwame Gyekye. Gyekye's position is that the tendency to think deeply about certain kinds of questions is a universal human propensity, and is the source of all philosophical ideas. The task of the professionally trained African philosopher is to lift ideas expressed on such questions from their cultural context and critically develop them. He writes:

> Regarding the difficulty of getting at indigenous ideas in the light of Africa's historical contact with Christianity and Islam, I wish to say that in Akan, as indeed in every African community, there are certain individuals who are steeped in the traditional lore. These individuals are regarded as wise persons in their own right. They stand out in their own communities and command the respect and esteem of their townsfolk. A researcher who goes to any Akan town or village would invariably be directed to such individuals; they are generally tradition bound in their intellectual and general outlooks. Some of them have had no formal education at all. (1987, 53)

In his book *An Essay on African Philosophical Thought—The Akan Conceptual Scheme,* Gyekye cites the medium-priest Kwaku Mframa, the elder Nana Boafo-Ansah, and other indigenous sources regarding traditional Akan beliefs about personal identity, the relationship between religion and ethics, the relationship between free will and responsibility, the nature of time and causality, etc.

Oruka, Sodipo and Hallen, and Gyekye see themselves as initiating dialogues that incorporate the analytical training of the professional philosopher with the critical reflections of the traditional sage. In such dialogues, it does not follow that European concepts must necessarily exert the dominant influence. African philosophers need not deny their Western training, nor need they depend on it as the only guide for their intellectual life.

Similar comments hold true for African literature. Although the concept of "the African" has emerged as a result of historical processes over the last few centuries, its contingent beginnings are no less real beginnings, which give rise to a focused consciousness. Abiola Irele has coined the term "African imagination" to reflect "the expression of Africans and people of African descent arising out of these historical determinations":

Despite the disproportionate attention paid to literature by Africans in the European languages, the primary areas of what I've called the African imagination is represented by the body of literature produced by, within, and for the traditional societies and indigenous cultures of Africa. This literature forms an essential part of what is generally considered the oral tradition in Africa. (Irele 1990, 53)

These comments apply no less to Africans in the diaspora than to Africans on the continent. Henry Louis Gates (1988), in his book *The Signifying Monkey,* identifies a tradition of interpretation and reinterpretation that is an essential element in African-American music and literature. If we were to mime Appiah's reasoning, this feature of African-American culture would be interpreted as only one of many adaptations of European hermeneutics. To his credit, Gates's accomplishment was to demonstrate in *"Signifying"* a hermeneutical principle of African origins that had maintained itself despite the rigors of slavery, colonization, and segregation.

Gates shows that the signifying monkey of African-American oral literature is the cultural progeny of the trickster gods of West Africa. He argues that the tradition of interpretation and reinterpretation, exemplified by the Yoruba deity Esu-elegbara, maintained its vitality among "traditional intellectuals" in the New World—individuals who maintained a connection with the vital cultural life of their communities. This would include storytellers, musicians, artists, and religious leaders—just those people who survived, not by a wholesale adoption of the European cultural tradition, but by syncretizing it with African cultural memes.

It is not clear why Appiah would want to deny African intellectuals independent access to endogenous African beliefs and practices. But, clearly, his views are not shared by many leading African and African-American philosophers and literary critics. Appiah makes much of the African intellectual's use of European languages and concepts to reject European hegonomy. But as I have shown, using the concept of race to oppose racism does not make one a racist. Likewise, using European concepts to reject European cultural imperialism does not make one wholly Eurocentric. To the contrary, the creative accommodation of indigenous African traditions to modern, Western-derived forms reflects a characteristic feature of its orally based literature (Irele 1990, 54; Gates 1988, chaps. 2, 3).

CONCLUSION

I have tried to show in this essay, (1) that contrary to Sartre and Appiah's claims, Senghor and Du Bois—with Crummell, Blyden, and Cesaire—opposed racism, not with another form of racism, but with racialism; (2)

that though racialist claims may in many cases be false, such claims are not nonsensical; (3) that the concept of race has both a biological and historical legitimacy; and (4) that African nativism (in both philosophical and nonphilosophical literature) is not necessarily a self-contradictory enterprise driven by European conceptions of African traditional culture. In all, I hope to have shown that Appiah's treatment of nativism, nationalism, and Negritude is seriously flawed.

Bibliography

Appiah, Anthony. *In My Father's House: Africa in the Philosophy of Culture.* New York: Oxford University Press, 1992.

Arnold, A. James. *Modernism and Negritude—The Poetry and Poetics of Aime' Cesaire.* Harvard University Press, Cambridge, 1981.

Bernal, Martin. *Black Athena.* New Brunswick, NJ: Rutgers University Press, 1987.

Biddiss, Michael D. *Father of Racist Ideology—The Social and Political Thought of Count Gobineau.* New York: Weybright & Talley, 1970.

Blyden, Edward W. *Christianity, Islam, and the Negro Race.* Edinburgh: Edinburgh University Press, 1967.

Campbell, Colin. *The Romantic Ethic and the Spirit of Consumerism.* London: Blackwell, 1987.

Dobzansky, Theodosius. *Mankind Evolving.* New York: Bantam Press, 1962.

Du Bois, W.E.B. *Dusk of Dawn.* New York: Harcourt Brace, 1940.

——— *The Crisis* (December, 1947)

Frederickson, George. *The Black Image in the White Mind.* Middletown, CT: Wesleyan University Press, 1971.

Gates, Henry. *The Signifying Monkey.* New York: Oxford University Press, 1988.

Griaule, Marcel. *Conversations with Ogotemmeli.* (Trans. of Dieud'eau, 1948) Oxford: Oxford University Press, 1965.

Gyeke, Kwame. *An Essay on African Philosophical Thought—The Akan Conceptual Scheme.* Cambridge: Cambridge University Press, 1987.

Hallen, B., and J. O. Sodipo. *Knowledge, Belief, and Witchcraft.* London: Ethnographica Press, 1986.

Irele, Abiola. "The African Imagination." *Research in African Literatures.* Special Issue on Critical Theory and African Literature. 21 no. 1, (Spring 1990), pp. 49–67.

Lewontin, R. C., Steven Rose, and Leon Kamin. *Not in Our Genes.* New York: Pantheon, 1984.

Nei, Masatoshi, and A. K. Roychoudhury. "Genetic Relationship and Evolution of Human Races." *Evolutionary Biology* 14 (1983): 1–56.

Oruka, H. Odera. *Sage Philosophy.* New York: E. J. Brill, 1990. "Philosophical Sagacity in African Philosophy." *The International Philosophical Quarterly* 23 no. 4 (December 1983): pp. 383–93.

Patterson, Orlando. *Slavery and Social Death.* Cambridge, Mass: Harvard University Press, 1982.

Rattray, R. S. *Ashanti Law and Constitution.* London: Oxford University Press, 1929.

Reed, John, and Clive Wake, eds. *Senghor Prose & Poetry.* New York: Oxford University Press, 1965.

Senghor, Leopold. "On Negritude: The Psychology of the African Negro." *Diogené* 37 (1962).

Sodipo, John. "Some Philosophical Aspects of the African Historical Experience." In *African Philosophy,* edited by Claude Sumner, Addis Ababa: Chamber Printing House, 1980.

Smith, Anthony. *The Human Pedigree.* London: George Allen & Unwin, 1975.

Williamson, Joel. *The Crucible of Race—Black White Relations in the American South Since Emancipation.* New York: Oxford University Press, 1984.

Africa and the Imperative of Philosophy: A Skeptical Consideration

Oyekan Owomoyela

Oyekan Owomoyela is a Nigerian critic and historian of traditional litera-ture currently teaching at the University of Nebraska. In this article, he summarizes the case against ethnophilosophy, as made by Towa, Wiredu, Hountondji, and others, and offers his own assessment. Ethnophilosophy is characterized as the reconstruction of the unconsciously held metaphysical beliefs and epistemological orientations of traditional African cultures. Ethnophilosophers assume that traditional African cultures were oral, unan-imist and uncritical, and argue that these characteristics should be seen as strengths rather than weaknesses.

The critics of ethnophilosophy insist, however, that philosophy is neces-sarily pluralistic and that ethnophilosophy has tended to valorize the very attributes used by racists to denigrate the African. Critics like Wiredu and Hountondji argue that ethnophilosophy can at best be a necessary condi-tion of African philosophy, but is not itself philosophy. Traditional beliefs can serve as a source of ideas about how we should position ourselves with respect to the present and future, but all beliefs should be subjected to crit-ical assessment and free discussion. Traditional beliefs should be no ex-ception.

Owomoyela attempts to rescue ethnophilosophy from the charges brought against it by its critics. He denies that ethnophilosophers need assume that traditional cultures were unanimist, he denies the necessity of writing as a precondition of philosophy, he denies that traditional wise men were uncritical, and he questions whether scientific development is necessary for solutions to many of Africa's current problems. Owomoyela does not believe that modern Europe's conquest of Africa is proof that mod-ern European morality is superior to traditional African morality. Instead, he suggests that many of the critics of ethnophilosophy may have been miseducated to the point of becoming Eurocentric, and he reaffirms the possibility that different cultures may produce different kinds of achieve-ments.

236

The African Studies Association in 1984 gave Paulin Hountondji a share in the Melville Herskovits award for the most significant Africanist publication for the previous year. The selection of Hountondji's book, *African Philosophy: Myth and Reality* (1983), suggests, logically, that the Association believes the book to be a significant contribution to African Studies. One might go even a step further and conclude that it indicates the Association's concurrence with the main premises and the general philosophical orientation of the author's arguments. This paper outlines some serious questions Hountondji and his fellow philosophers raise about what one's attitude to the African past should be and what criteria should dictate the course of development on the African continent.

Hountondji is perhaps the best known of the "professional philosophers."[1] As one would expect, each of the philosophers perceives the issues that will be raised in this discussion from a different perspective, even when they agree broadly on the critique of ethnophilosophy;[2] Hountondji has nevertheless emerged as the most articulate and representative in this regard, to the extent that his book has earned the title, "the 'bible' of anti-ethnophilosophers" (Mudimbe, 1985: 199). The focus of this essay will accordingly be on this important work, with occasional references, of course, to those of others, in particular the Ghanaian Kwasi Wiredu. This strategy has the attraction of straddling the divide between Anglophone and Francophone manifestations of the new philosophical attitudes.

To best understand what grounds there might be for objections to certain of the philosophers' positions, it is expedient that one isolate the several targets of their disparagement. Chief of these is ethnophilosophy, which Hountondji (1983: 34) defines as "an ethnological work with philosophical pretensions." This includes the works of all those who like Placide Tempels, Alexis Kagame, John Mbiti, and other ethnologists have attempted to articulate African philosophies or systems of thought. Another target is African cultures or traditions themselves, as distinct from whatever the ethnophilosophers or ethnologists might correctly or mistakenly have made of them. A third is what the philosophers see as the recidivism inherent in the attraction of some Africans to certain essential or residual traditional habits and a corresponding refusal on their part to Europeanize. The last is the discipline of African Studies, including its practitioners, which the philosophers represent as an unfortunate (to say the least) refusal to join, as Wiredu (1984: 153–54) puts it, in the general march towards development.

THE CASE AGAINST ETHNOPHILOSOPHY

Hountondji and other opponents of ethnophilosophy place the responsibility for its propagation on Placide Tempels. It was the Belgian cleric who, in his book *Bantu Philosophy* (1969), blazed the trail for Kagame,

Mbiti, and others towards the synthesizing of coherent philosophies from African traditions. For Hountondji and company what those scholars proffer as African philosophy is flawed in the mode of its supposed existence and in the manner of its articulation. Hountondji (1983: 56) complains: "More than once Tempels emphasizes that this philosophy is experienced but not thought and that its practitioners are, at best, only dimly conscious of it." The implication, Hountondji remarks, is that because the African is unaware of his philosophy he cannot very well express it and hence must look to the interpretive mediation of foreigners like Tempels (and their African followers, of course). He adds (1983: 57) that the image of the African as the unconscious, intuitive subscriber to a philosophy of which he is unaware makes him, in Eboussi-Boulaga's words, the "Monsieur Jourdain of philosophy."

Another objection of the philosophers to ethnophilosophy derives from its formulators' suggestion (inherent in the description of its various examples) that it is collectively held, or unanimist. Such formulations as "Bantu Philosophy," "African Philosophy," "*La philosophie bantou-rwandaise,*" and so forth suggest that all Bantu, all Africans, and all Rwandans espouse the respective philosophies attributed to them. The suggestion, says Hountondji (1983: 151), is an illusion consistent with the vision of anthropologists and ethnologists alike of "African village unanimity" and with their hankering for the "unique spectacle of a society without conflict, division or dissonance." True philosophy, Hountondji (1983: 179) asserts, results from individual intellectual engagement with the universe of experience, is pluralistic, and is subject to an "irreducible polysemy of discourse."

THE CASE AGAINST AFRICAN CULTURES

Quite apart from the disciplinary dispute about what is and what is not philosophy and what its proper mode of existence and the proper manner of its elaboration are or should be, Hountondji and the philosophers raise much larger questions. One concerns the adequacy of traditional African cultures. Whereas the case against ethnophilosophy could be construed as being against the misguided concoctions of foreigners and their African cohorts, the philosophers' pronouncements leave one with the certainty that the real object of their displeasure is African tradition and not what ethnophilosophers make of it.[3]

The philosophers' critique of African ways derives from a comparative evaluation of them, with modern European (or Western) ways as the norm. This is clearly evident in Wiredu's (1980: 1) description of the African way of life. He suggests two types of anachronism—the existence of "habits of thought and practice [that are] anachronistic within the development of a given society," and the anachronism of an entire society within the context of the whole world, resulting from the prevalence in the society of outmoded practices. Every society, he allows, is anachronistic to some degree. As far as Africa is concerned, however, he states: "the implications of calling a society 'underdeveloped', or in the suppositious synonym 'developing', is that it suffers from this malady in both ways." The same conviction explains Marcien Towa's sentiment, which Hountondji (1983: 172) echoes, that Africans must engage in "'revolutionary iconoclasm', a 'destruction of traditional idols' which will enable us to 'welcome and assimilate the spirit of Europe. . . .'"

The first defect of traditional African ways, as the philosophers perceive them, is the trait they have in common with ethnophilosophy. That trait is authoritarianism. In contrasting ethnophilosophy with genuine philosophy, Hountondji (1983: 83–84) explains that while true philosophy is a debate, a "pluralistic discourse, in which different interlocutors question one another within a generation or from one generation to another," the false discipline of ethnophilosophy, in this case as revealed by Ogotemmeli through Griaule[4] (but certainly also by Tempels and company), "aspires to confer a wisdom that is eternal, intangible, a closed system sprung from the depths of time and admitting of no discussion."

While the philosopher in this instance directs his barb at ethnophilosophy, further statements of his and by his colleagues reveal that their criticism applies as well to traditional African approaches to an understanding of the universe. For example, Wiredu (1980: 4) comments as follows on the "authoritarian odour" that suffuses African cultures: "Our social arrangements are shot through and through with the principle of unquestioning obedience to our superiors, which often meant elders. Hardly any premium was placed on curiosity in those of tender age, or independence of thought in those of more considerable years." For illustration he cites the abundance of proverbs in traditional African cultures which serve as immutable authority and the lack of other proverbs that encourage "originality and independence of thought." Elsewhere (Wiredu, 1984: 157), while conceding that certain African (specifically Akan) concepts of being are "more imaginative than those of some Western philosophers, he posits an essential difference between African and Western attitudes to their ontologies. That difference, he says, "is that the Western philosopher tries to argue for his thesis, clarifying his meaning and answering objections, known or anticipated; whereas the transmitter of folk conceptions merely says: 'This is what our ancestors said.'" The statement echoes Hountondji's (1983: 170) derision of the "official ideologue" who despite the confusion on the continent contents himself with the congratulatory declaration, "Alleluia, our ancestors have thought!"[5]

Another failing the philosophers impute to traditional African cultures is their innocence of the scientific spirit, a liability that forms the nucleus of a universe of ills. As they explain, closely tied to the lack of science is the lack of literacy, one explaining the other. Hountondji (1983: 99) describes the relationship as follows:

> The first precondition for a history of philosophy, the first precondition for philosophy as history, is . . . the existence of science as an organized material practice reflected in discourse. But one must go even further: the chief requirement of science itself is writing. It is difficult to imagine a scientific civilization that is not based on writing, difficult to imagine a scientific tradition in a society in which knowledge can be transmitted orally.

Similarly, Wiredu (1984: 151) says, "If a culture is both non-scientific and non-literate, then in some important respects it may be said to be backward in a rather deep sense."

Hountondji (1983: 103–104) offers some justification for valorizing writing at the expense of orality: "Oral tradition favors consolidation of knowledge into dogmatic, intangible systems, whereas archival transmission promotes better possibility of a critique of knowledge between individuals and from one generation to another." He goes on to argue that because those who must transmit knowledge orally are always fearful of forgetting, they are forced to "hoard their memories jealously, to recall them constantly, to repeat them continually, accumulating and heaping them up in a global wisdom, simultaneously present, always ready to be applied, perpetually available." A mind preoccupied with preserving knowledge is incapable of criticizing it, he continues; on the other hand, the memory that is liberated by archival storage can forget its acquisitions, provisionally question or reject them, knowing that it can always retrieve them whenever necessary. "By guaranteeing a permanent record, archives make actual memory superfluous and give full rein to the boldness of the mind," he concludes.

Pursuing the case for science, Wiredu (1980: 12–13) attributes certain unfortunate consequences to the persistence in African societies of "culturally ingrained attitudes" and a refusal to adopt logical, mathematical, analytical, experimental, or in other words, scientific, procedures where necessary. The retrograde attitudes, he suggests, explain "the weaknesses of traditional technology, warfare, architecture, medicine," and other ills that bedevil traditional life. Specifically, he cites automobile mechanics who would shun available precision instruments and rely on their intuition when tuning modern engines. In the realm of medicine he points to the influence of Africans' illogical, spiritistic conception of the universe, whereby the African abandons sober inquiry into the causes of diseases of mind and body and pursues instead "stories of malevolent witchcraft and necromancy." Moreover, he continues, many people, especially children, die from supposedly curative prescriptions that, however, have no scientific recommendation. For these reasons, he remarks, "any inclination to glorify the unanalytical cast of mind is not just retrograde; it is tragic."

Another example of irrational Africanism, according to Wiredu (1984: 154), is the prevalent practice (even among the educated) of pouring libations to spirits "in the belief that in this kind of way they can achieve development without losing their Africanness." His opprobrium, however, embraces more than the pouring of libations; it encompasses funerary rites in general, as witness his (1984: 155–56) characterization of funerals in Ghana:

> When a person dies there has first to be a burial ceremony on the third day; then on the eighth day there is a funeral celebration at which customary rites are performed; then forty days afterwards there is a fortieth day celebration (*adaduanan*). Strictly that is not the end. There are such occasions as the eightieth day and first anniversary celebrations. All these involve large alcohol-quaffing gatherings.

Already evident is the philosophers' conviction that Africans must discard their traditional ways in favor of modern European (or Western) ways in the name of development. Indeed, development is the powerful end that orients all their arguments, the end they believe that continued adherence to traditional ways will render unattainable. Thus, the case for the development of a valid African philosophy (in place of the impostor ethnophilosophy) is that philosophy makes science possible (Hountondji, 1983: 68), and science in turn makes development possible. As Wiredu (1980: 32) notes: "for my part, I take science to be the crucial factor in the transition from the traditional to the modern world." In another context Wiredu (1984: 153–54) writes:

> Modernization is the application of the results of modern science for the improvement of the conditions of human life. It is only the more visible side of development; it is the side that is more associated with the use of advanced technology and novel techniques in various areas of life such as agriculture, health, education and recreation.

Observing that "the quest for development, then, should be viewed as a continuing world-historical process in which all peoples, Western and non-Western alike, are engaged," he advises Africans not to view modernization as a foreign invasion but as a general march towards development that involves all humankind but has hitherto left them behind.

The mere fact that Europeans were able to colonize Africa, according to the philosophers, is evidence enough of the superiority of Europeanism over Africanism. Towa's recommendation that Africans welcome and assimilate the spirit of Europe, we might recall, is that in doing so they might absorb "the secret of her power and of her victory over us." Quoting Towa, Hountondji (1983: 172) further counsels Africans about the attitude they must adopt toward their past: "regard it cooly, critically, without complacency or self-satisfaction . . . [and] try to discover not our unrecognized greatness or nobility but the secret of our defeat by the West." Along the same lines Wiredu (1980: 61) asserts that "the African, who asks himself why it came about that everywhere on his continent other peoples were able so easily to put his people in bondage, is bound to realize that the trouble lies not in our biology but in certain aspects of our culture . . . : the lack of a developed scientific method, broadly speaking."

Another philosopher, the Nigerian Peter Bodunrin (1984: 7), criticizes those he describes as "political thinkers" for romanticizing the African past: "certainly not everything about our past was glorious. . . . A way of life which made it possible for our ancestors to be subjugated by a handful of Europeans cannot be described as totally glorious."

THE CASE AGAINST AFRICAN STUDIES AND STUDENTS OF AFRICA

The philosopher's opinion of the quality of African traditional thought inevitably colors his opinion of studies and Students of that subject. In this regard one should emphasize a significant difference between Hountondji and some of his colleagues. Peter Bodunrin (1984: 14), for example, believes that the African philosopher should acquaint himself with traditional beliefs as a possible quarry for ideas to improve impoverished Western philosophy. Also, Wiredu (1980: 16) interprets the venality rampant on the continent as evidence of the confusion of cultural influences that plague the modern African. He suggests that the cure might be a better familiarity with the traditional part of the cultural mix such that "clarity could begin at home." Similarly, Lancinay Keita (1984: 72) refers to the "cultural amnesia of the contemporary African whose knowledge of history and philosophy is limited to European thought systems. He blames the unfortunate situation on long centuries of the slave trade, colonialism, and the concomitant indoctrination of Africans. For Hountondji, however, the study of what he describes (1983: 67) as "so-called African subjects," rather than the universal "problematic" of philosophy, amounts to "folklorism," and, "a sort of collective cultural exhibitionism which compels the 'Third World' intellectual to 'defend and illustrate' the peculiarities of his tradition for the benefit of the Western public." The deceptive appearance of universal dialogue, he continues, only "encourages the worst kind of cultural particularism," because the particularities are only a delusion, and because the intellectuals who propagate them are impostors claiming to speak for their people, whereas the people are not even aware of the intellectuals' activities.

While Hountondji expresses opposition to the study of African traditional thought, he (Hountondji, 1983: 52) at the same time insists on
the philosopher's freedom to study non-African ideas and complains
about criticisms that might limit that freedom:

> Each and every African philosopher now feels duty-bound to reconstruct
> the thought of his forefathers, the collective *Weltanschauung* of his people.
> To do so, he feels obliged to make himself an ethnological expert on Afri-
> can customs. Anything he may produce in another vein, say on Plato or
> Marx, Confucius or Mao Tse-Tung, or in any general philosophical area un-
> connected with Africa, he regards as a sort of parenthesis in his thought, of
> which he must feel ashamed.

If he does not show shame, Hountondji adds, the critics pounce on him
and drag him back "to the straight and narrow path . . . of Africanism."
Hountondji (1983: 80) moreover attributes some devious (even sinister) motives to Africanists, both native and foreign. To the extent that
these ethnophilosophers define African habits of the heart and mind as
distinct from the European (and, therefore, in the philosophers' opinion
as inferior), their goal, he says, is actually the perpetuation of the African's status as "the 'absolute other' of the 'civilized' man." Criticizing
Aimé Césaire's paean to African non-technicality, Hountondji (1983: 159)
further alleges "a complicity between Third World nationalists and 'progressive' Western anthropologists. For years they will assist each other,
the former using the latter in support of their cultural claims, the latter
using the former to buttress their pluralistic thesis." Bronislaw Malinowski and Melville Herskovits are his prime example of "'progressive'
Western anthropologists," while Césaire and Senghor exemplify "Third
World nationalists." He seemingly approves of Césaire's brand of nationalism because it aims at political liberation. He (Hountondji, 1983: 159)
lambastes Senghor's cultural nationalism, on the other hand: "This gar-
rulous negrism . . . works as an alibi for evading the political problem of
national liberation. Hypertrophy of cultural nationalism generally serves
to compensate for the hypotrophy of political commitment."
Hountondji's low opinion of African Studies as a discipline has already surfaced in his description of African students of the African past as
cultural exhibitionists playing to the European gallery. He charges (1983:
52) that what Europe expects of Africans is that "we should offer her our
civilization as showpieces and alienate ourselves in a fictitious dialogue
with her, over the heads of our people." That, he asserts, is the ulterior
motive behind invitations that we establish African Studies and preserve
our cultural authenticity. "We forget too easily," he chides, "that African
Studies were invented by Europe and that the ethnographic sciences are
an integral part of the heritage of Europe, amounting to no more than a
passing episode in the theoretical tradition of the Western peoples."

By now it should be clear that the philosophers' strictures, certainly Hountondji's, apply not only to ethnophilosophy as a false discipline, but really to significant (perhaps even essential) aspects of African cultures, aspects the philosophers would have Africans abandon in order to "welcome and assimilate the spirit of Europe." Thus, not only ethnophilosophy but also African Studies and the recidivism it supposedly encourages are included in the pejorative description (Hountondji, 1983: 171) as "a powerful means of mystification in the hands of all who have a vested interest in discouraging intellectual initiative because it prompts not living thought in our peoples but simple pious ruminations on the past."

Finally, Hountondji (1983: 164) dismisses the notion of cultural pluralism as "a pretext for a conservative cultural practice." He notes also that "exotic" cultures are giving way to "the irreversible advent of a world civilization," and that cultural nationalists, instead of grasping the phenomenon, "simplify and trivialize it, emptying it of all real content by calling it 'acculturation'."

ETHNOPHILOSOPHY: INTUITIVENESS, UNANIMISM AND ANONYMITY

Philosophers are certainly entitled to debate the methodologies and parameters of their discipline. From that standpoint Hountondji is welcome to his views about the status and validity of ethnophilosophy.[6] Having granted the foregoing, however, one might take issue with his presentation of Placide Tempels' opinion regarding the degree of the African's conscious awareness of a philosophy, collective or otherwise, or of a system of thought. The cleric (Tempels, 1969: 21) thus states his case:

> We need not expect the first African who comes along, especially the young ones, to be able to give us a systematic exposition of his ontological system. None the less, this ontology exists; and it penetrates and informs all the thought of these primitives; it dominates and orientates all their behavior.

Further, in refuting Diertelen's contention that the "Ba Souto . . . do not indulge in reflective thought," Tempels (1969: 21, 23) adds, "Anyone who claims that primitive peoples possess no system of thought, excludes them thereby from the category of men. . . . I venture to think that the Bantu . . . live more than we do by Ideas and by following their own ideas."

There are grounds to object to Tempels' views and activities. He was undoubtedly a symbol of "the arrogance of Christianity" (Mudimbe, 1985: 157) that fueled the missionary efforts, and also a participant in the

European scheme to subjugate and exploit the Africans. Besides, his objective in synthesizing Bantu philosophy was to arrive at a more effective way of civilizing the savage. There is, on the other hand, some validity to his statement that not all Africans walk around with fully developed articulations of the beliefs that underlie their actions and choices readily available for presentation to inquirers. Besides, one could say the same of any people anywhere, as Robin Horton (1970: 171) indeed does with regard to "the modern Western layman." Furthermore, when Barry Halen and Harold Sodipo (1986) wanted to synthesize certain Yorùbá epistemological concepts they took great pains to identify the most reliable informants, the *onísègùn,* medicine men and custodians of ethnic mysteries, because not just any layman would do.

As for the contention that the ethnophilosophers present their readers with supposedly collective or unanimist pseudo-philosophies, one wonders if there could not be some body of shared conceptions of a philosophical nature that united cohesive groups. Whatever the case might be, however, John Ayoade (1984: 96) usefully observes that ideas of necessity originate from individual minds, a basic fact that cannot be lost on any thinker. Thus even when one attributes ideas or beliefs to whole communities one says no more thereby than that the ideas or beliefs have undergone the necessary communal proofing to be judged consistent with the group's ethos. The expression "Bantu Philosophy" no more means that all "Bantu" people necessarily subscribe to it any more than "Contemporary European Philosophy" suggests the adherence of all contemporary Europeans to the philosophy so described.[7]

The *apparent* trait of unanimism moreover is consistent with African usage. Students of traditional African societies are conversant with many instances of the de-emphasis of the cult of the individual. The reason is not necessarily that Africans do not believe in individualism. Any society that encourages heroism and worships it, as Africans certainly do, evidently encourages individual excellence. Traditionally, nevertheless, the individual composer of a song would not think of copyrighting or attaching his or her name to it, nor would the carver carve his name on his product. Whatever smacks of assertive possessiveness, even over one's undisputed possessions, runs counter to the traditional spirit. One finds expressions of the underlying principles of cooperation, communalism and self-effacement in such Yorùbá sayings as *Adaṣe ní hunni; ájọṣe kì í hunni* (Going it alone brings disaster; cooperating never brings disaster); *Kò mú tọwọ́ọ rẹ̀ wá kò gba tọwọ́ ẹni* (A person who does not contribute what he/she has has no claim to what one has); *Ẹnìkan kì í jẹ́ àwá dé* (No single person may say "here we are"); and *Aṣiwèrè èèyan ní nsọ pé irú òun kò si; irúu rèé pọ̀ o ju ẹgbàágbèje lo* (Only an idiot claims that there is no one like himself/herself; the world is full of people like him/her). To attach one's name to an object or an idea is to assert exclusive claim and proprietorship to it, whereas traditional society frowns on the implied possessiveness and ostentatious self-importance.[8] The Yorùbá user of proverbs resorts to them in order, among other reasons, to disclaim proprietorship of the wisdom they carry, and to attribute it instead to the elders. It would seem that the ethnophilosophers are in this regard closer in their expression to the African spirit than are the professional philosophers.

For the African, one might argue (to the extent that the generalization would permit), Truth has an independent existence and is not necessarily dependent for its validity on who voices it. If philosophers argue that their discipline has no absolutes but depends on personalities they limit its attractiveness to the African mind. The traditional manner of pursuing eternal verities, by detaching them from individual agents and liberating them from whatever sentiments one might harbor of their purveyors, is more attractive.

TRADITIONAL AFRICAN CULTURES

Before commenting on the various deficiencies the new philosophers charge to traditional African cultures one should remark on the use of language (by Wiredu for example) suggesting that certain traits are common to traditional Africans. The suggestion weakens their case against the unanimist implications of ethnophilosophy. Moreover, their arguments against traditional habits have a familiar ring to them. European commentators have long held that certain hereditary, cultural, and social traits explain Africa's backwardness in comparison with Europe and the West. For example, P. T. Bauer (1976: 78–79) criticizes the refusal of certain observers to apply the same explanations to unequal economic achievements (among societies and individuals) as they would to unequal athletic, political, artistic, and intellectual accomplishments—differences in personal qualities and motivations. He argues that relatively more authoritarian traditions of Africa, in comparison with those of the west, were probably responsible for the persistence in Africa of "attitudes and mores damaging to material advance." He goes on to list examples of the attitude (Bauer, 1976: 78–79):

> lack of interest in material advance, combined with resignation in the face of poverty; lack of initiative, self-reliance, and a sense of personal responsibility for the economic fortune of oneself and one's family; high leisure preference, together with a lassitude often found in tropical climates; preordained, unchanging and unchangeable universe; emphasis on performance of duties and acceptance of obligations, rather than on achievement or results, or assertion or even a recognition of personal rights; lack of sustained curiosity, experimentation and interest in change; belief in the effi-

cacy of supernatural and occult forces and their influence over one's destiny. . . .

Needless to say, other scholars (see Baran, 1957: 142–44, 163) see the source of the economic problems of the Third World differently.[9] Bauer's argument is familiar; to the extent that our philosophers share his opinions, one might legitimately wonder if they are not themselves guilty of setting up the African as "the 'absolute other' of the 'civilized' man."

One of Wiredu's examples of traditional ills is the authoritarianism evident in the abundance of proverbs which stifle youthful initiative and the absence of balancing ones that encourage it. Another supposed manifestation of authoritarianism is the African's refusal to seek new and original explanations for beliefs and phenomena, preferring instead to say that the ancestors had spoken and leaving matters at that. If Wiredu was sufficiently clear about African traditions he would be aware of a commonplace of proverb scholarship that is as true in Africa as elsewhere—within the same culture one is liable to find proverbs that will serve both sides in a contentious issue. John Messenger is perhaps the authority most cited for the unquestioned fiat of proverbs in Africa. In a celebrated article he claims (Messenger, 1965: 303–04) that in a certain Nigerian community skillful application of proverbs often decides issues in litigation. Fortunately he offers (Messenger, 1965: 302) the best refutation for that claim in the same article by noting that the judges take great pains to ascertain the facts, to the extent even of employing mediums because in theory at least their verdict might have life-and-death implications.

Incidentally, Wiredu himself (1980: 20–21) provides an argument to undercut his assertion about the authoritarianism of traditional cultures. Seeking to justify his criticism of African ways he pleads that his action is consistent with the openness of African systems to question:

> Those who seem to think that the criticism of traditional African philosophy is something akin to betrayal are actually more conservative than those among our elders who are real thinkers as distinct from mere repositories of traditional ideas. If you talk to some of them you soon discover that they are not afraid to criticize, reject, modify or add to traditional philosophical ideas.

If one considers, furthermore, that rather than the abject submissiveness and will-less servitude that characterizes Christian and Muslim approaches to their respective gods Africans adopt an almost brash assertiveness in their approach to theirs, one would conclude that people averse to authoritarianism in their gods would hardly tolerate it in mortals or their systems.

Africans might attribute opinions to ancestors, thereby implying that the opinions are ageless or immutable; common sense indicates, however, that "ancestors" cannot be taken in a literal sense. If we so took it we would need to determine who the ancestors were, when they lived, and, by implication, when original thinking ceased among Africans and why. New ideas surface all the time in Africa as elsewhere, and proverbs of very recent coinage exist. Attributing ideas to ancestors, therefore, only indicates a preference for *formal* self-effacement.

ILLITERACY

Hountondji argues that literacy is the precondition for philosophy, which is the precondition for science, which in turn is the precondition for technological advancement. It is not difficult to grant the point that things that are not somehow fixed may be impossible to define or measure precisely or difficult to manipulate. With regard to ideas, however, one cannot sustain an argument that unless they are fixed in writing they are not available to philosophy or reflection. If ideas are capable of transmission from one mind to another without the intermediary of documentation, then the receptive mind can be a reflective mind. Peter Bodunrin (1984: 10) concedes that "writing cannot be a precondition for philosophy," but he hedges by saying that writing is nevertheless important for the creation of a philosophical tradition. He thus aligns himself with Hountondji's assertion (1983: 106) that there might have been philosophers in traditional Africa, but not philosophy, because as far as philosophy is concerned "everything begins at the precise moment of transcription."

Hountondji further makes the interesting argument that Socrates gave birth to Greek philosophy only because his disciples committed his discourses to writing. One would conclude from it that Hountondji does not recognize the Pre-Socratics as philosophers, inasmuch as no one is sure that Thales wrote anything (Freemen, 1966: 50), nor Heraclitus, or Pythagoras for that matter (Wilbur and Allen, 1979; 60, 82). It appears that in this regard Hountondji is not in tune with the European philosophers he holds as his models.

One difficulty inherent in Hountondji's concession that Africans might very well have reflected seriously on the universe and their place in it, in other words philosophized, but yet produced no philosophy (because they did not record their thoughts)[10] is the complete subordination of the material to its medium. The proposition that Truth cannot exist except in a written mode seems to be an extreme form of materialism.

Without going into an elaborate discussion of the probable reasons for the preference in traditional Africa for non-literacy, since there is no doubt that some sort of writing was known and practiced in various parts of the continent before contact with Europe or even with Arabs,[11] one might suggest the unattractiveness of a medium that smacked of a secret code to communities that believed in universal participation in public life.[12] Furthermore, the Yorùbá proverbs, *Oyìnbó tó ṣe lẹ́ẹ̀di ló ṣèrésà* (The white man who made the pencil also made the eraser), and *Bí òní ti rí òla ò rí bẹ́ẹ̀, ní babàláwoó fi ndlfá lóróọrún* (Today is not necessarily a reliable preview for tomorrow, hence the diviner consults his oracle every fifth day), point to the preference for a medium that does not fix one in positions but permits a cleansing of the slate when and as necessary. The African perception of the fixity writing represents comes across quite clearly in the words of a fictional character infatuated with the European way, and, to some extent, alienated from the African. In Chinua Achebe's *No Longer at Ease* (1960: 120–21) the apostatic Isaak tells his son Obi:

> Our women make black patterns on their bodies with the juice of the *uli* tree. It was beautiful but it soon faded. If it lasted two market weeks it lasted a long time. But sometimes our elders spoke about *uli* that never faded, although no one had ever seen it. We see it today in the writing of the white man.

He goes on to explain that in the court records nothing ever changes or is alterable, because "'What is written is written'. It is *uli* that never fades." If philosophers argue, therefore, that traditional proverbs indicate the authoritarianism of traditional systems, one could very well riposte that documents, *uli* that never fades, exude their own sort of authoritarian and restrictive odor.[13]

Ruth Finnegan's observation (1970: 18–19) about the "detachment and relatively impersonal mode of transmission" that writing and printing represent is also worth noting. These qualities are consistent with the West's vending-machine culture, wherein human interactions, in official capacities especially (but not exclusively), reek strongly of automatism. African cultures tend in the opposite direction. Horton notes (1970: 137) that Africans adopt a "personal medium" as the basis of their world view. That personal emphasis has strong implications in their social arrangements. Which of the two tendencies one considers better depends on one's values.

Hountondji's dissertation on the debilitating effects of non-literacy contains other weaknesses. While one would grant that certain traditional bodies of knowledge or codifications, especially those connected with rituals, are so important as to require constant recall and repetition to obviate their loss through lapses of memory, one needs to stress the fact that those functions involve specialists and not the whole community. Indeed the materials concerned are very often secrets restricted to certain rather exclusive cultic fraternities. If all members of the community spent all their time frantically recalling and repeating essential bodies of knowledge there would be no point in establishing special occasions for festivals and performances for communal reacquaintance with the mores of the group. The fact is of course, that not only do the occasions exist, but they are so important that even group members who have wandered far and wide return home for them.[14]

Even more importantly, one could argue that contrary to Hountondji's scenario, people who inscribe the laws on parchments (or commit them to data banks) rather than on their hearts are more in danger of permanently losing them through forgetfulness or some sort of corruption. The complacency resulting from the certainty that the document is in safe storage somewhere does free the mind for other pursuits; but in time the disburdened mind might soon forget what the laws are, where they are stored, or even that they exist at all. Such is the genesis of "cultural amnesia."

SCIENCE

The philosophers' conception of science and technology as the panacea for what ails Africa deserves serious attention. Sober and reputable thinkers have convincingly discredited the usual opposition of the non-scientific, magical and superstitious traditional man and the scientific, pragmatic and rational Westerner. Bronislaw Malinowski (in Wilbur and Allen, 1979: 17) suggests that if science were defined after J. G. Crowther as "the system of behavior by which man acquires mastery over his environment," or even if it were represented as a theoretical enterprise, no people may be said to be entirely without science any more than it is without religion. On the other hand, if we took intuition to mean the absence of logical support for convictions or beliefs, and the substitution of "mythological thinking" for rationality, then one could argue, as Leo Apostel (1981: 17–18) does, that since even "mythological thinking" makes an attempt at proof, although proof of a different sort, Africans cannot be said to live by intuition alone.

Malinowski (1954: 17ff.) demonstrates, with particular reference to the Trobriand Islanders of Melanesia, that traditional peoples combine scientific and mystical approaches in dealing with their universe. In dealing with the known they rely on empirical knowledge whereas when confronted with the unknown they resort to magic. He (Malinowski, 1954: 28) points out that if one were to suggest to the Trobriander that he make his garden by magic alone he would smile at one's simplicity. He (Malinowski, 1954: 29–30) adds, "in canoe building empirical knowledge of material, of technology, and of certain principles of stability and hydrodynamics, function in company and close association with magic, each yet uncontaminated by the other." He (1954: 32) concludes that the traditional person "never relies on magic alone, while, on the contrary, he sometimes dispenses with it completely, as in fire-making and in a number of crafts and pursuits."

Robin Horton has also demonstrated the striking similarities between African traditional thought and modern science.[15] According to him (Horton, 70: 131) the Westerner is often unable to recognize the similarities, firstly because he is unfamiliar with the theoretical thinking of his own culture, and secondly because its African counterpart is expressed in a different idiom. Like Malinowski, Horton (1970: 135) argues that in dealing with the world of "common sense" the traditional African behaves according to the principles of causality. But when he is confronted by "gross incommensurability" he resorts to theory. His behavior is thus no different from that of the Western scientist, whereas his idiom is different.

The recent experiments of Barry Halen and Harold Sodipo (1986) on Yorùbá thought deserve some mention. They set out to bridge the gap between anthropologists and theoretical philosophers skeptical of anthropological reconstructions of traditional thought systems. In particular, they conducted an experiment in Yorùbá epistemology in order to arrive at its differences from or similarities to its English counterpart. They found (1986: 80–81), much to their surprise, that the Yorùbá insist on a more rigorous standard of proof than the English before they would classify any information as knowledge. They go on to comment (Halen and Sodipo, 1986: 81), "How ironic then, that the model of African thought systems produced by English-language culture should typify them as systems that treat second-hand information (oral tradition, 'book' knowledge, etc.) as though it were true, as though it were knowledge!" Hountondji (1983: 99) concedes that pre-colonial Africa "had undoubtedly amassed a wealth of true knowledge, of effective techniques which have been transmitted orally from generation to generation and continue to this day to ensure the livelihood of a large part of the population of our countryside and cities." Wiredu (1984: 153) also grants the existence of "the principle of rational evidence" in Africa, pointing to the application of knowledge of soils and seeds and meteorology to farming, and the preservation of communal harmony through the determination of conflicting claims on the basis of objective investigation. Despite these concessions, however, the philosophers argue that Africans must, in effect, develop science and technology that duplicate European models. That being the case, they seem open to the charge C. E. Ayres (1927: 13) makes against scientists, that they have substituted one form of folklore for another, inasmuch as their pursuit of science amounts to nothing short of "inviolable faith."

Ayres (1927: 19) further warns that "the prime mover in our recent developments is not that galaxy of noble truths which we call science, but the thoroughly mundane and immensely potent driving force of mechanical technology. Science is the handsome Doctor Jeckyll; machinery is Mr. Hyde—powerful and rather sinister." To the extent that our philosophers are infatuated with applicatory science, they seem, in comparison to Ayres, to be unphilosophical about science and technology; they have not seriously considered the ramifications of such products and by-products of science and technology as the neutron bomb, robotics and the marginalization of the working person, Kesterson, and Love Canal,[16] in order to determine whether or not science, in the final analysis, is a boon to humankind.

Before leaving the subject of science and the scientific spirit one should give some attention to Wiredu's criticism of the African habit of protracted funerals attended by the quaffing of liquor. The habit illustrates, in his view, the spiritistic manner in which the African approaches the understanding and solution of problems. Here again, unfortunately, Wiredu adopts the perspective of an outsider who lacks the insight Horton (for example) has demonstrated in this regard. Even Western medicine recognizes the need to attend to non-physiological disorders, the sort that bereavement might induce. In the West people at risk visit their analysts; in Africa the process of separation is protracted and cushioned with such festive socialization as would envelope the bereaved in the warm embrace of their extended kin. Ivan Karp's study of beer drinking among the Iteso makes valuable points that will help non-Africans and Africans suffering from "cultural amnesia" to understand the value of such social strategies. Karp (1980: 84) sees in them "mutual commensality," and argues that "beer is a symbol of diffuse solidarity and unencumbered sociability which expresses the ideal form of relations among men that Iteso would like to achieve." Having said that, one must, in fairness to Wiredu, acknowledge the unfortunate practice known in Nigeria as "spraying," meaning the mindless expenditure of (usually ill-gotten) wealth on social occasions. But one can blame even that on "cultural amnesia" and the undermining of traditional principles of accountability by colonialism and imperialism.

What Wiredu describes negatively as spiritism is not very different from what the Frankforts (1946: 5) describe rather positively as the traditional "I–Thou" relationship with the universe, in contrast with the modern "I–It" attitude. Each type has significant implications for its adherents' regard for human life and for nature. According to Francis Cornford (1957: vi), in contrast to the traditional reverential, reciprocative approach to nature, the scientific tendency seeks to master the world. In so doing it does away with what others consider most meaningful in nature; the gods and life itself are accordingly drummed out of Nature.

Finally, we must allow that despite their supposed irrationality and spiritism, traditional societies did manage to develop impressive pharmaceutics and psychiatry, for example,[17] and were by no means stagnant, despite their lack of "science and technology."

AFRICANIST AND AFRICAN STUDIES

One should not need to defend African Studies and Africanists against the imputations the philosopher make about their motives. Given the experiences of the last few centuries that have resulted in the "cultural amnesia" prevalent on the continent, the most urgent need for Africans would seem to be self-rediscovery. Thus, even if Europeans had not invented African Studies, Africans would have had to invent it. Mudimbe (1985: 208) properly places the African Studies movement in the process of African renascence, noting that its inception was part of the antithethical response to the earlier thesis: "all that is African is barbarous." He mentions also that the movement was highly influenced by Sheik Anta Diop, and has more recently earned the endorsement of such philosophers as Mabika Kalanda and Eboussi-Boulaga. For them, a thorough and dispassionate understanding of the African past is indispensable for effectively confronting the future.

Hountondji's suggestion that African Studies as a discipline is suspect because it was invented by Europeans and is, therefore, part of the European tradition, is strange. It is strange because it comes from someone whose central belief is that the only sort of philosophy fit for African attention is European style philosophy, and one who advocates the dissolution of African particularities (real or imaginary) in the emergent world civilization, meaning, of course, a cultural pax Europeana.

The philosophers' belief that the conquest of Africa by a handful of Europeans is the most persuasive argument for the abandonment of African ways strongly indicates their need for cultural rehabilitation. Apart from the cynicism of a might-makes-right, nothing-succeeds-like-success argument, it also shows evidence of alienation from the African spirit. Tradition tells us, for example, that when in the distant past Oduduwa invaded and conquered Ile-Ife, the ancestral home of the Yorùbá the indigenes formed the Ogbóni secret society whose function, according to Idowu (1963: 23–24), was "in all probability, to protect the indigenous institutions of the land from annihilation under the influence of the new regime." The result is that although today the Yorùbá accept Oduduwa as their ancestor, a measure of the success of the invader, the Ogbóni society remains one of the most powerful institutions of the land, a measure of the survival of indigenous mysteries and traditions. To represent what happened in Africa in the wake of European intervention as conquest by a handful of Europeans is, in any case, simplistic.

Long before Africans were colonized the Hebrews suffered a similar fate. They always relied, however, on the survival of a faithful remnant that would in more auspicious times reconstruct the essentials of Hebrewness. Even in the more recent era of colonization, Africans have not been the only peoples overrun by rampaging Europeans, but Africans are unique in their belief that their future lies in becoming, in thought, speech and habit, like their erstwhile colonizers. A true African philosophy would aim at reconciling Africans to Africaness, not at advocating dissolution in a European cultural mélange.

THE VALIDITY OF DISPARATE "FORMS"

"Suppose now," Wiredu (1980: 36) remarks, "that a critic should attribute what I have written to my particular educational background; I am bound to concede as much. In a certain obvious sense we are all children of our circumstances." His words are admirable and true. In this regard Wiredu and the philosophers are no different from other Africans raised in the era of colonialism, an era that continues in no small measure until the present day, nominal independence notwithstanding. Unfortunately, awareness of the mental conditioning does not always imply recognition of a need for deprogramming.

The philosophers sometimes betray unabashed Europhilia and an embarrassing insensitivity to racist nuances. Wiredu (1984: 157), for example, contrasts Africa with "other, better placed, parts of the world, [where] if you want to know the philosophy of the given people, you do not go to aged peasants or fetish priests or court personalities; you go to individual thinkers, in flesh, if possible, and in print." He (Wiredu, 1984: 152) gives examples of the "backward aspects of our culture" such as "assiduously participating in the pouring of libation to the spirits of our ancestors on ceremonial occasions, or frantically applauding imitation of the frenzied dancing of 'possessed' fetish priests. . . ." The disparaging references to "fetish priests" and their antics parallel Henry Odera's observation (in Hountondji, 1983: 60):

> What may be a superstition is paraded as "African religion," and the white world is expected to endorse that it is indeed a religion but an African religion. What in all cases is a mythology is paraded as "African philosophy," and again the white culture is expected to endorse that it is indeed a philosophy but an African philosophy.

They also parallel Hountondji's lament (1983: 74): "What a mockery it is to compare such ambitious philosophies [as produced by Plato,

Spinoza, and Hegel] and their scholarly surveys of the history of philosophy . . . with what anthropologists are today presenting as 'African systems of thought.'"

People so solicitous of the sensibilities of the white world and the white culture are in a poor position to accuse others, namely students of African traditions, of playing to the European gallery. They also cut a pathetic figure as worshippers of people who might have little use for them. Wiredu (1984: 159) correctly and wistfully observes that the African philosopher cannot take the same sort of pride in European philosophical achievements as a Western student of philosophy might. Indeed, he continues, "an African needs a certain level-headedness to touch some of these thinkers at all. Hume, for example, had absolutely no respect for black men. Nor was Marx, for another instance, particularly progressive in this respect." Yet the mentality that sees superstition and fetish priests in Africa while it sees religion and thinkers in Europe, that sees mythology and systems of thought in Africa while it sees philosophy in Europe, is kin to that which sees natives, savages and tribes in Africa while it sees citizens, civilized peoples and nations in Europe, even when the tribes are far more numerous than the nations.

The cause of the problem is miseducation (Wiredu's diagnosis is absolutely correct), and it will take a different sort of education to cure the new African of the hypnotic impulsion toward Westernism and the almost pathological conviction that African ways are important only as illustrations of things from which to distance oneself.

The basic monism of the African professional philosophers' position is obviously at variance with the pluralistic nature of the universe, which we observe in the divergencies all around us, in peoples, in fauna, in flora, and in planetary physical features. Many people would be dismayed if confronted with the possibility that in each of these classes of phenomena, one type might be selected for survival, because it has proved more acceptable in one respect than the others in that class, and all others consigned to extermination. The horse is a marvelous animal for its purposes, but one would neither wish the zebra a horse, nor wish all animals to become like horses.

More importantly, we should be mindful of the ultimate implications of the thought that one way of being and only that is desirable for all peoples. Many of the atrocities that have plagued human history have sprung from such thoughts, and Africans of all peoples forget that fact at their peril. We may allow ourselves to be impressed by the temporary success of European predation on the continent and elsewhere, but we would be perverse to see it as vindicating one and only one course of human development.

Henri Frankfort (1956: 3–18) in his discussion of the ancient civilizations of the Near East makes a persuasive case for cultural pluralism.

Each civilization, he says, has an individuality, a recognizable character, an identity which it maintains throughout its development. He calls it (Frankfort, 1956: 63) the form of the civilization, which is evident in "a certain coherence among its various manifestations, a certain consistency in its orientation, a certain cultural 'style' which shapes its political and its judicial institutions, its art as well as its literature, its religion as well as its morals." Although the form changes, partly as a result of inherent developmental imperatives and partly due to external influences, it is never destroyed. He takes issue with Toynbee's and Spengler's scientific view of civilization which proposes a uniform pattern of societal development from birth to death. In this view, "an imperialistic and socialistic order follows a traditional and hierarchical society; expanding technique and trade follow greatness in art, music, and literature as certainly as dispersal of the seeds follows the maturing of a plant which will never flower again" (Frankfort: 1956: 6).

Frankfort (1956: 14) further quotes Toynbee's comparison of civilizations to motor cars travelling along a one-way street, and his distinction between so-called primitive societies and civilizations: "Primitive societies . . . may be likened to people lying torpid upon a ledge on a mountainside, with a precipice below and a precipice above; civilizations may be likened to companions of these 'sleepers of Ephesus' who have just risen to their feet and have started to climb up the face of the cliff." Both images, Frankfort comments, suggest a "predetermined orientation and limitation of cultural endeavour." Toynbee, he continues (Frankfort, 1956: 14), believes there is a cliff to climb and a street to follow, whereas in truth,

> we see figures at rest or on the move in a cloudy space but know nothing about their relative position: we do not know which ledge is above or below which other ledge. Or again: we see motor cars moving, halting, or out of order. But we do not know whether they move in an alley, or on a four-drive highway, on an open plain, or within a circle—we do not even know whether there is an entrance or exit at all.

The perceptions and arguments of the professional philosophers inevitably show the consequences of what Mudimbe (1985: 150) describes as "silently depending on a Western episteme," and share the weaknesses of inauthenticity that are often associated with Négritude (Mudimbe, 1985: 170–71). Because our philosophers begin from the European model as a norm and criticize African cultures and habits accordingly, they need to take Frankfort's words (1956: 15) to heart to the effect that two divergent ways of life are not necessarily two attempts at doing the same thing, one attempt better than the other. "Bach was not trying to write like Beethoven and failing; Athens was not a relatively unsuccessful attempt to produce Rome."

Wiredu is correct to urge that clarity should begin at home. Accordingly, we must attend to a study and understanding of the form or forms of African civilizations, not simply so that we might make them serve as quarries to enrich European philosophical traditions but so that we might rediscover and resume our proper selves. Further, in order to rehabilitate our professional philosophers, African universities might need to absorb the discipline of philosophy into their institutes of African Studies. The philosophers would then have strong inducements to shed their present disdain for African Studies, and might even discover, as Frankfort (1956: 18) remarks, that "the values found in different civilizations are incommensurate."

CONCLUSION

The professional philosophers in Africa have raised many issues that one cannot adequately address in a short paper. The foregoing discussion has touched only glancingly on some of them. Certain points need stressing, however. The many references to the philosophers *en bloc* are not a suggestion that they form a monolithic group. Among those critical of ethnophilosophy, typically from Francophone countries, one finds notable differences of approach and opinion (see Mudimbe, 1986; 195–206); even individual philosophers do not remain fixed in stone in defense of their opinions, as Hountondji's modifications attest. Moreover, Anglophone philosophers tend to be more receptive to the philosophical possibilities of African traditions (Irele, 1983: 28–29) than are their Francophone colleagues. This greater receptiveness finds expression on the covers of their journal, *Second Order,* where they undertake to "regard inter-disciplinary boundaries as made for man, not man for them, and to watch out for growing points in their subject as it applies itself to new problems." Such an attitude avoids the paradox of making philosophy a closed discipline, and opens the way for the possibility of an equal dialogue between African thought and Western thought. Such a dialogue will undoubtedly be beneficial for both sides.

Notes

1. I use the term "professional philosophers" as Irele (1983: 8) does in his introduction to Hountondji's book to refer to the faculty of the departments of philosophy in some African universities.
2. Mudimbe's (1985) article is a most authoritative and comprehensive survey of the major developments to date on African thought. For a discussion of the various approaches to ethnophilosophy, see pages 179–202.

3. Wiredu (1984: 150–51) notes that "traditional thought," in its non-scientific characteristics, is inferior to "modern science-oriented thought" and is not an African peculiarity. Yet, he notes further, some people confuse African thought with traditional African thought, and fallaciously use that characteristic as one that distinguishes Africans from Westerners.

4. In Griaule's *Conversations With Ogotemmeli* (1965).

5. This misperception that Africans who live according to the old ways are disinclined to think for themselves seems widespread. In a generally perceptive discussion of the similarities and difference between traditional African societies and Western societies, Robin Horton (1974: 167) makes very much the same comment as do Wiredu and Hountondji, although for him the trait has another significance. In his view, "the standard justification of so much thought and action: 'That is what the old-time people told us,'" is an indication of traditional African preference for the past and corresponding dread of the future. See notes 13 and 14 below.

6. Abiola Irele (1983: 21) speaks of the anxiety of the "academic philosophers" to "remove their discipline from the shadow of the ideological preoccupations of African nationalism in order to affirm its independent, scientific character." It is fair at this point to note, as Irele (1983: 29–30) and V. Y. Mudimbe (1985: 202) have pointed out, that since the original publication of his views in French in 1976, Hountondji has responded to intense criticism of his positions by offering some clarifications. In two articles he (1981; 1982) moderates his total rejection of African thought as philosophical material (without abandoning his dismissal of the notion of a unanimist philosophy), and argues the political relevance of his case for contemporary Africa.

7. I refer here to I. M. Bochenski (1961), but there are several others that refute the notion that this sort of usage implies unanimism.

8. The suggested hubris is so alien to Yorùbá sensibilities that superstitions exist to discourage it. Accordingly, a person who shows such a trait invites envious agencies, human or non-human, to destroy the endowments he/she makes so much of. On the other hand astute manipulation of this cultural preference can be rewarding. A doctor who lived in Ibadan from the 1950s to the 1970s furthered his political ambitions by naming his luxurious car "Boys' Car" and handing the keys to any young man who wanted to drive it around. This is only one example of the ideal of possession in common.

9. Although Western intervention in other parts of the world could have been beneficial for them, Baran (1957: 141–42) writes, the manner of European exploitation made matters turn out differently: "that Western Europe left the rest of the world behind was . . . by no means a matter of fortuitous accident or of some racial peculiarities of different peo-

ples. It was actually determined by the nature of Western European . . . capitalist penetration of the outside world. . . . Western European visitors rapidly determined to extract the largest possible gains from the host countries, and to take their loot home. Thus they engaged in outright plunder thinly veiled as trade, seizing and removing tremendous wealth from the places of their penetration."

10. There is a clear difference between arguing that *Weltanschauung* is not philosophy, and saying that whatever is not written is not philosophy.

11. See Janheinz Jahn (1961: 185), and Owomoyela (1985: 4–5) for a discussion of this issue.

12. The professionals apparently wish to restrict the quest for Truth to a certified fraternity. That attempt is preposterous, because Africans would consider the notion that wisdom or the quest for it should be restricted to a class preposterous. Indeed, Africans would very likely see philisophizing as a profession ludicrous.

13. The points I have made in this section highlight the African's mindfulness of the inevitability of change, and even his making allowances for the necessity of change. These run counter to Robin Horton's (1970: 166–70) aforementioned image of the African as so petrified by the possibility of change that he cannot bear any thought of the future. See note 14 below.

14. Horton (1970: 168) erroneously interprets such recreative and commemorative occasions as expressions of Africans hankering for a golden age in the past, in contrast to Westerners' looking to the future for Utopia. He believes that for Africans the passage of time means the accumulation of pollution and declining fortune. That belief contradicts the obvious reverence they have for age, and flies in the face of direct expressions of the expectation that the norm is for people to increase in fortune, not the opposite. For example, the Yorùbá say, *Iwájú iwájú lọpá ẹbìtì nré si* (The staff of a snare ever springs forward), and *Ọlánrewájú là ngbọ́, a kì í gbọ́ Ọlánrẹhìn* (One hears only "Fortune surges ahead," never "Fortune fades away"). My view on the role of the traditional ceremonies in question are in line with those Victor Turner (1984) expressed in his article, "Liminality and the Performative Genres."

15. In the second part of his essay he details the dissimilarities between the two, making some valid and some controversial suggestions. The essay is important, however, at least in casting doubt on "most of the well-worn dichotomies used to conceptualize the difference between scientific and traditional religious thought" (Horton, 1970: 152).

16. The Kesterson Wild Life Refuge in northern California is a classic case of the scientific dilemma. The "refuge" has become so deadly for plant and animal life that rangers now have to find ways to keep wild life out of it. It became a deathtrap ironically because of the application of

scientific advances to agriculture. Love Canal and the dead lakes and streams of New England and elsewhere are also legacies of technology to humankind, as are, of course, the tons of nuclear waste that no one knows how to dispose of.

17. On January 6, 1981, the NOVA program broadcast by PBS was on "The Doctors of Nigeria"; it documented the impressive achievements of Yorùbá "native doctors" in the treatment of mental disorders, and also the on-going cooperative research in that area by traditional healers and modern psychiatrists.

References

Achebe, Chinua. 1960. *No Longer at Ease.* Conn.: Fawcett.

Apostel, Leo. 1981. *African Philosophy: Myth or Reality?* Gent, Belgium: Scientific Publishers, E Story-Scientia.

Ayoade, John A. A. 1984. "Time in Yoruba Thought," pp. 93–112 in Richard A. Wright (ed.) *African Philosophy: An Introduction.* Lanham: University Press of America.

Ayres, C. E. 1927. *Science: The False Messiah.* Indianapolis: The Bobbs-Merrill Company.

Baran, Paul A. 1957. *The Political Economy of Growth.* New York: Monthly Review Press.

Bauer, P. T. 1976. *Dissent on Development: Studies and Debates in Development.* Cambridge, Mass.: Harvard University Press.

Bochenski, I. M. 1961. *Contemporary European Philosophy.* Berkeley: University of California Press.

Bodunrin, P. O. 1984. "The Question of African Philosophy," pp. 1–24 in Richard A. Wright (ed.) *African Philosophy: An Introduction.* Lanham: University Press of America.

Cornford, Francis Macdonald. 1957. *From Religion to Philosophy.* New York: Harper & Row.

———— 1978. *Before and After Socrates.* Cambridge: The University Press.

Finnegan, Ruth. 1970. *Oral Literature in Africa.* Oxford: The Clarendon Press.

Frankfort, Henri, et al. 1946. *The Intellectual Adventure of Ancient Man: An Essay on Speculative Thought in the Ancient Near East.* Chicago: The University of Chicago Press.

———— 1956. *The Birth of Civilization in the Near East.* Garden City: Doubleday Anchor.

Freeman, Kathleen. 1966. *The Pre-Socratic Philosophers.* Cambridge, Mass.: Harvard University Press.

Griaule, M. 1965. *Conversations with Ogotemmeli: An Introduction to Dogon Religious Ideas.* London: Oxford University Press.

Hallen, Barry and J. O. Sodipo. 1986. *Knowledge, Belief & Witchcraft: Analytic Experiments in African Philosophy.* London: Ethnographica.

Horton, Robin. 1970. "African Traditional Thought and Western Science," pp. 131–71 in Bryan R. Wilson (ed.) *Rationality.* Oxford: Basil Blackwell.

―――― 1980. "Distances," *Recherche, Pédagogie et Culture* 49, IX: 27–33.

―――― 1981. "Que peut la Philosophie?" *Présence Africaine* 119: 47–71.

Hountondji, Paulin. 1983. *African Philosophy: Myth and Reality.* Bloomington: Indiana University Press.

Idowu, E. Bolaji. 1963. *Olodumare: God in Yoruba Belief.* New York: Praeger.

Irele, Abiola. 1983. "Introduction," in Paulin Hountondji. *African Philosophy: Myth and Reality.* Bloomington: Indiana University Press.

Jahn, Janheinz. 1961. *Muntu: An Outline of Neo-African Culture.* New York: Grove Press.

Kagame, Alexis. 1956. *La Philosophie Bantou- Rwandaise de l'Etre.* Brussels: Arsom.

Karp, Ivan. 1980. "Beer Drinking and Social Experience in an African Society: An Essay in Formal Sociology," pp. 83–119 in Ivan Karp and Charles S. Bird (eds.) *Explorations in African Systems of Thought.* Bloomington: Indiana University Press.

Keita, Lancinay. 1984. "The African Philosophical Tradition," pp. 57–76 in Richard A. Wright (ed.) *African Philosophy: An Introduction.* Lanham: University Press of America.

Malinowski, Bronislaw. 1954. *Magic, Science and Religion and Other Essays.* Garden City: Doubleday Anchor.

Mbiti, John S. 1969. *African Religion and Philosophy.* New York: Praeger.

Messenger, John C., Jr. 1965. "The Role of Proverbs in a Nigerian Judicial System," pp. 299–307 in Alan Dundes (ed.) *The Study of Folklore.* Englewood Cliffs, N.J.: Prentice Hall, Inc.

Mudimbe, V. Y. 1985. "African Gnosis," *The African Studies Review* 28, 2/3: 149–233.

Owomoyela, Oyekan. 1985. "Proverbs: Exploration of an African Philosophy of Social Communication," *Ba Shiru: A Journal of African Language and Literature* 12/1: 3–16.

Tempels, Placide. 1969. *Bantu Philosophy.* Paris: Présence Africaine.

Turner, Victor. 1984. "Liminality and the Performative Genres," pp. 19–41 in John J. MacAloon (ed.) *Rite, Drama, Festival, Spectacle: Rehearsals Toward a Theory of Cultural Performance.* Philadelphia: ISHI.

Wilbur, J. B. and H. J. Allen (eds.). 1979. *The World of the Early Greek Philosophers.* Buffalo: Prometheus Books.

Wiredu, Kwasi. 1980. *Philosophy and an African Culture.* Cambridge: The University Press.

Wiredu, J. E. 1984. "How Not to Compare African Thought with Western Thought," pp. 149–62 in Richard A. Wright (ed.) *African Philosophy: An Introduction.* Lanham: University Press of America.

Contemporary Thought in French Speaking Africa

Abiola Irele

Abiola Irele of Nigeria is currently a professor of modern languages at Ohio State University and editor of the journal Research in African Literatures *(Bloomington, IN: Indiana University Press). In this article, Professor Irele presents African philosophy as a search for an African identity. Europeans originally introduced the notion of a difference in kind between themselves and Africans as a way of justifying the exploitation of Africans in ways not allowed for Europeans.*

Africans in Europe and America were constantly confronted with the assumption of an essential difference between themselves and Europeans. And while many rejected this assumption, many others (both Africans and Europeans) accepted it not as a mark of inferiority but as a mark of value. Irele chronicles the valorization of this difference in the works of Edward Blyden, Leopold Senghor, and Cheikh Anta Diop, showing how different attributes ("emotion" or "matriarchy") were identified as the social manifestation of the African's difference from the European.

Irele presents various objections to the "ethnophilosophical enterprise" raised by the Francophone writers Albert Franklin, Stanislas Adotevi, Aime Cesaire, Frantz Fanon, Marcien Towa, and Paulin Hountondji. This is an especially useful survey because Anglophone audiences may not have been exposed to the work of many of those covered, such as Franklin, Adotevi, and Towa.

The final section reviews the work of Valentin Y. Mudimbe of Zaire, with special attention to his recent book The Invention of Africa: Gnosis, Philosophy, and the Order of Knowledge *(Bloomington, IN: Indiana University Press, 1988). Irele concludes with a warning against placing too great a reliance on the Western model of development and cautions Mudimbe against too great a reliance on the deconstructionist tendencies of Foucault and Derrida.*

In the introductory pages of his short book *Feuerbach and the End of German Philosophy,* Friedrich Engels provides an interesting testimony as to the impact which *The Essence of Christianity* had upon his and Karl Marx's generation of German intellectuals. Engels' testimony not only throws light on a significant moment in the development of the ideological system to which he made such an important contribution but also, in broader terms, illustrates the correlation between the political and social conditions of a historical period and the movement of ideas which it reflects. In the particular instance of mid-nineteenth century Germany, and with specific reference to the development of Marxism as a system of thought, Engels' testimony points to the realization among the young German intellectuals about the lack of a real correspondence between the idealism of established German philosophy, in particular its Hegelian brand, and the social and economic transformations that were then taking place. Feuerbach was thus an important stage in the reaction against Hegel of which Marx's dialectical materialism was to be, in one particular direction, a culmination. The full import of this reaction came then to be a profound transformation of the mental universe which would ultimately lead to a significant revolution of thought.[1]

I want to suggest in this essay that a comparable development in the realm of thought is taking place in Africa today, a development which, will, I believe, have implications for the way in which we as Africans perceive ourselves and our position in the modern world—for the way in which we not only conceive our collective historical being but also our possibilities within the historical process as it unfolds in our own time.

Put quite simply, this development involves a complete rethinking of the tenets and assumptions that have gone into the formation of African attitudes and found an articulation in the prevailing intellectual reaction to the colonial experience. The terms in which the investigation of the African experience has so far been carried on are being questioned and revised, and the set of problems perceived by an earlier generation of African and black intellectuals is now being supplanted by a new set of problems, raised by the younger generation. In other words, there is beginning to be a redefinition of what one might call the "African problematic," and this redefinition appears to be related to the changed realities of the contemporary African situation in the post-colonial era. A new perception of African problems is thus emerging, affecting as a consequence the mental processes which were implied in the emergence of the nationalist consciousness.

This development is most evident in the way the movement of ideas has been proceeding among French speaking African intellectuals. The clearest indication is provided here by the steady buildup of the reaction against the *Négritude* movement and the ideas it propagated, especially through the writings of Léopold Sédar Senghor. I propose therefore to examine this phenomenon, placing it in a perspective that sees it as an evolution, not so much in historical terms but rather as a process—a dialectic, if one prefers—having a certain coherence which derives from an immediate relation to the course of a general African experience.

When one considers the broad movement and the main points of emphasis in modern African thought,[2] it seems clear that it has so far been dominated by a single problem: that of identity. By this, I mean that, for generations of African intellectuals urged by the very pressures of the colonial experience to engage their intelligence upon the fact of this experience and to consider its implications for themselves and their fellow Africans, the central theme of their reflection has been that of self-definition in terms of being Africans. The intellectual response to European conquest and domination took the form of a long and sustained effort on the part of the Westernized elite to situate themselves anew in relation to their cultural and spiritual antecedents as defined by their African environment and to apprehend in themselves an essential African nature, supposedly obscured by the cultural and spiritual impositions of the dominant European civilization, but retaining a profound correspondence with their original sources of being.

Though often posed in these abstract terms, the problem of identity as perceived by these intellectuals was of course bound up with the historical encounter between Africa and Europe in terms of its concrete effects upon every African involved in this encounter. In particular, it was not divorced from the social interests of the rising African bourgeoisie. As the example of the Gold Coast intellectuals clearly indicates, cultural nationalism subserved immediate political and economic ambitions and provided a rationale for them.[3] But it is also important to consider that the prominence which African intellectuals have regularly given to the problem of identity has been a function of their cultural and psychological situation as a class. The African intellectual is indeed an individual at the meeting point of two cultures. It is probably safe to say that the successive generations of intellectuals who came to maturity within the colonial system experienced the contradictions of the system most directly as an intense psychological and moral tension, a tension they interpreted as a form of spiritual alienation. They tended therefore to subsume all the other concrete issues that made the objective reality of their situation—the political, social, and economic issues of colonial dependence—under the single problem of recovering a unified consciousness of the self.

We find the most vivid dramatization of this issue in Cheikh Hamidou Kane's novel, *L'Aventure Ambiguë,* whose hero, Samba Diallo, is the prototype in modern African literature of the Westernized African torn between two worlds and the conflict of values which each represents. In Kane's novel, the trauma of European conquest in the various areas of life

and expression within an African social formation is perceived ultimately in sole relation to a disruption in the hero's being and consciousness; thus, his existential plight represents the thematic focus, the significant structural level of the novel.[4] The example illustrates the way in
which the affective coloration of the intellectual reaction to colonialism
conditions, as it were, an idealist orientation in African thinking, which
comes to provide the terms of a whole discourse around the issue of
identity.

There was of course an objective dimension to the African intellectual's preoccupation with the problem of identity. Colonial domination
was not only a political fact but represented as well the imposition of
global constraint upon the colonized society; it also effected a general
reordering of life, producing social and cultural tensions that were reflected in the consciousness of the individual, and through the interpen-
etration of minds, in a collective cultural malaise. The so-called messianic movements in Africa as elsewhere attest to the comprehensive
nature of cultural resistance by the colonized. They define the more restricted form of reaction among the intellectuals, and it appears, in sociological terms, to be an articulated form of counteracculturation.

But if the quest for an original integrity of being came to dominate
African thinking, it was not only because it fulfilled a psychological need
but also because it served to answer the system of rationalizations by
which Western ideologues sought to justify European domination of
other races.[5] We know that the cultural argument was a prominent and
even central one in the imperialist ideology. It was directly from this argument that the implication was drawn as to the natural inferiority of the
African and by extension of the entire black race, and this supposedly
made its members fit to be subjugated. The myth of inferiority could not
but provoke an anxiety in the African intellectual who encountered it at
every turn as part of the process of his intellectual formation within the
colonial educational system and indeed as a regular feature of his colonial experience. More than this, the myth could not but induce in him a
process of self-exploration, touching upon the quality not only of his individual mental dispositions but also of the entire cultural and spiritual
inheritance in this African background. The implication here is that the
terms of reference for African self-reflection were determined by the fact
of its opposition to the ideology of imperialism. What has been called
modern African philosophy starts as a polemical form of thought, a coun-
terthesis, placed in historical and logical relation to the scheme of ideas
and representations by which the colonial system was sustained.

The sociological significance of modern African thought, in its preoccupation with the problem of identity as the intellectual focus of a
whole movement of counteracculturation, is thus complemented by its
ideological significance as the elaboration of a whole system of counter-

values. In its restatement of a formulation regarding the nature of the African—and of the black race in general—proposed by the racial ideology which went with European domination, the intellectual reaction of the African came to involve a comprehensive reassessment of the African universe in both its objective historical dimensions and in its inner spiritual qualities. The bent of this enterprise was clearly to give a new and positive significance to a world that had been devalued in real terms as a result of the Western negative appraisal of that world and of the race associated with it.

It has been necessary to recall these elements that define the framework of development of modern African thought in order to place the *Négritude* movement in its proper historical perspective. The special significance of *Négritude* resides first of all in the fact that it is the culmination of the process of self-reflection implied in the intellectual reaction to colonial domination and, secondly, in the particular quality of its formulation of what I've called the African problematic, that is, of a long-standing question about the place and role of the African in a world dominated by the West. The special significance to which I've called attention implies a progression in that the theory of *Négritude* gathers up into a focussed articulation the various strands of the process of African self-exploration, then ties them up into a unifying concept of African and black identity. To place this progression in a clear light, it is enough, I believe, to indicate the way in which Edward Wilmot Blyden's notion of the "African personality" is given complex elaboration in Senghor's *Négritude* and transformed into a fully fledged theory of African being.[6]

In considering *Négritude* itself, we need to distinguish between two acceptations of the term. In its first and general sense, the term refers to the phenomenon of black awakening, as a global response to the collective situation. Associated with this sense is Jean-Paul Sartre's definition of *Négritude* as "an affective attitude to the world,"[7] that is, a subjective disposition expressive of the black man's total apprehension of his peculiar situation. Sartre not only related the black man's apprehension to the historical conditions of his existence as a member of an oppressed race, but basing his analysis on the character of the black poetry in French which was the immediate occasion of his definition, he went on to give an active significance to the black *prise de conscience,* seeing in this the passage from an unreflected to a reflected mode of experience. It indicates therefore a collective revolutionary project destined to transform the conditions of the black man's existence and thus, ironically, to eliminate the need for a self-directed consciousness on the part of the black subject himself. We might say that Sartre's definition situates *Négritude* in a relative perspective and is intended to accord it a universalizing purpose.

The other sense of the term emerges from Senghor's formulation of

Négritude as a concept and can be considered a special case, a restricted sense within the general one. In effect, for Senghor, the term in its proper reference designates an attribute of the black man, specific to the race in its timeless constitution as a distinct branch of humanity. Senghor insists on the distinction between "subjective *Négritude*," which corresponds to Sartre's definition, and "objective *Négritude*," which denotes an African mode of life and values and the fundamental adherence of the black man's basic personality to this reality. *Négritude* in this sense seeks to grasp the singular wholeness of the varied "patterns of culture"[8] that characterize African societies as well as their derivations in the New World—that is, an underlying principle which may be said to define a common spirit of African civilization.[9] Along this range of references, the term points ultimately to the conception of a unique racial endowment of the black man.

There is a clear divergence between Sartre's historical conception of *Négritude* and the ethnic conception which emerges from Senghor's formulation. The point of remarking upon this divergence is to emphasize the motivation behind Senghor's thinking; it appears to be the need to differentiate the black man, to present him in his original bond with a determining structure of African civilization. The salient points of this theory are too well known to require exposition here, but we may remark upon three aspects which contribute to its coherence and give it significance.

To begin with, Senghor's *Négritude* rests upon a theory of culture. The observation already advanced in regard to Senghor's conception of the term indicates that the concept of *Négritude* is grounded in a firm correlation between race and culture. This is not to say that *Négritude* is a racial theory in the sense that it is an exclusive vision of a race and the way of life associated with it. There is, however, an explicit postulation of an intimate relationship between the biological constitution of the black race and the cultural works it has produced in history. For Senghor, culture has a racial character to the extent that culture is the effect of a total response by man to his environment, a response that involves his total being, including his organic constitution. The distinctive features of the various forms of African cultural expression derive from a long process of adjustment by man to the natural milieu of Africa; they represent a structure of equilibrium between the physical determinations of the environment and the human pressures, immediate and spiritual, upon the environment. The process of adjustment to the milieu left its impress on the African in such a way as to determine a racial character in all black men.[10] Senghor has often had recourse to certain notions of character study to distinguish the black race from the other races, to explain the observable differences between human groupings in terms not merely of their external aspects but of the common internal dispositions which they express and which affect modes of living. Whatever this approach is worth, the point remains that Senghor's theory of *Négritude* is predicated on the idea of a lively reciprocity between racial character as conditioned by an original formative milieu and the different cultural forms to be found in the world.

Senghor's purpose becomes all the more evident when we consider the second aspect of his theory, the fact that it involves an epistemology. One of the key ideas in Senghor's system is that of emotion, which he virtually erects into a category of knowledge and attributes to the African as a cardinal principle of his racial disposition. Senghor has devoted considerable attention to what he calls the "physiopsychology of the African."[11] He has sought to clarify what, in the very organic constitution of the African, makes for a distinct tonality in his comportment, in his manner of being. By identifying this element as a particular quality of emotion, Senghor postulates a distinct African mode of apprehension to which the neuroorganic equipment of the race (as shaped over the ages) predisposes the black man: a mode of "affective participation" by the black subject in the object of his experience.

It is easy to recognize here the influence of Lucien Lévy-Bruhl, but once again, the point of remarking upon this influence is to note Senghor's method of dealing with the French anthropologist's idea of "primitive mentality" by hardly assuming it on his own account while giving it a different connotation and even significance. For Senghor, each people, race, and civilization has its own manner of envisaging the world, and each manner is as valid ultimately as another. The African manner is rooted in the values of emotion rather than in the logical categories historically developed in the tradition of European rationalism, and it is as valid in its own terms as the European, hence his well-known dictum: "Emotion is African as Reason is Hellenic."[12]

The physiopsychology of the African, the result of his timeless insertion within a certain milieu and his organic adaptation to that milieu, thus conditions a distinctive mode of apprehension. That mode itself finds objective expression not only in characteristic cultural forms but also in the superstructural sphere of collective life in the realm of thought and values. The emotive disposition of the African, for example, appears as the principal factor in the pronounced mystical outlook of man in the African world, an intense religiosity that expresses a total grasp of life in the universe. At the imaginative and spiritual level of collective expression, this outlook receives an elaboration in those mythical representations and symbolic schemes which define a structure of being and consciousness. In proposing this view of African life, which also has implications for his interpretation of traditional forms of social organization in Africa, Senghor gives to his theory of *Négritude* the dimension of a cosmology.

For reasons which will become apparent later, it is important to draw attention to the contribution made by Father Placide Tempels' exposition of the so-called Bantu philosophy to the architecture of Senghor's theory. As is well known, Tempels extracted a coherent worldview from the mores of the Baluba (in present day Zaire) and attached this label to it. The crux of this philosophy is an ontology in which being is conceived not as a static notion but as a "vital force" and in which the universe is seen as an interrelation of forces within the whole realm of existence. According to this primordial scheme, everything that can be thought to exist is endowed with vital force and contingent upon certain factors that may intervene in the course of existence.[13]

It is not surprising that Tempels' theory features prominently in Senghor's *Négritude,* into which "Bantu philosophy" is integrated in such a way as to demonstrate a distinctive African form of spirituality. The attraction of Tempels' work resides not only in its apparent vindication of the African claim to an elevated system of thought but also in its providing a conceptual framework for this African mode of thought. The vitalist emphasis of Bantu philosophy ties in very well with the epistemology implicit in Senghor's *Négritude,* and its postulation of a hierarchy of forces attributes to the African a comprehensive world view which presupposes characteristic structures of mental projection. In his assimilation of Bantu philosophy into a general scheme of ideas concerning the nature of the African, Senghor's purpose is to present through *Négritude* an independent African system of thought, a distinctive African humanism.

In the preindependence period, *Négritude* was the dominant ideology in francophone Africa. Thanks to the personality of Senghor, it has maintained an ideological presence in the post-independence period, and the attacks that continue to be directed against it attest to its ongoing importance. The peculiar force of *Négritude* stems from the fact that it formed so comprehensive a system of ideas that, in one way or another, it responded to African interests in the colonial situation and thus came to serve as a significant ideological reference—in both a positive and a negative sense—for the intellectual activity of French speaking black intellectuals. We may even go further to observe that *Négritude* was the most complete expression of the African state of mind in relation to the colonial experience. The political and cultural aspects of nationalism in Africa must be taken together, in their intimate association, to achieve a full appreciation of the nationalist phenomenon itself, because the drive for political autonomy reflected the growth and consolidation of a confident awareness of the self. The specific contribution of *Négritude* to this development was to articulate, in the form of an all-encompassing concept of black identity, the sense of the African's separate cultural and spiritual inheritance.

Senghor's method, as we have seen, consisted in seeking a validation of this concept by reference to an "objective *Négritude*," of the African's collective cultural expression, as documented in the ethnographic literature devoted to African societies. Senghor's example inspired a line of development in French African intellectual activity that came to have important consequences for its subsequent direction. This line of development involved what amounts to an entire school of scholars, who, in the wake of Tempels, devoted their attention to the investigation and elucidation of traditional thought systems in an effort to derive from them a distinctive African philosophy.

The most notable effort in this connection was perhaps that of Alexis Kagame, who sought to follow up Tempels' work by verifying within his native Rwanda culture the Belgian missionary's theory of Bantu ontology. In his book *La Philosophie Bantu-Rwandaise de l'être,* published in 1956, Kagame adopted an original approach to the question. It consisted of analysing the Rwanda language in an effort to demonstrate the existence among its users of a different and more precise intelligence of the notion of being than the one that had been suggested by Tempels. Kagame pointed out that this notion was rendered in the abstract by the radical *ntu* and in its manifestations or modalities by four terms derived from it: *Umuntu,* which designated man, a being endowed with intelligence; *Ikintu,* anything without intelligence; *Ahantu,* space-time; and *Ukuntu,* modality, such as quantity, quality, and relation.[14] Kagame maintains that for the user of the language, these terms prescribe a universal order and correspond to the world. More, they represent not only an order of essences but also an order of concepts and thus provide an image of the mental structure which the language itself determines in its users. The ontology of the Rwanda is thus present in the grammatical structure and the semantic field proposed to them by their language; it has an effect on thought processes comparable to that of classical Greek on the pioneers of Western philosophy and in particular on Aristotle. Kagame goes on to claim that the Rwanda conception of the world based on this ontology is explicit, having found expression in the oral tradition of the people and constituting an effective factor of their indigenous forms of social organization and total cultural life. In a subsequent work, *La Philosophie Bantu Comparée,* Kagame recognizes the cultural unity of the area covered by the Bantu family of languages, not only in terms of their common use of classifiers but also in what he describes as "the mental organization of the symbol of ideas, the categorization of beings and whatever else exists, the conception of the world of the existence of what lies beyond.[15]

Kagame's exploration of the Bantu worldview takes him well beyond Tempels, whose theory of "vital force" he refutes; but he does appear to remain within the same perspective, for he too wants to establish the reality of a distinctive African mode of thought and existence. Quite apart from the theoretical merits of the case he makes, the ideological import of his point of view cannot be missed. It becomes even more manifest in the work of other francophone African scholars concerned with Bantu philosophy as a specific problem or as part of a general construction of an authentic African system equivalent to that of Western philosophy.[16] All this effort came in the wake of *Négritude* and reflects its spirit, its attempt to give a conceptual form to an immediately felt sense of African identity.

The same spirit animates the work of Cheikh Anta Diop, the foremost representative of another group of scholars whose activity runs parallel to that of the philosophers. This group may be described as the historical school of the *Négritude* movement. It may come as a surprise to see Cheikh Anta Diop associated in this way with Senghor, but the rapprochement is justified by the fact that his work takes its place and meaning from the same context of cultural nationalism as that in which *Négritude* was born; Diop occasionally even employs some of the latter's conceptual terms. In a more fundamental way, Diop's work addresses itself to the same problem of African identity which preoccupied writers in the *Négritude* tradition.

Diop has called his method "historical sociology," but no neat label can be attached to his approach, which involves a vast erudition and has its foundations in the natural sciences and the humanities. The range of his scholarship is evident in his first work, *Nations Nègres et culture,* which can be said to have attained the status of a classic in black intellectual circles.[17] It is easy to explain the success of this book, for it contains the most overt and vigorous challenge to the cultural argument of the imperialist ideology; its firm nationalist stand is still able to elicit a deep African response even today. As is well known, the primary objective of the book is to demonstrate the Negro origins of ancient Egyptian civilization and thus to refute the argument that the black race had produced no great world civilization; however, the discussion extends beyond an argument for this thesis to a demonstration of the continuity between ancient Egyptian civilization and the contemporary cultures of black Africa.

A full exposition of Diop's thesis cannot be undertaken here, but it is not without interest to chart the lines of his thinking for an understanding of its mechanisms and its course. It is essential in this respect to stress the fact that Diop's presentation of his thesis was in fact the intervention of an African in a debate, that had long been going on in Western scholarly circles, about the racial character of the ancient Egyptians. His contribution was motivated by a dissatisfaction with the point of view espoused by European scholars who seemed (to him) to have gone deliberately against the evidence in classifying the Egyptians among the white races. Diop attributes this point of view to the effect of racial prejudice against the black race and credits it with producing a falsification of history. An element of racial indignation thus permeates Diop's discussion, lending to his work a strong polemical tone which may not be thought compatible with objective scholarship, but which, under the circumstances, was necessitated by the force of the established ideas with which he was contending. Nevertheless, Diop does raise important issues of historical method in his ruthless assault upon the prevailing ideas, showing up the system of rationalizations by which they were constructed. The least that can be said is that *Nations nègres et culture* succeeds in reopening the whole question about the racial origin of ancient Egyptian civilization.

In two subsequent works, *Anteriorité des civilisations négres* and *Parenté génétique de l'Egyptien pharaonique et des langues négro-africaines,*[18] both of which must be seen as complementary to the first work, Diop further develops his arguments for considering ancient Egyptian civilization as essentially a creation of the black race; he does this by marshalling an array of evidence drawn from a formidably diverse range of special fields: archaeology, paleontology, physical anthropology, oesteology, classical European studies, historical and comparative linguistics, as well as the central field of Egyptology itself. It is impossible to judge the value of the evidence, internal and external, without some specialized knowledge in this vast area of scholarship. It is possible to note, however, that his examination of ancient Egyptian institutions and thought provides him with a cultural argument for postulating an essential affinity between the forms of social organization and the cosmology of the ancient Egyptians and those that appear to characterize the traditional African world. In this respect, he comes closest to Senghor, both in his vision of the African world as a unified whole and in his acquiescence with the theory of Tempels as regards the vitalist conception of the world. The cultural argument leads Diop to the following categorical affirmation:

> The identity of Egyptian culture and black culture could not be more evident. It is by reason of this essential identity of genius, culture and race that all black men can today legitimately link their culture to ancient Egypt and build a modern culture on that basis. It is a dynamic, modern contact with Egyptian antiquity that will enable Negroes to discover more and more each day the intimate relationship between all Blacks on the continent and the mother valley of the Nile. It is by means of this dynamic contact that the Negro will arrive at the profound conviction that these temples, these forests of columns, these bas-reliefs, these mathematics, this medicine, all this science, are indeed the works of his ancestors and that it incumbs upon him to recognize himself completely in them.[19]

For all the ideological flavor of this statement, it would be a limited view of Diop's purpose to see in this passage merely a simple reversal of established Western prejudices against the African and the black race. It is certainly true that Diop appears here at pains to demonstrate that Africans have had a past of great technical and intellectual achievement. Elsewhere, he makes the point that Western civilization owes an original debt to Africa through the direct influence of ancient Egypt on its early formation in classical Greece. But the real thrust of Diop's affirmation lies in another direction. The cultural argument is accessory to a much wider project: it serves to establish ancient Egyptian civilization as a retrospective reference and primordial model of African existence and endeavor. Diop's purpose is not merely to refute the theory of black inferiority by presenting the African in the image of technical man, *homo faber,* but more significantly to provide a broader perspective upon African collective experience and identity, this identity being defined not as an intangible entity of his racial being but as an effective presence in the world. In this perspective, the colonial experience itself is reduced to a mere interlude in a historical process that stretches back to an original time during the emergence of the race and forward to a creative future of new fulfillment.

Indeed, Diop can be said to have constructed a general model of history, stated in geosociological and ethnic terms, within which his particular conception of African development finds its place and meaning. In his book, *L'Unité culturelle de l'Afrique noire,* he reacts against the evolutionist view of human experience which, in the hands of Western scholars, almost invariably ascribes a superior position to the white race and to Western forms of cultural expression. Diop proceeds to a vast demarcation of the prehistoric and ancient world between the northern and southern races, using as a basis their different kinship structures. Thus, he associates the patriarchal system with the southern, arguing that the opposition is the effect of a primitive differentiation between the nomadic life of the former and the sedentary life of the latter. Diop develops this opposition throughout the full range of social institutions and value systems which he sees as characteristic of each race in its original determination. He arrives at the conclusion that the course of human history can be explained by the interaction, often marked by conflict, between the aggressive disposition and pessimistic world outlook of the northern races, conditioned by their prolonged nomadism, and the more peaceful inclinations and optimistic approach to the universe of the southern races, due to their much earlier sedentarization—in terms, that is, of the opposition between the divergent historical personalities incarnated in the two races.[20]

Few scholars would, I imagine, want to commit themselves to this ethnic conception of history, but it is essential to point out that in its actual exposition in Diop's book, it is not merely an opposition between North and South that is postulated, but in fact a relation; the manifestations in history of the two races are seen as two distinct currents, two related directions of a single universal historical process. As against the uni-lateral conception of Hegel and those Western scholars who have derived their philosophy of history from him, Diop proposes an all-embracing perspective to view the course of human development: a perspective that throws a new light upon Africa, grasped as an indivisible whole and upon its contribution to that development. As he says, "Historical science itself cannot shed all the light one might expect it to cast upon the past until it integrates the black component of humanity, in proportion to the role it has actually played in history, into its synthesis."[21]

We may conclude then that two clear moments emerge in the un-folding of Diop's ideological project. The first consists in the effort to es-tablish a historical and cultural connection between ancient Egypt and black Africa, in such a way as to give historical depth and resonance to the contemporary African consciousness. The second derives from the will to place the African continent and the black race firmly within the movement of universal history, to project the vision of a universal history in which Africa is profoundly involved.

The two currents I have tried to distinguish as the "philosophical" and the "historical" within the general movement of cultural nationalism among French speaking African intellectuals can be said to complement each other admirably, despite their divergence on certain points. Their common acceptance of a global reality of African identity, in whatever terms this is defined, and their common insistence upon its distinctive quality can be said to resolve their divergent points of view within a common vision of African existence. Both Senghor and Diop proceed by attaching a positive value to the objective difference between African and European civilizations at the moment of their historical confrontation; they take up, each in his own way, the ideological gauntlet thrown down by European racism and ethnocentrism. The differences between them appear, therefore, largely a matter of detail, or, more correctly, of per-spective, affecting areas of emphasis in each writer's effort to give body to his idea of Africa—to think through the vicissitudes of a disturbing history to a fundamental vision of African integrity.

The two currents represented by Senghor and Diop thus bear upon the same African problematic that had been created by the colonial ex-perience. It would be a simplification to say that the reaction against the trend of intellectual and ideological activity which they both represent arose immediately with the passing of the colonial era, but there can be no doubt that it has developed in amplitude largely as a function of the consequent change in attitudes and by direct reference to the new social and political realities of the post-colonial situation in Africa. The work-ings of the process leading to this development can be seen in the way the objections to *Négritude* have converged to define a new perspective upon African problems at the present moment.

The objections of *Négritude* have tended to focus not only on its explicit theoretical terms but also on what are taken to be the practical political and social implications of the theory. This double trend was established in the essay entitled "La Négritude: Réalité on mystification?"
published in 1956 by an African student, Albert Franklin, whose vigorous criticism anticipated practically all the arguments that were later developed against Senghor's theory by his adversaries.[22] Directing his critique specifically at Sartre's "Orhpée noir," Franklin attacked the French
philosopher's apparent endorsement of the image, offered in *Négritude*
poetry, of the black man as a nonrational being, disposed to mystic communion with nature rather than to a technical mastery of it. Franklin observed that such an image had no basis in reality, and even if it did, it
would not imply a fixed essence of African man but was to be seen rather
as an indication of the low state of technical development in traditional
African society—a state which could be transcended, giving way to a scientific and rational approach to the universe.

This argument has turned out to be the dominant line of attack on
Senghor's theory; it was first given a detailed elaboration by Stanislas
Adotévi in his book, *Négritude et négrologues,* which contains the most
comprehensive critique of *Négritude* so far published. Adotévi places
himself on a resolutely sociological plane from which to view the theory.
In this way he comes to reject what he regards as its static conception of
African cultural reality, resulting from an abstract schema that is out of
touch with the diversified forms of concrete life in the various African
societies:

> It presupposes a fixed essence of blackness that cannot be affected by the
> passage of time. In addition to this immutability is the idea of a specific na-
> ture that can not be confirmed in terms of sociological determinants, his-
> torical fluctuations, or geographical realities. It makes black men every-
> where and at all times into similar beings.[23]

It is not only Senghor's unified conception of African and black cultural expression that is called into question here but also the correlation
between race and culture on which it is founded, along with the biological underpinnings that are woven into the structure of his theory.
Adotévi specifically attacks this "biologism," which appears to him to be
so embedded in the ideological presuppositions of European racism as to
be no more than a restatement of them in terms which amount to an acquiescence with their negation of the black man.

As can be seen from the turn which Adotévi's critique finally takes,
the political objection to *Négritude* is accompanied by a certain radical
stance which does duty in the post-colonial context for the political nationalism of an earlier period and generation. It is in this context that
Frantz Fanon came to impinge so directly and so decisively on the de-

velopment of African thought. It is impossible to doubt that this influence has been dominant in the accentuation of radical thought in post-
colonial Africa generally and especially in the radical tone of an opposition to *Négritude* by which a significant section of the younger generation
of French African intellectuals can be recognized.

When one considers the effect of Fanon's thought on the ideological
temper of this generation, there is no little irony in the fact that the point
of departure for his entire reflection was *Négritude*—with the important
qualification that it was the profound impression made upon him by the
particular manifestation of its spirit in Aimé Césaire's work that impelled
him to this reflection. Césaire's brand of *Négritude* involves no elaborate
theory of blackness in a total and aggressive response to centuries of den-
igration and humiliation. The intense symbolism of aggression, which is
the hallmark of Césaire's poetry, not only gives expression to this affirmation in an extraordinary burst of poetic energy but it also offers a peculiar complexity of imagery which results from the transformation of a
deep structure of consciousness. Césaire's poetic expression thus becomes quite literally an affect: it involves a drama of consciousness, a
sloughing off process by which the complex of negative associations
through which the black subject has been forced to perceive himself is
overturned and transformed into a mode of mental liberation and, ultimately, of self-acceptance.[24]

This cursory examination of Césaire's poetry has been essential for
a placing of Fanon's development, because the psychological and moral
ferment of Césaire's consciousness, as revealed in his poetry, is the
hotbed in which Fanon's thought strikes its roots and issues. It is hardly
an exaggeration to say that Césaire's poetry provides the essential ground
plan for Fanon's reflection, which can be regarded as a transposition
(into ideological propositions) of the psychological processes and wider
implications at work in Césaire's poetry. It is indeed the general application of his understanding of these issues to the situation of the black man
that forms the subject of his first work, *Peau noire, masques blancs*.[25]
The book is a reflection upon the black subject's experience of himself
and of the world, as conditioned by his situation. It is, in a sense, a phenomenology of black existence. In simple psychological terms, Fanon in-
vestigates the way in which the introjection of social values is disturbed
in the case of the black subject placed within a sociopsychological field
dominated by the white paradigm. The conflict between the external fact
of his blackness and his internalization of a highly valorized symbolism
of whiteness creates a distortion of his self-image and installs within him
a profound neurosis, with repercussions upon his total mode of being.
Peau noire, masques blancs contains a diagnosis of the black condition
that is certainly more pertinent to the Afro-American and Caribbean experience than to the African, but it has a general relevance in that Fanon

offers a psychological (one might even say clinical) explanation for the sense of alienation suffered by the black man under white domination.

Fanon's active participation in the Algerian revolution widened his vision beyond the horizons of *Négritude* and provided a theater for the development of his ideas on a broader format. From the evidence of his testimony on the Algerian war of independence in *Sociologie d'une révolution*,[26] the Algerian insurrection was for him as much a political act, founded upon the moral requirements of an oppressed nation, as an occasion for the colonized natives to effect a reconstruction of their collective personality. The demands of the war, as Fanon recounts it, led to a profound inner transformation of the Algerians themselves—in the general mobilization of the physical and psychic energies of an entire people, old values inappropriate to the situation were swept away, new values created, presaging a new social order. The revolution thus took on the significance of an immense process of collective metamorphosis.

The pronounced psychological bias of Fanon's account of the Algerian revolution issues directly into the ethics of violence developed in the first chapter of his last book, *Les Damnés de la terre*.[27] It is essential to view his ideas on violence in their proper historical context as well as in the full perspective of the evolution of his thought. The mechanisms which Fanon brought to light in his analysis were first suggested to him by his reading of Césaire's poetry and later confirmed in the live context of the Algerian war. In this sense, he was doing no more than continuing the diagnosis of his first work, establishing a real correspondence between the symbolic projection and the physical exteriorization of the torment in the colonized subject's consciousness. His advocacy of violence against colonial domination appears therefore as a prescription, in the full medical sense of the word. His preoccupation with the psychiatric effects of colonial oppression, the distortions it creates within the colonized native, led him to see in the aggressive reaction against this oppression quite simply a therapeutic means of self-recreation for the colonized subject. Through the violence directed at his oppressor, the colonized subject remakes himself as a full human being, without any limiting qualifications to his human status and quality.

Fanon's ethics of violence has a pedigree within Western political thought, for Engels, George Sorel, and V. I. Lenin have all meditated upon the significance of violence in politics. But Fanon gives an original dimension to the question. In his view, the value of violence in the revolutionary situation lies not simply in ensuring the effectiveness of political action, not simply in being the "midwife of history," but in self-realization of the historical subject himself; it has to do with a vision of man creating his own identity in the effervescence of a progressive movement in history.

In its bearing upon *Négritude*, such a vision seems fully in accord with Sartre's emphasis upon the revolutionary significance of the movement, at least of the spirit of its poetic expression as exemplified by Césaire. Senghor's subsequent elaboration of the term into a concept of an African being informed by a living coherence of the traditional culture seems to have alienated Fanon. Indeed, Fanon displayed an insensitivity to the cultural thesis of African nationalism that may be imputed, not as might at first be thought to his West Indian background but rather to his cosmopolitanism. The Algerian experience seems indeed to have confirmed in him what looks like an aversion to traditional cultures to which he tended to attribute a factitious character, if not a retrograde significance. To Fanon's ingrained lack of sympathy for the cultural positions of *Négritude* was joined a political and ideological hostility directly related to his radical commitment. Fanon's sojourn in Ghana as FLN ambassador may well have strengthened this commitment, if it did not engender it. His observation of Kwame Nkrumah's Ghana opened his eyes and his mind to the contradictions inherent in the post-colonial situation, where a national bourgeoisie substitutes itself for the departed colonizer without undertaking an overhaul of the social structure to bring about a greater social justice. The Ghanaian experience can be said to have inspired his critique of the new ruling class in Africa, for a crucial chapter of his last book displays a remarkable prescience on the subject. The point that is relevant here, however, is that his dim view of the African bourgeoisie led him to discount both its preindependence nationalism and the cultural affirmation that went with it. In the post-colonial situation, the cultural theories of the bourgeoisie amounted, for him, to no more than a form of ideology, in the pejorative sense often given the word by Marx: a superstructural mask thrown over the class interests of the elites. Fanon's scant regard for this form of cultural expression emerges clearly from the following comment: "The substantiality of Negro-African culture is built around the people's struggle, not songs, poems, or folklore."[28]

Later in the same text, Fanon stresses his point with the converse of this statement: "One can hardly desire the spread of African culture unless one contributes concretely to that culture's conditions of existence—that is to say, to the liberation of the continent."[29]

Fanon's cultural ideas are linked to his radical critique of the new African bourgeoisie in such a way as to lead him to proffer a new and different conception of culture in the context of African development—a revolutionary conception which presents culture as the product of a collective enterprise involving the historical fortunes and destiny of the people. The significance of Fanon's cultural ideas attaches to the vision of a new, revolutionary humanism which he proposes, the mission he assigns to non-Western peoples "to create a new man." But it is easy to understand how his conception of culture and his wider projection into the

Third World does away with the traditional problematic of African thought, centered upon the issue of identity. Fanon transcends this issue and clears the path for a new direction of thought.

Fanon's work belongs to an established tradition of intellectual and ideological interest in black Africa on the part of New World Blacks, an interest which springs from the sense of a common historical predicament and which has created a pattern of reciprocal ideas and attitudes among black intellectuals on both sides of the Atlantic. His early preoccupation with the racial problem certainly arises from a sentiment of personal involvement, but his individual temperament and the peculiar inclination of his intellectual gifts made him respond to a new configuration of events, and that gave a new direction to his thinking. The result of Fanon's contribution was to leave the racial problem shorn of sentimentalities and the cultural issue raised along with it divested of the sublimities with which it had been adorned by his predecessors. The attitude he introduced into the debate on African problems, especially on the cultural question, amounts to a new realism; and the ideological spirit it has fostered now pervades the writings of that section of the francophone African intelligentsia which it is convenient to call the "new philosophers," represented notably by Marcien Towa and Paulin Hountondji.

The progression from the critique of *Négritude* to a new ideological position is clearly marked in the succession of three short books published by Towa. The first is a study of Senghor's poetry with the provocative title, *Léopold Sédar Senghor: Négritude ou servitude.*[30] Towa's analytical approach is, however, seriously compromised by his literal reading of a form which works through allusion and suggestion, by his fastening upon immediate denotations and missing the tense harmony of the structure of connotations in the poetic text. This insensitive approach in Towa's study serves an ideological purpose—to discredit the poetry and the theory of *Négritude,* which is assumed to be its sole reference. Towa attempts to place both the poetry and the theory in a direct and unilateral correspondence with Senghor's biography and his actual options in the real world, but apart from the doubtful value of the procedure in literary criticism, his obvious hostility to Senghor betrays him into distortions and simplifications which bear no relation either to the deeper meanings of Senghor's poetry or even to the verifiable facts of his political career. There is an obvious forcing of the radical tone in Towa's first book, and it largely invalidates his demonstration.

Towa is on a more even keel in his second book, *Essai sur la problématique philosophique dans l'Afrique actuelle,*[31] in which he leaves poetry alone to deal exclusively with ideas; the result is a remarkably coherent work whose argument ends by forcing conviction. His critique of *Négritude* is directed here against what we have called the philosophical current of the movement, the effort deriving from the inspiration of Tempels' *Bantu Philosophy* and sustained by recourse to Western anthropology as a means of demonstrating the existence of a distinctively African mode of philosophical thinking. Towa recognizes that the aim of this effort was to rehabilitate the African by a revaluation of his part, but he objects to the claim that it constitutes a philosophical enterprise. The procedure adopted by the adepts of *Négritude* in its philosophical garb consists (for Towa) in simply enlarging the concept of philosophy itself in order to include African cultural and mental productions within it. Philosophy in this sense becomes coextensive with culture in the ordinary sociological meaning of the word, and African philosophy becomes no more than an unreflective presentation of certain forms of cultural expression associated with traditional Africa, placed in opposition to Western forms and to a more strongly articulated tradition of Western philosophy. For Towa, this procedure is illegitimate from a strict methodological point of view, since it creates a terminological confusion between philosophy in its nature and function, and cultural anthropology or ethnology considered as a discipline; hence, he dubs this current of thought "ethnophilosophy." He points out the way in which this confusion is fostered by the equivocal character of the procedure:

> Ethnophilosophy objectively discusses beliefs, myths, rituals, and then suddenly transforms itself into a metaphysical profession of faith, without taking the trouble to either refute Western philosophy or present a rational justification for its adherence to African thought. (p. 31)

Beyond this terminological confusion, Towa discerns in the procedure of the ethnophilosophers an insufficient understanding of the objectives of philosophy, an inadequate grasp of its critical function in an open debate upon ideas and values. This leads him to a denunciation of what he regards as the dogmatic implications of appealing to the past to sanction African thought in the present. It is precisely here that the real direction of Towa's argument begins to emerge. The effort to resuscitate a heritage of values and a world view from the past is, he contends, irrelevant to present African preoccupations and aspirations: "An original African philosophy torn from the dark night of the past could not be, if it ever existed, but the expression of a situation that was itself in the past" (p. 35).

Elsewhere, Towa makes clear the sense he gives to this "relation to the world" by linking the cultural question with the problem of Africa's continued political and economic dependence upon Europe and with the general issue of the material underdevelopment of the continent. His critique of cultural nationalism in a situation of African weakness takes on the radical tone of Fanon: "Senghorian Negritude and the ethnophilosophy that seeks to extend its influence keep alive the illusion that Africa could contribute a 'spiritual supplement' to the European soul before European imperialism has been totally eliminated from Africa" (pp. 51–52).

Towa's echo of Fanon's cultural ideas gives them a new resonance by sounding them against a background of disillusionment with African independence and of a grim and lucid appraisal of the African situation, "For it is our deficiencies that now impose themselves upon our attention, not our wealth and our possibilities" (p. 39).

Towa's critique of *Négritude* and ethnophilosophy is thus bound up with an ideological and political position determined by a sombre awareness of contemporary realities in Africa, of the incapacity of cultural nationalism to effect a genuine transformation in the hoped for direction— of its irrelevance, in a word. The presiding idea in Towa's reflection develops with an implacable logic out of this awareness. The following passage, in which it is expressed, can be considered the most significant in the book:

> The desire to be one's self immediately leads to the proud reappropriation of one's past, because the essence of self is no more than the culmination of its past; however, when the past is examined and scrutinized lucidly, dispassionately, it reveals that contemporary subjugation can be explained by reference to the origins of the essence of the self, that is to say in the past of the self and nowhere else. (p. 41)

Nothing can be more explicit than this statement of a new mode of self perception. Here Towa is reversing the whole trend of African intellectual effort in the modern age, breaking with its entire framework of presuppositions and valuations. From this negative appraisal of the effort to affirm a specifically African and spiritual identity, Towa proceeds to a reformulation of the African problematic in terms that are more directly related to the requirements of the moment: "Therefore, as a warrant of our humanity, we propose to replace the search for originality and difference with a search for the avenues and means to power as the ineluctable condition for the affirmation of our humanity and our freedom" (p. 53).

Towa's position here implies an entirely new program of African intellectual activity, one no longer centered upon the question of African identity but upon that of our potential in the modern world. As he puts it more succinctly elsewhere: "What we need to become, not what we uniquely are, should determine our questions" (p. 56).

The complementary aspect of Towa's call for a renunciation of the self as constituted by the African past represents an opening toward new perspectives of thought and action. If the spirit of the traditional past is inoperative in the present, and if it is understood that the immersion of traditional man in that spirit is responsible for our conquest and domination by Europe, then we should seek out the secret of the power which overwhelmed us and ascertain the direction from which it came. Towa finds this secret in the European practice of rationality, the key to the scientific and technological progress which enabled Europe to master the world of nature and dominate the other populations of the universe: "Due to its close affinity with science and technology, European philosophy seems to be the source of European power; for that reason, it will help us bring about the revolution of consciousness that underlies the construction of our own power" (p. 68).

Towa assigns then to Western philosophy a practical function which amounts to its serving as an agent of development for African people after their experience of colonial domination. He is careful to specify that his argument does not imply "a journey to Canossa" by African culture but rather a total reassessment within radical perspectives of the conditions of African life, including a critical interrogation of the past. The advocacy of Western rationalism appears therefore as a tactical move to ensure a firmer hold by the African on the territory of his total being, but it implies nonetheless a revolution of being in the same sense in which Fanon had preached it—a total act of self-regeneration.

The fact that Towa is a professor of philosophy is not without interest for an appreciation of his ideas as developed in this essay, for not only does it reflect a professional concern for a rigorous demarcation of the area of his discipline but indeed a passionate faith in the effective significance of philosophy within the context of real life. This becomes even more apparent in his latest book *L'Idée d'une philosophie africaine,*[32] which represents a development on the preceding one on many points. The distinguishing theme of this book, however, is an effort to found the philosophical enterprise in Africa upon a tradition of critical thought within the continent itself.

Towa begins by developing, at greater length than in the earlier essay, his point that philosophy in its essential meaning is a critical activity, that the philosophical enterprise must be conducted as a reasoned mode of discourse rather than by reference to a general system of beliefs, ethical precepts, or symbolic constructions which, whatever their poetic force, do not contain within themselves any principle of verification. In order to oppose philosophy (considered as thought in its engagement with what he calls "the absolute") to myth and religion, Towa goes back to the distinction between wisdom derived from considered judgment and received opinion untested by reason. By proposing anew this classical dichotomy, Towa stresses the social significance of a philosophy that implies a liberation of minds and, as a consequence, of individuals in their social determinations.

He then argues for a consideration of the rational spirit manifest not only in ancient Egyptian thought—which, following Cheikh Anta Diop, he ascribes to Africa—but also in traditional folktales. The very fact that a major segment of these tales dramatizes social and moral conflicts gives them a critical function within the context of traditional life; hence, they become the mode of expression of an intelligence that constantly calls into question established value and institutions, including religious beliefs. Their philosophical value and status reside, therefore, in their function as a critical interrogation of the natural world and of social facts.

Against this background, Towa considers the general problem of the place and role of philosophy in Africa at the present time. He returns to his earlier preoccupation with philosophy as an agent of development. As he puts the matter, "The possibility for a philosophical renaissance in Africa is tied to its political and economic fate" (p. 51). Thus, projecting in schematic form a philosophy of history that derives its inspiration from Hegel, he relates the processes of thought itself to their objective manifestations and effects upon human life. Consequently, when he affirms that mind is activity, it becomes easy to understand his restatement of the correlation between philosophical activity—pure thought—and the logic of science and technological development, as well as his advocacy of Western rationalism as a means of accession to modernity.

In this book as in the earlier work, Towa's preoccupation with the possibility of an African philosophy, with the problem of philosophy itself, is commanded by immediate concerns of a political and ideological order. As he says, "Philosophy is essentially a relation between a theory and the demands of social life" (p. 112). In the particular development that he gives to this proposition, it implies a radical calling into question of the present structures in our contemporary societies as determined by the values, options, and practice of the ruling classes.

Towa's thinking is obviously tributary to Fanon's, but it has an originality all its own both in his manner of carrying the latter's ideas to their logical limits, thereby giving explicit conceptual form to their implications, and in his effort to place these ideas on a sound philosophical foundation. The marked ideological orientation of this effort makes for certain theoretical weaknesses which will be touched upon in my conclusion. For the moment, it is useful to point out a contradiction between his earlier stand against the methods of the ethnophilosophers and the procedure, adopted in his latest book, of attaching a philosophical significance to traditional folktales, simply on the basis of their critical function. It is obvious that such a value can be given to any form of imaginative expression within any culture as long as it fulfills a similar function, without compelling a recognition of its status as a form of philosophical thinking in the restricted, technical sense suggested by his own definition. It does seem, therefore, that Towa is attempting to attenuate the cutting effect of his earlier position—which, it should be noted in passing, assumes the existence of a distinctive mode of African thought, even if it rejects both the method of its exposition in ethnophilosophy and the relevance of the mode and its exposition to present African concerns. We might say then that Towa is attempting to put back with the left hand what he took away earlier with the right, a procedure that can only be justified at the cost of special pleading.

When we turn to Paulin Hountondji, we find a position that is much more uncompromising. His ideas are developed in a series of journal articles, the earliest of which appeared in 1969. Some of these were included in a volume, *Libertés,* published in Cotonou in 1973; but a more complete selection was later collected, revised, and placed together in the volume entitled *Sur la "philosophie africaine,"* published in Paris in 1977.[33] Hountondji's work thus predates and overlaps with that of Towa: their ideas coincide on many points, but Hountondji's critique is more comprehensive and his whole manner more emphatic, hence the greater impact his work seems to have made in French African intellectual circles.

Hountondji's ideas proceed from the same ideological reaction against *Négritude* as Towa's, from the same standpoint which links ethnophilosophy with the movement of cultural nationalism (of which *Négritude* is the theoretical expression). But as his various references to the movement indicate, he refuses to concede any positive significance to the effort to rehabilitate African culture. For him, the relationship between this movement and the colonial ideology it is intended to combat, reveals a peculiar ambiguity, a pathetic correspondence between the terms of African affirmation and the opposite system of ideas or representations proposed by the colonial ideology in its image of Africa. Thus, he observes,

> by desiring at all costs to compare ourselves to Europe . . . , we are still defining ourselves *in relation* to it; we make it our primary term of reference and ascribe the origin of our civilization's meaning to it. The nature of demonstration of this kind is to be essentially reversible: its terms can be reversed, transformed into their opposites, and cultural superiority can be transmuted into inferiority or vice versa, in the mythological space of an objectless comparison.[34]

The motivation of ethnophilosophy in its association with cultural nationalism renders its entire undertaking suspect: it accounts for the equivocation discernible in its procedures and formulations and compromises from the outset the very principle of its mode of discourse. This fundamental weakness affecting its conceptual framework becomes the object of Hountondji's critique, since the equivocal character of ethnophilosophy not only obscures its ideological motivation but has implications for a proper understanding of the nature and function of philosophy:

> Precisely for that reason, a political critique of ethnophilosophy could not possibly suffice; one must also provide a theoretical critique that transcends the changing practical effects of this discourse and attacks the con-

cepts on which they are based, for in the final analysis the ambiguity of these concepts explains the reversibility of its effects.[35]

One might say then that Hountondji undertakes a "critique of ethnophilosophical reason" in its conceptual constitution, a critique directed primarily against its manifestations in the work of the African practitioners of ethnophilosophy but also intended to affect the framework of concepts elaborated by Western ethnology and the value systems they imply, both of which seem to him to have insidiously made their way into the African formulations.

Hountondji's main line of attack proceeds from the categorical stand he takes against the notion of collective philosophy. His objection to ethnophilosophy concerns what he sees as its fixed attachment to the reconstruction of African worldviews and systems of thought whose common character is that they can be opposed to European ones. The collective philosophy derived in this way from African forms of cultural expression is unconscious and unreflective, merely deduced by the outside observer and assumed to be immanent in a culture and to serve both as the underlying principle of the mental processes of all its members and as a normative reference for moral and social life. Hountondji objects to what he considers the reductionist penchant of the ethnophilosophers, who throw a veil of uniformity over processes that are in reality diverse and by so doing perpetuate the image of African societies as a spontaneous adhesion of all their members to a common system of ideas and norms.

In order to illustrate the unfruitfulness of the dominant perspective of the ethnophilosophers, Hountondji undertakes, in the first three essays of *Sur la "philosophie africaine,"* a critical exposition of the ideas and methods of Tempels and his African successors. In view of his recognition of the quality and usefulness of Kagame's work, his critique of Kagame is particularly significant, for it illuminates Hountondji's own conception of philosophy. While conceding the fact that Kagame's approach shows a greater analytical rigor than that of Tempels, whose ideas it is intended to verify and correct, Hountondji objects to the terms of Kagame's formulation of Rwanda ontology and to his general perspective upon the idea of a collective philosophy. In the departures made by Kagame from Aristotle's scheme, Hountondji discerns distortion of the Greek philosopher's method—a distortion which produces an equivocal result. Kagame's attempt to derive the categories of Rwanda ontology from the grammatical structure of the language appears to Hountondji to constitute a misrepresentation of Aristotle's method, for the latter's purpose is not so much to explore the structures of the Greek language as to go beyond their factitious character and found language itself upon a universal and necessary order. It ought to be said at once that this criticism itself demonstrates a misunderstanding of Kagame's purpose, which is precisely to show that Aristotle's categories cannot be universal, since they are formulated within a language quite differently structured from Rwanda and to demonstrate, from the insight and vantage point afforded by a non-Western language, a different mode of representation of reality which is not simply inherent in the structures of the Rwanda language but explicit in its larger transformations in the oral tradition.[36]

But it is on this point that Hountondji's objection finally rests: the fact that Kagame professes to reconstruct a philosophy from the oral traditions which provide him with what he calls "institutionalized documents." For Hountondji, such a method is illegitimate not only because, by employing it, Kagame subscribes to a myth of collective philosophy but especially because these institutionalized documents themselves are by their nature anything but philosophical texts. By drawing upon them, Kagame commits a "confusion of genres"; he is merely projecting upon them a philosophical significance which they do not and cannot have. The combination in Kagame's work of analytical scruple and a recourse to the oral tradition for his demonstration results in something of a paradox for Hountondji: "This same scientific rigor prohibits one from arbitrarily projecting a *philosophical discourse* behind the products of language, which are themselves presented as anything but philosophy" (p. 30).

Again, it is evident that Hountondji's idea of a philosophical text does not correspond with that of Kagame, whose specialized knowledge of the very elaborate forms of Rwanda literature permits him to draw out of them a mode of thought that employs an imaginative key to represent the world and express a human apprehension of it.[37]

This divergence of view between Kagame and Hountondji on the proper status of oral tradition in the practice of philosophy in Africa points to a more fundamental disagreement about the nature of philosophy itself. On the basis of Hountondji's critique of Kagame, it becomes evident that the former is at pains to hold ethnophilosophy to a rigorous conception of the discipline, if it is to qualify as philosophy. For Hountondji, in effect, the assumptions and formulations of ethnophilosophy are contrary to the spirit of philosophy, which entails a conscious and explicit mode of discourse: "No more than any other philosophy, African philosophy could hardly be a collective vision of the world. It can not exist as philosophy except in the form of a confrontation between individual thoughts, a discussion, a debate" (p. 48). This requirement excludes any possibility of considering a reconstruction of African systems of thought as philosophy, of creating a distinctive African philosophy merely by the repetitive recall of an unconscious and implicit collective worldview, without submitting the elements of this worldview to critical treatment. Hountondji maintains that it is not a vision of the world that makes for philosophy, but its description, its mode of presentation; not the content, but the form of discourse. At best, philosophy can bear an African label by reason only of the existence of a body of explicit texts produced by Africans who are conscious of working within a regional tradition and of being engaged in a discussion which maintains an essential connection with the international philosophical community.

In a sense, the discussion presently under way contributes to the constitution of African philosophy considered from this point of view. Hountondji even remarks that African philosophy already exists in this sense, and he includes within it the work of the African ethnophilosophers whom he criticizes; in his view, they are in reality doing no more than providing an individual interpretation of what they take to be an African vision of the world, with each interpretation producing different and often conflicting results: "Incontestably philosophical, their only weakness was to work out mythically, under the guise of a collective philosophy, the philosophical form of their own discourse" (p. 22).

Hountondji seems to be moving here towards a formal definition of philosophy. However, in the most substantial essay of his collection, "La Philosophie et ses révolutions," he attempts to validate his conception of philosophy as a particular form of debate by affirming that philosophy is not a system in the sense of a closed structure of ideas—however coherent or grandiose that structure may be, as in the case of Hegel—but by its very nature a perpetual movement, a chain of responses from one individual philosopher to another across the ages, a progression in which the future direction of the philosophical enterprise cannot be determined, since it must keep open the perspectives of human thought. This observation leads him to affirm that structurally, in its substance, philosophy is historical, drawing its life from the evolution of a continuing debate regulated by a single preoccupation with verification, on which point philosophy shares a common nature with science. Here are his own words on the question:

> A philosophical or mathematical work can only be understood as a moment in a larger debate that sustains it and passes beyond it: it always refers to previous positions, either to refute them or to confirm and embellish them. It has no sense except in relation to that history—in relation to the terms of a debate which continually evolves and in which the only constant is an unvarying reference to the same object, to the same realm of experience, the definition of which is, moreover, determined during the course of that evolution. In short, scientific literature is historical through and through. (p. 100)

It has been necessary to quote this passage because it is surprising that, in expressing this point of view, Hountondji does not seem to have perceived its limitation. Even if we are to believe that history constitutes the essence of philosophy rather than serving simply as a contingent factor of its incarnation in Europe, there remains a difficulty. For when we roll back its process, by a kind of regressive method, we inevitably arrive at some point of departure in its evolution, and there we are left to wonder how this point, without an antecedent, can assume the character of philosophy. This difficulty is bypassed in Hountondji's discussion by his assimilation of philosophy into science, in contradistinction to mental projections of the imaginative kind. As we have seen in his critique of Kagame, Hountondji does not consider that the material with which ethnophilosophy operates—its sources and texts as provided by the oral tradition—belongs in the category of philosophical literature. The mere fact that they can and do frequently serve as vehicles of thought is not sufficient to class them within that category. The reason he adduces for his rejection is that philosophy forms part of scientific literature. As he says, "It shares the same life and evolves according to the same rhythm as mathematics, physics, chemistry, and linguistics" (p. 99).

Whatever one may think of this large claim for philosophy, it soon becomes plain that Hountondji is not using a metaphor, that his assimilation of philosophy to science is in fact a synonymy. For him, philosophy is in fact a second order of science in its empirical practice, nothing other than the form of its reflection: "Philosophical practice, or that particular form of theoretical practice that is commonly called philosophy, is inseparable from that other form of theoretical practice commonly called science" (p. 124).

The influence of Louis Althusser becomes apparent in the terminology and the turn of mind it suggests. In the immediate context of Hountondji's essay, it leads to his observation that no serious and meaningful philosophical enterprise can be undertaken in Africa without a comprehensive effort of scientific research and activity. "That which Africa needs first of all is not philosophy, but rather science," he declares (p. 124). And as part of the implication of his assimilation of philosophy to science, fundamental to all his thinking, is his restriction of the meaning of philosophy to theoretical analysis, which has for its corollary the exclusion of metaphysics and all kinds of pure speculation. It is important again to quote him fully on this:

> That sort of philosophy, that sort of theoretical research rigorously constructed on the basis of science, leaves us miles away from the concerns around which the myth of a so-called traditional African "philosophy" crystallized and evolved. It leaves us far from metaphysical problems about the origin of the world, the sense of life, the meaning of death, man's destiny, the reality of the after-life, the existence of God, mythology and everything else in which philosophical musings habitually take delight. (p. 124)

The statement here represents a frontal attack upon ethnophilosophy from within the principles of philosophy itself. It is not only a definition of the proper domain of philosophy—a definition which is, at the very least, controversial—but more significantly a vehement call for the application of a rigorous scientific method in African philosophy. Certainly a note of impatience often emerges in Hountondji's writing; it might be considered the emotional overtone of his intellectual reaction to the formulations of ethnophilosophy. His inclusion of Kagame within the trend he is reacting against appears to reveal his lack of a sense for proper discrimination, and it unquestionably does an injustice to the quality of the Rwanda priest's work, although it ought perhaps to be seen as an attempt to deal with the movement as a whole by attacking an exceptional case which, by its very quality, endorses a general trend to facility.

Marcien Towa and Paulin Hountondji meet on the common ground not only of their opposition to ethnophilosophy but also on the ground of their radical commitment to modernization in Africa. Both see ethnophilosophy as an expression of cultural nationalism that, no longer relevant to the African situation, actually constitutes a fruitless diversion from urgent tasks. As stated earlier in connection with Towa, the pronounced ideological hue of the work of the new philosophers raises a number of issues around which a lively controversy has in fact already begun. It will not be possible here to describe the details of this controversy,[38] but by way of conclusion, it is not without interest to remark upon some of the implications and effects of the countermovement they represent.

To start with, the rather preemptory tone of both Towa and Hountondji makes it difficult to discern in their work a concern for the necessary discriminations required in a debate of this kind. It is evident that Towa's attack on ethnophilosophy, motivated by a disaffection towards Senghor, has a passionate character that necessarily affects all arguments *ad hominem;* it is significant that in his last book he displays what amounts to an ambiguous attitude in relation to his earlier position on the question of tradition. Moreover, in their insistence upon the need for Africa to adopt a modern scientific spirit, both Towa and Hountondji are flogging a dead horse; the point itself has never been in doubt with the adepts of cultural nationalism. They take for dogma what is rather a general premise of ethnophilosophy—the possibility of deriving a valid alternative view of human life and experience from the traditional background, what Willie Abraham (who is attacked by Hountondji) calls a "paradigm."[39] It is true of course that reference to tradition and the past eventually acquired a moral value with Senghor and that Cheikh Anta Diop gave it a didactic significance; nonetheless, it is obvious that its essential aim is to restore to the African a sense of historical initiative from which colonial ideology diverted him.

Particularly in this regard the new philosophers lay themselves open to criticism. The implication of their position is to leave to African thought and effort no possible perspective other than a Western one. Their linkage of Western ideas and values with modernity and development does not entail an assessment of the inadequacies of Western civilization in all its ramifications—political, social, economic, cultural, and spiritual. It is not made clear in their writings why the rejection of the African past should not imply, as well, an assessment of the Western model in its objective and practical significance, a consideration of why there ought to be a retreat from judgment in regard to it. Their position seems therefore to be partial, in both senses of the word, leading to a disquieting restriction of thought and implying a limitation of the African's sense of creativity.

One is, of course, aware that this result is far from the intentions of both writers, but it is evident from the terms and processes of their thinking, especially in the case of Hountondji, that their position arises from an inflexible adherence to conventional Western canons. Hountondji's ideas on language, for example, are limited by a strictly Western conception of speech acts, and even then they lag behind the contemporary findings of linguistics; as a result, he advances views that are actually quite inaccurate. Similarly, in his latest book, Towa focuses upon the present significance of European thought, but in presenting its history he omits important details about the actual process of its development. It seems then that both these representatives of the new generation of French African intellectuals have been so impressed by the Western achievement that they feel obliged to offer it as a model for African development.

But for all their limitations, the strength of their passion is not in doubt. They are moved to take a position against the prevailing spirit of cultural nationalism by their commitment to a progressive vision of Africa. As against the noble idea of the past, which animates cultural nationalism, they are struck by the picture of Africa's present weakness. The disillusionment occasioned by present experience induces in them an acute sense of realism, which runs counter to the romanticism of their elders. They are the counterparts, in the domain of thought, of the new breed of African fiction writers, who are also disinclined to accept a complacent view of Africa. And what the Ouologuems, the Kouroumas, and the Fantoures are dramatizing in their novels, Towa and Hountondji are expressing with a relentless logic present as explicit, clear ideas.

We may discern in the phenomenon they represent—in its opposition to earlier movements, ideas, and attitudes—something of a conflict of generations. However, the more meaningful interpretation is to see it as the conflict between a resolutely unsentimental awareness of African difference (and of the real disadvantages it entails in the modern world) and a nostalgic attachment to that difference—a conflict reminiscent of the one between the modernists and the Slavophiles in prerevolutionary Russia.

It ought to be stressed, however, that the position of the new philosophers carries with it absolutely no hint of an inferiority complex in relation to Europe; there is no suggestion of self-contempt in their work. If anything, it reflects a new self-confidence capable of sustaining a critical examination of the African background. There is an irony here, for the new philosophers owe their new confidence to the effort of their predecessors, against whom they have now turned; it is indisputably an inheritance from their elders. If the younger generation of African intellectuals is able to feel unperturbed by the image of the African and the black race presented by the colonial ideology, if that image no longer wounds their self-awareness, it is surely because the intellectual and ideological battles have already been fought for them. As a result of those battles, African independence has become a reality; their problem is no longer to justify that reality but to determine what to do with it.

Finally, it is undeniable that the debate they have initiated has renewed the whole movement of African intellectual activity and given a new sense of urgency to ideological preoccupations in the contemporary context. Cultural nationalism was essentially retrospective in character, even if it involved a vision of the future; the current trend on the other hand is markedly prospective in nature. *Négritude* was and remains a limiting concept in the sense that it seeks to circumscribe an area of African being so as to mark it off from others, to define the frontiers of African identity and expression. The ambition of the new generation of French African intellectuals is precisely to extend those frontiers.

Notes

1. For a full discussion, see Shlomo Avineri, *The Social and Political Thought of Karl Marx* (Cambridge: Cambridge University Press, 1968).

2. See Robert July, *The Origins of Modern African Thought* (London: Faber and Faber, 1968).

3. The point emerges clearly from several studies, notably D. Kimble, *A Political History of Ghana* (Oxford: Clarendon Press, 1963); and July, *op. cit.*

4. See Abiola Irele, "Faith and Exile—Cheikh Hamidou Kane and the Theme of Alienation," in *The African Experience in Literature and Ideology* (London: Heinemann, 1980).

5. G.W.F. Hegel's *Philosophy of History*, in its general reference to non-Western peoples and its particular bearing on Africa, provides the most important intellectual foundation for the colonial ideology. It was on this foundation that classical anthropology sought to rationalize European domination of other races by presenting them as inherently inferior to the white race. This ideological thrust of classical anthropology found its culmination in Lucien Lévy-Bruhl, *La Mentalité primitive* (Paris: Li-

brairie Felix Alcan, 1922). For a general account of the relationship between anthropology and colonial ideology, see Gerard Leclerc, *Anthropologies et colonialisme* (Paris: Fayard, 1972).

6. Senghor made the acquaintance of Blyden's work only recently, as he admits in his preface to Hollis Lynch, ed., *Selected Letters of Edward Wilmot Blyden* (Millwood, N.Y.: KTO, 1978); however, the progression of ideas suggested here is real, inscribed in the logic of the development of modern African thought from the mid-nineteenth to the mid-twentieth century.

7. Jean-Paul Sartre, "Orphée noir," in *Situations III* (Paris: Gallimard, 1948); English translation by Samuel Allen, *Black Orpheus* (Paris: Présence Africaine and Black Orpheus, 1962).

8. The title of a well-known book by Ruth Benedict.

9. Léopold Sédar Senghor, "L'Esprit de la civilisation ou les lois de la culture négro-africaine" in *Présence Africaine,* 8–10 (1956): 56ff.

10. Léopold Sédar Senghor, *Les Fondements de l'africanité* (Paris: Présence Africaine, 1967).

11. Léopold Sédar Senghor, "L'esthéthique négro-africaine," in *Liberté I* (Paris: Editions du Seuil, 1964).

12. *Ibid.* I have translated "négro" here as "African" rather than the literal "Negro" or "black" in order to stress the fact that, in this context, Senghor's formula refers to a fact of civilization and is not intended to suggest that the black man is congenitally inaccessible to intellection. On this point, see Léopold Sédar Senghor, "Pour une philosophie négro-africaine," in *Ethiopiques,* 23 (1980); 5–32.

13. Placide Tempels, *La Philosophie bantoue* (Paris: Présence Africaine, 1949).

14. Alexis Kagame, *La Philosophie Bantu-Rwandaise de l'être* (Brussels: Académie Royale des Sciences Coloniales, 1956). Kagame's ideas were later to be popularized in Janheinz Jahn, *Muntu* (London: Faber and Faber, 1961).

15. Alexis Kagame, *La Philosophie Bantu comparée* (Paris: Présence Africaine, 1976), p. 56.

16. For a selection of representative works exemplifying this current, see the list of references in Paulin Hountondji, *Sur "la philosophie africaine"* (Paris: Maspero, 1977).

17. Cheikh Anta Diop, *Nation négres et culture* (Paris: Editions Africaines, 1955); 3d ed. (Paris: Présence Africaine, 1979). References are to the latter edition.

18. Cheikh Anta Diop, *Antériorité des civilisations négres: Mythe ou réalité* (Paris: Présence Africaine, 1967); Cheik Anta Diop, *Parenté génétique de l'egyptien pharaonique et des langues Négro-africaines* (Dakar: Nouvelles Editions Africaines, 1979).

19. Diop, *Nations négres,* p. 212.

20. Cheikh Anta Diop, *L'Unité culturelle de l'Afrique noire* (Paris: Présence Africaine, 1959).

21. Diop, *Antériorité,* p. 11. See also Lancina Keita, "Two Philosophies of African History: Hegel and Diop," in *Présence Africaine,* 91 (1974): 41–49.

22. Albert Franklin, "La Négritude: Réalité ou mystification," *Présence Africaine,* 14(1952): 287–303.

23. Stanislas Adotévi, *Négritude et négrologues* (Paris: Union Generale d'Editions, 1972), p. 45.

24. For a fuller discussion, see Abiola Irele, *Les Origines de le négritude à la Martinique: Sociologie de l'oeuvre poétique d'Aimé Césaire* (Unpublished doctoral thesis, University of Paris, 1966).

25. Frantz Fanon, *Peau noire, masques blancs* (Paris: Seuil, 1952).

26. Frantz Fanon, *Sociologie d'une révolution* (Paris: Maspero, 1966). First published in 1959 under the title *L'An v de la révolution algerienne.*

27. Frantz Fanon, *Les Damnés de la terre,* 3d ed. (Paris: Maspero, 1975).

28. Fanon, *Damnés,* p. 164.

29. *Ibid.,* p. 165.

30. Marcien Towa, *Léopold Sédar Senghor: Négritude ou servitude?* (Yaoundé: CLE, 1971). Page number of quotations are included in the text.

31. Marcien Towa, *Essai sur la problématique philosophique dans l'Afrique actuelle* (Yaoundé: CLE, 1971).

32. Marcien Towa, *L'Idée d'une philosophie africaine* (Yaoundé: CLE, 1979).

33. Paulin Hountondji, *Libertés* (Cotonou: Editions Renaissance, 1977); and Paulin Hountondji, *Sur la "philosophie africaine"* (Paris: Maspero, 1977).

34. Hountondji, *Libertés,* p. 36.

35. Hountondji, *Sur "la philosophie africaine,"* p. 241.

36. Kagame's approach to the question has been confirmed by the eminent French linguist, Emile Benveniste, in his essay "Catégories de pensée et catégories de langue," in *Problémes de linguistique generale* (Paris: Gallimard, 1966), pp. 63–74.

37. See Alexis Kagame, *La Poésie dynastique au Rwanda* (Brussels: Institut Royal Colonial Belge, 1951); and Andre Coupez and Thomas Kamanzi, eds., *Litterature de cour au Rwanda* (Oxford: Oxford University Press, 1970).

38. Hountondji's position has been challenged notably by Niamey Koffie, "L'Impensé de Towa et d'Hountondji," in Claude Summer, ed., *Philosophie africaine* (Addis-Ababa: N. P., 1980); and Olabiyi Yai, "Theorie et practique en philosophie africaine: Miséré de la philosophie speculative," in *Présence Africaine,* 108 (1978): 65–91. An abridged English version of the last named article appeared in *Second Order,* 2, 2 (1977).

39. Willie Abraham, *The Mind of Africa* (London: Weidenfeld and Nicholson, 1962).

ABIOLA IRELE

Concluding Remarks on Valentin Y. Mudimbe

There is a kind of crisis in African philosophy, resulting from the confusion between ideology and philosophy. Mudimbe's project is an attempt to resolve this crisis. In this sense, his work occupies a position relative to the critics of ethnophilosophy similar to the position of Dewey relative to Hegel. Mudimbe attempts to provide a new basis for thinking about, on, and in Africa.

Valentin Y. Mudimbe is a francophone African, originally from Zaire, who emigrated to the United States as a political refugee. He taught at Haverford College for some time, and now is a professor at Duke University. His best known book is *The Invention of Africa*. Mudimbe is not a professional philosopher, and his book is difficult to appraise, because his language is often oblique and inaccessible.

In a sense, his work is not philosophy as such but intellectual history, though certainly an intellectual history of the highest caliber. In this regard his work is, like that of Foucault, an archeology of literature. Using the antifoundationalist perspective of Foucault, philosophy for Mudimbe is purely discourse. Thus, it is not a question of deciding what is true but rather of exploring the contextual implications of the discourse. This is what Foucault means by the "archeology of knowledge." In like manner, Mudimbe is doing an archeology of discourse about the nature of African people. This archeology explores the margins, distribution, management, and control of discourse about African people and cultures.

At any particular point in time, one would then have a crystallization of these various discourses going on in society, which Foucault calls the *episteme*. Mudimbe sees the colonial background as the cornerstone of discourse centered on Africa. Colonialism stimulated a discourse on Africa that is now gathered in archives, and this "order of knowledge" legitimizes the existing system of power. As such, Mudimbe sees a homology between economic imperialism as a historical phenomena and what he calls "epistemological imperialism."

After the colonialist discourse, we have what Mudimbe calls a "discourse of succession." This "discourse of succession"—consisting of the work of ethnophilosophers such as Blyden and Senghor—is in opposition to the hegemony of Western rationality. What is premised is a valorization of otherness, a reversal of values applied to the terms introduced in colonialist discourse. What is negative is made positive. Thus, Senghor declares that emotion is African and reason is European. They account for two different modes of approach to the world, both valid.

Mudimbe's solution is to deconstruct the original source of ideas about the African. In one of his works, called *L'Ecart* (Paris: Presence Africaine, 1979), Mudimbe uses the image of getting out of an elevator that is going nowhere, where the elevator is meant to symbolize Western rationality, which proceeds without a direction. In a subsequent collection of essays, *L'Odeur du Pere: Essai sur des limites de la Science et de la Vie en Afrique Noire* (Paris: Presence Africaine, 1982), Mudimbe again suggests that the massive introduction of Western rationalism must be eliminated, the colonial father must be killed. In this way, Mudimbe advocates a kind of parricide, in which Africans must repudiate their conceptual progenitor. One means of doing this, he advocates, is for Africans to write in African languages—thereby exploiting and enlarging the conceptual possibilities of Africa's own cultures.

Following Foucault, truth itself ceases to be an object of interest, and Mudimbe proposes to focus only on the means by which truths are produced. This is why he does not speak of African philosophy, but of African gnosis—knowing rather than wisdom. Mudimbe's reliance on Foucault suggests that we should pull away from the Western system, for the West has set the terms of our discourse with it. Yet, Foucault himself is a part of the Western tradition. And the most serious objection to Mudimbe is that he accepts Foucault uncritically and does not interrogate Foucault as a part of the system Foucault condemns.

Foucault's aim is to demolish eighteenth-century humanism, to deconstruct it, to show that all that has happened is purely contingent, a fabric of discourse that could have been stitched together in many other different ways. Unfortunately, I find this to be but another form of skepticism, part of a philosophical tradition which, if pursued as in Foucault, engenders a kind of nihilism.

Moreover, I do not see that any necessary ground for repudiating Western rationality has been provided. It is not enough to say that Africans need a kind of conceptual autonomy. What we really want to know is whether the Western system provides useful ideas, and I do not see Foucault as having undermined that basic point. The project of Foucault, Derrida, and others has been to undermine, to disestablish the Enlightenment ideals of universal reason and universal equality. Of course, many have been betrayed by these ideas—by the difference between word and deed. Africans have suffered greatly from the derogatory insults of the Age of Enlightenment, but they have also benefited from the ideals of the Enlightenment. I believe we must separate the ideals of universal reason and equality from their historical implementation. We must, as it were, trust the tale and not the teller; for though the messenger be tainted, the message need not be.

Outside a rational system—and Foucault himself admits this point—there is no possibility of agreement. Each person cannot project his or her own subjectivity onto the world and pronounce reality to be what they see it to be. There seems to be no reason why Africans cannot subscribe to the notion of universal reason, indeed, contribute to it in perhaps unique ways. The idea of ratiocination did not originate in England and France. Rather, its primary source was the Greeks, as introduced by the Romans. And Sartre is no more likely to be a descendant of Socrates, or Putnam a descendant of Plato than am I or Mudimbe or Hountondji or Towa. It is therefore not obvious why African philosophers might not make just as unique and significant a contribution to the development of such ideals as have European philosophers.

There are many contributing to the discourse on African philosophy, and this is, of course, the minimal sense of philosophy. African philosophy is being created. Mudimbe represents the apex of a tremendous adventure, and it is in this sense that we must understand *The Invention of Africa.* Its contribution to the development of African philosophy manifests the original meaning of "invention," from the Latin *inventio* which means resourceful, creative, and generative.

SECTION II

Magic, Witchcraft, and Science

Belief in magic and witchcraft is common throughout Africa and is typically contrasted with the scientific orientation of modern Europe. This section begins with a much-cited article by Robin Horton on traditional African thought, in which he argues that the spiritual beings and forces of African belief systems are theoretical entities much as the elementary particles and fields (gravitational, electromagnetic, etc.) of modern scientific belief systems. In both traditional/mystical and modern/scientific belief systems, theoretical entities serve as a means of creating intelligible patterns between seemingly unrelated events. For Horton, the ancestors, gods, and other spiritual entities of traditional African thought are no less theoretical than the inert atoms and fields of modern European thought. Moreover, Horton suggests that spiritualistic ontologies may have had certain advantages in traditional settings in terms of facilitating psychosomatic interactions.

Following the view set forth in Evans-Prichard's classic *Witchcraft, Oracles, and Magic among the Azande* (Oxford: Clarendon Press, 1937), Horton argues that the primary difference between traditional African and modern European belief systems is that magical systems are closed while scientific systems are open. Many commentators have criticized Horton on this score, citing recent works in the philosophy and sociology of science showing normal scientific theories to be just as resistant to change as traditional spiritualistic beliefs. Recognizing that the open–closed distinction is not a viable way of distinguishing magical from scientific systems, Horton has in recent works proposed a more subtle analysis in which traditional belief systems appear more inclusive and accommodative, while modern Western belief systems appear more competitive and exclusive. (See Horton's *Patterns of Thought in Africa and the West.* Cambridge, England: Cambridge University Press, 1993.)

In his book *An Essay in African Philosophical Thought,* Kwame

Gyekye of Ghana occupies a middle ground between condemnation and acceptance of an ethnophilosophical approach to African philosophy. In the first half of the book, he mounts a blistering attack against unanimism in general and, in particular, the claim (by Mbiti) that Africans have a distinct concept of time. He goes on, however, to argue that there are many basic similarities between diverse African cultures, one of which is acceptance of a metaphysical framework that would allow for the existence of divination and extrasensory interactions.

In their book *Knowledge, Belief, and Witchcraft* (London: Ethnographica Press, 1986) Barry Hallen and J. O. Sodipo of Nigeria apply Quine's "Indeterminancy of Translation" thesis to the problem of translating concepts such as "knowledge," "belief," and "witchcraft" from English into the Yoruba equivalents of "mò," "gbàdó," and "àjé." It is shown that, though these Yoruba concepts are perhaps the closest equivalents to the preceding English concepts, the Yoruba concepts nonetheless have significant differences in meaning that the authors attempt to elaborate. In particular, they show that traditional sages recognize the existence of witchcraft, acknowledge that the power exercised by witches can be used for good or evil, and identify different degrees of the use and exercise of such powers.

In 1978, a special issue of *Second Order,* the official journal of the Nigerian Philosophical Association, was devoted to the topic of magic, witchcraft, and healing. In one of her articles in this collection, "On the Existence of Witches" Sophie Oluwole of Nigeria points out that many commentators acknowledge *the belief in the existence of witches* without thereby acknowledging *the existence of witches.* They know that many of their informants believe in the existence of witches without themselves believing in the existence of witches. Such investigators typically consider witches to be a reification of the belief in witches. Others, however, clearly believe in the existence of witches, and Oluwole denies that they can be ignored simply because Western science has not been able to empirically verify such claims. For Oluwole, if an individual were able to manifest witchcraft powers, then that should be sufficient to prove witchcraft real, even if explanations and causal mechanisms are unknown.

Oluwole cites work in parapsychology as a possible direction for evolving an explanatory model of witchcraft. This possibility had been elaborated by Albert G. Mosley in another article in the 1978 issue of *Second Order,* in which he argued that many of the claims of traditional magic and witchcraft could be accounted for using the notions of telepathy, clairvoyance, psychokinesis, and precognition. In that article, Mosley also presented the classical experimental evidence supporting the claims of parapsychology, and argued that Western scientists were emotionally biased against accepting the existence of such phenomena.

P. O. Bodunrin of Nigeria provides a critical response to the suggestion that extrasensory perception as studied in parapsychology is the source of belief in magic and witchcraft. His response is in line with that of Wiredu and Hountondji, insisting that traditional beliefs in magic and witchcraft as well as modern beliefs in extrasensory perception must be scrutinized and subjected to experimental verification before being accepted.

This section shows contemporary African philosophers grappling with notions that have an indigenous origin and content, and which continue to play a significant role in the life of a majority of the African population. Whether African notions of magic and witchcraft are more or less like similar European notions, and whether both can be explained scientifically by parapsychology, remains to be established. But it is clear that African philosophers are actively involved in debating and clarifying issues regarding the relationship between magic, witchcraft, and science.

African Traditional Thought and Western Science

Robin Horton

In this much cited article on traditional African thought, Robin Horton argues that, contrary to the usual characterization of traditional Africans as limited to a concrete orientation toward reality, the spiritual beings and forces of African belief systems are theoretical entities much as are the elementary particles and fields (gravitational, electromagnetic, etc.) of modern scientific belief systems. In both traditional/mystical and modern/scientific belief systems, appeal to theoretical entities is made when events occur in real life that cannot be explained by reference to commonsensical notions. For Horton, the ancestors, gods, and other spiritual entities of traditional African thought function to connect concrete events into intelligible patterns. Moreover, Horton suggests that spiritualistic ontologies may have certain advantages in traditional settings in terms of facilitating psychosomatic interactions.

Following the view set forth in Evans-Prichard's classic Witchcraft, Magic and Sorcery among the Azande, *Horton proposes that the primary difference between traditional African and modern scientific belief systems is that traditional African systems are closed, whereas modern scientific systems are open. Many commentators have criticized this view. Recent works in philosophy have shown how normal scientific activities are resistant to new conceptions. And recent works in anthropology have shown the extent to which African traditional beliefs readily combine with new conceptions to form novel syncretic unions. Recognizing that the open–closed distinction is not viable, Horton has in more recent works proposed a more subtle analysis in which traditional African belief systems appear more inclusive and accommodative while modern Western belief systems appear more competitive and exclusive. (See Horton's* Patterns of Thought in Africa and the West. *Cambridge, England: Cambridge University Press, 1993.) For a review of this issue, see Kwame A. Appiah, "Old Gods, New Worlds: Some Recent Work in the Philosophy of African Traditional Religion," in Floistad, G. (ed)* Contemporary Philosophy, vol 5: African Philosophy. *(Boston: Martinus Nijhoff Publishers, 1987) and Chapter six of D. A. Masolo,* African Philosophy in Search of Identity *(Bloomington, IN: Indiana University Press, 1994).*

FROM TRADITION TO SCIENCE*

Social anthropologists have often failed to understand traditional religious thought for two main reasons. First, many of them have been unfamiliar with the theoretical thinking of their own culture. This has deprived them of a vital key to understanding. For certain aspects of such thinking are the counterparts of those very features of traditional thought which they have tended to find most puzzling. Secondly, even those familiar with theoretical thinking in their own culture have failed to recognize its African equivalents, simply because they have been blinded by a difference of idiom. Like Consul Hutchinson wandering among the Bubis of Fernando Po, they have taken a language very remote from their own to be no language at all.

My approach is also guided by the conviction that an exhaustive exploration of features common to modern Western and traditional African thought should come before the enumeration of differences. By taking things in this order, we shall be less likely to mistake differences of idiom for differences of substance, and more likely to end up identifying those features which really do distinguish one kind of thought from the other.

Not surprisingly, perhaps, this approach has frequently been misunderstood. Several critics have objected that it tends to blur the undeniable distinction between traditional and scientific thinking; that indeed it presents traditional thinking as a species of science.[1] In order to clear up such misunderstandings, I propose to devote the second part of this paper to enumerating what I take to be the salient differences between traditional and scientific thinking and to suggesting a tentative explanation of these differences.

In consonance with this programme, I shall start by setting out a number of general propositions on the nature and functions of theoretical thinking. These propositions are derived, in the first instance, from my own training in Biology, Chemistry, and Philosophy of Science. But, as I shall show, they are highly relevant to traditional African religious

* This paper first appeared in a rather longer form in *Africa* XXXVII, Nos. 1 and 2 (January and April, 1967), pp. 50–71 and 155–87.
[1] See, for instance, John Beattie, 'Ritual and Social Change', *Journal of the Royal Anthropological Institute,* 1966, vol. 1, No. 1.

thinking. Indeed, they make sense of just those features of such thinking that anthropologists have often found most incomprehensible.

1. The Quest for Explanatory Theory Is Basically the Quest for Unity Underlying Apparent Diversity; for Simplicity Underlying Apparent Complexity; for Order Underlying Apparent Disorder; for Regularity Underlying Apparent Anomaly

Typically, this quest involves the elaboration of a scheme of entities or forces operating "behind" or "within" the world of common-sense observations. These entities must be of a limited number of kinds and their behaviour must be governed by a limited number of general principles. Such a theoretical scheme is linked to the world of everyday experience by statements identifying happenings within it with happenings in the everyday world. In the language of Philosophy of Science, such identification statements are known as Correspondence Rules. Explanations of observed happenings are generated from statements about the behaviour of entities in the theoretical scheme, plus Correspondence-Rule statements. In the sciences, well-known explanatory theories of this kind include the kinetic theory of gases, the planetary-atom theory of matter, the wave theory of light, and the cell theory of living organisms.

One of the perennial philosophical puzzles posed by explanations in terms of such theories derives from the Correspondence-Rule statements. In what sense can we really say that an increase of pressure in a gas "is" an increase in the velocity of a myriad tiny particles moving in an otherwise empty space? How can we say that a thing is at once itself and something quite different? A great variety of solutions has been proposed to this puzzle. The modern positivists have taken the view that it is the things of common sense that are real, while the "things" of theory are mere fictions useful in ordering the world of common sense. Locke, Planck, and others have taken the line that it is the "things" of theory that are real, while the things of the everyday world are mere appearances. Perhaps the most up-to-date line is that there are good reasons for conceding the reality both of common-sense things and of theoretical entities. Taking this line implies an admission that the "is" of Correspondence-Rule statements is neither the "is" of identity nor the "is" of class-membership. Rather, it stands for a unity-in-duality uniquely characteristic of the relation between the world of common sense and the world of theory.

What has all this got to do with the gods and spirits of traditional African religious thinking? Not very much, it may appear at first glance. Indeed, some modern writers deny that traditional religious thinking is in any serious sense theoretical thinking. In support of their denial they contrast the simplicity, regularity, and elegance of the theoretical schemas of the sciences with the unruly complexity and caprice of the world of gods and spirits.[2]

But this antithesis does not really accord with modern field-work data. It is true that, in a very superficial sense, African cosmologies tend towards proliferation. From the point of view of sheer number, the spirits of some cosmologies are virtually countless. But in this superficial sense we can point to the same tendency in Western cosmology, which for every common-sense unitary object gives us a myriad molecules. If, however, we recognize that the aim of theory is the demonstration of a limited number of *kinds* of entity or process underlying the diversity of experience, then the picture becomes very different. Indeed, one of the lessons of such recent studies of African cosmologies as Middleton's *Lugbara Religion,* Lienhardt's *Divinity and Experience,* Fortes's *Oedipus and Job,* and my own articles on Kalabari, is precisely that the gods of a given culture do form a scheme which interprets the vast diversity of everyday experience in terms of the action of a relatively few *kinds* of forces. Thus in Middleton's book, we see how all the various oppositions and conflicts in Lugbara experience are interpreted as so many manifestations of the single underlying opposition between ancestors and *adro* spirits. Again, in my own work, I have shown how nearly everything that happens in Kalabari life can be interpreted in terms of a scheme which postulates three basic *kinds* of forces: ancestors, heroes, and water-spirits.

The same body of modern work gives the lie to the old stereotype of the gods as capricious and irregular in their behavior. For it shows that each category of beings has its appointed functions in relation to the world of observable happenings. The gods may sometimes appear capricious to the unreflective ordinary man. But for the religious expert charged with the diagnosis of spiritual agencies at work behind observed events, a basic modicum of regularity in their behaviour is the major premiss on which his work depends. Like atoms, molecules, and waves, then, the gods serve to introduce unity into diversity, simplicity into complexity, order into disorder, regularity into anomaly.

Once we have grasped that this is their intellectual function, many of the puzzles formerly posed by "mystical thinking" disappear. Take the exasperated, wondering puzzlements of Lévy-Bruhl over his "primitive mentality." How could primitives believe that a visible, tangible object was at once its solid self and the manifestation of an immaterial being? How could a man literally see a spirit in a stone? These puzzles, raised so vividly by Lévy-Bruhl, have never been satisfactorily solved by anthropologists. 'Mystical thinking' has remained uncomfortably, indi-

---

[2] See Beattie, op. cit.

gestibly *sui generis.* And yet these questions of Lévy-Bruhl's have a very familiar ring in the context of European philosophy. Indeed, if we substitute atoms and molecules for gods and spirits, these turn out to be the very questions posed by modern scientific theory in the minds of Berkeley, Locke, Quine, and a whole host of European philosophers from Newton's time onwards.

Why is it that anthropologists have been unable to see this? One reason is that many of them move only in the common-sense world of Western culture, and are unfamiliar with its various theoretical worlds. But perhaps familiarity with Western theoretical thinking is not by itself enough. For a thoroughly unfamiliar idiom can still blind a man to a familiar form of thought. Because it prevents one from taking anything for granted, an unfamiliar idiom can help to show up all sorts of puzzles and problems inherent in an intellectual process which normally seems puzzle-free. But this very unfamiliarity can equally prevent us from seeing that the puzzles and problems are ones which crop up on our own doorstep. Thus it took a "mystical" theorist like Bishop Berkeley to see the problems posed by the materialistic theories of Newton and his successors; but he was never able to see that the same problems were raised by his own theoretical framework. Again, it takes materialistically inclined modern social anthropologists to see the problems posed by the "mystical" theories of traditional Africa; but, for the same reasons, such people can hardly be brought to see these very problems arising within their own theoretical framework.

2. Theory Places Things in a Causal Context Wider Than That Provided by Common Sense

When we say that theory displays the order and regularity underlying apparent disorder and irregularity, one of the things we mean is that it provides a causal context for apparently "wild" events. Putting things in a causal context is, of course, one of the jobs of common sense. But although it does this job well at a certain level, it seems to have limitations. Thus the principal tool of common sense is induction or "putting two and two together," the process of inference so beloved of the positivist philosophers. But a man can only "put two and two together" if he is looking in the right direction. And common sense furnishes him with a pair of horse-blinkers which severely limits the directions in which he can look. Thus common-sense thought looks for the antecedents of any happening amongst events adjacent in space and time: it abhors action at a distance. Again, common sense looks for the antecedents of a happening amongst events that are in some way commensurable with it. Common sense is at the root of the hard-dying dictum "like cause, like effect." Gross incommensurability defeats it.

Now one of the essential functions of theory is to help the mind transcend these limitations. And one of the most obvious achievements of modern scientific theory is its revelation of a whole array of causal connexions which are quite staggering to the eye of common sense. Think for instance of the connexion between two lumps of a rather ordinary looking metal, rushing towards each other with a certain acceleration, and a vast explosion capable of destroying thousands of people. Or think again of the connexion between small, innocuous water-snails and the disease of bilharziasis which can render whole populations lazy and inept.

Once again, we may ask what relevance all this has to traditional African religious thinking. And once again the stock answer may be "precious little." For a widely current view of such thinking still asserts that it is more interested in the supernatural causes of things than it is in their natural causes. This is a misinterpretation closely connected with the one we discussed in the previous section. Perhaps the best way to get rid of it is to consider the commonest case of the search for causes in traditional Africa—the diagnosis of disease. Through the length and breadth of the African continent, sick or afflicted people go to consult diviners as to the causes of their troubles. Usually, the answer they receive involves a god or other spiritual agency, and the remedy prescribed involves the propitiation or calling-off of this being. But this is very seldom the whole story. For the diviner who diagnoses the intervention of a spiritual agency is also expected to give some acceptable account of what moved the agency in question to intervene. And this account very commonly involves reference to some event in the world of visible, tangible happenings. Thus if a diviner diagnoses the action of witchcraft influence or lethal medicine spirits, it is usual for him to add something about the human hatred, jealousies, and misdeeds, that have brought such agencies into play. Or, if he diagnoses the wrath of an ancestor, it is usual for him to point to the human breach of kinship morality which has called down this wrath.

The situation here is not very different from that in which a puzzled American layman, seeing a large mushroom cloud on the horizon, consults a friend who happens to be a physicist. On the one hand, the physicist may refer him to theoretical entities. "Why this cloud?" "Well, a massive fusion of hydrogen nuclei has just taken place." Pushed further, however, the physicist is likely to refer to the assemblage and dropping of a bomb containing certain special substances. Substitute "disease" for "mushroom cloud," "spirit anger" for "massive fusion of hydrogen nuclei," and "breach of kinship morality" for "assemblage and dropping of a bomb," and we are back again with the diviner. In both cases reference to theoretical entities is used to link events in the visible, tangible world (natural effects) to their antecedents in the same world (natural causes).

To say of the traditional African thinker that he is interested in supernatural rather than natural causes makes little more sense, therefore, than to say of the physicist that he is interested in nuclear rather than natural causes. Both are making the same use of theory to transcend the limited vision of natural causes provided by common sense.

Granted this common preoccupation with natural causes, the fact remains that the causal link between disturbed social relations and disease or misfortune, so frequently postulated by traditional religious thought, is one which seems somewhat strange and alien to many Western medical scientists. Following the normal practice of historians of Western ideas, we can approach the problem of trying to understand this strange causal notion from two angles. First of all, we can inquire what influence a particular theoretical idiom has in moulding this and similar traditional notions. Secondly, we can inquire whether the range of experience available to members of traditional societies has influenced causal notions by throwing particular conjunctions of events into special prominence.

Theory, as I have said, places events in a wider causal context than that provided by common sense. But once a particular theoretical idiom has been adopted, it tends to direct people's attention towards certain kinds of causal linkage and away from others. Now most traditional African cultures have adopted a personal idiom as the basis of their attempt to understand the world. And once one has adopted such an idiom, it is a natural step to suppose that personal beings underpin, amongst other things, the life and strength of social groups. Now it is in the nature of a personal being who has his designs thwarted to visit retribution on those who thwart him. Where the designs involve maintaining the strength and unity of a social group, members of the group who disturb this unity are thwarters, and hence are ripe for punishment. Disease and misfortune are the punishment. Once a personal idiom has been adopted, then, those who use it become heavily predisposed towards seeing a nexus between social disturbance and individual affliction.

Are these traditional notions of cause merely artefacts of the prevailing theoretical idiom, fantasies with no basis in reality? Or are they responses to features of people's experience which in some sense are "really there"? My own feeling is that, although these notions are ones to which people are pre-disposed by the prevailing theoretical idiom, they also register certain important features of the objective situation.

Let us remind ourselves at this point that modern medical men, though long blinded to such things by the fantastic success of the germ theory of disease, are once more beginning to toy with the idea that disturbances in a person's social life can in fact contribute to a whole series of sicknesses, ranging from those commonly thought of as mental to many more commonly thought of as bodily. In making this rediscovery, however, the medical men have tended to associate it with the so-called "pressures of modern living." They have tended to imagine traditional societies as psychological paradises in which disease-producing mental stresses are at a minimum.

If life in modern industrial society contains sources of mental stress adequate to causing or exacerbating a wide range of sicknesses, so too does life in traditional village communities. Hence the need to approach traditional religious theories of the social causation of sickness with respect. Such respect and readiness to learn is, I suggest, particularly appropriate with regard to what is commonly known as mental disease. I say this because the grand theories of Western psychiatry have a notoriously insecure empirical base and are probably culture-bound to a high degree.

Even of those diseases in which the key factor is definitely an infecting micro-organism, I suggest, traditional religious theory has something to say which is worth listening to.

Over much of traditional Africa, let me repeat, we are dealing with small-scale, relatively self-contained communities. These are the sort of social units that, as my friend Dr. Oruwariye puts it, "have achieved equilibrium with their diseases." A given population and a given set of diseases have been co-existing over many generations. Natural selection has played a considerable part in developing human resistance to diseases such as malaria, typhoid, small-pox, dysentery, etc. In addition, those who survive the very high peri-natal mortality have probably acquired an extra resistance by the very fact of having lived through one of these diseases just after birth. In such circumstances, an adult who catches one of these (for Europeans) killer diseases has good chances both of life and of death. In the absence of antimalarials or antibiotics, what happens to him will depend very largely on other factors that add to or subtract from his considerable natural resistance. In these circumstances the traditional healer's efforts to cope with the situation by ferreting out and attempting to remedy stress-producing disturbances in the patient's social field is probably very relevant. Such efforts may seem to have a ludicrously marginal importance to a hospital doctor wielding a nivaquine bottle and treating a non-resistant European malaria patient. But they may be crucial where there is no nivaquine bottle and a considerable natural resistance to malaria.

After reflecting on these things the modern doctor may well take some of these traditional causal notions seriously enough to put them to the test. If the difficulties of testing can be overcome, and if the notions pass the test, he will end up by taking them over into his own body of beliefs. At the same time, however, he will be likely to reject the theoretical framework that enabled the traditional mind to form these notions in the first place.

This is fair enough; for although, as I have shown, the gods and spirits do perform an important theoretical job in pointing to certain interesting forms of causal connexion, they are probably not very useful as the basis of a wider view of the world. Nevertheless, there do seem to be few cases in which the theoretical framework of which they are the basis may have something to contribute to the theoretical framework of modern medicine. To take an example, there are several points at which Western psycho-analytic theory, with its apparatus of personalized mental entities, resembles traditional West African religious theory. More specifically, as I have suggested elsewhere,[3] there are striking resemblances between psycho-analytic ideas about the individual mind as a congeries of warring entities, and West African ideas, about the body as a meeting place of multiple souls. In both systems of belief, one personal entity is identified with the stream of consciousness, whilst the others operate as an "unconscious," sometimes co-operating with consciousness and sometimes at war with it. Now the more flexible psycho-analysts have long suspected that Freud's allocation of particular desires and fears to particular agencies of the mind may well be appropriate to certain cultures only. Thus his allocation of a great load of sexual desires and fears to the unconscious may well have been appropriate to the Viennese sub-culture he so largely dealt with, but it may not be appropriate to many other cultures. A study of West African soul theories, and of their allocation of particular desires and emotions to particular agencies of the mind, may well help the psycho-analyst to reformulate his theories in terms more appropriate to the local scene.

Modern Western medical scientists have long been distracted from noting the causal connexion between social disturbance and disease by the success of the germ theory. It would seem, indeed, that a conjunction of the germ theory, of the discovery of potent antibiotics and immunization techniques, and of conditions militating against the build-up of natural resistance to many killer infections, for long made it very difficult for scientists to see the importance of this connexion. Conversely, perhaps, a conjunction of no germ theory, no potent antibiotics, no immunization techniques, with conditions favouring the build-up of considerable natural resistance to killer infections, served to throw this same causal connexion into relief in the mind of the traditional healer. If one were asked to choose between germ theory innocent of psychosomatic insight and traditional psychosomatic theory innocent of ideas about infection, one would almost certainly choose the germ theory. For in terms of quantitative results it is clearly the more vital to human well-being. But it is salutary to remember that not all the profits are on one side.

[3] Robin Horton, 'Destiny and the Unconscious in West Africa', *Africa* XXXI, 2, 1961, pp. 110–16.

From what has been said in this section, it should be clear that one commonly accepted way of contrasting traditional religious thought with scientific thought is misleading. I am thinking here of the contrast between traditional religious thought as "non-empirical" with scientific thought as "empirical." In the first place, the contrast is misleading because traditional religious thought is no more nor less interested in the natural causes of things than is the theoretical thought of the sciences. Indeed, the intellectual function of its supernatural beings (as, too, that of atoms, waves, etc.) *is* the extension of people's vision of natural causes. In the second place, the contrast is misleading because traditional religious theory clearly does more than postulate causal connexions that bear no relation to experience. Some of the connexions it postulates are, by the standards of modern medical science, almost certainly real ones. To some extent, then, it successfully grasps reality.

I am not claiming traditional thought as a variety of scientific thought. In certain crucial respects, the two kinds of thought are related to experience in quite different ways, but it is not only where scientific method is in use that we find theories which both aim at grasping causal connexions and to some extent succeed in this aim. Scientific method is undoubtedly the surest and most efficient tool for arriving at beliefs that are successful in this respect; but it is not the only way of arriving at such beliefs. Given the basic process of theory-making, and an environmental stability which gives theory plenty of time to adjust to experience, a people's belief system may come, even in the absence of scientific method, to grasp at least some significant causal connexions which lie beyond the range of common sense. It is because traditional African religious beliefs demonstrate the truth of this that it seems apt to extend to them the label "empirical."

3. Common Sense and Theory Have Complementary Roles in Everyday Life

In the history of European thought there has often been opposition to a new theory on the ground that it threatens to break up and destroy the old, familiar world of common sense. Such was the eighteenth-century opposition to Newtonian corpuscular theory, which, so many people thought, was all set to "reduce" the warm, colourful beautiful world to a lifeless, colourless, wilderness of rapidly moving little balls. Not surprisingly, this eighteenth-century attack was led by people like Goethe and Blake—poets whose job was precisely to celebrate the glories of the world of common sense. Such, again, is the twentieth-century opposition to Behaviour Theory, which many people see as a threat to "reduce" human beings to animals or even to machines. Much recent Western Philosophy is a monotonous and poorly reasoned attempt to bludgeon us into believing that Behaviour Theory cannot possibly work. But just as the common-sense world of things and people remained remarkably un-scathed by the Newtonian revolution, so there is reason to think it will not be too seriously touched by the Behaviour-Theory revolution. In-deed, a lesson of the history of European thought is that, while theories come and theories go, the world of common sense remains very little changed.

One reason for this is perhaps that all theories take their departure from the world of things and people, and ultimately return us to it. In this context, to say that a good theory "reduces" something to something else is misleading. Ideally, a process of deduction from the premises of a theory should lead us back to statements which portray the common-sense world in its full richness. In so far as this richness is not restored, by so much does theory fail. Another reason for the persistence of the world of common sense is probably that, within the limits discussed in the last section, common-sense thinking is handier and more economical than theoretical thinking. It is only when one needs to transcend the lim-ited causal vision of common sense that one resorts to theory.

Take the example of an industrial chemist and his relationships with common salt. When he uses it in the house, his relationships with it are governed entirely by common sense. Invoking chemical theory to guide him in its domestic use would be like bringing up a pile-driver to hammer in a nail. Such theory may well lend no more colour to the chemist's domestic view of salt than it lends to the chemically unedu-cated rustic's view of the substance. When he uses it in his chemical fac-tory, however, common sense no longer suffices. The things he wants to do with it force him to place it in a wider causal context than common sense provides; and he can only do this by viewing it in the light of atomic theory. At this point, someone may ask: "And which does he think is the real salt; the salt of common sense or the salt of theory?" The answer, perhaps, is that both are equally real to him. For whatever the philosophers say, people develop a sense of reality about something to the extent that they use and act on language which implies that this something exists.

This discussion of common sense and theory in Western thought is very relevant to the understanding of traditional African religions. Early accounts of such religions stressed the ever-presence of the spirit world in the minds of men. Later on, fieldwork experience in African societies convinced most reporters that members of such societies attended to the spirit world rather intermittently.[4] Many modern criticisms of Lévy-Bruhl and other early theorists hinge on this observation. For the modern

---

[4] See for instance E. E. Evans-Pritchard, *Theories of Primitive Religion,* Oxford 1965, p. 88.

generation of social anthropologists, the big question has now become: "On what kinds of occasion do people ignore the spirit world, and on what kinds of occasion do they attend to it?"

In answer we need to recognize the essentially theoretical character of traditional religious thinking. And here our discussion of common sense and theory in European thought becomes relevant.

I suggest that in traditional Africa relations between common sense and theory are essentially the same as they are in Europe. That is, common sense is the handier and more economical tool for coping with a wide range of circumstances in everyday life. Nevertheless, there are certain circumstances that can only be coped with in terms of a wider causal vision than common sense provides. And in these circumstances there is a jump to theoretical thinking.

Let me give an example drawn from my own fieldwork among the Kalabari people of the Niger Delta. Kalabari recognize many different kinds of diseases, and have an array of herbal specifics with which to treat them. Sometimes a sick person will be treated by ordinary members of his family who recognize the disease and know the specifics. Sometimes the treatment will be carried out on the instructions of a native doctor. When sickness and treatment follow these lines the atmosphere is basically commonsensical. Often, there is little or no reference to spiritual agencies.

Sometimes, however, the sickness does not respond to treatment, and it becomes evident that the herbal specific used does not provide the whole answer. The native doctor may rediagnose and try another specific. But if this produces no result the suspicion will arise that "there is something else in this sickness." In other words, the perspective provided by common sense is too limited. It is at this stage that a diviner is likely to be called in (it may be the native doctor who started the treatment). Using ideas about various spiritual agencies, he will relate the sickness to a wider range of circumstances—often to disturbances in the sick man's general social life.

What we are describing here is generally referred to as a jump from common sense to mystical thinking. But, as we have seen, it is also, more significantly, a jump from common sense to theory. And here, as in Europe, the jump occurs at the point where the limited causal vision of common sense curtails its usefulness in dealing with the situation on hand.

4. Level of Theory Varies with Context

A person seeking to place some event in a wider causal context often has a choice of theories. Like the initial choice between common sense and theory, this choice too will depend on just how wide a context he wishes to bring into consideration. Where he is content to place the event in a relatively modest context, he will be content to use what is generally called a low-level theory—i.e. one that covers a relatively limited area of experience. Where he is more ambitious about context, he will make use of a higher-level theory—i.e. one that covers a larger area of experience. As the area covered by the lower-level theory is part of the area covered by the higher-level scheme, so too the entities postulated by the lower-level theory are seen as special manifestations of those postulated at the higher level. Hence they pose all the old problems of things which are at once themselves and at the same time manifestations of other quite different things.

It is typical of traditional African religious systems that they include, on the one hand, ideas about a multiplicity of spirits, and on the other hand, ideas about a single supreme being. Though the spirits are thought of as independent beings, they are also considered as so many manifestations of dependants of the supreme being. This conjunction of the many and the one has given rise to much discussion among students of comparative religion, and has evoked many ingenious theories. Most of these have boggled at the idea that polytheism and monotheism could coexist stably in a single system of thought. They have therefore tried to resolve the problem by supposing that the belief-systems in question are in transition from one type to the other. It is only recently, with the Nilotic studies of Evans-Pritchard and Lienhardt,[5] that the discussion has got anywhere near the point—which is that the many spirits and the one God play complementary roles in people's thinking. As Evans-Pritchard says: "A theistic religion need be neither monotheistic nor polytheistic. It may be both. It is the question of the level, or situation, of thought, rather than of exclusive types of thought."[6]

On the basis of material from the Nilotic peoples, and on that of material from such West African societies as Kalabari, Ibo, and Tallensi,[7] one can make a tentative suggestion about the respective roles of the many and the one in traditional African thought generally. In such thought, I suggest, the spirits provide the means of setting an event within a relatively limited causal context. They are the basis of a theoretical scheme which typically covers the thinker's own community and immediate environment. The supreme being, on the other hand, provides

---

[5] E. E. Evans-Pritchard, *Nuer Religion,* Oxford, 1956; Godfrey Lienhardt, *Divinity and Experience: The Religion of the Dinka,* London, 1961.

[6] Evans-Pritchard, op. cit., p. 316.

[7] Robin Horton, "The Kalabari World-View: An Outline and Interpretation," *Africa,* XXXII, 3, 1962, pp. 197–220; "A Hundred Years of Change in Kalabari Religion" (Unpublished paper for the University of Ife Conference on "The High God in Africa," December 1964); "God, Man, and the Land in a Northern Ibo Village Group," *Africa* XXVI, 1, 1956, pp. 17–28; M. Fortes, *The Web of Kinship among the Tallensi,* London, 1949, esp. pp. 21–22 and 219.

the means of setting an event within the widest possible context. For it is the basis of a theory of the origin and life course of the world seen as a whole.

In many (though by no means all) traditional African belief-systems, ideas about the spirits and actions based on such ideas are far more richly developed than ideas about the supreme being and actions based on them. In these cases, the idea of God seems more the pointer to a potential theory than the core of a seriously operative one. This perhaps is because social life in the communities involved is so parochial that their members seldom have to place events in the wider context that the idea of the supreme being purports to deal with. Nevertheless, the different levels of thinking are there in all these systems. It seems clear that they are related to one another in much the same way as are the different levels of theoretical thinking in the sciences. At this point the relation between the many spirits and the one God loses much of its aura of mystery. Indeed there turns out to be nothing peculiarly religious or "mystical" about it. For it is essentially the same as the relation between the homogeneous atoms and planetary systems of fundamental particles in the thinking of a chemist. It is a by-product of certain very general features of the way theories are used in explanation.

5. All Theory Breaks up the Unitary Objects of Common Sense into Aspects, Then Places the Resulting Elements in a Wider Causal Context. That Is, It First Abstracts and Analyses, Then Re-integrates

Commentators on scientific method have familiarized us with the way in which the theoretical schemas of the sciences break up the world of common-sense things in order to achieve a causal understanding which surpasses that of common sense. But it is only from the more recent studies of African cosmologies, where religious beliefs are shown in the context of the various everyday contingencies they are invoked to explain, that we have begun to see how traditional religious thought also operates by a similar process of abstraction, analysis, and reintegration. A good example is provided by Fortes's recent work on West African theories of the individual and his relation to society. Oldfashioned West African ethnographers showed the wide distribution of beliefs in what they called "multiple souls." They found that many West African belief-systems invested the individual with a multiplicity of spiritual agencies. The general impression they gave was one of an unruly fantasy at work. In his recent book,[8] however, Fortes takes the "multiple soul" beliefs of a single West African people (the Tallensi) and places them in the context

---

[8] Fortes, op. cit.

of everyday thought and behaviour. His exposition dispels much of the aura of fantasy.

Fortes describes three categories of spiritual agency especially concerned with the Tale individual. First comes the *segr*, which presides over the individual as a biological entity—over his sickness and health, his life and death. Then comes the *nuor yin*, a personification of the wishes expressed by the individual before his arrival on earth. The *nuor yin* appears specifically concerned with whether or not the individual has the personality traits necessary if he is to become an adequate member of Tale society. As Fortes puts it, evil *nuor yin* "serves to identify the fact of irremediable failure in the development of the individual to full social capacity." Good *nuor yin*, on the other hand, "identifies the fact of successful individual development along the road to full incorporation in society." Finally, in this trio of spiritual agencies, we have what Fortes calls the "*yin* ancestors." These are two or three out of the individual's total heritage of ancestors, who have been delegated to preside over his personal fortunes. *Yin* ancestors only attach themselves to an individual who has a good *nuor yin*. They are concerned with the fortunes of the person who has already proved himself to have the basic equipment for fitting into Tale society. Here we have a theoretical scheme which, in order to produce a deeper understanding of the varying fortunes of individuals in their society, breaks them down into three aspects by a simple but typical operation of abstraction and analysis.

Perhaps the most significant comment on Fortes' work in this field was pronounced, albeit involuntarily, by a reviewer of "Oedipus and Job."[9] "If any criticism of the presentation is to be made it is that Professor Fortes sometimes seems to achieve an almost mystical identification with the Tallensi world-view and leaves the unassimilated reader in some doubt about where to draw the line between Tallensi notions and Cambridge concepts!" Now the anthropologist has to find *some* concepts in his own language roughly appropriate to translating the "notions" of the people he studies. And in the case in question, perhaps only the lofty analytic "Cambridge" concepts did come anywhere near to congruence with Tallensi notions. This parallel between traditional African religious "notions" and Western sociological "abstractions" is by no means an isolated phenomenon. Think for instance of individual guardian spirits and group spirits—two very general categories of traditional African religious thought. Then think of those hardy Parsonian abstractions—psychological imperatives and sociological imperatives. It takes no great brilliance to see the resemblance.[10]

---

[9] R. E. Bradbury in *Man*, September 1959.

[10] Such parallels arouse the more uncomfortable thought that in all the theorizing we sociologists have done about the working of traditional African societies, we may often have done little more than translate indigenous African theories about such workings.

6. In Evolving a Theoretical Scheme, the Human Mind Seems Constrained to Draw Inspiration from Analogy between the Puzzling Observations to Be Explained and Certain Already Familiar Phenoma

In the genesis of a typical theory, the drawing of an analogy between the unfamiliar and the familiar is followed by the making of a model in which something akin to the familiar is postulated as the reality underlying the unfamiliar. Both modern Western and traditional African thought-products amply demonstrate the truth of this. Whether we look amongst atoms, electrons, and waves, or amongst gods, spirits, and entelechies, we find that theoretical notions nearly always have their roots in relatively homely everyday experiences, in analogies with the familiar.

What do we mean here by "familiar phenomena"? Above all, I suggest, we mean phenomena strongly associated in the mind of the observer with order and regularity. That theory should depend on analogy with things familiar in this sense follows from the very nature of explanation. Since the overriding aim of explanation is to disclose order and regularity underlying apparent chaos, the search for explanatory analogies must tend towards those areas of experience most closely associated with such qualities. Here, I think, we have a basis for indicating why explanations in modern Western culture tend to be couched in an impersonal idiom, while explanations in traditional African society tend to be couched in a personal idiom.

In complex, rapidly changing industrial societies the human scene is in flux. Order, regularity, predictability, simplicity, all these seem lamentably absent. It is in the world of inanimate things that such qualities are most readily seen. This is why many people can find themselves less at home with their fellow men than with things. And this too, I suggest, is why the mind in quest of explanatory analogies turns most readily to the inanimate. In the traditional societies of Africa, we find the situation reversed. The human scene is the locus *par excellence* of order, predictability, regularity. In the world of the inanimate, these qualities are far less evident. Here, being less at home with people than with things is unimaginable. And here, the mind in quest of explanatory analogies turns naturally to people and their relations.

7. Where Theory Is Founded on Analogy Between Puzzling Observations and Familiar Phenomena, It Is Generally Only a Limited Aspect of such Phenomena that Is Incorporated into the Resulting Model

Philosophers of science have often used the molecular (kinetic) theory of gases as an illustration of this feature of model-building. The molecular theory, of course, is based on an analogy with the behavior of fast-moving, spherical balls in various kinds of space. And the philosophers have pointed out that although many important properties of such balls have been incorporated into the definition of a molecule, other important properties such as colour and temperature have been omitted. They have been omitted because they have no explanatory function in relation to the observations that originally evoked the theory. Here, of course, we have another sense in which physical theory is based upon abstraction and abstract ideas. For concepts such as "molecule," "atom," "electron," "wave" are the result of a process in which the relevant features of certain prototype phenomena have been abstracted from the irrelevant features.

Many writers have considered this sort of abstraction to be one of the distinctive features of scientific thinking. But this, like so many other such distinctions, is a false one; for just the same process is at work in traditional African thought. Thus when traditional thought draws upon people and their social relations as the raw material of its theoretical models, it makes use of some dimensions of human life and neglects others. The definition of a god may omit any reference to his physical appearance, his diet, his mode of lodging, his children, his relations with his wives, and so on. Asking questions about such attributes is as inappropriate as asking questions about the colour of a molecule or the temperature of an electron. It is this omission of many dimensions of human life from the definition of the gods which gives them that rarefied, attenuated aura which we call "spiritual." But there is nothing peculiarly religious, mystical, or traditional about this "spirituality." It is the result of the same process of abstraction as the one we see at work in Western theoretical models: the process whereby features of the prototype phenomena which have explanatory relevance are incorporated into a theoretical schema, while features which lack such relevance are omitted.

8. A Theoretical Model, Once Built, Is Developed in Ways which Sometimes Obscure the Analogy on Which It Was Founded

In its raw, initial state, a model may come up quite quickly against data for which it cannot provide any explanatory coverage. Rather than scrap it out of hand, however, its users will tend to give it successive modifications in order to enlarge its coverage. Sodmetimes, such modifications will involve the drawing of further analogies with phenomena rather different from those which provided the initial inspiration for the model. Sometimes, they will merely involve "tinkering" with the model until it comes to fit the new observations. By comparison with the phenomena which provided its original inspiration, such a developed model not unnaturally seems to have a bizarre, hybrid air about it.

Examples of the development of theoretical models abound in the history of science. One of the best documented of these is provided by the modern atomic theory of matter. The foundations of this theory were laid by Rutherford, who based his original model upon an analogy between the passage of ray-beams through metal foil and the passage of comets through our planetary system. Rutherford's planetary model of the basic constituents of matter proved extremely useful in explanation. When it came up against recalcitrant data, therefore, the consensus of scientists was in favour of developing it rather than scrapping it. Each of several modifications of the model was a response to the demand for increased explanatory coverage. Each, however, removed the theoretical model one step further away from the familiar phenomena which had furnished its original inspiration.

In studying traditional African thought, alas, we scarcely ever have the historical depth available to the student of European thought. So we can make few direct observations on the development of its theoretical models. Nevertheless, these models often show just the same kinds of bizarre, hybrid features as the models of the scientists. Since they resemble the latter in so many other ways, it seems reasonable to suppose that these features are the result of a similar process of development in response to demands for further explanatory coverage. The validity of such a supposition is strengthened when we consider detailed instances: for these show how the bizarre features of particular models are indeed closely related to the nature of the observations that demand explanation.

Let me draw one example from my own field-work on Kalabari religious thought which I have outlined in earlier publications. Basic Kalabari religious beliefs involve three main categories of spirits: ancestors, heroes, and water-people. On the one hand, all three categories of spirits show many familiar features: emotions of pleasure and anger, friendships, enmities, marriages. Such features betray the fact that, up to a point, the spirits are fashioned in the image of ordinary Kalabari people. Beyond this point, however, they are bizarre in many ways. The ancestors, perhaps, remain closest to the image of ordinary people. But the heroes are decidedly odd. They are defined as having left no descendants, as having disappeared rather than died, and as having come in the first instance from outside the community. The water-spirits are still odder. They are said to be "like men, and also like pythons." To make sense of these oddities, let us start by sketching the relations of the various kinds of spirits to the world of everyday experience.

First, the ancestors. These are postulated as the forces underpinning the life and strength of the lineages, bringing misfortune to those who betray lineage values and fortune to those who promote them. Second, the heroes. These are the forces underpinning the life and strength of the community and its various institutions. They are also the forces underpinning human skill and maintaining its efficacy in the struggle against nature. Third, the water-spirits. On the one hand, these are the "owners" of the creeks and swamps, the guardians of the fish harvest, the forces of nature. On the other hand, they are the patrons of human individualism—in both its creative and its destructive forms. In short, they are the forces underpinning all that lies beyond the confines of the established social order.

We can look on ancestors, heroes, and water-spirits as the members of a triangle of forces. In this triangle, the relation of each member to the other two contains elements of separation and opposition as well as of co-operation. Thus by supporting lineages in rivalry against one another, the ancestors can work against the heroes in sapping the strength of the community; but in other contexts, by strengthening their several lineages, they can work with the heroes in contributing to village strength. Again, when they bring up storms, rough water, and sharks, the water-spirits work against the heroes by hampering the exercise of the village's productive skills; but when they produce calm water and an abundance of fish, they work just as powerfully with the heroes. Yet again, by fostering anti-social activity, the water-spirits can work against both heroes and ancestors; or, by supporting creativity and invention, they can enrich village life and so work with them.

In this triangle, then, we have a theoretical scheme in terms of which Kalabari can grasp and comprehend most of the many vicissitudes of their daily lives. Now it is at this point that the bizarre, paradoxical attributes of heroes and water-spirits begin to make sense: for a little inspection shows that such attributes serve to define each category of spirits in a way appropriate to its place in the total scheme. This is true, for example, of such attributes of the heroes as having left no human descendants, having disappeared instead of undergoing death and burial, and having come from outside the community. All these serve effectively to define the heroes as forces quite separate from the ancestors with their kinship involvements. Lack of descendants does this in an obvious way. Disappearance rather than death and burial performs the same function, especially when, as in Kalabari, lack of burial is almost synonymous with lack of kin. And arrival from outside the community again makes it clear that they cannot be placed in any lineage or kinship context. These attributes, in short, are integral to the definition of the heroes as forces contrasted with and potentially opposed to the ancestors. Again, the water-spirits are said to be "like men, and also like pythons"; and here too the paradoxical characterization is essential to defining their place in the triangle. The python is regarded as the most powerful of all the animals in the creeks, and is often said to be their father. But its power is seen as something very different from that of human beings—something "fearful" and "astonishing." The combination of human and python elements in the characterization of the water-people fits the latter perfectly for their own place in the triangle—as forces of the extra-social contrasted with and potentially opposed to both heroes and ancestors.

Another illuminating example of the theoretical significance of oddity is provided by Middleton's account of traditional Lugbara religious concepts.[11] According to Middleton, Lugbara belief features two main categories of spiritual agency—the ancestors and the *adro* spirits. Like the Kalabari ancestors, those of the Lugbara remain close to the image of ordinary people. The *adro,* however, are very odd indeed. They are cannibalistic and incestuous, and almost everything else that Lugbara ordinarily consider repulsive. They are commonly said to walk upside down—a graphic expression of their general perversity. Once again, these oddities fall into place when we look at the relations of the two categories of spirits to the world of experience. The ancestors, on the one hand, account for the settled world of human habitation and with the established social order organized on the basis of small lineages. The *adro,* on the other hand, are concerned with the uncultivated bush, and with all human activities which run counter to the established order of things. Like the Kalabari water-spirits, they are forces of the extra-social, whether in its natural or its human form. The contrast and opposition between ancestors and *adro* thus provides Lugbara with a theoretical schema in terms of which they can comprehend a whole series of oppositions and conflicts manifest in the world of their everyday experiences. Like the oddities of the Kalabari gods, those of the *adro* begin to make sense at this point. For it is the bizarre, perverse features of these spirits that serve to define their position in the theory—as forces contrasted with and opposed to the ancestors.

In both of these cases the demands of explanation result in a model whose structure is hybrid between that of the human social phenomena which provided its original inspiration, and that of the field of experience to which it is applied. In both cases, oddity is essential to explanatory function. Even in the absence of more direct historical evidence, these examples suggest that the theoretical models of traditional African thought are the products of developmental processes comparable to those affecting the models of the sciences.

In treating traditional African religious systems as theoretical models akin to those of the sciences, I have really done little more than take them at their face value. Although this approach may seem naïve and platitudinous compared to the sophisticated "things-are-never-what-they-seem" attitude more characteristic of the social anthropologist, it has certainly produced some surprising results. Above all, it has cast doubt on most of the well-worn dichotomies used to conceptualize the difference

---

[11] John Middleton, *Lugbara Religion: Ritual and Authority among an East African People,* London, 1960.

between scientific and traditional religious thought. Intellectual versus emotional; rational versus mystical; reality-oriented versus fantasy-oriented; causally oriented versus supernaturally oriented; empirical versus non-empirical; abstract versus concrete; analytical versus non-analytical: all of these are shown to be more or less inappropriate. If the reader is disturbed by this casting away of established distinctions, he will, I hope, accept it when he sees how far it can pave the way towards making sense of so much that previously appeared senseless.

One thing that may well continue to bother the reader is my playing down of the difference between non-personal and personal theory. For while I have provided what seems to me an adequate explanation of this difference, I have treated it as a surface difference concealing an underlying similarity of intellectual process. I must confess that I have used brevity of treatment here as a device to play down the gulf between the two kinds of theory. But I think this is amply justifiable in reaction to the more usual state of affairs, in which the difference is allowed to dominate all other features of the situation. Even familiarity with theoretical thinking in their own culture cannot help anthropologists who are dominated by this difference. For once so blinded, they can only see traditional religious thought as wholly other. With the bridge from their own thought-patterns to those of traditional Africa blocked, it is little wonder they can make no further headway.

The aim of my exposition has been to reopen this bridge. The point I have sought to make is that the difference between non-personal and personalized theories is more than anything else a difference in the idiom of the explanatory quest. Grasping this point is an essential preliminary to realizing how far the various established dichotomies used in this field are simply obstacles to understanding. Once it is grasped, a whole series of seemingly bizarre and senseless features of traditional thinking becomes immediately comprehensible. Until it is grasped, they remain essentially mysterious. Making the business of personal versus impersonal entities the crux of the difference between tradition and science not only blocks the understanding of tradition. It also draws a red herring across the path to an understanding of science.

All this is not to deny that science has progressed greatly through working in a non-personal theoretical idiom. Indeed, as one who has hankerings after behaviourism, I am inclined to believe that it is this idiom, and this idiom only, which will eventually lead to the triumph of science in the sphere of human affairs. What I am saying, however, is that this is more a reflection of the nature of reality than a clue to the essence of scientific method. For the progressive acquisition of knowledge, man needs both the right kind of theories *and* the right attitude to them. But it is only the latter which we call science. Indeed, as we shall see, any attempt to define science in terms of a particular kind of theory runs contrary to its very essence. Now, at last, I hope it will be evident why, in comparing African traditional thought with Western scientific thought, I have chosen to start with a review of continuities rather than with a statement of crucial differences. For although this order of procedure carries the risk of one's being understood to mean that traditional thought is a kind of science, it also carries the advantage of having the path clear of red herrings when one comes to tackle the question of differences.

THE "CLOSED" AND "OPEN" PREDICAMENTS

Turning, to the differences in African thought and Western science, I start by isolating one which strikes me as the key to all the others, and go on to suggest how the latter flow from it.

What I take to be the key difference is a very simple one. It is that in traditional cultures there is no developed awareness of alternatives to the established body of theoretical tenets; whereas in scientifically oriented cultures, such an awareness is highly developed. It is this difference we refer to when we say that traditional cultures are "closed" and scientifically oriented cultures "open."[12]

One important consequence of the lack of awareness of alternatives is very clearly spelled out by Evans-Pritchard in his pioneering work on Azande witchcraft beliefs. Thus he says:

> I have attempted to show how rhythm, mode of utterance, content of prophecies, and so forth, assist in creating faith in witch-doctors, but these are only some of the ways in which faith is supported, and do not entirely explain belief. Weight of tradition alone can do that. . . . There is no incentive to agnosticism. All their beliefs hang together, and were a Zande to give up faith in witch-doctorhood, he would have to surrender equally his faith in witchcraft and oracles. . . . In this web of belief every strand depends upon every other strand, *and a Zande cannot get out of its meshes because it is the only world he knows. The web is not an external structure in which he is enclosed. It is the texture of his thought and he cannot think that his thought is wrong.*[13]

[12] Philosophically minded readers will notice here some affinities with Karl Popper, who also makes the transition from a "closed" to an "open" predicament crucial for the take-off from tradition to science. For me, however, Popper obscures the issue by packing too many contracts into his definitions of "closed" and "open." Thus, for him, the transition from one predicament to the other implies not just a growth in the awareness of alternatives, but also a transition from communalism to individualism, and from ascribed status to achieved status. But as I hope to show in this essay, it is the awareness of alternatives which is crucial for the take-off into science. Not individualism or achieved status: for there are lots of societies where both of the latter are well developed, but which show no signs whatever of take-off. In the present context, therefore, my own narrower definition of "closed" and "open" seems more appropriate.

[13] E. E. Evans-Pritchard, *Witchcraft, Oracles and Magic among the Azande,* Oxford, 1936, p. 194.

And again:

> And yet Azande do not see that their oracles tell them nothing! Their blind-
> ness is not due to stupidity, for they display great ingenuity in explaining
> away the failure and inequalities of the poison oracle and experimental
> keenness in testing it. It is due rather to the fact that their intellectual inge-
> nuity and experimental keenness are conditioned by patterns of ritual be-
> haviour and mystical belief. Within the limits set by these patterns, they
> show great intelligence, but it cannot operate beyond these limits. Or, to
> put it in another way; *they reason excellently in the idiom of their beliefs,
> but they cannot reason outside, or against their beliefs because they have
> no other idiom in which to express their thoughts.*[14]

In other words, absence of any awareness of alternatives makes for an absolute acceptance of the established theoretical tenets, and removes any
possibility of questioning them. In these circumstances, the established
tenets invest the believer with a compelling force. It is this force which
we refer to when we talk of such tenets as sacred.

A second important consequence of lack of awareness of alternatives is that any challenge to established tenets is a threat of chaos, of the
cosmic abyss, and therefore evokes intense anxiety.

With developing awareness of alternatives, the established theoretical tenets come to seem less absolute in their validity, and lose something of their sacredness. At the same time, a challenge to these tenets is
no longer a horrific threat of chaos. For just as the tenets themselves have
lost some of their absolute validity, a challenge to them is no longer a
threat of absolute calamity. It can now be seen as nothing more threatening than an intimation that new tenets might profitably be tried. Where
these conditions begin to prevail, the stage is set for change from a traditional to a scientific outlook.

Here, then, we have two basic predicaments: the "closed"—characterized by lack of awareness of alternatives, sacredness of beliefs, and
anxiety about threats to them; and the "open"—characterized by awareness of alternatives, diminished sacredness of beliefs, and diminished
anxiety about threats to them.

Now, as I have said, I believe all the major differences between traditional and scientific outlooks can be understood in terms of these two
predicaments. In substantiating this, I should like to divide the differences into two groups: those directly connected with the presence or absence of a vision of alternatives; and those directly connected with the
presence or absence of anxiety about threats to the established beliefs.[15]

---

[14] Ibid., p. 338.

[15] In this abridged version of the paper only the former are discussed. For a discussion of differences connected with anxiety about threats to established beliefs the reader is
referred to the original version of the paper, in *Africa*, XXVII, No. 2, esp. pp. 167ff.

DIFFERENCES CONNECTED WITH THE PRESENCE OR ABSENCE OF A VISION OF ALTERNATIVES

(a) Magical versus Non-magical Attitude to Words

A central characteristic of nearly all the traditional African world-views we know of is an assumption about the power of words, uttered under appropriate circumstances, to bring into being the events or states they stand for.

The most striking examples of this assumption are to be found in creation mythologies where the supreme being is said to have formed the world out of chaos by uttering the names of all things in it. Such mythologies occur most notably in Ancient Egypt and among the peoples of the Western Sudan.

In traditional African cultures, to know the name of a being or thing is to have some degree of control over it. In the invocation of spirits, it is essential to call their names correctly; and the control which such correct calling gives is one reason why the true or "deep" names of gods are often withheld from strangers, and their utterance forbidden to all but a few whose business it is to use them in ritual. Similar ideas lie behind the very widespread traditional practice of using euphemisms to refer to such things as dangerous diseases and wild animals: for it is thought that use of the real names might secure their presence. Yet again, it is widely believed that harm can be done to a man by various operations performed on his name—for instance, by writing his name on a piece of paper and burning it.

Through a very wide range of traditional African belief and activity, it is possible to see an implicit assumption as to the magical power of words.

Now if we take into account what I have called the basic predicament of the traditional thinker, we can begin to see why this assumption should be so deeply entrenched in his daily life and thought. Briefly, no man can make contact with reality save through a screen of words. Hence no man can escape the tendency to see a unique and intimate link between words and things. For the traditional thinker this tendency has an overwhelming power. Since he can imagine no alternatives to his established system of concepts and words, the latter appear bound to reality in an absolute fashion. There is no way at all in which they can be seen as varying independently of the segments of reality they stand for. Hence they appear so integrally involved with their referents that any manipulation of the one self-evidently affects the other.

The scientist's attitude to words is, of course, quite opposite. He dismisses contemptuously any suggestion that words could have an immediate, magical power over the things they stand for. Indeed, he finds magical notions amongst the most absurd and alien trappings of traditional thought. Though he grants an enormous power to words, it is the indirect one of bringing control over things through the functions of explanation and prediction.

Why does the scientist reject the magician's view of words? One easy answer is that he has come to know better: magical behaviour has been found not to produce the results it claims to. Perhaps. But what scientist has ever bothered to put magic to the test? The answer is, none; because there are deeper grounds for rejection—grounds which make the idea of testing beside the point.

To see what these grounds are, let us return to the scientist's basic predicament—to his awareness of alternative idea-systems whose ways of classifying and interpreting the world are very different from his own. Now this changed awareness gives him two intellectual possibilities. Both are eminently thinkable; but one is intolerable, the other hopeful.

The first possibility is simply a continuance of the magical world-view. If ideas and words are inextricably bound up with reality, and if indeed they shape it and control it, then, a multiplicity of idea-systems means a multiplicity of realities, and a change of ideas means a change of things. But whereas there is nothing particularly absurd or inconsistent about this view, it is clearly intolerable in the extreme. For it means that the world is in the last analysis dependent on human whim, that the search for order is a folly, and that human beings can expect to find no sort of anchor in reality.

The second possibility takes hold as an escape from this horrific prospect. It is based on the faith that while ideas and words change, there must be some anchor, some constant reality. This faith leads to the modern view of words and reality as independent variables. With its advent, words come "unstuck from" reality and are no longer seen as acting magically upon it. Intellectually, this second possibility is neither more nor less respectable than the first. But it has the great advantage of being tolerable whilst the first is horrific.

That the outlook behind magic still remains an intellectual possibility in the scientifically oriented cultures of the modern West can be seen from its survival as a nagging undercurrent in the last 300 years of Western philosophy. This undercurrent generally goes under the labels of "Idealism" and "Solipsism"; and under these labels it is not immediately recognizable. But a deeper scrutiny reveals that the old outlook is there all right—albeit in a strange guise. True, Idealism does not say that words create, sustain, and have power over that which they represent. Rather, it says that material things are "in the mind." That is, the mind creates, sustains, and has power over matter. But the second view is little more than a post-Cartesian transposition of the first. Let me elaborate. Both in traditional African cosmologies and in European cosmologies before

Descartes, the modern distinction between "mind" and "matter" does not appear. Although everything in the universe is underpinned by spiritual forces, what moderns would call "mental activities" and "material things" are both part of a single reality, neither material nor immaterial. Thinking, conceiving, saying, etc. are described in terms or organs like heart and brain and actions like the uttering of words. Now when Descartes wrote his philosophical works, he crystallized a half-way phase in the transition from a personal to an impersonal cosmological idiom. Whilst "higher" human activities still remained under the aegis of a personalized theory, physical and biological events were brought under the aegis of impersonal theory. Hence thinking, conceiving, saying, etc. became manifestations of "mind," whilst all other happenings became manifestations of "matter." Hence whereas before Descartes we have "words over things," after him we have "mind over matter"—just a new disguise for the old view.

What I have said about this view being intellectually respectable but emotionally intolerable is borne out by the attitude to it of modern Western philosophers. Since they are duty bound to explore all the alternative possibilities of thought that lie within the grasp of their imaginations, these philosophers mention, nay even expound, the doctrines of Idealism and Solipsism. Invariably, too, they follow up their expositions with attempts at refutation. But such attempts are, just as invariably, a farce. Their character is summed up in G. E. Moore's desperate gesture, when challenged to prove the existence of a world outside his mind, of banging his hand with his fist and exclaiming: "It is there!" A gesture of faith rather than of reason, if ever there was one!

With the change from the "closed" to the "open" predicament, then, the outlook behind magic becomes intolerable; and to escape from it people espouse the view that words vary independently of reality. Smug rationalists who congratulate themselves on their freedom from magical thinking would do well to reflect on the nature of this freedom!

(b) Ideas-Bound-to-Occasions versus Ideas-Bound-to-Ideas

Many commentators on the idea-systems of traditional African cultures have stressed that, for members of these cultures, their thought does not appear as something distinct from and opposable to the realities that call it into action. Rather, particular passages of thought are bound to the particular occasions that evoke them.

Let us take an example. Someone becomes sick. The sickness proves intractable and the relatives call a diviner. The latter says the sickness is due to an ancestor who has been angered by the patient's bad behaviour towards his kinsmen. The diviner prescribes placatory offerings to the spirit and reconciliation with the kinsmen, and the patient is eventually cured. Now while this emergency is on, both the diviner and the patient's relatives may justify what they are doing by reference to some general statements about the kinds of circumstance which arouse ancestors to cause sickness. But theoretical statements of this kind are very much matters of occasion, not likely to be heard out of context or as part of a general discussion of "what we believe."

If ideas in traditional culture are seen as bound to occasions rather than to other ideas, the reason is one that we have already given in our discussion of magic. Since the member of such a culture can imagine no alternatives to his established system of ideas, the latter appear inexorably bound to the portions of reality they stand for. They cannot be seen as in any way opposable to reality.

In a scientifically oriented culture such as that of the Western anthropologist, things are very different. The very word "idea" has the connotation of something opposed to reality. Nor is it entirely coincidental that in such a culture the historian of ideas is considered to be the most unrealistic kind of historian. Not only are ideas dissociated in people's minds from the reality that occasions them: they are bound to other ideas, to form wholes and systems perceived as such. Belief-systems take shape not only as abstractions in the minds of anthropologists, but also as totalities in the minds of believers.

Here again, this change can be readily understood in terms of a change from the "closed" to the "open" predicament. A vision of alternative possibilities forces men to the faith that ideas somehow vary whilst reality remains constant. Ideas thus become detached from reality—nay, even in a sense opposed to it. Furthermore, such a vision, by giving the thinker an opportunity to "get outside" his own system, offers him a possibility of his coming to see it *as a system.*

(c) Unreflective versus Reflective Thinking

At this stage of the analysis there is no need for me to insist further on the essential rationality of traditional thought. I have already made it far too rational for the taste of most social anthropologists. And yet, there is a sense in which this thought includes among its accomplishments neither Logic or Philosophy.

Let me explain this, at first sight, rather shocking statement. It is true that most African traditional world-views are logically elaborated to a high degree. It is also true that, because of their eminently rational character, they are appropriately called "philosophies." But here I am using "Logic" and "Philosophy" in a more exact sense. By Logic, I mean thinking directed to answering the question: "What are the general rules by which we can distinguish good arguments from bad ones?" And by Philosophy, I mean thinking directed to answering the question: "On what grounds can we ever claim to know anything about the world?" Now Logic and Philosophy, in these restricted senses, are poorly developed in traditional Africa. Despite its elaborate and often penetrating cosmological, sociological, and psychological speculations, traditional thought has tended to get on with the work of explanation, without pausing for reflection upon the nature or rules of this work. Thinking once more of the "closed" predicament, we can readily see why these second-order intellectual activities should be virtually absent from traditional cultures. Briefly, the traditional thinker, because he is unable to imagine possible alternatives to his established theories and classifications, can never start to formulate generalized norms of reasoning and knowing. For only where there are alternatives can there be choice, and only where there is choice can there be norms governing it. As they are characteristically absent in traditional cultures, so Logic and Philosophy are characteristically present in all scientifically oriented cultures. Just as the "closed" predicament makes it impossible for them to appear, so the "open" predicament makes it inevitable that they must appear. For where the thinker can see the possibility of alternatives to his established idea-system, the question of choice at once arises, and the development of norms governing such choice cannot be far behind.[16]

(d) Mixed versus Segregated Motives

This contrast is very closely related to the preceding one. The goals of explanation and prediction are as powerfully present in traditional African cultures as they are in cultures where science has become institutionalized. In the absence of explicit norms of thought, however, we find them vigorously pursued but not explicitly reflect upon and defined. In these circumstances, there is little thought about their consistency or inconsistency with other goals and motives. Hence wherever we find a theoretical system with explanatory and predictive functions, we find other motives entering in and contributing to its development.

Despite their cognitive preoccupations, most African religious systems are powerfully influenced by what are commonly called "emotional needs"—i.e. needs for certain kinds of personal relationship. In Africa, as elsewhere, all social systems stimulate in their members a considerable diversity of such needs; but, having stimulated them, they often prove unwilling or unable to allow them full opportunities for satisfaction. In such situations the spirits function not only as theoretical entities but as surrogate people providing opportunities for the formation of ties forbidden in the purely human social field. The latter function they discharge

---

[16] See Ernest Gellner, *Thought and Change,* London, 1964, for a similar point exemplified in the Philosophy of Descartes p. 105.

in two ways. First, by providing non-human partners with whom people can take up relationships forbidden with other human beings. Second, though the mechanism of possession, by allowing people to "become" spirits and so to play roles *vis-à-vis* their fellow men which they are debarred from playing as ordinary human beings.

There is little doubt that because the theoretical entities of traditional thought happen to be people, they give particular scope for the working of emotional and aesthetic motives. Here, perhaps, we do have something about the personal idiom in theory that does militate indirectly against the taking up of a scientific attitude; for where there are powerful emotional and aesthetic loadings on a particular theoretical scheme, these must add to the difficulties of abandoning this scheme when cognitive goals press towards doing so. Once again, I should like to stress that the mere fact of switching from a personal to an impersonal idiom does not make anyone a scientist, and that one can be unscientific or scientific in either idiom. In this respect, nevertheless, the personal idiom does seem to present certain difficulties for the scientific attitude which the impersonal idiom does not.

Where the possibility of choice has stimulated the development of Logic, Philosophy, and norms of thought generally, the situation undergoes radical change. One theory is judged better than another with explicit reference to its efficacy in explanation and prediction. And as these ends become more clearly defined, it gets increasingly evident that no other ends are compatible with them. People come to see that if ideas are to be used as efficient tools of explanation and prediction, they must not be allowed to become tools of anything else. (This, of course, is the essence of the ideal of "objectivity.") Hence there grows up a great watchfulness against seduction by the emotional or aesthetic appeal of a theory.

DIFFERENCES CONNECTED WITH THE PRESENCE OR ABSENCE OF ANXIETY ABOUT THREATS TO THE ESTABLISHED BODY OF THEORY

(e) Protective versus Destructive Attitude towards Established Theory

Both in traditional Africa and in the science-oriented West, theoretical thought is vitally concerned with the prediction of events. But there are marked differences in reaction to predictive failure.

In the theoretical thought of the traditional cultures, there is a notable reluctance to register repeated failures of prediction and to act by attacking the beliefs involved. Instead, other current beliefs are utilized

in such a way as to "excuse" each failure as it occurs, and hence to protect the major theoretical assumptions on which prediction is based. This
use of *ad hoc* excuses is a phenomenon which social anthropologists
have christened "secondary elaboration."[17]

The process of secondary elaboration is most readily seen in association with the work of diviners and oracle-operators, who are concerned
with discovering the identity of the spiritual forces responsible for particular happenings in the visible, tangible world, and the reasons for
their activation. Typically, a sick man goes to a diviner, and is told that a
certain spiritual agency is "worrying" him. The diviner points to certain
of his past actions as having excited the spirit's anger, and indicates certain remedial actions which will appease this anger and restore health.
Should the client take the recommended remedial action and yet see no
improvement, he will be likely to conclude that the diviner was either
fraudulent or just incompetent, and to seek out another expert. The new
diviner will generally point to another spiritual agency and another set of
arousing circumstances as responsible for the man's condition, and will
recommend fresh remedial action. In addition, he will probably provide
some explanation of why the previous diviner failed to get at the truth.
He may corroborate the client's suspicions of fraud, or he may say that
the spirit involved maliciously "hid itself behind" another in such a way
that only the most skilled of diviners would have been able to detect it.
If after this the client should still see no improvement in his condition,
he will move on to yet another diviner—and so on, perhaps, until his
troubles culminate in death.

What is notable in all this is that the client never takes his repeated
failures as evidence against the existence of the various spiritual beings
named as responsible for his plight, or as evidence against the possibility
of making contact with such beings as diviners claim to do. Nor do members of the wider community in which he lives ever try to keep track of
the proportion of successes to failures in the remedial actions based on
their beliefs, with the aim of questioning these beliefs. At most, they
grumble about the dishonesty and wiles of many diviners, whilst maintaining their faith in the existence of some honest, competent practitioners.

In these traditional cultures, questioning of the beliefs on which di-
vining is based and weighing up of successes against failures are just not
among the paths that thought can take. They are blocked paths because
the thinkers involved are victims of the closed predicament. For them,
established beliefs have an absolute validity, and any threat to such be-

---

[17] The idea of secondary elaboration as a key feature of prescientific thought-systems
was put forward with great brilliance and insight by Evans-Pritchard in his *Witchcraft, Oracles and Magic*. All subsequent discussions, including the present one, are heavily indebted to his lead.

liefs is a horrific threat of chaos. Who is going to jump from the cosmic palm-tree when there is no hope of another perch to swing to?

Where the scientific outlook has become firmly entrenched, attitudes to established beliefs are very different. Much has been made of the scientist's essential scepticism towards established beliefs; and one must, I think, agree that this above all is what distinguishes him from the traditional thinker. But one must be careful here. The picture of the scientist in continuous readiness to scrap or demote established theory contains a dangerous exaggeration as well as an important truth. As an outstanding modern historian of the sciences has recently observed,[18] the typical scientist spends most of his time optimistically seeing how far he can push a new theory to cover an ever-widening horizon of experience. When he has difficulty in making the theory "fit," he is more likely to develop it in the ways described in Part I of this essay than to scrap it out of hand. And if it does palpably fail the occasional test, he may even put the failure down to dirty apparatus or mistaken meter-reading—rather like the oracle operator! And yet, the spirit behind the scientist's actions *is* very different. His pushing of a theory and his reluctance to scrap it are not due to any chilling intuition that if his theory fails him, chaos is at hand. Rather, they are due to the very knowledge that the theory is not something timeless and absolute. Precisely because he knows that the present theory came in at a certain epoch to replace a predecessor, and that its explanatory coverage is far better than that of the predecessor, he is reluctant to throw it away before giving it the benefit of every doubt, but this same knowledge makes for an acceptance of the theory which is far more qualified and far more watchful than that of the traditional thinker. The scientist is, as it were, always keeping account, balancing the successes of a theory against its failures. And when the failures start to come thick and fast, defence of the theory switches inexorably to attack on it.

If the record of a theory that has fallen under a cloud is poor in all circumstances, it is ruthlessly scrapped. The collective memory of the European scientific community is littered with the wreckage of the various unsatisfactory theories discarded over the last 500 years—the earth-centred theory of the universe, the circular theory of planetary motion, the phlogiston theory of chemical combination, the aether theory of wave propagation, and perhaps a hundred others. Often, however, it is found that a theoretical model once assumed to have universal validity in fact has a good predictive performance over a limited range of circumstances, but a poor performance outside this range. In such a case, the beliefs in question are still ruthlessly demoted; but instead of being thrown out altogether they are given a lesser status as limiting cases of more embrac-

[18] T. Kuhn, *The Structure of Scientific Revolutions,* Chicago, 1962.

ing generalities—still useful as lower-level models or guides to experience within restricted areas. This sort of demotion has been the fate of theoretical schemes like Newton's Laws of Motion (still used as a guide in many mundane affairs, including much of the business of modern rocketry) and the "Ball-and-Bond" theory of chemical combination.

This underlying readiness to scrap or demote established theories on the ground of poor predictive performance is perhaps the most important single feature of the scientific attitude. It is, I suggest, a direct outcome of the "open" predicament. For only when the thinker is able to see his established idea-system as one among many alternatives can he see his established ideas as things of less than absolute value. And only when he sees them thus can he see the scrapping of them as anything other than a horrific, irretrievable jump into chaos.

(f) Protective versus Destructive Attitude to the Category-System

If someone is asked to list typical features of traditional thinking, he is almost certain to mention the phenomenon known as "taboo." "Taboo" is the anthropological jargon for a reaction of horror and aversion to certain actions or happenings which are seen as monstrous and polluting. It is characteristic of the taboo reaction that people are unable to justify it in terms of ulterior reasons: tabooed events are simply bad in themselves. People take every possible step to prevent tabooed events from happening, and to isolate or expel them when they do occur.

Taboo has long been a mystery to anthropologists. Of the many explanations proposed, few have fitted more than a small selection of the instances observed. It is only recently that an anthropologist has placed the phenomenon in a more satisfactory perspective by the observation that in nearly every case of taboo reaction, the events and actions involved are ones which seriously defy the established lines of classification in the culture where they occur.[19]

Perhaps the most important occasion of taboo reaction in traditional African cultures is the commission of incest. Incest is one of the most flagrant defiances of the established category-system: for he who commits it treats a mother, daughter, or sister like a wife. Another common occasion for taboo reaction is the birth of twins. Here, the category distinction involved is that of human beings versus animals—multiple births being taken as characteristic of animals as opposed to men. Yet another very

---

[19] This observation may well prove to be a milestone in our understanding of traditional thought. It was first made some years ago by Mary Douglas, who has developed many of its implications in her book *Purity and Danger*. Though we clearly disagree on certain wider implications, the present discussion is deeply indebted to her insights.

generally tabooed object is the human corpse, which occupies, as it were, a classificatory no-man's land between the living and the inanimate. Equally widely tabooed are such human bodily excreta as faeces and menstrual blood, which occupy the same no-man's-land between the living and the inanimate.

Taboo reactions are often given to occurrences that are radically strange or new; for these too (almost by definition) fail to fit in to the established category system. A good example is furnished by a Kalabari story of the coming of the Europeans. The first white man, it is said, was seen by a fisherman who had gone down to the mouth of the estuary in his canoe. Panic-stricken, he raced home and told his people what he had seen: whereupon he and the rest of the town set out to purify themselves—that is, to rid themselves of the influence of the strange and monstrous thing that had intruded into their world.

A sort of global taboo reaction is often evoked by foreign lands. As the domains of so much that is strange and unassimilable to one's own categories, such lands are the abode *par excellence* of the monstrous and the abominable. The most vivid description we have of this is that given for the Lugbara by John Middleton.[20] For this East African people, the foreigner is the inverted perpetrator of all imaginable abominations from incest downwards. The more alien he is, the more abominable. Though the Lugbara attitude is extreme, many traditional cultures would seem to echo it in some degree.[21]

Just as the central tenets of the traditional theoretical system are defended against adverse experience by an elaborate array of excuses for predictive failure, so too the main classificatory distinctions of the system are defended by taboo avoidance reactions against any event that defies them. Since every system of belief implies a system of categories, and vice versa, secondary elaboration and taboo reaction are really opposite sides of the same coin.

From all this it follows that, like secondary elaboration, taboo reaction has no place among the reflexes of the scientist. For him, whatever defies or fails to fit in to the established category-system is not something horrifying, to be isolated or expelled. On the contrary, it is an intriguing "phenomenon"—a starting point and a challenge for the invention of new classifications and new theories. It is something every young research worker would like to have crop up in his field of observation— perhaps the first rung on the ladder of fame. If a biologist ever came across a child born with the head of a goat, he would be hard put to it to

---

[20] Middleton, op. cit.

[21] This association of foreign lands with chaos and pollution seems to be a universal of prescientific thought-systems. For this, see Mircea Eliade, *The Sacred and the Profane,* New York, 1961, esp. Chapter 1.

make his compassion cover his elation. And as for social anthropologists, one may guess that their secret dreams are of finding a whole community of men who sleep for preference with their mothers!

(g) The Passage of Time: Bad or Good?

In traditional Africa, methods of time-reckoning vary greatly from culture to culture. Within each culture, again, we find a plurality of time-scales used in different contexts. Thus there may be a major scale which locates events either before, during, or after the time of founding of the major institutions of the community: another scale which locates events by correlating them with the life-time of deceased ancestors: yet another which locates events by correlating them with the phases of the season cycle: and yet another which uses phases of the daily cycle.

Although these scales are seldom interrelated in any systematic way, they all serve to order events in before-after series. Further, they have the very general characteristic that *vis-à-vis* "after," "before" is usually valued positively, sometimes neutrally, and never negatively. Whatever the particular scale involved, then, the passage of time is seen as something deleterious or at best neutral.

Perhaps the most widespread, everyday instance of this attitude is the standard justification of so much thought and action: "That is what the old-time people told us." (It is usually this standard justification which is in the forefront of the anthropologist's mind when he applies the label "traditional culture.")

On the major time-scale of the typical traditional culture, things are thought of as having been better in the golden age of the founding heroes than they are today. On an important minor time-scale, the annual one, the end of the year is a time when everything in the cosmos is run-down and sluggish, overcome by an accumulation of defilement and pollution.

A corollary of this attitude to time is a rich development of activities designed to negate its passage by a "return to the beginning." Such activities characteristically depend on the magical premiss that a symbolic statement of some archetypal event can in a sense recreate that event and temporarily obliterate the passage of time which has elapsed since its original occurrence.[22]

These rites of recreation are to be seen at their most luxuriant in the ancient cultures of the Western Sudan—notably in those of the Bambara and Dogon. In such cultures, indeed, a great part of everyday activity is

---

[22] In these rites of recreation, traditional African thought shows its striking affinities with prescientific thought in many other parts of the world. The worldwide occurrence and meaning of such rites was first dealt with by Mircea Eliade in his *Myth of the Eternal Return*. A more recent treatment, from which the present analysis has profited greatly, is to be found in the chapter entitled "Le Temps Retrouvé" in Claude Lévi-Strauss, *La Pensée*.

said to have the ulterior significance of recreating archetypal events and acts. Thus the Dogon labouring in the fields recreates in his pattern of cultivation the emergence of the world from the cosmic egg. The builder of a homestead lays it out in a pattern that symbolically recreates the body of the culture-hero Nommo. Even relations between kin symbolize and recreate relations between the primal beings.[23]

One might well describe the Western Sudanic cultures as obsessed with the annulment of time to a degree unparalleled in Africa as a whole. Yet other, less spectacular, manifestations of the attempt to "get back to the beginning" are widely distributed over the continent. In the West African forest belt, for instance, the richly developed ritual dramas enacted in honour of departed heroes and ancestors have a strong recreative aspect. For by inducing these beings to possess specially selected media and thus, during festivals, to return temporarily to the company of men, such rituals are restoring things as they were in olden times.[24]

On the minor time-scale provided by the seasonal cycle, we find a similar widespread concern for recreation and renewal. Hence the important rites which mark the end of an old year and the beginning of a new one—rites which attempt to make the year new by a thoroughgoing process of purification of accumulated pollutions and defilements.

This widespread attempt to annul the passage of time seems closely linked to features of traditional thought which I have already reviewed. As I pointed out earlier, the new and the strange, in so far as they fail to fit into the established system of classification and theory, are intimations of chaos to be avoided as far as possible. Advancing time, with its inevitable element of non-repetitive change, is the vehicle *par excellence* of the new and the strange. Hence its effects must be annulled at all costs. Rites of renewal and recreation, then, have much in common with the processes of secondary elaboration and taboo behaviour. Indeed, their kinship with the latter can be seen in the idea that the passage of the year is essentially an accumulation of pollutions, which it is the function of the renewal rites to remove. In short, these rites are the third great defensive reflex of traditional thought.[25]

When we turn from the traditional thinker to the scientist, we find this whole valuation of temporal process turned upside down. Not for the scientist the idea of a golden age at the beginning of time—an age

[23] See M. Griaule, and G. Dieterlen, "The Dogon," in D. Forde (ed.), *African Worlds*, London, 1954, and M. Griaule, *Conversations with Ogotemmêli*, London, 1965 (translation of *Dieu d'Eau*).

[24] For some interesting remarks on this aspect of West African ritual dramas, see C. Tardits, "Religion, Epic, History: Notes on the Underlying Functions of Cults in Benin Civilizations," *Diogenes*, No. 37, 1962.

[25] Lévi-Strauss, I think, is making much the same point about rites of renewal when he talks of the continuous battle between prescientific classificatory systems and the nonrepetitive changes involved in the passage of time. See Lévi-Strauss, op. cit.

from which things have been steadily falling away. For him, the past is a bad old past, and the best things lie ahead. The passage of time brings inexorable progress. As C. P. Snow has put it aptly, all scientists have "the future in their bones."[26] Where the traditional thinker is busily trying to annul the passage of time, the scientist may almost be said to be trying frantically to hurry time up. For in his impassioned pursuit of the experimental method, he is striving after the creation of new situations which nature, if left to herself, would bring about slowly if ever at all.

Once again, the scientist's attitude can be understood in terms of the "open" predicament. For him, currently held ideas on a given subject are one possibility amongst many. Hence occurrences which threaten them are not the total, horrific threat that they would be for the traditional thinker. Hence time's burden of things new and strange does not hold the terrors that it holds for the traditionalist. Furthermore, the scientist's experience of the way in which successive theories, overthrown after exposure to adverse data, are replaced by ideas of ever greater predictive and explanatory power, leads almost inevitably to a very positive evaluation of time. Finally, we must remember that the "open" predicament, though it has made people able to tolerate threats to their beliefs, has not been able to supply them with anything comparable to the cosiness of the traditional thinker ensconced amidst his established theories. As an English medical student, newly exposed to the scientific attitude, put it:

> You seem to be as if when learning to skate, trying to find a nice hard piece of ice which you can stand upright on instead of learning how to move on it. You continue trying to find something, some foundation piece which will not move, whereas everything will move and you've got to learn to skate on it.[27]

The person who enjoys the moving world of the sciences, then, enjoys the exhilaration of the skater. But for many, this is a nervous, insecure sensation, which they would fain exchange for the womb-like warmth of the traditional theories and their defences. This lingering sense of insecurity gives a powerful attraction to the idea of progress. For by enabling people to cling to some hoped-for future state of perfect knowledge, it helps them live with a realization of the imperfection and transience of present theories.

Once formed, indeed, the idea of Progress becomes in itself one of the most powerful supports of the scientific attitude generally. For the faith that, come what may, new experience must lead to better theories,

[26] C. P. Snow, *The Two Cultures and the Scientific Revolution*, Cambridge, 1959, p. 10.
[27] M. L. Johnson Abercrombie, *The Anatomy of Judgement*, London, 1960, quoted on p. 131.

and that better theories must eventually give place to still better ones, provides the strongest possible incentive for a constant readiness to expose oneself to the strange and the disturbing, to scrap current frameworks of ideas, and to cast about for replacements.

Like the quest for purity of motive, however, the faith in progress is a double-edged weapon. For the lingering insecurity which is one of the roots of this faith leads all too often to an excessive fixation of hopes and desires on an imagined Utopian future. People cling to such a future in the same way that men in pre-scientific cultures cling to the past. And in doing so, they inevitably lose much of the traditionalist's ability to enjoy and glorify the moment he lives in. Even within the sciences, an excessive faith in progress can be dangerous. In sociology, for instance, it has led to a number of unfruitful theories of social evolution.

At this point, I should like to draw attention to a paradox inherent in the presentation of my subject. As a scientist, it is perhaps inevitable that I should at certain points give the impression that traditional African thought is a poor, shackled thing when compared with the thought of the sciences. Yet as a man, here I am living by choice in a still-heavily-traditional Africa rather than in the scientifically oriented Western subculture I was brought up in. Why? Well, there may be lots of queer, sinister, unacknowledged reasons. But one certain reason is the discovery of things lost at home. An intensely poetic quality in everyday life and thought, and a vivid enjoyment of the passing moment—both driven out of sophisticated Western life by the quest for purity of motive and the faith in progress. How necessary these are for the advance of science; but what a disaster they are when they run wild beyond their appropriate bounds! Though I largely disagree with the way in which the "Négritude" theorists have characterized the differences between traditional African and modern Western thought, when it get to this point I see very clearly what they are after.

In modern Western Europe and America the "open" predicament seems to have escaped precariousness through public acknowledgment of the practical utility of the sciences. It has achieved a secure foothold in the culture because its results maximize values shared by "closed-" and "open-" minded alike. Even here, however, the "open" predicament has nothing like a universal sway. On the contrary, it is almost a minority phenomenon. Outside the various academic disciplines in which it has been institutionalized, its hold is pitifully less than those who describe Western culture as "science-oriented" often like to think.

It is true that in modern Western culture, the theoretical models propounded by the professional scientists do, to some extent, become the intellectual furnishings of a very large sector of the population. The moderately educated layman typically shares with the scientist a general predilection for impersonal "it-" theory and a proper contempt for "thou-" theory. Garbled and watered-down though it may be, the atomic theory of matter is one of his standard possessions. But the layman's ground for accepting the models propounded by the scientist is often no different from the young African villager's ground for accepting the models propounded by one of his elders. In both cases the propounders are deferred to as the accredited agents of tradition. As for the rules which guide scientists themselves in the acceptance or rejection of models, these seldom become part of the intellectual equipment of members of the wider population. For all the apparent up-to-dateness of the content of his world-view, the modern Western layman is rarely more "open" or scientific in his outlook than is the traditional African villager.

An Essay on African Philosophical Thought—The Akan Conceptual Scheme

Kwame Gyekye

In the following excerpt, Kwame Gyekye, chair of the Department of Philosophy at the University of Ghana in Legon, argues that the tendency to ask similar questions and think deeply about them is a universal human propensity that is the source of philosophical ideas. Contrary to the position suggested by certain of Wiredu and Hountondji's pronouncements, these ideas need not be expressed in a written form but may be encoded in spoken proverbs, myths, art, sociopolitical institutions, and so on.

The task of the professionally trained African philosopher is to lift these ideational constructs from their original context and critically develop them. This Gyekye does by providing a penetrating examination of Akan proverbs and metaphysical beliefs. In the process, he cites many sources, including traditional wise men, Western anthropologists, and others. He opposes the relativistic claim that it is impossible for members of one culture to understand the ideas of another culture. On the other hand, he is especially concerned to show that philosophical ideas expressed within an African culture need not have as their source a foreign culture such as Islam or the West, but may derive instead from sources that are indigenous to that culture. His discussion of Akan concepts of personal identity, religion, ethics, causality, time, logic, destiny, free-will, responsibility, and so on exemplifies what he considers to be the proper methodology for the African philosopher—namely, to uncover and critically discuss ideas discernible in the cultures of sub-Saharan Africa concerning the nature of reality. Although he does not hold that there is one uniform perspective on reality that is identical in every African culture, he does identify some beliefs that appear to be widely held throughout sub-Saharan African cultures. However he insists that such beliefs need not be unique to Africa and may exist in other cultures as well. The following selection explores issues in meta-physics, epistemology, and social philosophy.

THE COMMUNITY OF CULTURAL ELEMENTS AND IDEAS

I wish now to present, in a nutshell, the worldviews, sociopolitical ideas, values, and institutions that can with a high degree of certainty be said to pervade the cultural systems of different African peoples. What I have done is to extract the common or rather pervasive elements and ideas in the cultures of African peoples as may be found in as many of the existing publications as I have been able to look at. Such pervasive cultural elements and ideas are the elements which constitute the basis for constructing African philosophy (using "philosophy" in the singular). In some cases the attempt to bring out the philosophical implications of beliefs, ideas, attitudes or practices has led to brief philosophical discussions; so that this section is not just a catalog of facts about African cultures. We may start, then, with the African metaphysic.

Metaphysics

Categories of Being in African Ontology A critical examination of the scholarly literature on traditional African religions shows that most African peoples do have a concept of God as the Supreme Being who created the whole universe out of nothing and who is the absolute ground of all being. Thus, Busia wrote: "The postulate of God is universal throughout Africa; it is a concept which is handed down as part of the culture."[1] After studying the concept of God held by nearly three hundred peoples in Africa, Mbiti concluded thus: "In all these societies, without a single exception, people have a notion of God as the Supreme Being."[2] The Supreme Being is held to be omnipotent, omniscient, and omnipresent. He is considered uncreated and eternal, attributes implying his transcendence. But transcendence is also implicit in African beliefs about God removing himself far from the world of humankind as a result of our misconduct. "It appears to be a widespread notion in Africa that at the beginning God and man lived together on earth and talked one to another; but that owing to misconduct of some sort on the part of man—or more frequently of a woman—God deserted the earth and went to live in the sky."[3] But God is also held by African peoples to be immanent in that He is "manifested in natural objects and phenomena, and they can turn to Him in acts of worship, at any place and any time."[4]

African ontology, however, is a pluralistic ontology that recognizes, besides the Supreme Being, other categories of being as well. These are the lesser spirits (variously referred to as spirits, deities, gods, nature gods, divinities), ancestors (that is, ancestral spirits), man, and the physical world of natural objects and phenomena. Mbiti observed: "Myriads of spirits are reported from every African people,"[5] and "the class of the spirits is an essential and integral part of African ontology."[6] The reality of the ancestral spirits is the basis of the so-called ancestor worship that has been considered by some as an important feature of African religion. Thus, Fortes wrote: "It has long been recognized that ancestor worship is a conspicuous feature of African religious systems."[7] And Parrinder observed: "Thus there is no doubt that ancestral spirits play a very large part in African thought; they are [so] prominent in the spiritual world."[8] The physical world is also considered real in African ontology.

Mbiti thought that in addition to these four entities in African ontology—namely, God, qua the Absolute Being, lesser spirits (consisting of superhuman beings and ancestral spirits), man, and, finally, the world of natural objects—"there seems to be a force, power or energy permeating the whole universe"[9] which, in his opinion, is to be added as a separate ontological category.[10] But although African ontology distinguishes four or five categories of being, yet it must not be supposed that these entities are on the same level of reality. For God, as the Supreme Being and the ground of all existence, must be categorically distinguished from the lesser spirits and the other beings that were his creations. The Supreme Being is held as the ultimate reality, which is inferable not only from the attributes ascribed to God,[11] but also from the religious attitude and behavior of African peoples, the majority of whose "prayers and invocations are addressed to God."[12] Moreover, in spontaneous religious outbursts references are made to the Supreme Being rather than to the lesser spirits.[13] The lesser spirits are thus on a lower level of reality. African ontology therefore is hierarchical,[14] with the Supreme Being at the apex and the world of natural objects and phenomena at the bottom.

African ontology appears to be essentially spiritualistic, although this does not imply a denial of the reality of the nonspiritual, empirical world. Conceptually, a distinction is made between the empirical and nonempirical (that is, spiritual) world. But this distinction is not projected onto the level of being, so that in terms of being both worlds are regarded as real. Thus, McVeigh stated: "Both the world of the seen and the unseen are realities."[15] And Mbiti observed that in African conceptions "the physical and spiritual are but two dimensions of one and the same universe."[16] Reality in African thought appears to be homogeneous.

Thus, just as African ontology is neither wholly pluralistic nor wholly monistic but possesses attributes of both, so it is neither idealistic—maintaining that what is real is only spirit, nor materialistic (naturalistic)—maintaining that what is real is only matter, but possesses attributes of both.

Causation African ontological structure constitutes the conceptual framework for explaining the notion of causality. Implicit in the hierarchical character of that structure is that a higher entity has the power to control a lower entity. Since man and the physical world are the lower entities of that hierarchy, occurrences in the physical world are causally explained by reference to supernatural powers, which are held to be the real or ultimate sources of action and change in the world. Wrote Mbiti:

> African peoples . . . feel and believe that all the various ills, misfortunes, accidents, tragedies . . . which they encounter or experience, are caused by the use of (this) mystical power. . . . It is here that we may understand, for example, that a bereaved mother whose child has died from malaria will not be satisfied with the scientific explanation. . . . She will wish to know why the mosquito stung her child and not somebody else's child. . . . Everything is caused by someone directly or through the use of mystical power.[17]

Elsewhere Mbiti wrote that "for many millions of African people" such phenomena, as the eclipse of the sun, "do not just happen without mystical, mythological, or spiritual causes. It is not enough for them to ask *why* or *how* this causes them to happen. In traditional life the *who questions and answers* are more important and meaningful than the *how questions and answers*."[18] McVeigh made reference to "the African concern with the deeper 'why' questions,"[19] and "the African tendency to seek immediately mystical answers."[20] In a book that deals specifically with eastern and southern African peoples, Monica Wilson referred to the dogmas regarding mystical power as "the explanation of good and evil fortune, the answer to 'Why did it happen to me?'"[21] She observed that in Africa scientific answers are regarded as incomplete, for science "cannot answer the question the Mpondo or Nyakyusa is primarily concerned with when his child dies: 'Why did it happen to me?' 'Who caused it?'"[22]

The evidence, then, is that causation is generally explained in terms of spirit, of mystical power. Scientific or empirical explanations, of which they are aware, are considered not profound enough to offer complete satisfaction. The notion of chance is the alternative to the African proclivity to the "why" and the "who" questions when the answers to the "how" and "what" questions are deemed unsatisfactory. But the Africans' conception of an orderly universe and their concern for ultimate causes lead them to reject the notion of chance. Consequently, in

African causal explanations the notion or chance does not have a significant place.[23]

Concept of the Person "Every culture produces a dogma of human personality, that is to say, an accepted formulation of the physical and psychical constitution of man." So wrote the renowned British anthropologist Meyer Fortes.[24] African systems of thought indeed teem with elaborate dogmas of the nature of the human being. The African philosophy of the person is, in my view, rigidly dualistic: The person consists of body and soul. However, the common conception of the soul varies widely in its details. In some cases the soul is conceived as having three or even more parts, as, for example, among the people of Dahomey;[25] others, such as the Dogon,[26] the Rwanda,[27] the Nupe and Gwari of northern Nigeria,[28] and the Yoruba,[29] conceive it as bipartite. Still others, like the Mende and the Shilluk,[30] have simpler conceptions of the soul.

The soul is understood as the immaterial part of a person that survives after death. The African belief in the soul—and hence in the dualistic nature of the person—leads directly to their conception of an ancestral world inhabited by departed souls. Thus the logical relation between the belief in the soul and the belief in the ancestral world is one of dependence: The latter belief depends on the former. It is the immaterial, undying part of a person, namely, the soul, that continues to live in the world of the ancestral spirits. Thus, McVeigh was right when he wrote: ". . . it is impossible to deny that African thought affirms the survival of the human personality (that is, soul) after death."[31] For this reason, "the Christian missionary," in McVeigh's view, "does not go to Africa to inform the people that there is a spiritual world or that the personality survives the grave. Africans know this from their own experience."[32] The psychophysical conception of a person common to African thought systems and the commonly observable phenomena of psychophysical therapeutics practiced in all African communities presuppose a belief in psychophysical causal interaction.

Concept of Fate (Destiny) As the absolute being and the ultimate ground of being in the African metaphysic, the Supreme Being constitutes the controlling principle in the world. This fact, together with others to be mentioned presently, is the basis of the belief in fate (or destiny) common in African thought systems. "Running through the African conception of God," observed McVeigh, "is a clear sense of fate or destiny."[33] Dickson also noted that "The concept of Destiny is quite widespread in Africa; certainly the literature on West Africa suggests that many of its peoples have some ideas which may be put down under the heading of Destiny."[34] Writing on the African ideas about the works of God, Mbiti said: "God not only continues to create physically, but He also *ordains the* *destiny* of His creatures, especially that of man."[35] Fortes, however, thought that the concept of fate is held only in the religions of West African people: "Indeed one of the characteristic marks of West African religions, as compared with other African religions (for example: East and South African Bantu religions) in which ancestor worship also plays a part, is the occurrence of the notion of Fate in them."[36] It is not true, however, that eastern and southern African religious lack the notion of fate. Mbiti, for instance, noted that "Similar notions of predestination are found among peoples like the Ila, Tswana, Bacongo, Barundi, Yao and others."[37] (These are peoples in eastern and southern Africa.)

The concept of fate must be implicit, in my view, in systems of thought, like the African, which postulate a creator who not only fashioned man and the world but also established the order of the world in which man lives. It makes sense logically to assume that if human beings were fashioned, then they were fashioned in such a way that would determine a number of things about them. This assumption therefore must have been a basis for the African belief in fate. Further, the repudiation of the notion of chance in African thought would seem to lead to the idea of fate. Thus, some other assumptions in African thought involve a general belief in fate.

What is not clear is whether fate is self-determined, that is, chosen or decided upon by the individual soul or divinely imposed. Some African peoples think that destiny is chosen by the individual whereas others think that it is conferred by the Supreme Being. Among the Yoruba the manner in which destiny comes to the individual is ambiguously conceived: In one way the individual "*chooses* his destiny"; in another he "*receives* his destiny," that is, from Olodumare (God): in yet another way "his destiny is *affixed* to him."[38] In the conceptions of the Rwandas, the Fon of Dahomey, the Lele of Kasai (southwestern Congo Kinshasa), and others, God decides the destiny of the individual.[39] However, whatever the source of the individual's destiny, the fact remains—as I pointed out in discussing the concept among the Akan (section 7.2.2)—that the individual enters the world with a predetermined destiny. The concept of fate in African thought appears to be quite complex and, like other concepts, stands in need of thorough analysis and explication.

The Problem of Evil Busia, to whose views I have already referred in my discussion of the problem of evil, claimed that the African concept of deity does not generate the problem of evil, for the sources of evil in the world are the lesser spirits and other supernatural forces. That is to say, God is not the source of evil. Mbiti asserted that "many [African] societies say categorically that God did not create what is evil, nor does He do any evil whatsoever . . . In nearly all African societies, it is thought that spirits are either the origin of evil, or agents of evil."[40] A few African peoples hold, however, that, in the words of McVeigh, God is "the explanation for what is good and evil in man's life."[41] Among such peoples are the Shilluk, Dinka, Nupe, Bacongo, and Vashona. The assumption of God as the source of evil in the world stems from the conception of God as the first principle and the ultimate ground of explanation for all existence. This of course raises the problem of evil, since God is also considered in African thought to be good[42] and omnipotent.

Most African peoples, however, deny that God is the source of evil. Does their view succeed in eliminating the problem of evil, as Busia and others claimed? Maquet, writing about the Rwanda, said: The century-old problem of evil in the world, particularly acute where there is a belief in the existence of a being who is omnipotent and infinitely good, has been solved by putting the responsibility for all evil and all suffering on agents other than *Imana* . . . *Imana* (God) himself does not cause any evil but he allows the causes of evil to act."[43] These agents or causes of evil, according to Maquet, are the "malevolent agencies of the invisible world,"[44] that is, evil spirits. Maquet is surely mistaken in maintaining that the fact that evil is traceable to evil spirits eliminates the problem of evil. For the questions I raised in discussing the problem of evil as it occurs in Akan thought (in section 7.4) are relevant here too. Thus even if it is the lesser spirits and not God which are held as the sources of evil, evil still remains a genuine problem for African philosophy and theology.

EPISTEMOLOGY: PARANORMAL COGNITION— AN IMPORTANT MODE OF KNOWING IN AFRICAN THOUGHT

Historically, Western epistemology has acknowledged two main sources of knowledge: reason (mind) and sense experience. The theories associated with these sources are known as rationalism and empiricism. Despite the activities of the Society for Psychical Research (founded in England in 1882) and despite much-publicized experiences in clairvoyance and telepathy—which are forms of extrasensory perception (ESP)—ESP has not been formally accepted as a form of knowing in the Western philosophy of knowledge. There are, to be sure, some individuals in Western societies who believe in ESP as a source of knowledge, but this is far from implying the recognition of ESP.

The case is different in African ways of knowing. Reason and sense experience are, to be sure, not unknown to African epistemology, even though, as in other areas, epistemological concepts in African thought have not been extensively investigated. In Akan thought, for instance, the well-known proverb

No one teaches a child God,
(*obi nkyerē abofra Nyame*)

implies that knowledge of God is intuitive and immediate,[45] rather than acquired through experience. Other proverbs indicate the Akan belief in innate ideas, such as

No one teaches blacksmithing to the son of a blacksmith.

No one teaches the leopard's child how to spring.[46]
(that is, it is born with that knowledge even though that knowledge is developed through experience).

Sense experience as a source of knowledge is also recognized in African thought. The Akan proverb

All things depend on experience,
(*nneēma nyinaa dan sua*)[47]

indicates the high regard the Akan thinkers have for knowledge based on experience.

But I wish to point out an important feature of African epistemology that makes it distinct from Western epistemology, namely, spirit mediumship, divination, and witchcraft. These modes of cognition are of course occasioned by means that differ from, but work alongside (*para*), the normal. Divination, witchcraft, and spirit mediumship are psychical phenomena common in all African communities. Middleton and Winter said: "Beliefs about witches and sorcerers have a worldwide distribution; *in Africa their occurrence is almost universal.*"[48] Evans-Pritchard wrote: ". . . most, perhaps all, African peoples have witchcraft or sorcery beliefs or both—in some degree."[49] Debrunner also noted that "Witchcraft beliefs are prominent all over Africa."[50] "With a few exceptions," writes Mbiti, "African systems of divination have not been carefully studied, though diviners and divinations are found in almost every community."[51] Spirit medium and spirit possession are just as widespread.[52] Parrinder observed that "Divination . . . is very popular in Africa."[53]

In African communities it is commonly believed that some individuals are born with certain abilities that are not acquired through experience. Diviners, traditional healers, and witches are believed to possess ESP with which they can perceive and communicate with supernatural entities. African thought maintains that perception does not wholly or exclusively occur through the physical senses, and that human beings are not entirely subject to the limitations of space and time. Telepathy, a form of ESP in which information originating in the mind of one person is sent to that of another; clairvoyance, in which people can see objects that are far away or otherwise hidden from sight; and precognition, in which people acquire information about the future—all these forms of Western parapsychology are, in the African context, aspects of divination and spirit mediumship, for the African diviner claims knowledge of the thoughts of other persons and of certain facts that has been acquired without the use of the normal senses. In Africa, this information is thought to be the result of the activities of discarnate minds, that is, spirits. Divination thus links the physical and the spiritual worlds, and in Africa (as perhaps elsewhere) there are numerous stories about individuals communicating with the dead, which, if true, would attest to survival after death.

Divination and spiritual mediumship are parapsychological phenomena and should, if possible, be investigated scientifically, for if they are found to be genuine, they might establish that the human mind is *not* material but a spiritual entity—a conclusion with obvious implications for epistemology and the philosophy of mind. In Africa, however, judging from the popularity of diviners and mediums and from the assiduity with which people in an African community seek certain kinds of knowledge from them, it can legitimately be claimed that paranormal cognition is recognized by and large as a mode of knowing.

Notes

1. K. A. Busia, *Africa in Search of Democracy,* (Praeger, New York, 1967), p. 5.

2. John S. Mbiti, *African Religions and Philosophy,* p. 37; also Malcolm J. McVeigh, *God in Africa,* p. 16; E. G. Parrinder, *African Traditional Religions* (Harper & Row, New York, 1962), pp. 32ff.

3. Edwin Smith (ed.), *African Ideas of God: A Symposium* (Edinburgh House Press, London, 1950), p. 7.

4. Mbiti, p. 43.

5. Ibid., p. 102; Also Parrinder, pp. 23, 43ff; McVeigh, pp. 32ff; Daryll Forde (ed.), *African Worlds* (Oxford University Press, Oxford, 1954); Monica Wilson, *Religion and the Transformation of Society* (Cambridge University Press, Cambridge, 1971), pp. 26–7.

6. Mbiti, p. 105.

7. M. Fortes, "Some Reflections on Ancestor Worship in Africa," in M. Fortes and G. Dieterlen (eds.), *African Systems of Thought* (Oxford University Press, Oxford, 1965), p. 122; also McVeigh, p. 34; Mbiti, p. 107ff.

8. Parrinder, p. 57. African scholars, however, argue that "ancestor worship" is a misnomer. Idowu, for instance, wrote that "ancestor worship" was not worship but only a veneration. E. Bolaji Idowu, *African Traditional Religion, A Definition* (SCM Press, London, 1973), pp. 178–89.

9. Mbiti, p. 21.

10. Ibid., p. 257.
11. Ibid., pp. 37–49.
12. Ibid., p. 80.
13. Ibid., pp. 55, 84–6; also Parrinder, p. 33.
14. McVeigh, p. 139.
15. Ibid., p. 103.
16. Mbiti, p. 74; also p. 97.
17. Ibid., pp. 261–2; also p. 222. See also Forde (ed.), *African Worlds,* pp. 8, 173; Robin Horton in Bryan R. Wilson, *Rationality,* p. 133.
18. John S. Mbiti, "The Capture of the Sun," in *Modern Science and Moral Values* (International Cultural Foundation, New York, 1983), p. 191; my italics.
19. McVeigh, p. 164.
20. Ibid., p. 230, n. 57.
21. Monica Wilson, p. 38.
22. Ibid., p. 141.
23. Forde (ed.), *African Worlds,* p. 168; McVeigh, p. 163; Mbiti, p. 262; J. O. Sodipo, "Notes on the Concept of Cause and Chance in Yoruba Traditional Thought," *Second Order,* Vol. II, No. 2, July 1973.
24. M. Fortes, "Some Reflections," p. 126.
25. Forde (ed.), *African Worlds,* p. 227.
26. Marcel Griaule, "The Idea of Person among the Dogon," in Simon Ottenberg and Phoebe Ottenberg (eds.), *Cultures and Societies of Africa* (Random House, New York, 1960), p. 366.
27. Forde (ed.), *African Worlds,* p. 174.
28. Ottenberg and Ottenberg (eds.), *Cultures and Societies,* p. 408.
29. E. Bolaji Idowu, *Olodumare,* pp. 169–70.
30. Forde (ed.), *African Worlds,* pp. 115, 155.
31. McVeigh, p. 26.
32. Ibid., p. 37.
33. Ibid., p. 130; also p. 144.
34. Kwesi A. Dickson, *Aspects of Religion and Life in Africa,* p. 3.
35. Mbiti, p. 52; my italics.
36. Fortes, *Job and Oedipus,* p. 19.
37. Mbiti, p. 52; also Forde (ed.), *African Worlds,* pp. 168ff.
38. Idowu, *Olodumare,* p. 173; italics in original.
39. Forde (ed.), *African Worlds,* pp. 9, 169, 228.
40. Mbiti, pp. 226–67; also Forde (ed.), *African Worlds,* pp. 43, 75.
41. McVeigh, pp. 128–9; also Forde (ed.), *African Worlds,* pp. 160–1.
42. Mbiti, p. 47; Forde (ed.), *African Worlds,* p. 169.
43. J. J. Maquet, "The Kingdom of Ruanda," in Forde (ed.), *African Worlds,* p. 172.
44. Ibid., p. 169.
45. W. E. Abraham, *The Mind of Africa,* p. 55; J. B. Danquah, *Akan Doc-*

trine of God, p. 153; C. A. Akrofi, *Twi Proverbs,* proverb no. 192.

46. Akrofi, *Twi Proverbs,* proverb No. 193; J. G. Christaller, *A Collection of 3,600 Twi Proverbs,* proverbs nos. 227–35; J. A. Annobil, *Proverbs and Their Explanations,* p. 88.

47. Christaller, *Proverbs,* proverb no. 2284; Akfrofi, *Twi Proverbs,* proverb no. 722.

48. John Middleton and E. H. Winter, *Witchcraft and Sorcery in East Africa* (Routledge and Kegan Paul, London, 1963), p. 1, et passim.

49. Ibid., p. vii.

50. H. Debrunner, *Witchcraft in Ghana,* p. 2.

51. Mbiti, p. 232.

52. Ibid., pp. 224ff; also J. H. M. Beattie and John Middleton (eds.), *Spirit Mediumship and Society in Africa* (Africana Publishing Corp., New York, 1969).

53. Parrinder, p. 119; also pp. 100–34.

Excerpts from Knowledge, Belief, and Witchcraft: Analytical Experiments in African Philosophy

Barry Hallen and J. O. Sodipo

While members of the philosophy department at Awolowo University in Ile-Ife, Nigeria, Professors Barry Hallen and J. O. Sodipo engaged in a long series of interviews with the traditional healers of a Yoruba village in order to elicit their understanding of key concepts within their belief system. The traditional healers (native doctors, herbalists) or oníṣẹ̀gùn interviewed were highly esteemed in their community as well as in the professional society of healers (ẹgbẹ́). Contrary to the generally accepted view of knowledge in oral cultures as based on authority and passed unchanged from generation to generation, Hallen and Sodipo found that the oníṣẹ̀gùn clearly distinguished belief from knowledge and exhibited a critical attitude towards received opinion.

In their book, they provide an extended exposition of W. V. Quine's controversial "Indeterminacy of Translation" thesis, which states that the theoretical terms of one culture can be mapped in different ways on the theoretical terms of a radically different culture, with no way of using empirical evidence to choose the best mapping. They test this thesis by examining the common practice of translating the Yoruba words "mọ̀" and "gbàgbọ́" into the English words "knowledge" and "belief," and they uncover significant differences in the way the two sets of words are understood.

In the last chapter of their book, they provide a similar examination of the practice of translating the Yoruba word "àjẹ́" into the English word "witch." Western commentators [eg., Geoffrey Parrinder, Witchcraft: European and African *(London: Faber and Faber, 1970), Lucy Mair,* Witchcraft *(London: Weidenfeld and Nicolson, 1969) and E. Evans-Prichard,* Witchcraft, Magic and Sorcery among the Azande *(Oxford: Clarendon Press,*

1937)] have promulgated a model in which healers and sorcerers use learnt techniques to manifest psychic powers whereas witches manifest such powers without benefit of learnt techniques. In contrast, Hallen and Sodipo show that the identification of "witches" in Western culture with women who cause harm by unlearned psychic means is not mirrored among the oníṣẹ̀gùn. The oníṣẹ̀gùn *accept the existence of "*àjẹ́*," but it is not an uncritical acceptance. Moreover, they identify different forms of the power that makes "*àjẹ́*" possible and clearly distinguish between its use for good and evil.*

For the Yoruba the essential elements of the person (*èniyàn*) when in the world are the body (*ara*), the vital spirit of that body, or soul (*èmí*), and the destiny (*orí*) that will determine every significant event during that particular lifetime. The concept of "*orí*" is an exceedingly complex and fascinating one, and a good deal of literature already exists on the subject. But all we need say of it here is that the same spirit (*èmí*) returns to the world an indefinite number of times, each time with a new destiny (*orí*) which it consciously, deliberately and *freely* chooses before being reborn.

Therefore, when the *oníṣẹ̀gùn* make a remark such as the following:

(20) The *àjẹ́* behaves according to how its *èmí* is. Not all of them do bad things.

what they also have in mind is that even after death, when existing only as *èmí*, the person is still a *moral* being with a character (*ìwà*) that may be assessed as good or bad. And it is this moral element that plays a significant role in influencing the kind of destiny (*orí*) the person will choose for his next lifetime. If he is a good person (*èníyàn rere*), he will choose a destiny that will entail his doing good things while in the world. If he is a bad person (*èníyàn burúkú*), he will choose one that entails the opposite, though he will see it as being to his benefit. This interpretation of Yoruba beliefs about life and afterlife is in part supported by the following statements:

(21) The *ìwà* of *àjẹ́* . . . there are some *àjẹ́* whose *ìwà* is good.
(22) It is inside your *ìwà* [character] that you bring out *èníyàn rere*. If he is a *babaláwo*[1] and you bring a child to him [because it has some problem], if

---

[1] For the meaning of this term see p. 1 [of original] above. However, when referring to themselves in discussion, the *oníṣẹ̀gùn* often use the terms "*oníṣẹ̀gùn*" and "*babaláwo*" interchangeably.

there are some people who are trying to be cruel to the child, he will drive them away. He will not allow them to come. As a *babaláwo* all his medicine will be answering (*jé*) [i.e. be effective]. If there is any *àjẹ́* who is going to disturb him, he will drive him away. He is *àjẹ́ rere, àlùjànún rere* and *èníyàn rere*. He will combine everything. If he is not a *babaláwo*, but if a *babaláwo* is making his medicine, he will not allow them [*èníyàn burúkú*] to spoil it, and he will tell the *babaláwo* to change his hand [i.e. how to improve his techniques so that they will not be fallible]. He will teach him. This is good *àlùjànún*.

We will undertake some explanation of the difficult term "*álùjànún*" a bit later on.[2] For the moment our interest centers on the expression "*àjẹ́ rere,*" good *àjẹ́*, in quotation 22 and its implied equivalent in quotation 20. Is it being used here in a metaphorical sense, as an expressive way of referring to an exceptionally talented individual? Or does it mean that there really can be *àjẹ́* who are neither malevolent nor anti-social, who in fact work for the positive betterment of mankind? The answer to this question may be obtained from the following:

(23) There are some who behave well, if they have chosen to be so from heaven. This type of *àjẹ́* will not associate themselves with others [*àjẹ́*] who are known to be bad.

(24) *Àjẹ́* is *èníyàn rere.* Not all the *àjẹ́* are *èníyàn burúkú.* There are some good ones.

(25) *Àjẹ́ rere* cannot do anything bad. He will be looking for good things. And he will not be eating blood.

And finally, a remark made in discussion with specific reference to the issue of whether it is possible for a *babaláwo/oníṣègùn* to be *àjẹ́, àlùjànún,* and *èníyàn rere* (a good person) at the same time:

(26) I said it was possible. The *babaláwo* who has *àlùjànún* and *àjẹ́*, their medicine will always answer (*je*) [i.e. work well]. He should have seen the *ìdí*[3] of what he wants to use the medicine for . . . As *àjẹ́* and *àlùjànún,* any medicine which I put my hands on must be good.

The answer to our original question, then, is that there definitely are many *àjẹ́* who are *good* persons; furthermore, that some of them are *oníṣègùn* or *babaláwo*, in fact the most powerful amongst the *oníṣègùn* or *babaláwo*. And since the gentlemen with whom we are holding our discussions are considered to be amongst the most powerful of the *oníṣègùn* in the area, the implication is definite and clear. Many amongst them are knowingly *àjẹ́*. But they dare not admit to it in an open and direct man-

---

[2] See p. 107.
[3] See p. 70 above, "*ìdí*" is a component of "*nwadi*" and a noun form of "bottom," "cause" or "reason."

ner. The closest they can come is to state it in the hypothetical manner found in the final sentence of quotation 26.

We have yet finally to conclude why this reluctance to admit to being *àjẹ́*, why the need for secrecy, exist. But before we get to this we must first say something about the concept of "*àlùjànún*":

(27) If you come to ask something from me now, I can tell you to go and come back. I will put that thing in mind (*okòn*[4]). And when I see (*riran*) it, if it is something that will not be possible, I will say so. If it is good, I will tell you to go there—that there is nothing [no problem]. It means that I've used the *ojú inú* (literally: 'inside' eye) to see (*wo*) it.

As is the case with *àjẹ́*, *àlùjànún* confers a certain power upon a person. In the above example, the closest English-language equivalent is perhaps "second sight," a kind of telepathic power (the "inside" eye) that allows a person to foresee the consequences of an action. People who are *àlùjànún* are therefore considered among the most powerful in Yoruba society.

IS THE *ÀJẸ́* A WITCH?

If one goes by the criteria, or model(s), of African witchcraft drawn up by Parrinder and Mair, the *àjẹ́* appear not to fit them in at least four important respects:

1. Many *àjẹ́* are men.
2. Many *oníṣègùn* are *àjẹ́*. According to Parrinder's model the *oníṣègùn* are one important professional group in Yoruba society who would be classed under the anachronistic heading of "witch-doctor." A person who is being troubled by *àjẹ́* will often go to an *oníṣègùn* for help with identifying the *àjẹ́*, and for counsel and medicine to counter their onslaught. But it is Parrinder who insists that the witch-doctor can*not* be a witch.[5]
3. Many *àjẹ́* use medicine to achieve their ends. Granted sometimes it may be because they are *oníṣègùn*, rather than that they are *àjẹ́*, that is the primary reason for their practising medicine. But it is clear that there are *àjẹ́* who are *neither oníṣègùn* nor *babaláwo*[6] and still make use of medicine to achieve their ends:

(28) If the *àjẹ́* learns the medicine for making rain, it will fall immediately. And if he wants to take [prevent] it, he will do this easily. They can do both easily.

[4] For the meaning of this term see p. 61 [of original] above.
[5] See p. 94 [of original] above.
[6] That there are *àjẹ́* who are neither *oníṣègùn* nor *babaláwo* is also indicated by the last three sentences of quotation 22 above.

(29) This can be done by means of medicine, especially if he is *àjẹ́* . . . he could use a medicine which would make it impossible for the leopard to see him. . . . These are the works of medicine.

(30) Persons, like *àjẹ́*. . . . are those who are responsible . . . If the "power-fuls" want to travel to somewhere like Lagos, they will be making a lot of preparation [i.e. medicine] in the afternoon. And when it is night time, they will tie all the medicine on their body. Then they will rise from the earth to the sky and they will be moving . . .

Parrinder has stated categorically that witchcraft must not be confused with sorcery. Witchcraft is a *purely* psychical phenomenon, and one who makes the mistake of associating it with the preparation or use of "magical" medicines is confusing the sorcerer, the good magician, the witch-doctor, or the wizard, with witchcraft proper. But, as the above quotations indicate, the Yoruba are either confused (a possibility we shall discuss in the final sub-section of this chapter) or attribute properties to the *àjẹ́* which do not suit Parrinder's model.

If the *àjẹ́* do make use of "magical" medicines, is this the source of their power? And if it is not medicine, what is? These are extremely difficult questions to answer, and have been from the very beginning. Thomas may attribute it to the occult, Parrinder to psychical power, and Mair to a mystical ability, but what precisely are these terms meant to convey other than that the basis for the power of witchcraft exceeds the boundaries of ordinary or scientific understanding and explanation. Witchcraft is *extra*ordinary. Witchcraft is *super*-natural.

Is it the same with the Yoruba *àjẹ́*? This is a question to which we can only give a partial and somewhat speculative answer, though to attempt even this we must first introduce a few more technical terms from the Yoruba conceptual system.

First, let us go back to the question of how a person first becomes *àjẹ́*. We have already made reference to the way *ẹ̀mí* chooses its destiny (*orí*) before coming to the world (i.e. being born), but let us now go over it a bit more carefully:

(31) They [the *àjẹ́*] are *èníyàn* (persons), just like you and me.

(32) You cannot use medicine to make *àjẹ́*.

(33) This is what they [*àjẹ́*] brought from heaven.

(34) *Ọlọ́run* (the supreme deity) put the *àṣẹ* on their destiny (*orí*).

(35) There are some *èníyàn* (persons) who are only *àjẹ́* and not the others [i.e. *àlùjànún*, etc.]. It depends upon the choice of individual.

When the individual (as *ẹ̀mí*) has chosen a new destiny (*orí*) he then appears before *Ọlọ́run*, the supreme deity, who uses his supreme power, the *àṣẹ*, to "fix" that destiny to the individual so that it will guide and channel the person's approaching lifetime in the world. Assumption to the power of *àjẹ́*, then, is something that is said to happen to a person before they are born into the physical world.

Secondly, although being *àjẹ́* is said to be the function of choosing a particular *orí*, the choice *of* that *orí* has serious consequences for the *ẹmí* or *inú* of the person who then comes into the world:

(36) There are some with two *ẹ̀mí*. *Àjẹ́* has two *ẹ̀mi*.

(37) *Àjẹ́* has two *inú*.

(38) They were born with them [people with two *inú*]. They do not simply come by them in the world. It is part of their destiny.

(39) In the most common use of the word (*nipata ki*) [the word referred to is *inú*], when we say that someone has got *inú* we mean that he is a good person (*omolúàbí*). In another way you can say that someone has got *inú* to mean that he has got [the power of] *àjẹ́*.

(40) It is his *ìwà* (character), because the *ìwà* is *inú*. All the things we do come out of *inú*.

(41) A person (*ènìyàn*) cannot have anything apart from the thing which is given to him in heaven . . . If the *inú* of someone is good, bad things will not have a place there. If we teach him to do bad things, he will not accept. Whenever a person is instigated to do bad things, if he agrees, this means that it is his own will.

Because of the peculiarities of their medicinal and theoretical systems, the *oníṣẹ̀gùn* have reason to be specially concerned with and interested in the *inú* of a person. *Inu* literally means "inside." It can also be used to refer to the stomach. But for purposes of our present exposition, rather than becoming involved with the intricacies of the medicinal system, it is sufficient to point out that *inú* and *ẹmí* are also sometimes used by them interchangeably (as may be inferred from quotations 37–39 above).

What does a second *ẹ̀mí* or *inú* enable the *àjẹ́* to do? This is perhaps the most difficult question of all to answer. As far as the stereotype is concerned, it certainly is the source of the powers of the *àjẹ́* when in the world.[7] And as a "vital spirit," *ẹmí/inú* is certainly more or other than material substance. As a second vital element, it is this *àjẹ́ ẹmi/inú* that the person can send out or use to go out and away from himself to accomplish those things that make him extraordinary.

This (coupled with quotation 33 above) would apparently indicate that the source of the power of the *àjẹ́* is not medicine. But it would be an error to therefore conclude that the power of *àjẹ́* has nothing to do with medicine, including what Parrinder would refer to as "magic." If *àjẹ́* makes medicine it is thought to be more powerful and more effective as medicine than what would be prepared by a person with no special power or ability. The exact nature of the causal connection between the

[7] As recounted on p. 102 [of original] above.

àjẹ́ and the power of its medicines still eludes us,[8] but there is not doubt but that it is there.

One further, possibly minor but still interesting, point about the powers of the *àjẹ́* is brought out by several remarks in which the *oníṣẹ̀gùn* compare them with those of the *àlùjànún*:

> (42) *Àjẹ́* cannot know what is going on in the next room, whereas *emèrè*[9] and *àlùjànún* can.
>
> (43) *Emèrè* can detect what a person has done in secret, but *àjẹ́* cannot.
>
> (44) If someone holds something in his [closed] hand, *emèrè* can identify what it is. But *àjẹ́* cannot.

"Paranormal perception," "clairvoyance," "telepathy" and even "mind-reading" are all rather technical English-language terms in the field sometimes referred to as parapsychology. On a more prosaic level that will enable us to avoid becoming entangled with the various theories underlying this controversial field of interest, what the above quotations seem to indicate (when coupled with quotation 27) is that, while the *àlùjànún* can both "send" (or "transmit") and "receive," the *àjẹ́* can only "send." This would mean that the power of the *àjẹ́* is demonstrated primarily by the ability to use the second *èmí/inú* to do something for it, even if it is distant from the body with which it is associated. The *àlùjànún*, however, in some manner for future researchers to look into, is able to know about (to receive information about) events that are going on distant from him *as well as* to do something about them, if he so chooses.

4. Many *àjẹ́* are neither evil nor malevolent. In fact many *àjẹ́* may be characterized as benevolent and eminently moral persons. Numerous remarks of the *oníṣẹ̀gùn* support these assertions (quotations 22, 23–25, 41, 42), and therefore they do not seem to require any further defence. But it is important to recall that, for Mair, an evil disposition and, for Parrinder, deliberate malice were important, sometimes even essential, characteristics of the witch.

In this sub-section we have drawn attention to four important respects in which Yoruba beliefs about the *àjẹ́* differ from the models of African witchcraft formulated by Parrinder and Mair, and to which the Yoruba are said by them to subscribe. We would therefore suggest that their models are inadequate, or at least incomplete, for providing an adequate basis for analysis and understanding of the *àjẹ́* phenomenon in Yoruba thought.

---

[8] Another reason for the problem of obtaining more specific information about this is the element of secrecy (*awo*) surrounding the making of medicines, in addition to that surrounding the powers of the *àjẹ́*. For further information about the role of secrecy in professional associations in Yoruba culture see Abimbola and Hallen 1978.

[9] Another apparent personality-type to which we shall make brief reference in the next subsection. For the moment the important things are what the *àjẹ́* cannot do rather than what the *emèrè* can do.

On the Existence of Witches

Sophie Oluwole

In this article, Dr. Sophie Oluwole of the Philosophy Department at the University of Lagos in Nigeria summarizes the many explanations Western social scientists have given for the African's belief in witchcraft. Dr. Oluwole points out how many investigators of witchcraft acknowledge the belief in the existence of witches without themselves believing in witches. Typically such investigators believe that witches are merely a fallacious reification of the socially accepted belief in witches. Others, however, accept the existence of witches as a fact and Oluwole denies that their beliefs can be dismissed simply because Western science has not been able to empirically verify those beliefs. The current requirements of empirical verification depend on the assumption that information can only be received by human beings through the recognized channels of the senses, and this assumption is subject to alteration in the future. As such, it is at best only a good working hypothesis for the present. Even if unable to provide adequate explanations or experimental demonstrations, if a believer is able to practically manifest the powers that make witchcraft possible, we would be justified in accepting its existence.

While she is critical of Western skepticism about witchcraft, Oluwole is equally critical of Africa's partiality to such claims. She challenges those who believe in witchcraft to contribute, not by merely repeating and codifying traditional beliefs, but also by exposing their mistakes. Insisting that the canons of current science cannot be accepted as inviolable, Oluwole insists equally that traditional beliefs cannot be accepted as unalterable truths.

When one considers the almost innumerable works on witchcraft and the overwhelming condemnation of it as the result of fantasy or illusion, there can be little wonder that a Nigerian psychologist recently asserted that "even now, manuals on whether witches exist have become encyclopaedic in bulk and lunatic in pedantry."[1] But when one comes across other works where the authors categorically assert the objective reality of witchcraft, then the feeling of wonder is increased. Both positions, since contradictory, cannot be true. It is of philosophical interest to examine both claims in order to find out which is more likely to be true, and to try to find a way of deciding which of the two positions is more logically justifiable.

My aim here is first to try to define what we mean by witchcraft. Then I shall look into each of the two positions on the nature of witchcraft. For each, I shall try to show where the judgment is misconceived, where the justifications offered are logically untenable and where some of the conclusions are invalidly derived. At the end I shall try to rectify these faults, clearly spelling out the justifications and consequences of the claim that witchcraft is real.

John Middleton and E. H. Winter define witchcraft as "a mystical and innate power which can be used by its possessor to harm other people."[2] Bringing out more clearly the salient features of witchcraft M. J. Field, in his *Search for Security,* said: 'The distinguishing feature of killing or harm by witchcraft is that it is wrought *by the silent, invisible projection of influence from the witch.* Witches are believed to be able to act at any distance."[3] (emphasis mine).

It is clear from the above that witchcraft is usually regarded as a peculiar power by virtue of which some people perform actions which the ordinary man cannot normally perform. The most unique and mysterious characteristic of this power being the claimed ability of the witch to affect her victims, or perform actions, without any physical contact and using no medicine. Thus, the late Professor Sir Edward Evans-Pritchard, one of the most renowned authors on witchcraft, introduced his famous book on the Azande with the observation that "Azande believe that some people are witches and can injure them by virtue of an inherent quality: a witch possesses no rites, utters no spell, and possesses no medicine. An act of witchcraft is a psychic act."[4] Finally, Mr. E. O. Eyo in a paper read almost a decade ago said:

> I, myself, do not believe that a man or woman is a witch in the supernatural sense except in so far as he or she is practically a social deviant or an unpleasant person within the community that believes in witches . . . what is correct is that it does exist, not in reality but only in the minds of some people. Witchcraft exists in fantasy in the minds of mentally sick people.[5]

One can go on almost indefinitely quoting extracts to show this general attitude towards witchcraft and witchcraft belief. Although there is no dispute about the fact that most primitive societies, including almost all African societies, believe in witchcraft, the attitude of authors from the "modern societies" can be summarized in the words of J. R. Crawford who asserts that "witchcraft is essentially a psychic act and is, objectively speaking, impossible."[6]

Now, what about those who claim that witchcraft is real? I let a few of them speak for themselves. Professor E. Bolaji Idowu, writing in an article titled "Challenge of Witchcraft," said:

> Do witches exist? I will assert categorically that there are witches in Africa; that they are as real as murderers, poisoners, and other categories of evil workers, overt or surreptitious. This, and not only imagination, is the basis of the strong belief in witchcraft.[7]

Professor John S. Mbiti, formerly Professor of Theology at Makerere University, writing on witchcraft, remarked:

> Every African who has grown up in the traditional environment will, no doubt, know something about this mystical power which often is experienced, or manifests itself, in the form of magic, divination, witchcraft and mysterious phenomena that seem to defy even immediate scientific explanation.[8]

Lastly Dr. D. E. Idoniboye of the Philosophy Department, University of Lagos, writes:

> The point I want to stress here is that when Africans talk of spirits in the sense I have been discussing, they are not speaking metaphorically nor are they propounding a myth. *Spirits are as real as tables and chairs, people and places.*[9]

These are but a few testimonies to show that despite Gillian Tindall's claim "that witchcraft today is virtually a dead issue in Europe . . ." and that it has ceased to be accepted either as a force of evil or as a rival of Christianity, most Africans not only continue to believe in it but some even go as far as trying to prove its reality.

The next question is, what exactly do these writers mean when they say either that witchcraft is real or unreal? The word "real" is one of the most problematic if not the most fundamental in philosophical discussions. From Thales through Socrates and Aristotle down to Hume and Russell, philosophers have endeavoured to spell out what distinguishes the real from the unreal. All we can do here is try to bring out the important features of "reality." When something is described as real, the first distinction that is commonly drawn is between the "real" as physical and the "unreal" as abstract. Hence quality, (e.g., redness) will be unreal in this sense while a chair will be real. Next, we speak of different levels of reality. Redness, for instance, is real because there are instances of red things in the world. Hence, although there is no tangible object which we can refer to as redness, philosophers still regard it as real in its own way, though having no objective independent existence.

Authors who deny the existence of witchcraft claim that witchcraft neither designates something tangible or observable nor does it refer to something that has an independent existence either in the sense of being actual or true, hence they label it an illusion. This, of course, as hinted above, does not rule out the possibility of witchcraft having a *metaphysical reality*. Furthermore, there has never been any doubt that many Africans believe in witchcraft, i.e., to them it has what Max Marwick calls a threatening reality, so much so that they project it to the level of reality as "actual" or true. This wrong projection, this lack of ability to separate the objects of the ordinary world of experience from those of the world of thought, is what western authors often refer to when they call witchcraft belief "a fallacy." This then is the position of those who say witchcraft is unreal; that there is nothing like witches.

Let us now discuss the views of those who claim that witchcraft is real. Dr. Idoniboye, in his article referred to above discusses how Africans use metaphysical explanation of the existence of spirits to express "their view of what is the case in the world around them." Clearly the African is postulating a metaphysical explanation. And although this explanation does not rule out the theory that *metaphysical assumption* can relate to factual situations, yet it does not automatically do so—it has to be shown that it is so. It may be true that to Africans, *ideas* of spirit, witches, etc., have "a threatening reality." This only establishes, in the language of Professor Bolaji Idowu, that "it is real that Africans believe in witchcraft." But it is not the *reality of the belief* that is under examination. No matter how vivid our ideas of spirits and witches, the vividness alone cannot vouchsafe for the objective self-existence of what is believed. If to Africans "spirit is real, as real as matter" it is only in their thought that there is no difference between the witch and matter. If Africans regard spirits as part of the furniture of the world and not merely as logical constructions out of certain unaccountable manifestations, it may simply be that the "universe of the African" is different from the objective one. It appears to me that Dr. Idoniboye is here ably arguing for the metaphysical (theoretical) reality of the concept of "spirits" *to the African.* He has not tried to establish the scientific basis of the belief. If his aim was to establish the latter, then the former is neither a necessary nor a sufficient basis for doing so. Reason demands that we ask for the logical as well as the "empirical" justifications of such belief. The latter part of Dr. Idoniboye's article was meant to illustrate the empirical rather than the metaphysical reality of witchcraft. And he went straight to the point when he said, "this is no sheer sentimentalism. Witchcraft is ever present with us." In support of this claim, Dr. Idoniboye relates an experience he had as a child.

When Professor Idowu asserts that "witches are as real as murderers and poisoners, etc.," it is quite evident that the type of reality he is claiming is an objective one (actual)—the practical efficacy of a power possessed *and used* by human beings just as poisoners effectively use medicine to kill. Thus, he wrote: "There is no doubt that there are persons of very strong character who can exude their personality and make it affect other persons. Witches and witchcraft are sufficiently real as to cause untold sufferings and innumerable deaths."[10]

This excursion into the claims of these authors is but an attempt to clearly spell out the kind of reality they are talking about, because in many cases, the authors seem to confuse metaphysical reality (the reality of a belief) with reality as stressing correspondence to what exists in nature or to all known or knowable facts. Hence, when in fact all they try to show is a theoretical reality, they seem to think that they have shown the reality of witchcraft in the sense of its corresponding to the facts.

On what grounds to proponents claim either that witchcraft is real or that it is unreal? Those who claim that witchcraft is unreal defend their position by saying that for anything to be real, it must be such that it is observable even if only in principle, that it is susceptible to observational test, i.e., observable through the five senses either with or without the aid of scientific equipment. There are some who say that science does not deny the possibility of other modes of knowledge beside the strictly observable. This may *nominally* be true but there is an onus of proof which this liberal claim puts on anyone who professes there are other modes. Not only must such a person be ready to describe and/or show how it works, he must also be prepared to tell us how we can share in his knowledge. Put in another way, the demand of those who deny reality to witchcraft is that anything that we designate as real must be either actual in the sense of conformity with what exists in nature, or true in the sense of fitting into a pattern, a model, a standard; in short into a system whose outline is already well known. Anyone who calls witchcraft as illusion seems to say that since it does not cohere with a body of known facts, it cannot itself be a fact. What methods, what tests, what observations could establish for example, that: "a man who has been DEMONSTRABLY asleep on a mat throughout the night has spent the (very) night feasting, or that a dead person who has clearly suffered no cannibalistic ravages has been slain through witchcraft?" The conclusion is therefore that anything that cannot be tested, observed, etc., is not real.

How do the African authors justify their belief that witchcraft is real? Apart from perhaps Mr. Okunzua, I do not know of any direct or indirect justification of this belief. It is true that many of them lay claim to the knowledge of witchcraft and witchcraft practices. Professor Idowu, for instance, seems to suggest the existence of another mode of knowledge apart from that obtained through the scientific method. In answer to his own question quoted above he said, "If so then we might as well close down all churches and places of worships, speak up and declare to the world that we have been all along babblers and chatterers, spendthrifts of our time." Mr. Okunzua postulates an astral plane on which witches operate. Apparently both of these authors seem to claim that witchcraft is a mystical power, a power that exists not in the same form as tangible phenomena. Dr. Idoniboye said explicitly that he was not interested in the *modus operandi* of witches. Although Professor Mbiti did not go into the discussion of the nature of witchcraft, yet he calls it a *mysterious power*. If asked, "How do you know that something not tangible, not scientifically provable is real? How, for instance, do you come to the conclusion that "a woman demonstrably asleep on her bed throughout the night is the cause of the mysterious death of her neighbour?," many African authors are silent on this all-important issue.

Although Professor Idowu did not tell us how he knows of witches' meetings, etc., Mr. Okunzua seems to have an answer when he held that witchcraft not being ordinary, witchery research cannot be ordinary. But then we can easily tell him that since most of us are ordinary men, and hence cannot have an access to the knowledge he claims, we are in no way obliged to accept his testimonies. Secondly, since he claims that witches operate on another plane, probably they belong to another world not quite the same as concerns us. There is a gap we cannot bridge and so we can neither verify not falsify his claims. To us they remain, in an important sense, "meaningless."

On the other hand, the claim that witchcraft is mysterious, is really an answer to the question: what is the nature of witchcraft? Whereas the question we are supposed to be answering is "How do you know there is this mystical power?" Probably one question presupposes the other but definitely they are not identical and hence must be answered differently. How does the African claim to know that this mysterious power is real? The answer is in some of the quotations above. In all cases, what the Africans seem to be saying is "We know it is real because there are innumerable occurrence that prove its practical efficacy." We experience it, and it is ever present with us, working in our presence." To substantiate this claim, Dr. Idoniboye relates a personal experience; Professor Idowu tells the story as told by one of the students in his University; and Professor Mbiti refers us to the records of the life experience of a white author, Mr. James Neal. All these incidents are referred to as the rational basis of the logical justification of the reality of witchcraft power. "A power that actually works is real," they all seem to be saying.

When the western authors say that a real object must be "actual, i.e., scientifically observable or testable even if only in principle" they are not propounding a myth, they are giving the canons of a method, their method of evaluation. And, as earlier noted, anyone who rejects these canons must be prepared to produce substitutes, not just any substitute but one which is as simple, and of the same explanatory power, as theirs. The most important fact to be stressed here, which scientists more often than not forget, is that these canons depend upon an assumption, an epistemological thesis yet to be proved, namely, the assumption adequately put by Professor J. B. Rhine when he said:

> It has been long a *common assumption* among the learned that nothing enters the human mind except by way of the sense. According to this *long-unquestioned doctrine* there is no way of direct communication between one mind and another and *no possible* means by which *reality* can be experienced except through the recognised channels of senses.[11] (emphasis mine).

There is no doubt that this is a rational assumption, a good working hypothesis, but because of the very fact that it is a hypothesis, we must constantly remind ourselves that it only expresses the canons of a kind of method and not a record of an eternal indubitable truth. By its very nature, its premise is open to doubt and question.

The true scientific attitude is that we must be prepared to adjust, to modify or even entirely abandon our hypothesis if there is enough evidence of uncompromising experience against it. If we leave this question open, we may at times discover that our standard is based on a prejudice and consequently fails to take cognizance of all available facts. If on the other hand we raise our hypothesis to the level of an indubitable fact, and use it to throw overboard anything that does not fit our pattern or standard, then, we should suspect the inadequacy of our standard—of failing to take into cognisance a number of things which may in fact be as natural as those we knew earlier on. So, rather than adjust our experience to suit our standard, science should really proceed *vice versa.*

If all Middleton and Winter mean when they describe "witchcraft as a mystical power" is that it is a "a power not yet understood," there would not be much ado; but to proceed the way Crawford did by saying "it is objectively speaking impossible" is to go beyond the limits of what a model, a pattern, a standard can legitimately be used to do. We can of course say: so far this piece of experience has peculiarities which make it different from the ones we are used to, or rather, that are common. Yet one is making an unsound logical leap by denying such an experience a reality just because of its non-conformity to known laws.

Regretably, scientists have recorded a poor history as far as this attitude is concerned. It is true that many times they have changed their views or positions and in such cases appear to be wonderfully open-minded. But apparently, scientists are interested only in the region of reality they *want* to be interested in. Where their curiosity should be aroused, they sometimes turn deaf ears. Although most scientists eventually accepted Einstein when he showed that Euclid's theorems and Newton's law of gravitation, hitherto regarded as indubitable, were both inadequate and in a sense untrue, it was not without some resistance. The history of science is punctuated with similar resistance to revolutionary discoveries. Scientists today hold their hypothesis as a sort of religious dogma, and many cling fanatically to it as if it were the last word on possible knowledge. Until scientists accept that they have not discovered an indubitable method of knowing what is real until they realise that science, being based on the generative theory of causal relationship which treats statistical evidence of succession as the basis of the hypothesis that a causal mechanism exists, is a direct consequence of our epistemological rather than an ontological requirement, so long will they give room for being accused of "intellectual fraud"—"fraud" for substituting the epistemic for the ontic. As a matter of fact, this demand, this scientific hypothesis, transcends experience. For nothing in our experience tells us that the real is only the scientifically provable. Our consent to the occurrence of mysteries confirms that *the mysterious is that which is not yet understood* but not that which is unknowable.

Hence, to declare something impossible just because "there is no place for it in contemporary science" is to present a logically invalid argument. If we are not careful, we shall be inadvertently committing ourselves to the presumptuous claim that "man, after some 400 years of scientific endeavour set in a universe with a time span of some 4,000,000,000 years, has discovered *all* the features of reality."[12] Yet it is only on this false assumption that science justifies its denial of the mysterious as anything real. And just as Socrates and his pupil Plato were so much impressed by the validity and "apparent certainty" of logic that they relegated empirical studies to the realm of illusion, so may scientists be intoxicated with the undeniable successes of science that they too are ready to brand as illusory anything that does not conform to their empirical dogma. Thus, they may shut the gates of their heaven to any experience which fails their test. No one denies that "any fact which can be checked, reproduced at will, varied and tested," in short, any fact that can be established through one or more of the experimental methods of science, takes on an enormously increased reality, yet the inability to check, reproduce, etc., may not be the result of the non-existence of what is studied but rather an evidence of the inadequacy of our present method of experiment. Future scientific progress may remove this inadequacy.

What then does one say about the African justification of his belief in this reality of witchcraft? Many writers have criticised attempts at the empirical justification by Africans as either fake or based on fallacious reasoning. First is the claim that many (if not all) of the stories and testimonies that are cited as evidences of the practical efficacy of witchcraft are make-belief, created to safeguard the existence of a traditional dogma. The few that are not fake are just ordinary occurrences whose real causes can be known if the primitive man knows a little of science. Ignorance, therefore, makes Africans postulate obscure mysterious causes for scientifically explainable occurrences. For instance, not knowing the real cause of some disease, they say "the witch has killed my child," etc. Some people "see" others as the cause of their misfortunes just because they are psychologically disturbed (e.g., the paranoid); others who confess to effecting these mysterious occurrences often are victims of different diseases of the mind like schizophrenia. People who claim to do things which in reality they did not do are people who need to assert themselves because of poor social status. This is especially true of the women whose social status in many African countries is a little above that of slaves. Another reason why the primitive man believes in the existence of witchcraft powers is because he has been indoctrinated right from youth. And finally any mysterious event whose occurrence cannot be dismissed in any of these ways are mere *accidents* or coincidences. Here the claim is that the primitive man postulates an occult power at work because "the idea of the unexplained," "the unknown" is abhorrent to him. In short, the verdict is that Africans see connections between different events where no such connections exist. They apply the *post hoc, ergo propter hoc* invalid argument pattern to their claims.

Listening to stories about the practices and meetings of witches, even the most credulous African at times finds it difficult to disagree with Professor Mbiti when he hinted that "in a non-scientific environment, belief of this type cannot be 'clean' from fear, falsehood, exaggeration, suspicion, fiction and irrationality."[13] In short, some of the criticisms of the belief and accusations of witchcraft seem not completely out of place. But rather than agree totally with Mbiti that these exaggeration, etc., are the results of an unscientific environment, I would add that they are part of man's natural reaction to the "unknown." In other words, it is a natural reaction to something that *seems* inexplicable. To substantiate his claims therefore the African needs not only show that his reasoning is not necessarily invalid, he must also be prepared to experimentally establish the causal relationship between an event and the witch supposed to be its cause. This he can do by showing that his belief has a basis in his experience or showing the practical efficacy of witchcraft.

But before we discuss this it is interesting to observe that no matter how sceptical one is, the honest observer can testify to Professor Idowu's and Professor Mbiti's claim that there are some events and occurrences, that cannot be explained in the language of modern science. I do not think that many scientists would deny the occurrence of *mysteries* as such, only they would want to dismiss them as coincidence or accidents. Yet the recognition of coincidences requires some degree of justification. As it is clear from the following quotes, Africans agree that these incidents refute every scientific explanation.

After dismissing as fraud and stressing the fallacious nature of the reasoning that leads to the primitive man's postulation of a mysterious power which he labels "witchcraft," Arthur S. Gregor notes:

> There is a side to magic, a dark shaded area we have not been able to penetrate. No investigator has been able to explain away some of the powers the shamans possess, and *there are witchcraft phenomena that refuse to yield to our cold Western analysis. 'Hay algo mas alla.'* "There is something beyond," as the Mexicans say. We may strip the magic from the magic, but the mystery remains[14] (emphasis mine)

Gregor's honesty of admitting that there is something to be explained is a step in the right direction. And although the tacit acceptance of a different possibility does not imply that we must accept just any explanation, it is much more faithful to the true scientific method, and it is far more likely to lead us to the truth in a much more convincing way than the sceptic's attitude of dismissing the unknown as accident or coincidence. Only an unbiased, honest study of these events can reveal the truth or falsity of the African position. Any explanation given by the Africans in support of their claim, must not only be logically sound, it must also be experimentally verifiable; it must have at least some bearing on experience, otherwise it would for ever remain a speculation and a fantasy.

Now let us examine the "evidence" advanced for the claim of the objective reality of witchcraft and then test the validity of the argument on which it is based:

> A fly is trapped in a stopped bottle . . . no amount of shaking would wake the witch; . . . the fly was released, and the sleeper awoke.
> —IDONIBOYE

> On this visit . . . the woman brought a cock and declared it was going to cause Obi's death . . . Obi jumped up and seized the cock, . . . managed to pluck out two feathers . . . The following morning everybody was amazed to see the feathers where Obi had placed them and the blood on the bed.
> —IDOWU

It is true that these and many other stories, being mostly testimonies, do not conclusively prove the existence of witchcraft. Yet it is equally difficult to dismiss some, such as those recorded by Mr. Neal or the results of some psychical researches, as fake. The point, therefore, is that just as it is fraudulent to assert the existence of a power whose nature we know nothing about, so also is it equally fraudulent to *deny the occurrence* of an experience just because we do not yet understand it. It is true that a philosopher worth that name would insist on the validity of arguments. Also no philosopher has any justification for dismissing an inference based on experience, no matter how bizarre that experience might be, just because it fails to comply with known limits of possible occurrence. The African inference, though its authors claim it is empirically justified, is what most western authors, for one reason or the other, regard as the application of the *post hoc, ergo poster hoc* invalid argument form.

But I think there are at least two or three methods through which the African can logically refute this derogatory comment. (1) First he can do this by giving an explanation of the nature and *modus operandi* of witchcraft power. (2) Short of this, he must be prepared to demonstrate a causal relationship between this postulated occult power and the mysterious event he cites to prove its practical efficacy. (3) Thirdly, he can try to prove his knowledge of the reality of this power by practically manipulating it. I think any one of these and not necessarily a conjunction of the three will give credence to his claim; for each is an acceptable method of scientific proof.

The first method is the most scientific, if it could be done. But how does one experimentally demonstrate a causal relationship between two events? Does this also entail adhering to the first method? My answer to the second question is an emphatic no. And without wasting our time, I quote from a renowned physicist.

> Physicists have been very pleased thus to be able to preserve the two great principles of conservation which had been threatened and although the neutrino has obstinately refused to divulge its existence to experimenters they nonetheless generally admitted its existence.[15]

Although one can assume the nature of a source of power, one does not necessarily need to have observed it before it is scientifically accepted as proved. In some cases it may not be observable, at least through the medium of modern scientific apparatus. Once we can establish a constantly conjoined occurrence, we have the right to suspect causal relationship. And to strengthen our suspicion we need to prove the constancy by many repetitions. The more times it is repeated, the greater our faith in its truth and reality. This directly involves the third method, which is based on K. Kuypers's assertion that part of the philosophy of science is that one does not understand something until one can make it oneself.[16] And I would think this is also true put the other way round, i.e. to make, at times, implies to understand.

Which of the three proofs must the African present before his assertions can be accepted within the logic of western science? I think his claims are based on methods (2) and (3). But claiming these is not enough, the African must be prepared to justify such claims. For although it is quite true that like all human beings Africans decide how they shall behave on the basis of their view of what is the case in the world around them; the ingenuity of the early Greek philosophers lies not in their ability to codify Greek cosmology but to show the "absurdities and interior confusions" they contain. More painfully perhaps, they had to throw away a great part of their cosmology and substitute in its place principles which to them *"lay wholly within the world of experience."* One of the methods of experimental inquiry suggested by J. S. Mill is the method of concomitant variation. This method may not be without any criticism but such criticism will equally be valid against many of the acceptable theories of science as we know them today. For example, if it is said that the knowledge of causes must be accompanied by a demonstration showing the connection between cause and effect, then one can answer in the words of K. Kuypers who noted:

> If this (knowledge of cause) is not the case as with natural bodies, then we do not know what constructions, and consequently there is no demonstration possible either, but instead *we must start from the effects* and seek to derive the possible causes from these.[17] (emphasis mine).

And I think this is exactly what physics did with the neutrino. If we are not so biased, not so prejudiced as to "deny the occurrence of something just because we have not ourselves experienced it (not that it cannot be experienced)" or suspect overall fraud just because we are die-hard sceptics then we may agree that it is possible that the African, through various experiences of the types listed above, can validly infer the existence of a mysterious power in the same way as the physicist inferred the existence of the neutrino. In both cases the student has not seen the phenomena but he sees their effects and from here seeks to derive the possible causes.

If the African can go on to strengthen his claim by applying the third method, (i.e., of manipulating this power) then his claims "take on an enormous amount of reality." There exists innumerable claims of different related powers of controlling and manipulating these occult powers. We have the magicians, the sorcerers, the native-doctors who claim knowledge of these powers. As in the case of stories and testimonies of witchcraft practices, many of these are of course spurious. But many Africans as well as scholars from the western world can testify to some apparently genuine powers of some of these people. Anyone who has read through the testimonies of Mr. Neal would likely find it difficult to dismiss Uncle Tetteh and Mallam Allarge as frauds.[18] The stories of the bilocational and dematerialistic powers of Harry Houdini (1874–1926) as recorded by J. R. Rhine in the *Encyclopaedia of the Unexplained* should leave a cold grip on all its readers. In short, Uncle Tetteh may not be able to explain in scientific terms the nature of the power he evokes and manipulates, nor how this power actually operates. Yet, apparently he can make it work *over and over again*; he can control it, he can use it, he can teach it to others. Well, in some cases may be science can do more than this by giving scientific explanation but then this is not a prerequisite of the acceptability of any claim to scientific knowledge.

Many writers, both Africans and non-Africans, have attempted different explanations of the nature and *modus operandi* of these mysterious powers. Some of these explanations are occult and hence hold very little-interest for philosophy. But quite philosophically interesting is the postulation that the mind can affect other minds either by a kind of physical or nonphysical radiation transmitted through brain waves. To be sure the theory raises some problems, but I do not think they are insurmountable. As philosophers, our first concern is not to spell out the *modus operandi* of witchcraft as such. At least it is not our first priority. Rather it is to try to show that the existence of witches cannot be ruled out on purely logical grounds.

Some have commented that traditionally the term 'witchcraft' connotes a supernatural, mysterious power, and that as such the possibility of a scientific explanation does not exist.[19] My answer to such an objection is that while it is true that some even now still believe that witchcraft is supernatural in the sense of "being beyond explanation" we may discover that they are in fact making a mistake. Secondly, to say something is mysterious does not automatically mean it is beyond explanation. At times all it means is that it is "not yet explained." So the possibility of an explanation may exist at least in the future. Above all, the African doctor or scientist does not regard witchcraft in any of these senses. He understands it well enough to be able to influence and manipulate it. More accurately, to him witchcraft is "paranormal."

Another objection is that if we accept these bizarre experiences as real, science, as we know it today, would have to undergo a radical change to incorporate them. Some of its basic laws and principles would have to be rethought. This, scientists think, is intellectually painful and should be resisted. As earlier on noted in this paper, this kind of resistance is not novel. But quite unfortunately the resistance has almost always been found to be based on emotion. I quite agree that nobody finds it pleasant to throw away a baby after nursing it for two or three centuries—as scientists have done science. Emotion, on the other hand, is not always a justifiable basis of resisting change. Furthermore, a discovery of a part of nature that does not obey the same laws as now formulated by scientists, does not necessarily imply a destruction of science. It may, in fact, only set a limit to the probably false notion of the uniformity of nature. We may even be able to retain this notion if we could work out a framework that can accommodate both of these apparently contradictory positions. But even if a destruction of the present assumptions of science is what results, the only legitimate care that should be taken is that we are not substituting a framework based on the whims and caprices of our minds. Hence, an "intellectual pain" can only be justified if it results, in this case, from a feeling that we have for so long erred by mistaking a part for the whole. The alternative, of course, is to avoid the pain by tenaciously holding on to what we know to be false. And although it is generally agreed that to err is human, self-deceit, we should also agree, is an unpardonable intellectual sin.

NOTES AND REFERENCES

1. Tunde Akingbola, "Do witches Really Exist?"; *Spear* (October, 1975), p. 15.

2. J. Middleton and E. H. Winter, *Witchcraft and Sorcery in East Africa* (London: Routledge and Kegan Paul, 1963), p. 3.

3. M. J. Field, *Search for Security* (London: Faber, 1960), pp. 36–37.

4. E. Evans-Pritchard, *Witchcraft, Oracles, and Magic Among the Azande* (Oxford: Clarendon Press, 1927), p. 21.

5. E. O. Eyo, "Witchcraft and Society" in *Proceedings of the Staff Seminar, African Studies Division, University of Lagos,* 1967.

6. J. R. Crawford, *Witchcraft and Sorcery in Rhodesia* (London: Oxford University Press, 1967), p. 40.

7. E. Bolaji Idowu, "The challenge of Witchcraft," *Orita: Ibadan Journal of Religious Studies,* IV, No. 1 (June 1970), p. 9.

8. John S. Mbiti, *African Religions and Philosophy* (London: Heinemann, 1969), p. 194.

9. D. E. Idoniboye, "The concept of 'Spirit' in African Metaphysics," *Second Order,* II, No. 1 (January 1973), p. 84.

10. Idowu, *Op cit.* p. 88.

11. J. B. Rhine, *New Frontiers of the Mind* (Greenwood, 1972), pp. 5–6.

12. J. R. Smythies, "Is ESP Possible?" in Smythie (ed.), *Science and ESP* (London: Routledge and Kegan Paul, 1967), p. 5.

13. Mbiti, *op. cit.* p. 202.

14. Arthur S. Gregor, *Witchcraft and Magic; The Supernatural World of Primitive Man* (New York: Scribner, 1972), p. 26.

15. Louis de Broglie, *Physics and Microphysics* (New York: Harper and Row, 1960), p. 33.

16. K. Kuypers, "The Relations Between Knowing and Making as an Epistemological Principle," *Philosophy and Phenomenological Research, No.* 1 (September, 1974), p. 69.

17. *Ibid.* pp. 69–70.

18. James H. Neal, *Juju in my Life* (London: George Harrap, 1966), Chapters 1 and 8.

19. For these and other useful suggestions, I am greatly indebted to Dr. P. O. Bodunrin, of the Philosophy Department, University of Ibadan, and my colleague, Dr. R. J. M. Lithown, of the Philosophy Department, University of Lagos.

Magic, Witchcraft, and ESP: A Defence of Scientific and Philosophical Skepticism

P. O. Bodunrin

P. O. Bodunrin, vice chancellor of Ondo State University and former head of the Department of Philosophy at the University of Ibadan in Nigeria, is one of the few African philosophers that has taken an openly skeptical stance towards the existence of parapsychological phenomena and their operation in traditional Africa. In response to suggestions by Albert Mosley, Sophie Oluwole, and others, that magic and witchcraft be understood as the display of psychic powers, Bodunrin criticizes both the anecdotal and the scientific evidence for the existence of psychic powers. The anecdotal evidence is unreliable because so many cases involve fraud, manipulation, and self-deception. And the scientific evidence lacks validity because its principle experimental demonstrations have proven to be unreplicable.

For Bodunrin, an essential feature of scientific evidence is that similar results should be obtained under similar circumstances. Thus, to satisfy scientific standards parapsychology would need to consistently produce specifiable paranormal effects under similar conditions. This would amount to what Bodunrin calls a "scientizing" of witchcraft and magic, reducing them to the concepts of parapsychology.

To date, parapsychology has not been able to produce experimental evidence that is consistently replicable. But even if parapsychological experiments were produced that were replicable, and magic and witchcraft were "scientized," Bodunrin argues that we still could not view traditional practitioners as having known what they were doing, for they would not have true beliefs about what they were doing.

Traditional practitioners believe in spiritual agencies, but if spirits don't exist (while telepathy, clairvoyance, psychokinesis, and precognition do exist) then traditional healers and witches do not know what they are doing, even if we allow, for the sake of argument, that they are able to manifest psychic abilities at higher rates than average.

Professor Albert Mosley and Mrs. S. B. Oluwole in their articles[1] attempt to defend those aspects of traditional and modern[2] metaphysics which posit the existence of non-material, and non-physical entities and forces. Mosley concentrates on magic which he defines as "accumulated sets of beliefs and techniques by means of which non-physical entities (or forces) can be used to achieve certain kinds of physically-manifested results . . . techniques for the use and enhancement of psi abilities."[3] Psi abilities include ESP of which four types—telepathy, clairvoyance, precognition and psychokinesis are identified by Rhine.[4] The reason why the authenticity of magic has been denied, Mosley argues, is that the existence of psi abilities has been questioned and the theoretical posits which supply the explanation for psi abilities have been generally rejected by the scientific community. These theoretical posits are metaphysical in nature, but "the existence of psi abilities (as indicated by ESP and psychokinesis), and the acceptance of the existence of magic is primarily a metaphysical one."[5] Mosley wishes to show that the reasons for the rejection of magic and of the existence of psi abilities are not sufficient and that the metaphysical posits upon which rest magic and the belief in psi abilities are rational, are indeed as rational as belief in certain kinds of theoretical entities in science.

Mrs. Oluwole concentrates on the phenomenon of witchcraft. In her article she wishes to spell out the justifications and consequences of the claim that witchcraft is real.[6] It is clear that if it can be shown that there is witchcraft, all we have to do to establish the existence of witches is to show that there are those who know how to exercise witchcraft powers, for witches are by definition "those who exercise witchcraft powers." As witches are generally conceived, it is claimed that they can affect their victims or perform actions, without any physical contact and using no medicine.[7] Those who deny the reality of witches and witchcraft deny that there can be action from a distance without any physical contact and using no medicine. To be able to have such effect would be in Mosley's own language to have psi ability and to belong to the small class of human beings which include medicine-men, witches, priests and rainmakers who know how and are able to tap the force, power, or energy permeating the whole universe.[8]

Why have the scientific community and many modern men refused to recognise the authentic existence of psi abilities and of men with psi abilities? According to Mosley, one reason is that the scientific community finds the whole thing intellectually uncomfortable in that it seems to contradict the immutable laws of physics, the fundamental ideas and principles on which modern science has been based.[9] One of the basic metaphysical assumptions behind the rise of modern science is that only physical forms of matter exist and that any event that occurs must be explicable in terms of the interaction of physical energy.[10] Another reason is the scientific empiricist's ideology according to which something (an entity or a fact) is to be accounted real, if and only if it is scientifically provable.[11] To be scientifically provable, according to Oluwole is to be experimentally demonstrable or demonstrable in principle.[12] Mosley on the other hand, thinks that abundant proof of the existence and exercise of psi abilities abound (e.g. in the Rhine and his Duke University group card experiments on ESP). He also thinks that there now exist scientific conceptions which make the existence of psi phenomena ESP and psychokinesis quite reasonable if not totally within the reach of imagination.[13] Reasonable explanations have also been offered, all of which scientists find unacceptable. Mrs. Oluwole, on the other hand, says that believers in witchcraft, and therefore in psi abilities, do not usually try to prove how something which cannot be scientifically demonstrated can be known to exist.[14] She dismisses explanations to the effect that witches are mystical entities occupying astral regions, or that as witches are not ordinary witchery research cannot be ordinary as uninteresting and perhaps meaningless.[15] He who believes in witches and witchcraft needs not only show the validity of his reasoning, he must also be prepared to EXPERIMENTALLY ESTABLISH [sic] the causal relationship between an event and the witch supposed to be its cause. In other words, to validate his position, *witchcraft efficacy must be established/establishable experimentally and* this, to me is the crux of the whole question.[16]

In effect then, Mosley is telling the scientific community, you should have understood this thing, what you need is to find a way of controlling and harnessing psi powers, while Mrs. Oluwole is saying the proofs can be given and I will give them. In one thing they seem to be agreed, viz, that what is needed is a scientific proof. And on this I agree with them, for if you want to convince the scientific community who are the sceptics in this matter, you have to speak their language, or if you are going to invent a new language you must teach them the grammar and syntax of your language. The kind of metaphysical change of mind Mosley is asking for is not possible until there has been an agreement on the facts and on just what are the problems needing explanation.

In this paper, I shall examine the nature of the evidence and explanation offered for the existence or occurrence of psi abilities. I shall argue that the evidence is not conclusive and that the explanations offered are unsatisfactory from the scientific and philosophical points of view.

Two sets of charges are levelled against the scientific community: one is that of an unpardonable incredulity and reticence and the other is that of using a double standard. What is being argued under the first charge is that when evidence has been collected in the normal scientific fashion, and the occurrences of psychic phenomena have been established under the usual laboratory conditions of controlled experimentation such as Professor J. B. Rhine and his Duke University group and others have done in the early 1930's, science has no reasonable grounds for disbelief. The only grounds for disbelief can only be prejudice—an anti-scientific scientific prejudice. Mosley and Oluwole are not the first to complain against a simple state of incredulity despite reported evidence of psychic powers (psi abilities). Henry Sidgwick in his Presidential Address to the British Society for Psychical Research on July 17, 1882, had complained of the same thing.[17] Research into psychic phenomena had begun at least 30 years before Sidgwick delivered his address. In the address he reports some progress. As men of undisputed scientific competence began to take part in the research, the occurrence of psychic phenomena was no longer being ruled out as conjuring tricks. Even the clergy was having a change of attitude as they had come to realise that if these modern marvels cannot be allowed the miracles reported in the bible and in church history cannot be allowed either.[18] What Sidgwick saw as lacking and what he saw as the goal of his society was the accumulation of sufficient evidence, and by sufficient evidence he means "evidence that will convince the scientific community."[19] What is lacking is not a scientific preparedness to accept psychic phenomena but lack of sufficient and convincing evidence for them. The facts have first of all to be established before explanatory hypotheses are posited. I believe that if there is still incredulity among scientists and philosophers, this is because they have not considered the evidence such as are adduced as sufficient to establish the claims being made. And it is useful to examine why the evidence is considered either insufficient or unconvincing.

Daniel Cohen sums it up neatly in *ESP: Science or Delusion.*[20]
Some of the reasons he gives are:

1. While the discovery in 1920 of electro-encephalography has shown that the brain does generate some electrical impulses and in theory it should be possible for one brain to receive and interpret the impulses from another brain no evidence has so far been adduced that this takes place.
2. In the experiments conducted by Dr. Rhine (whom Cohen describes as the "Pope of American ESP"), (*a*) no one scores well consistently, (*b*) three-quarters of those tested show no ESP ability, (*c*) the tests seemed to work well only in those cases where both the medium and the experimenter are both believers in ESP and (*d*), successful experiments are often not repeatable even with the same medium.

Now, (1) is not a serious objection as it may be argued that we just have not as yet discovered that such a thing happens. But objections (2) (*a*), (*c*) and (*d*) are worthy of note. If no one scores consistently high can we be sure that we are not dealing with chance occurrences? However, the Pearce-Pratt experiments in 1934 and those of Rhine on psychokinesis of the same year show that the chances of the mediums having the scores they had without psi abilities are one in several billions. While the average scores cannot on the theory of probability be attributed to chance, it could still be claimed to be a matter of chance on which occasion (at which particular attempt) a medium will make a correct guess since the medium himself does not *know* whether he is right. (I shall discuss the epistemological implications of this point towards the end of this essay.) Besides, we have to explain just how it is that such a small percentage of human beings have ESP powers. To explain this we would be forced to say that psi ability is not the universal possession of human beings, but the special gift of a few. The difficulty with this view is that it may lead us into mysticism. It may lead us into the very position that Sidgwick wants: that "we don't know," which is no explanation. If the tests seem to work well only in cases where the medium and the experimenter both believe in ESP, you cannot rule out self deception and hallucination. If the attempt is to convince the scientific community then it ought to work with the most out and out anti-ESP scientist. Repeatability is often demanded in scientific experiments. Again this is to rule out the possibility of chance, for even if the chances of a medium guessing the correct cards are one in a trillion, nevertheless, it is no use for scientific purposes if this experience cannot be repeated. But even if to make does not imply to understand, as Mrs. Oluwole wrongly suggests it does, (for it is possible for one to make, bring into being, what one does not understand), to make may lead to understanding. When we can repeat an occurrence, we can establish the cause of it. Common sense approach ignores those features of our experience which cannot be made the basis of fruitful generalisation.[21] Common sense also demands that in cases where strange occurrences, contrary to our every day experience are reported, we demand overwhelming evidence for our belief. A wise man must proportion his belief to the evidence, and the more strange the story we are invited to believe, the more sceptical we can be expected to be and the more is the weight of evidence required to gain belief. While there is perhaps some evidence that some people do have unusual ESP powers, the evidence is not yet enough to permit any useful generalisations about the phenomena and we must therefore scientifically and philosophically suspend our judgement.

The case with witchcraft is even less well established. We do not have any scientifically organised experiments as yet. Mrs. Oluwole admits this, that is why she is advocating that the existence of witchcraft must not only be shown to be logically tenable but that it must also be experimentally demonstrable. And although she seems to see the scientific attitude as a hindrance to fruitful research on witchcraft, yet, the methods of research which she goes on to advocate are essentially scientific. Mrs. Oluwole argues that the existence of witchcraft can be scientifically proved by the following three methods the positive result of any one of which would be sufficient to establish the claim that witchcraft is real and that witches exist:

1. We may give an explanation of the *modus operandi* of witchcraft power.
2. We may *experimentally establish* a causal relationship between the postulated occult power and the mysterious event he (the African) cites to prove its practical efficacy.
3. We may show a practical manipulation of witchcraft power.[22]

Let us look at these methods. The first method is what Oluwole calls the scientific method. Yes, it is the scientific method only if it means the method of dealing with an accepted authentic phenomenon.

A thing is deemed authentic if its existence has been demonstrated or if acceptance of its existence is necessitated by a theory whose truth is compelling. In the case in point, however such a procedure begs the question in that we are implicitly being asked to accept the existence of witchcraft power the *modus operandi* of which we wish to explain. If we observe a strange phenomenon surely we can postulate a range of possible explanations of it, but this would be far from identifying the explanation. Mrs. Oluwole maintains that the second method does not entail the first, you can demonstrate the existence of a phenomenon experimentally without being able to explain its *modus operandi*. In a way this is true; you can show a child a magnet as it attracts a nail and simply say the magnet attracts iron. In a trivial way, that would be to experimentally demonstrate that there is such a thing as one object having a magnetic power over another. You can do this without knowing the scientific explanation of what it is in one piece of metal that attracts another. If you can show this over and over again you can establish a constantly conjoined occurrence (whenever the magnet is put near the nail, the nail "moves" towards it and that the nail does not so move otherwise). The method of constant conjunction is applicable only when the occurrence of two events or two entities has already been established. The passage which Mrs. Oluwole quotes from Broglie on this is misapplied. You may postulate the existence of an entity of a certain sort if you find that there is no way you can explain a phenomenon without it. Although this may hold as an explanatory device, it is further experiment that can show that the postulation is correct. The evidence that has been given in support of witchcraft power consists of oral reports and reports of personal experiences. It is difficult to see how these reports could be tested (verified) by either of the methods so far discussed. I realise that Mosley complains about the refusal of scientists to accept subjective (personal) experience as evidence for the occurrence of psi abilities and inveighs against science for this.[23] But there are good reasons for the wariness in accepting reports of personal experience. It is partly because the subjective world of each of us seem to differ so much as to make impossible a fruitful generalisation. After Don Juan had administered some potion to Carlos Castaneda the latter had strange experiences—he saw himself existing in a disembodied state! What are we to make of it? Are we being asked to throw away the difference between objective and subjective reality? Certainly Carlos Castaneda was having some strange experiences—one cannot deny that, and there is a sense in which his experiences can be described as real, since it is not nothing he is experiencing. If I were to lift up my upper eyelids and press them against my eye balls I would experience double—I would see each line of this page on which I am writing double. Are they double because I experience them as double.

I have listened to people under the influence of mind-bending drugs (which they had taken in equal doses to get high) relate their experiences. They gave different accounts of their experiences. The experience of each is real, but it is not without good reason that we treat as objectively real only something which exists in our inter-subjective experience. My friends were in a state of fantasy. We cannot live in a world which goes in and out of existence; this is the kind of world Carlos Castaneda was made to experience. Reports of ESP and witchcraft power often come from people who are in some unusual state of mind, in sickness, in some anxiety or the like. Most of the occurrences moreover are spontaneous and not amenable to scientific experimentation of the sort Oluwole advocates. Sir Gilbert Murray testifies to this in a quote cited by Mosley. Worlds that go in and out of existence depending on the state of the perceiver are alogical worlds. When logic and experience conflict, we can resolve the conflict by pointing out the flaw in the logic or by deciding that experience is illusory.[24] In most of these cases, the verdict must be that experience is illusory until more evidence is available.

We now come to the third method prescribed by Oluwole: the method of making—of practically manipulating witchcraft power. Indeed, if we could demonstrate the efficacy of witchcraft power by manipulating it, we would have gone a long way in our understanding of the phenomenon. If Mallam Allarge does not know the *modus operandi* of the amulet he gave to Mr. Neal and the amulet works, this establishes that the amulet has worked *because of witchcraft power*. In this case, we would probably have to concede that something surprising has happened, especially if our experience is repeatable. What we cannot hasten to conclude is that the efficacy of the amulet is due to witchcraft power. What we have is a phenomenon that calls for explanation. But if we can successfully manipulate this power repeatedly, we might be able to discover the law(s) that govern(s) its behaviour without which we cannot claim to understand the phenomenon. Understanding is our aim, for it has never been disputed that there are strange occurrences such as are attributed to witchcraft power. The point in dispute is how one is to account for these occurrences. If we can discover the laws governing them, we would have succeeded in *"scienticising"* the whole affair; and witchcraft, if it could still be called by that name, would have turned to science. It is necessary to realise that the scepticism shown towards ESP and other forms of claims to psi abilities, including witchcraft, is no greater than scientists would show if someone were to announce the discovery of an anti-ageing vaccine.[25]

I now come to the second set of criticisms of the scientific attitude, namely, that science is guilty of double standards in that it is willing to accept unobservable theoretical entities as explanatory devices in science but unwilling to accept the same as proof for ESP and witchcraft. I think the essential questions we must ask ourselves here are: What is a theoretical entity in science? In what way do scientific postulates differ from those of "traditional metaphysics"? Both Mosley and Oluwole cite several instances of entities which for a long time were theoretical and unobserved but nevertheless accepted as real by scientists albeit not without reluctance.

A scientist postulates the existence of an entity when he notices a gap in the explanatory chain of a theory, i.e., when a theory demands it. An entity which cannot be observed to exist but whose existence *must* be assumed in order to make a theory work is a theoretical entity. Which entity to postulate is not arbitrary. You hypothesize the existence of a theoretical entity out of a background of other scientific theories that are known to be valid. And even then the existence of such an entity is hypothetical. It is when this hypothesis coupled with repeated observations has enabled us to make predictions that the existence is demonstrated. If we come across a case where things do not work we suspect the existence of a new factor hitherto unknown or not yet taken into account. Gaps in the well accepted explanatory theories of science together with a massive background of accumulated knowledge must have led to the postulation of the neutrino and of positrons. The theoretical entities in traditional metaphysics are *deus ex machina.* The validity of their postulation is not tested and their necessity not established. There is then this difference in the contexts of discovery between neutrinos and witchcraft. I think that both Mosley and Oluwole misconstrue the nature of science. The sort of scepticism they inveigh against science, science exercises on itself. We are guided by the principle of parsimony according to which one must not multiply entities beyond necessity. For most of the cases of reported witchcraft manifestations and ESP there exist scientific explanations. Should it turn out that we are dealing with utterly strange new phenomena inexplicable by any of the known laws of nature, we would have had something new in our hands. But it is research, it is experience that will teach us. Our knowledge of the laws of nature is based on experience. No respectable scientist, contrary to Mosley's claim, holds these laws as immutable. But no respectable scientist would abandon a theory that has worked for so long unless there are convincing reasons for doing so, and unless there is an advantage to be derived from so doing. If the existence of witches becomes established, science would not be thereby refuted. If there are things contrary to the known laws of science, it is through experience alone that we shall find out. As Hume states,

> it is experience that gives authority to human testimony, and it is the same experience which assures us of the laws of nature. When, therefore, these two kinds of experience are contrary (as ESP and witchcraft research may one day show) we have nothing to do but to substract the one from the other and embrace an opinion either on one side or the other with that assurance which arises from the remainder.[26]

Rather than refute science, what it would show is that experience has boiled over[27] making correction of our present formulas and ideas necessary. Science does not disregard inconvenient observations. Their occurrence always causes us to make some alteration in our system of hypotheses in spite of our desire to keep it intact,[28] in spite of our reticence and scepticism. Well-confirmed theories, like old soldiers, die hard.

In our time, rationality is judged by the standards of logic and science and what both science and logic demand are self-consistent procedures for the formation of beliefs. But

> the fact that the procedure, by reference to which we now determine whether a belief is rational, may subsequently forfeit our confidence does not detract from the rationality of adopting it now. For we define a rational belief as one which is arrived at by the methods which we now consider reliable. There is no absolute standard of rationality, just as there is no method of constructing hypotheses which is guaranteed to be reliable. We trust the methods of contemporary science because they have been successful in practice. If in future we were to adopt different methods then the beliefs which are now rational might become irrational from the standpoint of these new methods. But the fact that this is possible has no bearing on the fact that these beliefs are rational now.[29]

The question may now be asked: Even if scientific scepticism is justifiable in the case of the authenticity of the existence of witches and witchcraft, is it also justifiable in the case of the findings of Rhine and his group in respect of ESP? For in the latter case, the investigations were carried out according to scientific methods, methods which we now consider reliable, and by experimenters whose scientific competence is not in doubt. Must we not consider belief in ESP and the other psi abilities as rational? If so, why the scepticism? My answer is yes, the evidence is overwhelming. And Mosley and Oluwole (as indeed many before them) have shown that these beliefs are not irrational. The point, however, is that both science and philosophy (and I believe, most ordinary men) are interested not only in the rationality of their beliefs, they are also interested in holding *true beliefs*. Merely to show that a belief is rational is not sufficient to show that it is also true, for there could be two mutually inconsistent rational beliefs, but two mutually inconsistent beliefs cannot both be true. It is common place to accept a belief as true if it corresponds to the fact(s). The difficulty is that correspondence to facts cannot be used to establish the existence of psi abilities of the kinds we have been discussing in this paper without question begging. It cannot be used to verify the truth of beliefs in unknown entities or uncharted areas of experience. Unless we are out and out sceptics we each have a body of beliefs we hold as established truths. This constitutes our store of knowledge. When we come across a belief which is in conflict with this we accept it only if the consequences of rejecting it would be intellectually more disastrous than those of accepting it.[30] The test we use is one of coherence. We seek to understand a new phenomenon in order to extend the bounds of our knowledge to build a bridge of intelligible relation from the continent of our knowledge to the island we wish to include in it.[31] Our quest for understanding is an attempt to bring something unknown or imperfectly known into a sub-system of knowledge, and thus also into that larger system that forms the world of accepted beliefs.[32] Our system of beliefs must be coherent. The coherence of our system of beliefs does not guarantee the truth of the system, but an incoherent system of beliefs would not even have any chance of being true. Whatever explanation of the phenomena we call witchcraft, ESP, magic, and other psi abilities is offered must settle account with science which is today our most reliable test of experience. It is science that is likely to reveal the remaining secrets about this universe.

An interesting philosophical question is whether or not and in what sense the state of mind of a person with psi powers could be described as one of knowledge. In what sense, that is, can the witch, the clairvoyant, the magician and the traditional ontologists, be said to know what they claim to know or are able to do? It is generally agreed that for a claim to know that P is to be accepted as representing a state of knowledge, the following conditions must be satisfied. (1) It is necessary that P be true. For, suppose P is the claim that there are invisible intelligent beings on/in the Idanre hills. If such beings are not in fact in the Idanre hills no one could know that they are. No one could know what is not the case. (2) It is necessary that the person believes that P. Suppose I was merely repeating the popular belief to which I do not myself subscribe the slightest iota of accent, I could not be said to know that there are these beings in the Idanre hills, even if it was true that such beings *are* in the hills. Where there is no belief there is no knowledge. (3) I must be justified in my belief that P, that there are invisible intelligent beings in the Idanre hills. If my state of mind is to count as knowledge, my belief must not only be justifiable (by others or merely justifiable in principle) I myself must be able to give reasons for my belief. If this is not the case, one would be unable to distinguish between mere guesses and genuine knowledge. Someone who has correctly guessed the solution of a problem no matter how firmly he believes his solution cannot be said to be in a state of knowledge with respect to that solution. Edmund Gettier has shown that the three conditions here discussed may be satisfied in circumstances where we would be prepared to deny that we have an instance of knowledge.[33] What Gettier has shown is that these conditions are not necessary *and* sufficient for knowledge, not that they are not *necessary*. Attempts to show that they are not all necessary have so far been unsuccessful.[34] With this background, let us now examine some of the epistemological issues raised in discussions of witchcraft, magic, ESP, and traditional ontology.

Believers in witchcraft maintain that there are witches with all that that claim connotes. Those who believe in ESP, clairvoyance etc. believe that there are men who can exercise the psi abilities which those terms connote. Oluwole and Mosley have convincingly argued that there are no reasons of logic why such claims are necessarily false. No existential proposition could be necessarily false except it is such as deals with a relation of ideas or concepts. The assertion that there are round squares is necessarily false simply because of the incompatibility of the concepts of squareness and roundness. The assertion that there are spirits, or witches, or clairvoyants, or flying saucers, or dead-men-come-to-life is not necessarily false. It would be mistaken to deny the existence of any of these things on *a priori* grounds. Besides, it would seem that the examples of studies already cited in the literature on these matters have established that strange phenomena do occur. The interesting question from the point of view of both science and philosophy is not that these events do occur, but how we are to explain them? What are we to make of them? It is here that the traditionalist on the one hand and the scientist and philosophers on the other hold different views. Let us ignore for now questions of explanation and simply admit that the claims of the traditionalists pass the test of condition (1) i.e., that their claim is true. That their claim also passes condition (2) can also be granted without much ado. One might go so far as to say that this is what the whole issue rests upon. What about condition (3)?

Is the traditionalist's belief justifiable? What does "justifiable" here mean? Note, the question is not whether or note the belief of the traditionalist is justifiable in principle. It is not whether or not there are reasons why one may hold as true such beliefs as the traditionalists hold to be true. Parapsychology has in fact shown why one may hold as true various absurd and false beliefs. And it is not a question of the conceivability of the truth of the propositions of the traditional metaphysician. As pointed out above, since his assertions are not logical falsehoods, they could conceivably be true. And in order to determine whether or not the traditionalist is justified in his belief we cannot invent arguments for him; we must instead examine the reasons he gives for his beliefs. In deciding whether or not the traditionalist is justified in believing as true what he so believes, the pertinent question to ask him is: How do you know that your claim is true? We must here make some distinctions.

On the one hand, there is the scientific and philosophical sceptic who does not believe in the possibility of the existence of witches, clairvoyants etc. and/or in the exercise of the kind of powers attributed to them. On the other hand, there are the traditionalists who believe in the existence and exercise of the strange psychical powers that have formed the subject of our discussion in these essays. Among the latter group there are those who though not having, nor laying claim to, the ability to exercise psi abilities themselves, do, nevertheless, believe that others have them and can exercise such powers. There are also those who have or claim to have psi abilities (the mystics themselves).

The disagreement between the sceptic and the believer (the traditionalist) can be resolved. If, without any means of communication someone claims to know what my wife is doing at home at this moment, we can check the veracity of his claim by phoning home, by noting the precise moment at which he makes his claim and checking what the facts are later on. If someone claims to be able to tell us through some extraordinary means what will happen 100 years from now, we can at least record his predictions for those who will be in the world at that time to confirm or disconfirm. We can, in other words, use one of Rhine's methods (reported by Mosley in his paper) to convince the sceptic or to justify our own beliefs about persons who claim to have ESP and witchcraft powers. As admitted earlier, it seems that those who believe that some people have some extraordinary powers can justify their beliefs. It must be admitted however that witchcraft still awaits further investigations. Scientific and philosophical scepticism does not *at present* remain here.

That there are these special powers and that there are those who can exercise them is no more the interesting point of the dispute. The interesting point is the explanation of these phenomena. How are we to explain them? Surely, if these phenomena can stand the test of repeatability we may, as earlier argued, one day succeed in *scienticising* witchcraft and ESP. But does everything rest there? Even though we may in one sense ultimately gain a scientific understanding of the phenomena, one epistemological question remains; and I think this is where one main thrust of philosophical scepticism remains. Is the state of mind of the mystic one of knowledge? The question is whether or not he can justify his claim to knowledge (for it is assumed that he claims to have knowledge of his "art") just as other traditionalists can justify their knowledge claim? The difficulty is that the justification acceptable from others cannot be accepted from him. It will not be sufficient for him to demonstrate his ability. For reasons already stated, he has to be able to tell us precisely what is going on; he has to be able to explain his actions. It is here that the philosopher finds his explanation unsatisfactory. For what we are told is that his knowledge is indescribable. We just have to be like him to realise what he knows. His knowledge is incommunicable. He just knows what he knows and no justification of this knowledge is required for, no matter what, we cannot understand.

One common feature of replies of this type is that the knowledge has not come from experience and that it is not inferred from reason and/or experience. It is immediate and intuitive. The truth simply dawns on the mystic. Some even claim that it is only by direct awareness (by which they do not mean introspection) alone that one can penetrate the inner essence of things.[34] I do not deny the possibility of knowledge by direct awareness. We are directly acquainted with many things, or mental states for example. In a sense no one can understand my pain simply because it is in me and not in any one else. But what this means is that no one else can have direct acquaintance with my pain. Even if this is true, it is not true that no one else can know something about my pain. The mystic seems to be insisting that one cannot know something which one does not know by acquaintance. This is simply not true. We know many more things than we are, or are ever likely to be, acquainted, with. If the mystic's "knowledge" is really incommunicable he must admit that when he talks about what he knows, his language is not descriptive, or if it is, he is merely describing his own experience. Truth or falsity does not inhere in those experiences *qua* experiences. Knowledge, in the more interesting sense, goes beyond the description of personal experiences; these descriptions must be interpreted in relation to other experiences. We do these by means of bridge laws. That is the only way we can check the correctness of our interpretation. If the mystic's claim is that what he "knows" is absolutely transempirical the less he says about his thing the better. Such knowledge as he claims to have must be considered spurious. He himself is as helpless in this regard as the rest of mankind.[35]

Notes and References

1. Albert Mosley, "The Metaphysics of Magic: Practical and Philosophical Implications" and S. B. Oluwole, "On the Existence of Witches,"

both in this no. and vol. of *Second Order* hereafter referred to by author and page only.

2. "traditional and modern," because Albert Mosley does not intend to relate his discussion to African metaphysics alone although this is the occasion for his writing. The use of supernatural entities to explain psi abilities is not peculiar to African and/or traditional cultures.

3. *Mosley,* p. 1.

4. *Ibid.,* p. 5.

5. *Ibid.,* p. 14.

6. *Oluwole,* pp. 18ff

7. *Ibid.*

8. *Mosley.*

9. *Mosley,* p. 9 quoting one Waren Weaver in his (Weaver's) *Lady Luck: The Theory of Probability.*

10. *Mosley,* p. 1.

11. *Oluwole, passim.*

12. This is another formulation of the positivist's verifiability criterion which Mrs. Oluwole has earlier referred to.

13. *Mosley.*

14. *Oluwole,* One is led to expect a non-scientific way of proving the existence of witches in Oluwole, but the opposite is what in fact one finds!

15. *Ibid.*

16. *Ibid.*

17. From the *Proceedings of The Society for Psychical Research* extract in Robert Paul Wolff, *Philosophy: A Modern Encounter* (Englewood Cliffs, New Jersey: Prentice Hall Inc., 1976), pp. 165–170. Herward Carrington made the same complaint in 1931. See "Psychical Research" in Wolff, *op. cit.* pp. 176–178.

18. *Ibid.,* p. 168. Professor Idowu also realises the implications of disbelief in witchcraft and the existence of non-physical entities for Christian theology. See Professor Idowu's words quoted by Oluwole in her paper.

19. *Ibid.,* p. 168.

20. In *The Nation,* No. 19 (May 9, 1966), pp. 550–553; reprinted in Wolff *op. cit.* pp. 178–183.

21. A. J. Ayer, *Language Truth and Logic* (New York: Dover Publications Inc. 1946), p. 98.

22. *Oluwole.*

23. *Mosley,* pp., quoting Malinowski and Sir Gilbert Murray's experiences.

24. A. P. Cavendish in D. J. O'Connored., *A Critical History of Western Philosophy* (New York: The Free Press, 1964), p. 10.

25. Both Mosley and Oluwole cite examples of the initial rejection of theories that science later accepted.

26. David Hume, "On Miracles" in *Inquiry Concerning Human Understanding.* quoted in Paul Wolff, *op. cit.*, p. 208.

27. See Chapter Six of William James' *Pragmatism* quoted in Paul Wolff *op. cit.*, p. 220.

28. Ayer: *Language Truth and Logic*, p. 97.

29. *Ibid.*, p. 100.

30. Brand Blandshard, "Coherence as the Test and Nature of Truth" in Ernest Nagel and Richard B. Brandt (ed.,) *Meaning and Knowledge: Systematic Readings in Epistemology* (New York: Harcourt, Brace and World Inc., 1965), p. 144.

31. *Ibid.*, p. 145.

32. *Ibid.*, p. 145.

33. E. L. Gettier, "Is Justified True Belief Knowledge?" *Analysis*, 23 (1963), pp. 121–124.

34. This is a major theme of Hans Zehrer's *Man in This World* (London: Hodder and Stoughton, 1952).

35. Those who took Herbert Feigl's course, PHI 158: Theory of Knowledge, at the University of Minnesota in the autumn term of 1967 will recognise my indebtedness to him and to our discussions of trans-empirical knowledge.

SECTION III

Moral Philosophy and Aesthetics

The final section introduces four recent works that contrast the nature of moral and aesthetic values in traditional and modern African cultures (three previously unpublished). Well known for criticizing the unexamined and wholesale acceptance of traditional beliefs and practices, Kwasi Wiredu has also been in the forefront of African philosophers exploring traditional African worldviews for ideas that might be needed in solving Africa's current problems.

In his paper "Custom and Morality," Wiredu distinguishes customs from morals and argues that traditional Akan morality is based on "humanistic" concerns regarding the welfare and harmonization of the community while the Christian morality of modern Europe is based on supernatural authority. The philosopher Parker English and art historian Nancy Steele Hamme take issue with Wiredu on these claims. They use artifacts and legends to represent the traditional account of the spiritual origin of the authority of the *Asantehene* and the laws regarded as the basis of traditional Akan moral thought.

This excursion raises the question of the nature of the objects now called "works of traditional art." Clearly, the significance of the Golden Stool to traditional Akan people was not the same as its significance in a twentieth century museum. In his paper "Traditional African Aesthetics: A Philosophical Perspective," the Nigerian philosopher Innocent C. Onyewuenyi argues that the arts within traditional Africa, instead of being remote and valued for their uniqueness, were intimately involved with the practical realities of living. The American philosopher H. Gene Blocker continues this theme in his article "On the Distinction between Modern and Traditional African Aesthetics." For Blocker, the modern aesthetic attitude emphasizes detachment and "aesthetic distance" while the traditional aesthetic attitude emphasizes involvement and participation because aesthetic attitudes are relative to sociohistorical conditions, they change as conditions change.

▲ Custom and Morality: A Comparative Analysis of Some African and Western Conceptions of Morals

Kwasi Wiredu

While well-known for opposing the uncritical acceptance of traditional beliefs and practices, Kwasi Wiredu has also encouraged African philosophers to explore traditional African worldviews for ideas that might prove fruitful—even indispensable—in meeting Africa's current problems. This essay reflects the wide range of topics that Wiredu has written on.

In this article, Wiredu distinguishes between moral rules and customs, arguing that a rule is moral if its systematic nonobservance would bring about communal collapse. He further proposes that moral rules must harmonize the interests of the community. Because of their focus on harmonizing human interests within society, Wiredu views traditional Akan moral rules as humanistic. On the other hand, Wiredu discusses the Ten Commandments of Judaism and Christianity to show that Western morality, in contrast to traditional Akan morality, is justified by appeal to commandments and precepts issued by the supernatural authority of God.

In contrast to moral rules, customs may vary from place to place and time to time. They are meant to maximize social benefits, given the circumstances of time and place. Wiredu gives an interesting discussion of the relationship between commandments and taboos, and argues that rhetorical eloquence, respect for one's elders, polygamy, polyandry, premarital sex, and other social practices are examples of customs, not moral rules. Kwame Gyekye's An Essay on African Philosophical Thought: The Akan Conceptual Scheme *provides another analysis of the relationship between morality and religion in traditional African cultures.*

Contemporary African experience is marked by a certain intellectual anomaly. The African today, as a rule, lives in a cultural flux characterized by a confused interplay between an indigenous cultural heritage and a foreign cultural legacy of a colonial origin. Implicated at the deepest reaches of this cultural amalgam is the superimposition of Western conceptions of the good on African thought and conduct. The issues involved here are of the utmost existential urgency, for it may well be that many of the instabilities of contemporary African society are traceable to this circumstance.

But, first, to fundamentals. Rules are absolutely essential to human communities. At the very least there must be some linguistic rules—rules of syntax and semantics—for without some interaction you do not have the communion implied by the concept of community, and without language you do not have the communication presupposed by human interaction. Only a little reflection is required to see that there also has to be a whole host of other kinds of rules for defining, regulating, and facilitating interactions and relationships. For example, if we drive, we must have traffic rules; if we buy and sell, we must have rules not only to regulate these activities but also to define them in the first place, and so on, indefinitely.

The mention of rules of traffic and of commerce naturally brings to mind the concept of law. Laws are promulgated or acknowledged rules that are enforced or, at least, intended to be enforced by a recognized authority having sanctions, usually physical force, at its disposal. Laws are, of course, a feature of the *modus operandi* of governments. But there are other, more informal, rules such as are prescribed by custom, tradition, convention, fashion, and etiquette. Most likely, any human society will have rules of this sort whether or not it is organized in the manner of political governance. There is still, however, one category of rules of the most extreme importance to human society that we have not mentioned so far, at least, not explicitly. This is the category of moral rules. Morality and law do intersect, for some laws are simply moral rules formalized and backed up with the authority of the state. But there are also laws that are clearly not moral rules. Think of traffic rules, for example.

The question now is, How may we distinguish between moral rules and all the rest? This question is important because moral rules seem to have an *intrinsic* obligatoriness which is lacking in other kinds of rules. In warming up toward an answer it would perhaps help if we cleared up some points of usage. The word *moral* and its cognates are frequently used with such broad signification as to cover matters that might also be brought under custom, tradition, or even convention, all of which, for the sake of conceptual economy, might be called simply *custom*. Thus, in discussing the morals of a given people, one might mention such things as their rules of marriage and sex conduct generally, their manner of organizing mutual aid, their way of defining and evaluating success in life, their system of reward and punishment, and so forth. Considerations of this kind should certainly reveal a lot about their values, but the point is that not all those values are moral values.

Consider some particulars. Among the Akans of Ghana, a value is placed on beauty of speech that might well appear extraordinary to other people. Beauty of speech here refers not just to beauty of delivery but also, and more particularly, to a characteristic of speech deriving from both logical and rhetorical factors. Beautiful speech is one that develops a coherent and persuasive argument, clinching points—and this is cru-cial—with striking and decisive proverbs. Anybody not possessed of such a tongue can forget any ambitions of high office at the court of a tra-ditional Akan ruler. There is, surely, nothing immoral in adhering to much less proverbial criteria for this kind of recruitment.

Or consider a somewhat simpler case. In Akan society, one just does not address a person or group without first greeting them. Failure to ob-serve this rule is regarded as a very serious lapse from good behavior. Persistent default will cost any individual his or her reputation. A re-lated rule is this. If in the course of greeting people, one has occasion to shake hands with or wave to more than one person, one absolutely must always proceed from right to left. Again, nonconformity is regarded as an error so grave as to be capable of radically compromising a person's standing in the society. These rules are motivated by values that are not universal either generically or in terms of degree; they can hardly be called moral rules.

This should become apparent from the following thought experi-ment. Compare any of the rules just mentioned with the rule of truth telling. One cannot contemplate the latter for any length of time without a renewed sense of its unconditional imperativeness. An Akan living in Akanland is expected, as a matter of course, to observe, for example, Akan rules of greeting. It goes without saying that other people living in other lands need not feel any such obligation. On the other hand, whether you are a Ghanaian or an American or a Chinese or of any other nationality, race, or culture, truth telling is an indefeasible obligation on you. To trifle with such an imperative is, quite plainly, to be immoral in a very strict sense. It seems, then, that if we could elucidate the uncon-ditional or universal obligatoriness of moral rules, we would be able to make at least a start at drawing an illuminating distinction between rules of conduct that are moral in the strict sense and those that are not moral or are so only by courtesy of some linguistic idiom.

In this project it might be useful to start with another thought ex-periment. Let us revert to the rule of truth telling and ask ourselves if we can imagine any circumstances in which it might be feasible to base con-duct in human society on its reversal. To so much as pose this question is to realize that the answer must be "No!" Any such situation would be a situation of the breakdown of human community; for if truth telling were, by open common avowal, not binding, and everybody could tell lies without let or hindrance, no one could depend on anyone's word, and social life would become intolerably Hobbesian. By contrast, it is a visible fact that life without rules like the Akan rules of greeting mentioned above is not intolerable. This suggests the following condition for the identification of moral rules in the strict sense: A rule of conduct is not a moral rule unless its nonexistence or reversal would bring about the collapse of human community.

It should be observed that the kind of contra-truth-telling situation that we imagined a moment ago is not merely one in which many people tell lies in various circumstances. This, unfortunately, is the actual state of affairs in which we all live, move, and have our struggles. On the contrary, the imagined scenario is the more drastic one in which, to use Kantian language, the maxim "Tell lies whenever convenient" has become a universal rule of conduct. Apart from flirting a little with Kantian terminology, there is an obvious formal analogy between our emerging characterization of moral rules and Kant's use of his "categorical imperative" to the same purpose. In one formulation, the principle of the categorical imperative says, "Act only on that maxim through which you can at the same time will that it should become a universal law." Now, for Kant, the decisive consideration is that one cannot *consistently* will the maxim of an action that is contrary to good morals to be universalized. This elevation of pure consistency in the realm of morals is quite germane but still insufficient as the foundation of morals. If it were, the principle of noncontradiction would be the supreme law of morals, but it is not.

It is important, however, to note that the principle of noncontradiction satisfies the condition so far specified for moral rules. Certainly, if that principle were to be generally and studiously discarded—a scale of noncompliance not dreamed of by even the most enthusiastic paraconsistentist—there would no longer be any such thing as a human community, for communication would become impossible; and without communication, as we earlier saw, there is no human community. It follows that the condition in question is not a sufficient condition for a rule being a moral rule but only a necessary one.

How, then, may we attain sufficiency in the characterization of the rules of morality? What we need is, I think, to exhibit the necessary connection between morality and human interests. This connection almost leaps into the eye when we consider what sort of motivation might lead an individual to break a rule such as that of truth telling. This can only be the desire of the individual to pursue his or her own interests in deliberate indifference to the interests of others. Its short name is selfishness. The point becomes even more clear if we take concrete examples of moral imperatives such as "Do not steal" or "Do not pursue your neighbor's wife." It must dawn on us, from such considerations, that the rationale of a moral rule is the harmonization of the interests of the individual with the interests of others in society, and its motivation is the sympathetic appreciation of those interests, a frame of mind that facilitates the mind's ability to contemplate with equanimity the possible abridgement of one's own interests in deference to the interests of others. The rationale discloses the objective, and the motivation the subjective, aspects of morals; both aspects are essential to the constitution of morality. And this accounts for the important distinction between scrupulous action and a merely prudential one. An individual is not deserving of moral approbation merely because he or she did something that promotes the requisite harmony of interests; he or she has to have done it in the requisite spirit.

This last remark must again remind us of Kant. The sage insisted that doing your duty is not morally meritorious unless it is done out of respect for duty. But our depiction of morals has also an un-Kantian implication. Kant spurned any suggestion that human well-being could be the motto of the moral life. On the other hand, by our lights, human well-being is an irreducible presupposition of all morality. Not, of course, that every quest for human well-being is a moral enterprise; but every moral endeavor is a certain kind of quest for human well-being. It is the kind that seeks its objective through the empathetic harmonization of human interests. Empathetic or not, a certain minimum of harmonization of interests is indispensable to any tolerable form of human social existence. Hence morality, at least, on its objective side, is humanly essential. Herein lies the universal obligatoriness of moral rules.

Perhaps no one can be the ultimate authority on the origins of his or her opinions, but I find these thoughts on the necessary connection between morality and human well-being totally attuned to the moral thinking pervasive in the culture in which I was born and raised, namely, the culture of the Akans of Ghana. The first axiom of all Akan axiological thinking is that man or woman is the measure of all value. ("*Onipa na ohia*".) And every Akan maxim about the specifically moral values that I know, explicitly or implicitly, postulates the harmonization of interests as the means, and the securing of human well-being as the end, of all moral endeavor.

On the strength of the last remark, we may characterize Akan ethics as humanistic. In this, of course, the Akans are not unique. There are humanistic strands in Western ethical thought, too. But it is significant to note that there is also in the West, in contrast to the situation in Akan thought, a highly influential tradition of ethical supernaturalism. Indeed, if you take account of popular as well technical thought, it may justly be said that the dominant bent of Western ethics is nonhumanistic. I hasten to point out that I use the word *nonhumanistic* as the strict contradictory of *humanistic* in the sense just indicated. I do not mean *nonhumanistic* in the sense of wicked or anything like that. As for wickedness, I suspect that, by and large, it is evenly distributed among all the different tribes of humankind. It is, besides, worthy of note that not all nonhumanistic ethics in the West are supernaturalistic. Kant's ethics, for example, are sharply nonhumanistic; he expressly disavows any *necessary* connection between morality and human interests. Yet, his conception of morality is equally sharply nonsupernaturalistic. He defines moral worth, purely by the lights of human reason, in terms of respect for the categorical imperative. God, indeed, has a place in the total scheme of Kant's ethics, but only as the legislative and executive source of compensation, in the afterlife, for virtue unrequited in this life. God's very existence, incidentally, is ("from a practical point of view") established—believe it or not— by the alleged necessity of this eschatological compensation. As distinct from this kind of logically extrinsic status for God in ethics, ethical supernaturalism bases the very essence of morality on the will of God. On that view, what is morally right is, by definition, what is in accord with the will of God. This view of ethics is particularly popular, though not universal, among Christians. I have already remarked on its absence from Akan ethical thinking and will return to the point in due course.

Meanwhile, there is a judicious flexibility in humanistic ethics to which attention should be called at this point. It consists in the fact that from such an ethical standpoint it is easy to see that and to see why, although moral rules are unconditionally imperative, they are not necessarily exceptionless. Probably everyone has had his or her moral imagination teased by the following classical poser: What do you do if confronted by a sword-brandishing psychopath who inquires of your mother's whereabouts with the unambiguous purpose of promptly hacking her to pieces? By virtual common consent, moral uprightness does not require sacrificing your mother on the altar of truth-telling under this kind of duress. But on nonhumanistic premises it is not clear why not. On the other hand, if the moral end is the evenhanded securing of human interests, then some tempering with the truth in the harrowing encounter imagined is easily recognized as a rational adjustment of principle to special circumstance. The reason why such an adjustment does not smack of opportunistic casuistry is that it is obvious that everybody's interests are, on the whole, best served by withholding the truth in question from a lunatic on the rampage. It might be said, accordingly, that what we have here is only an exception to the rule of truth telling, not an overturning of it; and if the exception proves this rule, it is because in the very act of seeming to evade it we are, in fact, reaffirming its rationale. It emerges, by an obvious generalization, that moral rules are susceptible to exceptions but not to reversal, and the admissible exceptions can only be ones that uphold their rationale.

In Western philosophy, Kant is certainly one of the thinkers who had the strongest sense of the irreversibility of moral rules. But he seems to have conflated this irreversibility with exceptionlessness. He thus made himself an uninviting exception to the apparent consensus in regard to the permissibility of telling a lie to save one's mother in the terrible situation visualized a moment ago. As is well-known, he earnestly maintained, in the teeth of this specific example, that one is in duty bound to yield the truth, come what maniac may. I cannot help suspecting that the powerful mind of Kant was trapped into so irrational an inflexibility by the dead weight of his nonhumanistic approach to ethics.

But this is speculation. Let us return to the question of the distinction between custom and morality, this time more concretely. In the light of the foregoing discussion, it is clear that, for example, the Akan rule of greeting mentioned earlier is a rule of custom rather than of morality, strictly speaking. It is not unimportant on that account, but it lacks the unconditional obligatoriness of a moral rule; an honest person can envisage its absence from human social intercourse with composure. It is only putting the same point in different words to say that the obligatoriness of custom may be relative to a particular culture or society or to an even lesser grouping. Perhaps this might be called a form of relativism. If so, it will have to be recognized as a rather limited and atypical form of relativism that does not really conform to the acceptation of that word, for it does not rule out the possibility that the rationale of a custom might become interculturally appreciated once it has been situated in the context of its own habitat.

However, the question of rationale does not always arise in connection with custom. Some customs seem to originate in accidental or even subconscious circumstances. It may well be, for example, that the unique set of phonetic articulations used in a particular language out of the myriads of possibilities owes its origins to a process in which, as Ruth Benedict suggests in her classic "Anthropology and the Abnormal,"[1] accidental and subconscious factors play a decisive role. In regard to customs of such accidental origins, which are, I think, more important in the differentiation of cultures than the cross-culturally explicable ones, propriety or impropriety is even more strikingly relative to culture.

As an example of a cross-culturally intelligible custom, consider the rule of respect for elders. Probably every culture enjoins it with some degree of urgency. But the differences of degree from one society to another in this continuum of urgency can be extremely significant. One of the Ten Commandments says, "Honor thy father and thy mother: that thy days may be long upon the land which the Lord thy God giveth thee" (Exodus 20:12). From other bible stories, such as, for example, the story of the fate that befell the mischievous infants who made fun of an old man who seemed to be making heavy weather of walking up a trivial hill (remember the Almighty dispatched some wild beasts to devour them), one may safely generalize the quoted commandment into a pretty rigorous requirement of respect for those of ripe age. Now, this particular imperative is a major feature of the traditional Akan ethic. In this respect, therefore, there is an obvious similarity between Akan morals and the morals of ancient Judea, from where both the commandment and the story originate. In this same respect, however, there is a noticeable dissimilarity between the dictates of Akan and Judean morality, on the one hand, and those of, say American morality, on the other, as far as I can see. Notice, by the way, that in this paragraph I have used the concept of morals in its broad signification.

To return to the comparison of morals, it cannot be said, of course, that people are not expected to respect their elders in the United States of America. But the fact is that the deference that is considered to be due to age in Akan traditional society is much greater than is required in the American social environment. The difference is, indeed, so great that one might almost call it one of kind rather than of degree. In consequence, one can foresee quite serious disparities in the moral characterization of relevant actions, reactions, and attitudes. Thus, a traditional Akan elder freshly transported into American society would be likely to find the attitude of American youth to their elders to be marked, or more strictly, marred by an unbearable offhandedness; while, for their part, American youth in a converse shift of environment would be likely to feel that traditional Akan society demands nothing short of grovelling docility from the young in their relations with the old.

This difference is, in fact, easy to understand. Traditional Akan society, as presumably its Judean counterpart, was a society in which science, technology, and industry had not reached any very high level of development. In such societies, knowledge is likely to be, on the whole, more a possession of the old than of the young. Prestige and influence will naturally go along with knowledge, more especially, knowledge of a practical kind. Under such conditions, the high respect accorded to age is not gratuitous. The position is apt, however, to change in a highly industrialized, technological society. Respect for age is still in place, but it is unlikely to reach the high levels obtaining in a traditional society, nor, in view of the all-too-human tendency to overcompensation in major transitions of outlook, will it always reach a reasonable level.

In all this, what is of crucial significance is that the differences noted, whatever their explanation, appertain to custom rather than morality in the narrow sense. To repeat, this observation does not imply any diminution in the importance of custom as such. Still less does it imply that customs are necessarily inaccessible to transcultural evaluation from either a moral or utilitarian standpoint. Morality, in particular, can override anything, saving only its own rationale. Nevertheless, it is of the last consequence to realize that the merits or demerits of a particular custom may be independent of any specifically moral considerations. Many customs are, indeed, designed to achieve the well-being of given societies, and we may suppose that some do actually succeed in this. But in itself, this is not a moral fact. Furthermore, there is plenty of room for variability in the efficacy of customs. A custom that is good in one society may be the contrary in another. Or it may be good in a given society at a given time without being so in a changed era. Thus, for the same sorts of reasons as those previously rehearsed, the high respect demanded for age in Akan traditional society is giving rise to intergenerational tensions in contemporary semi-industrialized Akan society.

This susceptibility to being overtaken by changing time, place, or circumstance is one of the marks of custom as distinct from morality. Yet, because there is, as already remarked, a broad concept of morality within which custom is a moral topic, it has been easy for some students of the great variety of customs among the different cultures of the world to conclude that all morality is *relative* in the specific sense that moral rightness consists in being approved by a given culture, society, group, or epoch. This, of course, is an egregious error. Even with respect to custom, there are quite definite limits to relativity. Any custom that leads to needless suffering, for example, is bad wherever and whenever it exists. True, it may not be easy to show that a particular instance of suffering is needless, for the issue may be entangled in the web of a complex system of cosmological beliefs. But it is a fact of history that even the most entrenched belief systems can change under the pressure of recalcitrant facts.

An interesting thing about the confusion of the norms of custom, which may be relative to time, place, or circumstance, with the norms of morality, which are not, is that it has two sides of opposite attractions. The first consists in treating morality as if it is of a piece with custom, while the second consists in treating custom as if it is of a piece with morality. The relativist wades into the error by the first side, while a sanctimonious antirelativist is apt to tumble into the same error by the second.

Relativism seems to be enjoying something of a revival in recent philosophy. This is not due to any intrinsic intellectual merit of that standpoint. It is due, I think, to the fact that, ironically, antirelativism is liable, through a certain adulteration of logic with psychology, to be transformed into some form of authoritarian absolutism, which turns off many intellectuals who have their hearts in the right place. The transformation is roughly like this. From the fact that morality is not relative to culture or circumstance, it is inferred that it is not dependent on anything human. The way is then open to the antirelativist, full of a sense of the importance of morals, to suppose that morality is only correctly conceived from a divine or some suitably Olympian perspective. The thinkers or nonthinkers who thus align themselves with a point of view so infinitely superior to any merely human point of view easily gain a sense of infallibility (by association) in their own self-perception. Accordingly, their own norms of conduct are seen as ineluctable models of the right and the good in the sphere of all morals. The divergent ways of life of other individuals or peoples, except perhaps the most inconsequential, are therefore wrong, immoral, impermissible; they constitute an execrable affront to righteousness. It should now be clear how antirelativism, ill conceived, can become a particularly insidious enemy of that open-mindedness in the face of the diversity of ways of life among the different peoples of the world, which cultural pluralism seeks to foster.

Two misidentifications are touched on, explicitly or implicitly, in this diagnosis. There is the misidentification of the point of view of morality with some transcendent point of view, and there is the misidentification of good conduct with moral uprightness. I shall return to the first in more concrete terms later. Let me try, at this stage, to bring some concrete observations to bear on the second. It may be conceded at once, in apparent mitigation of the grossness of the error here in question, that it is not always easy to distinguish between custom and morality in specific cases. A particular case of considerable intercultural interest is the question of the legitimacy or illegitimacy of polygamy. It is well-known that in Africa and some other parts of the world polygamy is regarded as a legitimate marriage arrangement. On the other hand, the Christian missionaries who came to Africa to "save" our souls, perceiving the practice to be incompatible with their own norms of good conduct, condemned it inexorably as immoral and worked assiduously to eradicate it. They have had a measure of success in this. But there has been a certain superficiality about that success, which has been responsible for a kind of ethical schizophrenia in the consciousness of many of our people. However sincere the African convert has been in his avowal of the foreign faith, he has too often not been able to erase from all the recesses of his consciousness a predisposition to many of the cultural habits ingrained in him in the course of his domestic and community socialization. In the upshot, many noble and pious Africans have been known to operate a subtle compromise of an official monogamy supplemented with informal but quite stable and demographically significant amorous relationships. Needless to say, the "pagan" sections of our populations have never been able to view this dual system of behavior as anything but a somewhat amusing form of emergency pragmatism.

Be that as it may, the question is, How are we to analyze this whole situation from the point of view of the philosophy of morals? If, in keep-

ing with our earlier thought experiment, we consider whether circumstances are conceivable in which polygamy might come, everywhere, to
be seen as a more reasonable connubial institution than monogamy, little
imagination would be needed to conjure up a scenario to motivate an affirmative answer. Suppose, for example, that by some unanticipated combination of persisting causes women were to come to outnumber men by,
say, fifty to one. Make it a hundred to one or worse, if you foresee greater
resistance to the impending suggestion, which is that in such a state of
affairs to insist on a policy of one-man–one-wife would mean, as a matter of simple arithmetic that the overwhelming majority of women would
go through life in the most drastic sexual deprivation and, very probably,
in deep emotional distress on account of the inevitable frustration of
related instincts. Common decency would everywhere recommend
polygamy or something substantially similar to that system under such
conditions.

Or reverse the experiment. Imagine that, through equally inscrutable changes in the phenomena of our world, men come to outnumber
women by the aforementioned factor. Then, by similar and perhaps more
urgent considerations, good sense would urge an analogous revision of
marriage system: polyandry in place of monogamy! Rational flexibility
would be more urgent in this hypothetical case than in the previous one,
only because, if in the new circumstances the principle were to be
pressed that only one man could be the recipient of all the married at-
tentions of one woman, you could infallibly predict that the resultant
sexual and emotional famine among men would quickly drive them to a
war of all men against all men. An obvious general lesson here is that
rules of conduct were made for man or woman, not the other way round;
but a more particular lesson is that, purely in itself, the issue of polygamy versus its contraries is one of custom rather than morality in the
strict sense.

Again, from this last point, it cannot be inferred that polygamy enjoys any relativistic immunity from cross-cultural evaluation. On the
contrary, it can still, in principle, be scrutinized from, at least, a utilitarian point of view. And, in any case, as a human institution, its actual operation by any given group of persons will undoubtedly generate moral
issues. The point is only that the self-righteous blanket denunciation of
polygamy in Africa by the Christian missionaries was, if nothing else,
oblivious to philosophical considerations of considerable practical import. In fact, polygamy, like monogamy to be sure, is open to all sorts of
moral abuses from both sides of the relationship, and the Akans are extremely sensitive to this fact, as shown in their folklore, for example.
They have also been alive to the sociological implications of a changing
economy. The generality of Akans have perceived that industrialization,
even such as it has been, has brought in its trail conditions severely un-

congenial to polygamy, and the practice is currently on the wane. Practical considerations rather than moralistic preachments are what have proved really decisive. And this is as it should be, having regard both to the true nature of the issue and the humanistic basis of the Akan outlook on the rules of human conduct.

Industrialization, by the way, has made a morally more debatable inroad into another aspect of the Akan ethic. The word *communalist* might be used to characterize the bent of that ethic. This alludes to the fact that in that outlook the norms of morality are defined in terms of the adjustment of the interests of the individual to the interests of society rather than in terms of the adjustment of the interests of society to those of the individual. The latter way of viewing morality may be taken to be characteristic of individualism. From a logical point of view, pure morality still remains a constant in this variation of outlook; for, however the adjustment of interests is arrived at, its actual existence satisfies the objective conditions of morality. But psychologically, the accent on the community in a communalist orientation can provide an added incentive to the moral motivation. Unfortunately, the apparent concomitants of industrialization are eroding this mechanism for the reinforcement of morals.

The most threatening circumstance in this regard is the urbanization that has attended industrialization. African residents of large cities no longer have the benefits of either the support or the sanctions of the system of caring that was the mainstay of traditional community life. The circles of obligations, rights, and privileges, which irradiated from the center of household relations of kinship to the larger circumferences of lineage and clan affinities, provided a natural school for training in the practice of sympathetic impartiality, which, in its most generalized form, is the root of all moral virtue. The integration of individuality into community in African traditional society is so thoroughgoing that, as is too rarely noted, the very concept of a person has a normative layer of meaning. A person is not just an individual of human parentage, but also one evincing in his or her projects and achievements an adequate sense of social responsibility.[2] Bereft of the traditional underpinnings of this sense of responsibility, city dwellers are left with nothing but their basic sense of human sympathy in their moral dealings with the great numbers of strangers encountered in and out of the work environment. The well-known crime rate in the cities is proof of the limited capabilities of that moral equipment. Thus, by and large, industrialization seems to be proving deleterious to that system of communal caring and solidarity that was a strong point of traditional communalism. One of the greatest problems facing us in Africa is how to reap the benefits of industrialization without incurring the more unlovable of its apparent fallouts, such as the ethic of austere individualism.

When the Akan or, in general, the African traditional social outlook is described as *communalist,* is it unusual to contrast it with that of Western society by calling it *individualistic.* There is a certain obvious anthropological validity in this comparison. But some riders are necessary. First, it should be repeated that this does not disclose a difference with respect to the actual content of morality. Aside from the difference in the manner of viewing the adjustment of interests required by morality, the real difference between communalism and individualism has to do with custom and life-style rather than anything else. Although the notion of custom tends to evoke imageries of social practice, while life-style is more readily associated with individual lives, both are, conceptually, of a kind and are distinct from morality in the strict sense. While on this, it might be of some use to note that histories of Western ethics regularly allot generous space to certain classical portrayals of different life-styles. Aristotle's treatments of ethics, for example, or the discourses of the epicureans and the stoics, consist largely of (reasoned) recommendations of particular life-styles and only deal with questions of pure morality when they touch, relatively briefly, on such topics as justice. Had our communalist forebears preserved in print their thoughts on the same range of subjects, we may be sure that mutual aid would have loomed larger in their meditations than most of the concerns of the classical moralists.

Second, the distinction between communalism and individualism is one of degree only; a considerable value may attached to communality in individualistic societies, just as individuality is not necessarily trivialized within communalism. Finally, the two orientations can coexist in different sectors of the same society. Thus, for example, intimations of a communalist outlook are discernible in the life-styles of the rural folks of individualistic America.

Perhaps the sphere of conduct in which the conflict between Akan morals and Western morality, or more strictly, the Christian form of it, has been acutest is the sphere of sexual morality. Christianity, as it came to us in Africa through the missionaries, proscribed premarital sex as totally incompatible with morality. Contrast this with Akan conceptions of marriage. This is conceived of as a union in which the parties are a pair of individuals and their respective families, and the purpose is principally, though not exclusively, procreation. As such, it is not a relationship lightly to be entered into. Considerable mutual knowledge between both principals, including "carnal" knowledge, is regarded as a commonsense requirement. Indeed, prior intimacy is viewed not only as educative but also as pragmatic. Akan men and women usually seek visible signs of fertility before committing themselves to the union in question. Thus, far from something like pregnancy before marriage being looked on as a scandal, it is welcomed as an auspicious omen.

But a man does not just fall on a woman and impregnate her on the off chance of a possible marriage. The thing is governed by rigorous and well-structured rules. A man who takes a comprehensive fancy to a woman has, if his advances are reciprocated, to reveal the fact, in the first instance, to his own family and, in the second, to the woman's. To the latter, he goes in due time in the company of his father with offerings of schnapps and a message of the following tenor: The man has been very strongly impressed with your royal and would like to see a lot more of her. He has, in fact, been seeing her for a little while. This offering is only an earnest of his sentiments and intentions. All being well, he will come back later in due style. Meanwhile, he begs to suggest that if you look for her and you do not readily find her, you may check with him. Unless the woman's family, who, on their side, would already have done some research on the prospective suitor, have well-founded moral or medical objections to him, they will give their blessing to the association, knowing full well that the two will not stop short of sex, though, at this stage, there would be no absolute guarantee of marriage. Of course, if all goes well, the man will come again to seal the relationship with due ceremony.

On the other hand, if a man, heedless to custom, should unceremoniously put a woman in the family way—reckless individuals exist in all cultures—he would be declared to have "stolen" her and would be liable to quite severe fines and concerted and equally severe reprimands from all concerned on both kinship sides. The premarital arrangements just recounted are, obviously, radically different from anything that was officially countenanced in orthodox Christian circles. Still, in light of our distinction between custom and morality, there is no question but that what we have here are just different customs. To the Christian authorities, however, the Akan system involved living in sin.

It is a fact, of course, that in the last three decades or so orthodox Christian precepts of premarital chastity have been massively overtaken by "permissive" practices in Western society. For the time being, however, the significant difference between the Akan and Christian milieus remains, for it makes sense to speak of permissiveness in this connection only in environments where there is a background of previously authoritative commandments to the contrary. In Akan society, the practice in question is not permissive; it is the permitted. At all events this difference illustrates the kind of plurality of ways of life in the world that a reasonable mind ought to be able to contemplate without pique or panic.

So far we have not encountered any difference of morality in the strict sense between Akan and Western ways of life. This is not accidental. If the concern of morality is the harmonization of the interests of the individual with the interests of society, this is exactly what is to be expected, for none but the most brutish form of existence could be foreseen among any group of individuals who standardly disavowed and disregarded any such concerns. It is true that individuals and groups may differ in their degree of inclination or dedication to such aims; but this is a fact of practice, not of precept.

Nevertheless, without prejudice to the last reflection, there may be philosophically important differences in the ways in which various individuals, groups, or peoples conceive of morality in the strict sense; and I would like to comment on a difference of this sort between Akan and certain influential Western conceptions of morals. The Western intellectual situation is characterized by a great diversity of philosophic persuasions, and prudence dictates abstention from unqualified generalizations. Yet, there is a certain recognizable metaethical orientation in some very important forms of Christian thinking that might approximately be called orthodox. This is the understanding of ethics, which sees its basis in religion. Certainly, the influence of this way of viewing morality is very pervasive in popular Christian thinking and is, surely, not unconnected with the semantical fact that the adjective "un-Christian" imputes some measure of moral degeneracy. That this way of thinking about morality is popular, even if not universal, in Western society is undoubtedly a noteworthy fact about Western moral thinking. And in any case, the Christian evangelism that was brought to Africa was of this outlook.

In regard to this notion of the dependence of morality on religion, we encounter a rather striking contrast, for it does not even make sense in the Akan context. This brings us back to some matters previously touched on, namely, the antithesis in ethics between humanism, on the one hand, and antihumanism with its subspecies of supernaturalism, on the other. As noted earlier, in Akan thought, what is moral is, by definition, what promotes the well-being of society by way of the harmonization of interests. Logically, the existence of God is irrelevant to the essence of morality as so conceived. It is, indeed, a fact that the Akans, like *most* other African peoples, believe in the existence of a Supreme Being, who might be called God, provided this nomenclature in not taken to imply an identity of attributes with the Christian God. This Supreme Being is regarded as supremely good; but, from the Akan point of view, it would just be compounding ambiguity with obscurity to suggest that "good" here means anything other than what it means in mundane semantics. In particular, to say that "morally good" means "in conformity with the will of God" would leave it *logically* possible that the morally good could conceivably be at variance with the harmonious ordering of human interests, a veritable contradiction in Akan terms. Yet, in orthodox Christianity, specifically, this is the kind of dependence that morality is supposed to have on religion. The relation is not merely a motivational dependence; it is a conceptual one: moral rightness just connotes accordance with the will of God.

The only area of Akan thinking where any kind of rightness or wrongness is defined in this sort of way—that is, in terms of the will of an extra-human being—is the area of taboo. A taboo is a prohibition expressing the dislike of some extra-human being believed capable of punishing noncompliance with disasters, sometimes quite severe and widespread. The idea here is that what a taboo prohibits is *ipso facto* bad; it is not supposed to be prohibited because it is bad, rather, it is regarded as bad solely because it is thus prohibited.

Two observations are urgent at this point. First, in view of the humanistic conception of morals in Akan thinking, any concept of badness defined in terms of taboo falls outside the pale of morality in the strict sense. Second, there is evidence to suggest that taboo is not an irreducible category in the Akan system of norms of conduct. It is arguable that the taboos are a pedagogical expedient designed by our sages of old to concentrate ordinary minds on the path of desirable behavior.

Consider two frequently cited taboos of Akan society. One is, "Do not work your farm on Thursdays" and the other, "Never have sex in the bush." The taboo-style explanation of the first is that Thursday is the day after which the earth goddess is named. Her name is *Asaase Yaa*. The word *Asaase* means the earth, and *Yaa* is the first name given to any female born on Thursday. Thus, the two words together mean something like, "Madam Earth whose day is Thursday," and the madam apparently regards working on that day as an act of disrespect to her. Now, the Akans credit their ancestors not only with wisdom but also with ingenuity. Our ancestors are reputed generally to have had good practical reasons for their prescriptions and proscriptions. If so, one must suspect some lost rationale, in this case, perhaps communally regularized respite from toil.

We are on stronger grounds with respect to the second taboo. The common explanation is that bush sex is a pastime that the earth goddess simply finds insupportable and will punish with soil infertility. But why? After all, sex in the bedroom is as much a kind of commotion on some earth surface as sex in the bush. In fact, a practical rationale is not far to seek and is known to be proffered by those who do not rest content with the ideas of the populace. The freedom of unaccompanied females from unorthodox sexual invasion in isolated areas could hardly have been far from the motivation of the ancestors who laid down this rule. Other taboos would seem to be susceptible to similarly intelligible explanations.

Not only, then, are taboos not a component of the Akan system of morals, strictly so-called, but also they would seem not to constitute *as such* any *essential* part of the Akan repertoire of customs and usages. The rules themselves, of course, remain an ingredient of the Akan ethos, but the apparent irrationality of their genesis would seem to be dissolvable.

On the other hand, taboos seem to have quite a secure place in the orthodox Christian ethic alongside the moral rules proper. Take the decalogue again, and recall the following injunctions. (1) Thou shalt not kill. (2) Thou shalt not commit adultery. (3) Thou shalt not steal. (4) Thou shalt not bear false witness against they neighbor. (5) Thou shalt not covet they neighbor's house, thou shalt not covet they neighbor's wife, nor his manservant, nor his maidservant, nor his ox, nor his ass, nor anything that is thy neighbor's. (Exodus 20:13–17. Numbering not in biblical sequence.) Subject to reasonable qualifications with respect to the first and some refinements and updating here and there, these are straightforward moral rules in the narrow sense under our definition of morality. They, obviously, do not differentiate the Christian ethic from the Akan counterpart. In their essential meaning, all these rules can be effortlessly duplicated in the Akan stock of ethical sayings. Indeed, it is difficult to see how such moral truisms could differentiate the moralities of any pair of human groups.

Recall next the following: (6) Honor thy father and thy mother (etc.). (7) Thou shalt not take the name of the LORD thy God in vain (etc.). The first of this pair, as we have already discussed, is a custom—one that is invested with comparable importance in both traditional Judean and Akan society but is rather less touted in places such as the United States. The second is perhaps a special case of the first.

But, now, reflect on the remaining commandments, which run as follows. (8) Thou shalt have no other gods before me. (9) Thou shalt not make onto thee any graven image or any likeness of anything that is in heaven above or that is in the earth beneath or that is in the water under the earth. (10) Remember the sabbath day to keep it holy. These have all the distinctive marks of taboos. They are, as far as one can see, rules whose entire normative force consists in expressing the likes and dislikes of an extra-human being.

What do these taboos look like from the perspective of the Akan traditional worldview? Let us begin with the first two, namely, those prohibiting any trafficking in other gods. These are unlikely to convey much meaning to a traditional Akan. In his cosmology he believes that there exist, as *regular* parts of the world order fashioned out (not "created") by the Supreme Being, a great variety of extra-human beings and forces which are capable of aiding humans if properly tapped or approached. The more impersonal of these forces are, on this view, as intrinsic to the scheme of things in this world as electricity or rainfall, and the relatively personalized ones are viewed much like we view other minds, except that they are differently localized and, in some cases, are supposed to be endowed (by God) with striking powers. Thus it must sound very paradoxical indeed to the Akan to suggest that it could possibly occur to God to take offence at his dealings with those forces. Some of the more remarkable aspects of the Christian conversion of large masses of traditional Akans have to do with how they were persuaded to make verbal commitments to commandments such as the ones now under discussion. The fact, in any case, is that the traditional beliefs usually remained psychologically operative in spite of everything.

What of the taboo relating to the sabbath? This is likely to make some sense to the Akan, because in some ways it appears analogous to the Akan taboo against farm work on Thursdays. However, an important question immediately arises: Would the orthodox Christian take kindly to any attempt to find a practical, nonsupernaturalistic rationale for the sabbath commandment? If, as I suspect, the answer is likely to be "no," then this Christian taboo and the others are revealed as taboos in a more irreducible sense than the Akan ones.

The foregoing reflection has an even more remarkable implication for the characterization of Christian morals. If Christians do not shy away from calling moral rules in the strict sense commandments of God whose moral rightness logically consists in the sheer fact of being the will of God, it would follow, from the definition of taboo, that they reduce morality to the status of taboo. Such a reduction is, surely, unfortunate. It is fortunate, however, that in analyzing a set of rules of conduct, such as the Ten Commandments, one can, if one has a clear criterion for the purpose, separate custom from morality, and, even within custom, distinguish the rationally explicable elements from the normative surds. In this way, one is enabled to recognize in the ways of life of different peoples those ethical norms of universal applicability that underlie the possibility of orderly dialogue and interaction between different peoples, groups, or individuals, while, at the same time, understanding the basis of the great variety of norms by which people live.

On the preceding showing, it is apparent that the distinction between custom and morality is of more than a theoretic interest. Failure on the part of some benefactors of Africa to make or observe the distinction in all its subtlety has not served the continent well. But it is not only in Africa that the distinction can have practical consequences. Inattention to it can result, everywhere, in authoritarian moralism.

Endnotes

1. *Journal of General Psychology* 10 (1934).
2. This is the burden of Ifeanyi Menkiti's "Person and Community in African Traditional Thought," in *African Philosophy: An Introduction,* 3d ed., ed. Richard A. Wright (Lanham, MD: University Press of America, 1984).

Morality, Art, and African Philosophy: A Response to Wiredu

Parker English and Nancy Steele Hamme

In this article the philosopher Parker English and art historian Nancy Steele Hamme take issue with Wiredu's claim that the primary source of traditional Akan moral thought is humanistic, whereas the primary source of modern Western moral thought is spiritualistic. Acknowledging that no written records exist to adjudicate the claim, English and Hamme use instead the historical record found in the artifacts and legends produced by traditional Akan society. These traditional artifacts and legends recount the spiritual origin of the Asantehene and the seventy-seven laws regarded as the basis of traditional Akan moral thought. According to traditional accounts, the authority of the Asantehene derives from his ability to mediate between humans and spirits.

English and Hamme argue that Wiredu's characterization of modern Western morality as spiritualistic and traditional Akan morality as humanistic is mistaken. And they recommend, as Wiredu has recommended in the past, that we compare traditional African morality to traditional European morality, and modern African morality to modern European morality.

A more extensive version of English and Hamme's argument will be published in The Journal of Social Philosophy with a reply by Wiredu.

ART HISTORY AND TRADITIONAL
AFRICAN PHILOSOPHY

In a series of six recent works, the distinguished Akan philosopher Kwasi Wiredu argues that technological progress is apt to outstrip moral insight.[1] "Accordingly, the philosophical thought of a traditional (i.e., preliterate and nonindustrialized) society may hold some lessons of moral significance for a more industrialized society."[2] One surprising lesson Wiredu derives from his examination of traditional African culture is that Western moral thought is more "supernaturalistic" and less "humanistic" than is that of traditional Akans. Western moral thought is more supernaturalistic in that Westerners tend to justify their moral principles with what they suppose to be the will of God, especially as expressed in the Ten Commandments. In contrast, traditional Akans go so far as to deny that moral principles must accord with the will of God. Instead, traditional Akans regard "the harmonization of interests as the means, and the securing of human well being as the end of all moral endeavor."[3] There is a "necessary" connection between moral principles and human interests. This approach to moral principles is humanistic in that it emphasizes an evenhanded securing of human welfare together with a sympathetic appreciation of one another's interests. "Akan ethics is a humanistic ethics in the precise sense that it is founded exclusively on considerations having to do with human well-being and, contrary to widespread reports, has nothing to do, except very extrinsically, with religion."[4]

Wiredu is concerned with protecting this Akan tradition. His primary reason is that the Western/supernaturalistic alternative tends to be authoritarian. A person who takes the supernaturalistic approach to moral thought easily gains a sense of "infallibility" by virtue of conceiving his or her own viewpoint from a "divine perspective." Too often, this leads to unjustifiably overriding the will of one or more other people.

Wiredu's argument that Western moral thought is more supernaturalistic and authoritarian than is traditional Akan moral thought is significant in that it reverses the view of traditional Africa popularized by writers such as John Mbiti. "But precisely because religion became so deeply entrenched and institutionalized in all the different forms of [traditional] African life, it lost its ability to continue exercising supreme control and holding a position of absolute authority once new challenges and radical changes came upon African societies."[5] Nonetheless, it is notoriously difficult to make cross-cultural comparisons of concepts such as supernaturalism, humanism, and authoritarianism. "If I am reluctant to use the term *religion* without qualification, it is because religion in the contemporary West is, by and large, so different from what it is in traditional life that to report it in Western categories is as much to invite misunderstanding as to offer insight."[6]

In the limited space provided by this essay, we focus exclusively on traditional Akan moral thought. And we hope to show that there are very significant ways in which traditional Akan moral thought was indeed both supernaturalistic and authoritarian.

Of course, there is a major obstacle to investigating traditional Akan moral thought: There is no extensive written record of Akan moral principles during the precolonial period when traditional thought flourished relatively purely. Nonetheless, there is an extensive record. It exists in the art objects that traditional Akans treated as integral to moral education and enforcement.[7] Let us explain.

Art is a category term that originated in the cultural traditions of the West, expressing exclusively Western ideas. In a broader sense, however, art has come to mean something less Western-specific. Art, as we shall use the term, is to be regarded as "culturally significant meaning, skillfully encoded in an affecting sensuous medium."[8] It constitutes one of the ways in which the resources of the material environment are employed in the lives of people as social and communicative beings. The arts are also a collection of describable activities (and responses to these activities) based on the proclivity to "make special."[9]

In traditional oral societies, art also was used to facilitate or make palatable socially important behavior. This is especially true of ceremonies in which group values are expressed and transmitted. An oral tradition comprises a memorized body of information considered important for the perpetuation of the group. This includes the group's history, social organization, technical skills, and moral principles. As the only repository of important information, an oral tradition must be easily memorable. Hence, it is taught by a system of indoctrination that emphasizes obedience and deemphasizes the individuality of teachers, their instruments, and their students. Within an oral tradition, art is an adaptive necessity for this system of indoctrination. It is used as an encoding and mnemonic instrument to make important information more easily and accurately assimilable. As a result, even in the absence of written texts, essential aspects of culture are not lost, ignored, or dismissed. Instead, coded in nonliterate ways, they are integrated and expressed in socially shared symbols.[10]

Traditional Akan art, a body of material objects extant from the traditional cultures of the Akan, is a residue of events whose purpose was to impose on social individuals unforgettable patterns of essential knowledge and explanation. Functional objects such as robes, sandals, jewelry, staffs, swords, and umbrellas, for example, were elaborated to serve as regalia identifying the rank and function of their owner. In addition, traditional Akan artworks expressed ideas about political and moral relationships, especially as these latter related to the rank and function of the ruler.[11] Traditional artworks were also used to invoke messages from and actions by spiritual entities. This was not moral philosophy in the sense of a peer-reviewed sequence of written arguments deriving moral conclusions from moral laws. Rather, it was moral philosophy as a way of accommodating one's neighbors-for-life when they demanded certain actions and prohibited others under conditions that were highly flexible and subject to incompatible interpretations.[12] Art expressed moral philosophy for traditional Akans who were not constrained by the precise implications of writing, but who were nonetheless constrained by an evolving group consensus based around proverbs and myths. Often, a traditional art motif might refer directly to certain proverbs explicitly taught in association with this motif. Such motifs existed as enduring, material evidence not only of the proverbs themselves but also of the ways in which these proverbs were used.

Contemporary art history studies such motifs by using not only the literature of history and art criticism but also that of anthropology, economics, agronomy, sociology, religious studies, and other disciplines as needed. Art history situates a functional artifact within a specific cultural practice. It identifies significant events in the development and use of specific artifacts. It elucidates constraints on and conditions for the production of the beliefs associated with art–artifacts as these beliefs were created, circulated, and renegotiated within different historical moments.

In the next section, we take the approach of art history to identify how the most important traditional Akan art–artifacts display moral principles as these were related to supernaturalistic authoritarianism. We attempt to address the following questions: (1) To what extent did traditional Akans use beliefs about supernatural entities in teaching and enforcing their moral principles? (2) To what extent were priests and other specialists regarded as having unique access to knowledge about the socially relevant action of supernatural entities? (3) To what extent did specialists about supernatural entities serve as secular, political powers who could override the wills of other people?

TRADITIONAL AKAN ART AS MORAL PHILOSOPHY

Akan society and its attendant culture were, in the most literal sense, hacked out of nature. Throughout the sixteenth and early seventeenth centuries, in a recalcitrant tropical forest environment, a protracted investment of labor transformed the dominant mode of production from hunting and gathering to crop agriculture.[13] Sustainable crop agriculture was established through unremitting land clearing of the most difficult order, which to be successful, had to be carried on throughout several generations. This labor required vastly more social cooperation than did the previous economic labor of hunting and gathering. In particular, it divided labor into categories that had to be regulated by principles to which most people were voluntarily compliant: land clearing, land cultivation, livestock husbandry, structure building, tool making, container making, apparel making, administration, defense, and trade.[14] This social cooperation required that an individual's thought be disciplined by relatively unquestioning obedience to certain permissions and prohibitions controlling behavior within a social context. The development of an agricultural economy was thus the most significant determinant event in Akan history, at least before extensive trade with distant Africans and with Europeans. It also produced the indispensable base of food production on which a more formally structured social order would later be enlarged. This more formally structured social order itself evolved into the expansionistic eighteenth-century state as a strong and centralized authority became required for efficient interaction with traders from the rest of Africa and from Europe.[15]

"Culture, society and polity were brittle artifacts, inserted with enormous effort into the constantly encroaching anarchy of nature."[16] Consequently, traditional Akan societies evolved various instruments to profoundly condition an individual's understanding of the group's hard-won and fragile mastery over the environment. Traditional Akans were taught to believe that order within society was a concern that affected all. It required everyone's committed participation, just as had the communal creation of agriculture. In particular, traditional Akans were taught to believe that a person's sense of peace with the invisible world of spirits could be achieved only by cooperation and harmony with other members of human society. Thus, supernatural beliefs were an essential element in traditional Akan moral and social philosophy.

For traditional Akans, reality was a divine cosmic order fashioned by the high god, *Nyame* "by the very law of his own being."[17] Within this cosmic order was a set of subordinate orders composing one comprehensive universe. The natural order regulated physical, chemical, and biological events; the moral order regulated the conduct of human beings in society; the actions of entities within the supernatural order could be tapped and used by priests and other specialists for benefit or harm. All social rules were directed to an individual's maintaining harmony with each of the subordinate orders of which human beings were a part. "Religion for the Akan is a quest for harmony.... When this harmony is maintained things go well, otherwise there is chaos."[18] It was through sacrifices, offerings, prayer, and other social rituals, including those concerned with punishments, that this harmony was maintained, especially when a prohibition had been violated. Speaking specifically of the Asante, McCaskie remarks that until scholars "are prepared to accept anxiety as a 'cultural' fact—and one not obfuscated by something called religion—they will never be able to comprehend the indigenous reading of the fragility of history, or of the need for totemic devices to defuse irruptive disorder."[19]

How did the most important art objects function in traditional Akan cultures? Stools provide the best example. A stool served several functions for traditional Akans. It was sometimes used as a utilitarian object of rest; it was sometimes associated with rites of passage; it was some-times viewed as a sacred object imbued with the *sunsum* of its owner.[20] A stool was also sacred when used in ancestor veneration. In particular, contact with the ancestors was established and maintained through cere-monies involving the blackened stools of deceased chiefs, especially that of the *Asantehene,* paramount ruler for all traditional Asantes during Asante ascendancy.[21] Consequently, a royal stool was also a political symbol. As successor of the royal ancestors, only a chief could success-fully perform the various rites associated with the stool that were essen-tial for spiritual entities to support the welfare of all in his community.[22]

The political authority of all Akan chiefs rested on their being viewed as successors of those ancestors who had been the principal ac-tors in establishing Akan societies. The *Asantehene,* however, held supreme authority by virtue of holding the Golden Stool, the sacred shrine that housed the *sunsum* of the nation. Thus, any words of abuse uttered against the *Asantehene* reflected on the most important of the principal ancestors. This offense was punishable by death. So were adul-tery with any of the chief's wives, invoking a curse on the chief, theft of stool property, and assaults attempted by the chief's council against the chief. These were religious offenses that angered and threatened to es-trange the ancestral spirits and gods from the community, thereby putting at grave risk both spiritual harmony and societal well-being. "The Asante do not like to even speak of the *Asantehene,* still less to be questioned about him. When they have to talk about him, they do so in low tones, modulating gradually into whispers."[23]

The Golden Stool was understood by traditional Akans to be of spir-itual provenance. According to Asante oral traditions, the Golden Stool first appeared near the end of the seventeenth century. Osei Tutu, chief of Kumase (traditional capital of the Asante), successfully led an alliance of small states against the kingdom of Denkyira to whom they were subject. Osei Tutu thereby became the supreme ruler, the *Asantehene,* of the newly unified Akan nation whose spiritual center was the Golden Stool. According to Asante oral traditions, Osei Tutu's success resulted at least in part from the powerful magic of his priest, Komfo Anokye. Later, on a Friday, a great gathering was held at Kumase. There, Komfo Anokye brought down from the sky, "with darkness and in thunder, and in a thick cloud of white dust," a stool of solid gold, which floated to earth, alighting gently on Osei Tutu's knees. Komfo Anokye announced that all the strength and bravery of the Asante nation depended on the safety of the stool.[24]

As a precondition to producing the Golden Stool, however, Komfo Anokye had demanded that the blackened ancestral stools and the royal regalia of all the Akan member states be surrendered to him so that they could be buried in the Bantama River. This ensured that no item of regalia in the new kingdom could have a longer history than the Golden Stool and therefore take precedence over it. Komfo Anokye declared the stool must be fed at regular intervals so that it might not sicken and die, causing the Akan nation to perish also. Komfo Anokye then organized the military structure of Akan power and presented a formal constitution that outlined a code of seventy-seven laws to be observed by all. These laws are regarded as the basis for traditional Akan moral thought.[25]

In sum, traditional Akans, led by the Asante, constructed their social order and the moral code that supported it in response to their understanding of existence as fragile. By the time Osei Tutu was implementing Akan expansionist policies, the moral code had been given divine sanction and was embodied in a tangible, visual symbol, the Golden Stool. This moral code was upheld, protected, and passed on through those who held the sacred office of *Asantehene.* The authority of *Asantehenes* was legitimated by their superhuman ability to mediate between the world of spirits and that of humans so as to protect the entire nation. The Golden Stool not only was the object that contained the sacred essence of the Asante nation but also was a metaphor for the sacred office that administered and supported it.

Royal regalia such as robes, sandals, jewelry, staffs, swords, and umbrellas are another excellent example of how important art objects functioned in traditional Akan cultures. A very considerable body of these regalia derived in the eighteenth and nineteenth centuries with the growth of central government for the Akan. Each object obtained its own history, use, and significance.[26] By aggrandizing and validating the chief's position of leadership, these objects helped to run an empire without a large literate class. The royal regalia were not merely symbols of office, however. By virtue of their art motifs, they also served as the chronicles of history and as the evidence of traditional religion, cosmology, and social organization.

One of the most distinctive characteristics of royal regalia, and virtually all of traditional Akan visual arts, was the presentation of symbols, objects, or scenes directly related to traditional sayings and proverbs. Indeed, the relationship between art motifs and their verbal equivalents is often cited as one of the cornerstones of Akan aesthetics. While not exclusively an Akan phenomenon, in West Africa it is among the traditional Akan that this verbal–visual nexus was most highly developed.[27] One such motif appearing frequently on royal regalia deals with the continuity of the ruling matrilineage. It depicts one bird nesting and another bird resting above. The proverb is "When the kite is away, the hawk rests on its eggs." For the Akan, the birds are admired predators and are believed to come from the same family. The principal message here is that when the chief dies, there will be someone else from his matrilineage to take his place and guard the state.[28]

In numerous external and internal accounts of traditional Akan-land, death and the mortuary rituals that surround it figure prominently. Social anthropologists have demonstrated a general connection between beliefs about death and attendant funerary practices, on the one hand, and beliefs about sexuality and reproduction, on the other.[29] This is particularly true concerning the deaths of traditional *Asantehenes.* Such deaths led to reflection on higher-order social abstractions concerning increase, the fertility of the land, and that of its people. In turn, these reflections necessitated the introduction of measures to affirm and to renew the latter as goals. It should be clear that the initial and recurrent mortuary rituals for deceased *Asantehenes* functioned as expressive representations of basic beliefs within Asante experience.

The performance of funeral rites for a traditional *Asantehene* was complex, demanding, and prolonged because of the traditional Asante conception of afterlife. Traditional Asantes conceived afterlife as an extension or mirror of the prevailing hierarchies of lived existence. Thus, a deceased *Asantehene* was still an *Asantehene.* In afterlife he had the same status and role, together with the same needs and requirements—wives, servants, clothes, gold, food—as he had in his biological existence.[30] Providing these needs involved killing prisoners, slaves, subjects, and wives.[31] The most important thing to bear in mind here is that any error or oversight, neglect, or failure in the intricate performance of the royal funeral rites constituted a grave offense against the departed *Asantehene.* Without proper observance, he could not be fully incorporated into the world of spirits in a manner appropriate to him. If left with a lesser, ambiguous, or uncertain status, "he could withdraw his protective cooperation from society and instead remonstrate with it for its injurious abandonment and willful insult of him."[32]

A short paper such as this can do no more than present an overview of answers to the three questions we are using to explore supernaturalistic authoritarianism. As far as we can tell, however, both Akan and Western scholars are in wide agreement about the general thrust of these answers concerning traditional Akans. (1) Traditional Akans used beliefs about the authority and action of spiritual entities to an overwhelming extent in teaching and enforcing their moral principles. These beliefs were designed to influence people who typically viewed environmental order as fragile. The beliefs were meant to shape an individual's thought so that he or she could feel at peace with ever-present spiritual entities only if he or she cooperated in maintaining social harmony. This meant obedience to extant moral principles. (2) As successors to departed leaders, traditional chiefs (especially the *Asantehene*) were regarded as the living humans most able to intercede with spiritual entities for general social welfare. This was a primary source for the secular, political power of traditional chiefs. (3) By virtue of his apparent success in contacting spiritual entities, Komfo Anokye had the secular power to destroy the most important symbols of political authority in the Akan member states, their royal regalia. Likewise, he had the authority to present the seventy-seven laws that served as the basis of traditional Akan moral thought. Perhaps the most dramatic proof that specialists about supernatural entities held authoritarian control over traditional Akan societies, however, concerns the ritual killing involved in royal funerals. By virtue of their unique relationship with departed ancestors and other supernatural entities, chiefs had literally the power of life and death in secular matters. By virtue of their power in the world of supernatural entities, immediately deceased chiefs (especially the *Asantehene*) were regarded as still having immense power concerning life and death in their human communities. Consequently, royal princes and priests were licensed to ritually kill thousands of people during the extended funerals for chiefs and *Asantehenes*. If this does not count as overiding the welfare of individuals for spiritualistic purposes, then Wiredu needs to explain what would count as such.

Wiredu thinks the supernaturalistic type of moral thought imported into contemporary Akanland involves a self-validating notion of absolute truth about moral principles that has been appropriated by self-interested leaders. "[O]n the African continent there are everywhere groups privileged with direct access to *the* Truth, social and political; and woe betide those, who, not having eyes to see, do not at the very least stay silent."[33] Such leaders reinforce the traditional Akan respect for leadership so as to facilitate dogmatism in their followers. The leaders then develop authoritarian power to the point of stifling opponents by imprisoning them.

Our research so far indicates there is very little doubt that traditional Akan thought was much more supernaturalistic than is contemporary Akan thought when this is measured by the three questions used here. Whether or not traditional Akan thought was also more authoritarian in purely secular terms is more subject to debate, though the bulk of available evidence indicates it was. Space prevents our fully exploring why Wiredu might think contemporary Akans are actually more supernaturalistically authoritarian than were traditional Akans. One point is worth noting in brief, however. Wiredu is surely right that Westerners, during their colonization of Akanland, often claimed universalism and superiority for their own moral principles. Missionaries in particular often justified these claims by appealing to the authority of God as interpreted under their own self-validating opinions about the Bible. At the same time, however, Akans were encountering quite a different kind of Western authoritarianism in the persons of colonial bureaucrats. When facing Akan opposition, the bureaucrats relatively quickly dominated Akans by using economic, political, and military force. Consequently, many Akans perceived the colonial bureaucracy as concerned more with domination than with legitimation. "The formal agencies transferred to African hands were . . . alien in derivation, functionally conceived, bureaucratically designed, authoritarian in nature and primarily concerned with issues of domination rather than legitimacy."[34]

The significance of this point, however, is that supernaturalistic thought played no important role in the bureaucratic type of authoritarianism—this, even though the colonial bureaucracy was quite clearly self-serving. In contrast, the authoritarianism displayed by missionaries obviously did involve supernaturalistic thought. This was the authoritarianism of demanding that traditional beliefs about spiritual entities and the moral principles they endorsed be assimilated to Christian ones more than vice versa. But few traditional Akans viewed the missionaries as self-serving in ways that were significant and malignant. At worst, they viewed a few missionaries as patronizing or as inflexible concerning charitable endeavors sponsored by missionary societies.[35]

Finally, a reasonably complete challenge to Wiredu's view of supernaturalism and authoritarianism would contrast contemporary African moral thought with contemporary Western moral thought, following Wiredu's well-known suggestion that traditional African thought be compared with traditional Western thought.[36] We might find that supernaturalistic authoritarianism in Western moral thought has evolved in roughly the way this feature is now evolving in Akan moral thought.

Works Cited

Anderson, Richard. *Calliope's Sisters—A Comparative Study of Philosophies of Art.* Englewood Cliffs: Prentice Hall, 1990.

Antubam, Kofi. *Ghana's Heritage of Culture.* Leipzig: Koehler and Amelang, 1963.

Appiah, Kwame Anthony. *In My Father's House: Africa in the Philosophy of Culture.* New York: Oxford University Press, 1992.

Bloch, Maurice, and Jonathan Perry. *Death and the Regeneration of Life.* New York: Cambridge University Press, 1982.

Bowdich, T. E. *A Mission From Cape Coast Castle to Ashantee.* London: John Murray, 1819; 2d ed., 1873; reprinted, London: Frank Cass and Co., 1966.

Busia, Kofi A. *Position of the Chief in the Modern Political System of Ashanti.* London: Frank Cass and Co., 1968.

Cole, Herbert, and Doran Ross. *The Arts of Ghana.* Los Angeles: Museum of Cultural History, 1977.

Dissanayake, Ellen. *What Is Art For?* Seattle: University of Washington Press, 1988.

Dupuis, J. *Journal of a Residence in Ashantee.* London: Henry Coburn, 1824; reprinted, London: Frank Cass and Co., 1966.

Hauser, Arnold. *The Social History of Art.* vol. 1. New York: Vintage Books, 1959.

Kyerematen, A. A. Y. *The Panoply of Ghana.* New York: Praeger, 1964.

———. "Ashanti Royal Regalia: Their History and Function." Doctoral dissertation. Oxford, UK: Oxford University, 1966.

Mbiti, John. *African Religions and Philosophy.* Oxford, UK: Heinemann International, 1969.

McCaskie, Thomas C. "Komfo Anokye of Asante: Meaning and History in an African Society." *Journal of African History* 27 (1986): 319–46.

———. "Death and the Asantehene: A Historical Meditation." *Journal of African History* 30, no. 3 (1989): 417–44.

Opuku, Kofi Asare. "The World View of the Akan." *Tarikh* 7, no. 2 (1982): 48–73.

Otten, Charlotte, ed. *Anthropology and Art: Readings in Cross Cultural Aesthetics.* New York: The Natural History Press, 1971.

Pfeiffer, John. *The Creative Explosion: An Inquiry into the Origins of Art and Religion.* New York: Harper & Row, 1982.

Rattray, R. S. *Religion and Art in Ashanti.* Oxford, UK: The Clarendon Press, 1927.

Ross, Doran. "The Verbal Art of the Akan Linguist Staffs." *African Arts* 16, no. 1 (1982): 56–66.

Sarpong, Peter. *The Sacred Stools of the Akan.* Accra: Ghana Publishing Corporation, 1971.

Terray, Emmanuel. "Asante Imperialism and Gyaman Resistance." In *The Golden Stool: Studies of the Asante Center and Periphery,* edited by Enid Schildkraut. *Anthropological Papers of the American Museum of Natural History* 65, pt. 1 (1987): 245–51.

Ward, W. E. F. *A History of Ghana.* London: Allen & Unwin, 1948.

Wilkes, Ivor. "Land, Labour, Capital and the Forest Kingdom of the Asante: A Model of Early Change," In *The Evolution of Social Systems,* edited by J. Friedman and M. J. Rowlands. Pittsburgh: Pittsburgh University Press, 1977, 487–551.

Wiredu, Kwasi. *Philosophy and an African Culture.* Cambridge, UK: Cambridge University Press, 1980.

———. "How Not to Compare African Thought with Western Thought." In *African Philosophy,* edited by Richard Wright. Lanham, MD: University Press of America, 1984.

———. "Custom and Morality: A Comparative Analysis of Some African and Western Conceptions of Morals." Presented to the Greater Phila-

delphia Philosophy Consortium meeting at Rosemont College in November 1991a.

———. "On Defining African Philosophy." In *African Philosophy,* edited
by Tsenay Serequeberhan. New York: Paragon House, 1991b.

———. "Formulating Modern Thought in African Languages: Some Theoretical Considerations." In *The Surreptitious Speech,* edited by V. Y.
Mudimbe. Chicago: University of Chicago Press, 1992.

———. "African Philosophical Tradition: A Case Study of the Akan."
Philosophical Forum 24, nos. 1–3 (Fall–Spring), 1992–93: 35–62.

Notes

1. Akans are Twi-speakers now accounting for roughly 40% of the population of Ghana, living mainly in the south and center. The ascendance
of the Akan states (Adansi, Akim, Akwamu, Asante/Ashanti, Bono,
Denkyira, Fante, Gyaman, Sefwi, Twifo, Wasaw, etc.) was intimately related to the growth of trade. The region's gold, among other things, at-
tracted Mande-Dyula and Hausa traders as early as the fourteenth century; Portuguese, the first European traders arrived in 1471. Competition
for the economic benefits of trade with Europe as well as with the rest
of Africa encouraged the development of strong centralized chiefdoms
with effective military forces to control and defend the trade routes. The
Asante, who eventually gained dominance among the Akan during this
period, adopted and elaborated on both the technologies and the royal
symbols of their subject peoples. The Akan should thus be regarded as a
political-linguistic-cultural entity, not as a homogeneous kinship group
(Cole and Ross 1977, 6–7).

2. Wiredu 1991b, 98.

3. Wiredu 1991a, 7.

4. Wiredu 1992–93, 51.

5. Mbiti 1969, 266.

6. Appiah 1992, 108.

7. Antubam 1963, 151.

8. Anderson 1990, 238.

9. Dissanayake 1988.

10. Otten 1971, xi–xvi.

11. One example is the staff of office of the *akyeame,* or "linguists," perhaps more accurately described as the chief's counselors and spokesmen.
The staff, made from carved wood and gold leafed, has a carved finial
representing at least one proverbial saying. Although the staff itself is the
okyeame's badge of office, the carved finial almost always refers to the
chief or state. One of the most common finials is that of two men seated
at one table. The proverb cited is "The food is for the man who owns it
and not for the man who is hungry." The food is a metaphor for chief-

taincy, which belongs only to the one who occupies the stool (office of chief). See Ross 1982, 60.

12. Appiah 1992, 130–35.

13. Wilkes 1977.

14. Hauser 1959, 12–21.

15. We remarked in note 1 that the Akan state resulted primarily from Asante expansionism. When the Asante army invaded a neighboring state, whether to take possession of its wealth, its gold mines, its trade routes, or its labor force, the population had three options. They could fight the invaders, they could stay home and accept the Asante rule, or they could migrate. In the seventeenth century, the latter option generally led to the formation of a new state, as was the case with Gyaman. Consequently, the entire Twi-speaking area was divided up into states by the beginning of the eighteenth century. Vacant territories were no longer available for the would-be founders. Therefore, the vanquished communities that decided to migrate rather than accept Asante rule had to join an existing state and place themselves under the authority of its ruler. This was often considered preferable to a humiliating submission to their conquerors. Moreover, in an area where the "missing factor" was not land but population, the host-state was usually more than willing to receive the fugitives and to provide them not only with shelter but also with substantial immunities and privileges. This type of welcome helped to ensure the immigrants' integration into the community and their loyalty, particularly regarding military service, to the ruler. Many peripheral Akan states, such as Gyaman, were able to substantially increase their population by integrating refugees from the areas that had been conquered by the Asante.

This process of migration and hospitality deprived the Asante of the most important product from their victories, however. The significant factor was, indeed, not land, but people. There was no point in occupying wastelands or deserted gold mines. When faced with this result, the Asante had little choice but to present the host-ruler with an ultimatum to send back the refugees or to face war. In most cases, the ultimatum was rejected. A new war ensued, and produced new invasions, new migrations, new grants of hospitality, new ultimatums, and so on. The process did not end until the boundaries of the Twi-speaking world were reached. Beyond these boundaries, refugees were no longer integrated into hospitable societies. Rather, they were enslaved (Terray 1987).

16. McCaskie 1989, 421.

17. Wiredu, 1992–93, 42.

18. Opuku 1982, 63.

19. McCaskie 1986, 329–30.

20. Wiredu defines a person's *sunsum* as "the degree of impact which

that individual makes upon others by his sheer presence" (Wiredu 1992–93, 50).

21. Cf. Sarpong 1971.

22. Busia 1968, 96.

23. Busia 1968, 96.

24. Ward 1948, 119.

25. Busia 1968, 74; McCaskie 1986, 328; Kyerematen 1964, 115–16.

26. Kyerematen 1966.

27. Cole and Ross 1977, 9–12.

28. Cole and Ross 1977, 164.

29. Bloch and Perry, 1982.

30. Rattray 1927, 103, 182; McCaskie 1989, 428.

31. A notable example concerns the mortuary rituals for the *Asantehene* Kwaku Dua Panin, who died close to midnight on April 27, 1867. By sundown on April 28, more than 300 people had been killed by the royal princes. By custom, this killing was sanctioned as long as the *Asantehene's* body remained lying in state in the palace, often for as long as fifteen days. When Kwaku Dua Panin's corpse was given its "primary" burial, twenty-seven of his wives accompanied him in death. Overall estimates for the number killed range from 1,400 to 3,600 (McCaskie 1989, 428, 432–35). Bowdich (1819) reported that in 1809 the *Asantehene* Osei Tutu Kwame devoted 3,000 victims to the rituals of the queen mother Kwaadu Yaadom.

32. McCaskie 1989, 428; Dupuis 1824, 245.

33. Wiredu 1980, 96.

34. Appiah 1992, 164.

35. Another point worth noting is that Kwame Anthony Appiah, himself a distinguished Akan philosopher, disagrees with Wiredu about the relative amounts of authoritarianism in traditional and contemporary Akan societies (Appiah 1992, 170–71).

36. Wiredu 1984, 150–57.

Traditional African Aesthetics: A Philosophical Perspective

Innocent C. Onyewuenyi

Innocent Onyewuenyi is Professor of philosophy at the University of Nigeria, Nsukka. In this article, Onyewuenyi argues that traditional African aesthetic values have a very different orientation from modern Western aesthetic values. The primary objects of aesthetic appreciation in modern Western culture are removed from everyday life and preserved in museums as objects of contemplation. They are valued in proportion to how much they reflect the creativity and uniqueness of particular individuals. In contrast, the arts within traditional Africa were intimately involved with communal values and the practical realities of daily living. Building on Tempels' notion of an ontology of forces, Onyewuenyi concludes that traditional African aesthetic values were functional, depersonalized, contextualized, and embedded within communal activities.

This paper is an attempt to think differently from western aestheticians. It will essay to show that African aesthetic standards are different from the "accepted" standards of uniqueness and individuality; that African works of art, be they visual, musical, kinetic, or poetic are created as an answer to a problem and serve some practical end. It will also delineate the philosophical foundation for such differences, and finally propose the theory of African works of art as the Africans see it.

IS THERE AN AFRICAN AESTHETICS?

Before delving into the problem, we will first of all establish whether there is an African aesthetics or not. By way of definitions, we are told that aesthetics is that branch of philosophy which has tried to answer such questions as "What is Art?" "What is Beauty?" Dagobert Runes defines aesthetics traditionally as the branch of philosophy dealing with beauty or the beautiful, especially in art, and with taste and standards of value in judging art.[1] Accepting the above definitions as universal, there is an intellectual temptation to take the position that it is unnecessary and even futile to ask such a question. If aesthetics is universal, it is as ridiculous to talk of African aesthetics as it is to talk of African physics or African chemistry. The question may even be regarded as racially and nationally loaded, indicating an attempt to narrow the discipline of aesthetics in order to satisfy some racial or national whim.

A similar problem arose in my paper "Is There an African Philosophy?" where I showed that philosophizing is a universal experience and that

> What is generally agreed about philosophy is that it seeks to establish order among the various phenomena of the surrounding world and it traces their unity by reducing them to their simplest elements . . . that while these phenomena are the same in all cultures and societies, each culture traces the unity of these, synthesizes, or organizes them into a totality *based* on each culture's concept of life. . . . Hence it is that the order or unity the people of a culture establish is their own order, relative to their own conception of life in which everything around them becomes meaningful.[2]

If the above is accepted as true, then we have the basis for calling a philosophy (and by extension, aesthetics) European, Indian, American, African. We can and should talk of African aesthetics because the African culture has its own "standards of value in judging art"; its own "general principles" in explaining the value of any work of art. Africa has its own view of life which Dilthey regarded as the starting point of philosophy. Georg Misch summarizes Dilthey thus:

> Dilthey regarded life as the starting point of philosophy; life as actually lived and embodied or 'objectified' in the spiritual world we live in . . . Our knowledge of life is above all, contained in certain cultural and personal views of the world—which play a prominent part in philosophy as well as in religion and poetry.[3]

That philosophy of art is universal does not mean that all aestheticians should employ similar standards of value in judging art, similar general principles of explaining the value of any work of art. Neither does it

---

[1] Dagobert D. Runes, *Dictionary of Philosophy* (Totowa, NJ: Littlefield, Adams, 1966), p. 6.

[2] Innocent C. Onyewuenyi, "Is There An African Philosophy?" *Journal of African Studies*, 3 (Winter 1976/77), 513–528.

[3] Georg Misch, *The Dawn of Philosophy* (London, 1950), p. 47.

mean that all the rationally warrantable or objectively granted principles or methods must be identical or that they must establish similar truths. Two separate aesthetic standards of value or general principles, both being rational, can be opposed to one another.

Hegel underscores the cultural and relative aspect of philosophy when he said:

> But men do not at certain epochs merely philosophize in general. For there is a definite philosophy which arises among a people and the definite character which permeates all the other historical sides of the Spirit of the people, which is most intimately related to them, and which constitutes their foundation. The particular form of a philosophy is thus contemporaneous with a particular constitution of the people amongst whom it makes its appearance, with their institutions and forms of government, their morality, their social life and their capabilities, customs and enjoyments of the same.[4]

From the foregoing one may safely suggest that the general principles or standards of value of aesthetics, which is a branch of philosophy, are bound up intimately with a people's spirit and constitution, and are a factor in their life history, subject to the conditions of race, culture, and civilization.

One function of the arts is making explicit the images by which a society recognizes its own *values* and thus offering a means by which the members of a community may express and evaluate new elements in their lives. Furthermore, the arts afford a perspective on human experience as they are created to channel or express the powers of the super-human world on which men recognize their dependence. The Europeans/Americans and Africans evidently have different views of life here and hereafter; different conceptions of the powers of the super-human world to which they owe their existence, different ethical and moral values, different social institutions and forms of government—in short, different ideas of life and reality. Since the works of art, be they visual, musical, kinetic, or poetic are used "to convey the unfamiliar in the familiar, the abstract in the concrete, the discursive in the intuitive and the spiritual in the physical; in general to communicate the nonsensory through the sensory,"[5] it follows that the symbols must be culturally invested with the contents of their referents. Victor Uchendu may be quoted to round off these arguments in support of the issue of aesthetic relativity. He advised: "To know how a people view the world around them is to understand how they evaluate life, and a people's evaluation of life, both

[4] Georg Hegel, *Lectures on the History of Philosophy* (London, 1968), 1:53.
[5] Arthur Berndtson, *Art Expression and Beauty* (New York: Holt, Rinehart and Winston, 1969), p. 36.

temporal and non-temporal, provides them with a 'charter' of action, a guide to behaviour."[6]

. . . .

A BRIEF SURVEY OF AFRICAN ONTOLOGY

An adequate understanding of African ontology, especially in its conception of the nature of "reality" or "being" as dynamic, is fundamentally important to our discussion of African art appreciation. The essence of anything is conceived by the African as force. "There is no idea among Bantu of 'being' divorced from the idea of 'force'. Without the element of 'force', 'being' cannot be conceived. Force is the nature of being; force is being; being is force."[7] The concept of force or dynamism cancels out the idea of separate beings or substances which exist side by side independent one of another and which we have shown in our discussion of Western ontology to be responsible for individuality and uniqueness as standards or essence of art. Existence-in-relation, communalism, being-for-self-and-others sum up the African conception of life and reality.

> The African thought holds that created beings preserve a bond one with another, an intimate ontological relationship. There is an interaction of being with being. . . . This is more so among rational beings, known as Muntu which includes the living and the dead, Orishas and God.[8]

Because of this ontological relationship among beings, the African knows and feels himself to be in intimate and personal relationship with other forces acting above and below him in the hierarchy of forces.

A corollary to this relationship is the traditional African view of the world as one of extraordinary harmony, which Adebayo Adesanya explains as

> not simply a coherence of fact and faith, nor of reason and traditional beliefs, nor of reason and contingent facts, but a coherence of compatibility among all disciplines. A medical theory, e.g., which contradicted a theological conclusion was rejected as absurd and vice-versa. . . . Philosophy, theology, politics, social theory, landlaw, medicine, psychology, birth and burial, all find themselves logically concatenated in a system so tight that to subtract one item from the whole is to paralyse the structure of the whole.[9]

---

[6] Victor Uchendu. *The Igbo of Southeast Nigeria* (New York: 1965), p. 12.
[7] Tempels, *op. cit.,* p. 37.
[8] *Ibid.,* p. 104.
[9] Jahn, *op. cit.,* p. 96.

INFLUENCES ON AFRICAN AESTHETICS

Traditional African aesthetics, or interpretation, appreciation of works of art as a discipline in the body of African reality, cannot but fall in line with other theories and disciplines which "all find themselves logically concatenated" in the tight system of the African world-view; otherwise it would paralyze the whole structure of African life and being. Works of art, as expressions of ritual and religion, as clues to the temperament of the tribe and society, as language in a culture without writing, must do all these in service to the community whose ritual and religion they express, whose temperament they reveal, the being of whose ancestors they participate in. Its theory or standard of evaluation must conform to the theories of its sister disciplines and stem from identical metaphysical foundations. Hence African art is functional, community-oriented, depersonalized, contextualized, and embedded.

By functional and community-oriented we mean that African arts—visual, musical, kinetic or poetic—are designed to serve practical, meaningful purpose, beauty of appearance being secondary. All the same, "Functional beauty is also beauty,"[10] says Janheinz Jahn. A carving, for example, is aesthetically beautiful in the African standard if it functions well as stimulus in the worship of the deity, the community of worshippers being the judges. A mask, despite its "ugly" appearance, is judged beautiful and good if used correctly in the movement of the dance to depict the divine power with which it is imbued through the rhythmic incantations and sacrificial rites of the communal ceremonies. "Through his dance Efe has the power to please the witches and so turn their malevolent self-seeking power into a generous benevolence towards the community."[11]

If a sculpture of an ancestor for purposes of worship in an Igbo Society is scarified[12] and endowed with all the paraphernalia that combine to make a work aesthetically good, it would not be accepted by the Igbo and would have no aesthetic recognition simply because it is not true and meaningful. It does not fulfill the function which an Igbo society expects of it. For, the Igbos do not scarify their bodies, and the Muntu-face represented in such a sculpture cannot command their respect for a revered ancestor. Rather the same scarified Muntu-face may be aesthetically beautiful to the Yoruba or other tribes who culturally scarify their bodies.

---

[10] *Ibid.,* p. 174.

[11] Peggy Harper, "The Inter-Relation of the Arts in the Performance of Masquerades as an Expression of Oral Tradition in Nigeria," *Black Orpheus,* 4, No. 1 (1981), 3.

[12] To "scarify" means to adorn with indentations, scratches, or welts (on the skin).

The various African peoples have coined various basic forms for the "Muntu-face" but they all express the Muntu-face. Within one people the Muntu face is constant, for it is derived from their common ancestor, that *muzimu* who formed the physiognomy of his people. Thus the artist is not free to think out a Muntu-face for himself, according to his own conception. The Muntu to be represented must belong to his own people.[13]

When we say that African art is depersonalized we mean that the artist's concern is not to depict his own individual whims and feelings. He works from a background diametrically opposed to the Nietzschean expressionist influence about which Benn writes: "Our background was Nietzsche: his drive to tear apart one's inner nature with words, to express oneself, to formulate, to dazzle, to sparkle at any risk and without regard for the results."[14] He performs rather in such a way as to fulfill the ritual and social purposes of his community for whom the arts are meant to regulate the spiritual, political, and social forces within the community.

Speaking specifically about African poets, Janheinz Jahn testifies that

> In reality, the neo-African poet is not primarily concerned about his own ego. He is Muntu man who speaks and through the word conquers the world of things. His word is the more powerful the more he speaks in the name of his people living as well as dead. As a poet he is the representative of all, and as a representative he is a poet.[15]

Whether it is music, dancing, painting, poetry, etc., he cannot draw his own motifs, his themes, his obsessions from the very essence of his arts. The needs of the community determine the artist's production. His art is never "art for art's sake." He is responsible to his society. Hence the artists are "held in high esteem by the society because they supply those design needs as are vital to their spiritual and physical well-being. They are not as a rule separated or differentiated from the generality of their kindred people for whom they fashion tools and objects of belief."[16]

The foregoing emphasis on the depersonalization of the artist does not mean to rule out every professional freedom. While the artist is bound to adhere to the basic forms recognizable by the people, "the determinant of the first degree, the Muntu face for man, or the animal shape for beasts," he has some freedom with "the determinants of the second degree."[17] Thus he may indicate a chief by the coiffures, by the crown, or

[13] *Ibid.*, p. 162.
[14] *Ibid.*, p. 148. Ben Gottfried, Ch. 2, pp. 39ff.
[15] *Ibid.*, p. 142.
[16] Uche Okeke, *op. cit.*, p. 62.
[17] Jahn, *op. cit.*, p. 163.

by the dress, or he may set the figure on a horse—or he may even use foreign European insignia and medals that are proper to kings.

CONCLUSION

An attempt has been made in this paper to show the philosophical foundation of traditional African aesthetics vis-à-vis Western aesthetics and thereby the culturally relative interpretation of works of art. It has been shown that uniqueness and individuality are not, and need not be, the only basis for theories of aesthetics; that African works of art are functional, community-oriented and depersonalized, unlike Western art which is arbitrary, representative of the values and emotions of the artist, without reference to the cultural environment and the historical reality of the people. I would suggest that the misinterpretation of African works of art by western scholars of aesthetics is due to an ignorance of the cultural differences. . . .

On the Distinction between Modern and Traditional African Aesthetics

H. Gene Blocker

In this paper Gene Blocker of Ohio University takes an evolutionary approach to the concept of "aesthetic attitude," arguing that aesthetic experiences are relative to the level of sociohistorical development. The modern aesthetic attitude emphasizes detachment and "aesthetic distance," in which the artifact is reflected on and contemplated. In traditional societies, on the other hand, artifacts of symbolic import were imbedded in the practical activities of the society, making the traditional aesthetic experience vastly more participatory. But with the erosion of the historical conditions that made traditional life possible, there has been a concomitant erosion of the participatory attitude. More often than not, traditional techniques and motifs survive only by being lifted from their original contexts and reproduced as "art objects." Blocker suggests this may be necessary if the nation-states of Africa are to forge national identities, superseding those of tribal and clan origins. But Blocker cautions against making unanimist claims about the nature of aesthetic experiences in traditional societies. The fact that traditional artifacts and activities are primarily functional does not mean that there is no appreciation of their formal beauty.

The tradition of the "aesthetic attitude," or "aesthetic experience," beginning in the eighteenth century and continuing through the first half of the twentieth century, has been called into question from many sides— by analytic philosophers, such as George Dickie, who doubt the very existence of a peculiarly "aesthetic" experience, by neo-Marxist and other "political" theorists who accept the existence of traditional aesthetic experience but reject its apolitical pretense as a dishonest politics supporting the dominance of the status quo, and by "postmodernists," including "deconstructionists," who reject the pretense of artworks, aesthetically experienced, to symbolically interpret the world for us. In my own recent work considering the aesthetic experience of so-called "primitive" peoples (those who made and used traditional African wood carvings and pre-Columbian Meso-American ceramic objects, e.g.), and its contrast with the aesthetic experience appropriate to modern nation-states of the "developed" world,* I have come to see new, more compelling ways to defend the aesthetic attitude in a broader cultural context as a socially instituted kind of experience of works of art and objects of natural beauty that is peculiarly appropriate to a particular developmental stage of modernist culture. My approach is therefore developmental and evolutionary, urging that modern cultures arise from more "primitive" ones and that, correspondingly, the modern "aesthetic experience" evolves from a more "primitive" aesthetics.

Let us first look briefly at some of the more important implications of "aesthetic experience" for modern culture. The immediate consequence of the impersonal and nonutilitarian posture of the aesthetic attitude was to isolate the object of this aesthetic attention from its mundane, physical surroundings, transforming it into a self-contained whole, unconnected with the rest of the world, except, as we shall see shortly, symbolically. This is what Sartre calls the "unrealizing" function of aesthetic experience and what is often referred to as the "willing suspension of disbelief." To experience the novel, painting, or play aesthetically, one must realize that the events represented in these art works are "fictional," that is, that they are not contiguous with ordinary space–time physical reality. The unrealizing function of aesthetic experience is closely related to its "disinterestedness." To say that aesthetic perception is not concerned with practical consequences is just to say that in aesthetic experience we do not perceive the object as a real object with real consequences for us. It is the function of the arena, the picture frame, and the pedestal to transform and elevate the object from its ordinary space–time, which also ensures the adoption of the aesthetic attitude on the part of the audience, who may interact with and participate in the aesthetic "fiction" or "semblance," but only in aesthetically appropriate ways, whether as mere spectators, passively contemplating the aesthetic object, or more actively participating but within carefully defined aesthetic boundaries, separating fiction from reality. One may hiss and boo the villain, but one must not rush onto the stage to disarm him; one may weep for the hero's mortal wounds, but one must not call the doctor.

* *The Aesthetics of Primitive Art* (Lanham, MD: University Press of America, 1992).

As a result of this attitude of detachment and disinterestedness, the aesthetic attitude is generally more reflective or contemplative in orientation, and as a result of that, the object of aesthetic attention is generally understood "symbolically" to refer to meanings and significant content of a quite general though undefined sort. When I look at a tree, for example, from a pragmatic point of view, to see how much firewood it will yield, I see that object simply as an instance of the category *tree.* It is just a particular instance of a tree. But when I disengage myself from such practical concerns and look at the tree for its own sake, then, as Schopenhauer pointed out, my attention may be drawn to the general symbolic significance of the tree—as the link, for example, between heaven and earth, or the monumentality, quiet dignity, strength, and stability of the tree, or its protective aspect. It is no longer simply a member of the category *tree,* but an object that seems to partake of quite general and far-ranging meaning and significance.

Only by the "unrealizing" act of psychic "distance," in which beliefs are temporarily suspended, can one object come to represent something that it is not, especially where the object is concrete and what it represents is something quite general, such as rebirth and renewal, or the dialectical tension between creative and destructive forces. The epistemological paradox of the aesthetic attitude is that one is simultaneously aware of both the symbol and of what it symbolizes. The aesthetic attitude is composed of two contradictory states of mind held together in a dynamic tension—consciousness of the art object as existing in its own right and also as fused with and participating in what it symbolizes. The mystery of representation and impersonation is this simultaneous belief and disbelief in their identity and distinction. Those lines on paper become a generalized human face, but only if I know full well that they are not a face but only lines drawn on paper. The actor becomes Hamlet only if I know he is an actor playing the part of Hamlet.

The emotional interest in an object at this symbolic level can be very intense, indeed, especially because it involves an ordering of experience that is quite impossible in the chaos and confusion of everyday life. This symbolic meaning also transcends the concerns of a particular regional or ethnic group. Although we no longer worship Dionysius, we can still enjoy the plays of Sophocles and Euripides, which were once a part of that worship. We continue to appreciate the tragedy because our aesthetic attitude has detached it from its religious context and thereby transformed it into a potent, cross-cultural symbol that it was not for the original audience.

In precisely the same way, potent symbols in Soyinka's plays of Obatala and Ogun—Yoruba gods of creation and of war—transcend the ethnic borders of Yorubaland and become available on an aesthetic level to all Nigerians, whether Ibo, Tiv, Ishan, or Hausa, as well as to non-

Nigerians around the world. Furthermore, once the aesthetic dimension has emerged as an independent entity, it becomes possible to deliberately, self-consciously *create* symbolic meaning in art. Once we see that from within the gaze of the aesthetic attitude ordinary physical objects from everyday life take on symbolic meaning, it becomes possible to isolate, select, reorganize, and manipulate such symbolic content in deliberately constructed patterns; and these patterns will possess greater aesthetic intensity than objects of natural beauty because they are more tightly organized and unified. Thus, artists can create symbols that express and represent their society if they are able to disengage themselves from that society and look on it from a detached perspective.

Of course, the problem with the experience of aesthetic distance is that it appears excessively narrow and elitist, excluding any appreciation of art and beauty in most of the world's cultures—and even in European culture before the eighteenth century, or, at the earliest, the Renaissance. The reason most societies are excluded from this definition is that their interest in art is submerged in various nonaesthetic concerns, including religious, ceremonial, military, agricultural concerns, and so on. The Chiwara antelope carvings of the ancient Bambara of Ivory Coast, for example which today are so highly prized as art by European and contemporary collectors, were originally made to be used in ritual masquerage dances in the fields each year just before planting in celebration of the original ancestor spirits who taught the Bambara the arts of farming. Here the aesthetic dimension of sculpture, music, and dance is submerged within a predominantly religious and agricultural concern.

But, of course, to say that something is not exclusively or predominantly aesthetic is not to say that it is not aesthetic at all. If the aesthetic is a dimension of human experience, then we would expect to find it mixed in varying degrees with many other sorts of activities. It is true that in *our* society the mixture of nonaesthetic elements in the enjoyment of works of art is regarded as an inappropriate distraction not sanctioned by our collective aesthetic institutions and conventions, as opposed to "primitive" societies, where such mixture is the approved norm. Nonetheless, it does not follow that the aesthetic is entirely absent from the "primitive" perception; nor that it is entirely disapproved within the "primitive" society. Nor does it follow from the fact that the aesthetic is *different* from the religious or moral or ceremonial that it is necessarily or usually *opposed* to them. Obviously, in many cases the aesthetic quality of the accompanying music, dance, and plastic sculpture will *enhance* the religious import.

Many conceptual confusions and pitfalls surrounding the relationship of functional and aesthetic elements need to be clearly sorted out. Once these confusions are sorted out, I think it will be clear, as John Dewey said, that the aesthetic is a dimension in all human experience, present in varying forms and degrees in all peoples and in all societies, and that, as such, aesthetic experience is not the exclusive perogative of Western or European cultures. At the same time, I think it will also become clear that in the degree of its mixture with nonaesthetic elements, different *types* of aesthetics are possible. In this sense we will try to define the nature of a "primitive" aesthetics as a significantly different subset within the broader category or genus of aesthetics proper.

As we have seen, "primitive" artifacts are not made aesthetically *as* works of art. From this widely accepted fact, many writers on "primitive" art have concluded that traditional Africans and other "primitive" peoples have no aesthetic sense, no critical standards of taste, and no sense of the artistic worth of their own art. In my view this conclusion is unwarranted and represents a serious misunderstanding both of the nature of "primitive" art and also of our own aesthetic experience. In this paper, I argue that having an aesthetic sense is not synonymous with and does not require the socially accepted institution, which we know, of adopting in art contexts that degree of aesthetic perception that defines the modern "aesthetic attitude," and that while "primitive" peoples do not possess the latter, they most certainly do have aesthetic sensibilities. Similarly, I will argue that possessing critical standards for judging works of art is not synonymous with and does not require a theory of art criticism, and that while "primitive" peoples do not possess the latter, they do have and use critical standards in judging artworks.

These different types of aesthetic expression represent stages in a hierarchy in the sense that the latter presupposes the former, but not the reverse. There can be no verbalization of preference without some initial preference to start with. Nor can there be any institutionalized isolation of aesthetic experience from other types of experience unless there first exists some aesthetic experience to start with. Nor can social institutions select among preferences, channeling preferences into socially approved, "good taste," unless there are first preferences from which to accept and reject. And until there is verbalization, there can be no judgmental standards or criteria, and until standards appear, there can be no attempt to reconcile and order them, an effort that eventually leads to theories of art.

The fact that one level of aesthetic awareness is not present does not imply that none are present. The attempt to define the aesthetic attitude, as we have seen, is the attempt to locate that part of any experience that is aesthetic and discover what makes it so. It is not the discovery of a totally new kind of experience that is always and exclusively aesthetic and nothing else. Most aesthetic experience with artworks and objects of natural beauty is mixed with other elements and concerns. In Western aesthetic history, it is true that certain institutions surrounding the notion of "fine art" have indeed developed that foster the relatively sharper focusing on and therefore greater concentration of the aesthetic element as the accepted norm in the enjoyment of works of art. Nonetheless, as anyone with an interest in art surely knows, most encounters with works of art of whatever kind are always mixed, and the socially accepted norm is generally just that—an idealized norm.

It does not follow, therefore, that experiences that are not *primarily* aesthetic contain *no* aesthetic elements. Aesthetic and nonaesthetic elements need not be contradictory in every case but many often complement and enhance one another. Both a crucifix and a fragment of a saint's thigh bone are objects of religious worship, but the former requires an aesthetic character, which the latter does not. To convey its religious message, the crucifix must be carved or rendered to *look* a certain way, whereas a fragment of the saint's skeletal remains of any shape, size, or color whatever will serve equally well. Consequently, the crucifix may fail in a way the bone cannot through its visual appearance. As a result, the crucifix becomes a better candidate for becoming an art object within the perspective of the aesthetic attitude because it already *has* an aesthetic aspect, which the bone fragment does not, to be abstracted for aesthetic contemplation. Similarly, the music of the mass must *sound* solemn and profound if it is to accomplish its religious and devotional function.

This same principle seems to apply, at least in some cases, in "primitive" art. Certainly, there is evidence that it operates in much, though not all, West African art. Masks and figures worn atop the head, paraded, or carried in ritual dances will often only work if they have been fashioned to "look the part." The top portion of Yorubu Gelede Mask, for example, is designed to entertain and thus pacify evil witches, but if the masks are not visually entertaining, they can hardly be expected to do the job. This aesthetically subservient function would not be present or required, for example, in a stone fetish—that is, an ordinary stone covered with a thick patina of blood, oil, and other "medicines," which can have any shape or color whatever and indeed is usually not seen at all but, like the fragment of the saint's thigh bone, is enclosed in a shrine or other ritual container. In many, though not all, cases of religious art, then, an aesthetic role is present, and while it may be *secondary* to a religious function, it is nonetheless *necessary* to that predominantly religious function.

Finally, granted an underlying root-aesthetic concept common to both "primitive" aesthetics and our own aesthetic point of view, what differences exist between the two, and what are the strengths and weaknesses of each? In general, the main difference between the modern aesthetic attitude of the West and the aesthetic sense of "primitive" cultures concerns the *relative* ability and desire of separating aesthetic and nonaesthetic elements originally joined together and detaching the aesthetic more or less from the rest as one element having a character and value of its own. This relative separation is what makes it possible for the Buddhist to appreciate the crucifix; the atheist, the B Minor Mass; and the European, the awe, terror, and dignity of a tribal African mask. In addition to the ability of the aesthetic point of view to transform the object from a piece of religious paraphernalia into a symbol of far-ranging meaning to be contemplated and reflected on, the other great advantage of the modern aesthetic point of view is that it is not limited to a particular sociopolitical, tribal-religious setting. As Europeans increasingly begin to admire African art aesthetically, Africans' ritual participation in their own art is steadily declining. At the same time, however, with increasing education, Africans themselves are more and more adopting the modern aesthetic attitude toward their own art, with the result that *aesthetic* interest in their own art is gathering considerable momentum, especially in the ongoing search for "roots." In the rush to modernize, the tightly knit fabric of traditional tribal life disintegrates. Because the art is inseparable at that level from the religious and social pattern, the ritualistic art succumbs with the overall pattern of tribal life. Thus, the strength of the "primitive" aesthetic—its holistic integrity—proves to be its greatest weakness.

Yet other factors are at work in West Africa and other centers of "primitive" art in New Guinea, Northwest America, and the South Sea islands, which encourages the development of aesthetic consciousness, which in turn gives "primitive" art a new hold on life—albeit in the museum and on the stage rather than around the communal fire. The weakness of "primitive" aesthetics is precisely the strength of the modern "aesthetic attitude," and it is this aesthetic attitude, both in the West and among the educated elite in developing countries, which ironically ensures the survival of "primitive" art. As Africans, for example, relinquish their tribal identities in search of a new national identity, they turn increasingly to the university-trained young artists, such as Olayinka, Bruomah, Fakeye, and Twins Seven Seven, to inspire them with a new sense of national unity. Much of the new art in West African cities tries to recapture and preserve motifs of the tribal past, but self-consciously, deliberately, selecting and abstracting from the ritual practices of different secret societies and, indeed, from different tribes, which are then mixed and woven together into a new entertaining "art" product, self-consciously projecting a new, positive sense of national unity and regional pride.

In short, the new art can only succeed *as art* within a modern aesthetic consciousness, and "primitive" art survives only when it ceases to be the art of a "primitive" society. In much the same way, recently independent countries are making an effort to collect representative examples of the tribal art of their past for display in newly constructed art museums in the larger cities. The art is displayed to be viewed aesthetically, and its audiences come to view these pieces, in the museum and the theater, much as Western spectators do, as symbols of generalized aspects of their past to be contemplated aesthetically as sources of national and regional pride. The same carving can go through various stages from a predominantly religious icon to a work of art. The Egungun mask, for example, was once used as part of a sacred funerary ritual in which the spirit of the deceased spoke to surviving members of his or her family. Years later, the family converted to Christianity, and the mask was demoted to the status of a false idol, removed in shame, and hidden from view. At this point, the object could have been sold through a Muslim trader to a foreign art collector, or even destroyed as an act of faith in the new religion. But in this particular case, the piece remained in the family, largely forgotten, much as our grandparents' possessions often moulder away in our attics and basements, ignored and forgotten for decades, until they are rediscovered, often quite by accident. Many years later, after the country has become independent, a new emphasis by the Ministry of Culture is begun that changes the status of the mask once more, this time elevating it to the rank of a "work of art" and a "national treasure" as part of the program of nation building to instill feelings of pride and nationality in the people. And so the mask is dusted off and taken to the regional museum, where it is proudly placed on display for the enjoyment and education of museum goers.

As we have indicated, the result of the impact of European civilization on "primitive" societies was, among other things, to undermine the very fragile basis of "primitive" culture, including, of course, "primitive" art, interlocked as it was in the total fabric of family, agricultural, military, political, and religious aspects of "primitive" society. But as religious interest in "primitive" art by the indigenous peoples declined, two interesting things happened. First, as we have already pointed out, these same "primitive" peoples began to take a more aesthetic interest in their own art and to plan for its protection from exportation and for exhibition in newly constructed museums in the emerging independent nations formerly under colonial rule.

But the other than that happened was equally interesting. Under the impact of European culture, some of these "primitive" peoples began to evolve new art forms within a newly emerging modern "aesthetic" point of view. Newly colonialized "primitive" peoples began to respond to the interest that their European masters were taking in their "primitive," indigenous traditional crafts. As a result, in many cases, instead of declining, as might have been expected, modern versions of traditional art thrived under colonial administrations. By the turn of the present century, native Navaho blanket making had become a dying art. It was cheaper and easier for Native Americans to purchase brightly printed wool blankets from local "Anglo" traders than it was to spin, dye, and weave the wool—all by hand—into the traditional blankets. But at this critical moment, American tourists, settlers, and collectors expressed a great interest in these increasingly rare blankets as works of "primitive art," and what is probably more important, expressed their willingness to pay considerable sums (though seemingly small by today's standards) for the older blankets. Older tribal members who still remembered how to make such blankets were sought out and encouraged to reenter the manufacture of the blankets in the traditional manner, but this time, for "export" trade to tourists and "Anglo" collectors. Similarly, New Mexico traditional Amerindian pottery was rescued from a total replacement by cheaper metal and later plastic pots by an enthusiastic tourist market willing to pay the price for authentic "Indian-made" articles. Similarly, in Africa, carvers were encouraged to produce more and more wood carvings, not for their declining religious and ceremonial use in the indigenous society, but for export to the lucrative European market.

In many cases, this resulted in what was effectively new art forms. Despite the insistence of the European market on "authenticity," European preferences for some kinds of native art and for some individual pieces over others inevitably acted as a filter, influencing carvers and potters to produce more of what was wanted and less of what was being rejected. Eventually, a stable style developed within each of these transformed primitive art styles. It is only by comparing the expensive but beautiful New Mexican Amerindian blankets and pottery today with those made a hundred years ago that we can see this gradual evolution toward a steady and flourishing contemporary Indian tourist market.

In the early 1950s, a British missionary to Nigeria, Father Carroll, became concerned with what he correctly perceived were clear signs of the imminent demise of traditional Yoruba wood carving. Feeling some responsibility for the missionaries' role in this decline, Father Carroll sought to reverse the trend by reestablishing traditional carving centers in Nigeria. Under his direction, Lamidi Fakeye brought several of his nephews, Joseph and Ganiyu Fakeye, into the carving workshop, and their work, especially that of Lamidi Fakeye, now teaching in the School of Art at the University of Ife, became internationally well-known. Retaining key elements of the traditional Yoruba style, they expanded the traditional repertoire to include such utilitarian objects as bas relief doors, chests, tables, wall hangings, and to work in beautiful West African woods, such as Iroko and African mahogany, whose fine grain is not covered with vegetable dyes, as were the older sacred carvings, but, like modern European wood sculptures, preserved as part of the total aesthetic effect. Unlike the older, sacred carvings, the newer works are more concerned with secular, even anecdotal subjects depicting typical everyday scenes of village life. The carving has also become more polished and commercially more refined. Nonetheless, the style remains broadly and recognizably Yoruba. These works are not only sold to a growing tourist market abroad but are seen prominently displayed throughout Nigeria in hospitals, banks, universities, and government buildings.

In other cases, totally new artistic crafts have been introduced by Europeans, both to preserve local art and craft traditions and also to provide a means of economic support for the indigenous communities: thorn carvings in Nigeria, stone carvings among the Eskimo, silver and turquoise jewelry introduced by the Spanish in Mexico in the sixteenth century (as well as various lacquered wood and glazed ceramic styles introduced by Spanish missionaries throughout central Mexico and the Southwestern United States), and glass bead weaving introduced by the French missionaries among the Native North Americans, to name only a few. Sometimes this was more a matter of substituting new materials for older materials but also frequently introducing completely new art forms. Soon each became a stable art style entirely naturalized within that particular group of people and an expected source of income. In some cases, as with the slate carving among the Haida of North America, the new art was developed entirely for a foreign tourist trade. In other cases, as with the glass bead art of the Plains Indians and the silver and turquoise jewelry among the Indians of Mexico and the American Southwest, the new art became a source and a symbol of family wealth among the indigenous peoples themselves. Or, in the case of the lacquer and ceramic styles introduced by the Spanish missionaries in the sixteenth century, the new art forms became a permanent part of the everyday culture of the local people.

Thus, we can distinguish the relatively more integrated aesthetics of "primitive" cultures from the relatively more detached and abstracted and self-conscious aesthetics of the modern "aesthetic attitude" that evolves out of the former. Each has opposing strengths and weakness. The strength of the "primitive" aesthetics lays in its greater contextual integrity and audience involvement and participation, whereas the strength of the modern aesthetic attitude rests on its more contemplative and hence universalizing, nonparochial, symbolic nature. Contemporary West African countries provide interesting case studies of the transformation of the one into the other, with all the negative and positive connotations which that transformation inevitably involves.

Certainly, it does not follow that the greater the isolation of the aesthetic, the better. My interest has been to trace the development or emergence of the relatively more aesthetic from the relatively more functional, but this does not necessarily imply progress. Indeed, we have just distinguished between a relatively pure aesthetics and a relatively mixed aesthetics with opposing strengths and weaknesses. Where the aesthetic element is more thoroughly mixed with nonaesthetic concerns, as in the more traditional societies of West Africa a hundred years ago, there is a much greater sense of social and cultural integration and participation of the individual in the total cultural milieu than in the relatively pure aesthetic contexts, such as Europe since the eighteenth century, whose culture is more fragmented, disjointed, and the individual is relatively more alienated than in the former.

The isolation of the aesthetic also results in a semantic depletion of the religious beliefs, which tend to be taken less literally and seriously and more symbolically as the aesthetic dimension gains the upper hand. The religiously potent crucifix of Ibeji now merely decorates a study or museum shelf. On the other hand, the greater the aesthetic purity, the greater the possibilities for deliberately creating universal, cross-cultural symbolic meaning. Here, there is less literal belief but greater scope for self-conscious reflection and conscious manipulation of symbols.

Thus, the modern aesthetic attitude is more suited to pluralistic societies of the modern type in which individual freedom of expression, religion, and life-style is encouraged, and ethnic and tribal integrities give way to national objectives. In other words, whereas the more integrative, participatory aesthetics of the mixed mode is ideally suited to the tribal setting, a relatively pure aesthetic attitude is needed to forge national symbols of identity and aspiration in the modern developing nation-states.

Finally, one must be careful not to exaggerate the differences between traditional African and modern European aesthetic attitudes, as if they marked mutually exclusive domains. It is frequently claimed, for example, that Western aesthetics is a cerebrally detached concern with art for art's sake, whereas African aesthetics involves total participation and immersion. Both sides of the comparison are mistaken; the differences, as we have tried to show, are not categorical but a matter of degree. It would be as serious a mistake to ignore the element of aesthetic distance present in African traditional aesthetics as it would be to ignore the existence of audience participation in modern European aesthetics.